The Next Pope

EDWARD PENTIN

THE

NEXT
POPE

*The Leading
Cardinal Candidates*

SOPHIA INSTITUTE PRESS
Manchester, New Hampshire

Sophia Institute Press
Box 5284, Manchester, NH 03108
1-800-888-9344

www.SophiaInstitute.com

Sophia Institute Press® is a registered trademark of Sophia Institute.

paperback ISBN 978-1-64413-311-8

ebook ISBN 978-1-64413-312-5

Library of Congress Control Number: 2020938138

First printing

To Our Lady Queen of Apostles,
Virgin Most Prudent

PHOTO CREDITS

CONTENTS

ACKNOWLEDGMENTS

ALTHOUGH MY NAME APPEARS ON THE COVER of this book, this is actually the work of many hands and mine are truly the least of them. I would like to thank, first of all, those who wish to remain anonymous but who had the idea for this project, generously funded it, and organized the research over a number of years. Without them, their expertise, and their persistence, driven solely by their love of the Church and the Faith, *The Next Pope* would never have seen the light of day. Secondly, I would like to thank the researchers who also wish to remain anonymous but spent many hours scouring publications and online sites for information to make this book as valuable a resource as possible. Thirdly, I would like to thank Charlie McKinney and all the team at Sophia Institute Press for their great professionalism, patience, and commitment in publishing this book. Last, but not least, I express my gratitude to friends and colleagues who gave help and direction, including Roger McCaffrey, Diane Montagna, and others who shared their expertise and advice.

The Next Pope

INTRODUCTION

AT THE ELECTION OF A NEW POPE, we naturally tend to focus on the man in white appearing on the balcony of St. Peter's Basilica, but what of the many men around him dressed in red?

The pope is the Vicar of Christ, the bishop of Rome, the earthly spiritual leader of over a billion Catholic souls, and arguably the best-known, most influential, and widely revered moral and religious voice in the world. But the cardinals who elected him—among whom was the new pope until just a few moments earlier—are much less known.

Moreover, at a conclave, the election of a cardinal to lead the Catholic Church, it's usually not just the public who have little or no knowledge of a prospective pope. Perhaps, surprisingly, neither do the cardinals who are voting for him.[1] Unlike a political leadership contest, where the candidates are publicly scrutinized, often *ad nauseam*, few of us know much about these men who play an enormous, but sometimes unknown, role in the Church and the world.

---

[1] This has become especially pertinent in recent years as Pope Francis has chosen not to hold pre-consistory meetings during his pontificate, thereby lessening the chance of cardinals being able to become acquainted with one another. See "Pope Francis Decides Not to Hold Pre-Consistory Meeting of Cardinals," *National Catholic Register*, 17 November 2016, https://www.ncregister.com/blog/edward-pentin/pope-francis-decides-not-to-hold-pre-consistory-meeting-of-cardinals.

This book, therefore, aims to equip readers with a detailed knowledge of some of the cardinals considered to have the greatest likelihood of being elected pope. For this first edition, nineteen candidates are discussed in detail—ones whom I and others believe are currently *papabili*, that is, most likely to be elected pope. Of course, the next successor of Peter may be none of them. Cardinal Jorge Bergoglio was not on many papabile lists in 2013, as he was considered by most observers to be too old, especially after Benedict XVI had chosen to retire largely on age grounds. "*Chi entra papa in conclave, ne esce cardinale* [whoever enters a conclave as pope, leaves it as a cardinal]," so the Roman saying goes.[2] Still, the cardinals listed in this book are the ones whom most informed observers are discussing at the present time. It should also be pointed out that this book is slightly different from other pre-conclave journalistic prognostications in that it aims to provide detailed and generally more academic descriptions of the candidates who, in the words of St. Catherine of Siena, could potentially hold the office of "Sweet Christ on Earth." It is also not intended to be a commentary on any popes or their works, whether past or present.

Contemporary Church historian Miles Pattenden persuasively maintains that information is always a central concern for cardinals entering a conclave.[3] They need to be able to discern the righteous from the rogues, the saints from the schemers, the apostles from the bureaucrats. Because of the importance of their choice, and their future careers, cardinals have historically sought to be well informed about their colleagues' real and feigned beliefs and behaviors. In earlier eras, kings and princes, as well as the pope's vassals, had particular vested interests in who might ascend to the Chair of St. Peter. In our day of worldwide papal presence and influence, largely made possible by the media, I would argue it is important for all of us to be informed of who could be pope.

---

[2]   Technically, any baptized male can be elected pope. The last time a non-cardinal was elected was in 1378, when Urban VI was elected. Six non-cardinals have been elected pope in the history of the Church.

[3]   Miles Pattenden, *Electing the Pope in Early Modern Italy, 1450-1700* (Oxford, UK: Oxford University Press, 2017), 133-67.

Previously, at least as far back as the 1550s, cardinals were not limited to private discussions and correspondence about prospective popes. In the days leading up to a conclave, public notices and *libelli*, precursors to the newspaper, were posted in Rome. But rumor is always an untrustworthy informant. Indeed, "fake news" may be a new term, but lies, propaganda, and misdirection are as old as the serpent in the Garden of Eden. It was, therefore, left to diplomats and other trusted scribes to compile reliable biographies of the cardinals and to distribute them to interested parties. Manuscripts dating back to the sixteenth century serve as precedents for the present work.[4]

The Next Pope aims to be useful for cardinal-electors, the media, and everyone affected by the most influential religious leader on earth. In light of my experience as Rome correspondent for the *National Catholic Register*, I have tried to ensure that the cardinals are presented in charity and truth, offering what I hope is an accurate picture of what sort of man might one day fill the shoes of the Fisherman.

To help contextualize the profiles that follow, let us now look at the history of the cardinalate as well as its most important function — the election of a pope.

BRIEF HISTORY OF THE CARDINALATE

To understand the origins of the College of Cardinals, we can consider its roots in ancient Jewish practice. The Pentateuch records how God called Moses to serve as a bridge between humanity and Himself. Moses was simultaneously the head of Israel as well as the human voice of the Almighty (Ex 3:10-12). To Moses was given the power to teach and enforce God's Law; to pray and make sacrifices for Israel; to establish feasts, such as Passover; and to direct the decoration and building of the tent of worship. Moses also established a particular hierarchy among his collaborators. Following the Lord's orders, Moses ordained his brother Aaron as the high priest,

---

[4]   See ibid., 147.

established seventy elders to assist him, and also consecrated the men of the tribe of Levi to assist the priesthood (Lev 8; Num 11:16-17).

When Jesus Christ walked this earth, He, too, established a hierarchy, one evocative of the earlier order. He called to Him twelve apostles, who were consecrated to the Father's service through the Spirit and participated in His own life as His friends (Mt 10:1-4; Jn 17:17-19). He gave them power and authority to teach all that He taught, to cast out demons, to baptize, to anoint the sick, to forgive sins, and to celebrate the Holy Eucharist (Mt 10:5-15; 28:19-20; Mk 6:13; Jn 20:19-23). Christ also appointed seventy others. They are less central to the Gospel narratives and were given power for only some of the same acts, such as offering peace, preaching, and exorcizing demons (Lk 10:1-20). Whereas the Old Covenant priesthood was passed on through a bloodline, the priesthood of the New Covenant was passed on through sacramental ordination, as was the episcopate. After Christ ascended into heaven, therefore, the apostles extended their number by ordaining Matthias. According to the will of the Lord (although this is debated), they also added a new grade of Holy Orders by having the disciples of Christ select seven men to serve in the Church for liturgical and everyday needs: the first deacons.[5]

Within a very short time, the early Church began to distinguish between three distinct grades of Holy Orders: bishop, priest, and deacon. St. Clement, third bishop of Rome and successor to St. Peter (ca. A.D. 88), indicates that Catholic Holy Orders are somehow parallel to the Old Testament orders.[6] Hundreds of years later, St. Jerome affirms more clearly: "So that we can know that the apostolic traditions were taken from the Old Testament, positions which were occupied by Aaron, his sons, and the Levites in the temple, are now claimed by bishops, presbyters,

---

[5] Acts 6:1-6 records the founding of the diaconate, especially for the purpose of "serving at table" and distributing alms. Soon enough, we see the deacon Philip preaching, explaining Sacred Scripture, and administering Baptism (Acts 8:12, 30-38).

[6] Clement of Rome, *Letter to the Corinthians*, c. 40.

and deacons in the Church."[7] Eventually the pope's chief helpers, his "cardinal" assistants, would be associated with these three grades of orders, comprising cardinal-bishops, cardinal-priests, and cardinal-deacons.

Here is how that came about.

In continuity with the Mosaic and the apostolic recognition that rulers need delegates to assist them, St. Peter ordained seven deacons for the Diocese of Rome before his death, according to the ancient *Book of Pontiffs*.[8] From the earliest times, deacons played a particular role as assistant to the bishop—for example, by reading the Gospel during the sacred liturgy, distributing Holy Communion, and occasionally baptizing; they often came in groups of seven.[9] They were often associated with the lowest rank of Old Testament clergy, the Levites. Soon after St. Peter was martyred, Pope St. Clement created seven districts—later called "deaconries"—within Rome for administrative purposes; Pope Evaristus ordained seven deacons to bear witness to the pope's teachings; and in the third century Pope St. Fabianus appointed seven deacons to administer affairs within those regions, with the help of seven subdeacons and notaries.[10]

By the time of Pope St. Gregory the Great (540-604), the position "cardinal-deacon" was held by a deacon who exercised precedence over other deacons while being incardinated stably from another large parish

---

[7] Hieronymus, *Epistulae 121-154,* ed. I. Hilberg: *Corpus Scriptorum Ecclesiasticorum Latinorum* (CSEL), vol. 56 (Vienna: F. Tempsky, 1910), *Letter 146: To Evangelus,* 2, p. 312.

[8] *The Book of Pontiffs (Liber Pontificalis): The Ancient Biographies of the First Ninety Roman Bishops to AD 715,* trans. Raymond Davis, rev. ed. (Liverpool: Liverpool University Press, 2010), 2. Also, *The Book of the Popes (Liber Pontificalis) 1: To the Pontificate of Gregory 1,* trans. and ed. Louise Ropes Loomis (New York: Columbia University Press, 1916), 6. Loomis and other historians speculate that the work imposes a narrative to justify fifth-century ecclesiastical practices, including issues related to cardinals (see p. 7, n. 2). I read it as reflecting an oral tradition that was incompletely documented because of pre-Constantinian persecutions.

[9] See Loomis, *Book of the Popes,* 6n1.

[10] Ibid., 8, 10, 24.

or diocese.[11] Around the same period, eighteen monastic churches were associated with the expanded group of cardinal-deacons, whose work included distributing food and financial help to widows, orphans, and the poor from the alms collected by the pope.[12]

Because Rome was the preeminent diocese in the world, its clergy who were incardinated into an ancient church locale, including these deacons, took precedence over other clergy in the city and elsewhere.[13] To the senior cardinal-deacon was given the task of reading out and counting the votes in a conclave for the election of a pope: in 1515, Giovanni de'Medici "had the welcome task of announcing his own election."[14] After the Council of Trent, disputes about the rights of cardinals within Rome led to a decree that all cardinals, including cardinal-deacons, had "quasi-episcopal" status in their proper churches.[15] Due in part to confusion as to how a deacon could exercise quasi-episcopal powers and have jurisdictional precedence even over non-Roman bishops, the 1917 *Code of Canon Law*, canon 232, §1, stipulated that all cardinals were to be at least ordained priests. John XXIII decreed in 1962 that cardinals ordinarily are to be ordained bishops.[16] However, Paul VI removed from all cardinals the rights of jurisdiction and

---

[11] Stephan Kuttner, "Cardinalis: The History of a Canonical Concept," *Traditio* 3 (1945): 123-214 at 144.

[12] See Johannes Baptist Sägmüller, "Cardinal," in *The Catholic Encyclopedia*, vol. 3 (New York: Robert Appleton Company, 1908), http://www.newadvent.org/cathen/03333b.htm.

[13] Charles Augustine, *A Commentary on the New Code of Canon Law*, col. 2, 3rd ed. (St. Louis, Mo.: B. Herder, 1919), 228.

[14] Mary Hollingsworth, "Cardinals in Conclave," in *A Companion to the Early Modern Cardinal*, ed. Mary Hollingsworth et al. (Leiden: Brill, 2020), 58-70 at 67.

[15] Arnold Witte, "Cardinals and Their Titular Churches," in *A Companion to the Early Modern Cardinal*, 333-50 at 344.

[16] John XXIII, *Motu Proprio Cum Gravissima* (15 April 1962). This measure was directed to exclude deacons from the cardinalate, for he excepts cardinal-priests from this requirement; indeed, he made honorary cardinals out of a number of priests.

ownership over their titular parishes, thus making the differences among ranks more honorific than otherwise.[17]

Turning to cardinal-priests, now considered a higher dignity than the level of deacons, ancient tradition holds that St. Peter ordained ten priests and instructed St. Cletus, his eventual successor after Pope St. Linus, to ordain twenty-five men as priests for the Diocese of Rome.[18] Less than twenty years later, another pope divided the parish or "titular" churches in Rome among his priest collaborators.[19] Evidence indicates that the title "cardinal-priest" was given to presbyters who oversaw the ancient titular churches, and perhaps others, in a juridically stable way on behalf of the pope.[20] Around the year 306, Pope Evaristus clarified that priests in these churches had the power to administer Baptism, Penance, Eucharist, and the interment of martyrs there.[21] Augustine of Hippo attested to an established practice whereby the bishop of Rome would consult with a council of his presbyters regarding doctrinal and disciplinary matters. In a remarkable letter to Pope Boniface (418-422), he defended the decisions of the Roman clergy—almost certainly these cardinal-priests—under Zosimus, the previous pope (417-418), explaining that their patience with heretics was a sign of mercy, not prevarication.[22]

For assistance in pontifical liturgical duties, a pope in the fifth century established a rotation of cardinal-priests to celebrate Mass in the most important patriarchal basilicas: St. Peter's, St. Paul's, and St. Lawrence; St. Mary Major was added at some later point.[23] In the ninth century, a law

---

[17] Paul VI, *Motu Proprio Ad Hoc Usque Tempus* (15 April 1969).

[18] Loomis, *Book of the Popes*, 7.

[19] Ibid., 10. Also, Arnold Witte, "Cardinals and Their Titular Churches," 333-50. The "titular" churches were originally homes whose legal titles were held by pious laymen.

[20] Kuttner, "Cardinalis," 139-42.

[21] Ibid., 147. It may be that the original twenty-five parishes were reorganized at this time because of a loss of organization on account of persecutions. See Loomis, *Book of the Popes*, 38n3.

[22] See Augustinus Hipponensis, *Contra duas Epistolas Pelagianorum* (Against Two Letters of the Pelagians), lib. II, c. 3 (5) and c. 4 (8).

[23] Pope Simplicius (468-83); Kuttner, "Cardinalis," 147-8.

for cardinal-priests was promulgated, formalizing their roles as supervisors of ecclesiastical discipline and judges of law within their jurisdictions. Significantly, the document states that the pope stands in the place of Moses with his clemency, whereas *the cardinal-priests stand in the place of the seventy elders*, who judged cases under the authority of Moses.[24] They were also associated with the middle rank of Old Testament clergy—namely, the Temple priests. As precedence and functions morphed through time, by the twelfth century the Church of St. Mary Major had gained precedence over the other titular churches of cardinal-priests, who since then have formed the greater majority of the College of Cardinals.[25]

Cardinal-bishops are the first in rank, the smallest in number, and the last to be historically established.[26] All of the first apostles were bishops in their own right; they came to be heads of the ancient local churches that they established. The acute persecutions in Rome led the early popes to establish suffragan bishops to assist in pastoral duties throughout the city and its environs: a situation that distinguished the Roman church from nearly every other in the early Church.[27] St. Peter is reputed to have ordained three bishops, each of whom, in turn, would be his successor as supreme pontiff.[28]

According to ancient (pagan) Roman law, the prefect of the city (*Praefectus Urbis*) had jurisdiction over an area one hundred miles from the city, a large area where emperors and aristocrats made their estates known as the *suburbanum*, "the place under the City."[29] A similar administrative structure

---

[24] Promulgated by Pope John VIII (872-882). Johannes Dominicus Mansi, *Sacrorum Conciliorum*, vol. 17 (Venice: Atonium Zatta, 1772; repr. Paris: H. Welter, 1902), col. 247.

[25] Sägmüller, "Cardinal."

[26] For rank, see CIC/83 can. 350.1.

[27] Outside of Rome, the early norm was one bishop per diocese. Kuttner, "Cardinalis," 146.

[28] That is, Linus, Cletus, and Clement. Loomis, *Book of the Popes*, 6.

[29] See "Rome, surroundings of," in *The Oxford Dictionary of Late Antiquity*, ed. Oliver Nicholson, vol. 1: A-I (Oxford, UK: Oxford University Press, 2018), 1308.

was early adopted by the bishops of Rome, with suffragan bishoprics established in the "suburbicarian" sees, eventually comprising Ostia, Porto Santa Rufina, Albano, Sabina, Tusculum (Frascati), and Palestrina.[30] Augustine attests that the bishop of Ostia was the first to consecrate the bishop of Rome,[31] apparently a decision made by Pope Marcus in 336.[32] Over four hundred years later (769), Pope Stephen decided that these bishops, now designated with the title "cardinal," could be obliged to celebrate Holy Mass in his place at the Lateran Basilica.[33] By the early Middle Ages, the great reforming saint Peter Damian, cardinal-bishop of Ostia (1057-1072), called his brothers "cardinals of the Lateran Church," indicating an established recognition of their particular status and rank.[34] In 2018, Pope Francis created an anomalous situation by making four men cardinal-bishops despite their not possessing suburbicarian sees: Pietro Parolin, Leonardo Sandri, Marc Ouellet, and Fernando Filoni.[35]

By the late Middle Ages, the precedence of cardinal-bishops above all other members of the ecclesiastical hierarchy was recognized in ecumenical councils, with the cardinal-bishop of Ostia foremost.[36] It was only during the time of the Council of Trent, however, that Pope Paul IV finally formalized the practice that the cardinal-bishop of Ostia would also be the dean of the College of Cardinals.[37] Canon 237 of the 1917 *Code* specified that the dean would be whichever cardinal-bishop from a suburbicarian see was most senior—and it clarified that as *primus inter aequales* (first among

---

[30] See Can. 6 of the Council of Nicaea; Sägmüller, "Cardinal."
[31] Augustinus Hipponensis, *Breviculus collationis cum Donatistas* (Brief Collations with Donatists), pars. III, 16.29.
[32] Loomis, *Book of the Popes*, 72.
[33] Kuttner, "Cardinalis," 149.
[34] Ibid., 151-2.
[35] *Rescriptum* (29 June 2018). At least two are papabile by my calculations: Parolin and Ouellet.
[36] Bernward Schmidt, "Cardinals, Bishops, and Councils," in *A Companion to the Early Modern Cardinal*, 91-108 at 101.
[37] Paul IV, Bull *Cum Venerabiles* (22 August 1555). See Rudolf Hüls, *Kardinäle, Klerus und Kirchen Roms: 1049-1130* (Tübingen: Niemeyer/De Gruyter, 1977), 77-80.

equals) he would have no jurisdiction over his brother cardinals at all.[38] Following his tendency toward the democratization of the Church, Pope Paul VI declared that cardinals would elect their dean from among the cardinal-bishops holding suburbicarian offices; he would then receive the title "Cardinal Bishop of Ostia."[39] Perhaps in response to the unusual situation of Angelo Cardinal Sodano, who held power as secretary of state for fifteen years and then as dean of cardinals for fourteen years, Pope Francis has limited the term of dean to five years.[40]

Evidence of the cardinals considered as a group arises in 853, when Pope Leo IV called cardinals of all three ranks to assist him with decisions for the Diocese of Rome.[41] From that time forward, there is evidence that these cardinals were an established ecclesiastical division preeminent in subsequent Roman synods; within a couple of centuries, they expressly participated in papal government over the Church as cardinals and not simply according to their episcopal, presbyteral, or diaconal roles.[42] Whereas St. Ignatius of Antioch spoke in the first century of the bishop as standing in place of God, and the priests standing in place of the "senate of apostles,"[43] St. Peter Damian, nearly a thousand years later, referred to the entire group of cardinals as the "Senate of the Church," under the bishop of Rome, who stands in the place of the true Emperor

---

[38] See also CIC/83 can. 352.1.

[39] Paul VI, *Motu Proprio Sacro Cardinalium Consilio* (26 February 1965).

[40] Francis, *Motu Proprio Riguardante l'Ufficio del Decano del Collegio Cardinalizio* (21 December 2019).

[41] *The Lives of the Ninth-Century Popes (Liber Pontificalis): The Ancient Biographies of Ten Popes from A.D. 817-891*, trans. Raymond Davis (Liverpool: Liverpool University Press, 1995), 150-51. See Mansi, *Sacrorum Conciliorum*, vol. 14, cols. 1009-16.

[42] Barbara Bombi, "The Medieval Background of the Cardinal's Office," in *A Companion to the Early Modern Cardinal*, 9-22 at 10.

[43] Ignatius of Antioch, *Letter to Magnesians*, c. 6.1: συνεδρίου τῶν ἀποστόλων. The French translation accurately renders it *sénat des apôtres*. Ignace D'Antioche, Polycarpe de Smyrne, *Lettres, Martyre de Polycarpe*, ed. and trans. Thomas Camelot, 3rd ed. (Paris: Éditions du Cerf, 1958), 98.

of the world.[44] By around 1100, the group was referred to as the "College of Cardinals," a title that has persisted since then.[45] Increasingly the members of the College exercised jurisdiction over the rest of the Church, including other bishops and even secular rulers, and by serving with delegated papal authority in various matters. In this way, the College as a whole and its members were considered to be "papal assistants and *coadiutores*, whose power was directly invested by the pope," whom they elected.[46]

ROLES OF PRESENT-DAY CARDINALS

As seen in the historical considerations above, early on in the history of the Church, the pope gathered to himself various members of the Roman clergy to assist him in pastoral tasks that included administrative, legal, liturgical, and doctrinal work. In time, the group of cardinals who assisted him on a regular basis, even many times a week, formed the center of his "curia," modeled, in part, on the pre-Christian city council (Latin *curia*) that helped rule secular Rome and its environs.[47] This ecclesiastical organization has undergone changes through the centuries, noticeably since the Second Vatican Council's call to reshape the Roman Curia and Paul VI's implementation thereof.[48] Presently the Roman

---

[44] Peter Damian, *Letters 91-120*, trans. Owen J. Blum (Washington, D.C.: Catholic University of America Press, 1998), *Letter* 97, 82n22.

[45] Bombi, "The Medieval Background of the Cardinal's Office," 12.

[46] Ibid.

[47] See "City Councils and Councillors," in *The Oxford Dictionary of Late Antiquity*, vol. 1, 352.

[48] Second Vatican Council, Decree *Christus Dominus* (28 October 1965), 9: "The fathers of this sacred council, however, desire that these departments—which have furnished distinguished assistance to the Roman pontiff and the pastors of the Church—be reorganized and better adapted to the needs of the times." Paul VI, Apostolic Constitution *Regimini Ecclesiae Universae* (15 August 1967).

Curia is organized for the most part by the 1983 *Code of Canon Law* and John Paul II's Apostolic Constitution *Pastor Bonus*, which he notes was written in consultation with the entire College of Cardinals in two separate consistories, and with many extensive consultations of bishops, patriarchs of Oriental churches, and others.[49] Recently, the Vatican has indicated that Pope Francis intends a sweeping change with a new constitution entitled *Praedicate Evangelium* (Preach the Gospel), slated for promulgation in 2020.[50]

Undoubtedly the most important role of a cardinal is to elect a Roman pontiff, a theme treated below, but to understand these electors — a few of whom were themselves elected — we may take a wider view of their present-day roles. For centuries, Christians recognized the color red in clothing, whether liturgical or ceremonial, as symbolizing martyrdom; in 1245 Pope Innocent IV inaugurated the custom of giving cardinals red hats as their signature clothing — which lasted until Paul VI's abrogation of the practice in 1967.[51] In 1630, Urban VIII insisted that cardinals be addressed with the title "Your Eminence" (Italian *Sua Eminenza*), a custom that remains to this day.[52] Cardinals in previous ages were prominent as Princes of the Church, who, with their often enormous incomes and retinues, patronized exquisite paintings, music, and architecture, including their own tombs. In the extraordinary cases of Richelieu and Mazarin, and others like them, some cardinals forged the destinies of entire states. Perhaps in humbler positions, cardinals nevertheless play a significant part in the Church and the world even now. The general qualifications necessary for a man to be promoted as cardinal are laid

---

[49] John Paul II, Apostolic Constitution *Pastor Bonus* (28 June 1988), 6.

[50] Edward Pentin, "Draft of Vatican's New Curial Constitution Would Reform Lines of Authority," *National Catholic Register*, May 29, 2019, https://www.ncregister.com/daily-news/draft-of-vaticans-new-curial-constitution-would-reform-lines-of-authority.

[51] Carol M. Richardson, "The Cardinal's Wardrobe," in *A Companion to the Early Modern Cardinal*, 535-56 at 540-41.

[52] Sägmüller, "Cardinal."

out in Church law: they are to be "truly outstanding in doctrine, virtue, piety, and prudence in practical matters."[53]

All cardinals possess certain privileges by right, including: they can keep a private chapel with the Blessed Sacrament; they can hear confessions and preach anywhere in the world; they are not subject to any jurisdiction except that of the pope.[54] Now that cardinals no longer have jurisdiction over their suburbicarian or titular churches,[55] one may divide all cardinals into one of three groups: curial cardinals, who serve full-time and solely in the Roman Curia, cardinals who have full-time responsibilities as diocesan bishops, and cardinals with no jurisdiction who do not serve in the Curia.[56] Below I discuss the first two groups in turn.

Ordinarily the pope conducts the business of the universal Church by means of the Roman Curia, "which acts in his name and with his authority for the good and service of the Churches."[57] John Paul II underlines that the Roman Curia is an instrument of the pope; like a pen in the hand of a writer, it possesses "no force and no power apart from what it receives from the same Supreme Pastor."[58] Therefore, the cardinals work in the Curia in a "vicarious character," participating in the Petrine Office of the Roman pontiff.[59] Their cooperation with the pope helps guarantee Catholic unity — in the first place, unity of faith, and then unity of discipline, in communion with Christ.[60] Curial positions held by cardinals in the spring of 2020 include:

- Secretariat of State (Pietro Parolin)
- Congregation for the Doctrine of the Faith (Luis Ladaria Ferrer)

---

[53] CIC/83 can. 351.1.

[54] CIC/83 cans. 357.2, 967.1. Also, *Elenchus privilegiorum et facultatum S.R.E Cardinalium in re liturgica et canonica* (18 March 1999).

[55] CIC/83 can. 357.1

[56] See CIC/83 can. 356, which obliges all cardinals who are not diocesan bishops to dwell in Rome.

[57] CIC/83 can. 360.

[58] John Paul II, *Pastor Bonus* 7.

[59] Ibid., 8.

[60] Ibid., 10.

- Congregation for Bishops (Marc Ouellet)
- Congregation for Divine Worship (Robert Sarah)
- Congregation for the Evangelization of Peoples (Luis Tagle)
- Congregation for Catholic Education (Giuseppe Versaldi)
- Congregation for the Causes of Saints (Giovanni Becciu)
- Congregation for the Clergy (Beniamino Stella)
- Congregation for Institutes of Consecrated Life and Societies of Apostolic Life (João Bráz de Aviz)
- Congregation for the Oriental Churches (Leonardo Sandri)
- Dicastery for the Laity, the Family and Life (Kevin Farrell; also the Papal Camerlengo)
- Dicastery for Promoting Integral Human Development (Peter Turkson)
- Pontifical Council for Culture (Gianfranco Ravasi)
- Pontifical Council for Promoting Christian Unity (Kurt Koch)
- Office of Papal Charities/Papal Almoner (Konrad Krajewski)

This may seem like a fairly sizable number—there are other curial cardinals as well—but in reality, fewer than 20 percent of cardinal-electors, with power to cast a vote for the next pope, are solely curial cardinals. It should be noted that being the head of a curial position does not guarantee that one becomes a cardinal, as between 1940 and 1950, Pius XII did not elevate many prefects and presidents to the cardinalate.

By far, the large majority are cardinals who serve as full-time arch-bishops in dioceses around the world. Traditionally, cardinal-bishops, as seen in the historical section above, were those who held sees within the environs of Rome. As the Church grew, the pope began to desire that the archbishops of some important metropolitan areas be cardi-nals: these locations became known as "cardinalatial sees": a bishop appointed as its head would customarily receive the scarlet. In this way, cardinals had deep knowledge regarding the most important cit-ies and Catholic centers in the world, including Venice, Milan, Paris,

Santiago de Compostela, London, Cologne, Lisbon, Budapest, and later, Tokyo, New York, Washington, D.C., Bombay, and Mexico City, among many others. Being an archbishop of any particular see does not grant a right to the cardinalate, as Pope Francis has shown by not giving the red hat to the archbishops of Venice, Tokyo, Los Angeles, and Philadelphia.[61] Because large archbishoprics demand an enormous amount of attention, very few cardinals who lead them are also heads of curial offices — with the rare exceptions presently including Reinhard Marx, archbishop of Munich and coordinator for the Council for the Economy, and Oscar Rodríguez Maradiaga, archbishop of Tegucigalpa and coordinator of the Council of Cardinals.

ELECTING A POPE

In the early years of the Church, the acclamation of the faithful, united with that of the clergy, could canonize a saint or elect a man as bishop — even the bishop of Rome. Unfortunately, this process could be disorderly and was subject to mob manipulation by bad actors.[62] To rectify these significant defects and ensure a process as free as possible to follow the promptings of the Holy Spirit, the Church gradually developed more formal means for these decisions. The first major reform of papal elections took place in 1059, when Pope Nicholas II determined that the cardinal-bishops alone had the right to elect his successor, with the qualification that their

---

[61] Pope Francis has preferred to make cardinal those on the "peripheries," churchmen who lead smaller dioceses, or metropolitan dioceses in the global south, partly to reflect where the Church is growing fastest.

[62] Miles Pattenden notes that loud and sometimes violent Roman mobs put great pressure on cardinals in favor of different papal candidates — sometimes instigated by base promises of "bread and circuses." Many fifteenth- and sixteenth-century prelates blamed popular pressure for the Great Western Schism, which was precipitated by the cardinals' poor choice for pope. *Electing the Pope*, 116.

decision must be ratified by the other cardinals, the clergy, the people of Rome, and the Holy Roman Emperor.[63] St. Peter Damian, the famous reforming Benedictine of that time, wrote that the cardinal-bishops do the electing, other clergy give their assent, and the people are able to give their applause.[64]

A century later, Alexander III extended the right of election to all three orders of cardinals, requiring a two-thirds majority for validity.[65] During the interim between the death of the pope and the election of his successor, that is, the state *sedes vacans*, in which the Chair of St. Peter was empty, chaos could reign in Rome as the people tried to exploit the absence of a spiritual and temporal head of state.[66] To expedite a papal election, and to reduce outside influence, Gregory X established the conclave: cardinals were to live behind doors locked with a key (*cum clave*) until a majority agreed upon a successor to St. Peter.[67] It followed perhaps the most bizarre and farcical conclave ever to have taken place: the papal election of 1271, when the cardinal-electors, having struggled to decide on a pope for a year and a half because of the influence and interference of external powers, were locked up in the papal palace; the roof was removed, exposing them to the elements, their diet restricted, and the premises surrounded by soldiers. Some cardinals were taken ill as they were left exposed to the elements.[68]

Today, only the College of Cardinals possesses the prerogative to elect the sovereign pontiff, in accordance with the particular laws laid out for a conclave.[69] Cardinal-electors are those below the age of eighty, who are

63 Hollingsworth, "Cardinals in Conclave," 60.
64 Edward Pentin, "History of Conclaves: It's Grace That Sustains the Church," Zenit, 21 February 2013, https://edwardpentin.co.uk/history-of-conclaves-its-grace-that-sustains-the-church/.
65 Ibid.
66 Pattenden, *Electing the Pope*, 102-6, 114-32. Also, John M. Hunt, "Cardinals and the Vacant See," in *A Companion to the Early Modern Cardinal*, 322-32.
67 Hollingsworth, "Cardinals in Conclave," 60.
68 Edward Pentin, "History of Conclaves."
69 CIC/83 can. 349. These laws include the *Ordo Rituum Conclavis* (Order of Rites for a Conclave) (2000), and John Paul II, Apostolic Constitution

not gravely impeded from participation, although all unimpeded cardinals may take part in the pre-conclave preparatory meetings.[70]

The lead-up to a conclave begins with the vacancy of the Chair of St. Peter (*sede vacante*), which can occur only in two ways: through a pope's valid resignation or through his death.[71] The dean of the College of Cardinals has the responsibility to inform all the cardinals of the death of a pope and to convoke a conclave.[72] Cardinals outside of Rome are expected to return to the city as soon as possible and take up residence at the Domus Sanctae Marthae, erected by John Paul II for purposes of housing cardinals during a conclave, with rooms chosen by lot. The Sistine Chapel closes around this time, with security measures being taken to ensure that electronic surveillance cannot take place during the election, including jammers for radios and cell phones.

Prior to the conclave, a "general congregation" takes place over the days leading up to the conclave, in which all cardinals are free to participate. They discuss when a conclave is to start and hear interventions by cardinals regarding a variety of matters, such as the present needs of the Church, the state of the Curia and its work, improving the Curia and the Church's relation to the world, and so on (it was the vision for Church reform that Cardinal Jorge Bergoglio presented during these meetings that was the catalyst for his being elected Pope Francis).

The dean of the College is the ordinary presider over these congregations, and he is to ensure that each cardinal will place his hand on the Gospels and take an oath of fidelity to the rules of the conclave. Cardinals swear to maintain "rigorous secrecy with regard to all matters in any way related to the election of the Roman pontiff or those which, by their very

---

Universi Dominici Gregis (UDG) (22 February 1996), with modifications by Benedict XVI, Apostolic Letter Issued *Motu Proprio Normas Nonnullas* (*NN*) (22 February 2013).

[70] Grave impediments could include the inability to travel on account of serious sickness, incarceration, or a dictatorial regime.

[71] CIC/83 can. 332.2

[72] UDG 19.

nature, during the vacancy of the Apostolic See, call for the same secrecy."[73] Particular congregations also take place, consisting of cardinal-electors only, in which the Papal Camerlengo leads discussions and decisions of lesser matters. At least fifteen full days must elapse before the conclave begins, with a maximum of twenty days' lapse before the election.[74]

On the first day of the conclave, the cardinal-electors gather in St. Peter's Basilica to celebrate the Mass *Pro Eligendo Pontifice* (for the Election of a Pope). In 2005, Joseph Ratzinger, in his capacity as dean of the College of Cardinals, gave the homily for this Mass, utilizing the phrase "dictatorship of relativism," subsequently made famous.[75] When Benedict XVI abdicated, it was Cardinal Sodano who gave the homily before a large diplomatic corps, in a Mass that included the languages of Latin, Italian, English, French, Spanish, German, Swahili, and Malay.

Later that same first day, the cardinal-electors process to the Pauline Chapel within the Vatican and there implore the coming of the Holy Spirit to aid their electoral process. They also hear a brief exhortation from a preacher. From there, accompanied by music, they process to the Sistine Chapel. The cardinals then swear collectively an oath, which reads in part:

> We promise and swear to observe with the greatest fidelity and with all persons, clerical or lay, secrecy regarding everything that in any way relates to the election of the Roman Pontiff and regarding what occurs in the place of the election, directly or indirectly related to the results of the voting; we promise and swear not to break this secret in any way, either during or after the election of the new Pontiff, unless explicit authorization is granted by the same Pontiff; and never to lend support or favour to any interference, opposition or any other form of intervention, whereby

---

[73] UDG 12.

[74] NN 37.

[75] Joseph Ratzinger, Mass *Pro Eligendo Pontifice*, "Homily of His Eminence Card. Joseph Ratzinger Dean of the College of Cardinals" (18 April 2005).

secular authorities of whatever order and degree or any group of people or individuals might wish to intervene in the election of the Roman Pontiff.[76]

After this, each individually, with a hand on the Gospels, pledges his oath to the same.

The cardinal-electors are to refrain from all contact with the outside world during the election: no shared messages, no newspapers, no radio, no television.[77] In 2013, shortly before he stepped down, Benedict XVI introduced the penalty of automatic (*latae sententiae*) excommunication for anyone violating this norm of confidentiality.[78]

Another homily is given, and the voting begins.

Often the first vote is purely ceremonial, a way for cardinals to honor particular members of the College who, though distinguished, are not considered papabile (electable as pope). From that point on, the voting is scheduled to be two sessions a day, with two rounds of voting per session (four rounds total per day).

The cardinals select three fellow cardinals to count the votes, three others to check the counts, and three, if necessary, to collect ballots from those who, from infirmity, are unable to walk to the high altar. Each able cardinal writes on a ballot the name of his choice for pope, then walks to the high altar. There, under the painting of the Last Judgment by Michelangelo, he says aloud, "I call as my witness Christ the Lord, who will be my judge, that my vote is given to the one who before God I think should be elected."[79] The cardinal then places the ballot into the proper receptacle, bows to the altar, and returns to his place.

Once the ballots have been placed in the receptacle, they are mixed up and then counted aloud. If the number does not equal that of the electors, the ballots are burned. If the number is accurate, the ballots are taken out

---

[76] UDG 53.
[77] UDG 57.
[78] NN 55.
[79] UDG 66.

singly, noted by two cardinals, and then announced in a loud, clear voice by a third cardinal.

For a man to be validly elected pope, he must receive two-thirds of the votes.

During the election, some candidates will gain support; others will lose it. And if the leading candidates in the first vote fail to win a two-thirds majority after several ballots, support will be transferred to someone else. Pope St. John XXIII once described how candidates bob up and down during votes "like peas in a pot of boiling water." A cardinal may keep climbing up until he is near the two-thirds majority but then fade, as people conclude he does not have the numbers and switch to someone else. He may later reemerge when other candidates similarly lose favor.[80]

Various laws are established to avoid unduly prolonging a conclave if no clear candidate emerges, and if no result emerges after three days (the usual length of modern conclaves), voting is suspended for a day of "prayer, reflection and dialogue."[81]

After each vote, the ballots are burned, and the smoke coming out of the chimney above the Sistine Chapel is black if the vote is inconclusive, white if a new successor of Peter has been elected.[82]

PAPAL QUALITIES

Most books and treatises that have been written about popes have focused on the nature and the extent of papal authority, what a pope can properly govern. Far fewer are about *how* a pope should govern and what sort of

---

[80] Edward Pentin, "Cardinals Prepare to Elect Next Pope with Clear Favorites in Mind," *Newsmax*, 11 March 2013, https://www.newsmax.com/newsfront/conclave-pope-cardinals-favorites/2013/03/11/id/494084/.

[81] *NN* 75.

[82] Frederic J. Baumgartner argues that the use of distinct colors of smoke is of recent origin: *Behind Locked Doors: A History of the Papal Elections* (New York: Palgrave Macmillan, 2005), 241-45.

qualities a cardinal should have to be worthy of the papacy. What sources we have are telling.

The bishop of Rome is the successor to St. Peter, not to Christ; he is the Vicar of Christ on earth, not a substitute for Him. Consequently, the figure of St. Peter in Sacred Scripture can teach us much about the qualities necessary for a virtuous pope. After His Resurrection, Jesus approached Peter, who had betrayed Him, and asked, "Do you love me?" He then commanded the apostle, "Tend my sheep, feed my sheep" (see Jn 21:15-17). These words manifest some of the fundamental virtues necessary in the heart of a future pope. A pope should be one whose love for Christ extends to all the members of Christ's Mystical Body, the "flock" of which Christ is the Good Shepherd. Unlike a politician whose focus is exclusively on this life, a pope's primary role is helping to shepherd millions of souls safely to the next. His charity, therefore, should be such that he can "tend" the flock through the kingly role of governance, and "feed" the sheep through the priestly role of sanctifying in the liturgy and through the prophetic role of teaching sound doctrine.[83] St. Peter offers a development of these themes, exhorting those ordained to the priesthood, "Tend the flock of God that is your charge, not by constraint but willingly, not for shameful gain but eagerly, not as domineering over those in your charge but being examples to the flock. And when the chief Shepherd is manifested you will obtain the unfading crown of glory" (1 Pet 5:2-4). In addition, the pope, as one who will be girded by another and carried to places he does not wish to go, must be humble and docile to the plans of divine providence (Jn 21:18). As successor to Peter, the "rock" upon whom the visible Church was founded (Mt 16:18), the Roman pontiff needs to be strong in character and in faith. As one who holds the "keys to the kingdom of heaven," who can "bind and loose" (Mt 16:19), the pope is to be one who judges justly, tempered

---

[83] All bishops should have these qualities, but the pope preeminently: "By divine institution, Bishops succeed the Apostles through the Holy Spirit who is given to them. They are constituted pastors in the Church, to be teachers of doctrine, and the priests of sacred worship and the ministers of governance" (CIC/83 can. 375).

with mercy, in light of the true good of souls and their eternal salvation. He is also to confirm the faithful in the Faith of the Church, handed down by tradition, and watch over respect for orthodoxy—duties that, in sum, amount to Peter's primary role: to maintain the unity of the Church.

All people on earth are called to be saints, but sanctity is apportioned differently according to different vocations. When his monastic disciple was elected as Pope Eugenius III (1145), St. Bernard of Clairvaux decided to continue his instruction with a treatise on how to be a saintly pope, titled *On Consideration*. The Cistercian monk's advice was to echo in the ears of popes throughout the centuries. Benedict XIV (1740-58) appraised the treatise so highly that he considered it to be the rule by which papal sanctity is measured, and in his treatise on the canonization of saints he summarized the "golden advice" of St. Bernard.[84] The chief points, which follow, give a clue as to what to look for in cardinals considered *papabile*.

1. The pope must not be wholly absorbed in activity but should remember that his principle work is to edify the Church, to pray, and to teach the people.
2. Above all other virtues, a pope must cultivate humility: "By the amount you are raised above others, even more should your humility be manifest."[85]
3. A pope's zeal should regard his personal sanctity, and not worldly honors.

---

[84] See Benedetto XIV (Prosper Lambertini), *De Servorum Dei Beatificatione et Beatorum Canonizatione* (La beatificazione dei Servi di Dio e la Canonizzazione dei Beati III/2) (Vatican: Libreria Editrice Vaticana, 2017), no. 3, pp. 51-55. In English: Benedict XIV, *On Heroic Virtue: A Portion of the Treatise of Benedict XIV on the Beatification and Canonization of the Servants of God*, vol. 2, (London: Thomas Richardson and Son, 1851), no. 3, pp. 97-100.

[85] Bernard, *In libris de consideratione*, lib. 2, c. 6, col. 246, no. 13. In English: *Saint Bernard: On Consideration*, trans. George Lewis (Oxford, UK: Clarendon Press, 1908). This was clearly stated in the phrase used during the former ceremony of papal enthronement: *Sic transit gloria mundi* (1409-1963).

4. A pope should have friends known for their goodness.
5. Because power structures more easily receive good men than make men good, the pope should strive to promote those who have proven virtue.
6. In dealing with the wicked, the pope should turn his face against them: "Let him dread the spirit of your anger who is not afraid of man.... Let him dread your prayers who has despised your admonition."[86]

Benedict XIV notes a seventh characteristic, underlined by the Council of Trent:

7. A pope should choose cardinals from the men most eminent in learning and virtue, ones who are good and well-qualified pastors.[87]

From St. Robert Bellarmine, himself a cardinal, this lesson results:

8. A pope should appoint good bishops, see that they fulfill their duties, and, if necessary, compel them.

Finally, from the ancient oath that popes would make upon assuming the office of the bishop of Rome, more may be learned:

9. Popes are to have zeal for the propagation of the Catholic Faith, for the encouragement and restoration of ecclesiastical discipline, and the defense of the rights of the Holy See.

Seeing the great virtue necessary for a man to be a good and holy pontiff, St. Robert Bellarmine lamented on April 25, 1605, before a conclave, that he could not think of a single candidate who was suited to become bishop of Rome. He wrote in a private letter:

We are about to enter into a conclave again, and we have need of much prayer, for I do not see a single person in the Sacred College

[86] Ibid., lib. 4, c. 4, col. 450.
[87] See Trent, Session 24, *in decreto Reform.*, c. 1.

[of Cardinals] that possesses the qualities [necessary]. And what is worse, no one is looking for such a person. It seems to me that for the Vicar of Christ, we are not looking for someone who knows the will of God, that is, who is well-versed in Sacred Scripture; instead [we are looking] only for one who knows the will of Justinian [the legislator] and other similar authors. We are looking for a good temporal prince, not a holy bishop who truly spends himself for the good of souls.[88]

In light of this dismal outlook, one might wonder what role the Holy Spirit plays in all of this. Certainly divine help is invoked before voting, but is each pope truly "God's choice"? Shortly after the publication of John Paul II's new rules regarding papal elections, this question was put to Cardinal Ratzinger. He replied:

I would not say so, in the sense that the Holy Spirit picks out the pope.... I would say that the Spirit does not exactly take control of the affair, but rather like a good educator, as it were, leaves us much space, much freedom, without entirely abandoning us. Thus the Spirit's role should be understood in a much more elastic sense, not that he dictates the candidate for whom one must vote. Probably the only assurance he offers is that the thing cannot be totally ruined.

With historical realism, he concluded: "There are too many contrary instances of popes the Holy Spirit obviously would not have picked!"[89]

One old saying about papal elections is that a "fat pope follows a thin one," meaning a newly elected pontiff will probably be the opposite in vision to his predecessor, or perhaps more liberal than the conservative pope he replaces, and vice versa. Another old saying about conclaves is that a

---

88   Quoted in Peter Godman, *The Saint as Censor: Robert Bellarmine between Inquisition and Index* (Leiden: Brill Academic, 2000), 190n139. My translation.

89   Quoted in John Allen, "A Quick Course in 'Conclave 101,'" *National Catholic Reporter*, 15 February 2013, https://www.ncronline.org/blogs/all-things-catholic/quick-course-conclave-101.

man walks into a conclave as pope but leaves as cardinal. In other words, expectations are often overturned. Even the fact that a pope appoints the large majority of cardinals does not guarantee that they will elect someone like him; sometimes to the contrary. Whoever may be chosen, and however much or little the cardinal-electors listen to God in their choice, the man becomes pope at the moment he verbally accepts their vote. Shortly thereafter, the senior cardinal-deacon announces to the world:

Annuntio vobis gaudium magnum;
    (I announce to you a great joy)

habemus Papam!
    (we have a Pope)

A NOTE ON THE TEXT

⊢————————————————————⊣

A FEW WORDS TO HELP THE READER TO NAVIGATE THIS TEXT.

First, it should be noted that the text is derived from the research of a number of scholars from all over the world. These professionals were independent, unaffiliated with any news group, ecclesiastical institution, social-change organization, or the "Red Hat Project" that has an alternative purpose.[90] This is, therefore, the fruit of collaboration with many who, out of great love for the Church, toiled to see this project to fruition. The entire project, which I joined in its latter stages, has taken a number of years to complete.

Second, a work that covers the biography and thinking of public figures whose writings and work span a variety of languages and many decades is an ambitious project that entails an enormous amount of research. Even with the best of efforts, a work such as this will necessarily be imperfect and incomplete. Nevertheless, we have worked to ensure that the most pertinent facts are included and that the assessments are well founded. Researchers' findings are documented and footnoted as much as possible.

Third, the organization of *The Next Pope* calls for some explanation. Because this book is not a simple collection of biographies, it does not follow a narrative form in which anecdote and witty aphorism are prominent. Likewise, because this book is much more than an encyclopedia

---

[90]   See Better Church Governance, https://betterchurchgovernance.org.

entry on each cardinal, it contains some details and assessments not to be found elsewhere. This book is meant, above all, to be a tool by which a future pope may be known in regard to what matters most—namely, in his work as an ordained bishop of the Catholic Church. The Second Vatican Council's Constitution *Lumen Gentium* reminds us: "Episcopal consecration, together with the office of sanctifying, also confers the office of teaching and of governing" (21). Christ Himself possessed and exercised these offices to the most perfect degree.

Consequently, each profile in this book begins with only a very brief biography of the main features of a cardinal's ecclesiastical life. It is then divided into three sections, which summarize the threefold office (*munus*) of a successor to the apostles: (1) priest, with its role of sanctifying; (2) king, with its role of governing; (3) prophet, with its role of teaching. The *sanctifying* office will focus on how a cardinal celebrates Holy Mass; what devotions and prayers he favors publicly; what means he takes to lead others to holiness. The *governing* office considers administrative roles of the cardinal; how he led a diocese, if he had one; what notable executive decisions he has made. The *teaching* office addresses the teachings of the cardinal, especially on controverted topics. Often the section on teaching is the longest, because it best reveals the true character and belief of the individual. You will be able to ascertain where each cardinal stands on crucial and topical areas such as the liturgy, the Church's moral teaching, right-to-life issues, priestly celibacy, migration, *Humanae Vitae*, and women deacons. At the end of each biography, I provide a summary that tries to encapsulate the cardinal's overall reputation in order to encourage the reader to consider carefully the details of his life.

The *papabili* are listed in alphabetical order.

THE
CARDINALS

Papal Electors, Potential Popes

ANGELO CARDINAL BAGNASCO

"Christ My Hope"

Born: 14 January 1943
Pontevico, Brescia, Italy
Nationality: Italian
Title: President, Council of the Bishops' Conferences
of Europe; Archbishop Emeritus of Genoa

BIOGRAPHY

Born during World War II and raised in Genoa, Italy, Angelo Bagnasco was attracted to the priesthood as a young altar boy; this experience later served him well in his extensive pastoral experience. His family was working-class and wanted him to become an accountant. Angelo, however, wanted to become a priest, and his parish priest helped his parents to accept his vocation. Cardinal Giuseppe Siri, himself once a candidate for the papacy, ordained Bagnasco a priest on June 29, 1966, less than a year after the close of the Second Vatican

Council. Rather than go down a bureaucratic route in the Church, Siri ensured that Bagnasco was with the people of the diocese, with a focus on ministering to youth. For over twenty years, Bagnasco served as an assistant parish priest in Genoa, ten years of which he also taught at a seminary. For many years, he worked with university students and secondary school students, including the Scouts, helping supply for their pastoral needs. Later, he continued similar work, directing the catechetical office for the Diocese of Genoa.

In 1998, he received episcopal consecration from Archbishop Dionigi Tettamanzi. Bagnasco gained intimate knowledge of Italy through his unique appointment as archbishop of the Military Ordinariate of Italy in 2003, a post which he held until being moved to Genoa as archbishop in 2006, and through his appointment by Benedict XVI as president of the Italian Episcopal Conference from 2007 to 2012. The widespread respect he enjoys among his fellow bishops was manifested in their electing him president of the Council of the Bishops' Conferences of Europe in 2016. Now over seventy-five years of age and known as a man of acute intelligence, high culture, profound compassion, and intense spirituality, Cardinal Bagnasco is a figure who retains national and international significance.[91]

SANCTIFYING OFFICE

Centrality of the Eucharist
"The Eucharist is the beating heart of the Church and of the People of God," Cardinal Bagnasco said as Pope Francis' special envoy to the Italian National Eucharistic Congress in 2016.

[91] Marco Ansaldo, "The Church after Bagnasco, Five Running Names," *La Repubblica*, 30 January 2020, https://genova.repubblica.it/cronaca/ 2020/01/30/news/la_chiesa_dopo_bagnasco_cinque_nomi_in_corsa- 247103434/?rss; Gianni Cardinale, "When the Pope Calls, One Answers," *30 Days* (February 2007), https://web.archive.org/web/20070519215654/ http://www.30giorni.it/us/articolo.asp?id=13527; "Bagnasco Card. Angelo," Vatican, http://press.vatican.va/content/salastampa/en/documentation/ cardinali_biografie/cardinali_bio_bagnasco_a.html.

His appearance was itself unusual, given that it was the first time since the Second Vatican Council that the pope did not himself attend a Eucharistic Congress held in Italy.[92] "Charity, missions, and works of mercy are born out of the Eucharist."[93] This teaching accords with that of the *Catechism of the Catholic Church* (CCC), that the Eucharist is "the source and summit of the Christian life" (1324).

In his homily at the conclusion of a January 2010 meeting of the permanent council of the Italian Bishops' Conference, Bagnasco spoke of the importance of the liturgy and devotion to the Eucharistic Jesus.[94] He noted that everything ultimately springs forth from and returns to the Eucharist. "The divine Eucharist, the heart of the life and mission of the Church, vivifies our speech and makes our pastoral concern fruitful; it introduces our humble persons into the liturgy of Heaven; it purifies and restores everything as a gesture of love."[95] Only by participating in the Word of God made flesh are our words able to echo the Divine Word. "Only in assiduousness in his school, as docile and loving disciples, will we be able to be, in turn, an echo of the supreme Teacher, a voice of the Word that saves," Bagnasco cautioned.[96]

Importance of Prayer

In a 2010 interview with *L'Osservatore Romano*, Cardinal Bagnasco said that prayer is a weapon against conforming to the dominant modern culture.[97] "Prayer is contact with God, and God is truth." "Certainly we need

---

[92]   Andrea Gagliarducci, "What is the 'Beating Heart' of the Church? The Eucharist," Catholic News Agency, 21 September 2016, https://www.catholicnewsagency.com/news/what-is-the-beating-heart-of-the-church-the-eucharist-90721.

[93]   Ibid.

[94]   "Cardinal's Homily at Italian Bishops' Meeting," Zenit, 29 January 2011, https://zenit.org/articles/cardinal-s-homily-at-italian-bishops-meeting/.

[95]   Ibid.

[96]   Ibid.

[97]   "Cardinal Bagnasco: God's Truth Is Weapon against Dominant Culture," Catholic News Agency, 21 August 2010, https://www.catholicnewsagency.

to dedicate time to prayer, each according to his own vocation, and draw close to those means that the liturgy and especially the Lord have put at our disposal: The Gospel, the book of Psalms and all of the other practices of piety." These are all ways that "help us to find the truth of God and of man."[98]

The Extraordinary Form

In a speech opening the Sixty-Third General Assembly of the Italian Bishops' Conference on May 23, 2011, Cardinal Bagnasco promised that the Italian bishops would correctly apply Pope Benedict XVI's *Summorum Pontificum* as well as the 2011 instruction on its implementation, *Universae Ecclesiae*. Bagnasco noted that the intent of those documents was a "harmonious recovery of the entire liturgical heritage of the universal Church in each diocese."[99]

Bagnasco has himself celebrated the Tridentine Mass and defended its continued celebration.[100] While he is supportive of those who wish to celebrate the Extraordinary Form of the Roman Rite, Bagnasco also has cautioned that harmony between individual local churches and the universal Church should not be disturbed over liturgical practices and disputes.[101]

---

com/news/cardinal-bagnasco-prayer-to-find-gods-truth-is-weapon-against-dominant-culture.

[98] Ibid.

[99] "Cardinal Angelo Bagnasco: Old Mass Is Treasure to Rediscover," *Kath.net*, 24 May 2011, http://www.kath.net/news/31567 (translated from German).

[100] "363 Cardinals and Bishops Who've Said the Latin Mass Since Summorum Pontificum," *A Catholic Life* (blog), 22 September 2014, https://acatholiclife.blogspot.com/2014/09/363-cardinals-and-bishops-whove-said.html; Filip Mazurczak, "Pope Francis, New Cardinals, and European Bishops' Leaders," *Catholic World Report*, 17 October 2016, https://www.catholicworldreport.com/2016/10/17/pope-francis-new-cardinals-and-european-bishops-leaders/.

[101] "Old Mass Is Treasure."

GOVERNING OFFICE

Cardinal Bagnasco has held many governing positions within the Italian Church over the course of his priestly ministry. After teaching courses on metaphysics and contemporary atheism at the Theological Faculty of Northern Italy for almost twenty years, in 1998 he was appointed a bishop for the Diocese of Pesaro, where he served until being appointed the military ordinary of Italy in 2003. Since 2006, he has served as archbishop of Genoa. In 2007, Bagnasco was elevated to the cardinalate by Pope Benedict XVI. Since then, he has served in the Curia as a member of the Congregations for the Oriental Churches and for Divine Worship and the Discipline of the Sacraments. Beginning in 2007, he served for ten years as president of the Italian Bishops' Conference, chosen by the pope (as all the country's conference presidents are), at that time Benedict XVI. Since 2016, Bagnasco has served as president of the Council of the Bishops' Conferences of Europe.[102]

Addressing Sexual Abuse

Bagnasco has spoken of the need to address sexual abuse within the Church without excuses or cover-ups.[103] He urged the Church not to fall back on the "tendency to dredge up excuses for the actions of certain clergy members," and that the Church need not fear the truth, "even when it is painful," and should not hide or cover up abuse.[104] "It is appropriate, then, that we all return to calling things by their names at all times, to identify evil in all of its gravity and in the multiplicity of its manifestations."[105] In 2010, the Italian bishops revealed that about one hundred cases of clergy sexual

---

[102] "Bagnasco Card. Angelo."

[103] "Holy Father Accepts No Excuses for Clerical Abuse, Affirms Cardinal," Catholic News Agency, 25 March 2010, https://www.catholicnewsagency.com/news/holy_father_accepts_no_excuses_for_clerical_abuse_affirms_cardinal.

[104] Ibid.

[105] Ibid.

abuse had been processed in Italian Church courts over the past decade.[106] Cardinal Bagnasco, then serving as president of the conference, said that the Church has never sought to underestimate the severity of the sex abuse crisis and that it would do everything it could always to merit the trust of the Catholic laity.[107] He affirmed that "a person who abuses minors needs to be concurrently brought to justice and receive treatment and mercy," but also that "healing cannot replace punishment, let alone remit the sin."[108] Responding to reporters' questions, Bagnasco acknowledged it is "possible that there have been cover-ups of sex abuse in Italy, too." But he added that if the Church ever verified the cover-up of a case of clerical sexual abuse, it would clearly condemn such concealment as being "something that is wrong and which must be corrected and overcome."[109]

Financial Transparency

The cardinal has also stressed the importance of transparency in Church finances. In 2011, he spoke at an Italian convention for diocesan finance workers and emphasized the "absolutely decisive importance of transparency" in society today.[110] "When we speak of transparency, it doesn't just mean highlighting honesty and correctness but a clear administration of assets that can be verified by all," the cardinal continued. The success of donations to the Church depends on the ability of the faithful to track what their charitable giving is being used for. The credibility of the Church

---

[106] Carol Glatz, "Italians Handled 100 Sex Abuse Cases in Past Decade," *National Catholic Reporter*, 26 May 2010, https://www.ncronline.org/news/accountability/italians-handled-100-sex-abuse-cases-past-decade.

[107] Ibid.

[108] Ibid.

[109] Carol Glatz, "Abuse Scandal Must Inspire Purification, Justice, Pope Tells Bishops," Catholic News Service, 28 May 2010, http://www.catholicnews.com/services/englishnews/2010/abuse-scandal-must-inspire-purification-justice-pope-tells-bishops-cns-1002232.cfm.

[110] "Transparency in Church Finances Gives the Faithful Satisfaction, Says Cardinal," Vatican Radio, 17 February 2011, http://www.archivioradiovaticana.va/storico/2011/02/17/transparency_in_church_finances_gives_the_faithful_satisfaction,_says/in2-463003.

is never damaged by the clarity of its behavior, the cardinal added, noting that if real transparency "exists in every parish, the faithful will no longer look at the offering as a type of duty, but donating will become a great joy because each will live with the satisfaction of doing something good and concrete" for the Church.[111]

Pope Benedict XVI appointed Bagnasco to the Congregation for Bishops, which is responsible for the cultivation of new bishops around the world. He was not reconfirmed to that role when Francis began his pontificate.[112] Pope Francis also removed Bagnasco from his post in the Congregation for Divine Worship and the Discipline of the Sacraments in 2016—at the same time the pope removed a number of other Benedict XVI–appointed members of the congregation who were generally favorable toward Cardinal Sarah (then prefect of the congregation) and his vision for liturgical reform.

TEACHING OFFICE

Defending the Church in the Public Square

Cardinal Bagnasco has been especially keen to address conflicts between modern culture and Church teaching, particularly in his role as head of the Italian Bishops' Conference and, more recently, as president of the European bishops' conference.

Throughout his ministry, Cardinal Bagnasco has firmly upheld the right of the Church to offer guidance to the public on matters of moral principle that might affect judgments about public policy, generally not shying away from taking public stances on political issues implicating matters of moral principle. He has argued that those who exercise public authority have a duty to uphold certain nonnegotiable values, and private

[111] Ibid.
[112] "Shuffle of Bishops, Non-Renewal of Burke and Rigali, Raise Eyebrows," *Inside the Vatican*, 1 January 2014, https://insidethevatican.com/news/lead-story/shuffle-bishops-non-renewal-burke-rigali-raise-eyebrows/.

citizens should take those values into account when voting in elections and weighing public policies. In a 2011 homily, for example, Bagnasco emphasized that the "moral issue in politics, as in all other realms of public and private life, is grave and urgent, and does not refer only to persons but also to structures and legislation."[113] Those who have "particular responsibilities in public life, in any way and at any level ... have an imperative need [for conversion to and fidelity to moral values]—more than others—knowing that, through their actions, they propose cultural models that are destined to become dominant."[114] The whole of society needs to become a place "where values are breathed."[115]

In 2008, while presenting an inaugural address at the meeting of the Italian Bishops' Conference permanent council meeting, Bagnasco challenged the notion that elections are not "a field that is relevant to the Church as such."[116] He echoed Benedict XVI's admonition while speaking at a previous meeting of bishops in Verona that "the risk of political and legislative choices that contradict the fundamental values and anthropological principles and ethical roots at the nature of human beings" should be countered with determination.[117] All citizens are called to make decisions in light of "fundamental values ... that have always constituted the very being of the human person," including "the protection of human life, in every stage, from conception to natural death" and "the promotion of the family founded on marriage, without introducing other forms of unions into public law that would contribute to destabilizing marriage, confusing its special characteristics and its irreplaceable social role."[118]

---

[113] "Ethics in Politics Is Urgent," *Secular Franciscan*, 29 August 2011.

[114] Ibid.

[115] Ibid.

[116] "Non-Negotiables Should Be Voting Criteria, Says Prelate," Zenit, 13 March 2008, https://zenit.org/articles/non-negotiables-should-be-voting-criteria-says-prelate/.

[117] Ibid.

[118] Ibid.

In affirming universal values that "can often be discovered by reason," the Church greatly values the good of reason and defends it "from both rationalistic tendencies, that try to restrict its horizons, and from the presumption of certain fideism that easily avoids the hard work of thinking."[119] Bagnasco emphasized the Second Vatican Council's teaching in *Gaudium et Spes* and recalled the Council's teaching on what Bagnasco called "non-negotiable risks" that undermine the good of the person — including everything that is opposed to life itself, "such as every type of homicide, genocide, abortion, euthanasia, even voluntary suicide."[120]

Bagnasco has urged Catholics to be more active in the public square, telling *L'Osservatore Romano* in 2008 that "Catholics must bring the contribution of spiritual and ethical values into the public square."[121] In doing so, Bagnasco explained, Catholics do not impose a religious vision of society, but rather propose universal truths. "The presence (in the public square) must be assumed by Catholics with greater persuasiveness and a greater capacity to respectfully explain our convictions, knowing that they come both from the Gospel and from a common understanding of the value of life."[122]

Upon being appointed by Pope Benedict XVI as president of the Italian Bishops' Conference in 2007, Cardinal Bagnasco said in an interview with *Il Messaggero* that the Church is not motivated, in its ministry in the public square, by self-interest or hegemony — rather, Catholics speak "about the value of the human person, and in this field, the Church has much to say."[123] Furthermore, in an interview with *Il Giornale*, Bagnasco

---

[119]   Ibid.

[120]   Ibid.

[121]   Elise Harris, "How Europe's Bishops Plan to Guide the Church through Murky Waters," Catholic News Agency, 13 October 2016, https://www.catholicnewsagency.com/news/how-europes-bishops-plan-to-guide-the-church-through-murky-waters-39942.

[122]   Ibid.

[123]   "Italy: Archbishop Angelo Bagnasco Succeeds Cardinal Ruini," FSSPX News, 13 May 2020, https://fsspx.news/en/news-events/news/italy-archbishop-angelo-bagnasco-succeeds-cardinal-ruini-21569.

explained the relationship between church and state: "Secularity is the autonomy of the civil and political domain in relation to the religious domain, but not in relation to the moral domain."[124]

Defending the Faith in the Public Square

Bagnasco sees Christian morality and gospel values (including those truths contained in the natural law) as universal, common values and essential foundations of the political order. He holds that it is a Christian duty to leaven the public square with Christian values. As a professor who taught about modern atheism, Bagnasco is attentive to the ways in which modern culture poses problems for people of faith. He has said that "no one is exempt" from the influences of the world that push for conformity to the dominant culture.[125] Bagnasco noted, in a 2010 interview with *L'Osservatore Romano*, that Pope Benedict XVI himself "calls the faithful back to a greater awareness" of the fact that the Church lives amid a dictatorship of relativism, and that "no one is exempt from this climate of possible contamination that could impoverish the faith."[126] Catholics need to be vigilant and should be "in the world" but not "of the world," meaning that Catholics must resist the dominant cultural currents while nevertheless being "exposed to all of the pressures and tensions and prodding that we know."[127] Living in the world but living by faith in a God who loves us, the cardinal continued, is the way Catholics should witness in the public square. "We need to truly believe that God loves us: (a truth) which holds the power to change our life."[128] When Catholics foster this interior conversion of heart and live their faith with conviction in the public square, Christian morality can better be upheld.

Cardinal Bagnasco has not shied away from espousing the Faith in the public square. After becoming president of the Italian Bishops' Conference

---

124 Ibid.
125 "God's Truth Is Weapon."
126 Ibid.
127 Ibid.
128 Ibid.

in 2007, Bagnasco led a campaign against an Italian government proposal legally to recognize homosexual civil unions.[129] Then-Archbishop Bagnasco was assigned police bodyguards after threatening graffiti appeared on his cathedral and other buildings. Later, activists mailed a bullet to the archdiocesan office accompanied by a picture of Bagnasco with a Nazi swastika scratched into the image.[130] These threats did not deter him from speaking truth in the public square.

In 2016, in his address opening that year's general assembly of the Italian bishops, Bagnasco publicly resisted continued legislative efforts to recognize same-sex civil unions; he stressed that the law passed by the Italian Parliament "certifies an equivalence" between civil unions and marriage.[131] While the law affirmed that civil unions and marriages are distinct things, Cardinal Bagnasco argued that those differences "are only tricks of terminology or juridical artifacts, which can be easily bypassed."[132] Bagnasco saw the civil union law as an intermediate step "on the path to the final strike, which will eventually include the approval of surrogate motherhood, a practice that exploits women, taking advantage of their poverty," to supply children for same-sex couples.[133]

In his address, Bagnasco quoted at length from Pope Francis' statements on the nature of marriage and the family. He quoted the pope's joint declaration with Russian Orthodox Patriarch Kirill of Moscow, wherein the bishops said "the family is based on marriage, an act of freely given and faithful love between a man and a woman.... We regret that other forms of

---

[129] Gudrun Schultz, "Threats Escalate with Bullet Mailed to Italian Cardinal Opposing Same-Sex Civil Unions," LifeSite News, 30 April 2007, https://www.lifesitenews.com/news/threats-escalate-with-bullet-mailed-to-italian-cardinal-opposing-same-sex-c.

[130] Ibid.

[131] Harris, "Murky Waters."

[132] Andrea Gagliarducci, "Top Italian Cardinal Throws Punch at New Civil Unions Law," Catholic News Agency, 18 May 2016, https://www.catholicnewsagency.com/news/top-italian-bishop-throws-punch-at-new-civil-unions-law-39976.

[133] Ibid.

cohabitation have been placed on the same level as this union, while the concept, consecrated in the biblical tradition, of paternity and maternity as the distinct vocation of man and woman in marriage is being banished from the public conscience."[134] Bagnasco further quoted Pope Francis' remarks from a November 17, 2014, colloquium that "children have a right to grow up in a family with a father and a mother capable of creating a suitable environment for the child's growth and emotional development."[135]

In closing, Cardinal Bagnasco expressed his frustration: "It cannot be understood why these clear statements from Pope Francis, which the bishops often reiterate, are kept under silence, as if the pope had never said or written them."[136] The Italian bishops intended to "underscore the pope's statements, so that they can turn into effective commitment."[137]

Canceled Prayer Reparation for "Gay Pride"

Despite his clear positions, Bagnasco surprised many in 2019 when he canceled three separate public prayers of reparation for a "gay pride" parade scheduled to take place in Genoa and gave no explanation for his decision.[138]

Importance of the Family

The foundational importance of the family is a theme that Cardinal Bagnasco sounds frequently. In a 2010 homily, while celebrating the solemnity of the Madonna della Guardia at the shrine in Liguria at the top of Mount Figogna, Bagnasco reflected on the family as the "womb of life."[139]

---

[134] Ibid.

[135] Ibid.

[136] Ibid.

[137] Ibid.

[138] Edward Pentin, "Cardinal Bagnasco Cancels Prayers of Reparation for 'Gay Pride' Parade," *National Catholic Register*, 19 June 2019, http://www.ncregister.com/blog/edward-pentin/italian-cardinal-cancels-prayers-of-reparation-for-gay-pride-parade.

[139] "Cardinal Angelo Bagnasco: A Culture without Children and the Elderly Is Warped," Catholic Online, 31 October 2010, https://www.catholic.org/news/international/europe/story.php?id=38045.

He spoke of the troubling trends reflected by Italy's negative birthrate and warned that "demographic balance is not only necessary for the physical survival of a community—which without children has no future—but is also a condition for that alliance between generations that is essential for a normal democratic dialectic."[140] Negative birthrates reflect a serious cultural catastrophe, the cardinal said, and foster educational poverty—because the presence of young people causes all of us, not just parents, to come out of ourselves and engage in important discussions. "A society without babies and children, just as a society without the elderly, is seriously mutilated and unable to function."[141]

The Holy Family is the model for family life. When we ponder the Holy Family or gaze upon the sacred image of Our Lady with the Child, Bagnasco said, we can envision what life in Nazareth was like: "They lived in absolute simplicity, in the joyful toil of daily work, at home and in the carpenter's shop; they lived the life of the village, relationships with their next door neighbors, participation in worship, the presence of God." The Holy Family teaches us "of a profound and positive adherence to life as a gift that is given and which is not our absolute property."[142] The cardinal contrasted that image of family life with the dynamic of family life today. Bagnasco explained that modern couples and families collapse before "the blows of life and of relationships." He continued: "The efforts of every day seem tedious and without meaning, hence unbearable. The future loses value and polish, the present is emphasized for what it promises of immediate satisfaction."[143]

A society that prizes immediate satisfaction is bound to see effects such as negative birthrates, Bagnasco said. A culture that worships immediate gratification will also fail to see the value of fidelity in relationships and family life, the cardinal explained. In this context, "fidelity is

---

[140] Ibid.
[141] Ibid.
[142] Ibid.
[143] Ibid.

understood as something repetitive, tedious, deprived of thrills."[144] But in truth, fidelity allows love to grow and become something much more substantial than an initial feeling of effervescence. "In this growth, the daily repetition of so many little and great duties, of so many actions that seem grey, is like the tranquil and continuous rain that bathes the earth and fertilizes it. It is not the storm of great passions and impetuous transports that make one grow or that measure the substance of love, but daily and humble fidelity is the sign of love."[145]

As families grow in fidelity and love, they serve as the most fundamental "school of humanity and faith."[146] It is within the context of family life that one first learns to love by being loved, to trust in oneself and others, to discover beauty in different stages in life, to see the value of acceptance, humility, reliability, and the power of forgiveness given and received. The family teaches the Faith through daily prayer together, "participation in Sunday Mass, liturgical festivities with their traditions, pilgrimages to shrines, sacred images in the homes." Ultimately, healthy family life gives us reasons to trust in the future, because we know it is impossible for "a mother [to] turn away from the gaze of her children."[147]

Blessed Virgin Mary

Mary is the model mother. In his homily in Fatima celebrating the hundredth anniversary of Our Mother's June apparitions, Bagnasco praised Mary for keeping the Faith intact and explained that "the Blessed Virgin Mary, with the persistent patience of a Mother, always returns to preserve our faith and brings us back to the light of Jesus."[148] When preaching a homily on the occasion of the 126th anniversary of the birth of St. Padre

---

[144] Ibid.

[145] Ibid.

[146] Ibid.

[147] Ibid.

[148] Angelo Cardinal Bagnasco, "Cardinal Bagnasco at Fatima for Vigil of June Apparition: The Message of Fatima 'Illuminates the Faith,'" Fidem in Terra — Faith on Earth, 20 June 2017, http://fideminterra.blogspot.com/2017/07/cardinal-bagnasco-at-fatima-for-vigil.html.

Pio, Cardinal Bagnasco praised the saint's devotion to the Blessed Mother.[149] He called our love for the Virgin "not just a devotion, it is a program of life, it is a program of holiness."[150] Man's heart, Bagnasco said, always remains in need of maternal tenderness—a person whom he can resort to and confide in, who can comfort him, and who can help him to regain trust and courage.[151] There is no better person man can turn to than "the Mother of God and ours," the cardinal said. "The Holy Virgin is the anchor in the storm, the port in fatigue, the star that orients, the gaze that includes, the hand that raises and accompanies. In whatever situation we find ourselves, we must not be discouraged or fearful: let us look at Mary."[152]

Conscientious Objection

In 2009, Bagnasco implored Italian doctors to exercise their right to conscientious objection after Italian health-care officials approved the sale of the emergency abortion drug RU-486, calling for "an end to corruption and injustice."[153] The cardinal lamented that where there is no respect for human life "from conception in its fragility and later during its course, society is less human. That the right of the strongest thus prevails is bitter."[154] At the root of a society that does not value human life, Bagnasco noted, "is an individualistic culture, hidden under respect for the freedom of women," who "in reality experience a tragedy, live in suffering and worry; when a truly human culture ought to take care of them."[155]

---

[149] Angelo Card. Bagnasco, "The Preparation of a Saint," Archdiocese of Genoa, 25 May 2013, http://www.chiesadigenova.it/pls/genova/v3_s2ew_consultazione.mostra_paginawap?id_pagina=362612&attiva_menu=0&nohtml=0 (translated from Italian).

[150] Ibid.

[151] Ibid.

[152] Ibid.

[153] Harris, "Murky Waters."

[154] "Cardinal Bagnasco Encourages Conscientious Objection to RU-486," Catholic News Agency, 4 August 2009, https://www.catholicnewsagency.com/news/cardinal_bagnasco_encourages_conscientious_objection_to_ru486.

[155] Ibid.

Humanae Vitae

In a speech at a conference marking the fiftieth anniversary of Pope Paul VI's Encyclical *Humanae Vitae* reaffirming the Church's constant teaching that contraception is always immoral, Cardinal Bagnasco remarked on the clarity of the pope's message.[156] Bagnasco noted that the pope correctly explained the "inseparable relationship between the unitive and the procreative ends" of marriage.[157] Marital love is to be a "total, faithful, indissoluble gift that gives life: it is fruitful. To break this plot, to disfigure love ... means to reduce people—oneself and the other—to an instrument of pleasure."[158] Bagnasco reaffirmed the encyclical's teaching that artificial contraception is to be always excluded and that natural means of regulating procreation using the woman's fertility cycle, such as natural family planning, can be employed licitly.[159]

Amoris Laetitia

Cardinal Bagnasco has firmly opposed the "Kasper Proposal" to allow access to Communion for the divorced and "remarried" on a case-by-case basis. Indeed, Bagnasco opposed such ideas long before the controversy came to head with the publication of *Amoris Laetitia* and the 2014 Synod of Bishops on the Family. In 2008, Bagnasco said it was impossible for divorced-and-"remarried" Catholics to receive the Eucharist, a fact that "does not depend on an external disposition but rather comes from the interior of the sacrament of the Eucharist itself, the sacrament of the perennial unity between the love of Christ and humanity."[160] He said some Catholics who are separated from their spouses suffer from the difficulty of the situation,

---

[156] Card. Angelo Bagnasco, "Fiftieth Anniversary of the Encyclical *Humanae Vitae*," Archdiocese of Genoa, 13 October 2018.

[157] Ibid.

[158] Ibid.

[159] Ibid.

[160] "Cardinal Bagnasco: Impossible for Divorced and Remarried to Receive Communion," Catholic News Agency, 24 June 2008, https://www.catholic-newsagency.com/news/cardinal_bagnasco_impossible_for_divorced_and_remarried_to_receive_communion.

yet "nonetheless live in fidelity to the indissolubility of the sacrament [of marriage] and desire to meet and pray together, to exchange experiences and encourage one another."[161] The "maternity of the Church" can be expressed in other ways than by admitting those who are living in ways that violate the indissolubility of marriage to the sacrament of Holy Communion.[162] However, the cardinal chose to keep silent over the *dubia*—five questions that four cardinals put to Pope Francis in late 2016 that aimed to clear up ambiguities many saw in the text of *Amoris Laetitia*, especially over the issue of Holy Communion for civilly "remarried" divorcees.

On Euthanasia

Cardinal Bagnasco has spoken out against euthanasia and assisted suicide. These practices are the result, he says, of "a world order without God."[163] He explained, "Only without God do we reach this point [where the terminally ill are euthanized], as we have no more criteria for love and for living together, for loving others. Without God, we do not follow the rationale of love, but we rather follow the different rationale of effectiveness and of wellbeing at all costs."[164]

Persecuted Christians

The persecution of Christians around the world is also the result of "a world order without God."[165] "Even today," Bagnasco said in 2016, "Christians experience martyrdom," not only in the classical sense, but also in new forms, "refined, but not less cruel; legalized, but not less unjust," such as the legal practice of killing Christians in countries such as Pakistan, where blasphemy laws allow such injustices.[166] This "world order without God" is partially a result of Europe's forgetting its own past, such that it now

---

[161] Ibid.
[162] Ibid.
[163] Harris, "Murky Waters."
[164] Gagliarducci, "What Is the 'Beating Heart' of the Church?"
[165] Harris, "Murky Waters."
[166] Ibid.

considers Christianity divisive, and of a world which "in the name of values like equality, tolerance and rights" effectively marginalizes Christianity.[167]

Europe's Christian Roots

As president of the Council of the Bishops' Conferences of Europe, Bagnasco has had a unique platform to address what he views as the deep problems facing the continent. Europe has forgotten its roots, which were formed by three cities: Jerusalem, Athens, and Rome.[168] Europe's roots are Christian.[169] The "world order without God" that is wreaking havoc on human lives, Bagnasco argues, gained steam from the cultural revolution of 1968, which included the sexual revolution.[170] The dismantling of Western culture wrought by this revolution "made the human being ever more individualistic and less related with others; hence, always more alone. . . . This is how people are made weak. And a society of weak people is a weak society."[171] Bagnasco argues that Europe is a weak society and that it has marginalized Christianity out of fear, forgetful of the fact that the light of the gospel created European civilization and its humanism. "The crisis of the world is above all a spiritual crisis," Bagnasco explains, and the solution to the crisis, therefore, lies in a return to faith and a new embrace of the Christian gospel.[172]

[167] Ibid.
[168] Andrea Gagliarducci, "Cardinal Bagnasco: 'The Church, Bulwark against the World Order without God,'" Catholic News Agency, 10 April 2017, https://www.acistampa.com/story/cardinale-bagnasco-la-chiesa-baluardo-contro-lordine-mondiale-senza-dio-5787 (translated from Italian).
[169] Ibid.
[170] Andrea Gagliarducci, "European Church Launches Re-evangelization Mission," Monday Vatican, 9 October 2017, http://www.mondayvatican.com/vatican/european-church-launches-re-evangelization-mission.
[171] Ibid.
[172] Andrea Gagliarducci, "Bagnasco's Complaint: 'We Want a World Order without God,'" Catholic News Agency, 10 August 2016, https://www.aci-stampa.com/story/la-denuncia-di-bagnasco-si-vuole-un-ordine-mondiale-senza-dio-3966 (translated from Italian).

Priestly Celibacy

Bagnasco would not welcome a departure from the discipline of celibacy for Latin-Rite Catholic priests. The Italian Bishops' Conference in 2010 voted against allowing Romanian Catholic priests, who are permitted to marry, to exercise their ministry in Italy.[173] In a September 13, 2010, letter from Bagnasco to Lucian Muresan, Major Archbishop of the Romanian Catholic Church, explaining the Italian Bishops' Conference decision not to allow the presence of married Romanian Catholic priests in Italy, the cardinal said that the conference had determined that "at present and in general, there is not 'just and reasonable cause' to justify the granting of the dispensation" allowing those priests to exercise their ministry in Italy.[174] Cardinal Bagnasco cited the importance of "protecting ecclesiastical celibacy" and the need to "prevent confusion among the faithful" in explaining to Muresan the decision to exclude married Romanian Catholic priests from ministry in Italy.[175]

Male Priesthood

Bagnasco upholds the Church's teaching that only men can receive Holy Orders. In 2014, the Church of England voted to allow female bishops, creating insurmountable difficulties in ecumenical efforts to bring that ecclesial community closer to the Roman Catholic Church. When asked about the Anglican development, Cardinal Bagnasco responded that the Catholic Church's view on female priests was clear and that "everyone knows what [the Church] thinks."[176] Cardinal Bagnasco's traditional views on all-male priesthood and the importance of celibacy for Latin-Rite priests strongly

---

[173] "Italian Catholic Episcopal Conference Vetoes Married Priests," *Orthocath* (blog), 2 March 2011, https://orthocath.wordpress.com/2011/03/02/italian-catholic-episcopal-conference-vetoes-married-priests/.

[174] Ibid.

[175] Ibid.

[176] Josephine McKenna, "Vatican Editor Says England's Female Bishops Vote 'Complicates' Relations," *U.S. Catholic*, 15 July 2014, https://www.uscatholic.org/news/201407/vatican-editor-says-england%E2%80%99s-female-bishops-vote-%E2%80%98complicates%E2%80%99-relations-29135.

suggest that he opposes the possibility of ordaining women deacons. No statement of Bagnasco's views on whether homosexuals are to be admitted to the priesthood has been found.

Relations with Judaism

Cardinal Bagnasco does not see the evangelization of Jews as appropriate. In September 2009, Bagnasco met with two Italian rabbis to extend his greetings to all Italian Jews and wish them a happy Jewish new year.[177] In a statement from the Italian Bishops' Conference following the meeting, the bishops (with Bagnasco then their head) noted, "There has been no change in the attitude of the Catholic Church towards the Jewish people, especially since the Second Vatican Council. Thus, the Italian Bishops' Conference reiterates that it is not the Catholic Church's intention to work actively for the conversion of the Jews."[178]

Evangelization

This special relationship between the Catholic Church and the Jewish people is not the standard approach of Catholics to evangelization.

Speaking to reporters in Poland during the 2018 Plenary Assembly of the Council of the Bishops' Conferences of Europe, Bagnasco was asked about the importance of Europe's retaining its Christian roots and transmitting the Faith to its young people in the midst of secularization.[179] The cardinal emphasized the urgent need to evangelize not only non-Catholics

177 "Cardinal Bagnasco Meets with the President of the Italian Rabbinical Assembly and Chief Rabbi of the Jewish Community of Rome; Resumes Common Celebration of the Day for Hebrew-Christian Reflection on January 17," Agenzia Fides, 23 September 2009, http://www.fides.org/en/news/25022-EU-ROPE_ITALY_Cardinal_Bagnasco_meets_with_the_President_of_the_Italian_Rabbinical_Assembly_and_Chief_Rabbi_of_the_Jewish_Community_of_Rome_resumes_common_celebration_of_the_Day_for_Hebrew_Christian_reflection_on_January_17.

178 Ibid.

179 Deborah Castellano Lubov, "Feature: Cardinal Bagnasco to Zenit: 'If Church Didn't Proclaim Gospel Today in Every Way Possible, She Wouldn't Be Faithful to Gospel of the Young,'" Zenit, 18 September

but Catholics, and especially young people, as well. "If the Church did not announce the Gospel today in every possible way, she would not be faithful to the Gospel and would not be faithful to the young," he said.[180] While our culture "impels us to be individualists, separated from each other, as individuals, as groups and as states, despite all this, and in fact, precisely because of all this, there is an ever greater need to proclaim the hope that is Jesus, who has made us a new people."[181] Individualistic and liberal culture dissolves relationships, and the result is "not a greater happiness, it is not a more supportive society, but it is a more divided society, anguish, bewilderment."[182] All people desire relationship, desire community—this is the "profound desire of the heart of every person, to whom the Church must respond."[183] In evangelizing and in announcing Christ's good news, the cardinal stressed, "we must recover the relational dimension and therefore the community dimension, that individualistic and liberal culture attack and want to dissolve."[184] This evangelization is the duty not only of clergy but of laity also.[185]

The work of evangelization is rooted in Sacred Scripture as its source. Cardinal Bagnasco has preached on the gratuitous nature of God's revelation of Himself to man. In his pastoral letter to the Archdiocese of Genoa for 2007, Bagnasco cited *Dei Verbum* in explaining that the first part of the Mass nourishes us with Word of God because "God out of the abundance of His love speaks to men as friends and lives among them, so that He may invite and take them into fellowship with Himself."[186] The Word of Scripture, he continued, narrates the works of God and contains

---

2018, https://zenit.org/articles/feature-cardinal-bagnasco-of-genoa-after-morandi-bridge-collapse-says-we-must-not-give-into-discouragement/.

[180] Ibid.

[181] Ibid.

[182] Ibid.

[183] Ibid.

[184] Ibid.

[185] Ibid.

[186] Angelo Cardinal Bagnasco, "'This Is My Body': Pastoral Letter 2007-2008," Archdiocese of Genoa, 1 October 2007, http://www.chiesadigenova.

"a unique efficacy that no human word, though high, possesses."[187] The cardinal has also hosted a seminar for diocesan clergy on the Second Vatican Council's Dogmatic Constitution *Dei Verbum* and its reception in the Apostolic Exhortation *Verbum Domini*.[188]

The importance of evangelization is tied to the Church's desire that as many as possible might be saved and enjoy beatific life with the Holy Trinity in God's Kingdom. Cardinal Bagnasco noted in a 2012 homily celebrating All Souls' Day that "faith saves us from the perspective that death coincides with our annihilation, a prospect that would make our actions vain because, if we live only to end up in nothingness, we live only for the present moment."[189] Bagnasco explained that we all must come to feel the need for salvation and to believe, as we say we do in the Apostles' Creed, in the resurrection of the flesh and eternal life.[190]

Rejection of Universalism

Bagnasco evidently rejects universalism. He has said that, when a person dies, his immortal soul presents itself before the Most High to give an account of his life, "hoping to hear the words of Christ: 'Come, good and faithful servant.'"[191] We all hope for salvation, the cardinal said, but we must take good care of our spirit to make us fit to enjoy the Kingdom.[192]

---

it/pls/genova/v3_s2ew_consultazione.mostra_paginawap?id_pagina=362608&attiva_menu=0&nohtml=0 (translated from Italian).

[187] Ibid.

[188] "Refresher Meeting for the Clergy," Archdiocese of Genoa, 6 March 2014, http://www.chiesadigenova.it/pls/genova/v3_s2ew_consultazione.mostra_pagina?id_pagina=363588 (translated from Italian).

[189] Angelo Card. Bagnasco, "I Believe in the Resurrection of the Flesh and Eternal Life," Archdiocese of Genoa, 2 November 2013, http://www.chiesa-digenova.it/pls/genova/v3_s2ew_consultazione.mostra_paginawap?id_pagina=362640&attiva_menu=0&nohtml=0 (translated from Italian).

[190] Ibid.

[191] Ibid.

[192] Ibid.

He has also warned in homilies of God's "severe" judgment of those who persist in sin.[193]

Islam

When French priest Fr. Jacques Hamel was stabbed to death in his church by an Islamist terrorist in 2016, Italy's Islamic Religious Community sent delegates to attend Catholic Masses throughout Italy to show solidarity. The community explained in a statement, "We feel it is essential at this time with this greeting from the Muslims of Italy to give a concrete signal of profound respect for the sacredness of the rites, the ministers and the places of worship of the Christian faith."[194] The presence of Muslims at Catholic Masses caused some controversy, with criticism coming from both Muslim and Catholic quarters.[195] Cardinal Bagnasco was "baffled" by these criticisms, explaining that he did not understand them.[196] "The presence [of Muslims at Mass] aimed to be a condemnation, a clear, absolute signal of distance by all those who do not accept any form of violence for any reasons, never mind religious," Bagnasco explained.[197] He stated that he was pleased by the show of solidarity from Muslims in Italy and that after Fr. Hamel had been murdered, the Italian bishops asked for help from the Islamic community "because we believe that the best reaction is that of a united condemnation [of terrorism] without hesitation."[198]

---

[193] Angelo Card. Bagnsaco, "The Easter Joy," Archdiocese of Genoa, 19 April 2014, http://www.chiesadigenova.it/pls/genova/v3_s2ew_consultazione. mostra_paginawap?id_pagina=363788&attiva_menu=0&nohtml=0 (referring specifically to those who lead children into sin) (translated from Italian).

[194] Alberto Carosa, "Controversy in Italy over Muslim Participation in Masses Said for Murdered French Priest," *Catholic World Report*, 9 August 2016, https://www.catholicworldreport.com/2016/08/09/controversy-in-italy-over-muslim-participation-in-masses-said-for-murdered-french-priest/.

[195] Ibid.

[196] Ibid.

[197] Ibid.

[198] Ibid.

Islam and Persecution

As mentioned above, Bagnasco has forcefully decried the persecution of Christians around the world by Muslims. In 2015, Bagnasco noted that the "cull of Christians continues" in the Middle East and Africa, where it "seems somebody has decided to uproot them to cleanse the territory."[199] He asked, "Why, we ask the western world, why not raise one's voice over so much ferocity and injustice?"[200] The cardinal's question was presumably aimed at those Catholics who fear that condemning extreme, militant Islamists might undercut positive achievements that have been attained in Catholic-Muslim dialogue.

After a terrorist attack in Paris in November 2015 left more than 130 people dead, Bagnasco called on the Muslim world to "loudly disassociate itself" from ISIS.[201] He added, "I am sure that not the whole Muslim world approves of these acts of brutality, but dissenters seem to lack the strength to explicitly condemn them and distance themselves from them."[202] Bagnasco argues that "the Islamic world is very pluralistic," and that they "have no single authority."[203] The cardinal has condemned Islamic fundamentalism and challenged Muslims around the world to demonstrate the compatibility of their religion with Christian civilization by forcefully condemning acts of terror such as those carried out

---

[199] "West Silent on 'Cull' of Christians—Italian Bishops' Head," *ANSA*, 30 September 2015, http://www.ansa.it/english/news/2015/09/30/west-silent-on-cull-of-christians-italian-bishops-head_836ceb82-9893-4b74-93d5-e28eee53c7d7.html.

[200] Ibid.

[201] Romeo Hontiveros, "Italian Cardinal Angelo Bagnasco Calls on Muslims to Publicly Condemn ISIS," PagadianDiocese.org, 16 November 2015, http://www.pagadiandiocese.org/2015/11/16/italian-cardinal-angelo-bagnasco-calls-on-muslims-to-publicly-condemn-isis/.

[202] Ibid.

[203] Alessandro Cassinis, "Bagnsaco : 'There Is No Religious War. From Islam I Would Like a Strong Condemnation,'" *Il Secolo XIX*, 15 November 2015, http://www.ilsecoloxix.it/p/italia/2015/11/15/ASEczAR-bagnasco_condanna_religione.shtml (translated from Italian).

by ISIS. Bagnasco was one of the Church's most committed defenders of Pope Benedict's 2006 Regensburg address, which raised the issue of Islam and violence.[204]

IMMIGRATION AND CATHOLIC SOCIAL THOUGHT

Cardinal Bagnasco has taken a balanced public stance on immigration, one that accords with the teachings of the *Catechism* and of the Church's Magisterium.

In a 2018 interview with *La Stampa,* Bagnasco spoke about current immigration policies in Italy.[205] He noted that immigration is an "epochal phenomenon that does not seem bound to end rapidly, if it ends" and recalled important criteria "which are not only Christian, but humanitarian," regarding the welcoming of immigrants.[206] One such criterion is solidarity. He noted that while immigration policies should be governed at a general level by these criteria, tackling the phenomenon in practice requires "prudence, balance and wisdom."[207] In 2016, Bagnasco said that the ongoing movement from the poor global south to the rich global north is "irreversible," but also that the differing realities of each country in Europe make a uniform response of the Church in Europe (and of political actors in Europe) to the refugee crisis impossible.[208] Building on the

[204] Sandro Magister, "The Bishops of Italy Have a New Leader: Angelo Bagnasco," chiesa.espressonline.it, 8 March 2007, http://chiesa.espresso. repubblica.it/articolo/125361%26eng%3Dy.html.

[205] Bruno Viani, "Bagnasco: Enough with Electoral Slogans, Welcoming Is a Value, We Need Prudence and Wisdom," *La Stampa,* 4 June 2018, https://www.lastampa.it/vatican-insider/en/2018/06/04/news/bagnasco-enough-with-electoral-slogans-welcoming-is-a-value-we-need-prudence-and-wisdom-1.34022100.

[206] Ibid.

[207] Ibid.

[208] Inés San Martín, "Europe's Bishops Call Unified Line on Refugee Crisis 'Impossible,'" *Crux,* 3 May 2016, https://cruxnow.com/church/2016/05/03/

comments of Cardinal Erdő (with whom he was addressing the media), Bagnasco said that one cannot make quick judgments about an individual country's decision to build a fence or wall to regulate immigration, for example.[209] The Church's mission, Bagnasco explained, "is to announce the Gospel and its values, certainly not to give political or operational indications."[210] The Church is not a geopolitical expert, he said, and its pastors are tasked first and foremost with proclaiming the gospel of Jesus Christ, not delivering public-policy solutions.

The cardinal noted a difference between the "welcoming stage" during an emergency, when refugees need a roof over their heads and food and clothing provided, and the stage of "integration," which implies on the part of immigrants "the will to stay in a country, respecting [its] cultures and the laws."[211] "You can't live in the welcoming stage forever," the cardinal added, "because this becomes welfare and it isn't good for anyone."[212]

In 2011, Bagnasco observed that the influx of migrants from North Africa to Italy was too much for Italy to handle on its own. While it is important to foster a spirit of welcome and to provide aid to migrants and refugees, there is a tipping point beyond which a nation's resources are spread too thin. Bagnasco explained that immigration emergencies in Europe stem from long-standing global inequities that cannot be solved simply by policing borders.[213] "It's an illusion to think that one can live in peace, keeping at a distance young populations that are burdened by deprivation and that are legitimately trying to satisfy their hunger," the cardinal said.[214] "Policies of true cooperation" are needed to create

---

europes-bishops-call-unified-line-on-refugee-crisis-impossible/.

[209] See ibid.

[210] Ibid.

[211] Ibid.

[212] Ibid.

[213] John Thavis, "Italy's Immigration Puts Church Teaching to Test," *National Catholic Reporter*, 8 April 2011, https://www.ncronline.org/news/italys-immigration-puts-church-teaching-test.

[214] Ibid.

situations in which these people will not feel the need to leave their homeland, he added.[215]

SUMMARY

Known as generally a fervent defender of orthodox Church teaching in the public square, Cardinal Angelo Bagnasco has held many positions of governance and leadership in the Italian Church and currently leads a council of European bishops' conferences.

A conservative and disciple of the kind of Church leadership espoused by Benedict XVI and John Paul II, as president of Italy's bishops' conference the cardinal fought hard for the Faith and the Church's moral teaching in the political arena, at one point requiring bodyguards for his personal protection. He views witnessing to Christian values in the public square, including the protection of human life from conception until natural death, as a matter of Christian duty.

Cardinal Bagnasco has firmly upheld *Humanae Vitae*, and opposed the "Kasper Proposal" to allow Holy Communion to "remarried" divorcees in some cases, although he did not publicly voice his support for the *dubia*. He has strongly opposed homosexual civil unions but recently lacked clarity on homosexual issues more generally.

He rejects universalism, opposes an end to mandatory priestly celibacy and women deacons, and has spoken out against persecution of Christians. He has defended Europe's Christian roots and frequently addressed the clerical sexual abuse crisis, urging an end to cover-ups. He has called for more transparency in Church finances.

Cardinal Bagnasco has upheld the Eucharist and the importance of the liturgy and pledged to apply correctly the Extraordinary Form of the Roman Rite.

---

[215]   Ibid.

Mild mannered, reliable, and discreet, Angelo Bagnasco is viewed as a potential pope, should voting cardinals wish for the papacy to return to its traditional Italian occupant and prefer a safe pair of conservative hands after the internal Church ructions of the Francis years.

SERVICE TO THE CHURCH

Ordination to the Priesthood: 29 June 1966
Ordination to the Episcopate: 7 February 1998
Elevation to the College of Cardinals: 24 November 2007

Education
- 1966: Archdiocesan Seminary of Genoa, Italy; Classics
- 1979: University of Genoa, Italy; Doctorate in Philosophy

Assignments
- 1966-1998: Priest, Archdiocese of Genoa, Italy
- 1980-1998: Episcopal vicar and spiritual director, Archdiocesan Seminary of Genoa
- 1995-1997: Professor of metaphysics and contemporary atheism, Theological Faculty of Northern Italy
- 1998-2000: Bishop, Diocese of Pesaro, Italy
- 2000-2003: Archbishop, Archdiocese of Pesaro, Italy
- 2003-2006: Archbishop, Military Ordinariate of Italy
- 2006-present: Archbishop, Archdiocese of Genoa, Italy
- 2007-2017: President, Italian Episcopal Conference
- 2007-present: Cardinal-priest of Gran Madre di Dio
- 2014: Delegate, 2014 Extraordinary Synod on the Family
- 2015: Delegate, 2015 Ordinary Synod on the Family
- 2016-present: President, Council of the Bishops' Conferences of Europe

Roman Curia
- 2008-2013: Congregation for Bishops
- 2008-2016: Congregation for Divine Worship and the Discipline of the Sacraments
- 2008-present: Congregation for the Oriental Churches

RAYMOND LEO CARDINAL BURKE

"According to Your Heart"

Born: 30 June 1948
Richland Center, Wisconsin, USA
Nationality: American
Title: Patron of the Sovereign Military Order of Malta

BIOGRAPHY

The youngest of six children in a family closely connected to its Irish immigrant roots, Raymond Burke grew up on a rural dairy farm in the American Midwest. He recalls with fondness the instruction in the Catholic Faith that he received from his parents, an Irish Catholic father and an American Baptist mother who converted to the Faith after meeting her husband.[216] His father died of a brain tumor when Raymond was eight. After time as a Basselin scholar seminarian at the Catholic University of America in the United States, he was sent to Rome, where he studied at the Jesuits' Pontifical Gregorian University, which counts more popes as graduates than any other university in the world. In 1975, on the Solemnity of Sts. Peter and Paul, June 29, he was ordained a priest by Paul VI. After a few years of pastoral work and teaching, he was sent back to the Gregorian, where he completed a doctorate in canon law before returning in 1983 to the Diocese of La Crosse, Wisconsin, where he served as moderator of the Curia and vice chancellor. John Paul II called Burke back to Rome a third time in 1989 to serve the Apostolic Signatura as the first American appointed defender of the bond. At this time, Burke also taught canon law at his alma mater.

In 1995, Burke was ordained bishop by John Paul II and appointed as bishop of La Crosse. During his tenure, Bishop Burke conceived of building a great shrine dedicated to Our Lady of Guadalupe, patroness of the Americas. It was finally dedicated in 2008, by which time he had been archbishop of Saint Louis, Missouri, for five years. Amid his many pastoral duties, he continued publishing scholarly works. Widely recognized as an expert in canon law, Burke was brought back to Rome a fourth time when Benedict XVI appointed him prefect of the Supreme Tribunal of the Apostolic Signatura, effectively the Church's "supreme court." He was elevated to cardinal in 2010, and since then he has continued his work in canon law among many other apostolates.[217] In 2014, Cardinal

---

[216] Michael Otto, "Faith Flourished on Farm for US Cardinal," *NZ Catholic*, 15 November 2018, https://www.nzcatholic.org.nz/2018/11/15/faith-flourished-on-farm-for-us-cardinal/.

[217] John J. Coughlin, "Burke, Cardinal Raymond Leo (1948-)," in *Encyclopedia of Catholic Social Thought, Social Science, and Social Policy: Supplement*, ed. Michael L. Coulter et al. (Lanham, Md.: Scarecrow Press, 2012), 38-39; David Kerr, "Cardinal Burke Talks about Rome, the Mass, Canon Law and U.S. Culture," *National Catholic Register*, 28 November 2011, https://www.ncregister.com/daily-news/cardinal-burke-talks-about-rome-the-mass-canon-law-and-u.s.-culture.

Burke's term at the Apostolic Signatura ended, and instead of renewing it, Pope Francis appointed him patron of the Sovereign Military Order of Malta. In 2017, Pope Francis returned him to the Apostolic Signatura as a member to allow him to serve as one of the court's judges when needed.[218]

SANCTIFYING OFFICE

The Liturgy

"The liturgy is the highest and most perfect expression of our life in Christ and in the Church," Cardinal Raymond Burke said in a 2017 interview.[219]

He is convinced that "the crisis in the life of the Church is principally a crisis of the liturgy."[220] More particularly, "the aspect [of the liturgy] most in crisis is sacrality itself, the transcendence of the liturgical act, the encounter of heaven and earth and the action of Christ himself, through the priest who offers the Eucharistic Sacrifice."[221] The danger to be avoided, according to Burke, is "anthropocentrism, a concept of the liturgy … as a creation (or invention) of our own."[222]

His book *Divine Love Made Flesh: The Holy Eucharist as the Sacrament of Charity* is the fruit of the weekly instructions that he gave through diocesan newspapers, subsequently published in Italian, Polish, French, Croatian, and Portuguese. Cardinal Burke personally presided over book-launching tours in Italy, England, France, Croatia, Poland, Brazil, and

---

[218] Edward Pentin, "Cardinal Burke on His New Appointment to Church's Highest Court," *National Catholic Register*, 3 October 2017, https://www.ncregister.com/blog/edward-pentin/cardinal-burke-explains-his-new-appointment-to-churchs-highest-court.

[219] Aurelio Porfiri, "Exclusive Interview With Cardinal Raymond Burke (1) – Faith And Tradition," *O Clarim*, 15 December 2017, http://www.oclarim.com.mo/en/2017/12/15/exclusive-interview-with-cardinal-raymond-burke-1-faith-and-tradition/#more-10221.

[220] Ibid.

[221] Ibid.

[222] Ibid.

Portugal. During these international trips, the programs were packed to standing room only, with many young people attending.

Devotion to Our Lady

Burke has often spoken of his devotion to the Blessed Virgin Mary and says he was inspired by this devotion to build a shrine to the Virgin of Guadalupe, patroness of the Americas, in La Crosse, Wisconsin. The classical structure was built in the tradition of pilgrimage churches, high in the hills outside a city, at a cost of $25 million.[223] The cardinal said that he considered the shrine, completed in 2008, to be "one of the most important works that Our Lord has asked me to undertake. The initial inspiration was a response to a situation which I saw, first as priest, then as Bishop. The situation is a hunger to know God, and to love Him, a hunger to which Our Blessed Mother responds in a particular way, leading us to the only place where that hunger can be satisfied."[224] The Shrine of Our Lady of Guadalupe is the center for the Marian Catechist Apostolate, founded by the Servant of God Fr. John A. Hardon, S.J., and established by Burke as a Public Association of the Faithful of the Diocese. Since 2000, Cardinal Burke has served as episcopal moderator and international director for the Marian Catechist Apostolate.

Promotion of the Extraordinary Form

Cardinal Burke promoted the careful implementation of the *Motu Proprio Summorum Pontificum* (2007) with a view to accomplishing the ends proposed by Pope Benedict XVI. Connected to his desire to promote a worthy celebration of the liturgy, the cardinal established the Institute of Sacred Music in the Archdiocese of Saint Louis. The new institute was established, the cardinal explained, "to assist me in providing a fuller cultivation of Sacred Music for the celebration of the complete Roman Rite."

---

223   Ibid.

224   "Cardinal Burke's Inspiration for the Shrine," YouTube video, 1:11, posted 10 April 2017, by Shrine of Our Lady of Guadalupe, https://www.guadalupeshrine.org/inspiration-for-the-shrine.

Cardinal Burke enthusiastically supported the liturgical reforms proposed by Robert Cardinal Sarah in 2017—namely, a call for the priest to face God (*ad orientem*) during Mass and for the faithful to receive Christ in the Eucharist on the tongue while kneeling (see Cardinal Sarah's profile for more on this initiative). These should take priority, Cardinal Burke said.[225] On another occasion, he lamented the abandonment of "Gregorian Chant ... the music proper to the Church, and also the organ, which as the [Second Vatican] Council says, is the instrument most adapted to divine worship."[226] He considers the Ordinary and Extraordinary Forms of the Roman Rite to be equally valid.

Despite criticism from some quarters of the Church, Cardinal Burke willingly adopts the liturgical vestments of the Extraordinary Form, such as the cappa magna, a voluminous red vestment with a long train. He stresses that such vesture has nothing to do with personal tastes or proclivities of the cardinal or bishop, or of his self-aggrandizement, but are meant to draw the faithful's attention "to the divine nature of action, that it is Christ, seated in glory at the right hand of the Father, Who, through the ministry of the priest in the Sacred Liturgy, is acting to heal and sanctify us." He says the "fact that beautiful cloth and lace is employed in the vesture is an expression of the Church's faith that, in the Sacred Liturgy, heaven really comes to earth." Having experienced the "great harm" caused by liturgical abuses over the years, the cardinal says he has "always tried to do whatever is indicated in the liturgical books."

Promoter of Vocations

Cardinal Burke has been an active promotor and effective attractor of vocations. As bishop of La Crosse, he established the Holy Cross Seminary House of Formation in 1996 for high-school-aged boys and the Mater Redemptoris Convent and House of Formation in 2000 for high-school-aged

---

[225] Ibid.

[226] "Aurelio Porfiri Interviews Cardinal Burke," *O Clarim*, 31 December 2017, https://www.oclarim.com.mo/en/2017/12/15/exclusive-interview-with-cardinal-raymond-burke-1-faith-and-tradition/.

girls. Burke also invited the Institute of Christ the King Sovereign Priest to run a parish, their first in the United States.[227] In 2002, he enabled the foundation of the Canons Regular of the New Jerusalem, an Augustinian institute dedicated to promoting traditional liturgy.[228] He also greatly supported the local diocesan seminary, including the custom that, every day after lunch, a seminarian would join him at his residence for a long walk, during which they would discuss anything the seminarian wanted, including spiritual direction. Under Cardinal Burke's direction, there was an increase in the number of seminarians for the Archdiocese of Saint Louis, so much so that plans were in place to expand the seminary but were postponed once he was called to Rome.

Cardinal Burke is a devotee of St. Gianna Beretta Molla, having developed a special friendship with the saint's husband and family and actively promoted the saint's life and charism. As bishop of La Crosse and later archbishop of Saint Louis, Burke encountered many couples who sought his counsel because they were not able to conceive. He began promoting St. Gianna as a recourse, giving blessings with a relic and promoting novenas and other devotions to the saint. As a result of the large number of the couples able to conceive, he established an annual "Gianna Baby" Mass to recognize the many babies conceived through St. Gianna's intercession.

Devotion to the Sacred Heart of Jesus

In every parish of the Diocese of La Crosse, in particular during 2001, Cardinal Burke promoted the Enthronement of the Sacred Heart of Jesus. Copies of an icon of the Sacred Heart were made available throughout the diocese to create a sense of unity between the parishes and the family homes. Pastors and laity were given extensive doctrinal and practical instruction in preparation for the Enthronement at the cathedral. In the

---

[227] Michael J. Matt, "More Trouble for TLM, Institute of Christ the King in La Crosse," *Remnant*, 5 October 2013, http://www.remnantnewspaper.com/Archives/2013-0815-mjm-institute-christ-king-la-crosse.htm.

[228] "History of the Canons," Canons Regular of the New Jerusalem, n.d., https://www.canonsregular.com/index.php/who-we-are/history.

Archdiocese of Saint Louis, Cardinal Burke created and installed a shrine to the Sacred Heart of Jesus in the cathedral basilica of Saint Louis, during which he solemnly consecrated the archdiocese to the Sacred Heart of Jesus.

Since coming to reside in Rome, Cardinal Burke has continued to support efforts to promote traditional liturgy.[229] He has been invited by laypeople worldwide to give many spiritual conferences and celebrate the Mass in the Extraordinary Form.

The cardinal fervently prays for all who ask him, and keeps in his pocket batches of prayer cards, which he goes through each day, asking for the intercession of whichever patron saint is relevant to a particular need.

GOVERNING OFFICE

La Crosse

Then-Bishop Burke served as Ordinary of La Crosse from 1994 to 2003. His diocese included two hundred thousand persons spread across fifteen thousand square miles of mostly farmland.[230] During his tenure, he "consolidated the Catholic schools of seven cities in his diocese into unified school systems," closing a number of schools.[231] As part of the reform, Burke "dramatically raised the wages of many teachers by standardizing salaries," and he also standardized tuition and curricula.[232] Also notably, then-Bishop Burke ordered Catholics of his diocese not to participate in a

---

[229] "Congratulations to Cardinal-Designate Raymond L. Burke," Institute of Christ the King Sovereign, 23 October 2010, http://www.institute-christ-king.org/109-congratulations-to-cardinal-designate-raymond-l-burke.

[230] Ron Harris, "Bishop Burke Doesn't Mind 'Taking the Heat'," *La Crosse Tribune*, 7 December 2003, https://lacrossetribune.com/news/bishop-burke-doesn-t-mind-taking-the-heat/article_59aeea80-e30a-5935-9015-5e3654d1425f.html.

[231] Ibid.

[232] Ibid.

fundraising drive to combat hunger because it was run by an organization that pays for contraception in developing countries.[233]

Catholic Lawmakers and Abortion

As bishop of La Crosse, Cardinal Burke convoked a diocesan synod (June 11-14, 2000) so that "the whole Body of Christ in the Diocese may be more fully equipped to cooperate with the inspiration of the Holy Spirit in carrying out the work of the New Evangelization at the sunset of the Second Christian Millennium and the dawn of the Third Christian Millennium."

Appointed archbishop of Saint Louis in December 2003, Burke continued to make news by speaking out in defense of the Faith. In February 2004, applying a policy he had first implemented in La Crosse,[234] he forbade Catholic presidential candidate and abortion supporter John Kerry from receiving Communion while campaigning in the archdiocese.[235] Drawing on canon law and a 1998 document of the U.S. bishops, he said in a statement that, as his "fundamental responsibility" as a bishop was to safeguard and promote respect for human life, it was his duty "to explain, persuade, correct and admonish those in leadership positions who contradict the Gospel of life through their action and policies." He called on all Catholic legislators of his diocese to uphold the inviolable dignity of all human life.[236]

---

[233] Ibid.

[234] William R. Wineke, "Madison Bishop Says He Agrees with La Crosse Bishop, but May Not Follow Suit," *Journal Times*, 23 January 2004, https://journaltimes.com/news/state-and-regional/madison-bishop-says-he-agrees-with-la-crosse-bishop-but/article_c4eb8401-847a-59c4-825d-a12b0d0d4e9b.html.

[235] David Paul Kuhn, "Kerry's Communion Controversy," CBS News, 6 April 2004, https://www.cbsnews.com/news/kerrys-communion-controversy/.

[236] Cardinal Raymond L. Burke, "Notification to State and Federal Lawmakers in the Diocese of La Crosse," Catholic Culture, 8 January 2004, https://www.catholicculture.org/culture/library/view.cfm?recnum=5565; Dan Rossini, "Archbishop Defends His Actions," *Compass*, 23 January 2004, https://www.thecompassnews.org/compass/2004-01-23/news2.shtml.

Following the controversy, a number of prelates and other clerics asked Burke if he could prepare a study addressing the Church's position and history on the issue. Burke complied and his study was published in the *Periodica de Re Canonica* of the Pontifical Gregorian University, titled "The Discipline regarding the Denial of Holy Communion to Those Obstinately Persevering in Manifest Grave Sin." Using documented examples from Church history and doctrine, the study clearly outlines the perennial history of this practice. It has never been refuted.[237]

In 2020, Burke defended a priest who denied Holy Communion to Joe Biden, a Catholic Democratic presidential contender who openly supported abortion and other policies not in line with Church teaching. "What the priest did in South Carolina was right and just—would that more priests would act in a similar manner!" Burke said.[238] He said he could name eighty to one hundred Catholic legislators who regularly vote in favor of abortion and called it a "major scandal." In the same interview, the cardinal also commended a priest for denying Holy Communion to a lesbian judge in Michigan who was "married" to her female partner. At the same time, Burke criticized pro-LGBT Jesuit Fr. James Martin for calling the priest's actions "discrimination." The cardinal said "it is clear to me that Father Martin does not teach the Catholic Faith in these matters."

Parish Governance and Church Closures
In 2004, Burke sought to bring a parish with an irregular governance arrangement back into conformity with canon-law norms. Making no headway, he transferred the parish's priests and ministry elsewhere. After

---

[237] *Periodica de Re Canonica* 96 (2007): 3-58, Marian Catechist Apostolate, 2007, https://mariancatechist.com/cardinal-burke-on-canon-915/.

[238] Michael W. Chapman, "Cardinal Burke: Denying Communion to Joe Biden Was 'Right and Just,'" CNS News, 13 January 2020, https://www.cnsnews.com/blog/michael-w-chapman/cdl-burke-denying-communion-joe-biden-was-right-and-just.

publishing a warning,[239] Burke issued an interdict against the lay board.[240] When the lay board proceeded to hire a priest from another diocese, that priest's bishop suspended him, and then-Archbishop Burke declared the priest and lay board members guilty of schism and therefore automatically excommunicated.[241] Burke canonically closed the parish, formally separating it from the Catholic Church.

Later asked about how to approach church closures, Burke emphasized the importance of following church procedures and having a just reason for the closures. He said that reason should be determined based on a review of all relevant factual information and should be well documented.[242] Regarding closures for lack of resources, the cardinal noted that, although "the existence of churches depends on the generosity of the laity . . . the bishop and the priests have to provide as best they can for the spiritual needs of the parishioners with the material goods that they have available."[243]

Handling Diocesan Scandals

In 2008, Archbishop Burke ordered the interdiction of Louise Lears, a Sister of Charity in his archdiocese. In November 2007, Sr. Lears had participated in the ordination of two women as "Roman Catholic Womenpriests."

[239] Tim Townsend, "Archbishop Threatens to Withhold Sacraments," BishopAccountability.org, 5 January 2005, http://www.bishop-accountability. org/news2005_01_06/2005_01_05_Townsend_ArchbishopThreatens.htm.

[240] "Deadline to Comply with Church Law Official Ends for St. Louis Parish," Catholic News Agency, 10 February 2005, https://www.catholicnewsa-gency.com/news/deadline_to_comply_with_church_law_officially_ends_ for_st._louis_parish.

[241] "Schismatic St. Louis Parish Loses Appeal to Vatican," Catholic News Agency, 29 May 2008, https://www.catholicnewsagency.com/news/ schismatic_st._louis_parish_loses_appeal_to_vatican.

[242] George P. Matysek Jr., "Hew to Canon Law When Closing Churches, Cardinal Burke Says," Catholic News Service, 9 May 2014, http://www. catholicnews.com/services/englishnews/2014/hew-to-canon-law-when-closing-churches-cardinal-burke-says.cfm.

[243] Ibid.

Following the ceremony, the archbishop informed those responsible that they had incurred excommunication and opened a canonical process against Sr. Lears.[244]

In 2007, Archbishop Burke said that out of pastoral necessity he had to oppose a benefit concert for a local Catholic hospital because it featured singer Sheryl Crow, a well-known abortion activist. He said her appearance would be "an affront to the identity and mission of the medical center, dedicated as it is to the service of life and Christ's healing mission."[245]

Apostolic Signatura

In 2008, Pope Benedict XVI named Cardinal Burke prefect of the Supreme Tribunal of the Apostolic Signatura, the Church's highest court. This appointment was the culmination of a career in canon law that began with doctoral studies—and an influential doctoral dissertation—at the Pontifical Gregorian University in Rome, followed by a position as the first American defender of the bond at the Signatura, and then an appointment on the same tribunal.[246]

Two years after his judicial appointment, Pope Benedict named Raymond Burke a cardinal. When Pope Francis came into office, he left Burke in his position until the end of the usual five-year term. Although the pope did not renew Burke's prefecture in 2014, no public commentary suggested that the nonrenewal resulted from incompetence. Instead, performance-specific commentary tended to be positive, as when a canon

---

[244] Sandro Magister, "There Can Be No Women 'Priests' in the Catholic Church," Catholic Online, 6 August 2008, https://www.catholic.org/news/international/europe/story.php?id=28812.

[245] "Burke Opposes Sheryl Crow Concert Out of Pastoral Necessity," Catholic News Agency, 26 April 2007, https://www.catholicnewsagency.com/news/archbishop_burke_opposes_sheryl_crow_concert_out_of_pastoral_necessity.

[246] Joan Frawley Desmond, "Cardinal Burke Officially Transferred from Apostolic Signatura," *National Catholic Register*, 8 November 2014, http://www.ncregister.com/daily-news/cardinal-burke-officially-transferred-from-apostolic-signature.

lawyer praised the cardinal for his "involvement in the publication of . . . Signatura decisions on a variety of issues," which "has been very important in providing canon lawyers with models for canonical jurisprudence in these situations."[247] The pope's re-nomination of Burke to membership (but not leadership) of the Signatura in 2017 is significant. As John Allen's *Crux* judged the matter: "Few have ever disputed [Burke's] abilities as an expert on canon law."[248]

Guam Case, Sexual Abuse Crisis

In February 2017, the Congregation for the Doctrine of the Faith requested that Cardinal Burke preside over a five-judge tribunal hearing the penal case of Anthony Apuron, archbishop of Agaña (Guam). Allegations that Archbishop Apuron committed sexual abuse of altar servers in the 1970s had led to civil lawsuits and considerable controversy in Guam. In March 2018, the tribunal issued a verdict finding Apuron "guilty of certain of the accusations" and sentenced him to removal from office and prohibition from living in Guam.[249] The tribunal's words, the lack of a penalty of laicization, and reports from sources close to Apuron suggest that the archbishop was not convicted of all charges.[250] Still, Apuron lodged an appeal, which Pope Francis personally administered.[251] The second tribunal upheld the first tribunal's verdict, definitively finding Apuron "guilty of delicts against the Sixth Commandment with minors" and modifying the sentence only to

[247] Ibid.

[248] Crux Staff, "Pope Re-Ups Cardinal Raymond Burke at Vatican's Supreme Court," *Crux*, 30 September 2017, https://cruxnow.com/vatican/2017/09/30/pope-re-ups-cardinal-raymond-burke-vaticans-supreme-court/.

[249] Joshua J. McElwee, "Vatican Verdict against Guam Archbishop Likely Not for Sexual Abuse, Say Canon Lawyers," *National Catholic Reporter*, 3 April 2018, https://www.ncronline.org/news/accountability/vatican-verdict-against-guam-archbishop-likely-not-sexual-abuse-say-canon.

[250] JD Flynn, "Analysis: Gregory, Apuron, 'Zero Tolerance,' and Pontifical Secrets," Catholic News Agency, 4 April 2019, https://www.catholicnewsagency.com/news/analysis-gregory-apuron-zero-tolerance-and-pontifical-secrets-46673.

[251] Ibid.

add that Apuron shall not live in Guam "even temporarily" and shall not display episcopal insignia.[252]

Judicial positions aside, Cardinal Burke understands that the office of cardinal includes the duty "in certain situations ... to say what he truly thinks to the Pope."[253] Thus, beyond presiding over a canonical trial of sexual abuse allegations, he has also shared views on the general issue, which he deems "possibly one of the worst crises that [the Catholic Church in the U.S. has] ever experienced."[254] Clericalism is an insufficient explanation of clerical sexual sin: "It would be clericalism that would protect or even promote priests who are doing evil things." In his experience, the evil acts themselves are not "done through some kind of clerical mentality."[255] Rather, clerics "simply had an amoral weakness, and it wasn't properly corrected, and they didn't use the proper spiritual means to remain chaste and perfectly continent."[256] The central cause of the crisis, in the cardinal's view, is the Church's failure to make clear that "homosexual acts are evil ... always and everywhere."[257] To move forward, "there needs to be an open recognition that we have a very grave problem

---

[252] Press Release from the Congregation for the Doctrine of the Faith, Holy See Press Office, 4 April 2019, http://press.vatican.va/content/salastampa/en/bollettino/pubblico/2019/04/04/190404c.html?fbclid=IwAR2_wsYoYP-gbSHe9lRWCR74YMnaS-3fYF4uSCb_C70YAe_y1QZbYs-GQeJc.

[253] Jean-Marie Guénois, "Le Figaro on the Vatican 'Secret War' — Cardinal Burke's interview to *Le Figaro*," *Rorate Caeli*, 20 December 2014, https://rorate-caeli.blogspot.com/2014/12/le-figaro-on-vatican-secret-war.html.

[254] "Cardinal Burke: We Face a Grave Crisis, Touching the Heart of the Church," Catholic News Agency, 16 August 2018, https://www.catholic-newsagency.com/news/cardinal-burke-we-face-a-grave-crisis-touching-the-heart-of-the-church-99840.

[255] Krystina Kratiuk, "Card. Burke: Church without Enemies? A Diabolical Vision!," Polonia Christiana, 26 October 2018, https://www.eng.pch24.pl/card--burke--church-without-enemies--a-diabolical-vision-,63729,i.html.

[256] Ibid.

[257] Ibid.

of a homosexual culture in the Church, especially among the clergy and the hierarchy, that needs to be addressed honestly and efficaciously."[258]

Cardinal Burke maintains that the Church should return to something like the 1917 formulation of canon law regarding clerical sexual sins; he does not think that new procedures need be implemented; rather, proper procedures are there, have been for centuries, and should be used today.[259] "Where we discover that the appropriate action has not been taken, then ... that bishop has to be corrected, and if the bishop has failed very grievously, then he would simply have to be removed."[260] That said, "it's the responsibility of the Holy Father, not the conference of bishops, to investigate bishops."[261]

Synodality and Papal Power

Burke opposes limiting the power of the pope by synod or synodality. In his view, a synod is "a meeting of bishops to assist the pope to see how to teach the Faith more effectively and how to promote a more faithful Christian life in accordance with the discipline of the Church."[262] Burke does not oppose such synods, nor does he oppose consultation with the College of Cardinals. Indeed, he thinks the College, which has not met since 2014, should be called together more frequently so that the cardinals

---

[258] Michael W. Chapman, "Cardinal Burke: 'We Have a Very Grave Problem of a Homosexual Culture in the Church,'" CNS News, 17 August 2018, https://www.cnsnews.com/blog/michael-w-chapman/cdl-burke-we-have-very-grave-problem-homosexual-culture-church.

[259] "World Over—Cardinal Raymond Burke on the Abuse Crisis with Raymond Arroyo," YouTube video, 29:38, posted 16 August 2018 by EWTN, https://www.youtube.com/watch?v=hxtSafC2VOg.

[260] Ibid.

[261] Ibid.

[262] Bree A. Dail, "Cdl. Burke: 'Synodality' Suggests Some Kind of 'New Church' Where Pope's Authority Is Destroyed," LifeSite News, 4 December 2018, https://www.lifesitenews.com/news/cdl.-burke-synodality-suggests-some-kind-of-new-church-where-popes-authorit.

may advise the pope and meet each other before the next conclave.[263] But Burke distinguishes proper synods and meetings of the College from "synodality," which is, in his view, a term without clear meaning. It seems to him to be used "as a kind of political tool to suddenly promote ideas that weren't even discussed in [a] synod itself," which is "not honest."[264] Burke also opposes the term's use "to suggest some kind of new church which is democratic and in which the authority of the Roman Pontiff is relativized and diminished—if not destroyed."[265]

In the cardinal's view, a pope should resist or reverse the diminution of proper papal power, though it may be "licit" to call for a pope's resignation. Indeed, "anyone can make [such a request] in the face of whatever pastor that errs greatly in the fulfillment of his office,"[266] although "the facts need to be verified."[267] Thus, to Archbishop Carlo Maria Viganò's call for Pope Francis' resignation, Burke responded, "Each declaration must be subject to investigation, according to the Church's time-tried procedural law."[268]

In Burke's view, the Roman pontiff has "the fullness of power to safeguard and to promote the transmission of the truths of the faith, the beauty of the sacred liturgy, the goodness of her discipline, but not to govern the Church as some kind of self-made autocrat."[269] Burke understands papal

---

[263] Tess Livingstone, "We Don't Talk Any More: US Cardinal," *Il Sismografo* (blog), 22 October 2018, https://ilsismografo.blogspot.com/2018/10/australia-we-dont-talk-any-more-us.html.

[264] Dail, "Synodality."

[265] Ibid.

[266] Gerard O'Connell, "Cardinal Burke: It is 'licit' to call for the resignation of Pope Francis," *America*, 29 August 2018, https://www.americamagazine.org/faith/2018/08/29/cardinal-burke-it-licit-call-resignation-pope-francis.

[267] Ibid.

[268] John-Henry Westen, "Cardinal Burke Responds to Former US Nuncio's Explosive Letter about Pope Francis," LifeSite News, 26 August 2018, https://www.lifesitenews.com/news/cardinal-burke-responds-to-former-us-nuncios-explosive-letter-about-pope-fr.

[269] Claire Chretien, "'Nonsense' : Cardinal Burke Rebukes Fr. Rosica for Saying Francis Is above Scripture," LifeSite News, 16 August 2018, https://www.lifesitenews.com/news/cardinal-burke-nonsense-for-fr.-rosica-to-say-church-is-ruled-by-individual.

authority and Church authority generally as founded on the authority of Jesus Christ, Holy Scripture,[270] and Catholic tradition.[271] The mission of both Church and pope is "the salvation of souls."[272] Thus, although "Peter ... [is] the principle of the unity of the Church throughout the world,"[273] nevertheless "any act of a Pope that undermines the salvific mission of Christ in the Church, whether it be a heretical act or a sinful act in itself, is simply void from the point of view of the Petrine Office."[274]

Approach to Society of Saint Pius X

Cardinal Burke has said that reconciliation with the Society of Saint Pius X would "really [be] a gift for the whole Church" and that the fraternity has "the Catholic faith and the love of the sacred liturgy."[275] On the other hand, he has insisted that the SSPX is "in schism" and its priests remain in "de facto excommunication." He characterized the pope's recent indults—allowing SSPX priests to hear confessions and officiate at weddings if no other priest is available and the local bishop approves—as an "anomaly"

---

270 The cardinal's expressed view of the authority of "the word of God" as "divinely revealed," with a reference to *Dei Verbum*, suggests that he accepts the inerrancy of Scripture. Edward Pentin, "Cardinal Burke Addresses the 'Dubia' One Year After Their Publication," *National Catholic Register*, 14 November 2017, http://www.ncregister.com/blog/edward-pentin/cardinal-burke-addresses-the-dubia-one-year-after-their-publication.

271 Ibid.

272 Edward Pentin, "Cardinal Burke: Scalfari Episode 'Went Beyond What Is Tolerable,'" *National Catholic Register*, 4 April 2018, http://www.ncregister.com/blog/edward-pentin/cardinal-burke-scalfari-episode-went-beyond-what-is-tolerable.

273 CWR Staff, "Cardinal Burke: It Is a 'Source of Anguish' to Hear Suggestions 'That I Would Lead a Schism,'" *Catholic World Report*, 22 January 2018, https://www.catholicworldreport.com/2018/01/22/cardinal-burke-it-is-a-source-of-anguish-to-hear-suggestions-that-i-would-lead-a-schism/.

274 Pentin, "Scalfari Episode."

275 Francis X. Rocca, "Cardinal Burke Optimistic on Reconciliation with SSPX," Catholic News Service, 15 June 2012, http://www.catholicnews.com/services/englishnews/2012/cardinal-burke-optimistic-on-reconciliation-with-sspx.cfm.

and warned that it is not "a good sign to receive sacraments" from SSPX clergy.[276]

If there are two themes in Cardinal Burke's exercise of governance, they are vigorous exercise of his office, as he understands it, and rigorous attention to the law. In defense of the latter in San Francisco in 2017, Burke asserted:

> Canon law is not in contrast with the many works of divine grace in the Church but rather assures that the work of divine grace will be received into souls formed in accord with the mind and heart of Christ.... We do not study and respect the law for its own sake but for the sake of the sacred realities which it safeguards and fosters. We serve the justice which is the minimal and irreplaceable requirement of divine love.[277]

Order of Malta Controversy

In 2016, as patron of the Order of Malta, Cardinal Burke found himself embroiled in a controversy involving the order's third-ranking official, Grand Chancellor Albrecht Freiherr von Boeselager. Cardinal Burke's task as patron was to promote relations between the Holy See and the Knights and to keep the Holy Father informed about spiritual and religious aspects of the order.

Cardinal Burke was present when the order's Grand Master, Fra' Matthew Festing, dismissed Boeselager as Grand Chancellor at a meeting on December 6, 2016, accusing him of being ultimately responsible for the distribution of contraceptives through the order's humanitarian agency, Malteser International.

---

[276] Christina Niles, "Cdl Burke: SSPX In Schism," Church Militant, 2 October 2017, https://www.churchmilitant.com/news/article/cdl-burke-sspx-in-schism.

[277] Valerie Schmalz, "Cardinal Raymond Burke Draws a Crowd at San Francisco Mass," *Catholic San Francisco*, 23 March 2017, https://catholic-sf.org/news/cardinal-raymond-burke-draws-a-crowd-at-san-francisco-mass-1.

At the meeting, Cardinal Burke made it clear that distribution of contraceptives was unacceptable. Some alleged that Burke had told Boeselager that the pope had instructed him to tell him to resign, but the cardinal firmly denied this. He was nevertheless acting on views shared by Pope Francis in a confidential December 1 letter, later made public by WikiLeaks, in which the pope had told Burke he would be "very disappointed" if it transpired that such distributions had been taking place and Burke had not "intervened to end such things."[278]

Cardinal Burke, however, found himself in the midst of an internal war within the order, one side wishing to modernize it along more secular lines (Boeselager and his allies), and the other holding to orthodoxy and tradition (mostly professed Knights). Burke naturally aligned with the latter.[279]

In response to Boeselager's dismissal, Cardinal Pietro Parolin, the Vatican secretary of state,[280] established a five-member commission of inquiry. Within a month of the commission's formation, Parolin declared Boeselager innocent of all wrongdoing.[281] The pope subsequently ordered

---

[278] Edward Pentin, "Wikileaks Publishes Crucial Papal Letter on Order of Malta Affair," *National Catholic Register*, 30 January 2019, https://www.ncregister.com/blog/edward-pentin/wikileaks-publishes-crucial-papal-letter-on-order-of-malta-affair

[279] The dispute was also seen as a microcosm of the crisis in the Vatican and wider Church, added to which was the order's considerable financial resources, some hidden in a shady Swiss trust, unknown to Festing, and which became apparent only around the time of the dispute.

[280] See Cardinal Parolin's profile for more details on his role in the affair.

[281] The audience transcription makes clear that while Boeselager claimed that the findings of the commission established by Festing were inaccurate, when challenged by Burke at the December 6, 2016, meeting to explain why he, Boeselager, had not requested corrections to the document throughout 2016 or provided materials to disprove its investigative conclusions, Boeselager had no response. This, Burke is reported to have said, did not surprise him, for had heard Boeselager himself vocalize a justification for precisely the dubious questions in practice—a justification that the commission also asserts was invoked by MI personnel in defense of the dubious practice. See Maike Hickson, "Leaked Report of Cardinal

Boeselager reinstated, stripped Burke of all prerogatives and duties with respect to the order (he retained the title of patron), announced the appointment of a new papal delegate to the order, and declared that the Holy See would oversee a review of the order and guide its reorientation. In January 2017, Francis dismissed Festing.

Burke was persistently accused of exceeding his mandate and of falsely saying that the pope instructed him to tell Boeselager to resign, accusations he always denied. The pope's confidential December 1 letter, revealed by WikiLeaks two years later, confirmed Burke's account of events.

TEACHING OFFICE

Call to Holiness

Cardinal Burke embraces the Second Vatican Council's emphasis on the universal call to holiness—that every Christian, by dint of Baptism, is called to be a saint. He affirms that "divine grace which helps even the weakest and the most tried human subject to attain a heroic degree of virtue, if he or she only cooperates with divine grace."[282]

On the other hand, he has stated plainly that "immortality of the soul and hell" are truths and the denials of these truths are "heretical ideas." [283] He thinks that souls can (be taught to) go in the right or wrong direction—and the right way is Christ: "In Christ is realized the right order of all things, the union of heaven and earth, as God the Father intended from the beginning," for "it is the obedience of God the Son Incarnate

Burke Audience Reveals Background on Malta Crisis," *One Peter Five*, 28 April 2017, https://onepeterfive.com/leaked-report-of-cardinal-burke-audience-reveals-background-on-malta-crisis/.

[282] Pete Baklinski, "Cardinal Burke: Catholics Must Let Christ Reign as King in Face of 'Apostasy' within Church," LifeSite News, 18 May 2018, https://www.lifesitenews.com/news/cardinal-burke-catholics-must-allow-christ-to-reign-as-king-in-face-of-apos.

[283] Pentin, "Scalfari Episode."

which reestablishes, restores, the original communion of man with God and, therefore, peace in the world."[284]

Importance of the Sacraments

For "visible and effective signs of our incorporation into Christ and His Church," Burke turns to the sacraments, "in and by which the Church publicly professes and actuates her faith."[285] In His Eminence's view, however, "the decisive criterion for admission to the sacraments has always been the coherence of a person's way of life with the teachings of Jesus."[286] More than just "the absence of a person's subjective culpability" is necessary.[287] Instead, one should avoid publicly living in a state of sin and actually adhere to objective morality.[288] Burke holds that admission to the sacraments depends, in part, on living in actual accordance with the natural law and, at a minimum, avoiding those violations that constitute mortal sin.[289]

His convictions in this regard have led him to speak up frequently in defense of the sacraments, especially the Eucharist. For example, before, during, and after the 2014 and 2015 synods on the family, Burke vehemently resisted the "Kasper Proposal" on allowing some divorced and civilly "remarried" persons engaging in sexual relations to receive Holy Communion. He insisted that allowing such an exception for people the Church considers to be living in an objective state of adultery would

---

[284] Baklinski, "Let Christ Reign."

[285] Pentin, "Burke Addresses the 'Dubia.'"

[286] Ibid.

[287] Ibid.

[288] Charles Collins, "Cardinal Burke Says He Is 'Sympathetic' to Marriage Difficulties," *Crux*, 2 April 2017, https://cruxnow.com/vatican/2017/04/02/cardinal-burke-says-sympathetic-marriage-difficulties/.

[289] Jeanne Smits, "Exclusive Interview: Cardinal Burke Says Confusion Spreading Among Catholics 'in an Alarming Way,'" LifeSite News, 24 March 2015, https://www.lifesitenews.com/news/exclusive-interview-cardinal-burke-says-confusion-spreading-among-catholics.

represent a "fundamental" break in Catholic teaching.[290] He contributed to the 2014 book *Remaining in the Truth of Christ*, defending the sacrament of Marriage in light of the "Kasper Proposal" and would later be one of the four cardinals to issue the *dubia*, seeking clarification of Pope Francis' 2016 Apostolic Exhortation *Amoris Laetitia*, which appeared to offer such an opening (see the section on relations with Pope Francis, below). He reaffirmed his position on the issue in 2018.[291]

The Family and the Natural Moral Law

According to Cardinal Burke, "not to speak about the natural law is to deny reason."[292] In this light, he has taught emphatically that absolute moral norms "that prohibit intrinsically evil acts and that are binding without exceptions" exist.[293] "With intrinsically evil acts," he has further explained, "no discernment of circumstances or intentions is necessary."[294] These intrinsically evil acts that are never morally justified include abortion,[295]

---

[290] "Cardinal Burke: Communion for divorced/remarried would be 'fundamental' break from Church teaching," Catholic Culture, 3 December 2015, https://www.catholicculture.org/news/headlines/index.cfm?storyid=26853

[291] Joshua J. McElwee, "Cardinal Critics of Francis Reaffirm No Communion for Divorced, Remarried," *National Catholic Reporter*, 7 April 2018, https://www.ncronline.org/news/vatican/cardinal-critics-francis-reaffirm-no-communion-divorced-remarried.

[292] Claire Chretien, "Cardinal Burke: Gender Theory Is 'Madness,' Transgender Bathrooms 'Inhuman,'" LifeSite News, 1 August 2016, https://www.lifesitenews.com/news/cardinal-burke-gender-theory-is-madness-men-going-in-womens-bathrooms-is-in.

[293] Brother André Marie, "The Five Dubia of the Four Cardinals," *Catholicism.org*, 19 November 2016, https://catholicism.org/the-five-dubia-of-the-four-cardinals.html.

[294] Edward Pentin, "Full Text and Explanatory Notes of Cardinals' Questions on 'Amoris Laetitia,'" *National Catholic Register*, 14 November 2016, http://www.ncregister.com/blog/edward-pentin/full-text-and-explanatory-notes-of-cardinals-questions-on-amoris-laetitia.

[295] "The Church's teaching on the intrinsic evil of procured abortion forbids the destruction of human beings from the moment of fertilization through every state of their development." Most Reverend Raymond L. Burke,

embryo-destruction,[296] euthanasia,[297] contraception,[298] cloning,[299] and any sexual act outside of marriage[300] (with marriage defined as "an exclusive and lifelong union of one man and one woman, which of its very nature cooperates with God in the creation of new human life").[301] The cardinal

---

Pastoral Letter *Our Civic Responsibility for the Common Good* (1 October 2004), 12. See also Pentin, "Burke Addresses the 'Dubia.'"

[296] "It is intrinsically evil to destroy human embryos, even for some intended good.... The Holy Father further reminds us that the solemn duty to protect human life extends also to 'living human embryos and fetuses sometimes specifically "produced" for [experimentation] by *in vitro* fertilization either to be used as "biological material" or as *providers of organs or tissues for transplants* in the treatment of certain diseases.'" Burke, *Our Civic Responsibility*, 12-13.

[297] "Another intrinsic moral evil which seemingly is growing in acceptability in our society is euthanasia, 'an action or omission which, of itself or by intention, causes death in order to eliminate suffering' (*Catechism of the Catholic Church* no. 2277).... It is important to distinguish euthanasia from: (1) the legitimate decision 'to forgo ... medical procedures which no longer correspond the real situation of the patient ...; and (2) the legitimate decision to use 'various types of painkillers and sedatives for easing the patient's pain when this involves risk of shortening life' (*Evangelium vitae*, no. 65b-c)." Ibid. See also Pentin, "Burke Addresses the 'Dubia.'"

[298] John-Henry Westen, "Vatican Cardinal: Contraception 'Is Fundamentally an Anti-Life Act,'" LifeSite News, 12 June 2013, https://www.lifesitenews.com/news/vatican-cardinal-contraception-is-fundamentally-an-anti-life-act.

[299] "Human cloning, for any reason, is 'in opposition to the dignity both of human procreation and of the conjugal union' (*Donum vitae*, I, no. 6), inasmuch as it reduces procreation to a species of manufacture, and treats human life as a product of human artifice." Burke, *Our Civic Responsibility*, 14.

[300] "Cardinal Burke ... We Face a Grave Crisis, Touching the Heart of the Church," *Wanderer*, 26 August 2018, http://thewandererpress.com/catholic/news/featured-today/cardinal-burke-we-face-a-grave-crisis-touching-the-heart-of-the-church/.

[301] Cardinal Burke, "On Our Civic Responsibility for the Common Good," Catholic Action for Faith and Family, 2018, https://www.catholicaction.org/on_our_civic_responsibility_for_the_common_good.

has distinguished all of these acts from war and the death penalty, which, he taught in 2004, "can rarely be justified, [but] are not intrinsically evil."[302]

Burke maintains that these (and other) moral principles must guide and govern social as well as individual action. In social matters, he affirms the primacy of the right to life and the family founded upon marriage: "In the long tradition of not only the Church's thinking but also of philosophical reason … the fundamental question has to be the question of human life itself … and of its cradle, its source, in the union of man and woman in marriage."[303] Burke defends this prioritization in two ways. First, life and marriage are foundational social conditions on which other social conditions depend.[304] Second, attacks on such goods, as discussed above, tend to be intrinsically evil acts, contrary to absolute negative norms.[305] By contrast, other social questions may not involve intrinsically evil acts, but rather implicate positive moral norms, which, in the cardinal's teaching, do not "bind without exception."[306]

The cardinal suggests that an initial locus for social action is the family itself. "Parents today must be especially vigilant in instructing their children in the truth about human sexuality and in safeguarding them from all of the false messages regarding human sexuality conveyed in the schools and by the communications media."[307] Burke has affirmed that same-sex attraction is "not right" and not to be encouraged,[308] even

---

[302] Ibid.

[303] Pete Baklinski, "Cardinal Burke on Push for U.S. Bishops to Shift Priorities: Life Always Comes Before Immigration, Poverty," LifeSite News, 1 September 2016, https://www.lifesitenews.com/news/ cardinal-burke-on-u.s.-bishops-shifting-priorities-life-issues-always-come.

[304] Cardinal Burke, "On Our Civic Responsibility."

[305] Ibid.

[306] Pentin, "Cardinals' Questions."

[307] Izabella Parowicz, "Cardinal Burke on Faith, the Right to Life, and the Family: English Exclusive," LifeSite News, 20 March 2014, https://www. lifesitenews.com/news/english-exclusive-cardinal-burke-on-faith-the-right-to-life-and-the-family.

[308] "Cardinal-Designate Raymond Burke Discussing Homosexual 'Marriage,'" YouTube video, 3:33, posted 27 October 2010 by Catholic Actions, https://

while reiterating the human dignity of persons who experience such attraction and calling for compassion toward such persons.[309] More broadly, Burke holds that "gender theory" is to be rejected as "an attack on [the] truth" about marriage, and he has insisted that the "twofold expression of the human person is ... male and female."[310] The cardinal would have parents teach instead the Church's tradition, which "offers a powerful model of true femininity in the Blessed Virgin Mary and in many female saints"[311] and, "especially through the devotion to St. Joseph ... stress[es] the manly character of the man who sacrifices his life for the sake of the home, who prepares with chivalry to defend his wife and his children and who works to provide the livelihood for the family."[312]

---

www.youtube.com/watch?v=r6Hls4562qE. The cardinal may not have publicly and directly addressed guidelines for admission to the seminary, but he has welcomed a "development" away from "a period of time when men who were ... confused about their own sexual identity had entered the priesthood." Mike Tighe, "Burke Contends Feminism Marginalizes Men, Fosters Abuse," La Crosse Tribune, 9 January 2015, https://lacrossetribune.com/news/local/burke-contends-feminism-marginalizes-men-fosters-abuse/article_4b8405ef-d64c-59d5-a55e-96bad102ca16.html. Also, he has called for a "homosexual culture" within the Church to be "purified at the root." Thomas McKenna, "Cardinal Burke Addresses the Clergy Scandal," Catholic Action, 16 August 2018, https://www.catholicaction.org/cardinal_burke_addresses_the_clergy_scandal.

309   Ibid.
310   Chretien, "Gender Theory is 'Madness.'"
311   Parowicz, "Cardinal Burke on Faith."
312   "Cardinal Raymond Leo Burke on the Catholic 'Man-Crisis' and What to Do about It," The New Emangelization, 5 January 2015, https://www.newemangelization.com/uncategorized/cardinal-raymond-leo-burke-on-the-catholic-man-crisis-and-what-to-do-about-it/. Obviously, Cardinal Burke does not think that marriage is the exclusive vocation for either men or women. See, e.g., "Cardinal Burke: Respond to the Lord with All Your Heart! Discerning a Religious Vocation to the Priesthood or Religious Life," YouTube video, 2:18, posted 13 December 2017 by 2SPetrvs, https://www.youtube.com/watch?v=eqUcEJVmwHE; Carrie Gress, "Got Debt and a Religious Vocation?," Catholic World Report, 16 December 2013, https://www.catholicworldreport.com/2013/12/16/got-debt-and-a-religious-vocation/.

Burke sees upholding and not diluting the fullness of Church doctrine as central to true Christian compassion, as evidenced in the case of Eric Hess when Burke was bishop of La Crosse. Hess had been living a violently pro-homosexual lifestyle of twelve years and decided to leave the Church, but three years later he gave up that life and returned to the Church on the basis of Burke's example and steadfastness to the moral law. Burke had never ceased praying for him.[313]

For Burke, all moral truth must be advanced in the public square. Citing Christ's example as an answer to Cain's question, he affirms that "we are our 'brother's keeper.' We are responsible for the good of all our brothers and sisters in our nation and in the world, without boundaries."[314] That is, "we are bound by the moral law to act with respect for the rights of others and to promote the common good."[315] More specifically, "we are morally bound in conscience to choose leaders at all levels of government, who will best serve the common good."[316] That choice should be guided by the moral priorities previously mentioned, such that, in the cardinal's view, consideration of life and marriage must come before consideration of poverty, immigration, and the environment, important as those issues are.[317]

---

[313] Hess boxed up all of his crucifixes and Bibles and left them at the office of Bishop Burke, along with a letter renouncing his Catholic Faith. Burke knew that the fact that Hess had left the items at the office signified that he was not certain of what he was doing and continued to pray for him. After Hess had a mystical experience, he returned to the Church and went to thank Burke for his prayers and collect his box of devotions. "While some malign Archbishop Burke for his fidelity to God, Church and all souls, I say that he is a true shepherd of the faithful and a present-day Athanasius," Hess wrote. "I tell you that he remains a mentor and an inspiration to me." Eric Hess, "Coming Out of Sodom," Catholic Culture, https://www.catholicculture.org/culture/library/view.cfm?recnum=8106

[314] Burke, "On Our Civic Responsibility."

[315] Ibid.

[316] Ibid.

[317] Baklinski, "Shift Priorities"; see also Burke, *Our Civic Responsibility*, 14-16. On the particular matter of immigration, Burke has opposed separation

Church and State

Cardinal Burke has also offered thoughts about the relationship between church and state. He holds that "Christians who do not pretend to govern the civil state by means of the Church at the same time are called to give an heroic public witness to the truth of the moral law, of the law of God."[318] Thus, he affirms both that "the Kingship of Christ is, by nature, universal, that is, it extends to all men, to the whole world,"[319] and also that all persons should be free to exercise religious faith "as long as it's not against good order."[320]

Cardinal Burke has said he has often drawn inspiration from the life and work of St. Thomas More, the patron saint of lawyers, statesmen, and politicians, especially in view of temptations and pressures to conform to the world.[321] He has also often been willing to lend his support to Catholics courageously defending the Faith in the public square. Sometimes this has caused controversy, particularly on the political left,

---

of small children from immigrant parents and affirmed that refugees must be taken in. On the other hand, His Eminence would distinguish refugees from immigrants who migrate for "their own advancement," and he thinks addressing the latter case involves more complex policy judgments by many nations. "Cardinal Raymond Burke Shares His Views On Migration Issues," YouTube video, 4:17, posted 19 June 2018 by EWTN, https://www.youtube.com/watch?v=lHhbJwykenQ.

[318] Baklinski, "Let Christ Reign."

[319] Ibid.

[320] David Gibson, "US Cardinal Says 'Christian Nations' in West Must Counter Islamic Influx," Religion News Service, 21 July 2016, https://religionnews.com/2016/07/21/us-cardinal-says-christian-nations-in-west-must-counter-islamic-influx/.

[321] David Kerr, "Cardinal Raymond Burke Pays Tribute to St. Thomas More," Catholic News Agency, 22 June 2011, https://www.catholicnewsagency.com/news/cardinal-raymond-burke-pays-tribute-to-st.-thomas-more. In October 2017, the cardinal venerated the relic of the head of St. Thomas More at St. Dunstan's Parish, Canterbury, England. Edward Pentin, "Cardinal Burke Venerates Relic of the Head of Thomas More," National Catholic Register, 17 October 2017, https://www.ncregister.com/blog/edward-pentin/cardinal-burke-venerates-relic-of-the-head-of-st.-thomas-more.

as when he appeared to support, and then distanced himself from, U.S. President Donald Trump's former chief strategist Stephen K. Bannon.[322] Such alliances, including with Italy's rightist former deputy prime minister Matteo Salvini, reflect Burke's willingness to stand by Catholic politicians for as long as he believes they are acting coherently with the Faith and promoting the common good.

Islam

Burke has expressed serious concerns about Islam, which he does not think is simply "a religion like the Catholic faith or the Jewish faith"[323] nor indeed a religion with "the same God" as Christianity.[324] One particular concern for the cardinal is that when Muslims "become the majority in any country they have the duty to submit the whole population to Shariah."[325] In the cardinal's eyes, "we have to insist … [that] our country is not free to become a Muslim state."[326]

Priestly Celibacy, Women Priests

Cardinal Burke has emphasized in many public pronouncements the requirements of the priestly office. He responded to self-proclaimed ordinations of female priests as acts "in contradiction to the perennial, constant, and infallible teaching of the Catholic Church."[327] He has taught that clerical celibacy is "something more than a discipline" because "it has to do

322 Philip Pullella, "Conservative Vatican Cardinal Withdraws Support for Steve Bannon," Reuters, 26 June 2019, https://www.reuters.com/article/us-vatican-bannon/conservative-vatican-cardinal-withdraws-support-for-steve-bannon-idUSKCN1TR2UT.

323 Ibid.

324 Joseph Pronechen, "Cardinal Burke Speaks on Attendance Drops, Liturgy, Ad Orientem and Islam," *National Catholic Register*, 6 September 2016, http://www.ncregister.com/blog/joseph-pronechen/cardinal-burke-speaks-on-attendance-drops-iturgy-ad-orientem-and-islam1.

325 Gibson, "Islamic Influx."

326 Ibid.

327 "St. Louis Archbishop Excommunicates Three for Attempted Women's Ordination," Catholic News Agency, 15 March 2008,

with the example of Christ Himself," because it has been "from the earlier centuries … understood as being most fitting for [the Church's] priests," and because it received "very solid reaffirmation" from a world Synod of Bishops in the 1960s.[328] As a less certain matter, the cardinal also favors exclusively male altar service to promote male engagement with the Mass and the Faith and to encourage priestly vocations.[329] Such measures would, in his judgment, strengthen the Church.

Crisis in the Church

In a 2020 interview, Cardinal Burke lamented the internal squabbles in the Church that had heightened during Francis' pontificate and said that at the center of such internal strife was a "fundamental misunderstanding about the Church herself and about the papacy, about the College of Bishops and Tradition."[330]

Strengthening the Church is much needed, in Burke's view, because "antinomianism embedded in civil society has unfortunately infected post-[Vatican II] ecclesial life."[331] Not least because of "an attitude of indifference toward Church discipline, if not even hostility," it has come about that "the reforms of ecclesial life which were hoped for

---

https://www.catholicnewsagency.com/news/st._louis_archbishop_excommunicates_three_for_attempted_womens_ordination.

[328] "Exclusive: Cardinal Burke Interview with Rorate Caeli," *Rorate Caeli*, 2 March 2015, https://rorate-caeli.blogspot.com/2015/03/exclusive-cardinal-burke-interview-with.html; see also "Card. Burke—Sacred Heart and Celibacy—Continued—5/8—CONF 295," YouTube video, 33:58, posted 15 November 2016 by Franciscan Friars, https://www.youtube.com/watch?v=8NSmeOYndU4.

[329] "Catholic 'Man-Crisis.'"

[330] Edward Pentin, "Cardinal Burke: Disputes over Doctrine Sapping Church's Energy to Evangelize," *National Catholic Register*, 6 March 2020, https://www.ncregister.com/daily-news/cardinal-burke-discusses-querida-amazonia.

[331] Francis X. Rocca, "Cardinal Burke: Vatican II Betrayed By Breakdown of Church Discipline," *National Catholic Reporter*, 25 October 2012, https://www.ncronline.org/news/parish/cardinal-burke-vatican-ii-betrayed-breakdown-church-discipline.

by the Council fathers were … in a certain sense, hindered if not betrayed."[332] Among the damage, the cardinal believes, is apostasy as prophesied by Our Lady at Fatima: "There has been a practical apostasy from the faith with regard to all the questions involving human sexuality."[333]

He believes that because "the Church itself seems to be confused," and because "one may have the feeling that the Church gives the appearance of being unwilling to obey the mandates of Our Lord," it may be that "we have arrived at the End Times."[334] That is, our times "realistically seem to be apocalyptic," and "clearly, the present situation of the world cannot continue without leading to total annihilation."[335]

In 2017, on the centenary of Our Lady of Fatima's first apparition to the three shepherd children, Cardinal Burke issued a call for the Catholic faithful to "work for the consecration of Russia to the Immaculate Heart of Mary."[336]

In the meantime, Burke has urged Catholics not to "worry whether these times are apocalyptic or not, but to remain faithful, generous and courageous in serving Christ in His Mystical Body, the Church."[337]

The cardinal has issued many statements and declarations in defense of the Church's doctrine; for instance, in June 2019, when he co-wrote a

---

[332] Ibid.

[333] "*World Over* — Abuse Crisis."

[334] Paolo Gambi, "'Perhaps We Have Arrived at the End Times': An Interview with Cardinal Burke," *Catholic Herald*, 30 November 2017, https://catholicherald.co.uk/perhaps-we-have-arrived-at-the-end-times-an-interview-with-cardinal-burke/.

[335] Pete Baklinski, "'Confusion and Error' from Catholic Leaders May Be Sign of End Times: Cardinal Burke," LifeSite News, 8 August 2017, https://www.lifesitenews.com/news/confusion-division-in-church-shows-we-may-be-in-the-end-times-cardinal-burk.

[336] John-Henry Westen, "Cardinal Burke calls for Consecration of Russia to Immaculate Heart of Mary," LifeSite News, 19 March 2017, https://www.lifesitenews.com/news/breaking-cardinal-burke-calls-for-consecration-of-russia-to-immaculate-hear.

[337] Ibid.

"Declaration of Truths," an eight-page document reaffirming the Church's perennial teaching on a range of key doctrines, from the Eucharist and marriage, to capital punishment and clerical celibacy. The document was written in response to concerns about prevailing ambiguities and contradictions during the Francis pontificate.[338]

Cardinal Burke's critics call him a "rigorist" for whom the Catholic community is "simply riddled through with confused souls, and there is error everywhere" and where he sees confusion, they see an "openness to new ways of expressing the faith."[339] In contrast, his supporters argue that he sees the Church how it really is, that he identifies the errors in the light of the gospel and the Church's perennial teaching, and is merely upholding the truths of the Faith.

Responding to the crisis, he advises prayer for an increase in faith, study of the Faith, and fellowship with others.[340] He encourages flight to the Blessed Virgin for her maternal intercession, to St. Joseph daily, and to St. Michael throughout the day.[341] He requests prayers for all cardinals and particularly for the pope, through the intercession of St. Peter.[342] In his view, Catholics must "safeguard especially our faith in the Petrine Office and our love for the Successor of Saint Peter, Pope Francis."[343]

---

[338] "The Church of the living God—the pillar and the bulwark of the truth (1 Tim. 3:15) —Declaration of the truths relating to some of the most common errors in the life of the Church of our time," https://www.ncregister.com/images/uploads/Declaration_Truths_Errors_final_version_clean.pdf.

[339] "Editorial: Cardinal Burke Is a Living Symbol of a Failed Version of Church," *National Catholic Reporter*, 31 July 2019, https://www.ncronline.org/news/accountability/editorial-cardinal-burke-living-symbol-failed-version-church.

[340] Ibid.

[341] Ibid.

[342] Ibid.

[343] Ibid.

Use of the Media

To promote his teaching office, Cardinal Burke has begun to make use of modern media, employing a full-time spokeswoman, creating his own website to post messages, homilies, and presentations (www.cardinalburke.com), and opening a Twitter account.

During the coronavirus outbreak, Cardinal Burke used his website to issue messages of support to the faithful. He urged churches and chapels to stay open for prayer, noting that "without the help of God, we are indeed lost." Reflecting on the crisis, he observed how far society is from God, that "there is no question that great evils like pestilence are an effect of original sin and of our actual sins," but also that God will never leave us and urged the faithful to have recourse to Him, if not through the sacraments, then through prayer and spiritual communion.[344]

RELATIONSHIP WITH POPE FRANCIS

Under Pope Benedict XVI, Cardinal Burke held numerous positions of significant influence in the Curia. Since the start of the present papacy,[345]

---

[344] Cardinal Raymond Burke, "Message on the Combat against the Coronavirus, COVID-19," Cardinal Raymond Burke, 21 March 2020, https://www.cardinalburke.com/presentations/combat-against-coronavirus.

[345] Cardinal Burke has rejected claims that Pope Benedict's resignation was invalid or incomplete or that Benedict tried to bifurcate or expand the office. Diane Montagna, "Did Benedict Really Resign? Gänswein, Burke and Brandmüller Weigh In," LifeSite News, 14 February 2019, https://www.lifesitenews.com/news/did-benedict-really-resign-gaenswein-burke-and-brandmueller-weigh-in. According to Burke, "it would be difficult to say it's not valid" (ibid.). Not only does His Eminence doubt that Pope Benedict intended to alter the papacy, but any intent to do so would be "fantasy," and Burke does not think that such "mistaken notions," if held, would "redound to non-abdication of the Petrine office" (ibid.). Further: "Whatever [Pope Benedict] may have theoretically thought about the papacy, the reality is what is expressed in the Church's discipline. He withdrew his will to be the Vicar of Christ on earth, and therefore he

the cardinal's responsibilities have decreased. In 2013, he ceased to be a member of the Congregation for Bishops[346] and the Congregation for the Causes of Saints.[347] In November 2014, following the October 2014 Extraordinary Synod on the Family and earlier rumors that Cardinal Burke would be removed as prefect of the Apostolic Signatura,[348] Pope Francis reassigned Burke from that position to be patron of the Sovereign Military Order of Malta when his five-year term as prefect ended.[349]

In 2015, Pope Francis reappointed Cardinal Burke to the Congregation for the Causes of Saints.[350]

In late 2016, Cardinal Burke played an indirect role in the removal of the Sovereign Military Order of Malta's Grand Chancellor (see above).[351]

---

ceased to be the Vicar of Christ on earth" (ibid.). Thus, in Cardinal Burke's view, Pope Benedict XVI ceased to be pope in 2013 — and indeed, Burke thinks, someone who is not pope should avoid the use of titles or dress that may suggest otherwise (ibid.).

[346] Francis X. Rocca, "Pope Removes Cardinal Burke from Vatican Post," *National Catholic Reporter*, 10 November 2014, https://www.ncronline. org/news/vatican/pope-removes-cardinal-burke-vatican-post.

[347] "Cardinal Burke Has Now Also Been Removed from the Congregation of the Causes of the Saints," *The Badger Catholic* (blog), 19 December 2013, http://badgercatholic.blogspot.com/2013/12/cardinal-burke-has-now-also-been.html.

[348] Sandro Magister, "Vatican Diary / Exile to Malta for Cardinal Burke," chiesa.espressonline.it, 17 September 2014, http://chiesa.espresso.repubblica.it/articolo/1350870bdc4.html?eng=y.

[349] Joan Frawley Desmond, "Cardinal Burke Officially Transferred from Apostolic Signatura," *National Catholic Register*, 8 November 2014, http://www.ncregister.com/daily-news/cardinal-burke-officially-transferred-from-apostolic-signature.

[350] UCatholic, "Cardinal Burke Brought Back into Roman Curia by Pope Francis," Ave Maria Radio, 29 September 2015, https://avemariaradio. net/cardinal-burke-brought-back-into-roman-curia-by-pope-francis/.

[351] Austen Ivereigh, "Knights of Malta Chief Says It Was Burke Who Asked Official to Resign," *Crux*, 15 February 2017, https:// cruxnow.com/analysis/2017/02/15/knights-malta-chief-says-burke-asked-official-resign/; Edward Pentin, "Cardinal Burke Firmly Rejects Account by Order of Malta's Acting Head," *National Catholic*

Pope Francis appointed a special delegate to take over the governing duties of the patron of the Sovereign Military Order of Malta, while leaving Cardinal Burke in that office.[352] Later in 2017, Pope Francis reappointed Cardinal Burke to the Apostolic Signatura as a member.[353]

Amoris Laetitia

On April 8, 2016, Pope Francis published *Amoris Laetitia*, his apostolic exhortation on the 2014 and 2015 synods on the family. On September 19, 2016, Cardinal Burke and three other cardinals submitted to the pope formal questions, *dubia*, seeking clarification on five points of *Amoris Laetitia*, primarily to ascertain if previous teachings still applied. The main area of concern related to whether "remarried" divorcees could receive Holy Communion, but the scope of the *dubia* also included other questions related to the moral law.[354]

After personal delivery of the letter containing their *dubia* to the papal residence and to the Congregation for the Doctrine of the Faith, they received "no acknowledgment" or any response to them, and so were "given to understand that there would be no response to these questions."[355] The four cardinals then judged that they were "obliged, in

---

Register, 18 February 2017, http://www.ncregister.com/blog/edward-pentin/cardinal-burke-explains-his-mission-to-guam.

[352] Steve Skojec, "Controversial Grand Chancellor of the Knights of Malta Loses in Court," *One Peter Five,* 13 September 2017, https://onepeterfive.com/controversial-grand-chancellor-of-the-knights-of-malta-loses-in-court/.

[353] Edward Pentin, "Cardinal Burke on His New Appointment to Church's Highest Court," *National Catholic Register,* 3 October 2017, http://www.ncregister.com/blog/edward-pentin/cardinal-burke-explains-his-new-appointment-to-churchs-highest-court.

[354] Cardinal Burke had also regularly expressed his concerns about the Holy Communion for remarried divorcees issue, most notably in the book *Remaining in the Truth of Christ* (Ignatius Press, 2014).

[355] Edward Pentin, "Pope Francis' Comments to Reuters on the Dubia Incomplete," *National Catholic Register,* 21 June 2018, http://www.ncregister.com/blog/edward-pentin/pope-francis-comments-to-reuters-on-the-dubia-incomplete.

conscience as cardinals, to publish the *dubia*, on Nov. 14, 2016, so that the faithful would be aware of these serious questions touching upon the salvation of souls."[356] Burke has fervently defended these actions as carried out "according to the long-standing practice of the Church."[357] Immediately following the publication of the *dubia*, the pope removed the cardinal as a member of the Congregation for Divine Worship.[358]

In June 2018, Pope Francis said in a public interview that he heard about the cardinals' letter "from the newspapers ... a way of doing things that is, let's say, not ecclesial, but we all make mistakes."[359] The pope has yet to respond directly to the questions posed in the *dubia*. Cardinal Burke has suggested that, if he received no response from the pope, he would issue a formal correction of the pope. He has not yet taken any public action of that sort.[360]

Archbishop Viganò

In August 2018, Archbishop Carlo Maria Viganò released an eleven-page testament alleging, *inter alia*, that Pope Francis learned about sexual abuse by Theodore (then-Cardinal) McCarrick on June 23, 2013, but continued to cover for him and even allowed him to have more responsibilities.[361] Of these allegations Cardinal Burke said: "The declarations made by a prelate of the authority of Archbishop Carlo Maria Viganò must be totally taken

---

[356] Ibid.

[357] Ibid.; see also, e.g., Pentin, "Burke Addresses the 'Dubia.'"

[358] Joshua J. McElwee, "Vatican Confirms Francis Did Not Renew Terms of Burke, Pell on Worship Congregation," *National Catholic Reporter*, 22 November 2016, https://www.ncronline.org/blogs/ncr-today/vatican-confirms-removal-burke-pell-worship-congregation.

[359] Philip Pullella, "Exclusive — Pope Criticizes Trump Administration Policy on Migrant Family Separation," Reuters, 20 June 2018, https://af.reuters.com/article/worldNews/idAFKBN1JG0YG.

[360] Pentin, "Burke Addresses the 'Dubia.'"

[361] Edward Pentin, "Ex-Nuncio Accuses Pope Francis of Failing to Act on McCarrick's Abuse," *National Catholic Register*, 25 August 2018, http://www.ncregister.com/daily-news/ex-nuncio-accuses-pope-francis-of-failing-to-act-on-mccarricks-abuse.

to heart by those responsible in the Church."[362] Burke has also called for further investigation of the Viganò testimony. According to Cardinal Burke, "[Archbishop Viganò's] request for resignation is . . . licit; anyone can make it in the face of whatever pastor that errs greatly in the fulfillment of his office, but the facts need to be verified."[363]

Holy See–China Relations

Burke criticized the Vatican's September 22, 2018, provisional agreement with China regarding the appointment of Chinese bishops. According to the deal, the Vatican lifted excommunication on bishops appointed by the Chinese government without Vatican approval.[364] Other precise details remain unclear. For example, the status of underground bishops loyal to the Vatican, the Vatican's future relationship with Taiwan, and the appointment process for future Chinese bishops had not yet been specified. Cardinal Burke considers the agreement "absolutely unconscionable" and "a betrayal of so many confessors and martyrs who suffered for years and years and were put to death" by the Chinese Communist Party.[365] In his view, "there is no question that the Chinese government is absolutely hostile to the Catholic faith and any Christian faith and they want to destroy it. In China the religion is China."[366]

---

[362] John-Henry Westen, "Cardinal Burke Responds to Former US Nuncio's Explosive Letter about Pope Francis," LifeSite News, 26 August 2018, https://www.lifesitenews.com/news/cardinal-burke-responds-to-former-us-nuncios-explosive-letter-about-pope-fr.

[363] Gerard O'Connell, "Cardinal Burke: It Is 'Licit' to Call for the Resignation of Pope Francis," *America*, 29 August 2018, https://www.americamagazine.org/faith/2018/08/29/cardinal-burke-it-licit-call-resignation-pope-francis.

[364] Jason Horowitz and Ian Johnson, "China and Vatican Reach Deal on Appointment of Bishops," *New York Times*, 22 September 2018, https://www.nytimes.com/2018/09/22/world/asia/china-vatican-bishops.html.

[365] Lisa Bourne, "Cardinal Burke Calls Vatican Deal with China 'Unconscionable,'" LifeSite News, 22 October 2018, https://www.lifesitenews.com/news/cardinal-burke-calls-vatican-deal-with-china-unconscionable.

[366] Kratiuk, "Church without Enemies?"

Amazon Synod

In March 2020, Burke said that, although it had good aspects, he found the pope's Post-Synodal Apostolic Exhortation *Querida Amazonia* "troubling," as it contained passages that "gravely contradict theological truths."[367] He said there was a clear agenda to keep married priests and a female diaconate on the table, despite the document appearing to reject them, and he was disturbed by the diminishment of the Pachamama controversy in the document. "We never incorporate anything into the sacred liturgy unless we know very certainly that it is coherent with the worship of God," he said.

Before the synod, he and Bishop Athanasius Schneider of Astana, Kazakhstan, issued an eight-page declaration warning against "six theological errors and heresies" they said were contained in the synod's working document, and called for a forty-day period of prayer and fasting to prevent them from being approved.[368]

Throughout the episodes described here, Cardinal Burke has clearly had differences with this pontificate, but he has always sought to draw careful distinctions between his relationship with the pope as a person and the Petrine Office. He has avoided speculation about the pope's motives in changing Burke's offices[369] and insists instead that his actions during this papacy are not "contra–Pope Francis."[370] He asserts "we must always distinguish the body of the man who is the Roman Pontiff from the body of the Roman Pontiff, that is, from the man who exercises the office of St. Peter in the Church."[371] He also stresses that "any expression

[367] Pentin, "Disputes over Doctrine."
[368] Edward Pentin, "Cardinal Burke, Bishop Schneider Announce Crusade of Prayer and Fasting," *National Catholic Register*, 12 September 2019, https://www.ncregister.com/blog/edward-pentin/crusade.
[369] See, e.g., "Burke Confirms: Yes, Pope Has Demoted Me," *Rorate Caeli*, 17 October 2014, https://rorate-caeli.blogspot.com/2014/10/burke-confirms-yes-pope-has-demoted-me.html.
[370] CWR Staff, "Source of Anguish."
[371] Pentin, "Scalfari Episode."

of doctrine or practice that is not in conformity with the Divine Revelation, contained in the Holy Scriptures and in the Tradition of the Church, cannot constitute an authentic exercise of the Apostolic or Petrine ministry and must be rejected by the faithful."[372]

Cardinal Burke states that his mission is to "defend the Catholic faith, and that means defending the Office of Peter to which the Pope has succeeded."[373] Whatever the implications of these views, he insists:

> I will never be part of any schism, even if I should be punished within the Church for what I in good conscience am trying to do to teach the Catholic faith and to defend it as I am obliged to do, first of all as a Christian but even more so as a Bishop and a Cardinal of the Church. I will never abandon the Catholic Church, because it is the Church founded by Our Lord Jesus Christ, who established Peter as the Head of the Apostolic College, as the principle of the unity [of] the Church throughout the world—and once we no longer have faith in our Lord's abiding presence in the Church, also through the Petrine Office, we cease to be Catholic, and we enter into that whole world of unending divisions among Christians.[374]

SUMMARY

Widely recognized as one of the Church's foremost experts in canon law, Raymond Burke is also known worldwide for his international apostolic work, including his support for right-to-life causes, the Extraordinary Form of the liturgy, and his devotion to the Holy Eucharist and the Sacred Heart.

[372] Hannah Brockhaus, "Cardinal Burke: Pope's Authority Is Derived Only from Obedience to God," Catholic News Agency, 7 April 2018, https://www.catholicnewsagency.com/news/cardinal-burke-popes-authority-is-derived-only-from-obedience-to-god-67420.

[373] CWR Staff, "Source of Anguish."

[374] Ibid.

Cardinal Burke's devotion to the Blessed Virgin was manifested in his successful project to build the Shrine of Our Lady of Guadalupe in La Crosse, Wisconsin. As a diocesan bishop, he promoted the growth of religious life within his diocese and enforced discipline when necessary. He has been especially firm in defending both the sacrality of the sacraments and the inviolability of all human life, most notably withholding Holy Communion from Catholic legislators who promote abortion.

In his curial experience as previous prefect of the Apostolic Signatura, as well as other curial appointments, he has manifested a commitment to implementing the teachings of the Church in accordance with Catholic tradition and the Second Vatican Council but purposely resisted entering into petty games within the Curia, adhering instead to applying Church law with fairness and justice.

Cardinal Burke is known for his fidelity to the revealed doctrine of the Church, a characteristic that, at times, has provoked vociferous criticism from those within the Church who often cannot accept those teachings. He has responded with meekness and prayer while remaining steadfast to his convictions, leading many of the faithful to look to him for guidance when they have doubts or are confused about the Church's leadership. Those of sound formation see a bishop who is reliably Catholic, who can resolve issues of faith, be they doctrinal or canonical. And despite his being stripped of almost every ecclesiastical role with the exception of bishop and cardinal, often they will seek out Cardinal Burke when they visit Rome — a sign, some believe, of both his personal sanctity and the *sensus fidelium* in action. He makes time to see visitors if he is available and freely imparts his advice. Ever willing to promote the good of souls and society, he has given his name to many Catholic groups, associations, educational institutes, and projects that work toward those ends. He has latterly made use of the digital media to promote his teaching office.

Critics have accused the cardinal of opposing Pope Francis, or of being too critical and negative. He himself sees his role as being supportive and in a positive light, always by drawing on faith and reason. He stresses that his concerns over recent documents or decisions coming from the Vatican stem from his care for souls; his commitment to Church doctrine, which he sees as inextricably tied to such care; and his love for the Holy Father and the Petrine Office. He insists that the role of every cardinal is to support the office of the Roman pontiff, which includes offering counsel and doctrinal assistance when needed. A point of reference for the faithful worldwide who look for a voice of clarity from cardinals on matters facing the Church today, Cardinal Burke is known as a reliable proponent of orthodoxy and traditional Catholic piety.

SERVICE TO THE CHURCH

Ordination to the Priesthood: 29 June 1975
Ordination to the Episcopate: 6 January 1995
Elevation to the College of Cardinals: 20 November 2010

Education
1962-1968: Holy Cross Seminary, La Crosse, Wisconsin
1968-1970: Catholic University of America,
Washington, D.C.; Philosophy (Ph.B., Ph.L.)
1971-1975: Pontifical Gregorian University,
Rome; Theology (B.S.T., M.A.)
1980-1984: Pontifical Gregorian University,
Rome; Canon law (J.C.L., J.C.D.)

Assignments
- 1975-1980: Religion teacher, Aquinas High School
- 1984-1989: Moderator of the Curia and Vice Chancellor, Diocese of La Crosse
- 1989-1994: Defender of the Bond, Supreme Tribunal of the Apostolic Signatura
- 1994-2003: Bishop, Diocese of La Crosse

- 2003-2008: Archbishop, Archdiocese of Saint Louis
- 2006-2008: Member, Supreme Tribunal of the Apostolic Signatura
- 2008-present: Member, Pontifical Council for Legislative Texts
- 2008-2013: Member, Congregation for the Clergy
- 2008-2014: Prefect, Supreme Tribunal of the Apostolic Signatura
- 2008-2014: President, Commission for Advocates
- 2009-2013: Member, Congregation for Bishops
- 2010-2016: Member, Congregation for Divine Worship and the Discipline of the Sacraments
- 2010-2013: Member, Congregation for the Causes of Saints
- 2010-present: Cardinal-deacon of Sant'Agata dei Goti
- 2011-2014: Member, Council of Cardinals and Bishops, Relations with States, Secretariat of State
- 2012: President, Commission for Controversies, Thirteenth Ordinary Synod of Bishops
- 2014-present: Patron of Sovereign Military Order of Malta (without responsibilities since 2017)
- 2015-present: Member, Congregation for the Causes of Saints
- 2017-present: Member, Supreme Tribunal of the Apostolic Signatura

Membership
- Congregation for the Causes of Saints
- Pontifical Council for Legislative Texts
- Supreme Tribunal of the Apostolic Signatura

Additional Positions

- President, Board of Directors, Shrine of Our Lady of Guadalupe, La Crosse, Wisconsin, USA
- International Director, Marian Catechist Apostolate
- Episcopal Adviser, Catholic Action for Faith and Family
- Episcopal Adviser, Catholic Healthcare International

DOMINIK JAROSLAV CARDINAL DUKA, O.P.

"In the Spirit of Truth"

Born: 26 April 1943
Hradec Králové, Bohemia and Moravia (now Czech Republic)
Nationality: Czech
Title: Archbishop of Prague

BIOGRAPHY

The son of a soldier, Jaroslav Duka grew up in Bohemia, now incorporated into the Czech Republic, under the harsh policies of communism. During the brief "Prague Spring" of 1968, he entered the Dominican Order and was given the name Dominik. After his ordination to the priesthood in 1970, he defied laws of religious suppression and wore his habit in public. Despite persecution, he worked as an underground priest and novice master and as a designer in an automobile factory until he was arrested in 1981 for offering Mass illegally and publishing uncensored books. While in prison for fifteen months, he shared his cell with Václav Havel, the playwright and eventual president of Czechoslovakia and the Czech Republic, and celebrated Mass under the ruse of a chess tournament.[375]

In 1986, he was superior of the Dominican Province, and in 1998 received episcopal ordination. In 1989, the Velvet Revolution, led by Havel and aided by Duka, peacefully dissolved communism in Czechoslovakia. After that, the Dominican friar increasingly served as a visible leader nationally and internationally—for example, as vice president of the Union of European Conferences of Major Superiors from 1992 to 1996. In 2000, he became Catholic primate of the Czech Republic; and from 2000 to 2004, he was vice president of the Czech Bishops' Conference. Since then, he has served as a bridge between the Holy See and his native country, helping to facilitate the return of Church property previously stolen by the communist government. In 2010, Benedict XVI appointed him archbishop of Prague and, in 2012, elevated him to the College of Cardinals. As a biblical scholar, he has served on a number of theological faculties, commissions, and boards.[376]

SANCTIFYING OFFICE

Teaching the Eucharist

The Czech Republic is now mainly an atheist country, and Cardinal Duka has worked to help make the Church's teaching on the Eucharist understandable. "The celebration of the Body and Blood of Our Lord

---

[375] Michael Zantovsky, *Havel: A Life* (Great Britain: Atlantic Books, 2014).

[376] See "Duka: From Dissent to the Moral Reconstruction of the Czech Republic," *La Stampa*, 15 February 2012, https://www.lastampa.it/vatican-insider/en/2012/02/15/news/duka-from-dissent-to-the-moral-reconstruction-of-the-czech-republic-1.36500296. Also, Markéta Hulpachová, "Cardinal Duka Sheds Light on Church Restitution Controversy," *Prague Post Magazine*, 12 September 2012, https://web.archive.org/web/20170517000214/http://www.praguepost.com/news/14244-cardinal-duka-Sheds-light-on-church-restitution-controversy.html.

tells us that God is the Father of all nations and every nation, and is our Savior and Redeemer,"[377] Cardinal Duka pointed out on the feast of Corpus Christi in 2015, referencing the Old Testament texts of the Israelites' wandering in the wilderness. They were a people brought to freedom by God.

"If anyone wants to discuss the Eucharist, he should know the Bible and philosophy,"[378] Duka said in response to doubts about the rationality of Transubstantiation. Catholics in the Middle Ages understood that "participation in the Eucharist isn't cannibalistic, but part of the great mystery in which God gives Himself for man."[379] When asked about the meaning of the procession of the Holy Sacrament, Duka explained that the Holy Sacrament "is not a symbol of Catholic triumphalism, but a confession of faith in Him who made a covenant at the cost of dying and shedding His blood."[380] "The most beautiful moment is actually the celebration of the Eucharist, it cannot stand comparison with anything."[381]

At the start of a Eucharistic Congress in 2015, Duka said, "The Eucharist is a gift, but also food for the journey of life, the sacrifice of the Lamb, the sacrifice of the righteous Abel, the forefather of Abraham and of the priest Melchizedek, the sacrifice of the new and everlasting."[382]

He further emphasized the gratuitous nature of the Eucharist when he argued in a 2009 interview that, since every person is sinful, seeing

---

[377] Dominik Cardinal Duka, O.P., "Preaching on God's Body," DominikDuka.cz, 8 June 2015, www.dominikduka.cz/kazaniK/kazani-na-bozi-telo-2015/ (translated from Czech).

[378] Ibid.

[379] Ibid.

[380] Ibid.

[381] Dominik Cardinal Duka, O.P., "Interview for *Catholic Weekly*," interview by Jiri Machane, DominikDuka.cz, 8 May 2015, www.dominikduka.cz/rozhovory-menu/rozhovor-pro-katolicky-tydenik/ (translated from Czech).

[382] Dominik Cardinal Duka, O.P., "Greetings at the National Eucharistic Congress 2015," DominikDuka.cz, www.dominikduka.cz/prednasky-proslovy/pozdrav-na-narodnim-eucharistickem-kongresu-2015/ (translated from Czech).

the Eucharist as in any way a reward for one's performance denies the power of the Eucharist.[383] On other occasions, Duka has implied that the understanding of the sacraments as unmerited gifts is undermined by contemporary practice, as "for all sacraments, we have compulsory preparation, somehow forgetting that the ancient Church had mystagogic catechesis, that it spoke to the catechumen of the effects of the sacrament after he was baptized," whereas now it seems Baptism has become "a difficult test in which I must prove myself to be baptized."[384] In emphasizing that the Eucharist is the way to Christ, Duka has said: "The Eucharist says I am a man who must go to Christ — to Someone, not to something; to the One who is, who transcends me but wants to lead me. I belong to Christ; therefore I accept Him as my life teacher, as food and drink for the journey, and I will reach the great community of Jesus' friends, His great flock, which He leads as a shepherd."[385]

Throughout his writings, Duka focuses on the commandment of love and invites us not to act immediately as an enforcer of rules but to go back to the essence of our Faith and realize that, in the Eucharist, Christ welcomes and strengthens us. "The One who during His Last Supper gave us, as a parting gift, the law of real love, explaining that the one who gives his life for his friends has the greatest love, teaches us to live with others and for others,"[386] Duka has taught. "Jesus Himself urges you to create God's kingdom of peace and love, truth and true freedom."[387]

---

[383] Dominik Cardinal Duka, O.P., "Interview on the Eucharist," interview by Milan Badal, DominikDuka.cz, 16 October 2015, www.dominikduka.cz/rozhovory-menu/rozhovor-o-eucharistii/ (translated from Czech).

[384] Ibid. See also Dominik Cardinal Duka, O.P., "Eucharistic Congress as Meeting with Christ," DominikDuka.cz, 17 October 2015, www.dominikduka.cz/vyjadreni/eucharisticky-kongres-jako-setkani-s-kristem (translated from Czech).

[385] Ibid.

[386] Dominik Cardinal Duka, O.P., "New Year's Shepherd's Leaf," DominikDuka.cz, 1 January 2015, www.dominikduka.cz/kazaniK/novo-rocni-pastyrsky-list/ (translated from Czech).

[387] Dominik Cardinal Duka, O.P., "Pastoral Word on the Sunday of Divine Mercy," DominikDuka.cz, 28 April 2019, www.dominikduka.cz/kazaniK/

Duka reminds us that "it is necessary to realize the great moment of the Eucharistic mystery and the presence of Christ in the sacraments."[388] He once recalled the story of a child who was not baptized attending Holy Communion without considering it as inappropriate. When a priest found out, he was terrified, to which Duka remarked: There is something called the "baptism of desire, which is supposed to rid us of anxiety so that we do not turn God into a mere policeman or judge."[389] In another speech, Duka reemphasized this, saying: "Where the Eucharist, the new and eternal covenant, is celebrated, there is an open friendly embrace for us, for you, for all." He references Moses' Ten Commandments and Jesus' commandment of love — a covenant that establishes friendship between God and man in Jesus Christ, the High Priest of the New Covenant.[390]

On the Traditional Latin Mass

Answering a question regarding Latin liturgy, Duka explained he has nothing against it or against chanting but urges recognition that liturgy is not an exhibition of baroque art. "I think that it is necessary to follow the history of the liturgy and the Council of Trent itself.... Liturgy is not rites; liturgy is life. The Tridentine liturgy would be a living liturgy only if we lived in Tridentine times in all its consequences, with its spirituality and its political order."[391]

Cardinal Duka regularly expresses his appreciation for traditional liturgy and the importance of rubrics to any sound liturgical celebration. But he often qualifies that appreciation by subordinating liturgical

---

pastyrske-slovo-na-nedeli-boziho-milosrdenstvi-2019/ (translated from Czech).

[388] Duka, "Interview for *Catholic Weekly*."

[389] Ibid.

[390] Duka, "Greetings."

[391] Dominik Cardinal Duka, O.P., "I'm Not a Diplomat or Dissident ...," interview with Petr Prihoda, DominikDuka.cz, 1 July 2010, www.dominikduka. cz/rozhovory-menu/nejsem-diplomatem-ani-disidentem/ (translated from Czech).

forms to a deeper spirit. In the 2005 Synod on the Eucharist as "Source and Summit of the Life and Mission of the Church," for example, Duka spoke on the Eucharistic liturgy:

> Many of us are convinced that a "Tridentine liturgy" and a "liturgy after Vatican Council II" exist. This is not true. There are different liturgies, and liturgical developments have always existed. We must have great consideration and respect for the liturgy of the Oriental Church, but also for the new developments in the "Latin liturgy." When the Byzantine liturgy was elaborated, to give honor to Christ, imperial court ceremonial was used, while maintaining, at the same time, faithfulness to the mystery of the Son of God. In this sense, different ways of venerating Christ in Asia, Africa, and Europe should be allowed. The difference between the Latin and the Byzantine liturgy is deeper than the one between the "Tridentine Rite" and the "liturgy of Zaire"![392]

Duka has further argued that: "Study on the history of the Liturgy and of the Sacraments also encourages new liturgical action. Everything cannot be lowered to an over-meticulous observance of rubrics. We also need to appreciate the deep meaning inherent in the liturgy, and that flows from it."[393]

GOVERNING OFFICE

Early Years as a Dominican

Dominik Duka entered the Order of Preachers (Dominicans) in 1968. Communists at the time controlled what was then Czechoslovakia, and

---

[392] Holy See Press Office, "XI Ordinary General Assembly of the Synod of Bishops," Vatican, 7 October 2005, www.vatican.va/news_services/press/sinodo/documents/bollettino_21_xi-ordinaria-2005/02_inglese/b11_02.html#-.

[393] Ibid.

entering the Dominican Order was illegal. Duka had been a priest for only five years when his state permit as a so-called "spiritual administrator" was withdrawn. As a result, he worked in a Skoda automobile factory for fourteen years. During this time, Duka served as the Dominicans' provincial vicar, taught and organized events for Dominican seminarians, and set up a clandestine religious-studies center. Because organizing such "religious activities" was not permitted by the regime, Duka was sentenced to fifteen months in prison at Plzeň-Bory. He remained provincial vicar and was later appointed superior of the Dominican Province, then president of the Czech Dominican Conference of Major Superiors, and finally vice president of the Dominican Union of European Conferences of Major Superiors. Duka also taught biblical theology at Palacký University (Olomouc, Czech Republic) before receiving his first episcopal assignment in 1998.

Hometown Bishop

Duka was appointed ordinary of his hometown, Hradec Králové, on June 6, 1998, and was installed on September 26 of that year. During his time as bishop of Hradec Králové, Duka founded a theological institute in Skuteč. In 2002, he convoked the second diocesan Eucharistic Congress. He published the new statutes of the Holy Spirit Cathedral Chapter and appointed nine canons. From 2000 to 2004 he was vice president of the Czech Bishops' Conference.

Archbishop of Prague

On February 13, 2010, Pope Benedict XVI appointed Duka archbishop of Prague. On his appointment, Duka said: "The Church must engage in a dialogue with society and must seek reconciliation with it. Twenty years ago, we were euphoric about freedom; today we live in an economic and financial crisis, and also to a certain extent in a crisis of values. So the tasks are going to be a little more difficult. But thanks to everything that's been done, it will not be a journey into the unknown."[394]

[394] "Profiles of the New Cardinals," *Inside the Vatican*, https://insidethevatican. com/news/lead-story/profiles-of-the-new-cardinals/.

Duka identified two focal points of his pastoral agenda: working with young people and opening up the Church to society.[395] Regarding the latter, Duka said, "The Church should respond more readily to the questions of today's world. Religious questions and answers must be put and answered in a comprehensible language and correspond to a higher level of people's education; and so that young people can recognize themselves in these reports so that they can better orient themselves in an increasingly contradictory world."[396] Duka furthermore said that "one of the ideas to think about for the Church is undoubtedly how to engage young people in liturgical and religious life in order to fit their mentality."[397] Currently, Duka's diocese (thanks, in part, to a large Slovak population) is one of the youngest in the Czech Republic—according to Duka, mostly "because of the new Prague quarters and areas with modern technologies. New Church buildings and community centers are being built there; even Bavarian Bishops envy us."[398]

Duka has also focused on bringing people closer together in pursuit of his dream: "I have a great dream: to make people behave together kindly throughout the year as they did at Christmas."[399]

Religious Education

Duka continues to stress the importance of religious education and teaching, to counteract the moral state of society.[400] He made a major contribution to

---

[395] Jan Gazdík, "Duka: The Archbishop Was Supposed to Be Someone Younger Who Could Better Bear the Pressure," *Indes.Cz*, 15 February 2010, www.idnes.cz/zpravy/domaci/duka-arcibiskupem-mel-byt-nekdo-mladsi-kdo-lepe-ponese-tlak.A100215_072307_domaci_klu (translated from Czech).

[396] Ibid.

[397] Ibid.

[398] Jaroslav Daniska, "The Church Cannot Only Think of Itself," *Svet krestanstva*, 1 January 2018, https://svetkrestanstva.postoj.sk/29523/cirkev-nemoze-mysliet-iba-na-seba (translated from Czech).

[399] Jan Gazdík, "Someone Younger."

[400] Dominik Cardinal Duka, O.P., "Shepherd's Letter to New Year 2017," DominikDuka.cz, 3 January 2017, www.dominikduka.cz/prednasky-proslovy/pastyrsky-list-k-novemu-roku-novy/ (translated from Czech).

translating the Jerusalem Bible into Czech.[401] As chairman of the Catholic Biblical Federation, Duka tries to contribute to the potential to evangelize contemporary European culture through, for example, innovative Bible studies aiming to provide a proper understanding of Holy Scripture for all those interested in reading the Bible.[402]

Elevation to Cardinal

The announcement that Duka would be elevated to cardinal led to protests within the Czech Catholic Church. The reason was that Duka is widely seen as too political, tied too closely to the Czech presidents. In a country where as many as 90 percent of the people are religiously indifferent or atheistic and where even the small minority of persons who are Catholic are divided in their opinions of his pastoral leadership, Duka is aware of the difficulty of speaking in plain terms about the demands of the Catholic Faith and of moral truth.[403] He often tries to create a beachhead for the Church in an unbelieving society by speaking on a wide range of issues, indicating therein the meaningfulness of human life and dignity and the place of Christ therein.

Indeed, on the day he was installed as archbishop of Prague, Duka said that "this cathedral became a symbol of Czech statehood. . . . Above the cathedral, there was never a foreign flag, no swastika, no red flag

---

[401] "DUKA Card. Dominik, O.P.," Vatican, https://press.vatican.va/content/ salastampa/en/documentation/cardinali_biografie/cardinali_bio_duka_d. html.

[402] Dominik Cardinal Duka, O.P., "Letter to Bible Day," DominikDuka.cz, 15 November 2015, www.dominikduka.cz/vyjadreni/dopis-ke-dni-bible/ (translated from Czech).

[403] Tom Jones, "Prague Archbishop Duka to Be Elevated to Cardinal amid Protests at Home," *Ceska Pozice*, 18 February 2012, http://ceskapozice. lidovky.cz/prague-archbishop-duka-to-be-elevated-to-cardinal-amid-protests-at-home-1zb-/tema.aspx?c=A120217_180006_pozice_57224. See also: Dominik Cardinal Duka, O.P., "Religion in Secularized Society," DominikDuka.cz, 7 October 2010, www.dominikduka.cz/prednasky-proslovy/nabozenstvi-v-sekularizovane-spolecnosti/ (translated from Czech).

with a sickle and a hammer. Even in the occupied castle there has always been an island of God and our freedom.... These figures show that the Church is not just a dedicated religious institution or a carrier of moral principles. It is part of the nation's organism and also carries hope and courage for the future as an example of selfless love.... I will continue to work with the government and the institutions of our state in the spirit of genuine interest in the constant bloom of our nation and society, where the family is the foundation of civil and religious community, where education and training have an ethical dimension and a religious aspect. To do so, I am bound by the Christian faith, the legacy of this cathedral, but also the life and sacrifice of my predecessors at the Holy See."[404]

In 2018 Duka turned seventy-five, and he sent the customary resignation letter to the pope, who asked him to stay on as archbishop of Prague.[405]

TEACHING OFFICE

Holy Scripture

Duka taught theology to Czech Dominican seminarists and was a biblical theology lecturer at Palacký University (Olomouc, Czech Republic). He also made a major contribution to translating the Jerusalem Bible into Czech. As a Bible scholar, Duka has written extensively on this topic. He has stated: "From the very beginnings to the present day, inspiration has

---

[404] Dominik Cardinal Duka, O.P., "Homily on the Day of Taking Office," DominikDuka.cz, 3 June 2010, www.dominikduka.cz/kazaniK/homilie-v-den-prevzeti-uradu/ (translated from Czech).

[405] "Duka to Keep Post of Prague Archbishop Despite Turning 75," *Prague Daily Monitor*, 10 May 2018, www.praguemonitor.com/2018/05/10/duka-keep-post-prague-archbishop-despite-turning-75.

been witnessed by the universal and constant Church tradition. The oldest Fathers of the Church call the Holy Scripture '*Oracula Dei dictatas a Spiritu Sancto.*' The Holy Spirit uses the writer as an instrument .... The Church's teaching office, in its various decrees of the assemblies and in various other documents, shows us the continuity of faith in inspiration."[406] Duka especially references Pope Pius XII's Encyclical *Divino Afflante Spiritu* and the Dogmatic Constitution *Dei Verbum*. The latter brings us "to use the term 'truthfulness'—the truthfulness of the Bible, the truthfulness of God's revelation," Duka explains.[407]

When speaking on a radio show in 2016, Duka stressed his commitment to popular instruction. "I'm not a doctor; I'm not a philosopher. Yet let me make a few remarks that will be spoken not in scientific and precise language, but in words that everyone can understand."[408] Duka was a member of the working class for a large part of his life. During this period, he clandestinely taught the Dominicans. He was also engaged in the publication of unauthorized *samizdat* literature (an activity that landed him in jail). As cardinal, Archbishop Duka maintains a blog and writes columns and is a frequent guest on radio shows and in other colloquial forums. With his "common folk" language he approaches different audiences and has the opportunity to address a wide range of issues. The contacts he made during his time in prison also strengthen his bonds with the government.

---

[406] Dominik Cardinal Duka, O.P., *Úvod do Písma sv. Starého zákona* (Prague: Editio Sti. Aegidii, 1992), excerpts available online, see: Dominik Cardinal Duka, O.P., "Úvod do Písma sv. Starého zákona," *Farnost.Katolik.cz*, http://farnost.katolik.cz/lanskroun/library/udps1.htm (translated from Czech).

[407] Ibid.

[408] Dominik Cardinal Duka, O.P., "About Not Dying: Commentary on the Effort to Introduce Euthanasia," DominikDuka.cz, 2 July 2016, www.dominikduka.cz/vyjadreni/o-nemirani-komentar-ke-snaze-o-zavedeni-euthanasie/ (translated from Czech).

Reason and Religious Freedom

On the day Duka was installed as archbishop of Prague, he addressed in his homily both the need for rational argumentation (especially needed in the mainly atheist Czech Republic) and the freedom of religion provided by democracy: "To proclaim the Gospel means to preach life and hope for life.... Unbelief helps us, like [Christ's] disciples, not to forget the need for rational argumentation in religious life. Faith is not the fruit of fantasy, passion, or ideological imperative. It is a free and reasonable reflection of a mature person. The gospel is for everyone. Here, the perspective of a genuine democracy has been opened, relying on rationality, not the seduction of pleasing offers."[409]

Valuing Laity

Duka praised the effort of his predecessor, Cardinal Miloslav Vlk, to improve the position of laypeople in the Church. "We are going to need capable professionals. Not every church in Europe has so many laypeople working for the Church as we do. And I am especially mentioning the number of women." Duka stresses that although a "priest needs to be a professional in his spiritual work, in his vocation and profession, in all other areas (where, in fact, he is considered a layperson), there are situations when the professionals can step in—people who know the fields of economics, construction, culture, or media. And we thus can have a great female adviser, chancellor, or catechist."[410]

Given the moral state of Czech society, Duka has stressed the difficult task of spreading knowledge about Church teaching and asked for the help of fellow priests, deacons, religious, and, above all, parents and catechists, in the years to come. Although "we criticize the whole society and the political sphere, the moral state of society, we lament that decency and interest in others are disappearing. Let us admit that it is, above all, our task, as Christians, as the Church [to spread the

---

[409] Duka, "Homily on the Day of Taking Office."
[410] Duka, "Interview for *Catholic Weekly*."

gospel]!"[411] Duka pointed out that "our main task has been and remains pastoralism and evangelism."[412] Further, he noted, "There is no need for bishops and priests constantly to remind the public of what the Church, the pope, or the Bible is saying. We should enter life by saying: this is right, good, useful; this is true. This is how we need to transform the presence of the Church in our country. We will not do much with mere statements and resolutions. This is the last resort. We are supposed to be present in our own place and patiently, often even humbly, co-create the life of society."[413]

RENEWAL OF POLITICS

"The renewal of politics can be achieved only by restoring [its] relationship to truth," Duka maintains.[414] He has focused most keenly, perhaps, on the family as a social pillar. "Only in the family will we learn solidarity, subsidiarity, relation to truth. But in what state are our families today? What will the new generation get [from today's family]? If the family is not the foundation of our society, but, on the contrary, the mentality of individualism, it cannot go well. It is a violation of the person's identity and personality.... It destroys [society], when everyone promotes only himself and his rights. It will distort political life."[415]

[411] Dominik Cardinal Duka, O.P., "Shepherd's Letter to New Year 2017," DominikDuka.cz, 3 January 2017, www.dominikduka.cz/prednasky-pro-slovy/pastyrsky-list-k-novemu-roku-novy/ (translated from Czech).

[412] Dominik Cardinal Duka, O.P., "Letter to My Co-Workers," DominikDuka.cz, 4 January 2012, www.dominikduka.cz/vyjadreni/list-mym-spolupra-covnikum/ (translated from Czech).

[413] Duka, "I'm Not a Diplomat."

[414] Daniska, "Church Cannot Only Think of Itself."

[415] Ibid.

Communism versus the Family

In his contribution to the Ignatius Press book *Eleven Cardinals Speak on Marriage and the Family: Essays from a Pastoral Viewpoint*, Duka starts by underlining that communism—as he experienced it in the Czech Republic—has played a big part in the destruction of the family. In his essay, Duka states that the significance of this ideological pressure that has demeaned and besmirched the family for a long time cannot be underestimated. "The family has been pilloried as an exploitative institution, as a place that oppresses spontaneity and destroys hedonistic desire, individual liberty, and so on," he states.[416] He goes on to say that, in his opinion, "the current crisis of the family is closely connected with the destruction of anthropology, that is, of our understanding of human beings as such."[417] Duka explains that it is already difficult for Catholics to consider the concept of man created in God's image given that God is invisible, unimaginable, and unfathomable. The concept of man is even more complex for those who live in the religious indifference of this postmodern era.

Duka underlined that in times of oppression and persecution of the family and all it stands for, strength and consolation can be found in studying the biblical foundations of our Faith. These clearly tell us that "father and mother are irreplaceable" because "father, mother, the deepest relationships, the deepest feelings of which man is capable, are the image of Him-who-is, in other words, of the living, *being* God."[418] Love, however, must be an "active element," he adds. The "priority of God's love commits man not to be satisfied with his own love but principally with making a gift of himself to the other."[419]

Duka stresses that the "current debasement of the word 'love' shows that true love has been replaced by mere eroticism without

---

[416] Winfried Aymans, *Eleven Cardinals Speak on Marriage and the Family: Essays from a Pastoral Viewpoint* (San Francisco: Ignatius Press, 2015).

[417] Ibid.

[418] Ibid.

[419] Ibid.

the dimension of friendship and gift."[420] This is especially true, Duka explains further, since nowadays someone's "word" does not seem to be worth anything anymore. When speaking about the subject of divorce, Duka elaborates that this indeed is not keeping one's word, not being faithful to one's oath, and, in fact, is not only "the spouses' denial of each other" but even worse, the denial "of who they themselves are."[421] Duka dares us to remember that "the Cross is the exaltation of keeping one's word, of the oath that God gave to mankind, of the God who trusts man."[422]

On Amoris Laetitia *and the* Dubia

When expressing his opinion on the four cardinals' *dubia*, Duka said he understood the motives of the cardinals, but did not explicitly reject or support them. He stated that the main topic of *Amoris Laetitia* is the family as such and that in *Amoris Laetitia* the pope formulates his thoughts and offers his thoughts for consideration, rather than defining infallible dogma ex cathedra.[423]

Similarly, Duka's focus on "keeping one's oath" and his references to the Eucharist as the new and eternal covenant provide some reason to believe that he opposes Communion for the divorced and "remarried." In a blog post from 2014, Duka said of a divorced person who is civilly "remarried": "He actually lives in sin with someone he is not lawfully married to" and thus "cannot approach to receive the Eucharist."[424]

---

[420] Ibid.

[421] Ibid.

[422] Ibid.

[423] Dominik Cardinal Duka, O.P., "Meeting with the Non-European Pope: Reflection on the Papacy," *Aktualne.cz*, 20 November 2017, http://blog.aktualne.cz/blogy/dominik-duka.php?itemid=30411 (translated from Czech).

[424] Dominik Cardinal Duka, O.P., "Marriage and Sacred Marriage," DominikDuka.cz, 20 October 2014, www.dominikduka.cz/vyjadreni/manzelstvi-a-posvatne-manzelstvi/ (translated from Czech).

Priestly Celibacy

In response to a journalist who mentioned that German theologians linked the sexual scandals in the Church to celibacy, Duka said: "Celibacy is voluntary. Somebody makes the decision to live celibate as a priest in the same way somebody else decides to marry. And we see examples of people morally failing in both matrimony and in celibacy." Duka furthermore explained that there are strong tendencies to misrepresent this topic in Western Europe. "Sometimes people blame celibacy as the cause of the shortage of priests. This, however, is not the main cause in a great part of Europe. We can see priest shortages in churches that allow priests to marry and even in those where women can become priests as well. All churches have the same problem. We have a Church tradition of celibacy, backed by the theological meaning in which the priesthood is understood as the representation of Christ. I would not change this tradition."[425]

Moral Norms and the Right to Life

On teaching moral norms more generally, Duka underlines that there is a reason for the Church authorities to formulate norms and defend them, since "the attitude of the Church is to strive for perfection." He states that he is aware that not everybody is able to live according to this attitude and that the conditions of our lives are not perfect either.[426] This, however, does not justify changing the rules, so to speak, because, after all, the reason behind the formulated Church rules and teachings has not changed. Duka underlined this standpoint when addressing the issue of contraception in response to a banner aimed against the March for Life that read: "Protected Sex is Not a Crime":

[425] Veronika Lehovcová Suchá, "Duka: Contraceptives Should Be Addressed Individually by Confessors," *Aktualne.cz*, 18 February 2011, https://zpravy. aktualne.cz/domaci/duka-antikoncepci-maji-zpovednici-resit-individualne/ r~i:article:691334/ (translated from Czech).

[426] Ibid.

Many things and attitudes are not a crime, but that doesn't mean they are right. I don't intend to [trivialize] this topic that the media usually pays a lot of attention to. I merely want to mention that sex that is open to creating life, sex that portrays mutual love and enrichment, is something that, according to the teaching of the Catholic Church, belongs to the relationship of a man and a woman joined in holy Matrimony. Protected sex might easily become an expression of selfishness, unwillingness to accept children, an expression of separating sex from real love.[427]

Duka has often condemned abortion. "Our message to the world is: human life is not a dream, it is not a comedy, not a mere experience, and it is meaningful in every form. The problem we call abortion will not disappear when we ban it by law," Duka said at the 2016 March for Life. He emphasized that education and social climate play a major role in the choice for abortion. "Once upon a time, as a nation, we have been persuaded of what is untruthful," he said and thanked those who have the courage to defend human life. "Man is created in the image of God, he is alive, even when his life is finished, murdered."[428]

Duka regularly takes part in the traditional March for Life, not only because of the thousands of babies being killed but also because of the absolute disregard for human life and its value. Duka has written about this topic many times. In one of his blog posts, he wrote:

If we kill unborn children, I dare say it is a greater terror and disaster than the recent terrorist attacks. We talk about hundreds of dead people with horror but forget about the thousands of dead children. Atheists, who criticize the March for Life, should rather get to know

[427] Dominik Cardinal Duka, O.P., "Perverted Progress and Killing Children," *Aktualne.cz*, 8 April 2016, http://blog.aktualne.cz/blogy/dominik-duka.php?itemid=27198 (translated from Czech).
[428] Dominik Cardinal Duka, O.P., "Preaching from the March for Life 2016," DominikDuka.cz, 2 April 2016, www.dominikduka.cz/kazaniK/kazani-z-pochodu-za-zivot-2016 (translated from Czech).

the fact that we do not force our opinions on anybody, we don't make people lose their jobs over it, and we don't shoot the doctors at the abortion clinics. We only offer the view of believers who accept life as a gift. Not only their own life, but the lives of all people. And they want to treat life with dignity and gratitude in the interest of the future generation that we believe has the right to live.[429]

He added: "We used to think about children as the future of the family. Now we think only about controlling birth rates, and the science continues to search for more means that would make it easier." [430]

Duka also references the paradox that many families today claim that they cannot afford a child or another child for economic reasons, whereas our grandparents, who certainly lived in much poorer circumstances, had five, eight, or more children. The question that is really at the heart of it all is whether we can still make out what is really important in life (parental care, love, and time dedicated to children rather than computers, cell phones, brand-name clothing, and vacations at sea), Duka says.[431] He also stressed the importance of providing a system of counseling and social facilities for mothers with children.[432]

Devotion to Our Lady

Duka situated the differences between man and woman within God's creative plan.[433] "The first pages of the Bible say that God created man

[429] Duka, "Perverted Progress."

[430] Suchá, "Contraceptives Should Be Addressed."

[431] Dominik Cardinal Duka, O.P., "Children Are Our Wealth," *Radiozurnal*, 16 September 2012, https://radiozurnal.rozhlas.cz/dominik-duka-deti-jsou-nase-bohatstvi-6265740 (translated from Czech).

[432] Dominik Cardinal Duka, O.P., "The Responses to the Abortion Debate," DominikDuka.cz, 6 May 2016, www.dominikduka.cz/vyjadreni/k-ohlasum-debaty-o-potratech (translated from Czech).

[433] Dominik Cardinal Duka, O.P., "Do Women Belong Only to the Kitchen? Asks Cardinal Dominik Duka," *Radiozurnal*, 23 August 2014, https://radiozurnal.rozhlas.cz/patri-zeny-jen-do-kuchyne-pta-se-kardinal-dominik-duka-6266042 (translated from Czech).

as man and woman.... Not long ago, I could see a snippet of a foreign documentary that demonstrated equality, but also the difference between a man and a woman, or vice versa, between a woman and a man. I think this difference is human society, culture, but also richer life. I can hardly imagine the validity of the claim that the difference between a man and a woman is only in education and in the cultural tradition. For I am a positivist and a realist. I cannot imagine or dare to deny the reality of exact sciences. Yet I ask where the fighting stance or class struggle between the sexes was born. Who sent the woman to the kitchen to hold *only* the wooden spoon?... The prototype of Christian womanhood is the Virgin Mary.... I have never seen a picture or sculpture on which St. Anne taught the Virgin Mary how to cook, sew socks, iron, or clean, but I *have* seen her being taught to read."[434]

Duka furthermore reminds us that "the figure of a woman appears on the pages of the Old Testament in a unique and unrepeatable role, where a woman, a virgin, a young girl, becomes the mother of hope of salvation."[435]

"Marian reverence is not merely a testimony of history and art in our regions, but it is above all an important element of our spiritual life," Duka said in a 2013 homily.[436] He underlined that "we always find Our Lady alongside Christ in all crucial and vital moments."[437] Duka reminds us that Mary is "the Mother of Christian Unity, the Queen of Peace, the Mediator of All Graces. Throughout the year we will approach her as the Virgin of the Mighty and the Refuge of Sinners. We are under her protection, and

---

[434] Ibid.

[435] Dominik Cardinal Duka, O.P., "Sermons of Mariazell," DominikDuka. cz, 16 August 2013, www.dominikduka.cz/kazaniK/kazani-z-mariazell/ (translated from Czech).

[436] Dominik Cardinal Duka, O.P., "Sermon at the Pilgrimage of Men, Piekary on May 26, 2013," DominikDuka.cz, 26 May 2013, www.dominikduka.cz/ kazaniK/kazani-na-pouti-muzu-piekary-26-kvetna-2013/ (translated from Czech).

[437] Ibid.

her Son, Jesus, who was sacrificed for us, *goes* with us. God the Father *is* with us and the Holy Spirit *connects* us."[438]

Euthanasia

Duka expressed his opposition to euthanasia in these terms: How could a doctor, on the one hand, "swear in one form or another to some version of Hippocrates' oath that he will heal patients, not kill them," especially since most doctors, despite their "philosophy or religion, [are] usually aware that being a doctor is not just a job, but a profession, even a mission," while, on the other hand, eliminating disabled children, the elderly, and those who are heavily treated without hope of recovery, as is the case in, for example, the Netherlands?[439]

"This issue is related to the value of human life," Duka stated. "Which life is more valuable — a young, happy, and healthy person? Or an old, helpless, immobile, or disabled person who has already done his job and will not bring anything else? If today some philosophers, even theologians, claim that human life can be of different value, the gate to hell opens. Of course, it will be nicely decorated with acceptable terminology."[440]

Duka is pleased with the attitude of the Czech doctors who, on the left and the right, state that euthanasia is not the right way. "Thanks for common sense, thanks for humanity and for a professional medical and healing approach to a disease that threatens mankind: inhuman stupidity,"[441] Duka stated in response.

---

[438] Dominik Cardinal Duka, O.P., "To Keep Our Civilization away from the Wind Like Fallen Leaves," *Aktualne.cz*, 1 March 2016, http://blog.aktualne. cz/blogy/dominik-duka.php?itemid=26502 (translated from Czech).

[439] Dominik Cardinal Duka, O.P., "About Not Dying: Commentary on the Effort to Introduce Euthanasia," DominikDuka.cz, 26 July 2016, www. dominikduka.cz/vyjadreni/o-nemirani-komentar-ke-snaze-o-zavedeni-euthanasie/ (translated from Czech).

[440] Ibid.

[441] Ibid.

Same-Sex "Marriage"

Duka has several times denounced homosexual "marriage" and adoption by same-sex couples.[442] The Church "defends the biological function of the family."[443] When Duka was bishop of Hradec Králové, he criticized the legal recognition of same-sex registered partnerships during the legislative process in 2006.[444] Regarding the adoption of children by same-sex couples and the use of surrogacy, Duka stated: "A child does not become a gift, but a human right, a claim, to satisfy the desire of adult people," leading to the "complete emptying and re-defining of the terms 'human' and 'human dignity'.... It is my duty to raise my voice when the dignity of human life is compromised under the masquerade of the claims."

Duka also wrote a letter to the Prague mayor to "reconsider carefully the patronage of the Prague Pride festival," because it "promotes an unbound lifestyle that is not responsible, dignified, or beautiful."[445] When LGBTQ Catholics asked Duka for special pastoral care for their

---

[442] "I would like to draw attention to a document that refutes the now frequently repeated (and misguided) argument that 'marriage for all is fair,' that this is only a minor adjustment that will not hurt anyone but will help others, or that children with parents of the same sex will be just as fine (or perhaps even better) than in classic families or institutions (the myth of orphanages full of unhappy children is very well refuted by Tomáš Zdechovský on his blog, https://zdechovsky.blog.idnes.cz/blog.aspx?c=672899)." Dominik Cardinal Duka, O.P., Facebook, 6 December 2018, www.facebook.com/dominik.duka.3/posts/2544734515567216. See also Dominik Cardinal Duka, O.P., "Full Development in Marriage," *Aktualne.cz*, 17 August 2013, http://blog.aktualne.cz/blogy/dominik-duka.php?itemid=20742.

[443] Dominik Cardinal Duka, O.P., "We Can No Longer Make Concessions," interview with Czech Primas, DominikDuka.cz, 17 April 2014, www.dominikduka.cz/rozhovory-menu/breznovy-rozhovor-pro-denik-pravo/ (translated from Czech).

[444] "Archbishop Duka Asks the Mayor to Consider the Patronage of Homosexuals," *Novinky.cz*, 11 August 2011, www.novinky.cz/domaci/241493-arcibiskup-duka-zada-primatora-aby-zvazil-zastitu-homosexualum.html (translated from Czech).

[445] "Archbishop Duka Asks the Mayor."

community, he turned them down because categorical pastoral care is given only to closed communities "that don't have any possibility to attend the Mass or to participate in general pastoral care.... LGBTQ Catholics are full-fledged citizens of the Czech Republic and welcomed as Catholic Christians. As such, the doors of our Masses are open, provided they respect the basic conditions required by the Christian ethics and by canon law. In this sense, our hearts and the doors of our churches are open," Duka said.[446]

Migrants and Refugees

When Duka celebrated Mass on the feast day of St. Wenceslas, patron saint of the Czech Republic, in 2017, he drew much attention for one of his intercessions: "We pray for refugees and migrants. May they have the strength to return to the lands of their fathers; may they become a new hope for their nations and rebuild their cities, where they may live in peace."[447] Some critics viewed this intercessory prayer (in combination with his homily) as an exhibition of excessive nationalism and a rejection of migrants, but Duka explained that the European refugee crisis is "merely a consequence of unsolved problems." "The current reception of refugees requires, on the basis of historical experience, not a multicultural approach but a way of inculturation that respects human dignity as well as the rights and traditions of host countries," Duka said.[448]

Duka has also criticized "momentary treatments of the problem that proved not to be useful—for example, those of 2015 Europe or UN

---

[446] Dominik Cardinal Duka, O.P., "Answer Logos CR and LGBT Catholics," DominikDuka.cz, 11 August 2017, www.dominikduka.cz/vyjadreni/odpoved-hnuti-logos-cr-a-lgbt-katolikum/ (translated from Czech).

[447] Dominik Cardinal Duka, O.P., "St. Wenceslas Sermon 2017," DominikDuka.cz, 28 September 2017, www.dominikduka.cz/kazaniK/svatovaclavske-kazani-2017/ (translated from Czech).

[448] Ibid.

debates."[449] He explained that it is accordingly necessary to use peace-keeping forces and to bring peace to the regions where the clashes take place and from which the migrants come. "It is not possible to take everybody in; it would lead to the collapse of Europe."[450] He finds it "as extremist and irresponsible to say: 'Not even one of them' as it is to proclaim: 'We can take everybody in.'"[451] Among other things, Duka urged people also to think of the monetary implications and the issue of integration.[452] That is why Duka stated that "together with open arms, vigilance is in place" and that he feels that "the right to the life and safety of our families and the citizens of this country is superior to other rights."[453]

[449] Dominik Cardinal Duka, O.P., "Poll on the Phenomenon of Migration," DominikDuka.cz, 6 August 2018, www.dominikduka.cz/vyjadreni/anketa-k-fenomenu-migrace/ (translated from Czech).

[450] Dominik Cardinal Duka, O.P., "Halik Is a Minority in the Church, Most of Them Are in Favor of Me," interview by Daniel Kaiser, *Echo24.cz*, 27 June 2017, https://m.echo24.cz/a/iB85V/duka-halik-je-v-cirkvi-mensina-vetsina-souzni-se-mnou, (translated from Czech). See also Dominik Cardinal Duka, O.P., "CBK Opinion on the Migration Crisis," DominikDuka.cz, 22 April 2016, www.dominikduka.cz/vyjadreni/stanovisko-cbk-k-migracni-krizi.

[451] Jana Bendova, "Cardinal Again under Fire. You Won't Get a Man for Good When You Beat Him, Says Dominik Duka," *Reflex*, 21 February 2018, www.reflex.cz/clanek/rozhovory/85234/kardinal-opet-pod-palbou-neziskate-cloveka-pro-dobro-kdyz-ho-budete-tlouct-rika-dominik-duka.html (translated from Czech).

[452] See Dominik Cardinal Duka, O.P., "Interview for Lidove Noviny," interview by Katerina Surmanova and Ondrej Koutnik, DominikDuka.cz, 9 May 2016, www.dominikduka.cz/rozhovory-menu/rozhovor-pro-lidove-noviny/. See also Dominik Cardinal Duka, O.P., "Conference Religion and Migration," DominikDuka.cz, 22 February 2017, www.dominikduka.cz/prednasky-proslovy/konference-nabozenstvi-a-migrace/ (translated from Czech).

[453] Dominik Cardinal Duka, "What Do I Expect as an Ordinary Christian from Refugees," *Aktualne.cz*, 7 September 2015, http://blog.aktualne.cz/blogy/dominik-duka.php?itemid=25888 (translated from Czech).

Islam

Duka has tried to avoid the often-linked issues of migration and fear of Islam. In one of his interviews for *Echo Weekly Journal*, the interviewer said it looked as if Duka was building up to the conclusion that we must stop the Muslim migrant wave into Europe but then did not voice this conclusion, to which Duka responded: "You're right, but I quote you a Church Father: 'I'm a man, I'm a Christian, I'm a Catholic.' This means that all people have a common ground that should allow us to accept the other and not make him an enemy. Therefore, I say: If we take in the migrants, we must insist on our rules."[454] Earlier in the interview, Duka had stated, "While we have one God with Islam, we differ in its conception. Islam does not know what Christianity knows, that is, the division and autonomy of the spiritual and civil spheres.... Protests... often take place with weapons in hand. [Immigrants] must be clearly given the principles, and we must really talk to those who come. There is fear in Western societies."[455]

Related to the topic of Christian ethics is the fact that world peace is "threatened by terrorist attacks in European countries," which was discussed by Duka in his 2016 new year's message.[456] Duka also cited Pope Francis, who said in an interview for *La Croix*: "We must admit there are some violent tendencies in Islam." Duka added, "Of course, there are tendencies to interpret Islam in a modern view, but Badal is essentially right.[457] What are we waiting for? Why does nobody say that

---

[454] Duka, "Halik Is a Minority."

[455] Ibid.

[456] Duka, "To Keep Our Civilization."

[457] Fr. Milan Badal was Duka's secretary until his death in March 2019. Badal claimed that we cannot distinguish between Islam and Islamism and that Islam is radical as such. He claimed that Muslims' inner duty is to outnumber Christians and proclaim their laws everywhere. See Simao, "Duka's Personal Secretary Died; Priest Badal Criticized Islam and Worked in the Council of CT," *Blesk.cz*, 24 March 2019, www.blesk.cz (translated from Czech).

there are almost twenty Surahs in Quran that are absolutely intolerant and militant? Fourteen centuries of Quran with a history of heavy fighting."[458]

Duka has nonetheless spoken forcefully about the tension between Islam and European democracy, even quoting Cardinal Bernardin Gantin, who — when answering a question about whether we need to be worried about more Muslims in Europe — said about Muslims that "as long as there are 5 percent in society, there are no problems. When they are 15 percent, they will come up with demands that they want to occupy certain key places in society with their people. And as soon as they reach 25 percent, they will enforce Sharia law and seek to take over government."[459]

DUKA AND POLITICS

Duka's ability to get along with Czech politicians, including some whom he knew during communist rule and who were (in a sense) accomplices to his imprisonment, spurred much critical discussion when his appointment as archbishop of Prague and primate of Bohemia became public.

Duka has stated that, as archbishop, he has to play a more political role and has to deal sometimes more with "political" issues than episcopal duties. In one of his interviews, Duka compared his function to being a church clerk and stated that he envied his auxiliary bishops for really being able to perform episcopal pastoral work.[460] His political gifts have at least been put to good use in addressing three large tasks presented to him when he became archbishop: the property settlement between the state and the Church,[461] arranging an international treaty between

---

[458] Duka, "Halik Is a Minority."
[459] Ibid.
[460] Duka, "Interview for *Catholic Weekly*."
[461] Although there is pressure to revise the property settlement.

the Czech Republic and the Vatican,[462] and finding a solution for the controversial ownership of St. Vitus Cathedral.

Duka is on a first-name basis with a number of influential politicians (including the Czech presidents) and has the ability to think out of the box and come up with solutions that are not only acceptable, but even beneficial, to all parties involved. These traits have helped Duka with two issues thus far.[463] Just months after becoming archbishop, he managed to agree on a resolution regarding St. Vitus Cathedral. This solution—as the declaration regarding its care states—builds "on the common belief that the cathedral ... is a national spiritual, cultural, and state symbol and is led by the intention to create a permanent foundation for the development of good relations between the state and the Church."[464] Duka said in this regard: "I believe that the agreement of the president of the Republic and the Prague archbishop [joint care for the cathedral by state and church] is an expression of our common will to ensure reliable and harmonious mutual cooperation in the care of the cathedral and its preservation for future generations."[465]

Regarding Church restitutions after confiscation by the communists (the Czech government agreed in 2012 to a compensation plan over thirty years), Duka has indicated that he agrees that "what was stolen is to be returned," and he knows that "according to the Constitutional Court's finding, the churches could defend themselves in court"; but he believed

---

[462] The international relation with the Holy See still needs to be resolved.

[463] Dominik Cardinal Duka, O.P., "Annual Report on the Life of the Czech Church," DominikDuka.cz, 21 September 2015, www.dominikduka.cz/prednasky-proslovy/vyrocni-zprava-o-zivote-ceske-cirkve/ (translated from Czech).

[464] Dominik Cardinal Duka, O.P., "Text of the Solemn Declaration on the Common Care of the Cathedral," DominikDuka.cz, 3 June 2010, www.dominikduka.cz/dokumenty/text-slavnostniho-prohlaseni-o-spolecne-peci-o-katedralu/ (translated from Czech).

[465] Dominik Cardinal Duka, O.P., "Statement of the Archbishop of Prague on the Agreement on Mutual Care of the Cathedral," DominikDuka.cz, 3 June 2010, www.dominikduka.cz/vyjadreni/prohlaseni-prazskeho-arcibiskupa-k-dohode-o-vzajemne-peci-o-katedralu/ (translated from Czech).

this course of action "would not benefit anyone."[466] Instead, Duka opted for the diplomatic route and came up with a framework for the gradual implementation of restitution, thereby ushering in a new period for the Church in the Czech Republic.[467]

As to the unresolved matter: the Czech Republic is one of the last European countries not to have a concordat with the Vatican. Following a recent visit from Czech dignitaries to the Vatican, however, it seems this issue may also be resolved shortly.[468]

Regarding politics and the Church, Duka has said in an interview that "churches cannot play the role of political parties." He said he could "understand that every one of us, when he is interested in the life of society, which is right, has to say some things. But we must be very careful not to divide society." Media coverage, he said, "is looking for conflict and contrast because then people are interested."[469]

Duka has said he believes his role is "to respect everyone in the Church and not to split it."[470] He explained his attitude by saying: "You will not gain a person for the good if you beat him.... As a Church leader, I consider it necessary to be wherever something positive is happening or where a certain opinion needs to be said. But I do not consider the Church to replace the role of critical media and political parties."[471]

This attitude comes to the fore in another quote from Duka in which he states that "whoever leaves you, even if you cannot help him, must not leave sadly and without encouragement. And when you speak to a

---

466 Danica Klein, "The Church Does Not Want Billions for Free; This Can Do for You," Zpravy.Tiscali.cz, 25 January 2019, https://zpravy.tiscali.cz/ cirkev-nechce-miliardy-zadarmo-tohle-pro-vas-muze-vykonat-117914 (translated from Czech).
467 Duka, "Annual Report."
468 "Pope Receives Czech Parliament Chairmen," Chamber of Deputies Parliament of the Czech Republic, 22 March 2019, http://public.psp.cz/en/ sqw/cms.sqw?z=12614.
469 Duka, "Interview for Lidove Noviny."
470 Duka, "Halik Is a Minority."
471 Bendova, "Cardinal Again under Fire."

priest, you must never let the priest be offended by you. You can reproach him rightly but never offend him. This principle should apply not only in the Church but also in family and society."[472]

As Duka said in an interview: "We must create an environment of cooperation in the spirit of the service of society. It is, above all, a spiritual ministry, but the Church speaks not only of the salvation of souls but also of the salvation of man. Hand in hand with the form of worship and proclamation of the gospel goes charity! We are supposed to help society in this area especially where the state cannot do so well."[473]

SUMMARY

Dominik Jaroslav Duka is considered orthodox and pro-life but not rule-focused, someone with a down-to-earth faith who believes the Church must dialogue with society.

He has expressed appreciation for traditional liturgy and also welcomes developments in the Novus Ordo; he is open to different liturgies and rites but is against meticulous observation of rubrics.

He favors finding a new language for the Church to relate to today's world, and places a premium on education. Cardinal Duka has called for greater lay involvement in the Church, especially of women, and prefers pastoralism and evangelization rather than statements and resolutions.

He has cultivated close relations with the Czech political class, partly due to his dedication to restitution of Church property confiscated by the communists. This has led some to see him as too political—excessively allied to the country's presidents and readily aligning the Church with the Czech nation. Others argue that he handles matters of state with acuity and prudence, using his influential position

---

[472] Daniska, "Church Cannot Only Think of Itself."
[473] Klein, "The Church Does Not Want Billions."

to serve the gospel and educate a predominantly atheist nation in the Faith. He frequently upholds the importance of the family as society's foundation.

Cardinal Duka said he understood the motives of the *dubia* cardinals but did not explicitly support or reject their initiative. He is against changing priestly celibacy, is a proponent of traditional morality, and has often condemned abortion. He firmly opposes euthanasia and same-sex "marriage" and has nuanced views on refugees and migrants. He does not see the Church as a replacement for political parties or the media but does see the Church's role as saving man from temporal suffering and destitution as well as being an instrument of eternal salvation.

As a cardinal who suffered economic deprivation under communist state control, but later rose to the challenge of leading his flock through a time of transition and prevalent atheism, Cardinal Duka would bring a dose of realism to the papacy.

SERVICE TO THE CHURCH

Ordination to the Priesthood: 22 June 1970
Ordination to the Episcopate: 26 September 1998
Elevation to the College of Cardinals: 18 February 2012

Education
- 1965-1970: Cyril and Methodius Theological Faculty, Litoměřice, Czech Republic
- 1979: Pontifical Theological Faculty of St. John the Baptist, Warsaw, Poland (LTh)

Assignments[474]

- 1968-1970: Novice, Order of Friars Preachers (Dominicans)
- 1970-1975: Parish priest
- 1975-1986: Provincial vicar, Dominican Order
- 1975-1989: Skoda Car Designer, Plzeň, Czech Republic
- 1976-1981: Professor of theology, Czech Dominican Seminary
- 1981-1982: Prisoner at Plzeň-Bory, jailed for performing "religious activities"
- 1986-1998: Superior, Dominican Province
- 1989-1992: President, Conference of Dominican Major Superiors of the Czech Republic
- 1989: Secretary, Czech Conference of Higher Religious Representatives
- 1990-1998: Professor of biblical theology, Palacký University, Olomouc, Czech Republic
- 1990-1998: Member, Czech Accreditation Commission
- 1992-1996: Vice president, Union of European Conferences of Dominican Major Superiors
- 1992-1996: Vice president, European KVPP Union
- 1998-2010: Bishop, Diocese of Hradec Králové, Czech Republic
- 2000-2004: Vice president, Czech Bishops' Conference
- 2004-2008: Apostolic administrator, Litoměřice, Czech Republic
- 2010- present: Archbishop, Archdiocese of Prague, Czech Republic
- 2010: Grand chancellor, Prague Faculty of Theology
- 2010: President, Czech Bishops' Conference

---

[474] Curriculum vitae: Dominik Jaroslav Cardinal Duka, O.P., DominikDuka.cz, www.dominikduka.cz/zivotopis/.

Additional Positions

- Member, Czech Ethical Forum
- Member, Scientific Council of the Theology Faculty of Prague
- President, Administrative Council of the Catholic Biblical Society and of the Center for Biblical Studies
- Member, Confederation of Political Prisoners
- Assistant Editor, *Salve* and *Communio* magazines

Roman Curia

- 2012-present: Member, Congregation for the Institutes of Consecrated Life and Societies of Apostolic Life
- Member, Pontifical Council for Justice and Peace

NOLI RECUSARE LABOREM

WILLEM JACOBUS (WIM) CARDINAL EIJK

"Do Not Refuse the Work"

Born: 22 June 1953
Duivendrecht, the Netherlands
Nationality: Dutch
Title: Archbishop of Utrecht

BIOGRAPHY

Willem Eijk's reputed ability to bridge diverse ways of thought comes in part from his childhood, having been raised by a Protestant father and a Catholic mother. He completed initial medical studies in 1978 at the University of Amsterdam and immediately entered the major seminary while focusing on medical ethics at the University of Leiden and working as a physician of internal medicine. In 1985, he was ordained a priest and, while serving as a chaplain, obtained a doctorate in medicine, with a thesis that responded to Dutch euthanasia practices. In 1990, Eijk was sent by his bishop to Rome, where he obtained a license in moral theology and a doctorate in philosophy at the University of St. Thomas Aquinas (the Angelicum). He also earned a degree from the Lateran University. Subsequently, Eijk taught moral theology in the Netherlands and in Switzerland; he also cofounded an association that promotes medical ethics, and he served on the International Theological Commission (1997-2000).

In 1999, Eijk was ordained a bishop and served the Diocese of Groningen-Leeuwarden for seven years as ordinary. Much of Eijk's work as a bishop has been in response to the increasing secularization and loss of faith in Dutch society — stressful work that possibly affected his health. In 2001, he suffered a subdural hematoma (cerebral hemorrhage); after a period of rest, he recovered and resumed his duties.[475] Benedict XVI appointed Eijk the metropolitan archbishop of Utrecht in 2007. In the midst of his episcopal duties, Eijk coedited a manual of Catholic medical ethics, published in 2010, and was elected president of the Netherlands' Episcopal Conference the following year. He has served as an esteemed member of the Pontifical Academy for Life and was reelected a member in 2017. In 2012, Benedict XVI created Eijk a cardinal-priest.

SANCTIFYING OFFICE

The Eucharist

"Through the sacrament of the Eucharist we are united with Jesus; thus, with God Himself and therefore with His infinite love. The Eucharist, Jesus Himself, is our pledge of eternal life and God's eternal love. Anyone

---

[475] Paolo De Groot-Testoni, "Cardinal Designate Eijk: Doctor, Defender of Life," Zenit, 14 February 2012, https://zenit.org/articles/cardinal-designate-eijk-doctor-defender-of-life/.

who, through the Eucharist, lets his love be supplemented by God's love, can love God and his neighbor as Jesus has shown us." So wrote the cardinal in a column published on the website of the Archdiocese of Utrecht.[476]

Eijk affirms that the Eucharist is "the source and summit of the Christian life."[477] From this source all our actions should flow. "If we serve God and our fellow human beings, then the Sunday Eucharist is embedded in our lives. Like the woman pouring a bottle of precious balm over the head or feet of Jesus in Bethany, may we present the best we have to our Lord, and may we serve the poor with the same generosity."[478]

In 2012, Eijk published a substantial pastoral letter on the Eucharist, reflecting on the value and significance of the celebration of the Holy Eucharist.[479] In this letter, he wrote that "if you realize that Christ

---

[476] Willem Jacobus Cardinal Eijk, "Love Imitated by Jesus: A Superhuman Requirement?," Diocese of Utrecht, June 2011, www.aartsbisdom.nl/home/organisatie/aartsbisschop/columns/liefde-in-navolging-van-jezus-een-bovenmenselijke-eis/ (translated from Dutch).

[477] CCC 1324. Willem Jacobus Cardinal Eijk, *Experience the Eucharist (Again) as the Beating Heart of the Life of Faith*, Diocese of Utrecht, 23 June 2019, www.aartsbisdom.nl/wp-content/uploads/2019/06/Pastorale-brief-b.g.v.-het-Jaar-van-de-Eucharistie.pdf (translated from Dutch).

[478] Willem Jacobus Cardinal Eijk, *Living with Christ: Pastoral Letter on the Eucharist*, Diocese of Utrecht, 22 February 2012, www.aartsbisdom.nl/wp-content/uploads/2017/07/Leven-met-Christus-Pastorale-brief-over-de-Eucharistie.pdf (translated from Dutch).

[479] Ibid. Eijk's pastoral letter followed up a pastoral-liturgical policy note from 2011 and builds on Eijk's online columns (see www.aartsbisdom.nl/home/organisatie/aartsbisschop/columns/) and his 2010 pastoral letter *Why Priests?* (www.aartsbisdom.nl/wp-content/uploads/2017/07/waarom-priesters-A5-def-versie-internet.pdf) (translated from Dutch). These were then followed up by an additional letter responding to violations of the liturgical regulations laid down in canon law and in *Redemptionis Sacramentum*. See Willem Jacobus Cardinal Eijk, "About Celebrating the Holy Eucharist," RK Documenten, 5 March 2012, www.rkdocumenten.nl/rkdocs/index.php?mi=600 &doc=4546. See also Willem Jacobus Cardinal Eijk, "About Certain Components of the Holy Eucharist: And the Duties

Himself is present in the Host, you cannot help but worship Him in the Host. In worship, we may dwell on the way Christ wants to be present in this world: He is there, as vulnerable as bread, with the surrender of love, in silence."[480] Eijk announced the Year of the Eucharist starting on December 1, 2019, in anticipation of which an additional pastoral letter on the Eucharist was published.[481]

In response to criticism for celebrating Mass *ad orientem* — or, as someone said, "turning his back on the people" — Eijk said: "I do not celebrate Mass with my back to the people; I say it by turning my face toward Christ, toward the tabernacle, so that ... together with the people, we are truly turned toward Christ. I no longer celebrate with my back turned to Christ but looking at Christ, who is present under the sacrament of the Eucharist in the tabernacle."[482]

Evangelization amid Secularization

Bold in facing reality, Eijk has distinguished himself from many prelates by directly addressing widespread secularization and loss of faith in the West. In an interview with Vatican Radio, he noted: "In the 1950s, ninety percent of Catholics still went to church every Sunday. Now, it's only five percent."[483] In his 2015 message for Lent, he spoke about the need

Specific to the Priest or the Deacon and Duties That a Pastoral Worker or Other Lay Minister in the Holy Eucharist Can Perform," RK Documenten, 7 March 2012, www.rkdocumenten.nl/rkdocs/index.php?mi=600&doc=4541.

[480] Eijk, *Living with Christ.*

[481] Eijk, *Experience the Eucharist.*

[482] Jeanne Smits, "Interview: Dutch Cardinal Willem Eijk Answers Questions on Crisis in Church, Loss of Faith," LifeSite News, 15 May 2019, www.lifesitenews.com/news/dutch-cardinal-willem-eijk-answers-questions-on-crisis-in-church-loss-of-faith.

[483] "Visita ad Limina dei vescovi olandesi. Il card. Eijk: diminuisce la quantità dei fedeli ma non la qualità," Radio Vaticana, 2 December 2013, https://web.archive.org/web/20151010005456/http://it.radiovaticana.va/storico/2013/12/02/visita_ad_limina_dei_vescovi_olandesi._il_card._eijk_diminuisce_la/it1-751740; Hilary White, "Dutch Bishops Tell Pope the

to close a vast number of churches in Holland, a reality that many have found painful. He wrote that, as a result of the mistakes made by the local Church after the Second Vatican Council and the *actual abandonment of evangelization*, the number of the faithful has drastically decreased in recent decades. In response to this situation, which sometimes leads to bitterness for the laity, the cardinal has encouraged them to bring more people into the Catholic fold through evangelization and catechetical efforts.[484] Similarly, seeing how few young people were engaging in the Church in Holland and abroad, in 2009 Eijk launched a worldwide Twitter campaign for vocations.[485]

As bishop of Groningen and then as archbishop in Utrecht, Eijk helped lead a number of pilgrimages to Lourdes. He noted: "Many seminarians have told me that they discovered their vocation in Lourdes. So you can see how much we owe to the Virgin Mary! Her intercession is incredibly fruitful."[486]

Devotion to Our Lady

Eijk has a marked devotion to the Blessed Virgin Mary. On May 13, 2017, the cardinal dedicated all Dutch dioceses to the Immaculate Heart of Mary. During his homily, he spoke of Mary's message in Fatima: "The first was a vision of hell and the call to prayer, repentance and penance to save souls and bring them to eternal salvation. The existence of hell was (and is) denied by many Christians and not, or hardly, raised by

---

Church Is Collapsing as They Face Hundreds of Closures," LifeSite News, 5 December 2013, https://www.lifesitenews.com/news/dutch-bishops-tell-pope-the-church-is-collapsing-as-they-face-hundreds-of-c.

[484] "Card. Eijk for Lent about a Future Without Churches," Vatican Radio, 24 February 2015, http://www.archivioradiovaticana.va/storico/2015/02/24/kard_eijk_o_przysz%C5%82o%C5%9Bci_bez_ko%C5%9Bcio%C5%82%C3%B3w/pl-1125477 (translated from Dutch).

[485] Tom McFeely, "Tweeting for Vocations," *National Catholic Register*, 22 June 2009, https://www.ncregister.com/blog/staff-bloggers/tweeting_for_vocations.

[486] Smits, "Eijk Answers Questions on Crisis."

Christian proclaimers in preaching or catechesis. However, Mary's grave warning must be taken seriously."[487] He wrote that Mary, though often misinterpreted, was a "powerful and firm woman."[488] The humility Mary speaks of in her Magnificat "is also not a false modesty, but a sense of reality with regard to the actual relationships we—as humans—have with God and fellow human beings." "Mary consciously chooses to make herself humble and small, so that she can serve God and us. Because of our innate selfishness, we often think too highly of ourselves, causing us to give little heed for what God or fellow human beings have to say or ask us to do." He added: "We also need this inner obedience in order to be able to hear what our fellow human beings deeply need and want. Without this inner obedience, it is impossible to serve God or our fellow man."[489] He said: "No one other than Mary can take us by the hand in prayer. She is the figure of the Church.... She is our most beautiful example, including in prayer, and that is why it is so good to pray [the Rosary] in union with her."[490]

Speaking of his own vocation, and his episcopal motto, "Do Not Refuse the Work," he explained:

> The priest who helped me on the path of my vocation—and to whom I therefore owe eternal gratitude—told me: "Wim, you have the duty to hold on: it is the virtue of perseverance." He told me that most people can't do it: "If you hold on, you'll see that you'll win."

---

487 Willem Jacobus Cardinal Eijk, "Maastricht, Onze-Lieve-Vrouwe-Basiliek, Vespers, 13 mei 2017, Toewijding van de Nederlandse bisdommen aan het Onbevlekt Hart van Maria," Roman Catholic Church in the Netherlands, 13 May 2017, www.rkkerk.nl/wp-content/uploads/2017/05/Homilie-Kardinaal-Eijk-Maastricht-Mariavesper-2017-05-13-def.pdf (translated from Dutch).

488 Willem Jacobus Cardinal Eijk, "Mary: Source of Hope," Diocese of Utrecht, October 2010, www.aartsbisdom.nl/home/organisatie/aartsbisschop/columns/maria-bron-van-hoop/, (translated from Dutch).

489 Ibid.

490 Smits, "Eijk Answers Questions on Crisis."

He concluded by describing his own determination: "I will never forget that [advice]. Keep going. Continue. Continue to proclaim the faith.... I am still in good spirits, I have an ardent faith, and I also always believe in the power of the Lord: He triumphs. Christus vincit. Not we, but He in us."[491]

Church Crisis

Cardinal Eijk is concerned about confusion in the Church and society that he attributes to an overload of information, but he believes it is important to continue to trust that the Holy Spirit is guiding the Church and that the faithful will later see what God meant by it. He also believes the current time is one of "great purification" for the Church. "The quantity of people who are believing is getting smaller, but the quality is getting higher. People are more believing, the people who go to Church are praying people," he said in 2019.[492]

GOVERNING OFFICE

As a Young Bishop

Eijk's first episcopal assignment (1999) was to the Diocese of Groningen.[493] With 115,000 Catholics, it was geographically the largest diocese in the Netherlands, but the smallest in terms of Catholic population.[494]

---

[491] Ibid.

[492] Edward Pentin, "Dutch Cardinal on Gender Ideology: It Sets the World 'Against the Christian Faith,'" *National Catholic Register,* 17 May 2019, https://www.ncregister.com/daily-news/dutch-cardinal-on-gender-ideology-it-sets-the-world-against-the-christian-f.

[493] Situated in the northern part of the Netherlands, it includes the provinces of Groningen, Friesland, Drenthe, and the Noordoostpolder part of the Flevoland province. See also "Dioceses," Roman Catholic Church in the Netherlands, www.rkkerk.nl/kerk/bisdommen/.

[494] Janneke Schuurman, "The Steadfast North," *NRC,* 9 November 2002, www.nrc.nl/nieuws/2002/11/09 /het-standvastige-noorden-7613447-a1323236 (translated from Dutch).

Eijk had a rough start in Groningen. Just weeks after his appointment, the press went from being eager to find out who Eijk was,[495] to attacking his views on sexual morality as "extremely conservative and inflexible."[496] These attacks relied substantially on unpublished notes of lectures given by Eijk, and the identity of their source was never revealed. Nonetheless, they were examined by the Dutch public prosecutors' national expertise center for justice, to decide whether criminal prosecution based on discrimination against homosexuals should be initiated.[497] (The prosecutor decided that there was no reason for a criminal investigation against Eijk.)[498]

In response to the commotion surrounding his appointment, Eijk clarified that the Catholic Church does not condemn anyone and that he would not either. He asserted, however, that "the Catholic Church has an ethical vision that is not always understood in today's culture."[499]

---

[495] "Hollands Dagboek: Wim Eijk," NRC, 31 July 1999, www.nrc.nl/ nieuws/1999/07/31/hollands-dagboek-wim-eijk-7456810-a109247.

[496] See Karin De Mik, "Bishop: 'Gays Can't Love,'" NCR, 18 August 1999, http://retro.nrc.nl/W2/Nieuws/1999/08/18/Vp/05.html; "Bishop Eijk Finds Homosexuality A Neurotic Disorder," De Telegraaf, 18 August 1999 https://krant.telegraaf.nl/krant/archief/19990818/teksten/bin.homobisschop.html (translated from Dutch).

[497] Enk Muller, "Justice Examines Eijk's Views on Gays," De Volkskrant, 31 August 1999, www.volkskrant.nl/mensen/justitie-onderzoekt-eijksopvattingen-over-homo-s~b1611eaa/.

[498] There was no criminal investigation because of discrimination against homosexuals since it was ruled that there was no intention to disregard the dignity of homosexuals and Eijk's notes did not meet the so-called publicity requirement. Hence, Eijk's moral theology lecture notes were ruled to fall outside the scope of criminal law. See "Bishop Eijk's Tract Falls outside Criminal Law," Trouw, 7 September 1999, www.trouw.nl/home/ traktaat-van-bisschop-eijk-valt-buiten-de-strafwet~ac0f920d/ (translated from Dutch).

[499] Willem Jacobus Cardinal Eijk, "Letter from the Newly Appointed Bishop of Groningen to His Faithful," Katholiek Nieuwsblad, 10 September 1999, https://web.archive.org/web/20050427170730/http://www.katholiek nieuwsblad.nl/actueel/kn1650b.htm (translated from Dutch). See also: Steven Derix, "Eijk: Messages about Me Give a One-Sided View," NRC, 1

Protests and Setbacks

Eijk's consecration as bishop of Groningen took place as planned on November 6, 1999. It was, however, marked by protestors outside the church and important dignitaries refusing to attend the ceremony or the congratulatory reception afterward.[500]

Eijk chose as his motto *Noli Recusare Laborem*, which he translates as: "Do not refuse the work or suffering and endeavors associated with the proclamation of the Christian faith according to the teachings of the Church in our time." Eijk chose this variation on the words St. Martin of Tours used to address Christ shortly before his death, to expresses his desire to take on the same attitude of St. Martin to continue to work for Christ. [501]

In a 2018 speech, Eijk mentioned a number of times when he particularly needed this attitude, including the four months between his appointment and his consecration in 1999, when Eijk received daily complaints and threats. "Some [even] tried to intimidate me in such a way as to try to get me to renounce my appointment as bishop."[502]

In January 2001, Eijk suffered a brain hemorrhage. After returning to work a few months later (mid 2002), he began experiencing severe facial pains, which again prevented him from working.[503] Of this period in

September 1999, http://retro.nrc.nl/W2/Nieuws/1999/09/01/Vp/02.html.

[500] Steven Derix, "Becoming a Bishop Is Not Easy," *NRC*, 8 November 1999, www.nrc.nl/nieuws/1999/11 /08/bisschop-worden-is-niet-gemakkelijk-7469540-a629446 (translated from Dutch).

[501] "Cardinal Eijk Receives Italian Culture Prize," RK Documenten, 29 October 2018, www.rkdocumenten.nl/rkdocs/index.php?mi=680&nws=4332 (translated from Dutch).

[502] Willem Jacobus Cardinal Eijk, "Speech on the Occasion of the Award of the Culture Prize 'San Jose Sanchez del Rio Martire' by the Giuseppe Sciacca Foundation to Cardinal Eijk," Diocese of Utrecht, 27 October 2018, www.aartsbisdom.nl/wp-content/uploads/2018/10/Premio-Sciacca-Ned-2018-10-27.pdf.

[503] Schuurman, "The Steadfast North."

Eijk's life, Bishop Van den Hende[504] wrote that, for "Eijk, born and raised in Amsterdam, the church of the Diocese of Groningen was completely new. He worked very quickly by visiting parishes and meeting people from the entire diocese. Eijk showed great commitment and insight. His motto, *Do Not Refuse the Work*, suits him very well."[505]

Correcting Abuses, Starting Initiatives

Eijk's work in the Groningen Diocese included correcting certain liberties introduced during the stewardship of the previous bishop in the 1960s and 1970s. These misguided practices included intercommunion between Catholics and Protestants, the ministry of the sacraments by pastoral workers, and the inordinate involvement of lay churchgoers in the organization of the liturgy. Eijk's work in this regard was supported by younger priests and more conservative Catholics but was sharply opposed by some pastoral workers, older priests, liberal Catholics, and ecumenical and Protestant pastors.[506]

Over the course of his eight years in the Diocese of Groningen-Leeuwarden,[507] Eijk undertook a number of initiatives that were well received overall.[508] These included initiatives aimed at young people, the establishment of a diocesan youth platform, and the organization of a diocesan altar-servers day. Additionally, Eijk undertook a large reorganization of the diocese.[509] He abolished the deanery structure in lieu

---

504 Eijk's vicar from 2000 to 2006.

505 Bishop Hans Van Den Hende, "Response of Bishop Van Den Hende to Appointment of New Archbishop of Utrecht Msgr. Eijk," Bisdom Breda, 11 December 2007, www.bisdomvanbreda.nl/nieuws/reactie-bisschop-van-den-hende-op-benoeming-nieuwe-aartsbisschop-van-utrecht-mgr-eijk/ (translated from Dutch).

506 Schuurman, "The Steadfast North."

507 Since 2005, the diocese has been called Groningen-Leeuwarden.

508 Marieke van Twillert and Herman Amelink, "The Monsignor Is Strict with Himself and Others," *NRC*, 14 July 2008, www.nrc.nl/nieuws/2008/07/14/de-monseigneur-is-streng-voor-zichzelf-en-anderen-11572541-a975292.

509 "Response of Bishop Van Den Hende."

of the formation of vicariates. He relocated the diocesan bishop's house to a location that also housed the diocesan office. And, in the course of his efforts, Eijk managed to make the Groningen-Leeuwarden Diocese financially healthy again.[510]

Eijk encouraged believers to renew their prayer lives and undertook a pilgrimage to Rome with nine hundred members of his diocese in the context of the Year of St. Boniface, in 2004 (the 1,250th anniversary of the saint's martyrdom). To replenish the number of priests in the diocese, Eijk invited the religious community Misionéros de Cristo Maestro from Colombia to establish two communities of priests and seminarians to serve the Groningen Diocese.[511] For men considering the priesthood, Eijk also organized "convent retreats" where, in a climate of silence and prayer, questions regarding life and faith could be discussed. During his time as bishop, the number of priestly vocations increased.[512]

As the bishop responsible for education within the Dutch Bishops' Conference, Eijk contributed to the merger that resulted in the establishment of the Vatican-recognized Faculty of Catholic Theology (now called Tilburg School of Catholic Theology [TSCT]) on January 1, 2007.[513] As grand chancellor, Eijk acts as the representative of the Roman Catholic

---

[510] "Bisschop Eijk New Archbishop Utrecht," *COC Nederland*, 10 December 2007, www.coc.nl/geloof-cultuur/bisschop-eijk-nieuwe-aartsbisschop-utrecht.

[511] "Colombian Priests at Work," *RTV Drenthe*, 5 June 2007, www.rtvdrenthe.nl/nieuws/17967/ Colombiaanse-priesters-aan-werk. See also "Colombian Congregation Settles in Groningen," *Trouw*, 5 June 2007, www.trouw.nl/home/colombiaanse-congregatie-vestigt-zich-in-groningen˜a3eb436a/ (translated from Dutch).

[512] Tjebbe T. De Jong, *Katholiek leven in Noord-Nederland 1956-2006: vijftig jaar bisdom Groningen* (Catholic Life in the Northern Netherlands 1956-2006: Fifty Years of the Diocese of Groningen) (Groningen: Uitgeverij Verloren, 2006), 136.

[513] "Location Utrecht: Tilburg School of Catholic Theology," Tilburg University, www.tilburguniversity.edu. See also Th.C.M. Hoogenboom, "Pastoraal jaarverslag van het Aartsbisdom Utrecht 2012," Diocese of Utrecht, 22 April 2013, www.aartsbisdom.nl/ wp-content/uploads/2017/09/Pastoraal-jaarverslag-2012-Aartsbisdom-Utrecht.pdf.

Church, and is obligated to preserve the integrity of the Christian message taught at the TSCT. He was also responsible for the reorganization that took place in wake of the merger.[514] When a number of outspoken LGBT-supporting faculty members were not granted a position within the TSCT, Eijk was accused of abusing his powers in order to "purge" faculty members.[515]

Archbishop of Utrecht

In December 2007, Pope Benedict XVI announced Eijk's appointment as archbishop of Utrecht. Once again, a media circus ensued.[516] This time, however, and mainly because of the financial reorganizations needed within the archdiocese and the success Eijk had had in reorganizing the Groningen-Leeuwarden Diocese, several well-respected bishops spoke out in Eijk's support. The ruckus quickly subsided.

Eijk took the unusual step of refusing to serve (as he would have been expected to) as chair of the Dutch Bishops' Conference. The reasons behind this included the enormous financial reorganization that awaited him in the archdiocese, the fact that he first wanted to concentrate on getting to know his new diocese, and his continuing administration of the Diocese of Groningen-Leeuwarden.[517]

---

[514] "Eijk Willem Jacobus (Wim) (1953-)," *Den katolske kirke*, 7 March 2008, www.katolsk.no/biografier/utenriks/eijk.

[515] "Roman Catholic Church Purifies New Training," *COC Nederland*, 19 January 2007, www.coc.nl/geloof-cultuur/rk-kerk-zuivert-nieuwe-opleiding (translated from Dutch).

[516] "Bishop Eijk New Archbishop Utrecht."

[517] This lasted for nearly a year, until September 2008, when Bishop De Korte became bishop of the Diocese of Groningen-Leeuwarden. See: "Eijk Willem Jacobus (Wim) (1953-)." Bishop Van Luyn of the Rotterdam Diocese was then chosen to replace Cardinal Simonis as chair of the Dutch Bishops' Conference. Upon Van Luyn being granted his resignation as bishop of Rotterdam, Eijk replaced Bishop Van Luyn as chair of the Dutch Bishops' Conference in 2011. See "Mgr. Eijk New Chairman Bishops' Conference," Diocese of Utrecht, 21 June 2011, www.aartsbisdom.nl/mgr-eijk-nieuwe-voorzitter-bisschoppenconferentie/. In 2016,

Addressing Sexual Abuse

Shortly after his appointment as archbishop, Eijk had to deal with the challenges presented by past clerical sexual abuse. This took an enormous toll on him, as well as on the Dutch Catholic Church. After the cardinal put in place a special inquiry committee, a foundation was established to set up various programs to process and examine the thousands of complaints.[518] In 2016, Eijk publicly apologized again on behalf of the Dutch Catholic Church for the abuse that had taken place and promised to report to the government on a yearly basis regarding the handling of new complaints.[519]

Emphasis on Good Catechesis, Formation

During his time as bishop and archbishop, Eijk has emphasized the necessity of good catechesis, which he sees as especially needed as catechesis almost vanished from the Netherlands after Vatican II.[520]

It is of great importance that Catholics dare to stand up for their Faith. After all, we live in a time when faith is often dismissed as irrelevant and believers as ignorant or even retarded. If we want to

---

however, after a term of five years, Eijk again relinquished his right to chair the Dutch Bishops' Conference and was succeeded by his old vicar, then bishop of Rotterdam, Van den Hende. See "Eijk Resigns Chair of Bishops' Conference," *Katholiek.nl*, 26 January 2016, www.katholiek.nl/actueel/eijk-legt-voorzitterschap-bisschoppenconferentie-neer/.

[518] "Research into the Sexual Abuse of Minors in the Roman Catholic Church," Voormalig onderzoek RK, https://voormaligonderzoekrk.nl/. See also Tom Heneghan, "Report Affirms Dutch Church Handling of Abuse Cases," *Tablet*, 2 January 2018, https://www.thetablet.co.uk/news/8322/report-affirms-dutch-church-handling-of-abuse-cases.

[519] Piet H. de Jong, "Cardinal Eijk Goes Deeply into the Dust," *Nederlands Dagblad*, 29 June 2016, www.nd.nl/nieuws /geloof/kardinaal-eijk-gaat-diep-door-stof.1839279.lynkx.

[520] See Willem Jacobus Cardinal Eijk, "Can Divorced and Civilly Remarried Persons Receive Communion?," *One Peter Five*, 13 July 2017, https://onepeterfive.com/can-divorced-civilly-remarried-persons-receive-communion/. See also Eijk, *Living with Christ*.

be effective missionaries in such difficult circumstances, we must proclaim loudly and clearly what our Faith is. This requires courage and also a thorough knowledge of the Faith. Only with this can we carry out the assignment that Jesus gave His disciples: "Go therefore and make disciples of all nations" (Matt. 28:19). That missionary call applies to all of us and is still solid as a rock. A personal relationship with Jesus, a living prayer life, and good catechesis form the joint foundation of this.[521]

Eijk has also emphasized parents' duty to transmit the Faith to their children and to bring their children to Mass. In a recent interview, Eijk said:

> We see a whole swarm of young people who also bring their children — these young people often have families — so the Mass is also very lively, because from time to time we see a child starting to run, scream, cry, or whatever — all this really doesn't matter. But these children, even if they do not understand what is being said, already see something of the respect shown by their parents; for example, during the Eucharistic prayer, during the Consecration, when they remain in complete silence. Children see it, and what you see, what you learn from your parents as a child, you never forget. What we learn later, we sometimes forget.... Hence, the very great importance of·this period for learning the Faith.[522]

Eijk has often stressed the importance of personal prayer, reflection on our actions, and, in particular, reading the Bible. He reiterated this in a homily at the symposium celebrating fifty years since Vatican II and the start of the Year of Faith: "The Council fathers of Vatican II wanted

---

[521] Willem Jacobus Cardinal Eijk, "Good Catechesis as the Foundation of Our Mission," Diocese of Utrecht, February 2015, www.aartsbisdom.nl/home/ organisatie/aartsbisschop/columns/goede-catechese-als-fundament-missie/ (translated from Dutch).

[522] Smits, "Eijk Answers Questions on Crisis."

to go back to the sources of faith: the Bible and the life of the Church in the first centuries. That is why the Council has given a boost to the study of the Bible and to the use of the Bible by laymen, ... in particular in the Dogmatic Constitution *Dei Verbum*."[523]

TEACHING OFFICE

Steadfast Defender of Sexual Morality

In the 1990s, Eijk taught moral theology[524] and held fast to the Church's teaching on sexual morality, bringing him some criticism. Just one year before he was appointed bishop of Groningen in 1999, homosexuals were allowed to enter into a so-called legal registered partnership in the Netherlands, which granted nearly identical civil legal rights as compared with civil marriage.[525]

Many homosexuals publicly protested against his appointment as bishop at the time. Eijk's brain hemorrhage in 2001 may have been brought on by the commotion surrounding his earlier published views on homosexuality. He did not speak out when same-sex civil "marriage" was legalized in 2001. On the publication of a midterm review for the 2014 Extraordinary General Assembly of the Synod of Bishops, which seemed remarkably mild regarding homosexuality, Eijk held a press conference to clarify that the midterm review was just that, a report of "what has been said and thus can also be the opinion of the minority." Eijk emphasized that the opinion of the majority — including Pope Francis — was not to

---

[523] Willem Jacobus Cardinal Eijk, "50th Anniversary Opening Vatican II," Roman Catholic Church in the Netherlands, 12 October 2012, www.rkkerk.nl/wp-content/uploads/2017/03/KD-2012-3-lezingen-symposium-vijftig-jaar-vaticanum-ii.pdf (translated from Dutch).

[524] Eijk, "Award of the Culture Prize."

[525] The Dutch Civil Code was amended on 21 December 2000 (with effect per 1 April 2001), allowing two people from the same or opposite sex to enter into a civil marriage.

deviate from Church teaching. Eijk reiterated the need for pastoral care that is able to bring homosexuals to a gospel-based path of life. And about that path of life Eijk was also very clear: "Homosexuals must hold themselves to abstinence."[526]

Communion for Divorced and "Remarried" and Intercommunion

In a 2015 essay, Eijk elaborated on marital and sexual morality and said that the "question of whether divorced and civilly 'remarried' persons can receive Communion is intrinsically joined to other questions of marital and sexual morality."[527] As to the principal question, Eijk stated: "In the 1970s, various theologians discussed this problem, without there being any precise pronouncement in this regard by the Magisterium of the Church. Nevertheless, there are loci theologici for this in Sacred Scripture and in the constant tradition of the Church that rule out the admission of the divorced and 'remarried' to Holy Communion." Church teaching, he said, "has always been clear and decisive about the indissolubility of a ratified and consummated marriage and about the absolute prohibition of divorce followed by a new marriage."[528]

Eijk focused on the fundamental analogy between the relationship of Christ and the Church, on the one hand, and the relationship of two spouses on the other. In both relationships, the parties "mutually give and accept one another."[529] "This gift is total, which also implies its definitive and therefore irrevocable character. The totality of the reciprocal gift of the spouses implies that it includes both the spiritual and the material dimension—not merely on the level of intention or emotion, but also encompasses the physical level, including sexual relations." In this respect, Eijk underlined the importance of a correct, nondualist anthropology

---

[526] "Cardinal Eijk: 'Gays Must Abide By The Abstention,'" COC Nederland, 17 October 2014, www.coc.nl/geloof-cultuur/kardinaal-eijk-homos-moeten-zich-houden-aan-de-onthouding (translated from Dutch).

[527] Eijk, "Can Divorced and Civilly Remarried Persons Receive Communion?"

[528] Ibid.

[529] CIC/83 can. 1057 §2.

that considers the physical dimension, too, as being intrinsic to the human person.[530]

In a 2015 essay, Eijk emphasized that those who are divorced and civilly "remarried" stand guilty of the sin of adultery and so have lost "the grace of justification already received and [are] unworthy to receive Communion, unless [they have] repented of the sin, confessed it, and no longer [commit] it."[531] He noted that Catholics are not obligated to receive Holy Communion in every Eucharistic celebration.[532] The person desiring to receive Holy Communion must be in the state whereby he may receive the graces given in the sacrament.[533]

Eijk received considerable international attention after he published an open letter in May 2019 in which he stated that Pope Francis needed to give clarity on intercommunion—a matter some had linked to the ambiguities over civilly "remarried" divorcees receiving Holy Communion. Eijk wrote that the pontiff's failure to give German bishops proper directives, based on the clear doctrine and practice of the Church, indicated a drift toward apostasy from the truth and, quoting the *Catechism*, possibly a sign and precursor of the End Times.[534]

Eijk explained the fundamental reason why a divorced and "remarried" person cannot receive Communion, saying, "the love of spouses is taken up

---

[530] See Eijk, "Can Divorced and Civilly Remarried Persons Receive Communion?" See also Willem Jacobus Cardinal Eijk, "Lustrum Symposium Foundation Medical Ethics: November 29, 2003—Self-Determination: Limited or Unlimited?," Juristenvereniging Pro Vita, 11 July 2015, https://provita.nl/publicaties/lustrumsymposium-stichting-medische-ethiek-29-november-2003-zelfbeschikkingsrecht-begrensd-of-onbegrensd-mgr-dr-w-j-eijk/ (translated from Dutch).

[531] Aymans, *Eleven Cardinals Speak on Marriage*. See also Eijk, "Can Divorced and Civilly Remarried Persons Receive Communion?"

[532] Except for the celebrating priest. Eijk, *Living with Christ*.

[533] Eijk, "About Certain Components of the Holy Eucharist."

[534] Willem Jacobus Cardinal Eijk, "Pope Francis Needed to Give Clarity on Intercommunion," *National Catholic Register*, 7 May 2018, www.ncregister.com/blog/edward-pentin/cardinal-eijk-pope-needed-to-give-clarity-to-german-bishops-on-intercommuni.

into the charity of Christ Himself, that is, into the reciprocal giving between Him and the Church. The mutual gift between Christ and the Church is made present in the Eucharist, through which we share more intensely in this gift, that is, in His suffering, death, and Resurrection. Adultery—and therefore also a divorce followed by a new civil marriage—violates the totality of the reciprocal gift between spouses at the spiritual, emotional, and physical level and, consequently, is incompatible with the total, reciprocal gift between Christ and the Church, to which the gift of the spouses is analogous and into which it should be taken up."[535]

Humanae Vitae

Eijk applied the same analogy to the use of contraceptives: "The argument against the use of contraceptives is that their obstruction of the gift of maternity and the gift of paternity through the conjugal act makes the spouses' reciprocal gift and therefore the totality of the gift itself incomplete at the physical level."[536] In a lecture about Pope Paul VI's Encyclical *Humanae Vitae*, Eijk clarified that this encyclical, once regarded as a bone of contention, is nowadays "increasingly recognized as a prophetic document" (see his further comments on contraception below).[537]

"The inalienable dignity of the human person, created by God in His image, in which natural moral law should be rooted, ought also to be the foundation of human laws," Eijk stated in another interview. "As soon as the civil law offers an opening, however minimal, to an act that violates

---

[535] Eijk, "Can Divorced and Civilly Remarried Persons Receive Communion?"

[536] Ibid.

[537] Willem Jacobus Cardinal Eijk, "*Humanae Vitae*: Half a Century of Stumbling Block or a Prophetic Document?," Diocese of Utrecht, 6 March 2018, www.aartsbisdom.nl/wp-content/uploads/2018/03/Groningen-Humanae-vitae-2018-03-06-lezing-zv-def2.pdf (translated from Dutch). See also "Cardinal Eijk at International Doctors' Congress," Diocese of Utrecht, 1 June 2018, www.aartsbisdom.nl/kardinaal-eijk-bij-internationaal-artsencongres/.

the dignity of the human person, there will be a risk of undermining all respect for this dignity."[538]

Catholics in the Public Square

Eijk has noted that "some judgments of the European Court of Human Rights make it more difficult for individuals to openly express their Christian views on a number of ethical issues. The same also happens with countries that want to take Christian principles into account in their legislation but are blocked by judgments from the court." Eijk stressed, however, that "it is not the 'one Europe' as such that is the culprit, but the absence of ideals, values, and norms, which also has an effect on legislation and case law."[539]

When asked if he agrees that it seems many Catholics involved in politics may have forgotten the so-called "nonnegotiable principles" such as the defense of life and the natural family, Eijk firstly referred to paragraphs 73 and 74 of John Paul II's 1995 Encyclical Letter *Evangelium Vitae*, which permits Catholic politicians under certain conditions to vote for a law, even if they are dealing with an intrinsically unjust law, in an attempt to prevent the acceptance of a still more permissive law. However, Eijk said, "It may be asked whether they have truly followed all of the conditions as mentioned in *Evangelium Vitae* and if their vote may truly be interpreted as a contribution to the common good." He added: "Apart from the fact that many Catholic politicians today may be less effectively prepared to dialogue on nonnegotiable principles in order to arrive at an ethically justifiable compromise, I fear that many of them no

[538] Lorenzo Bertocchi, "Crisis of Faith, Holland Report," *Il Timone*, March 2018, www.iltimone.org/articoli-riviste/crisi-della-fede-olanda-a-rapporto/ (translated from Italian). Available online in English at Maike Hickson, "Cardinal Eijk on Euthanasia, Gender Theory, Homosexuality, and Marriage," *One Peter Five*, 2 March 2018, https://onepeterfive.com/cardinal-eijk-euthanasia-gender-theory-homosexuality-marriage/.

[539] Willem Jacobus Cardinal Eijk, "The Church's Care for Europe," Diocese of Utrecht, October 2012, www.aartsbisdom.nl/home/organisatie/aartsbisschop/columns/de-zorg-van-de-kerk-voor-europa/ (translated from Dutch).

longer even see these things as nonnegotiable."[540] Eijk underscored that "human laws must correspond to the natural moral law, which safeguards the dignity of the person and which derives from the order which God has given to His creation."[541]

Upholding the Right to Life

Regarding the dignity of persons, Eijk has continuously spoken out against abortion, stating that it is an "intrinsic evil."[542] "With the acceptance of abortion, the boundary has been broken, which is indicated by the fundamental norm that human persons cannot be degraded to an object of use. Once this hurdle has been taken, it is no longer clear why that would not be permitted in other situations. It is clear that genuine human dignity begins with respect for the intrinsic dignity of the unborn.... Holy Scripture makes it clear that life is a gift from the Creator, which is under His special protection because man is created in God's image and likeness.... Life not only a gift but also a task: it is the fundamental 'talent' that is needed to develop our other talents for the benefit of the Kingdom of God."[543]

Since his days as a young doctor, Eijk has strongly opposed euthanasia (which later came to include the so-called Groningen Protocol[544] and

---

[540] Ibid.

[541] Ibid.

[542] Willem Jacobus Cardinal Eijk, "Chapter IV: Abortion and the Ethical Status of the Embryo," Katholieke Stichting Medische Ethiek, 23 March 1994, https://medische-ethiek.nl/hoofdstuk-iv-abortus-en-de-ethische-status-van-het-embryo (translated from Dutch).

[543] Ibid.

[544] An agreement between neonatologists and the attorney for the city of Groningen, according to which a doctor who ended the life of a handi-capped newborn baby would not be able to be prosecuted, provided that he had respected a series of cautionary requests. From this local protocol, a regulation was created at the national level for the suppression of life of handicapped newborn children.

assisted suicide[545]). Eijk earned his 1987 medical Ph.D. with a dissertation about euthanasia and has since written numerous publications on the issue, including the very thorough 2010 *Manual of Catholic Medical Ethics*.[546] The manual provides a comprehensive Catholic overview of the major topics encountered in today's medical practice. Eijk, along with his coauthors, explains how the Church's position on the aforementioned issues is just and why opposing views do not do justice to human dignity.

He has spoken out strongly against gender theory,[547] saying exposing its errors is "of the utmost urgency" because it undermines the roles of mothers, fathers, and married spouses, impairs the biological relationship between parents and children, and harms the ability to share the Church's teachings about God as a Holy Trinity. Eijk believes it sets the world "against the Christian faith," is an ideology rooted in "radical feminism," and is being spread under the term "gender equality." He also sees it as linked to contraception.[548]

---

[545] In October 2016, the Dutch government announced that it wanted to develop a new law that would make assisted suicide—not necessarily by a doctor—possible for people who are not suffering from any kind of psychiatric or somatic illness, but who are of the opinion that, due to feelings of loneliness, old age, or a reduced mobility, their life is "accomplished," that is, it no longer has any sense in being lived and thus may be ended.

[546] W.J. Eijk and L.J.M. Hendriks, *Handboek katholieke medische ethiek : verantwoorde gezondheidszorg vanuit katholiek perspectief* (Almere: Parthenon, 2010). English edition: W.J. Eijk, and M.R. Berg. *Manual of Catholic Medical Ethics: Responsible Healthcare from a Catholic Perspective* (Ballarat: Connor Court Publishing, 2014).

[547] Deborah Gyapong, "Cardinal Willem Eijk Says Gender Theory 'Radically Contradicts the Church's Teaching' and Undermines the Roles of Mothers and Fathers," *Catholic Register*, 21 May 2019 https://www.catholicregister. org/home/international/item/29531-cardinal-willem-eijk-says-gender-theory-radically-contradicts-the-church-s-teaching-and-undermines-the-roles-of-mothers-and-fathers.

[548] Edward Pentin, "Dutch Cardinal on Gender Ideology: It Sets the World 'Against the Christian Faith,'" *National Catholic Register*, 17 May 2019, https://www.ncregister.com/daily-news/dutch-cardinal-on-gender-ideology-it-sets-the-world-against-the-christian-f.

Contraception

In the Netherlands, many laws that violate the dignity of the human person came into effect starting in the 1960s. Eijk wrote that "after the introduction of hormonal contraception in 1964, the problem of unwanted pregnancies arose, for which procured abortion was prescribed as a remedy."

> The majority of young women use the pill starting at age 13-14 through the initiative of their parents, who are afraid that their daughters will get pregnant. Thus, Holland remains very proud of having relatively few adolescent pregnancies. This situation also generates a problem with the formation of youth, because the widespread use of the pill at such a young age does not help with the formation of the virtue of chastity, that is, the integration of impulses and sexual feelings into a mutual total gift of self which is done in marriage, or in a celibate life.[549]

Priestly Celibacy

Eijk often received the suggestion to solve the "problem" of the limited number of Dutch priests by abolishing celibacy for priests. In his 2010 pastoral letter *Why Priests?*, Eijk explained that "there is much discussion in the Church in our country about sacred ministry: what can a clergyman do that a pastoral worker cannot? Why can men be admitted to the ordinations [viz., of the diaconate and the priesthood] and women not? Why does a priest have to live celibate? In all these discussions, the content and meaning of the priesthood are often hidden in the background." In his letter, Eijk invited his readers to "view priests through eyes of faith, not focusing on what is or is not allowed, but to think about questions such as: Why do we need priests? What is the purpose of the priesthood? Why would one become a priest?"[550]

---

[549] Ibid.
[550] Eijk, *Why Priests?*

With reference to the Congregation for the Clergy's document *The Priest and the Third Christian Millennium* and John Paul II's Post-Synodal Apostolic Exhortation *Pastores Dabo Vobis*, Eijk explained in his letter why celibacy is inseparable from the priesthood.[551] In a 2018 interview, Eijk explicitly stated: "With [the implementation of '*viri probati*'[552]], priestly celibacy would be lost, [and with it], a splendid and fruitful centuries-long tradition of the Latin Church."[553]

Migrants and Refugees

In their 2015 Advent letter dealing with the refugee situation in Europe, Dutch bishops stated their concerns regarding the "refugee crisis" and the impact that large groups of refugees would have on their society. Such a challenged required "a realistic answer from those who bear political responsibility, from the churches and from civil society organizations, [who] together bear responsibility for living together well and for the general welfare."[554]

They expressed opposition to all forms of discrimination and xenophobia, because it disregards and violates the deepest dignity of every person, and stressed that Christians have a duty to help refugees, "to lend our fellow human beings in need a helping hand." They said refugees "may be asked to cooperate" so their arrival "does not disrupt our society," and that government should "develop and enforce a fair asylum policy that serves and promotes the common good, in particular cohesion in our society."[555]

---

[551] Ibid.

[552] The debated proposal to allow married men "of proven character" to be ordained to the priesthood.

[553] Francesco Boezi, "Cardinal: 'EU Does Not Show Solidarity with Italy on Migrants,'" *Il Giornale*, 13 December 2018, www.ilgiornale.it/news/cronache/cardinale-sui-migranti-lue-non-mostra-solidariet-allitalia-1615839.html (translated from Italian).

[554] Ibid.

[555] Ibid.

In a December 2018 interview, Eijk repeated that "migrants, in turn, have obligations toward the well-being of the country they seek refuge in and they must respect universal values, such as the inviolability of the human person." He stressed the importance of Europeans' being hospitable, "but we also have to take into account what a society can handle." Regarding economic migrants, Eijk said "the government is not obliged to grant a residence permit to every migrant, certainly not to economic migrants. They are necessary for the well-being of their country of origin."[556]

Eijk has commented relatively little on the refugee crisis, other than to say that refugees may not disrupt Dutch society. During a lecture titled "Blood Witnesses: Martyrdom through the Ages" celebrating the fact that St. Boniface came to the Netherlands thirteen hundred years ago, Eijk was asked about the difference between Christian and Muslim martyrs. Eijk explained that there is a fundamental difference between "Islamic martyrdom," which "is an active thing; killing others. With Christians it's about suffering." "Boniface called on his companions not to pick up arms, to remain faithful as a Christian and to die that way."[557]

Threat of Secularization, Hyperindividualism

From numerous letters, lectures, interviews, and teachings, it seems that Eijk sees the current secularization and "hyperindividualism" as the most potent threats to Christian life and values. The issues of how to "combat" secularization and how to evangelize a post-Christian society are his main

---

[556] KN Editorial Staff, "Cardinal Eijk Happy with 'Poor but Independent Church,'" *Katholiek Nieuwsblad*, 15 December 2018, www.kn.nl/nieuws/wereldkerk/kardinaal-eijk-blij-met-arme-maar-onafhankelijke-kerk/ (translated from Dutch).

[557] Jan van Reenen, "Cardinal Eijk: Martyrdom in Christianity Differs from Islam," *Reformatorisch Dagblad*, 24 June 2016, https://www.rd.nl/kardinaal-eijk-martelaarschap-in-christendom-verschilt-van-islam-1.709179 (translated from Dutch).

focal points.[558] In a 2012 column, for example, Eijk wrote that the majority in Western Europe has become spiritually blind in the last fifty years and that it does not seem to matter anymore what one believes. "In addition to this culture, evangelizing is also complicated by the idea that faith and reason exclude each other and the misconception that religions in themselves are the causes of violence, discord and war."[559]

Eijk stressed that what we believe impacts not only our image of God but also our understanding of human dignity and our view of the world. "The Triune God loves every human being without exception."[560] Eijk has underlined that "for Muslims, for example, God is one Person, a being who maintains distance from the world, who, supremely powerful, as absolute ruler, thrones in absolute loneliness above the world. It is precisely the belief in one God in Three Persons that makes God so approachable to us and is the most characteristic of our Christian faith."[561]

---

[558] Willem Jacobus Cardinal Eijk, "Religious Capital: The Ability to Be a Church," Diocese of Utrecht, 26 November 2015, www.aartsbisdom.nl/wp-content/uploads/2017/07/ABN-AMRO-Beheer-van-religieus-vermogen-2015-11-26.pdf. See also "Cardinal Eijk Preaches to Chrismamis about Sacrifices," Diocese of Utrecht, 29 March 2018, www.aartsbisdom.nl/kardinaal-eijk-preekt-chrismamis-offers/. See also Willem Jacobus Cardinal Eijk, "'On the Road to Easter with Christ: Letter for the Forty Days of 2018,'" Diocese of Utrecht, 14 February 2018, www.aartsbisdom.nl/wp-content/uploads/2018/02/2018-02-09-Vastenbrief-2018-kardinaal-Eijk.pdf.

[559] Willem Jacobus Cardinal Eijk, "Day of Judaism in the Shul in Enschede," Diocese of Utrecht, 17 January 2018, www.aartsbisdom.nl/wp-content/uploads/2018/01/Dag-van-het-Jodendom-Enschede-2018-01-17-def.pdf (translated from Dutch).

[560] Willem Jacobus Cardinal Eijk, "It Does Matter What You Believe," Diocese of Utrecht, 1 September 2012, www.aartsbisdom.nl/home/organisatie/aartsbisschop/columns/het-maakt-wel-degelijk-uit-wat-je-gelooft/ (translated from Dutch).

[561] Willem Jacobus Cardinal Eijk, "Sanctuary, Trinity Sunday," Diocese of Utrecht, 27 May 2018, www.aartsbisdom.nl/wp-content/uploads/2018/06/2018-05-27-Heiligdomsvaart-Drievuldigheid-B.pdf (translated from Dutch).

The Last Things

Eijk noted that "many are concerned by all the signs of climate change" and "people are frightened by the notion of the end of the world." "But people fail to see we are already in the final age of the world. And because we do not know when the end of the world will come, we are called to be vigilant."[562]

In a recent interview, Eijk emphasized: "The first secret, about hell, well, I think it's really a secret that remains highly relevant for our time. That's our duty: to make sure, because we are in charge of announcing the Catholic Faith, that people don't end up in hell, and to warn them about it. In this regard, we can sincerely ask ourselves if we do this often enough. Because when we talk about hell, that often arouses many emotions. Yet I think we really have a duty to do so." [563]

In the same interview, Eijk also spoke of the doctrine of universal salvation: "Yes, it is true that Christ wants to save all men, but you have to open yourself up to it. So there is a condition attached to it, and salvation is therefore not automatic. You really have to choose Christ."[564]

REORGANIZING THE CHURCH IN A POST-CHRISTIAN SOCIETY

Cardinal Eijk has had to make hard decisions, which presiding over a church in steep decline requires of its leaders.

In a time when fewer than 5 percent of Dutch who call themselves Catholic still go to Mass,[565] Eijk has been forced to close many churches.

---

[562] Willem Jacobus Cardinal Eijk, "What Can We Still Do for Deceased Fellow Humans?," Diocese of Utrecht, November 2015, www.aartsbis-dom.nl/home/organisatie/aartsbisschop/columns/kunnen-we-overleden-medemensen-nog-betekenen/ (translated from Dutch).

[563] Smits, "Eijk Answers Questions on Crisis."

[564] Ibid.

[565] Ibid.

When he became archbishop in 2008, the archdiocese had 312 parish churches.[566] In 2014 Eijk predicted that when he turns seventy-five in 2028, there will be 20 parishes with one or two churches left in each. In a 2018 interview, Eijk stated that even that is too optimistic.[567] Regarding the entirety of the Netherlands, Eijk indicated in 2013 that he expected that in 2025 two-thirds of all Dutch churches would be closed.[568]

These grim prognoses have provoked much opposition. Petitions have been sent to both Pope Benedict XVI and Pope Francis, urging them to halt Eijk's reorganization efforts. Indeed, both liberal and conservative Catholics have heavily criticized Eijk.[569] His response has been: "Sometimes you can keep things together only by being decisive. I don't have an extremely popular message. But I'm not out for the popularity prize."[570]

"It pains me when a church has to close," he has said. "But I said it before: in the shrinking process that the Church is going through, we must not cling to buildings; that is not our salvation.... Our Faith is linked not to a building but to God."[571] Eijk even planned to close his own cathedral in Utrecht, but mainly thanks to a lobby by the parishioners

---

[566] Twillert and Amelink, "Monsignor Is Strict."

[567] "The Shepherd Loses His Flock," Diocese of Utrecht, September 2018, www.aartsbisdom.nl/wp-content/uploads/2018/09/Interview-De-Gelder-lander-def.pdf (translated from Dutch).

[568] "Ten Misunderstandings about Church Closure in the Archdiocese of Utrecht," Diocese of Utrecht, 4 March 2015, www.aartsbisdom.nl/tien-misverstanden-kerksluiting-aartsbisdom-utrecht/.

[569] Hans Kuitert, "'Gap between Eijk and Other Bishops,'" *De Telegraaf*, 24 February 2015, www.telegraaf.nl/ nieuws/858835/kloof-tussen-eijk-en-anderebisschoppen?utm_source=google&utm_medium=organic.

[570] Enzo van Steenbergen, "'God Blesses No Way of Compromise,'" *NRC.nl*, 17 February 2012, www.nrc.nl /nieuws/2012/02/17/god-zegent-geen-weg-van-compromissen-12167619-a242543 (translated from Dutch).

[571] Eijk, "Religious Capital."

it was recently announced that a financial plan has been made that will allow the cathedral to stay open.[572]

Eijk has explained many times that reorganization is the only option.

We see parish finances drowning in red numbers. You have to see it this way: 10 percent of the parishes are rich, 10 percent of the parishes are simply bankrupt. The maintenance costs of the churches are too high for them. Even if they cut back their entire pastoral team, they still have a financial shortage. The other 80 percent isn't yet bankrupt but doesn't have great numbers either. We have arranged a meeting between the diocese staff and the parish boards. There were conversations with our economist. The question was: What can you keep open in the long term? What do we need to do to ensure "black numbers"? It is said that the bishop is always talking about money. But money is a condition for pastoral care. If you cannot pay your bills, both the first and second reading will be read by the bailiff.[573]

Eijk steadily maintains that, although there is a shortage of priests within the Dutch church and the duties of the remaining priests have consequently increased, priestly duties will *not* be assigned to those not ordained.[574] Neither that shortage, nor parishioner preferences, nor the desire to create a lower threshold to get people to attend Mass is ever a valid ground for deviation from the liturgy.[575]

Because of the dearth of priests in the Netherlands, the Eucharist is, unfortunately, no longer being celebrated in every church every Sunday. Eijk stated that it is a "great loss if believers do not regularly hear and pray

---

[572] "Cardinal Eijk: St. Catherine's Cathedral Remains Open!," *MariaBode. nl*, 2 March 2019, www.mariabode.nl/ bisdomnieuws/kardinaal-eijk-sint-catharinakathedraal-blijft-open/.

[573] "The Shepherd Loses His Flock."

[574] Ibid.

[575] Eijk, "About Certain Components of the Holy Eucharist."

along with the prayers prayed when the Eucharist is celebrated," which makes "it more difficult to discover the richness of the Eucharist."[576]

Although Eijk has said that closing churches "cuts through [his] soul,"[577] he looks at the bright side of the massive reorganization within the archdiocese. "It may seem contradictory, but closing (superfluous) churches is building the Church of the future." "For example, seven declining religious communities with little church attendance and hardly any activities, have been transformed into one lively religious community with high church attendance and new initiatives."[578]

Eijk says that he seeks to emulate the attitude of St. Martin. "I had to proceed to pastoral and financial reorganization in my current archdiocese, where in the first year I had to dismiss two-thirds of the curia staff in order to prevent the archdiocese from going bankrupt. The reorganizations have, however, also led to the emergence of new pastoral initiatives: the strengthening of the position of the priest, a new pastoral youth program, and—thanks to the, albeit modest, growth in the number of seminarians—I was able to reopen the archdiocese's seminary in 2014."[579]

Eijk has reminded the faithful "'not [to] let our hearts become troubled or dull.' We must remember these words every day, because no matter how big or small the Church becomes, the Lord is with us. And He will probably surprise us! Remember the words of Jesus in Luke (18:27): 'What is impossible with men is possible with God.'"[580]

---

[576] Eijk, *Living with Christ*.

[577] Ibid.

[578] Ibid.

[579] Eijk had been forced to close the seminary in 2010. See: "Archdiocese of Utrecht: Priest Training Back in Utrecht," Roman Catholic Church in the Netherlands, 4 April 2014, www.rkkerk. nl/aartsbisdom-utrecht-priester-opleiding-terug-in-utrecht/. See also Eijk, "Award of the Culture Prize"; "Cardinal Eijk Receives Italian Culture Prize," RK Documenten, 29 October 2018, www.rkdocumenten.nl/rkdocs/index.php?mi=680&nws=4332; Twillert and Amelink, "Monsignor Is Strict" (translated from Dutch).

[580] Willem Jacobus Cardinal Eijk, "The Members of the Pastoral Teams; the Board Members of the Parishes," Diocese of Utrecht, 5 October

"It is true that the numbers [viz., of churchgoers] are decreasing, but I sometimes say: the quantity is constantly decreasing, but the quality is increasing.... The community has become small, but it is also a stronger community.... I am still in good spirits, I have an ardent faith, and I also always believe in the power of the Lord: He triumphs. *Christus vincit.* Not we, but He in us."[581]

In conclusion, Eijk says of himself:

I sometimes compare a bishop today to a meteorologist who is concerned with climate change. And the religious climate in the Netherlands is deteriorating; a real storm front is approaching. A bishop has many duties, but pretending good weather is coming is not part of that. My warning about the shrinking church, however, does not mean passively waiting for the future. Certainly not. In these individualistic times we must show that a church community has added value. But at the same time, we have to prepare for what is possible and what is partly already there. I say possible, because sometimes a storm diminishes at the last moment or takes a different track. But we also have to take into account the possibility that we will be affected.[582]

SUMMARY

After the Second Vatican Council, the Dutch Church was one of the most radicalized; it is now in a free fall of secularization and parish closures. In the midst of that difficult situation, Cardinal Willem Eijk has worked to bring the light of Christ to his people and the world.

2018, www.aartsbisdom.nl/wp-content/uploads/2018/10/2018-10-05-Brief-kardinaal-Eijk-aan-teams-en-besturen.pdf (translated from Dutch).

[581] Smits, "Eijk Answers Questions on Crisis."

[582] "Shepherd Loses His Flock"; see also "Ten Misunderstandings."

He is widely seen as solidly orthodox and pro-life, and his apostolic initiatives have focused on reviving love of the Eucharist and the Blessed Virgin Mary, family catechesis, and personal evangelization. Eijk's experience as a physician and a moral theologian has given him tools to address cutting-edge issues that have life-or-death consequences, including euthanasia and in vitro fertilization.

Although he has had the unpleasant task of closing many parishes in Holland, an undertaking that has attracted considerable criticism from all quarters, he has done so primarily at the request of the local Church itself and in dialogue with those affected by these decisions. He has not been deterred by the unpopularity that such actions have brought him.

Clear and uncompromising when it comes to the Church's teachings, Eijk manifests a love of Catholic truth even when it is unpopular, as seen in his willingness to defend *Humanae Vitae* and to uphold the indissolubility of marriage as only between one man and one woman and the privileged place for the conjugal act. Likewise, his insistence on Christ's teaching regarding an all-male, celibate priesthood has been a sign of contradiction for some. While having compassion on refugees and emphasizing the need to care for them, especially for Christians fleeing persecution, Eijk has said that economic migrants often are obliged to build up their native countries; and they have obligations to the country into which they immigrate. He has also spoken with clarity about fundamental differences between Islam and Christianity.

Over the years, Eijk has become used to sometimes vehement criticism for his unabashed adherence to the Catholic Faith in all its facets, but he nevertheless provides an example for pastors who desire to "feed the flock" given them by Christ, no matter what wolves may be prowling around.

SERVICE TO THE CHURCH

Ordination to the Priesthood: 1 June 1985
Ordination to the Episcopate: 6 November 1999
Elevation to the College of Cardinals: 18 February 2012

Education

- 1971-1978: University of Amsterdam, Netherlands; Medicine
- 1979-1985: Rolduc Seminary, the Netherlands
- 1979-1987: Leiden University, the Netherlands; Medical Ethics (Ph.D.)
- 1987-1990: Pontifical University of St. Thomas Aquinas, Rome; Philosophy (Ph.D.)
- 1990: Pontifical Lateran University, Rome; Theology (LTh)

Assignments

- 1984-1987: Deacon/priest, Diocese of Roermond, Netherlands
- 1990-1999: Professor of moral theology, Seminaries of the Diocese of Roermond and 's-Hertogenbosch and MEDO Institute for Marriage and Family Theology, Netherlands
- 1992-2000: Advisory board member, Association of Dutch Physicians
- 1993-1997: Board member, Legal Association Pro Vita, Netherlands
- 1993-present: Cofounder and chairman, Medical Ethics Foundation, Netherlands
- 1996-1999: Chairman of the Ethics Committee, St. Camillus Nursing Home, Netherlands
- 1996-1999: Professor of moral theology, Pontifical Faculty of Theology, Lugano, Switzerland

- 1999-2008: Bishop, Diocese of Groningen (since 2005, Groningen-Leeuwarden), Netherlands
- 1999-present: Consultant for medical-ethical questions, Dutch Bishops' Conference
- 2001-present: Consultant for the sector of vocations and studies for ecclesiastical offices, Dutch Bishops' Conference
- 2007-present: Vice grand chancellor, Tilburg School of Catholic Theology, Netherlands
- 2008-present: Archbishop, Archdiocese of Utrecht, Netherlands
- 2011-2016: Chair, Dutch Bishops' Conference

Roman Curia

- 1997-1999: Member, International Theological Commission.
- 2001-present: Member of the Scientific Council of the Faculty of Bioethics, Pontifical Athenaeum Regina Apostolorum
- 2004, 2010-present: Ordinary member, Pontifical Academy for Life
- 2005-2010: Member of the directive board, Pontifical Academy for Life
- 2008-2012: Member, Pontifical Council for Culture
- 2008-2017: Member, Congregation for the Clergy
- 2012-present: Member, Congregation for Catholic Education
- 2014-2017: Member, Pontifical Council for the Laity

PÉTER CARDINAL ERDŐ

"In the Beginning There Was Nothing but Grace"

Born: 25 June 1952
Budapest, Hungary
Nationality: Hungarian
Title: Archbishop of Esztergom-Budapest

BIOGRAPHY

The eldest of six children, Péter Erdő was raised by deeply Catholic parents in a family in which the Faith was "woven into the fabric of our life."[583] He grew up under communism, and when he was four, his family was forced to flee with just the clothes on their backs after invading troops burned

---

[583] Robert B. Moynihan and Viktoria Somogyi, *Guarding the Flame: The Challenges Facing the Church in the 21st Century: A Conversation with Cardinal Peter Erdo* (Charlotte, NC: TAN Books, 2019), 3.

down their family home in 1956. He then experienced various degrees of discrimination on account of his Faith. He was educated at a Piarist boys' school in Budapest. The "reality of God" began to attract the young Péter Erdő as an altar boy, giving meaning and direction to his life. He entered the seminary after much prayer, believing that helping people toward salvation was so important that it required dedicating one's whole life to it.[584]

After his ordination to the priesthood in 1975—which he calls one of the three happiest moments in his life—he spent two years in parish service before being sent to Rome, where he earned degrees in theology and canon law at the Pontifical Lateran University (1980). In the following years, he taught on various faculties of canon law and theology in Hungary and abroad, including Buenos Aires, while serving as an ecclesiastical clerk and judge.[585] During this time, he published manuals and articles on canon law. He was a research fellow at the University of California, Berkeley in 1995 to 1996. For some time, he was rector of the Hungarian College in Rome, while teaching at the Gregorian and Lateran Universities. John Paul II consecrated Erdő bishop in 2000 and made him primate of all Hungary as ordinary of the Esztergom-Budapest Archdiocese in 2003. Erdő was elevated to the cardinalate the same year.

Speaking German, Italian, French, Spanish, English, and his native Hungarian, Erdő was elected president of the Hungarian Catholic Episcopal Conference in 2005 and, in the same year, president of the Council of European Episcopal Conferences (CCEE). The esteem he holds among his episcopal colleagues was shown in his reelection to the CCEE in 2011 as well as his appointment to help oversee the Secretariat of State's "Second Section," which is responsible for diplomatic relations.[586] Since 2003 he has participated in all the assemblies of the

---

[584] Ibid.

[585] Paul Badde, "Peter Erdo, a Peter on the Horizon of History," *Welt*, 22 February 2013, https://www.welt.de/politik/ausland/article113829273/Peter-Erdo-ein-Petrus-am-Horizont-der-Geschichte.html.

[586] John L. Allen Jr., "Papabile of the Day: The Men Who Could Be Pope," *National Catholic Reporter*, 24 February 2013, https://www.ncronline.org/blogs/ncr-today/papabile-day-men-who-could-be-pope-5.

Synod of Bishops, with the special honor given by Pope Francis to serve as relator for the synods of 2014 and 2015. He is the author of more than 250 articles and 25 books.[587]

SANCTIFYING OFFICE

Approach to the Liturgy

Cardinal Erdő once described the liturgy as a "beautiful work" and views many developments in liturgy ushered in by the Second Vatican Council, such as the change from Latin to the vernacular, as continuous with tradition.[588]

For him, "continuity has remained,"[589] and he especially welcomes the Council's revision of Mass readings. The Tridentine Mass, which usually has only two readings—the Epistle and the Gospel—neglected the Old Testament. But Erdő believes that the Old Testament readings help worshippers to understand better the Christian way, especially given that "the history of salvation of the New Testament appears already in prefigured form" in the Old Testament.[590] Although Erdő has thus welcomed the "rediscovery of the Old Testament," he nevertheless acknowledges that "there are few priests or theologians who can explain these texts well."[591] The cardinal prefers the Ordinary Form of the Mass but is willing to permit the Extraordinary Form and will support it if called to do so.

In keeping with his appreciation of the expanded use of Scripture in the post–Vatican II liturgy, Erdő emphasizes the duty of priests given in the *Code of Canon Law* to explain Holy Scripture in their Sunday homilies. He is critical of homilies that turn into a "free discourse on

---

[587] "Erdo Card. Peter," Vatican, http://press.vatican.va/content/salastampa/en/documentation/cardinali_biografie/cardinali_bio_erdo_p.html.

[588] Moynihan and Somogyi, *Guarding the Flame*.

[589] Ibid.

[590] Ibid.

[591] Ibid.

any topic" and desires that priests explain "all the mysteries of salvation throughout the course of the three-year cycle."[592]

The Eucharist

According to Cardinal Erdő, the Christian priesthood and the Eucharist are "closely related"—or better, "inextricably linked"—to each other. The priest can discover "the beauty and power" of his vocation only when he "really worships the Eucharist as the supreme and most dignified gift of Christ, in which his redeeming sacrifice itself becomes present."[593] There is only one High Priest, Jesus Christ, and the priest himself, through the sacrament of Holy Orders, shares in this one priesthood. Erdő's understanding of the role of the priest in the liturgy reflects the words of St. Pope Paul VI: that priests should celebrate the Mass every day with such dignity and devotion that not only they but *all* the faithful become partakers in the fruits of Christ's redemption on the Cross.[594]

The Priesthood

The sacrament of Holy Orders bestows on the priest the grace to act *in persona Christi* and the indelible character that empowers him to perform valid sacraments. There is an inextricable bond between the priest, the Church, and the Eucharist: "Without holy ordination, there is no Church because there is no Eucharist, and without the Eucharist, there is no Church."[595]

Cardinal Erdő emphasizes the importance for any priestly ministry to have Christ as the center: "But God's grace can be especially effective if people feel that [priests] are really in love with God and consider him the center of [their] lives."[596]

---

[592] Ibid.
[593] "Peter Erdő's Homily and Introductory Words," Esztergom-Budapest Archdiocese, 29 March 2018, https://www.esztergomi-ersekseg.hu/media/beszedek/olajszentelesi-szentmise-szent-istvan-bazilikaban-2113 (translated from Hungarian).
[594] Ibid.
[595] Moynihan and Somogyi, *Guarding the Flame.*
[596] "Peter Erdő's Homily."

Erdő does not suggest making celibacy optional for the Latin-Rite priests but, rather, emphasizes the value of the celibate way of life by pointing to the example that Jesus Christ Himself left His disciples: "We come to know the real Jesus Christ through the Gospels, [and] we know that he had a celibate life, he had a life totally consecrated to God, and he also recommend this chastity to those of his disciples who were able to understand."[597] Erdő acknowledges that celibacy is handled differently in the Eastern tradition. He nevertheless points out that though there are married priests in the Orthodox churches, those churches still maintain the tradition of ordaining bishops chosen only from the group of celibate priests. There is, furthermore, a strong monastic tradition in these churches that have a great appreciation for the ideal of celibacy.

The cardinal admits that chastity and celibacy are not easy ways of life and require a special grace of God. But he sees "an internal spiritual relationship" between the "apostolic mission, the episcopal and the priestly mission, and the celibate life."[598] He also refers to the teaching of St. Paul, who recommends chastity and celibacy "in order to give oneself completely to this ministry and to not be divided."[599]

Erdő defends the hierarchical structure of the Church as instituted by Christ, with its threefold office structure consisting of the bishop, the priest, and the deacon, but he emphasizes the servant character of that structure, stressing again and again the pope's title as "servant of the servants of God."

The clergy have received special graces through Holy Orders, not only to lead but also to teach and to sanctify, graces that enable them to execute tasks that, according to Erdő, are reserved to them—first and foremost, of course, the celebration of the Eucharist, but also other tasks, such as giving homilies. Erdő counters demands for more democracy in the Church by emphasizing that the Church is not a democracy but

---

[597] Moynihan and Somogyi, *Guarding the Flame.*
[598] Ibid.
[599] Ibid.

rather a "Christocracy,"[600] with Jesus ruling because He is its head. The Church must follow Christ's example and cannot act on its own authority.

GOVERNING OFFICE

Early Ministry

Cardinal Erdő exhibited a pastoral heart from the beginning of his discernment of the priesthood: "Helping people in the most important thing, in the matter of salvation," was the driving force behind his decision to become a priest.[601]

Erdő's first assignment was in the coal-mining town of Dorog. He described it as a "mission place," a place that had lived on old tradition but had not offered a religious education in its schools for a long time. In Dorog, Erdő found religion to be distant.[602] There, he worked with various church groups, visited the hospital, and helped out in neighboring parishes. His ministry was constrained by communist regulations that allowed religious activities only in the church building itself. In spite of these constraints, Erdő retains good memories of this assignment. Around the same time, he began working as defender of the bond at the diocesan tribunal of the Archdiocese of Esztergom-Budapest.

Erdő was appointed a bishop in 1999, while he was in Rome working as an expert priest of the synod for Europe. From the very beginning of his episcopacy, according to an anecdote he remembers, the expression of God's mercy has accompanied him.[603] His coat of arms bears the motto "In the Beginning There Was Nothing but Grace." Only a few years

---

[600] Peter Erdő, *Csak a Kegyelem* (Budapest: Cairo Publisher, 2003), 77.

[601] Moynihan and Somogyi, *Guarding the Flame.*

[602] Erdő, *Csak a Kegyelem*, 22.

[603] He remembers that at the end of that synod, preparing for the procession to enter St. Peter's Basilica, the president of the Hungarian conference of bishops asked him if he would be ordained a bishop, the choir was singing "Misericordias Domini in aeternum cantabo" (I will sing the mercies of the Lord forever). Moynihan and Somogyi, *Guarding the Flame.*

later, Erdő became archbishop of Esztergom-Budapest and thus primate of Hungary.

Cardinal Erdő takes very seriously the many duties the *Code of Canon Law* ascribes to the office of the bishop. He also places great trust in the providence of God and knows that in the end, it is Christ who acts.

Evangelization and Youth

Notwithstanding the many important practical problems people now face, such as those affecting marital and family life as well as social solidarity more generally, Cardinal Erdő maintains that the "people today have a hunger and thirst for Christ," that "the world is in need of hope: of the hope of Christ."[604] He therefore emphasizes the need for a new evangelization, because the gospel message, grounded in the person of Jesus Christ, must never be lost. According to Erdő, it is particularly the task of parish communities and of ecclesial movements to "open to the world around them, to nonbelievers, to those who are in need of the Good News of Jesus Christ."[605]

With regard to youths and young adults, Cardinal Erdő notes that many "are afraid of existential choices" such as marriage, career, or priestly or religious vocations. With this in mind, he set up specialized programs in his archdiocese to work with the youth. These programs aim at both catechesis and marriage preparation.

Having recognized both the need and the desire for a new evangelization, Erdő reintroduced at the parish level old traditions that echoed religious practice before the communist era.[606] He furthermore "tried to deepen the conviction and zeal" of those working at the parish level: priests, deacons, religious—and also laypeople.[607] He then encouraged

---

[604] "Primate of Hungary on New Evangelization in Europe (Part 1 of 2)," Catholic Online, 24 November 2005, http://www.catholic.org/featured/headline.php?ID=2788.

[605] Ibid.

[606] For example, mission crosses.

[607] Moynihan and Somogyi, *Guarding the Flame*.

parishes to open their doors, in an effort to "get in touch, even through the local media, with non-believers who were not familiar with the Church."[608]

Mission is a central element of Cardinal Erdő's pastoral work. In the early 2000s, for example, Budapest sent a large delegation to take part in missionary work in five other European cities, aimed at reviving the cities' religious roots. Great mission celebrations in various cities, processions with the Blessed Sacrament, penance days in different churches, and other initiatives were meant to evangelize or reevangelize the people in his diocese and in the country.

Attracting Vocations

Another urgent problem Cardinal Erdő has dealt with is the decreasing number of priests in Hungary. The Archdiocese of Esztergom-Budapest in particular suffers from a priest shortage that is severe even compared with other dioceses in Hungary. The urban public transportation system and the compact nature of the area enable the faithful to find their way to other parishes that offer Mass when their parish does not. But the shortage is still so acute that cluster parishes have been established, and priests from foreign countries have been invited to come to Budapest.[609]

Migrants and Refugees

Due to its geographical location in the heart of Europe, Hungary has long experience with migrants and travelers, and it was a major crossroads during the recent surge of peoples from the Middle East. Cardinal Erdő has addressed this issue at various times, indicating a balanced approach, with strong emphases on the just limits of any country's obligations to accept new residents and the obligations of immigrants to respect the laws and traditions of the host country.

---

[608] Ibid.
[609] Erdő, *Csak a Kegyelem*, 55.

On the one hand, Erdő affirms that every human being has the "sacrosanct right to try to survive,"[610] which means that in cases of life-threatening natural disasters or economic or political instabilities in their home countries, people have the right to try to find a safe haven. But Erdő is also very much aware of the challenges of immigration. Alongside his recognition of the basic human right to leave one's home country in order to find a better place to live, he also offers a realistic assessment of the challenges posed by large influxes of immigrants to certain European countries. He warns that the capacity of countries to integrate refugees without endangering their own political stability and public order is limited: "You cannot tell the Europeans that they are obliged to allow the whole world into their countries, because that would break down the public order."[611] The cardinal, therefore, pleads for a "true balance between the key elements of solidarity and mercy."[612]

In a 2016 homily, Erdő explicitly linked the Christian duty to help refugees and people in need to the Bible and especially to the Fourth Commandment. He mentioned that the "act of mercy must be seen in the context of parental responsibilities and love in the family" and "helping parents, children, brothers, and sisters does not stop at the boundaries of family and kinship, but must also be open to other people who suffer."[613]

Integration, Erdő argues, means primarily "respect for the laws, first of all, in the country that one has come to" and also "respect for the institutions."[614] Erdő's convictions about immigration and integration were tested in 2015, when Hungary became the focal point of the refugee crisis in Europe. Hundreds of thousands of refugees,

---

[610] Moynihan and Somogyi, *Guarding the Flame*.

[611] Ibid.

[612] Ibid.

[613] Péter Erdő, "Péter Erdő's Second Sacrament of Mercy," *Magyar Kurír*, 28 February 2016, https://www.magyarkurir.hu/hirek/erdo-peter-masodik-szentbeszede-az-irgalmassagrol.

[614] Ibid.

especially from Syria but also from other countries facing civil wars, were stranded in Budapest and other major cities on their way to Germany, France, and elsewhere. While at first, Erdő refused to open parishes for refugees, pointing to legal obstacles and stating that "we would become human smugglers if we'd taken in refugees,"[615] he revised this statement after an audience with Pope Francis. Erdő then declared: "We will readily and happily follow [the pope's] advice on taking in and helping refugees."[616]

Persecuted Christians and Islam

Erdő especially emphasizes the Christian duty to care and pray for persecuted Christians fleeing from their homelands, reminding the faithful that "we are closely associated with the persecuted Christians.... We see Christ's disciples in them."[617]

Cardinal Erdő seems to hold a benign view of Islam, or at least of the prospect of significant Muslim immigration to Hungary. Responding in an interview in 2015 to reports of widespread fear of Islam and even of a creeping invasion of Muslims into Europe (and of concerns that Islam is incompatible with Western values and traditions), Erdő pointed to Hungary's history and its long experience with the religion. He thinks there are "signs of nervousness with regard to the presence of Islamic communities in Western countries" but also argues that this nervousness "is unjustified."[618] The reason for this nervousness is not to be found in

[615] Eszter Neuberger, "The Hungarian Lutheran Church Opens Its Doors to Refugees," *New Eastern Europe*, 15 October 2017, http://neweasterneurope.eu/2017/10/15/hungarian-lutheran-churches-open-door-refugees/.

[616] Philip Pullella, "Love and Loathing Greets Pope's Appeal for Parishes to Host Refugees," Reuters, 10 September 2015, https://www.reuters.com/article/us-europe-migrants-pope/love-and-loathing-greet-popes-appeal-for-parishes-to-host-refugees-idUSKCN0RA27A20150910.

[617] Peter Erdő, "Speech at the opening of the Ecumenical Prayer Week," *Esztergom-Budapest Archdiocese*, 21 January 2018, https://www.esztergomi-ersekseg.hu/media/beszedek/beszed-okumenikus-imahet-megnyitojan-1573.

[618] Ibid.

Islam but, rather, in the fact that many people "have become uncertain of their own identity."[619] That Westerners' sense that their own identity has become uncertain through relativism and individualism has led, Erdő maintains, to inordinate fear when these people face minorities with a strong sense of their own identity.

Ecumenical Relations

The necessity of knowing one's own Faith seems to be, for Erdő, the prerequisite for dealing with other faith communities. His attitude toward the Orthodox is very positive. He points to the large communion and the many common beliefs the Catholic and the Orthodox churches share, and he worked personally on the preparation of the Catholic-Orthodox Forum, a network of European Orthodox churches and all the bishops' conferences of Europe.[620] Although he complains about tendencies in several Protestant communities to "move very quickly away from their own traditions," Erdő nevertheless acknowledges the merits of these communities and values dialogue with them.[621]

The cardinal also supports dialogue with non-Christian religions, emphasizing the value of the Second Vatican Council's Declaration on Religious Freedom *Dignitatis Humanae*. Erdő underscores, however, that this dialogue must not lead to an attitude of indifference and a leveling of all religious beliefs.[622] It is important not to abandon one's own Catholic beliefs but to have "constructive fidelity to Christian roots, respectful toward the convictions of each individual."[623]

---

[619] Ibid.
[620] Ibid.
[621] Ibid.
[622] Erdő, *Csak a Kegyelem*, 94.
[623] Moynihan and Somogyi, *Guarding the Flame*.

GENERAL RELATOR

Among the many responsible positions he has held, one of the most publicly recognized was when he served as general relator—essentially chief organizer—for both the 2014 and 2015 synods on the family. As it is sometimes a post given to a prelate whom the pope sees as a potential successor, the cardinal had to contend with various attempts by persons inside and outside the synod to manipulate the meeting along heterodox lines. The most visible evidence of this occurred with the first synod's midterm *relatio* (report). Although it was supposed to summarize the participants' interventions thus far, it included the comment that "homosexuals have gifts and qualities to offer the Christian community" and asked whether Christian communities were "capable" of accepting their orientation "without compromising" Church teaching.[624] Those and other passages in the text about welcoming nonmarital unions upset the synod fathers, as they did not reflect what they were saying and were sent out to the media before they had seen them, with the presumed intent of steering the media narrative to say the Church had significantly changed its position on such matters (some media reports called it a "stunning" change).[625] The report carried Erdő's signature, but he distanced himself afterward at a press conference, pointing to the special secretary of the synod, Archbishop Bruno Forte, as the true author of the most controversial passages.[626] It was also

---

[624] Frank Rocca, "Family Synod Midterm Report: Welcome Gays, Nonmarital Unions," Catholic News Service, 13 October 2014, https://www.catholicnews.com/services/englishnews/2014/family-synod-midterm-report-welcome-gays-nonmarital-unions.cfm

[625] Edward Pentin, "Synod Secretariat: 'Relatio' Is Just a Working Document," *National Catholic Register*, 1 October 2014, https://www.ncregister.com/daily-news/synod-secretariat-relatio-is-a-working-document-only.

[626] "Cardinal on His Own Report's Paragraphs on Homosexuality: 'Ask *Him!* I Didn't Write This, The Author Must Know What He Meant!,'" *Rorate Caeli*, 13 October 2014, https://rorate-caeli.blogspot.com/2014/10/cardinal-on-his-own-reports-paragraphs.html.

alleged that Erdő had been browbeaten to write his introductory report for that synod to be structured in a way he did not initially support.[627] But by the next synod the following year, Vaticanist Sandro Magister said he had "learned his lesson" and produced "by his own pen" an introductory talk of "crystalline clarity and of impeccable adherence to the perennial doctrine of the Church, which has brought not a little surprise and irritation to the innovators."[628]

TEACHING OFFICE

Experience in Education

Cardinal Erdő has spent many years of his priesthood as a teacher. After obtaining a degree in canon law from the Pontifical Lateran University in Rome, he returned to Hungary and was sent by his bishop to Esztergom in order to teach canon law, Church history, and moral theology in the local seminary.[629] He also taught at the Pázmány Péter Catholic University, where he eventually became rector.

After the new *Code of Canon Law* was promulgated in 1983, Erdő worked on its translation into Hungarian, eventually publishing a bilingual edition with annotations. He has also written an instructional book and several articles about canon law and its history.[630] He admits that he "loves to teach" and that the passing on of ideas, thoughts, and knowledge gives him "a great feeling."[631]

---

[627] Edward Pentin, *The Rigging of a Vatican Synod* (San Francisco: Ignatius Press, 2015).

[628] Sandro Magister, "Synod. First Shot on Target Comes from the Conservatives," chiesa.espressonline.it, 8 October 2015 http://chiesa.espresso.repubblica.it/articolo/1351150bdc4.html?eng=y.

[629] Ibid.

[630] Ibid.

[631] Erdő, *Csak a Kegyelem*, 33.

Centrality of Christ and Moral Norms

The central element of the Catholic Faith is, for Cardinal Erdő, the personal encounter with Jesus Christ: "What does it mean to be a Christian? A personal relationship with Jesus Christ, Our Lord and God." And for him, this Jesus of Nazareth is not a mythological figure but a historical person, true God and true man. "There is a historical way to His teaching and to His works."[632] Like the disciples who only through meeting with the resurrected Christ began to understand and have their hearts filled with joy, so it is through our encounter that Jesus Christ "confronts us again and again with the question of what is really good for man."[633]

He stresses that this foundation is especially important for the Church as it faces the "grave crisis" of "relativism" in secular society, a society that is "increasingly unable to say something is 'right' or 'wrong', 'true' or 'false.'"[634]

For Cardinal Erdő, it is clear that "law, morals, and religion prove to form an organic whole."[635]

The philosophical developments at the beginning of the nineteenth century relating to ideas of relativity and the unknowability or negation of natural law have led to "separation of law from so-called natural morals."[636] According to Erdő, it was exactly this separation of law from objective moral norms that "led to horrible abuses in Nazi Germany,"[637]

---

[632] "Preaching by Cardinal Péter Erdő, Primate of Hungary, at the Funeral of Cardinal Joachim Meisner on 15 July 2017 in Cologne," German Bishops' Conference, 15 July 2017, https://www.dbk.de/de/nc/presse/aktuelles/meldung/predigt-von-kardinal-peter-erdoe-primas-von-ungarn-in-der-beisetzungsfeier-von-kardinal-joachim-mei/detail/ (translated from German).

[633] "Peter Erdő's Homily on Easter Sunday," Esztergom-Budapest Archdiocese, 1 April 2018, https://www.esztergomi-ersekseg.hu/media/erdo-peter-szent-beszede-husvet-vasarnapjan-2133 (translated from Hungarian).

[634] Péter Erdő, "Religion and Church in the Secular State," Esztergom-Budapest Archdiocese, 29 January 2018, https://www.esztergomi-ersekseg.hu/media/beszedek/vallas-es-egyhaz-vilagi-allamban.

[635] Ibid.

[636] Ibid.

[637] Ibid.

as was demonstrated in the trials of Nuremberg, where "it was not easy to convict people whose actions were based on current, but immoral laws."[638]

Erdő holds that a legal system cannot function on its own, detached from objective moral norms. In socialist societies, the regimes worked assiduously to promote voluntary obedience to the laws of the regime, but without any form of religious legitimization or "recognition of natural law." Socialist morals, in the end, only resembled the current penal code.[639] Erdő explains that "if the content of morals is simply the penal code, then these kinds of morals will barely be able to strengthen the authority of the laws."[640]

Erdő argues that any state decision about the question of what is good for mankind has to be based on natural law and a worldview open to religion. Any state that rejects these principles or tries to replace these principles with other ideologies risks the people's loss of "trust in the ... institutions."[641] Politicians need these fundamental and unchangeable principles even in democracies, because "the majority can end up with wrong or harmful decisions, especially if the concept of the common good becomes uncertain, because there is no consensus even on the anthropological foundations of law."[642]

Religious Freedom versus Communism

Erdő lived through the transition in Hungary from a communist regime to a democracy. He highlights the important role religion has played in filling the gap after the collapse of the communist ideology. This role was explicitly manifested in the new constitution of Hungary, which recognizes "churches, denominations, and religious communities [as] entities

---

[638] Ibid.
[639] Moynihan and Somogyi, *Guarding the Flame.*
[640] Ibid.
[641] Erdő, "Religion and Church."
[642] Ibid.

of prominent importance, capable of creating values and communities."[643] The cardinal prioritizes religious freedom. "The Church must by its very nature be free because it has a mission from Jesus Christ and not just a commission from some political authority."[644]

In the 1990s, after Hungary had become a democratic state, Erdő was involved in preparatory work on religious freedom, and as a member of the ecclesiastical delegation, he contributed to the preparation of several agreements between Hungary and the Holy See defining the relationship between the state and the Church in the country.

Erdő argues that the theory of separation of church and state has led, in many cases, to a hostile separation in which an ideological state excludes religion. He points to communist countries in particular but also considers secularism to be such an ideology. Erdő even seems to question situations in which the separation between church and state is peaceful and cooperative because, even then, the state can require "that Churches and religious communities obey the laws," which "supposes that society has a broader ideological horizon on which laws are established."[645]

Given the emergence of relativism mentioned above and the separation of legal norms from natural law, Erdő raises the question "What is the basis of the law?"[646] Democratic processes of majority decision-making are not adequate because even majorities can make decisions that are wrong or harmful. Erdő also doubts those who would place their hope "in an independent judge, who passes a just verdict on a fair legal basis," given that in societies that have replaced natural law and religious views with hostile ideologies, there is an "uncertainty surrounding the concept of the common good and doubts about fair treatment on the part of the authorities."[647]

---

[643] Ibid.
[644] Ibid.
[645] Moynihan and Somogyi, *Guarding the Flame.*
[646] Ibid.
[647] Ibid.

Erdő concurs fully with Pope Francis' warning about detaching human rights from their deeper roots.[648] He argues that "fundamental rights, or the so-called human rights, should be based on an existing reality and on a certain morality, not simply on a majority decision of a body. That is, they have to have a content base too, not just a formal basis."[649]

The foundation for Christian morality and values lies in the Bible. Jesus not only "left us his teaching, which was then written down," but also "respected the Holy Scriptures, . . . read in the synagogue . . . and explained the Holy Scriptures."[650] The Bible is God's way of communicating with humanity, and, as such, "we must not give up on this knowledge."[651]

Qualified Universalism

Cardinal Erdő denies universalism—the idea that all of humankind is already saved. But he nevertheless believes that everybody *can* be saved. It is from revelation that we know that every human being is called to a relationship with God. But Erdő also points out that this does not mean that all of our choices must ultimately lead to God. Human beings, by sinning, can turn away from or even deny God. This denial is not final during this life: there is always the possibility of repenting and returning to God.[652] Erdő believes that everybody can become a member of God's people. Jesus came in order to heal the wounds of sin and temptation and gave the Church this power to forgive sins. But there can be no forgiveness without sorrow. Mankind must cooperate to be able to participate in

---

[648] "Address of Pope Francis to the Council of Europe," Vatican, 25 November 2014, http://w2.vatican.va/content/francesco/en/speeches/2014/november/documents/papa-francesco_20141125_strasburgo-consiglio-europa.html.

[649] Moynihan and Somogyi, *Guarding the Flame.*

[650] Ibid.

[651] Ibid.

[652] Erdő, *Csak a Kegyelem,* 101.

the fruits of redemption.[653] Ultimately, it is only through Jesus Christ that humankind will find the way to God.[654]

Defender of Marriage and the Family

Erdő was appointed by Pope Francis as relator general at the Ordinary General Assembly of the Synod of Bishops in 2015, responsible for providing a concise introductory statement of the topic of the synod and summarizing the debates for a closing document. In the introductory report for the Synod on the Family in 2015, Erdő confirmed the indissolubility of marriage by referring to the teaching of Jesus Christ in the Gospels and of the apostle Paul in his letters.[655] He also sees it as "the mission of the Church" to accompany those "who live in problematic marital or family situations."[656]

With regard to admission to the sacraments, he distinguishes between two groups. On the one side are the separated and the divorced who have not "remarried," who can find support by the Church on "a path of pardon and possibly of reconciliation" and who can "find in the Eucharist the nourishment they need to sustain them in their present state of life."[657] On the other side are those who are divorced and civilly "remarried," whom Erdő wants to offer pastoral accompaniment while leaving "no doubt about the truth of the indissolubility of marriage taught by Jesus Christ himself." The pardon offered through the mercy of God must go hand in hand with conversion. According to the cardinal, it is not due to the breaking up of the first marriage but rather due to the cohabiting

---

[653] Peter Erdő, "Chrism Mass in St. Stephen's Basilica," Esztergom-Budapest Archdiocese, 29 March 2018, https://www.esztergomi-ersekseg.hu/media/olajszentelesi-szentmise-szent-istvan-bazilikaban-2113 (translated from Hungarian).

[654] Erdő, Csak a Kegyelem, 83.

[655] Peter Erdő, "Introductory Report for the Synod on the Family," Catholic News Agency, 6 October 2015, https://www.catholicnewsagency.com/news/full-text-of-cardinal-erdos-introductory-report-for-the-synod-on-the-family-67404.

[656] Ibid.

[657] Ibid.

in the second relationship that these couples cannot have access to the Eucharist. Erdő argues that this is not an "arbitrary prohibition" meant to prevent these couples from a full integration into the ecclesial community and from access to the sacraments, but rather "an intrinsic demand of varied situations and relationships."[658]

Erdő supports and affirms the teaching of Pope John Paul II in *Familiaris Consortio* that divorced-and-"remarried" couples who cannot end their relationship because of their children can have access to the sacrament of Penance and the Eucharist only *if* they "practice continence by the strength of grace" and live a "relationship of mutual help and friendship."[659] Erdő also points to this encyclical for illustrations of other ways to integrate such couples into the ecclesial community "apart from admission to the Eucharist."[660]

The principle guiding all of Erdő's thinking about pastoral solutions to this problem is that fidelity to the indissolubility of marriage cannot be linked to the practical recognition of the goodness of concrete situations that are opposite and therefore irreconcilable. Indeed, Erdő strikingly affirms the nonnegotiable quality of basic moral norms. He emphasizes that "between true and false, between good and evil, in fact, there is no graduality" and that "even if some forms of cohabitation bring in themselves certain positive aspects, this does not imply that they can be presented as good."[661] He continues: "This means that in objective truth good and evil are not given gradually (*gradualness of the law*), while at the subjective level the *law of graduality* can take place.... The human act, in fact, is good when it is good in every aspect."[662]

In the same document, Cardinal Erdő also addresses the issue of the Church's attitude toward persons with homosexual tendencies. Following the Church's teaching, the cardinal emphasizes how important it

---

[658] Ibid.
[659] Ibid.
[660] Ibid.
[661] Ibid.
[662] Ibid.

is to avoid any sign of unjust discrimination and to receive "men and women with a homosexual tendency … with respect and sensitivity." Erdő firmly reiterates the position of the Church: that "there are absolutely no grounds for considering homosexual unions to be in any way similar or even remotely analogous to God's plan for marriage and family."[663]

Erdő understands the challenges facing persons with same-sex attractions. While he clearly affirms the Church's teaching that same-sex unions can in no way be accepted as "similar or remotely analogous to God's plan for marriage and family," he also sees the need for special care for persons who experience same-sex attraction and encourages dioceses and parishes to set up pastoral programs to accompany same-sex-attracted persons and their families.[664]

Humanae Vitae *and Life Issues*

Cardinal Erdő is a staunch defender of the unitive and procreative ends of marriage, seeing "openness to life as an intrinsic requirement of conjugal love." He warns of the dangers of an "individualistic vision of procreation" which manifests itself on both the social level (for example, the ongoing sharp fall in European birth rates) and the individual level.[665] Erdő points to the documents of the Magisterium on this question, especially to the message of the Encyclical *Humanae Vitae*. He emphasizes the importance of making them known so that people can rediscover the Church's teaching on married love, its rejection of artificial birth control, and its promotion of a culture of life.[666]

Erdő is a staunch defender of the unconditional dignity of every human life, from the moment of conception until natural death. He considers every human life to be "a blessing."[667] When Pope Francis in 2016

---

[663] Ibid.

[664] Ibid.

[665] Ibid.

[666] Ibid.

[667] Gedö Agnes, "*Formularium Ecclesiae Strigoniensis*: Interview with Cardinal Peter Erdő and Peter Tusor," Vatican News, 13 November 2018, https://www.

announced that every priest would be able to forgive the sin of having an abortion, a decision which was originally limited to the duration of the Year of Mercy, Cardinal Erdő welcomed the decision, considering it as a great "pastoral help" and an "expression of mercy."[668] At the same time, he reiterated the inerrant teaching of the Church and emphasized that the pope's decision did not change the theological considerations about the grave sinfulness of abortion.

This view influences his opinion regarding the death penalty, which is unconstitutional in Hungary. In an interview, Erdő referred to the *Catechism of the Catholic Church*, according to which a state has the duty to protect its citizens. But he emphasized that nowadays "it is possible for the state to protect its citizens against the most serious crimes without having to apply the death penalty." He furthermore added for consideration the many cases in which it was detected after the execution that the convicted was, in fact, innocent. He sees this as "such a great inhumanity, so great a sin and a mistake, that it must be avoided." He continued that even in states that "might not be able to effectively provide imprisonment" and therefore might rely on the death penalty, "the use of the death penalty is also more likely to lead to inhumanity and injustice."[669]

Our Lady

Cardinal Erdő has a very strong devotion to Mary and has often publicly preached on the need to emulate her. From his childhood on, he has prayed the Rosary. He even describes how, during his time of military service, he

---

vaticannews.va/hu/vilag/news/2018-11/erdo-peter-tusor-peter-formularium-ecclesiae-strigoniensis.html (translated from Hungarian).

[668] "Péter Erdő: The Practice in Hungary Is Confirmed by Pope Francis," *Breuerpress International*, 23 November 2016, http://www.breuerpress.com/2016/11/23/erdo-peter-a-magyarorszagi-gyakorlatot-megerositi-ferenc-papa-rendelkezese/ (translated from Hungarian).

[669] "Peter Erdő: The Death Penalty Must Be Avoided," *Népszava*, 21 May 2015, https://nepszava.hu/1057962_erdo-peter-a-halalbuntetest-mindenkeppen-el-kell-kerulni (translated from Hungarian).

would pray the Rosary during the long hours of the night watch, using only his fingers or other aids to count, since it was forbidden to carry rosaries.[670] His coat of arms shows the Virgin Mother sitting with Jesus Christ in her arms—a visual depiction of Mary's title as "seat of wisdom." In many homilies, he focuses on Mary's motherhood. Mary is not only the mother of Jesus Christ but also *our* mother in faith. She plays a special role in the Hungarian church: tradition has it that King Stephen offered his crown to her, dedicating thereby the whole country to her. This is the foundation for honoring Mary as the patron saint of Hungary.[671]

Reaction to Coronavirus

During the pandemic, Cardinal Erdő composed a prayer to be recited in every home; the prayer gave thanks to the Lord; expressed trust in Him; petitioned for an antidote; called on the Lord to strengthen faith, hope, and charity in the faithful; and asked Him to have mercy on His people.[672] The prayer was well received in Hungary and went viral on social media.

THE HUNGARIAN TRANSFORMATION FROM COMMUNISM TO DEMOCRACY

Cardinal Erdő's attitude toward ideologies has been shaped first by his exposure to communism while living under a totalitarian regime and then by his experience during Hungary's transition from communism to liberal democracy. Both experiences have made Erdő very cautious about ideologies

---

[670] Moynihan and Somogyi, *Guarding the Flame.*

[671] "Cardinal Péter Erdő's Homily in Rome at the Feast of Our Lady of the Cloister," Esztergom-Budapest Archdiocese, 10 October 2017, https://www.esztergomi-ersekseg.hu/media/beszedek/erdo-peter-biboros-homiliaja-rom-aban-magyarok-nagyasszony-kapolna-bucsujan (translated from Hungarian).

[672] Giuseppe Rusconi, "Coronavirus riflessioni; la preghiera del Cardinale Erdoe," Rossoporpora, 19 March 2020, https://www.rossoporpora.org/rubriche/italia/933-coronavirus-riflessioni-la-preghiera-del-cardinale-erdoe.html.

and have led him to emphasize in a particular way the need for refocusing society on its Christian roots and on Christian morals.

Erdő remembers that growing up under a regime that essentially tried to control people completely brought many hardships—especially for his family, which was, due to its adherence to the Catholic Faith, under suspicion of the state. Erdő's parents were not able to enjoy the careers they wanted because they were "too Catholic," and his father was downgraded at his workplace after Erdő was ordained to the priesthood.[673]

Cardinal Erdő witnessed the Hungarian Revolution of 1956 and recalls how, when he entered the seminary, it was not surprising for him to learn that the communist regime had infiltrated the seminary with spies. For him, the communist ideology never seemed attractive. He witnessed the end of the Cold War and the peaceful revolution in his home country after he had returned from his work in Rome.

When Erdő became archbishop of Esztergom-Budapest, and therefore primate of Hungary, he obtained an office formerly held by the heroic Cardinal József Mindszenty, a staunch opponent of communism who was several times imprisoned by the regime and had to live in exile in the American embassy for more than ten years after the failed revolution in 1956. Erdő considers being a successor to this fighter for freedom a "great honor."[674]

Despite being such a strong opponent of communism, Cardinal Erdő acknowledges that, after the defeat of the communist regime at the end of the 1980s, developments in Hungary have been ambiguous and that the country has certainly "not arrived in paradise."[675]

Interestingly, Erdő notes that the situation of the Catholic Church with regard to church attendance and vocations has not dramatically changed between the end of the 1980s and the early 2010s. He admits that "today we have almost the same pastoral result but with far greater commitment at the institutional level because we also have schools, we have many

---

[673] Moynihan and Somogyi, *Guarding the Flame.*
[674] Ibid.
[675] Ibid.

facilities, many expenses, but the bottom line remains the same." The Hungarian church of today is in much greater competition in the context of the greater freedom that was won after the fall of communism.[676]

The years under the communist regime led to a "deformation of society and people's mentality," even though the Church was not frequently openly and directly persecuted (with exceptions, of course, including that the regime banned the teaching of religion in schools when Erdő was young).[677]

This deformation led people to turn "too much toward individualism, concentrating all their attention on personal well-being," and causing them to become accustomed "to short-term reasoning without thinking about the 'greater future,' having lost their great ideals."[678] Erdő constantly warns that if the country's newly won freedom is understood only as "freedom from," detached from any Christian foundation, this freedom will not lead to true happiness.

For Erdő, the solution can be only in a strong adherence to religion, because

> religion, and especially the Judeo-Christian religion, is not simply a collection of moral rules, but so much more than this. It allows a personal relationship with the Absolute, the Almighty, who appears as a Creator in the context of the universe, whose wisdom and word (logos) penetrates the whole world. This means that our relationship with reality does not require an arbitrary pursuit in a meaningless or unknowable medium, but it fits into the context of an ultimate wisdom and love.[679]

---

[676] Ibid.

[677] Viktoria Somogyi, "Cardinal Peter Erdo on the Church in Hungary (Part 1)," Zenit, 5 October 2005, https://zenit.org/articles/cardinal-peter-erdo-on-the-church-in-hungary-part-1/.

[678] Ibid.

[679] Peter Erdő, "Religion and Church in the Secular State," *Esztergom-Budapest Archdiocese*, 29 January 2018, https://www.esztergomi-ersekseg.hu/media/beszedek/vallas-es-egyhaz-vilagi-allamban (translated from Hungarian).

Erdő emphasizes that in a time marked by rapid changes and ideological pluralism, "we cannot grow weary of proclaiming basic moral values," and these objective moral values must be applied in all walks of life.[680]

SUMMARY

Formed through the crucible of communist suffering, Cardinal Péter Erdő is widely regarded as a great intellect and a man of culture. A prolific and supremely well-read author, Erdő is also a proficient teacher and highly accomplished canonist and Scripture scholar. He has a love for the post–Vatican II liturgy, especially its emphasis on Old Testament readings; but although he prefers the Ordinary Form of the Mass, he is willing to permit the Extraordinary Form and will support it if called to do so. He sees the Eucharist and the priesthood as closely related and is opposed to optional celibacy for priests. A defender of the hierarchical structure of the Church with its threefold office structure of bishop, priest, and deacon, he is a priest with a pastoral heart for whom the importance of salvation was the driving force for being ordained. He has placed great emphasis on the New Evangelization and ministering to youth. Missionary work is central to his pastoral approach, and he has shown great concern for the Church's vocation crisis. Cautious, risk averse, and conservative by nature, Erdő was one of the Church's youngest cardinals when John Paul II elevated him to the College of Cardinals in 2003.

On political issues such as immigration, an issue that Hungary has been grappling with for some years, the cardinal has conveyed a balanced approach, recognizing the right to migrate but also aware of dangers of integrating refugees without endangering political stability. A true balance between solidarity and mercy must be struck, he believes. The cardinal is concerned about persecuted Christians ("We see Christ's disciples in them") and yet has a largely benign view of Islam. Erdő

[680] Ibid.

takes a very positive attitude toward the Orthodox church and keenly supports dialogue with non-Christian religions, emphasizing the value of *Dignitatis Humanae*.

Cardinal Erdő has spent many years of his priesthood as a teacher—a profession for which he has a great fondness. He frequently underlines the importance of having a personal relationship with Christ, something he sees as important for the Church as it faces a grave crisis because of secularism and relativism. He firmly upholds the existence of natural law and his experience of communism has taught him the importance religion can play in filling the void left by the collapse of a political ideology, and that only a personal relationship with Christ brings true freedom and happiness.

He denies universalism, the idea that all are saved, but nevertheless believes that all *can* be saved. Ultimately, he believes, only through Jesus Christ can mankind find its way to God. He is in favor of pastoral accompaniment for "remarried" divorcees but only if there is "no doubt" about the Church's teaching on the indissolubility of marriage. He is firmly against the acceptance of homosexual unions but favors pastoral support for those suffering same-sex attraction. He upholds *Humanae Vitae*, is strongly pro-life, and has a fervent Marian devotion.

SERVICE TO THE CHURCH

Ordination to the Priesthood: 18 June 1975
Ordination to the Episcopate: 6 January 2000
Elevation to the College of Cardinals: 21 October 2003

Education

- 1975-1976: Péter Pázmány Catholic University; Doctorate in theology
- 1977-1980: Pontifical Lateran University; Doctorate in canon law

Assignments

- 1975-1977: Parochial vicar, Dorog
- 1980-1986: Professor of theology, Seminary of Esztergom
- 1986-1988: Lecturer, Pontifical Gregorian University
- 1988-2002: Visiting professor, Pontifical Gregorian University
- 1988-2002: Professor of canon law, Péter Pázmány Catholic University
- 1998-2003: Rector, Péter Pázmány Catholic University
- 2000-2003: Auxiliary Bishop of Székesfehérvár
- 2003-present: Archbishop of Esztergom-Budapest
- 2005-2010: President of the Hungarian Episcopal Conference
- 2006-2016: President of the Council of Episcopal Conferences of Europe

Membership

- Secretariat of State (Second Section)
- Congregation for Catholic Education
- Congregation for Divine Worship and the Discipline of the Sacraments
- Pontifical Council for Legislative Texts
- Pontifical Council for Culture
- Supreme Tribunal of the Apostolic Signatura
- XIII Ordinary Council of the Secretariat General of the Synod of Bishops

GERHARD LUDWIG CARDINAL MÜLLER

"Jesus Is Lord"

Born: 31 December 1947
Mainz, Germany
Nationality: German
Title: Prefect emeritus, Congregation for the Doctrine of the Faith

BIOGRAPHY

The son of an automobile-industry worker, Gerhard Müller was born in Mainz, Germany, and brought up in a devout Catholic family. He began his studies in Mainz and continued studies in philosophy and theology in Munich and Freiburg im Breisgau. In 1977, Müller earned a doctorate, having written his dissertation on the Protestant Dietrich Bonhoeffer's contribution to ecumenical sacramental theology. His doctoral adviser was Professor, later Cardinal, Karl Lehmann, a student of Karl Rahner. The next year, in 1978, Müller was ordained a priest and began teaching in secondary schools while serving three parishes in the Mainz Diocese. His intellectual apostolate continued in 1985, when he became professor in Freiburg im Breisgau; the following year, Müller took up the chair of dogmatic theology at the Ludwig Maximilian University in Munich.[681] For the next sixteen years, Müller taught in Munich as well as in many other universities, while assisting at a local parish. From 1998 to 2003, he was a member of the International Theological Commission.

In 2002, John Paul II appointed him bishop of Regensburg—the diocese in which Joseph Ratzinger had once taught—Müller began his apostolic work there in 2003. During his tenure as bishop, he engaged in many works to develop the diocese while serving on various congregations and councils in the Holy See. In 2012, Müller took up residence in Rome when Benedict XVI appointed him prefect of the Congregation for the Doctrine of the Faith (CDF), which meant that *ex officio* he was also president of the Pontifical Biblical Commission, the International Theological Commission, and the Pontifical Commission *Ecclesia Dei*. Pope Francis created Müller a cardinal-deacon in 2014 but declined to renew his five-year term as head of the CDF in 2017. Since leaving the CDF, Müller has gained an even more public and prominent standing, continuing his multilingual publications and expanding his apostolate around the globe.

SANCTIFYING OFFICE

Doctrinal Importance

As a scholar of no small stature, Cardinal Müller's approach to holiness is deeply informed by his theological positions. Much of his apostolic work in the sanctifying office has been in the context of his theological and administrative roles, some of which are addressed below in the "governing office."

[681] "Gerhard Card. Müller, Prefect of the Congregation for the Doctrine of the Faith," Vatican, http://www.vatican.va/roman_curia/congregations/ cfaith/muller/rc_con_cfaith_doc_20160519_biografia-muller_en.html.

Regarding his acting principle for service to souls, he has said: "Doctrine and pastoral care are the same thing. Jesus Christ as pastor and Jesus Christ as teacher with his word are not two different people."[682]

Thus, perhaps even more than for other bishops, it is important to consider Müller's priestly role alongside his teachings directly pertinent to practices of sanctity. His lack of training in scholastic theology has led to difficulties in some quarters in reconciling his positions with those of the Church as taught through the centuries.

His episcopal motto, *Dominus Iesus* (Jesus Is Lord), is the oldest declaration of faith in the New Testament and is a "confession of the divinity of Christ," Müller explained in 2012. This confession, he said, "constitutes Christian identity."[683]

Devotion to the Eucharist

Cardinal Müller has encouraged devotion to the Holy Eucharist in a number of ways. While bishop of Regensburg, in 2004 he revived the six-hundred-year-old Kötzting "Whitsun Ride" (Kötztinger Pfingstritt) by reestablishing the event as a Eucharistic procession. To this day, the event attracts up to forty thousand people every year.[684] In 2005, Müller participated in the Synod of Bishops on "The Eucharist, Source and Culmination of the Life and Mission of the Church," during which he was able to draw upon his 2002 book, *Die Messe: Quelle christlichen Lebens*.[685] In that book, when

---

[682] Catholic News Service, "Not Understanding Church Teaching on Marriage Is Not an Excuse to Change It, Says Cardinal," *Catholic Herald*, 27 February 2014, https://web.archive.org/web/20140614130933/http://www.catholicherald.co.uk/news/2014/02/27/just-because-we-dont-understand-church-teaching-does-not-mean-we-should-change-it-says-cardinal.

[683] "Interview with H.E. Archbishop Gerhard Ludwig Müller," interview by Edward Pentin, *National Catholic Register / Catholic Herald*, 13 September 2012, http://www.vatican.va/roman_curia/congregations/cfaith/muller/rc_con_cfaith_doc_20120913_interview-muller_en.html.

[684] See "Bad Kötzting Whit Ride," *Bavaria*, https://www.bavaria.by/experiences/city-country-culture/traditions-customs/bad-koetzting-whit-ride/.

[685] Gerhard Müller, *Die Messe: Quelle christlichen Lebens* [The Mass: the source of Christian life] (Augsburg: Sankt Ulrich Verlag, 2002).

speaking about Holy Communion and the Body and Blood of Christ, he states:

> In reality, "Body and Blood of Christ" do not mean the material components of the man Jesus during His lifetime or in His transfigured corporeality. Rather, body and blood here mean the presence of Christ in the sign of the medium of bread and wine, which [presence] is made communicable in the here and now of sense-bound human perception.... In other words, the conversion of substance means that bread and wine go from being natural vehicles of communication to being a new way of supernatural communication between God and man, with the goal of mediating salvation, which occurred in Jesus Christ in a real historical way. Christ, then, is really present in an objective sense.[686]

He indicates that he intends to explain the doctrine of Transubstantiation but wants to explain it without recourse to the Aristotelian philosophical distinction between substance and accidents.[687] Elsewhere he more clearly affirms the doctrine of the Real Presence of Jesus in the Eucharist alongside other traditional doctrines, including "the sacrificial character of the Mass [and] the necessity of an ordained priest, without whom there is no Eucharist."[688]

---

[686] Müller, *Die Messe*, 139, 141. My translation. Original: In Wirklichkeit bedeuten Leib und Blut Christi nicht die materiellen Bestandteile des Menschen Jesus während seiner Lebenszeit oder in der verklärten Leiblichkeit. Leib und Blut bedeuten hier vielmehr Gegenwart Christi im Zeichen des Mediums von Brot und Wein, die im Hier und Jetzt sinnengebundener menschlicher Wahrnehmung kommunizierbar wird.... In der Wesensverwandlung geht es also darum, daß Brot und Wein aus natürlichen Medien der Kommunikation zum neuen Weg einer übernatürlichen Kommunikation werden zwischen Gott und der Menschheit, mit dem Ziel der Vermittlung des Heils, das in Jesus Christus sich real-geschichtlich ereignet hat. Christus ist also real gegenwärtig in einem objektiven Sinn.

[687] See *Die Messe*, 196.

[688] Gerhard Cardinal Müller, *The Power of Truth: The Challenges to Catholic Doctrine and Morals Today* (San Francisco: Ignatius Press, 2019), Kindle ed., 653.

Regarding his personal celebration of the liturgy, he prefers for himself to celebrate the Ordinary Form of the Mass. Nevertheless, Müller has also helped promote other noble forms. In 2016, for instance, he joined principal celebrants Cardinals William Levada and Donald Wuerl in the consecration of Steven Lopes as the first bishop of the Personal Ordinariate of the Chair of Saint Peter, a Catholic institution that retains elements of Anglican patrimony in its life and liturgy.[689]

Views on the Blessed Virgin Mary

The Blessed Virgin Mary, for Müller, is a "missionary of love," who teaches us about the gratuitous love of God and leads us on the path of sanctity to a happiness that is purely a gift.[690] We should turn to Mary in our need, Cardinal Müller recommends. In response to the coronavirus "social distancing" and quarantine that took place all over the world in April 2020, he gave the following spiritual advice in a Facebook post:

> In this period of undoubted suffering many of us are forced to stay home. This limitation, however, can be transformed … into a moment of particular grace if we find time to renew our intimacy with the Lord, by listening to His word, with personal prayer and with the meditation of the saving mysteries contained in the Via Crucis and in the recitation of the Rosary.[691]

---

[689] "Cardinal Müller in Texas for Consecration of Ordinariate Bishop," Vatican Radio, 3 February 2016, http://www.archivioradiovaticana.va/storico/2016/02/03/cardinal_m%C3%BCller_in_texas_consecration_of_ordinariate_bishop/en-1205660,

[690] "Homily of Card. Muller in the Cathedral of Avila on the Solemnity of the Immaculate Conception of the Blessed Virgin Mary," Vatican, 8 December 2014, http://www.vatican.va/roman_curia/congregations/cfaith/muller/rc_con_cfaith_doc_20141208_omelia-avila_sp.html (translated from Spanish).

[691] Edizioni Cantagalli, "La Preghiera per l'Italia del Card. Gerhard L. Müller," Facebook, 30 March 2020, https://www.facebook.com/cantagalliedizioni/videos/691255831646153/.

He went on to say that those in isolation "can take on a commitment to intercede for those in need." Müller then described that, after his daily celebration of Holy Mass, he prays to God, through the intercession of the Blessed Virgin Mary, "asking for the grace of consolation for those afflicted by pain, for strength of spirit for all who help them and for blessings for those who, in various ways, guarantee a constant service for the common good."[692]

The perpetual virginity of Mary, a Catholic dogma, became a point of discussion when Müller was appointed prefect of the CDF. Some accused him of having diverged from the Catholic Faith regarding the manner in which Mary remained a virgin even *during* Christ's birth. Müller argues that the doctrine does not refer to "deviating [from] physiological particularities during the natural birth process (such as the non-opening of the birth canal, the non-injuring of the hymen, and the absence of labor pains)," for the doctrine is not centered on "physiological and empirically verifiable somatic details." Rather, for Mary, "the passive conditions of birth are integrated into this personal relationship [with her Son] and intrinsically determined by it."[693] This position appears to run contrary to a widespread theological consensus, namely, that Mary's virginity during the birth of Christ includes a spiritual dimension as well as a miraculous physical integrity that was unharmed.[694] Even if he departs from perennial theological consensus, however, Müller is not denying Mary's perpetual

---

692 William Mahoney, "Cdl. Gerhard Müller: 'Time to Renew Our Intimacy with the Lord,'" Church Militant, 1 April 2020, https://www.churchmilitant.com/news/article/using-lockdown-to-grow-in-holiness.

693 Gerhard Ludwig Müller, *Katholische Dogmatik*, 10th ed. (Freiburg: Herder Verlag GmbH, 2016), 492. Original: Es geht nicht um abweichende physiologische Besonderheiten in dem natürlichen Vorgang der Geburt (wie etwa die Nichteröffnung der Geburtswege, die Nichtverletzung des Jungfernhäutchen und der nicht eingetretenen Geburtsschmerzen).... Der Inhalt der Glaubensaussage bezieht sich also nicht auf physiologisch und empirisch verifizierbare somatische Details.

694 See the discussion in Thomas Aquinas, *Summa Theologica*, III, q. 28, art. 2.

virginity, but only discussing a non-defined concern regarding the precise manner in which Christ's birth took place.[695]

Dominus Iesus *versus Interreligous Dialogue*

While acknowledging a valuable role for interreligious dialogue, Müller has clarified that one must distinguish between dialogue per se and common prayer among religious adherents. Such distinctions can easily become blurred—for instance, in the Abrahamic Family Houses[696] that are being established worldwide by the Higher Committee of Human Fraternity, the first of which is being built in Abu Dhabi with Pope Francis' encouragement.[697] Although these houses indicate separate worship spaces, nevertheless the system itself assumes a sort of equality among the religions. In contrast, Müller insists: "We [Christians] cannot pray like or with Muslims."[698] This is because "the faithful of Islam are not adopted children of God by the grace of Christ, but only his subjects."[699] Müller explained this in his 2019 *Manifesto of Faith*, saying, "The distinction of the three persons in the divine unity (CCC 254)

---

[695] It should be noted that Müller quotes Karl Rahner in support of his position: "Virginitas in Partu," in *Theological Investigations*, vol. 4, trans. Kevin Smyth (Baltimore, Md.: Helicon Press, 1966), 162. Rahner holds that the dogma does not provide certain and universally binding details regarding the manner of Christ's virginal birth.

[696] The three Abrahamic religions: Judaism, Christianity, and Islam.

[697] Sophie Tremblay and Jessie Gretener, "Mosque, Church and Synagogue to Share Home in Abu Dhabi," CNN, 26 September 2019, https://edition.cnn.com/2019/09/26/middleeast/uae-abu-dhabi-the-abrahamic-family-house-ctw-intl/index.html.

[698] Gerhard Cardinal Müller, "La Preghiera, dono di Dio," Lectio magistralis: Sezione di Verona della Società Internazionale Tommaso d'Aquino, 17 May 2019, https://www.dropbox.com/s/drzhztfk8zma1jd/La%20 Preghiera%2C%20dono%20di%20Dio_card%20MULLER_17maggio 2019.pdf?dl=0; quoted in Martin M. Barillas, "Former Vatican Head of Doctrine: Christians 'Cannot Pray Like or with Muslims,'" LifeSite News, 21 May 2019, https://www.lifesitenews.com/news/former-vatican-head-of-doctrine-christians-cannot-pray-like-or-with-muslims.

[699] Ibid.

marks a fundamental difference in the belief in God and the image of man from that of other religions. Religions disagree precisely over this belief in Jesus the Christ."[700]

GOVERNING OFFICE

Bishop of Regensburg

As bishop of Regensburg from 2003 to 2012, Gerhard Müller engaged in a number of activities aimed at improving the life of the local Church. Apostolic initiatives include Müller's collaboration with the Emmanuel Community to carry out a city mission in 2008, which fanned out to other city parishes the year after. This initiative ended up involving more than a thousand volunteers who helped make the Catholic Faith a point of reference in dialogue. In order to help residents and tourists alike, Müller also introduced and supported the Inner City Counseling (*Innenstadtseelsorge*) project in the center of Regensburg.[701]

Müller was also willing to correct what he saw as Protestant-like teaching and decision-making on the diocesan, deanery, and parish levels, promoted chiefly by three groups: the Central Committee of German Catholics (Zentralkomitee der deutschen Katholiken [ZdK]), the Action Circle Regensburg (Aktionskreis Regensburg [AkR]), and We Are Church (Wir sind Kirche). The groups reacted with multiple attempts to ruin his reputation. Here is how that came about.

Tackling Dissent in Regensburg

From 2004 to 2005, Bishop Müller got to know the Diocese of Regensburg, under his care, by making a pastoral visitation of its eight regions. Finding widespread Protestantization under the guise of "the Spirit of Vatican II" and "democracy," with participants in the three groups named above in

---

[700] Gerhard Cardinal Müller, *Manifesto of Faith*, 10 February 2019, https://manifestooffaith.com/media/manifesto-of-faith.pdf
[701] "Gerhard Card. Müller."

favor of laypeople effectively running parishes as well as women's ordination, Müller reorganized lay cooperation to correct for their aberrations. He corrected some participants, including both laity and priests, firing one theologian, withdrawing from another the permission to teach, returning the leadership roles to the clergy, and even exacting financial penalties, as is allowed in canon law.[702] In response, the layman Hans Maier, chairman of the ZdK, appealed against Müller's decisions arguing they were contrary to canon law.[703] The Congregation for Clergy, however, decided in 2006 that Müller was fully within his authority as bishop to make those changes. After a further appeal, the Apostolic Signatura sided with Müller and definitively closed the case in 2007.[704] These events influenced Müller, who would later say:

> After many years' pastoral experience of many kinds, I think perhaps it is time to deepen the concept of the "pastoral method". I for one tend to have little confidence in an insistence that the solution to the secularization of a diocese or a parish lies in the application of a new pastoral theory or that "now the liturgy should be reconfigured in this new way to be credible and participative." Behind these declarations, it is not hard to find a line of reasoning based on simply human postulates that, proposing laboratory pastoral recipes, is pursuing the ingenuous aspiration of solving all problems.... Especially

---

[702] Christopher Wenzel, "Sexual Abuse: Bishop of Regensburg in the Crossfire," *Welt*, 15 September 2007, https://www.welt.de/regionales/muenchen/article1183916/Regensburger-Bischof-im-Kreuzfeuer.html. Also, Christian Eckl, "Contradictions between the court and the diocese," *Regensburger Wochenblatt*, 4 October 2007, http://www.trennungsvaeter.de/presse/07/Wochenblatt_041007.htm.

[703] Editorial, "ZdK President Meyer: Reorganization in Regensburg Is an Infringement," Zentralkomitee der deutschen Katholiken, 16 November 2005, https://www.zdk.de/veroeffentlichungen/pressemeldungen/detail/ZdK-Praesident-Meyer-Neuordnung-in-Regensburg-ist-Rechtsverletzung-317k/.

[704] Editorial, "Regensburg Council Reform from Rome Finally Confirmed," *Kath.net*, 13 March 2007, http://kath.net/news/16216.

today, when our societies are under the influence of such an aggressive secularism, the mission has to give priority to divine grace.[705]

Addressing Sexual Abuse

Connected to Müller's relations with activist lay groups in his diocese are accusations that he failed to address adequately the abuse of minors perpetrated by clergy there. One of the chief issues regards Fr. Peter Kramer. In 1999, four years before Müller became bishop of Regensburg, Kramer had been arrested, tried, and found guilty of abuse of boys and was sentenced to a three-year probation by a civil judge. From 2001 to 2003, Kramer worked as a "supply priest" with the permission of his therapist. He completed his probation in 2003, whereupon the therapist did not recommend that his probation period be extended. That same year, Müller began his apostolic work as bishop, and he received a report that, from a therapeutic point of view, Kramer could be appointed pastor of a parish. Meanwhile, Müller and his staff discussed with the judge whether Kramer could be returned to full-time parish work, receiving indications that he could. Müller therefore appointed Kramer to a parish in Riekofen, without revealing Kramer's past. The priest began abusing boys almost immediately. The abuse continued for three years in secret until Müller learned of it and removed Kramer from ministry. Instead of apologizing, Müller wrote a letter explaining why he thought his decisions were reasonable; this was not well received.[706] When laity later complained about Müller's handling and negligence, and news outlets began reporting on this, the bishop said that he suffered from a *Diffamierungskampagne* — "a defamation campaign."[707]

[705] Gerhard Cardinal Müller with Carlos Granados, *The Cardinal Müller Report: An Exclusive Interview on the State of the Church*, trans. Richard Goodyear (San Francisco: Ignatius Press, 2017), 87, 88.

[706] See the thorough report on this by Leon J. Podles, "Peter Kramer: A Case Study of Sexual Abuse," Crossland Foundation, 1 April 2008, http://www.crosslandfoundation.org/case-studies/files/Kramer-Case-Study.pdf.

[707] Editorial, "Diocese of Regensburg Criticizes Defamation Campaign in the Kramer Case," *Kath.net*, 14 March 2008, http://www.kath.net/news/19314.

According to Müller, he deserves no blame regarding abuse matters, for there is a documented chronology that he initiated investigations into sexual abuse of minors as soon as he became aware of the issue.[708] In 2011, the criminologist Christian Pfeiffer was hired in conjunction with the diocese to investigate clerical sexual abuse of minors. In 2013, after Müller resigned his work for Regensburg and took up residence in Rome as prefect for the CDF, Pfeiffer's study was canceled. Precisely why is a matter of dispute. According to Pfeiffer, Bishop Gerhard Müller was largely responsible for this cancellation, as Müller, along with Cardinal Marx, wanted to change the contract and replace it with a new one that favored censorship.[709] Fr. Hans Langendörfer, secretary of the German Bishops' Conference, disagreed, arguing that the contract was canceled not for purposes of censorship but because Pfeiffer wanted to keep on permanent record tapes and interviews and make them available to a wide variety of researchers without adequately protecting the data, whereas the bishops—not only Müller, but all of them—wanted the data more protected and not for public consumption.[710] Müller also worked to dismantle Pfeiffer's arguments, pointing out

[708] Karl Birkenseer, "Domspatzen Scandal: Müller Sees No Basis for Allegations," *Passauer Neue Presse*, 19 July 2017, https://www.pnp.de/nachrichten/bayern/Domspatzen-Skandal-Mueller-sieht-keine-Basis-fuer-Anschuldigungen-2588896.html (translated from German). The reliability of this chronology is disputed. Editorial, "Fuchssche Legendenbildung," Regensburg-digital, 29 December 2016, https://www.regensburg-digital.de/fuchssche-legendenbildung/29122016/.

[709] Felix Bohr and Ann-Katrin Müller, "Too Many Believe That the Abuse Is God's Will," *Der Spiegel*, 14 September 2018, https://www.spiegel.de/panorama/katholische-kirche-kriminologe-christian-pfeiffer-ueber-missbrauch-in-der-kirche-a-00000000-0002-0001-0000-000159428627 (translated from German).

[710] Christiane Kaess, "Secretary of the Bishops' Conference: No Control or Censorship," *Deutschlandfunk*, 10 January 2013, https://www.deutschlandfunk.de/sekretaer-der-bischofskonferenz-keine-kontrolle-oder-zensur.694.de.html?dram:article_id=233746.

that the investigator blamed clerical celibacy for the abuse and argued for a freer exercise of sexuality.[711]

In 2015, the AkR—a lay group noted above that had been disciplined by Müller for its Protestantization—lobbed a formal complaint against the former bishop of Regensburg, alleging that he failed to exercise responsibility for sexual abuses in the diocese. The same year, an independent study of the diocese's actions was begun by Günther Perottoni, head of the Regensburg branch of the Weißen Ring, and lawyer Ulrich Weber, who had volunteered for this victim-protection organization since 2006.[712] In 2017, Weber wrote in his final report that Müller was responsible for the "strategic, organizational, and communicative weaknesses" in the process of investigations initiated in 2012 while he was still bishop.[713] Some of this, Weber notes, included abuse of more than five hundred boys in the choir led by Msgr. Georg Ratzinger, brother of Joseph Ratzinger (Benedict XVI). Although Msgr. Ratzinger has not been accused of abuse himself, and has not been accused of knowing about it, nevertheless at the very least he appears to have been negligent in protecting the boys.[714] Müller has said that Weber's report is inaccurate, and he called upon state officials to apologize for damaging his good name.[715]

[711] Maike Hickson, "Cardinal Müller Responds to Allegations of Leniency in Cover-Up Abuse Cases," LifeSite News, 17 September 2018, https://www.lifesitenews.com/blogs/cardinal-mueller-responds-to-allegations-of-leniency-in-cover-up-abuse-case.

[712] Stefan Aigner, "A 'Victim Advocate' in the Shallows of the Diocese," Regensburg-digital, 27 April 2015, https://www.regensburg-digital.de/ein-opferanwalt-in-den-untiefen-des-bistums/27042015/.

[713] Paul Badde and Gernot Facius, "Targeted Discrediting of the Catholic Church," Welt, 1 February 2013, https://www.welt.de/politik/deutschland/article113313904/Gezielte-Diskreditierung-der-katholische-Kirche.html.

[714] Editorial, "Over 500 Cathedral Sparrows Mistreated—Criticism of Ratzinger and Muller," Passauer Neue Presse, 18 July 2017, https://www.pnp.de/nachrichten/bayern/Ueber-500-Domspatzen-misshandelt-Kritik-an-Ratzinger-und-Mueller-2587107.html.

[715] Birkenseer, "Domspatzen Scandal."

In 2017, abuse survivor Marie Collins resigned from the Pontifical Commission for the Protection of Minors. Among her reasons were criticisms of the CDF, at the time headed by Cardinal Müller, and an apparent refusal of the CDF to reply to letters from victims of abuse.[716] Cardinal Müller responded by saying it was a "misunderstanding" to think his office "could deal with all the dioceses and religious orders in the world." He added that the congregation asks bishops to respond and to pass on information saying that the CDF would do all that is possible to bring about justice.[717]

Closing Controversial Pregnancy Centers

In Regensburg, Bishop Müller placed more power into the hands of the clergy than the laity, and in 2005, he reformed ecclesial structures with the aim of bringing governance more in line with the *Code of Canon Law*. Also as bishop in 2011, he closed Donum Vitae pregnancy centers on Benedict XVI's instruction, as they were involved in abortion counseling. That same year, Müller barred Hans Maier, former head of the largest German lay Catholic organization, the ZdK, from using a diocesan center to promote his memoirs because Maier had supported the Donum Vitae association.[718]

---

[716] John Allen, "Why Survivor's Exit from Papal Panel May Be a Blessing in Disguise," *Crux*, 1 March 2017, https://cruxnow.com/analysis/2017/03/survivors-exit-papal-panel-may-blessing-disguise/. See also Greg Daly, "Vatican Commission Support 'Validates' Resignation—Collins," *Irish Catholic*, 30 March 2017, https://web.archive.org/web/20170405195834/http://irishcatholic.ie/article/vatican-commission-support-%E2%80%98validates%E2%80%99-resignation-%E2%80%93-collins.

[717] Joshua J. McElwee, "Cardinal Muller Responds to Collins and Defends Not Answering Survivors' Letters," *National Catholic Reporter*, 6 March 2017, https://www.ncronline.org/news/accountability/cardinal-muller-responds-collins-and-defends-not-responding-survivors-letters.

[718] "Bishop Prohibits Former ZdK President from Presenting Books Because of Donum Vitae," Domradio.de, 13 May 2011, https://www.domradio.de/nachrichten/2011-05-13/bischof-untersagt-buchvorstellung-von-ehemaligem-zdk-praesidenten.

Administrative Skills and Finance

Cardinal Müller was not noted for his administrative skills at the CDF, and his approach to finances is mixed.

Germany's Church tax has been the subject of much discussion, often blamed for weakening the Church's witness by encouraging compromise with the state and deterring what Benedict XVI called *Entweltlichung* (unworldliness).

Müller, like Benedict XVI, is believed to have opposed a German bishops' 2012 decree that effectively barred German Catholics from participating in the life of the Church if they had not paid the tax. However, he does not wish to see the levy necessarily ended. Although clearly not happy with the state of the German Church and its frequent compromises with secular values (he said in 2019 that the Church's assets are not there to "fatten officials" and to "rent a platform for people's vanities"),[719] he believes less money will not resolve the Church's problems and notes that most of the money goes to Catholic hospitals and other needed social work.

As CDF prefect, the cardinal participated in the two synods on the family (2014 and 2015), and was a member of the German language group that was crucial in passing a proposition that would later permit "remarried" divorcees to receive Holy Communion in some cases. Müller's role in the group's voting in favor of the proposition is unclear: according to Cardinal Reinhard Marx, the group "unanimously" voted in support of the proposal on the grounds that it was Thomistic, and therefore implied that the CDF prefect had lent his weight to it. Two years later, however, Cardinal Müller said he never gave the proposal his consent.[720]

---

[719] Cardinal Müller: Church Money Not 'for the Fattening of Officials,'" Domradio.de, 24 December 2019, https://www.domradio.de/themen/glaube/2019-12-24/unerleuchtete-papstverehrung-kardinal-mueller-kirchengeld-nicht-fuer-maesten-von-funktionaeren.

[720] Maike Hickson, "Cardinal Müller Suggests He Had Not Voted for the Unanimous German Report at 2015 Family Synod," *One Peter Five*, 16 October 2017, https://onepeterfive.com/cardinal-muller-suggests-not-voted-unanimous-german-report-2015-family-synod/.

TEACHING OFFICE

Scholarly Output

With more than five hundred publications to his name, Gerhard Müller's scholarly and popular output manifests his serious commitment to the teaching office of a bishop. He states:

> For me there were never contradictions between being a priest and study. I was always convinced that the Catholic faith corresponds to the highest intellectual exigencies.... We must never fear intellectual confrontation; we don't have a blind faith, but faith cannot be reduced in a rationalistic way. I hope that everyone will have an experience similar to mine: that of identifying themselves in a simple way and without problems with the Catholic faith and of practicing it.[721]

Cardinal Müller has received numerous international accolades for his scholarship. In 2001, he became a member of the Pontifical Academy of St. Thomas Aquinas and a year later was made a correspondent member of the theological section of the Real Academia de Doctores de España in Madrid. He has been granted the title *Dottore Honoris Causa* by three Polish Catholic universities (Lublin, 2004; Warsaw, 2007; and Wrocław, 2015) and an honorary doctorate from the University of Lima in Peru.

He has published in many fields, including ecumenism, modern theology, the theology of revelation, theological hermeneutics, and ecclesiology. Among his most widely known works is his *Katholische Dogmatik: Für Studium und Praxis der Theologie* published by Herder.

Because of the great number of topics that Müller has covered, often in detail, only some of the most salient or controversial are covered here.

---

[721] Zenit Staff, "Archbishop Müller on Faith, the Curia and His Own Upbringing," Zenit, 25 July 2012, https://zenit.org/articles/archbishop-muller-on-faith-the-curia-and-his-own-upbringing/.

Views on Liberation Theology

Given Cardinal Müller's present reputation for orthodoxy, even conservatism, it may be a surprise to some that he has defended a "correct" liberation theology.[722]

His engagement with that controversial sphere began in 1988 when he was invited to participate in a seminar run by Gustavo Gutiérrez, one of the founders of liberation theology. Already the CDF had twice written about this theme with the important documents *Instruction on Certain Aspects of the "Theology of Liberation"* (1984) and *Instruction on Christian Freedom and Liberation* (1986), as well as corrections of Leonardo Boff's book on "militant ecclesiology" (1985). While accepting those interventions and recognizing that Catholic theology should not mix with "the doctrine of Marxist self-redemption," Müller freely admits, "A Catholic child of Mainz has social passion in his blood, and I am proud of it."[723] For fifteen years, he spent up to three months out of twelve in South America, especially Peru and Argentina, in simple conditions, teaching and learning about liberation theology.

Müller became such friends with Gutiérrez that they coauthored a book meant to clarify matters: *On the Side of the Poor: The Theology of Liberation* (2015). In the work, Müller argues, "People should not be suspicious of liberation theology in all of its forms simply because of its use of some Marxist ideas. Instead, they should investigate Marxism as an appropriation and secularization of the basic convictions of the Christian theology of history and eschatology."[724] According to him, "liberation theology fundamentally differentiates itself from Marxism on the basis of its foundation in a theological anthropology,"[725] such that an adequate theology of liberation has significant ties to French *nouvelle théologie* and Karl Rahner's thought: "When liberation theology is set in relation to the theologies of de Lubac and Rahner, questions

---

[722] Ibid.

[723] Ibid.

[724] Gerhard Cardinal Müller and Gustavo Gutiérrez, *On the Side of the Poor: The Theology of Liberation*, trans. Robert A. Krieg (Maryknoll, NY: Orbis Books, 2015), Kindle ed., location 1591 of 2822.

[725] Ibid.

about it and objections to it resolve themselves."[726] Müller repeated the same position in his work *The Cardinal Müller Report: An Exclusive Interview on the State of the Church*, with Carlos Granados (BAC, 2016/Ignatius Press, 2017). Having an admitted great friendship with Gutiérrez, Müller arranged a Mass in which they concelebrated with Pope Francis.[727]

Priestly Celibacy

The issue of priestly celibacy has also received attention from Cardinal Müller. In recent times, he has appeared to oppose the much-discussed proposal to ordain *viri probati* (proven married men) to the priesthood in the Latin Church, which is seen as a solution to vocation shortages. In an interview with the Italian newspaper *La Repubblica*, he made headlines by saying, "Not even the pope can abolish priestly celibacy."[728] He recalled the 692 synod of Trullo in which the emperor attempted to force the Church to abolish celibacy; Müller noted that celibacy is "not a law that can be changed at will" because it has "deep roots in the sacrament of orders." He explains, "The priest is the representative of Christ the Bridegroom; he lives a living spirituality that cannot be changed," and furthermore, "the tradition of the Church is not a game that can be shaped at will."[729] However, it was noted in the Amazon synod, in which this issue was openly discussed, that in 1991 Müller had given a talk in which he showed himself in favor of retaining celibacy while also ordaining married men.[730] Recalling a meeting in which he participated in 1988, he said:

---

[726] Ibid., 1647.

[727] Joshua J. McElwee, "Francis Reveals He Concelebrated Mass with Cardinal Muller and Gustavo Gutierrez," *National Catholic Reporter*, 14 February 2019, https://www.ncronline.org/news/theology/francis-reveals-he-con-celebrated-mass-cardinal-muller-and-gustavo-gutierrez.

[728] Paolo Rodari, "Cardinal Müller: 'Not Even the Pope Can Abolish the Celibacy of Priests,'" *La Repubblica*, 9 October 2019, https://rep.repub-blica.it/pwa/intervista/2019/10/09/news/mu_ller_nemmeno_il_papa_puo_abolire_il_celibato_dei_preti_-238138284/.

[729] Ibid.

[730] Gerhard Müller, "Priestertum und Zölibat. Reflexionen nach einem Besuch in Südamerika," in Josef Sayer and Werner Tzscheetzsch, eds., "*Pastoral*

Celibate priests are necessary for the priesthood. It must, however, be possible to ordain religiously proven and theologically educated family fathers, not only in remote areas but also in huge city parishes, so that basic pastoral and liturgical practices can continue to be celebrated.... A new concept of this kind would not contradict the Church's tradition, as loyalty to tradition does not mean that the Church is only committed to past history but, on the contrary, far more to future history.[731]

Significantly, in his statements regarding the tradition of priestly celibacy since 1991 or 1992, Müller has not entirely retracted his earlier reasoning. Instead, he has emphasized the value of celibacy as the "norm," while arguing that the introduction of married priests "would unquestionably mean the end of celibacy," which would be unacceptable.[732]

Women's Ordination

Regarding female ordination, Müller has consistently held that it is contrary to Catholic faith and practice. His work *Priestertum und Diakonat* (2000) — *Priesthood and Diaconate* (2002) — is something of a classic.[733] In it, Müller argued that the diaconate is the first essential grade of the sacrament of Holy Orders, such that women cannot be ordained. Although deacons do not act *in persona Christi capitis*, "in the person of Christ the

---

der Befreiung": Eindrücke einer praktisch-theologischen Forschungsreise nach Peru (Skriptenreihe der Akademie Altenberg 2, 1991), 98-101.

[731] Müller, "Priestertum und Zölibat. Reflexionen nach einem Besuch in Südamerika," quoted and translated in Christa Pongratz-Lippitt, "Müller Once Favoured Ordination of Married Men," *Tablet*, 28 October 2019, https://www.thetablet.co.uk/news/12164/m-ller-once-favoured-ordination-of-married-men.

[732] Müller and Granados, *The Cardinal Müller Report*, location 1306.

[733] Full titles: *Priestertum und Diakonat: Der Empfänger des Weihesakramentes in schöpfungstheologischer und christologischer Perspektive; Sammlung Horizonte NF 33* (Freiburg, 2000). English revision and trans., *Priesthood and Diaconate: The Recipient of the Sacrament of Holy Orders from the Perspective of Creation Theology and Christology* (San Francisco: Ignatius Press, 2002).

head," but as Christ was a servant, nevertheless, such a configuration to Christ is reserved to men alone by tradition and as a sign of the Bridegroom who is united to His Bride, the Church. Müller's work greatly influenced the International Theological Commission, whose subcommittee, which included Christoph Schönborn, had examined the question of women deacons from 1992 to 1997. Cardinal Ratzinger reconfigured the commission to include Gerhard Müller and Luis Tagle; after examining the issue, the commission produced the document *From the Diakonia of Christ to the Diakonia of the Apostles* (2002). Phyllis Zagano, an American author who strongly supports women deacons, notes that the ITC document borrows heavily from Müller's unattributed work.[734]

Significantly, Müller's views regarding the diaconate influenced and cohered so strongly with those of Ratzinger that Benedict XVI changed canon law to reflect that theology more closely.[735] Protestant professor Thomas Schirrmacher holds that when Pope Francis decided to explore the question of women's ordination, Müller refused to head yet another commission on the issue: "He rejected it; he saw it as an entrance door for the topic of the ordination of women."[736] He repeated his opposition to a female diaconate after news that the pope had decided in April 2020 to set up a second commission to discuss the subject (the third such commission

---

[734] Phyllis Zagano, "Catholic Women Deacons: Past Arguments and Future Possibilities," in *Deaconesses: The Ordination of Women and Orthodox Theology*, ed. Petros Vassiliadis et al. (Tyne, UK: Cambridge Scholars Publishing, 2018), 493.

[735] See Benedict XVI, "*Motu Proprio Omnium in Mentem*" (26 October 2009), promulgating that canon 1009 should read, "Those who are constituted in the order of the episcopate or the presbyterate receive the mission and capacity to act in the person of Christ the Head, whereas deacons are empowered to serve the People of God in the ministries of the liturgy, the word and charity."

[736] Maike Hickson, "German Protestant Theologian: Cardinal Müller Refused to Head Up Female Deacon Commission," *One Peter Five*, 31 August 2017, https://onepeterfive.com/german-protestant-theologian-cardinal-muller-refused-head-female-deacon-commission/.

in recent years). "Women cannot become priests," he said, "because this is excluded by the nature of the Sacrament of Holy Orders."[737]

But aside from a female diaconate, Müller has no problem with women having greater roles in the Church, nor women as extraordinary ministers of the Eucharist, nor girls as altar servers.

Approach to Defense of Doctrine

On his appointment as CDF prefect, Müller said he saw the Church "not as a fortress but rather a sacrament, a sign, a symbol and an instrument for the salvation of all people." He added that the congregation's role is, above all, to support the mission of the Church, which today means defending the Faith "from the assault of secularism and materialism, which denies the transcendent dimension of human existence and therefore distorts the ethical, moral and intellectual orientation of society."[738]

Müller sees the Faith as offering the greatest alternative to the culture of death as Christians promote the culture of life and of hope. But he also believes that the Church should accept all that is good and true about contemporary society while upholding the family as a prophetic witness to society. In fact, he has never seen himself as a "conservative" and rails against such a label. Rather he sees himself and his theology as fully consistent with the Second Vatican Council while recognizing problems with liberal theology.

In a 2017 interview with the *National Catholic Register*, he said: "All my life, after the Second Vatican Council, I've noticed that those who support so-called progressivism never have theological arguments. The only method they have is to discredit other persons, calling them 'conservative'—and this changes the real point, which is the reality of the faith, and not in your personal subjective, psychological disposition."[739]

---

[737] Maike Hickson, "'Women Cannot Become Priests': Cardinal Müller," LifeSite News, 14 April 2020, https://www.lifesitenews.com/mobile/blogs/women-cannot-become-priests-cdl-mueller-reacts-to-popes-new-commission-to-study-female-ordination?__twitter_impression=true.

[738] "Interview with H.E. Archbishop Gerhard Ludwig Müller."

[739] Edward Pentin, "Cardinal Müller Speaks Out on 'Amoris Laetitia,' the Dubia and the Vatican," *National Catholic Register*, 9 October 2017, https://

"By 'conservative,' what do they mean?" he continued. "Theologically it's not possible to be conservative or progressive. These are absurd categories: Neither conservatism nor progressivism has anything to do with the Catholic faith. They're political, polemical, rhetorical forms. The only sense of these categories is discrediting other persons."[740]

Human Fraternity Document

In May 2020, Cardinal Müller endorsed Pope Francis' controversial 2019 Document on Human Fraternity, which some Catholic scholars say contains heresy. Writing in the journal *Communio*, Müller argued that the document had led neither the pope nor the grand imam of al-Azhar, the joint signatory, "to give up their own creed" and that it "does not open the door to dogmatic and ethical relativism."[741] For more on the controversy surrounding the document, see Cardinal Parolin's profile.

Second Vatican Council

Respected for his theological expertise and seen as a true believer, Cardinal Müller is what a source called a "dyed-in-the-wool Vatican II prelate." He has said the problems that followed the Council "were not caused by the Council" and that the "secularist mentality" that followed it "had nothing to do with the Council."[742] Secularism was promoted in the nineteenth century by "liberals who denied the supernatural law," and so the "waves of secularism began to undermine the Church long before the Council."[743]

He is not a theological trailblazer or one who holds to a Hegelian approach to theology in the mold of fellow German cardinal Walter Kasper, but

---

www.ncregister.com/daily-news/cardinal-mller-discusses-the-cdf-the-curia-and-amoris-laetitia.

[740] Ibid.

[741] Jules Gomes, "Ex-Muslims Unmask Abu Dhabi 'Deception,'" Church Militant, 27 May 2020, https://www.churchmilitant.com/news/article/converts-counter-cardinal-on-abu-dhabi-deception.

[742] "Interview with H.E. Archbishop Gerhard Ludwig Müller."

[743] Ibid.

he does see himself as a theological innovator, as his views on Mary's virginity and liberation theology indicate. Politically, however, he is a conservative.

Müller has taken a hard line against the traditional Society of Saint Pius X, both as bishop of Regensburg and later as CDF prefect, when he was also president of the Pontifical Commission *Ecclesia Dei*—the body charged with regularizing the SSPX. In 2012, he accused them of developing ideas that "formed into an ideology" which they then use to "judge all things." He has rejected their emphasis on the liturgy, saying that more than one form can be celebrated. He also has rejected their views of Vatican II, saying their reasons for opposing the Council arise from "the use of terminology." But the Church "never contradicted herself," he said. Just before he left the CDF in 2017, Müller sent a letter to the SSPX with Pope Francis' approval, halting talks with the Vatican.[744]

Cardinal Müller has been a strong critic of the German Church's synodal path (2020-2021), which aims to tackle key issues arising from the clerical sex abuse crisis, but which critics say is aimed at having the Church align with the times and essentially Protestantize or even secularize the Church. He compared the process to the 1933 Enabling Act, when the Weimar Republic gave sweeping powers to Adolf Hitler. Müller said the synodal path was similarly a "self-appointed assembly, which is not authorized by God, nor by the people it is supposed to represent."[745]

Coronavirus

In May 2020, Cardinal Müller put his name to an appeal expressing concern about global measures being implemented to stem the coronavirus pandemic, and calling for "inalienable rights of citizens and their fundamental

---

[744] Christian Lassale, "Rome: The Decisive Effects of the Letter from the Deans and Friendly Communities," medias-catholique.info, 3 July 2017, https://medias-catholique.info/rome-les-effets-decisifs-de-la-lettre-des-doyens-et-des-communautes-amies/8711.

[745] KNA International, "Cardinal Mueller Criticized for His Nazi Comparison of Germany's Synodal Way Process," *America*, 6 February 2020, https://www.americamagazine.org/faith/2020/02/06/cardinal-mueller-criticized-his-nazi-comparison-germanys-synodal-way-process.

freedoms" to be respected. The appeal, whose signatories included Cardinal Joseph Zen Ze-kiun, Robert Kennedy Jr., and a number of doctors, lawyers, and journalists, said that the coronavirus was a "pretext" to deprive the faithful of Mass and, among other aims, impose a world government. The appeal, issued on May 7, 2020, had been drafted by Archbishop Carlo Maria Viganò, a former apostolic nuncio and strong critic of Pope Francis.[746]

Some German bishops, including the head of the country's bishops' conference, distanced themselves from the appeal, while others thought bishops were departing from their field of expertise by signing such petitions. Cardinal Müller stood by his decision to endorse it, criticizing the state-driven suspension of public Masses, and the hierarchy's cooperation, as "a very serious thing" and revealing that "secularist thinking has entered the Church." He said those who have a different opinion are today considered "conspiracy theorists," adding that some within the Church used the text "to make indignant capital against their supposed opponents."[747]

RELATIONSHIP WITH RATZINGER/ BENEDICT XVI AND FRANCIS

Papal Defender

Since Pope Francis' election, Cardinal Müller has sought to defend Francis and his actions personally while being vociferously critical of numerous aspects of his pontificate that have departed or appeared to depart from sound theology and ecclesiology.

---

[746] Edward Pentin, "Cardinals, Bishops Sign Appeal against Coronavirus Restrictions," *National Catholic Register*, 7 May 2020, https://www.ncregister.com/blog/edward-pentin/four-cardinals-several-bishops-sign-appeal-against-coronavirus-restrictions.

[747] Maike Hickson, "Cardinal Müller and Bishop Schneider Defend Signing Archbishop Viganò's Corona Crisis Appeal," LifeSite News, 12 May 2020, https://www.lifesitenews.com/blogs/cardinal-mueller-and-bishop-schneider-defend-signing-archbishop-viganos-corona-crisis-appeal.

In a 2017 interview, Cardinal Müller defended Francis' controversial Apostolic Exhortation *Amoris Laetitia*, saying it "must clearly be interpreted in the light of the whole doctrine of the Church." Müller also emphasized the importance of upholding the structure of the Catholic Church, due to the fact that many bishops began to interpret the publication according to their own understanding.[748]

Commentary about *Amoris Laetitia* from some Catholic leaders claimed the publication was a way for the Church to change Church doctrine to allow individuals who are divorced and "remarried" to receive Holy Communion.[749] However, Cardinal Müller noted if the pope's publication "had wanted to eliminate such a deeply rooted and significant discipline, it would have said so clearly and presented supporting reasons."[750]

Manifesto of Faith

In February 2019, Cardinal Müller delivered a *Manifesto of Faith* to remind bishops, priests, religious, and laypeople of the Catholic Church about the truth of revelation.[751]

Written in response to requests from "many bishops, priests, religious and laypeople," the testimony of Catholic doctrine covered Christology, ecclesiology, sacraments, morality, and eschatology. It was aimed at providing clarification in the context of a pontificate whose pronouncements many faithful had found at times confusing, disorienting, and inconsistent with Church teaching, and amid what Müller said was a "growing danger" that people are "missing the path to eternal life."

---

[748] CWR Staff, "The Truth Is Not Up for Negotiation," *Catholic World Report*, 4 February 2017, https://www.catholicworldreport.com/2017/02/04/the-truth-is-not-up-for-negotiation/.

[749] "Müller on Amoris Laetitia: The Church Is Called to Promote a 'Culture of the Family,'" Catholic News Agency, 12 May 2016, https://www.catholicnewsagency.com/news/mller-on-amoris-laetitia-the-church-is-called-to-promote-a-culture-of-the-family-62360.

[750] Ibid.

[751] Gerhard Cardinal Müller, *Manifesto of Faith*, https://manifestooffaith.com/media/manifesto-of-faith.pdf.

Müller heavily references the *Catechism of the Catholic Church* throughout the manifesto, and, within discussion of the sacraments, notes that individuals conscious of a grave sin, including "divorced and civilly 'remarried' persons, whose sacramental marriage exists before God, as well as those Christians who are not in full communion with the Catholic Faith and the Church," must receive the sacrament of Reconciliation before receiving Communion.[752]

He warns against bishops and priests keeping silent about hard truths of the Faith, saying that to do so is "the greatest deception," which the *Catechism* "vigorously" warned about as possibly presaging the rise of the antichrist—echoing what Cardinal Willem Eijk had said a year earlier. Quoting St. Paul's Second Letter to Timothy, he exhorts bishops and priests to "preach the Word in season and out of season" for there will come a time when "sound doctrine" will not be endured, but people will have "itching ears."[753]

Responding to the Dubia

Müller has also urged against issuing a fraternal correction of the pope while encouraging a papal answer to the *dubia*. "What the Church needs in this serious situation is not more polarization and polemics, but more dialogue and reciprocal confidence," he said in 2017. "The Successor of St. Peter deserves full respect for his person and divine mandate, and, on the other hand, his honest critics deserve a convincing answer."[754]

He said a possible solution could be for the pope to have a group of cardinals "begin a theological disputation with some prominent representatives of the *dubia* and the 'corrections' about the different and sometimes

---

[752] Catholic News Agency, "Cardinal Müller Is Following the Path of Martin Luther with New Manifesto, Cardinal Kasper Says," *Catholic Register*, 11 February 2019, https://www.catholicregister.org/home/international/item/28954-cardinal-mueller-is-following-the-path-of-martin-luther-with-new-manifesto-cardinal-kasper-says.

[753] Edward Pentin, "Cardinal Müller Issues 'Manifesto of Faith,'" *National Catholic Register*, 8 February 2019, https://www.ncregister.com/blog/edward-pentin/cardinal-mueller-issues-manifesto-of-faith.

[754] Pentin, "Müller Speaks Out on 'Amoris Laetitia.'"

controversial interpretation of some statements in Chapter 8 of *Amoris Laetitia*."[755]

As with most of his comments about Francis' pontificate and Francis himself, Müller seeks to provide a conciliatory rather than a critical voice, usually by simply reasserting what the Church has always taught. Genuinely concerned that the pontificate exists in a kind of theological and ecclesiological vacuum, lacking basic knowledge of crucial concepts, he has tried in his own way to offer basic correctives.

But his efforts at conciliation also confounded some, as in 2017, when, as CDF prefect, he played down what many viewed as problems with *Amoris Laetitia*, telling an Italian television program that the document posed "no danger to the faith" and so a fraternal correction was not necessary, and criticizing the four "*dubia* Cardinals" for making their appeal to the pope for clarification public.[756]

The cardinal became significantly more critical of the pontificate after he left the CDF, saying he shared the opinion of the *dubia* and arguing that it would have been better if Francis had had an audience with the four cardinals before their publication rather than have the "spectacle of a trial of strength" that followed.[757]

Refusal to Criticize Pope Francis

The cardinal has always remained respectful of Francis and instead attributed the problems to the courtiers around the pope, "careerists and opportunists," as he calls them, who were always sowing discord and had besmirched the cardinal's name.[758] And even though the CDF had become essentially superfluous under Francis, who, despite his lack of theological expertise, relied on his own courtiers and ghost writers and hardly consulted

---

[755] Ibid.

[756] Edward Pentin, "Cardinal Müller's TV Interview Causes Bewilderment," *National Catholic Register*, 8 January 2017, https://www.ncregister.com/blog/edward-pentin/cardinal-muellers-tv-interview-causes-bewilderment.

[757] Pentin, "Müller Speaks Out on 'Amoris Laetitia.'"

[758] Ibid.

the congregation on drafting or checking papal documents, Müller refused to be drawn into public criticism.

Furthermore, as a German cardinal theologian who had reached the pinnacle of an ecclesiastical career only to have it suddenly ended five years before retirement age and without any real explanation, Müller adamantly refused to criticize the pope publicly. In his 2017 interview with the *National Catholic Register* he said:

> The important thing is that we have to love the Church because she is the Bride of Christ. Loving her means that we sometimes have to suffer with her, because in her members she is not perfect, and so we remain loyal despite the disappointments. In the end, it is how we appear in the eyes of God that matters, rather than how we are regarded by men.[759]

Although he was highly critical of the Amazon synod both before and during the 2019 meeting, Cardinal Müller was quick to praise *Querida Amazonia*, Pope Francis' post-synodal apostolic exhortation on the gathering, calling it a "document of reconciliation." Although some leading figures, such as Cardinal Raymond Burke, criticized it for not definitively closing the door to married priests and women deacons (the text appeared to rule them out, but Francis' aides said these were still on the table), Müller praised the document for its "personal and attractive tone," and added it was "a pastoral letter of prophetic power."[760]

One of the rare moments when he did make his grievances known was when the pope, without any explanation, ordered Müller to dismiss three of his priest officials at the CDF, all reputed to be highly proficient.[761] Müller

---

[759] Ibid.

[760] Cardinal Gerhard Müller, "Cardinal Müller: 'Querida Amazonia' Is a Document of Reconciliation," *National Catholic Register*, 12 February 2020, https://www.ncregister.com/blog/edward-pentin/cardinal-mueller-querida-amazonia-is-a-document-of-reconciliation.

[761] Jan Bentz, "Report: Pope Francis Ordered Cardinal Müller to Dismiss Three Priests from Doctrinal Office," LifeSite News, 3 January 2016, https://www.lifesitenews.com/news/

strongly resisted and went to see the pope in person to try to reverse the decision but did not succeed. After leaving the CDF, he called the dismissals "unacceptable."[762] The episode, his friends say, revealed Müller's strong sense of loyalty to both collaborators and friends—and to the pope, whom he reluctantly obeyed.

Relationship with Benedict XVI

Müller's relationship with Pope Emeritus Benedict XVI has naturally been close, given their past history and their theological kinship. Müller also headed the diocese with close connections to Joseph Ratzinger, and Benedict appointed Müller CDF prefect. Müller also worked closely with Cardinal Joseph Ratzinger on the International Theological Commission when Ratzinger was president.

In 2008, when Müller was bishop of Regensburg, Pope Benedict XVI personally entrusted him with the publication of his *Collected Writings* of sixteen volumes. To ensure the undertaking was carried out properly, Bishop Müller founded in Regensburg the Pope Benedict XVI Institute, whose main task has been to collect and publish the works of Joseph Ratzinger in their entirety, including previously unedited writings.[763]

Benedict appointed Müller CDF prefect in 2012, raising him to archbishop—an appointment that he said did not surprise him because he had been a member of the CDF for a number of years and had been a professor of dogmatics for many years before that.[764] Francis elevated him to the College of Cardinals in 2014.

francis-boots-three-priests-out-of-cdf.-why-i-am-the-pope-i-do-not-need-to.

[762] Delia Gallagher, "Former Top Vatican Official Strikes Back at Pope," CNN, 12 July 2017 https://edition.cnn.com/2017/07/11/world/muller-pope-strikes-back/index.html.

[763] "Complete Works of Joseph Ratzinger To Be Published in German," Catholic News Agency, 22 October 2008, https://www.catholicnewsagency.com/news/complete_works_of_joseph_ratzinger_to_be_published_in_german.

[764] "Interview with H.E. Archbishop Gerhard Ludwig Müller."

Müller has often come to Benedict's defense, most recently praising the former pope's assessment of the clerical sexual abuse crisis issued just before a Vatican summit on the issue in 2019, and denying any rift between Benedict and Francis.[765]

SUMMARY

Intelligent and honest, Cardinal Gerhard Müller is a decisive and down-to-earth leader who will act courageously when necessary. Respected as a theologian, he is not as conservative as his media persona would appear, and he himself dislikes the label, preferring to consider himself as simply "Catholic." Formed under the tutelage of liberal German theologians such as the former head of the country's bishops, Cardinal Karl Lehmann, Müller rose through the Church's ranks with the support of Benedict XVI to reach one of the Church's loftiest positions—prefect of the CDF—before Francis chose not to renew his mandate for another five years in 2017.

Although liturgy is not his priority, he considers doctrine and pastoral care of equal importance, and he has encouraged Eucharistic devotion in a number of ways. He struggled to act coherently in the early years of the sexual abuse crisis but has been forthright on the issue since, and as bishop of Regensburg, he acted firmly and decisively with dissenting groups. He is regarded as politically conservative.

Generally viewed as theologically orthodox rather than ideological like some of his fellow German theologians, Müller has nevertheless been unorthodox in some of his teaching, such as on Transubstantiation; and though he does not deny the dogma of the perpetual virginity of Mary, he offered teaching that ran contrary to widespread theological consensus.

---

[765] Claire Giangravè, "Former Vatican Doctrine Czar Says Rift between Benedict XVI and Francis Is Impossible," *Crux*, 15 April 2019, https://cruxnow.com/vatican/2019/04/former-vatican-doctrine-czar-says-rift-between-benedict-xvi-and-francis-is-impossible/.

He also courted controversy through his interest in liberation theology, which he tried to separate from its Marxist interpretation. Otherwise, he mostly takes traditional positions, strongly opposing a female diaconate and resisting changes to priestly celibacy in the Latin Rite, although he once favored exceptions to the latter in the 1990s. Ardently supportive of the teachings of Vatican II and quite modern in his outlook, he has taken a hard line against the traditional Society of Saint Pius X.

Independent-minded, Gerhard Müller is regarded as an intensely loyal friend and collaborator who has striven to avoid criticizing Pope Francis, even in private, though he has many questions about this pontificate, whose faults he mostly ascribes to Francis' courtiers. An honest broker, knowledgeable, well read, and "without a scintilla of nastiness," according to an associate, Müller is a natural leader, unafraid to lead and make tough decisions.

SERVICE TO THE CHURCH

Ordination to the Priesthood: 11 February 1978
Ordination to the Episcopate: 24 November 2002
Elevation to the College of Cardinals: 22 February 2014

Education
- Mainz, Munich and Freiburg im Breisgau; Philosophy and theology
- 1977: Doctorate in Theology

Assignments
- 1978-1982: Parochial vicar at Klein-Krotzenburg, Bürstadt and Offenbach
- 1986-2002: Professor of dogmatic theology at the Catholic Theological Faculty of the "Ludwig-Maximilians Universitat," Munich

- 1990: Member of the Commission for the Doctrine of the Faith of the German Bishops' Conference
- 1998-2003: Member of the International Theological Commission
- 1999: Peritus to the Vatican's Synod of European Bishops
- 2001: Peritus to the international bishops' synod in Rome, "The Bishop as Servant of the Gospel of Jesus Christ for World Hope"
- 2012-2017: Prefect of the Congregation for the Doctrine of the Faith
- 2012-2017: President of the Pontifical Commission *Ecclesia Dei*
- 2012-2017: President of the Pontifical Biblical Commission of the International Theological Commission

Membership
- Congregation for the Oriental Churches
- Congregation for Catholic Education
- Congregation for Institutes of Consecrated Life and Societies of Apostolic Life
- Pontifical Council for Promoting Christian Unity
- Pontifical Council for Legislative Texts
- Pontifical Council for Culture

WILFRID FOX CARDINAL NAPIER, O.F.M.

"Peace and Goodness"

Born: 8 March 1941
Swartberg, South Africa
Nationality: South African
Title: Archbishop of Durban

BIOGRAPHY

Wilfrid Napier's Catholic education is deeply rooted in care for the marginalized.[766] One of seven children, he left South Africa as a young man, encountered the Franciscans in Ireland, and soon joined their order. In

---

[766] "SA's Cardinal Turns 75," *Southern Cross* (9-15 March 2016): 1, https://issuu.com/scross/docs/160309.

1964, he completed a degree in Latin and English at the University of Galway, Ireland. From there, he was sent to the University of Louvain, where he earned a master's degree in philosophy and theology. Returning to South Africa, Napier was ordained a priest in 1970 and, for eight years, served in rural areas near Kokstad. In the 1980s, he worked closely with the archbishop of Durban, eventually succeeding him with two terms as president of the South African Catholic Bishops' Conference.

In the 1990s, Napier worked to foster dialogue amid civil unrest in his country, and in 1991 he was present at the signing of the South African Peace Accord. In 1992, he was appointed archbishop of Durban. Reputedly fluent in six languages, he was created a cardinal by John Paul II in 2001. His engagement with modern social media has helped establish his reputation worldwide in recent years as a cardinal willing to name wrongs publicly in society.[767] He participated in the 2014 Synod of Bishops and was the president delegate of the 2015 Synod of Bishops that focused on the mission of the family.

SANCTIFYING OFFICE

Importance of the Eucharist

Because of his understanding of the Mass as central to the Catholic Faith, Wilfrid Cardinal Napier has prioritized teaching the faithful how to prepare for Mass. In a recent bulletin to his archdiocese, Napier stated that "the Eucharist is, or should be, the central pillar of our Faith and Christian life."[768] He encouraged his flock to "make the Church truly the House of God" [769] by "preparing to worship the Father, receive the Body and Blood

---

[767] Barbara Ludman and Paul Stober, eds., *The Mail and Guardian A-Z of South African Politics: The Essential Handbook* (Johannesburg: Jacana Media, 2004), 97-8.

[768] Cardinal Wilfrid Napier, "Cardinal's Corner," *Catholic News Bulletin* (June 2018): 37, http://www.catholic-dbn.org.za/june-2018-bulletin/.

[769] Ibid.

of the Son, and be filled with the Holy Spirit when leaving the House of God after Mass."[770] He continued:

> Even where the Tabernacle is in a most prominent place, many Catholics talk and converse as if they were in a hall, not the "House of God!" Often they carry on long conversations, completely un-concerned that there are people nearby who have come to pray, or meditate, or simply sit in the presence of God in His House![771]

Cardinal Napier understands devotion to the Eucharist as a sign of commitment to the priestly vocation. In a 2018 homily, he warned that "drifting away from the Eucharist"[772] is a sign of lukewarmness in the priestly vocation and that a sign of zeal is "when priests start speaking about the Eucharist [and] they become noticeably energized and upbeat."[773] He challenged all priests to offer themselves at each Mass, stating that each "priest is more than a presider, more than a social activist";[774] rather, the "holiness for the priest begins when he becomes the sacrifice that he offers."[775]

The cardinal also emphasized the role of the deacon in the Mass and encouraged priests, deacons, and parish liturgy committees to consult and implement the appropriate rubrics, rules, and guidelines.

Women Deacons

It does not seem that Napier has directly addressed the issue of women deacons. He has engaged, however, with a group who advocated for ordination of women. In response to a protest by the Women's Ordination South Africa group in 2001, Cardinal Napier denied the statement put forward by the group—namely, that Pope John Paul II had said "Catholics might

---

[770] Ibid.

[771] Ibid.

[772] Letters Editor, "Cardinal Napier's Warning to Priests and Are We Wandering From the Proper Mass?," *Southern Cross*, 21 April 2018, https://www.scross.co.za/2018/04/are-we-wandering-from-the-proper-mass/.

[773] Ibid.

[774] Ibid.

[775] Ibid.

no longer even speak about the question of Catholic women priests."[776] Rather, Napier understood the pope's view to be that he "did not have the competence to make a decision on the question of women in the priesthood."[777] From these comments, the cardinal seems to indicate that the pope cannot alter the reservation of ordination to men.

Critical of the Extraordinary Form

Cardinal Napier has been critical of the Mass in the Extraordinary Form of the Roman Rite. In a recent tweet replying to a photo of a Mass in the Extraordinary Form, Cardinal Napier stated:

> Looking at this picture reminds me of my childhood some 70 years ago. That was a time when there was a universe between the Clergy especially Bishops and Lay Faithful! Some might call it the age of supreme Clericalism. To me it's a reminder of what we should never ever be again![778]

In response to a critical reply on Twitter, Cardinal Napier stated that "Jesus was not in the Temple where similar sacred liturgy was celebrated."[779] Rather, "he was with the people especially those considered to be outcasts or even worse sinners!"[780] Napier stated that he did not "want the Mass to become a great spectacle, but a memory of Christ's saving death!"[781] From these comments, it is clear that the cardinal prefers the Novus Ordo because he views it as a better reflection of the active participation of the lay faithful in the liturgy as called for by the Second Vatican Council:

> Thank God I live and minister in the Church in Africa, where Christians focus on the need for God pure and simple, where active

---

[776] "Catholic Women Call for Ordination," *IOL*, 11 April 2001, https://www.iol.co.za/news/south-africa/catholic-women-call-for-ordination-64060.

[777] Ibid.

[778] Cardinal Napier (@CardinalNapier), Twitter, 30 September 2018, 1:05 a.m., https://twitter.com/cardinalnapier/status/1046264763800580096.

[779] Ibid.

[780] Ibid.

[781] Ibid.

participation is valued more than what this debate is centered on, vestments and aloofness from the Faithful, the Lay Faithful in particular.... I don't begrudge those who find meaning in the "old time religion"! My plea is that you respect and give freedom to those who follow the mind of the Church as reflected in the Popes who have led the Church through the reforms of the Liturgy! [782]

Inculturation

In discussing the liturgy, Cardinal Napier has also engaged with the difficult, but necessary, process of inculturation. It is not clear where the cardinal draws the boundaries of inculturation. But he has clearly echoed Pope Paul VI's challenge to make the Catholic Faith more authentically African and the African people more authentically Catholic. In a 2003 interview, Cardinal Napier commented that one would "be surprised at how little of Rome there is in the Roman Catholic Church in South Africa." [783] For Napier, "the Gospel would become irrelevant" [784] if one did not consider "the way people understand it from their own cultural point of view and express their religiosity through the rituals of the Church." [785] The same interviewer commented that the cardinal emphasized "that the essence of the Catholic faith is not affected by the process of inculturation, merely the way people express themselves." [786]

Addressing Liturgical Abuse

During his tenure as president of the South African Catholic Bishops' Conference (SACBC), Cardinal Napier promptly responded to a warning from the Roman Curia on certain nonsacramental practices occurring in his diocese.

---

[782] Ibid.
[783] "African Traditions Help Catholic Church Grow in South Africa," Episcopal News Service, 13 June 2003, https://www.episcopalchurch.org/library/article/african-traditions-help-catholic-church-grow-south-africa.
[784] Ibid.
[785] Ibid.
[786] Ibid. In this discussion of inculturation, the cardinal did not comment more generally on the inerrancy of Scripture or his views on the historicity of the Gospels.

In 2008, Archbishop Ranjith, at that time secretary of the Congregation for Divine Worship and the Discipline of the Sacraments, wrote to the SACBC concerning services in which lay faithful were anointed with "oil of gladness" during healing services. Archbishop Ranjith called for "proper catechesis and sacramental discipline"[787] and noted that the "use of any other oil or any other 'anointing' than those found in the approved liturgical books must be considered proscribed and subject to ecclesiastical penalties."[788] In response, the SACBC responded and published a statement on blessed oils, distinguishing essential oils from blessed oils and concluding that "the bishops are from now on limiting the blessing and use of this blessed oil to priests alone."[789]

GOVERNING OFFICE

Attentive Pastor

During Napier's time as cardinal-archbishop of Durban, the number of Catholics decreased from just over 7 percent of the population in 1990 to just over 4 percent in 2016.[790] The number of priestly vocations increased during that time.[791]

Napier is an attentive pastor to his diocese. He writes in a diocesan bulletin quarterly on pertinent issues affecting his flock.[792] The cardinal has spearheaded and supported many diocesan pastoral initiatives, including

---

[787] "Vatican Official Cautions Against S. African 'Oil of Gladness' Services," Catholic News Agency, 19 October 2008, https://www.catholic-newsagency.com/news/vatican_official_cautions_against_s._african_oil_of_gladness_services.

[788] Ibid.

[789] "Bishops' Rules for Blessed Oil," *Southern Cross*, 15 November 2015, https://www.scross.co.za/2015/11/bishops-rules-for-blessed-oil/.

[790] "Archdiocese of Durban," Catholic Hierarchy, http://www.catholic-hierarchy.org/diocese/ddurb.html#info.

[791] Ibid.

[792] Archdiocese of Durban, *Catholic News Bulletin*, http://www.catholic-dbn.org.za/category/bulletins/.

a refugee pastoral care program,[793] a streetwise rescue and rehabilitation project, the Right to Live campaign, and other educational, health, and outreach programs.[794] Cardinal Napier also helped to spearhead a mini World Youth Day with the SACBC in 2017.[795] He has spoken to the wider public about the "very strong sense that they need God"[796] among the African people. In responding to the rising secularism in the West and what the West could learn from Africa, Napier stated the following:

> What can Europe and the West learn from us? That is very difficult to say because the global culture tends to dominate so much that most of the time we are learning from you how to become more self-reliant or even self-sufficient, which is a short jump away from saying, "I don't really need God!" You can and should learn how to recognize your need for God! Perhaps the West could and would be open to learn from us if it spent more time looking at what really makes us human beings more truly the image and likeness of God.[797]

Financial Probity

Cardinal Napier has also taken active steps to deal with the financial issues in the Church—both in his local diocese and on a global level. In 2015, Cardinal Napier suspended a priest in his diocese for financial mismanagement and stated that "transparency and accountability is essential, and it is the reason for this course of action."[798] Cardinal Napier's decision was

---

[793] Staff Writers, "Cardinal Wilfrid Napier, the Cool Hand Cardinal from Africa," *Catholic Weekly*, 27 May 2015, https://www.catholicweekly.com.au/cardinal-wilfrid-napier-the-cool-hand-cardinal-from-africa/.

[794] Zulu Missions, "Catholic Archdiocese of Durban," 2016, https://zulumissions.co.za/about-us/#1454775736709-4cc69a70-caa5.

[795] Cardinal Wilfrid Napier, "Cardinal's Corner," *Catholic News Bulletin* (October 2017): 66, http://www.catholic-dbn.org.za/october-2017-bulletin/.

[796] Roland Noé, "Napier: 'Expect a Strong Reaffirmation of the Church's Teaching,'" *Kath.net*, 19 November 2015, https://www.kath.net/news/52940.

[797] Ibid.

[798] Nabeelah Shaikh, "Priest Suspended over R3 Million," *IOL*, 1 November 2015, https://www.iol.co.za/news/priest-suspended-over-r3-million-1938728.

unpopular among some in his diocese. He explained that the Church was following proper procedures, as "there was a clear indication that [the priest in question] had mismanaged a large amount of money."[799] Cardinal Napier stated that it was "an amount of money that I will never make in my lifetime"[800] and that "it was my responsibility to follow the protocols."[801]

As a member of the Council for the Economy, Napier has been an active participant in the reform of the Vatican Bank. He observed that "everyone knows ... the way that the Vatican Bank was being represented in the media, the way it couldn't account for some of its actions." Reform was undoubtedly needed: "A person must have come back from living on the moon, maybe, if they think there wasn't any need for reforms of the Vatican."[802] He has only expressed public support for financial reform but little or no criticism.

Collegiality and Synodality
Cardinal Napier believes that collegiality and synodality are central to effective Church reform. He views the leadership of the Church as a single community and has stated that bishops must be "walking together ... in a joint effort to make the Church a change-maker in modern society."[803] During his participation in the 2014 and 2015 synods, Cardinal Napier called for bishops to take a more unified approach, being united both to each other and to the pope. He stated that "it's more about ourselves being one, from the bishops down."[804] It is about being sure that "the bishops of the Church ... [are] united under the Holy Father and not divided into factions."[805]

[799] Ibid.
[800] Ibid.
[801] Ibid.
[802] "Cool Hand Cardinal."
[803] Matt Hadro, "What the Struggle against Apartheid Taught Cardinal Napier," Catholic News Agency, 22 February 2016, https://www.catholicnewsagency.com/news/how-the-struggle-against-apartheid-taught-cardinal-napier-the-value-of-collegiality-97417.
[804] Ibid.
[805] Ibid.

Napier has challenged the actions of the Roman Curia and his brother bishops where he deemed it necessary to do so. He has openly criticized the synodal processes as well as the documents summarizing synod meetings. During the 2018 Synod on Youth, for example, the cardinal criticized the *Instrumentum Laboris* (the synod's working document) for being "Eurocentric."[806] Cardinal Napier stated that the document did not account for a range of issues affecting the African Church and youth, including the mass migration of young Africans, exploitation of resources, and the phenomenon that young Africans are looking for "Jesus and looking for answers to their problems."[807]

In his role as president delegate to the 2015 Synod on the Family, Cardinal Napier sent a letter to Pope Francis (and to other cardinals) to express his concern about the composition of the drafting committee for the final report of the synod.[808] Cardinal Napier was not so much challenging the pope's right to appoint members of a drafting committee as he was concerned that, in order to give "a fair expression of what the Synod is about, [such as] what the Church in Africa really would like to see happening,"[809] there should be a change in the composition of the drafting committee.

In addition, Cardinal Napier criticized *Instrumentum Laboris* and the 2014 Synod on the Family for casting a positive light on actions that

---

[806] Deborah Castellano Lubov, "FEATURE: Cardinal Napier Explains 3 Inadequacies in Instrumentum Laboris for Addressing African Realities," Zenit, 15 October 2018, https://zenit.org/articles/cardinal-napier-explains-3-inadequacies-in-instrumentum-laboris-for-addressing-african-issues/.

[807] JD Flynn/CNA, "Cardinal Napier: Parishes, Learn from Youth Synod; Synod, Hear African Voices," *National Catholic Register*, 15 October 2018, http://www.ncregister.com/daily-news/cardinal-napier-parishes-learn-from-youth-synod-synod-hear-african-voices.

[808] Crux Staff, "Cardinals Clash on Doubts about Process at the Synod of Bishops," *Crux*, 12 October 2015, https://cruxnow.com/church/2015/10/12/cardinals-clash-on-doubts-about-process-at-the-synod-of-bishops/.

[809] Ibid.

were directly contrary to the Church's teaching. In a 2015 interview, the cardinal stated:

> Now, how can you in an official document of the Church be giving positive qualities to something that is in direct contradiction to the Church's teaching—Jesus's teaching.... For instance, cohabitation was presented as if it was a good kind of preparation for marriage or a good alternative to marriage. No, you can't do that and be talking about the sacrament of marriage in the same breath.[810]

He also criticized the *Relatio Post Disceptationem*, a summary document issued halfway through the 2014 Synod on the Family, asserting that "the message has gone out and it's not a true message."[811] In an interview with the press, Napier said that "whatever we say hereafter is going to be as if we're doing some damage control."[812] Cardinal Napier's criticism of the synod document was based on his "dissatisfaction" that elements said by individual synod members were inserted into the document "as if they really do reflect the feeling of the whole synod" and had been "made to be the message of the synod."[813] He also endorsed the 2015 book *Rigging of a Vatican Synod: An Investigation into Alleged Manipulation at the Extraordinary Synod on the Family* which showed how various attempts were made to push through heterodox agendas, such as admission to Holy Communion of civilly "remarried" divorcees and encouragement that the Church show greater acceptance of homosexuality—an issue that remains a particular social taboo in Africa.[814]

---

[810] "Cool Hand Cardinal."

[811] Joshua J. McElwee, "Napier on Synod Document: 'The Message Has Gone Out and It's Not a True Message,'" *National Catholic Reporter*, 14 October 2014, https://www.ncronline.org/news/vatican/napier-synod-document-message-has-gone-out-and-its-not-true-message.

[812] Ibid.

[813] Ibid.

[814] Edward Pentin, *The Rigging of a Vatican Synod: An Investigation into Alleged Manipulation at the Extraordinary Synod on the Family* (San Francisco: Ignatius Press, 2015).

Addressing Sexual Abuse

Various media outlets have asked the cardinal to speak directly about the sex abuse scandal in the Church. In response to a question from EWTN on the root cause of the scandal, the cardinal said "we let the model bar slip"[815] after the Second Vatican Council, when priests were released from very strict rules "of etiquette, of behavior"[816] which, in the opinion of the cardinal, produced an overreaction.[817] In a tweet regarding the problem of homosexuality in the priesthood, the cardinal seemed to indicate that he would weed out homosexual candidates for the priesthood early on during the selection process.[818]

In an interview with Stephen Nolan of the BBC, the cardinal described pedophilia as a "psychological condition or disorder ... not a criminal condition."[819] Cardinal Napier shared that he knew "at least two of the priests who became pedophiles who had themselves been abused as children."[820] Napier rebutted the generalization that the Church had "mishandled" cases of clerical sexual abuse and spoke of his experience dealing with complaints of sexual abuse in his diocese.[821] He explained

[815] EWTN, "'We Let the Bar Slip'—ENN 2018-11-27," YouTube video 3:58, posted 28 November 2018, https://www.youtube.com/watch?v=snCB4GhYsDU.

[816] Ibid.

[817] Ibid.

[818] Cardinal Napier (@CardinalNapier), "Wasn't this the problem with sending abuse offenders to treatment centres for these to root the evil tendencies out of them?" Twitter, 22 December 2018, 3:45 p.m., https://twitter.com/CardinalNapier/status/1076579625810169856. It is worth noting that the cardinal has not commented on the current debate in the Catholic Church around priestly celibacy.

[819] Cardinal Wilfrid Napier, "'Paedophilia Is Illness'—Cardinal Wilfrid Napier," BBC News, 16 March 2013, https://www.bbc.com/news/av/world-21810692/paedophilia-is-illness-cardinal-wilfrid-napier.

[820] Ibid.

[821] Cavan Sieczkowski, "Cardinal Wilfrid Fox Napier Suggests Pedophilia Not a Crime, but an Illness," *Huffpost*, 18 March 2013, https://www.huffingtonpost.com/2013/03/18/cardinal-wilfrid-fox-napier-pedophilia-not-a-crime-illness_n_2900941.html; Stephen Nolan, "Paedophilia Is

that he followed the protocols in place at the time.[822] The cardinal seems to prefer a case-by-case approach to the culpability of each accused abuser. During the interview, Napier stated that he could not determine the culpability of abused pedophiles, but that those persons should not be criminally punished in the same way as those abusers who acted with full agency.[823] He protested: "Don't tell me that those people are criminally responsible like someone who chooses something like that.... [I] don't think you can really take the position ... that that person deserves to be punished."[824]

After these comments sparked a critical response, Cardinal Napier issued an apology on Twitter "to victims of child abuse offended by my misstatement of what was and still is my concern about all abused, including the abused abuser."[825] He said that it was "the supreme irony"[826] since he had "raised the issue of the abused abuser"[827] and now stood "accused of insensitivity to the sufferings of the abused."[828]

In a recent bulletin to his archdiocese, Napier referred to the Church's sex abuse scandal and called for prayer and fasting to cast out the evil that has penetrated the Church:

> Given the deep-seated nature of the evil that has been perpetrated, there seems to be only one thing to do. After apologizing profusely to the victim/survivors, to their family and communities, we have to

an 'Illness, Not A Criminal Condition,'" BBC Radio 5, 16 March 2013, https://www.bbc.co.uk/programmes/p016fbgr.

[822] Ibid.

[823] Ibid.

[824] Ibid.

[825] James Legge, "South African Cardinal Who Said Paedophilia Is 'Not a Criminal Condition' Apologises for Offence," *Independent*, 18 March 2013, https://www.independent.co.uk/news/world/africa/south-african-cardinal-who-said-paedophilia-is-not-a-criminal-condition-apologises-for-offence-8539345.html.

[826] Ibid.

[827] Ibid.

[828] Ibid.

apply the remedy which Jesus himself applied to his Disciples when they were at a loss as to how to caste out a particularly stubborn demon. Our demon seems to be just as stubborn and just as difficult to caste out. "This kind can be caste out only by prayer and fasting!"[829]

Instructing his diocese not to tell others "especially Pope Francis, what to do," Cardinal Napier called for "all who care for their Church to follow the advice of Jesus—fast and pray!"[830]

TEACHING OFFICE

Tweeting Cardinal

Napier is an avid user of Twitter—despite its being rather an anarchical forum given to insults and provocation—to share candid opinions about social and moral issues affecting the Church today. For example, the cardinal reacted against the call for Catholics to apologize for their treatment of gay people after the shooting massacre at an Orlando gay club.[831] He stated his disapproval by tweeting "God help us! Next we'll have to apologize for teaching that adultery is a sin! Political Correctness (PC) is today's major heresy!"[832]

In addition, Napier publicly criticized the BBC for promoting homosexuality in a series of tweets in 2017.[833] As part of his support of the Catholic Church's pastoral role in helping same-sex-attracted people to

---

[829] Cardinal Napier, "Ad Intra Challenges," *Catholic News Bulletin* (August 2018): 54, http://www.catholic-dbn.org.za/august-2018-bulletin/.

[830] Ibid.

[831] David Gibson, "South African Cardinal Calls US Abortion Rate a Black 'Genocide,'" *Crux*, 5 July 2016, https://cruxnow.com/global-church/2016/07/05/south-african-cardinal-calls-us-abortion-rate-black-genocide/.

[832] Cardinal Napier (@CardinalNapier), Twitter, 25 June 2016, 12:27 p.m., https://twitter.com/CardinalNapier/status/746741516572450820.

[833] Staff Reporter, "Cardinal Napier: BBC Is Determined to Undermine Christian Values," *Catholic Herald*, 23 August 2017, https://catholicherald.co.uk/cardinal-napier-bbc-is-determined-to-undermine-christian-values/.

live chastely, Cardinal Napier tweeted his approval of two Catholics who have written against the pro-LGBTQ stance taken by some members of the Catholic Church.[834]

Defending the Family

As a delegate and participant in two synods on the family, Napier has also taken a keen interest in the social and cultural problems that erode the traditional family. He has called for the Catholic Church to help bolster and strengthen good marriages. In an article written by the cardinal in 2018 on the vocation of men, he states:

> So, in its ministry the Church is to set up the original order for marriage and family life as the benchmark for all relationships between men and women. This requires each man to embrace fully his chosen state in life. If it is marriage and fatherhood then he must be an equal partner and complement his wife especially in their common vocation of procreating and raising a family.[835]

After the interview about the Church's abuse scandal with the BBC (see above), Cardinal Napier was questioned by various media organizations on a range of social and moral issues. According to Napier, same-sex "marriages" go against "reason and revelation." In responding to the journalists' reaction to this statement, the cardinal seemed to say that the Church has exceptionless moral norms and "if we don't articulate this as the Church, it means we have to shut up shop."[836] Again the cardinal

---

[834] Romeo Hontiveros, "Cardinal Wilfrid Napier Subtly Rebukes Fr. James Martin's Pro-Gay Agenda," PagadianDiocese.org, 12 February 2018, http://www.pagadiandiocese.org/2018/02/12/cardinal-wilfrid-napier-subtly-rebukes-fr-james-martins-pro-gay-agenda/.

[835] Cardinal Wilfrid Napier, O.F.M., "Men Must Embrace Their Chosen Life," *Southern Cross,* 18 January 2017, https://www.scross.co.za/2017/01/men-must-embrace-their-chosen-life/.

[836] Staff Writer, "Napier: I Don't Know Any Gays," *Mail & Guardian,* 12 April 2013, https://mg.co.za/article/2013-04-12-00-napier-an-explanation-for-everything.

criticized the culture of political correctness, stating that "freedom of expression seems to work if you say what is deemed to be politically acceptable."[837]

For Cardinal Napier, the Church's position that same-sex "marriage" goes against human reason is based on the difference between men and women, who "were made differently, they were made to complement each other."[838] By virtue of these differences "men and women were made to create life together."[839] As a result, Cardinal Napier stated that same-sex "marriage" is "radically wrong"[840] because it is "devoid of the concept of bringing life into earth."[841] Napier continued by stating that "as far as church is concerned, sexual activity is for within the confines of marriage; for procreation and the building up of the relationship between the couple."[842] He sternly warned that one "can't practice in the Catholic Church if you aren't married and are sexually active."[843]

Cardinal Napier has also called for the Church to introduce a program of "accompanying marriages—for four, five, maybe 10 years,"[844] in the hope that if the Church accompanies couples, it will "avoid the pitfalls of broken marriages and divorce and needing to address this question of civilly 'remarried' Catholics being admitted to [reception of] the Eucharist."[845]

Communion for "Remarried" Divorcees

Another attack on the traditional family in Africa is the problem of polygamy. In a 2014 interview, Cardinal Napier clearly stated that Communion for divorced-and-"remarried" Catholics, whom he referred to as successive

[837] Ibid.
[838] Ibid.
[839] Ibid.
[840] Ibid.
[841] Ibid.
[842] Ibid.
[843] Ibid.
[844] "Cool Hand Cardinal."
[845] Ibid.

polygamists,[846] should not be permitted. Napier made the point that if divorced-and-"remarried" Catholics are permitted to receive Communion, the Catholic Church would have no ground to refuse Communion to those in polygamous relationships.[847] He called for those divorced-and-"remarried" Catholics to "carry the cross of Christ"[848] even if the world is telling them that the softer option is always preferable.[849]

Resisting Ideological Colonization

Speaking about the 2014 synod, Cardinal Napier signaled his disapproval of Western aid organizations' pressuring African countries to adopt policies that reflect anti-marriage and anti-family ideologies. He explained that the outcome of the synod would have a real impact on the traditional family in African countries.

It is clear that Napier is committed to certain nonnegotiable moral norms even when they prove unpopular. For the cardinal, relevance in the world is secondary to the Church's mission of conveying certain truths. He says: "It's not about whether the Church is relevant. It's that the message it's committed to conveying is more than relevant—that God created us for a very special purpose which He's entrusted to us."[850]

HIV and AIDS

The cardinal has also addressed the scourge of HIV and AIDS in Africa. He has been consistently critical of the practice of using condoms to prevent the spread of the disease.[851] Napier stated that the African bishops "regard

---

[846] Catholic News Service, "Cardinal Napier: Communion and Polygamy," YouTube video, 2:20, posted 8 October 2014, https://www.youtube.com/watch?v=U12-JT_pwKI.

[847] Ibid.

[848] Ibid.

[849] Ibid.

[850] "I Don't Know Any Gays."

[851] "South African Catholic Church Condemns Condom Use to Prevent HIV Spread," Kaiser Health News, 28 January 2005, https://khn.org/morning-breakout/dr00027847/.

the widespread and indiscriminate promotion of condoms as an immoral and misguided weapon in the battle against HIV/AIDS."[852] Napier sees value in "proclaim[ing] our message loud and clear"[853] because delivering the message clearly "will strengthen the moral fiber of our countries."[854] "Abstain and be faithful is the human and Christian way of overcoming AIDS. Abstain from sex before marriage and be faithful to your spouse within marriage. This is the answer which Christ gives us." [855]

Napier distinguishes, however, between programs that use condoms to reduce the spread of HIV and AIDS and married couples who use them because of a discordant HIV/AIDS status. In such cases, Cardinal Napier makes it clear that "there is a real danger that the healthy partner will contract this killer disease,"[856] and, as a result, "the Church accepts that everyone has the right to defend one's life against mortal danger, this would include using appropriate means and course of action."[857]

Right-to-Life Issues

For the cardinal, the demands of the common good on those who govern give rise to a duty to protect life. Napier appears not to have publicly commented on euthanasia. But the following statement illustrates his broad understanding of what it means to be pro-life:

> This means that in seeking to meet the demands of the common good, the government must set out clearly the measures it can and will take to ensure that its citizens have shelter, security, food,

---

[852] AP Archive, "African Bishops Reject Use of Condoms in Fight against AIDS," YouTube video, 2:13, posted 23 July 2014 by AP Archive, https://www.youtube.com/watch?v=HeOnmekj2QI.

[853] Ibid.

[854] Ibid.

[855] Ibid.

[856] Ibid.

[857] Ibid.

clothing, healthcare; but its first priority is to respect, protect, defend, enhance and promote human life.[858]

Napier is a fierce critic of the practice of abortion and has publicly criticized institutions that provide abortions.[859] In 2016, he highlighted the extremely high number of abortions carried out on black women, commenting that "it starts to look like genocide."[860] He has also criticized the Obama administration for funding abortions in Africa.[861] From these comments it is clear that, for the cardinal, abortion is never morally permissible.

Migrants and Refugees

Napier has not advocated a policy of giving permanent residency to all migrants to South Africa, citing in part the justified concerns of those impoverished already living there. The cardinal has identified what he calls the root cause of the problem of xenophobic violence in South Africa: poverty. He explained that "when the majority of people live in poverty there is always a temptation to take it out on the even more disadvantaged."[862] In discussing

[858] Cardinal Wilfrid Napier, O.F.M., "Commit to the Common Good," *Southern Cross*, 23 September 2017, https://www.scross.co.za/2017/09/commit-to-the-common-good/.

[859] Cardinal Napier (@CardinalNapier), "I like the ring of #SayNopeTo-MarieStopes the abortion agency that is killing tens of thousands of unborn Babies in Africa including South Africa," Twitter, 7 December 2018, 11:36 a.m., https://twitter.com/CardinalNapier/status/1071080909112336384; "1/3 Guttmacher Institute estimates that since 1973 USA has aborted 57 million+ babies! Isn't this something we should be apologizing for?," Twitter, 1 July 2016, 11:54 p.m., https://twitter.com/CardinalNapier/status/749088895430561794.

[860] Danny David, "South African Cardinal: U.S. Abortion Is 'Genocide' of African-Americans," *Live Action*, 6 July 2016, https://www.liveaction.org/news/south-african-cardinal-u-s-abortion-genocide-black-people/.

[861] Thomas D. Williams, "Obama Admin 'Funded Illegal Abortions in Africa' Says African Cardinal in Farewell," Breitbart, 11 January 2017, https://www.breitbart.com/politics/2017/01/11/obama-admin-funded-illegal-abortions-africa-says-african-cardinal-farewell/.

[862] "AFRICA/SOUTH AMERICA — 'Much of What Pope Francis Said Concerns the Whole of Africa' Cardinal Napier Archbishop of Durban

the problem of xenophobia in South Africa, Cardinal Napier explained that the source of tension was often from migration and the perceived threat of new immigrants. While Napier did not make any comments on appropriate immigration policy more generally, he did say the following:

> So, I feel for the local people who feel that their job opportunities, their housing opportunities; their education and all these other things that they ardently desire to have in a better way than they may be having at present, that these may be denied them because of foreigners that come in. [863]

Islam and Interreligious Dialogue

As part of his work to combat poverty in South Africa, Napier has participated in interreligious dialogue in his diocese. He carried out joint activities with Islamic leaders in his role as archbishop of Durban,[864] including a joint Muslim-Christian initiative for the homeless,[865] and acted as chair of an interfaith panel discussion during the Durban climate-change talks.[866] The tension between religious groups has also been highlighted by the SACBC,

---

Remarks," *Agenzia Fides*, 3 December 2015, http://www.fides.org/en/news/59034-AFRICA_SOUTH_AFRICA_Much_of_what_Pope_Francis_said_concerns_the_whole_of_Africa_Cardinal_Napier_Archbishop_of_Durban_remarks.

863   "Cool Hand Cardinal."

864   Cardinal Napier (@CardinalNapier), "... Denis Hurley Centre AGM for Trustees and Supporters of the Centre, including Buddhist leader, Islamic leader, several Christian leaders and score of Parishioners," Twitter, 5 February 2018, 2:42 a.m., https://twitter.com/CardinalNapier/status/960418223387705345; Russell Pollitt, S.J., "Bishops Meet with Other Faith Leaders," *Spotlight Africa*, 29 January 2018, https://spotlight.africa/2018/01/29/bishops-meet-with-other-faith-leaders/.

865   DBN Archdiocese, "DHC—Joint Muslim-Christian Initiative for the Homeless," Catholic Archdiocese of Durban, 25 June 2015, http://www.catholic-dbn.org.za/dhc-joint-muslim-christian-initiative-for-the-homeless/.

866   Martina Liebsch, "Durban Talks: Climate Justice and Food Security," Caritas, 12 December 2011, https://www.caritas.org/2011/12/durban-talks-climate-justice-and-food-security/.

which, for example, wrote about the religious persecution of Christians in Iraq in its August 2014 bulletin:

> As Catholic bishops of Southern Africa, we beg for religious tolerance in Iraq.... The utter destruction of ancient dioceses, vibrant parishes and faithful families because of their loyalty to faith is a crime against humanity. We also bear in our hearts those other religious traditions of Iraq who suffer the same fate as the Christian community.[867]

The statement expressed admiration for "many of the great religious teachings of Islam, particularly their care for the poor and the needy."[868] At a 2016 interfaith meeting at a mosque in Durban, the cardinal stated that "all our religions teach us acceptance, respect and love"[869] and that it was most important to "find renewal and reform in improving our relations between people like us gathered here today."[870] Cardinal Napier has not publicly identified any deep theological incompatibility between Islam and Christianity. He has rather drawn attention to a distinction between faithful Muslims and those driven by extremism.[871]

Evangelization

Napier has been an active advocate of continuous evangelization efforts in his diocese. During the 2016 Year of Mercy, he called for his diocese to address the urgent task of evangelization:

---

[867] "Statement on Iraq," *Catholic Archdiocese of Durban Newsletter* 1, no. 7 (11 August 2014): 2, http://www.catholic-dbn.org.za/wp-content/uploads/2014/09/Arch-Dbn-Newsletter-Aug-2014.pdf.

[868] Ibid.

[869] Arthi Sanpath, "Call for Unity on Eve of Ramadaan," *IOL*, 4 June 2016, https://www.iol.co.za/news/south-africa/kwazulu-natal/call-for-unity-on-eve-of-ramadaan-2030471.

[870] Ibid.

[871] In the same statement, the bishops "call on faithful Muslims who believe in our common humanity to plead with those driven by extremism to cease their oppression of deeply religious communities and to seek that peace which Islam itself endeavors to promote." See "Statement on Iraq," *Catholic Archdiocese of Durban Newsletter*, 2.

But what of those who don't know God, or His Son, Jesus? That's where you and I come in! It is our task to spread the message of God's mercy. And through the Missions—the work of every religious, and every lay person, and friends like you who support the Missions, this can be accomplished.[872]

The cardinal encouraged his flock to ask Our Lady to intercede in their evangelization efforts. Although he did not comment on the role of Our Lady as a model for women in family life, Napier did state that she is a source of inspiration for the evangelization mission of all Catholics. He explained that

moved by the Spirit, she welcomed the Word of life in the depths of her humble faith. May the Virgin Mother help us to say our own "yes", conscious of the urgent need to make the Good News of Jesus resound in our time. May she obtain for us renewed zeal in bringing to everyone the Good News of the life that is victorious over death. May she intercede for us so that we can acquire the holy audacity needed to discover new ways to bring the gift of salvation to every man and woman.[873]

It is clear that Napier understands the Catholic Church as containing the fullness of the truth and a corresponding divine law. In his own words:

The justice of God means you must keep his law, but when you've broken that law, how does his mercy come into play? That, I think, is the dilemma that we are having to handle and we have to keep that before us leading up to the synod, at the synod and beyond the synod.[874]

---

[872] Mission Office, "The 'Year of Mercy,' Zulu Missions," Catholic Archdiocese of Durban, 5 March 2016, https://zulumissions.co.za/message-from-cardinal-napier/.

[873] Archdiocese of Durban, *Catholic News Bulletin: Pope's Message for World Mission Sunday* (Durban: Archdiocese of Durban, 2017), http://www.catholic-dbn.org.za/wp-content/uploads/2017/10/september-2017-bulletin.pdf.

[874] Carol Glatz, "Cardinals Say Synod on Family Will Seek to Balance Truth, God's Mercy," *Catholic Courier*, 25 February 2014, https://catholiccourier.com/articles/cardinals-say-synod-on-family-will-seek-to-balance-truth-gods-mercy.

As any believer, of whatever faith, will readily affirm, you cannot ask for and expect to receive God's blessing unless you are willing and committed to submit to His will; in particular as it is expressed in His Commandments.[875]

OPPOSING APARTHEID

Cardinal Napier worked to end the apartheid regime while speaking out against the revenge and violence that the some in the liberation forces were advocating.[876] In the late 1970s, the South African bishops issued a declaration that stated that "the Catholic Church in South Africa [was] lagging behind in witness to the Gospel in matters of social justice."[877] After the declaration was made, Napier found inspiration in his episcopal motto, *Pax et Bonum*, which became "a call to do whatever is necessary to ensure that the joys and hopes … especially of those who are poor … would be heeded."[878] Thus encouraged, Napier got involved in mediation work during the struggles against the apartheid regime. For example, he took part in the work of the Patriotic Front and the Rustenburg Conference of Churches.[879] He explained that collegiality, defined as "the

[875] Admin, "Speaking the truth will set our country free," *Gateway News*, 31 January 2013, http://gatewaynews.co.za/speaking-the-truth-will-set-our-country-free/.

[876] Catholic University of America, "Cardinal Wilfrid Napier talks about Reconciliation in Southern Africa," YouTube video, 56:48, posted 19 February 2016, https://www.youtube.com/watch?v=Zur8USrH5jY.

[877] Hadro, "Struggle against Apartheid."

[878] Catholic University of America, "Reconciliation in Southern Africa."

[879] Ibid. The Patriotic Front was a collaboration between the African National Congress and the Pan-Africanist Congress, South Africa's two largest liberation movements during the apartheid regime. The Rustenburg Conference of Churches was an ecumenical conference of 230 delegates from 80 churches and 40 other church-related groups that met and made a declaration on "the unequivocal rejection of apartheid as a sin" and

participation of Bishops in the government of the Catholic Church in collaboration with the Pope,"[880] was a crucial tool in fighting apartheid. During the struggle, Napier explained that his initial aim was to "facilitate a consultation, which would engage every Church member in the search for the best way to ... remove apartheid thinking, speaking and acting from society [and] ... in the first instance from the Church's own day to day life."[881] This consultation took place between bishops as well as between the bishops and the laity and was "the basic strength of the Catholic Church and the foundation stone"[882] for the important and crucial role that it played in ending the regime.

Napier noted that the Catholic Church did not simply issue a simple statement or declaration expressing the Church's social teaching. The Church, instead, successfully moved from "statements and declarations against apartheid to trendsetting policies and transforming actions within the Church itself."[883] One example cited by Napier was the Church's reaction to the June 1976 Soweto student uprising. In Napier's words, "the Bishops formulated and then began immediately implementing their 'Declaration of Commitment on Social Justice and Race Relations within the Church' in all Catholic institutions";[884] this led to a strategy of noncompliance that was spearheaded by the opening of "Catholic schools

---

acknowledged that churches had played a "heretical part in the policy of apartheid which has led to such extreme suffering for so many in our land." See David B. Ottaway, "S. African Sects Condemn Apartheid," *Washington Post*, 10 November 1990, https://www.washingtonpost.com/archive/politics/1990/11/10/s-african-sects-condemn-apartheid/357b7403-bfef-4c18-a3b4-f1db1f278242/?utm_term=.00ac19a243e8.

[880] Wilfrid Cardinal Napier, "What Made Synod 2014 and 2015 So Interesting?: Collegiality and Synodality!" *Jurist* 6, no. 2 (2016): 327-38, doi:10.1353/jur.2016.0021.

[881] Ibid.

[882] Ibid.

[883] Ibid.

[884] Ibid.

to students of all races—which contrasted with the government's policy of segregation at the time."[885]

Napier admitted that there was a "racial mindset and attitude of Catholics ... as a result of generations of indoctrination and division on the basis of race."[886] To tackle this deeply embedded mindset, Napier commented that the Catholics of South Africa "needed a paradigm shift to bring them to recognise that each and every person has equally dignity and worth."[887] This shift is still taking place, and Napier has spoken in many forums about the importance of ongoing race reconciliation in South Africa, urging each group to "go beyond themselves."[888] He has spoken recently about the developments in South Africa after the fall of the apartheid regime and criticized the ANC government for not substantially improving the education system that existed under the apartheid regime. For Napier, there is still much more work to be done in the area of democracy and education in South Africa.[889]

Napier has clearly stated that the mission of the Church in South Africa goes beyond ending racial segregation. The Church's mission is to transform hearts and minds. As a result, the cardinal called for the Church in South Africa to be a "Community Serving God, Humanity, and All Creation,"[890] committed to Christ's missionary mandate. In Napier's words, "we are not a community focused only on removing the evil effects of colonialism and apartheid." We are "rather committed to becoming a community of those baptized to be the images of God, by introducing all men and women into the community of those who live God's life of community in the Trinity."[891]

---

[885] Hadro, "Struggle against Apartheid."

[886] Napier, "What Made Synod 2014 and 2015 So Interesting?"

[887] Ibid.

[888] Catholic University of America, "Napier Talks about Reconciliation."

[889] James Orillion, "South Africa's Cardinal Napier Reflects on Vatican Finances," St. Joseph Catholic Church, 9 September 2014, https://stjoerayne.org/2014/09/09/south-africas-cardinal-napier-reflects-on-vatican-finances/.

[890] Cardinal Wilfrid Napier, "Cardinal's Corner," *Catholic News Bulletin* (March 2018): 10, http://www.catholic-dbn.org.za/march-2018-bulletin/.

[891] Cardinal Wilfrid Napier, "Cardinal's Corner," *Catholic News Bulletin* (June 2018): 39, http://www.catholic-dbn.org.za/june-2018-bulletin/.

SUMMARY

Considered a slightly progressive-leaning centrist from the global south, Cardinal Wilfrid Napier has been on papabile lists since the conclave of 2005. Our research shows that concerning the liturgy, he has a devotion to the Eucharist, values reverence in church, and sees a drifting away from the Eucharist as a sign of lukewarmness in priests. He is a firm proponent of the Novus Ordo because he sees it as a better reflection of lay participation envisioned at Vatican II. He has been publicly critical of the Extraordinary Form of the Roman Rite, once equating the traditional Mass to a bygone age of "supreme clericalism."

Cardinal Napier has a reputation of being an attentive pastor and is a keen user of Twitter to vent sometimes frank and unguarded opinions. The cardinal has often been a vocal supporter of Francis and believes synodality and collegiality—two of the central themes of this pontificate—are important for Church reform. But he has also been publicly critical of some aspects of this pontificate, notably aspects of the family synod of 2014 and the working document of the 2018 youth synod, where his interventions tended to be in defense of Africa against the imposition of Western secular values, especially on life issues, and in support of traditional marriage in the face of polygamy and the push to allow "remarried" divorcees to receive Holy Communion. He believes the West can learn from Africa, especially what the faithful of the continent can teach about seeing man created in the image and likeness of God.

Cardinal Napier is fiercely pro-life and has been especially vocal against abortion, ideological colonization, and same-sex unions. He has been consistent in his opposition to condom use to prevent the spread of HIV and AIDS. He has blamed the sex abuse crisis partly on the period after the Second Vatican Council and has said he would filter out homosexual candidates from the priesthood early on in the selection process. Although he has made mistakes in presenting the abuse crisis in the media, he has not been accused of abuse himself or of its cover-up.

Cardinal Napier favors a sensible immigration policy that is welcoming while protecting host countries or regions and has often spoken up for the poor and against poverty. The cardinal actively engaged in anti-apartheid work but has also been critical of the ruling ANC government in the areas of democracy and education.

Despite Cardinal Napier's having turned seventy-five in 2016, as of April 2020 Pope Francis had retained him as archbishop of Durban, and the cardinal continues to be a member of the Vatican's Council for the Economy, an indication of Francis' trust in the cardinal's commitment to financial probity.

SERVICE TO THE CHURCH

Ordination to the Priesthood: 25 July 1970, Order of Friars Minor
Ordination to the Episcopate: 28 February 1981
Elevation to the College of Cardinals: 21 February 2001[892]

Education
- Novitiate, Franciscan Friary, Killarney, Ireland
- 1964: University College, Galway; Latin and English (B.A.)
- 1970: Catholic University of Louvain; philosophy and theology (M.A.)
- 1995: University College, Galway; Honorary Doctor of Laws

---

[892] Cardinal Napier submitted his resignation at the age of seventy-five, as required by canon law. Pope Francis asked the cardinal to continue in his position. Erin Carelse, "Pope Asks Cardinal Napier to Stay on in Durban," *Southern Cross*, 25 April 2018, https://www.scross.co.za/2018/04/pope-asks-cardinal-napier-to-stay-on-in-durban/.

Assignments

- 1970-1981: Priest, Parish of Lusikisiki
- 1978: Apostolic administrator, Diocese of Kokstad
- 1981: Bishop, Diocese of Kokstad
- 1987-1994: President, South African Catholic Bishops' Conference
- 1992: Archbishop, Archdiocese of Durban
- 1994-2008: Apostolic administrator, Diocese of Umzimkulu
- 1999-2008: President, South African Catholic Bishops' Conference
- 2001-present: Cardinal-priest, Titular Church, San Francesco d'Assisi ad Acilia
- 2009: President delegate, Second Special Assembly for Africa of the Synod of Bishops
- 2014: Participant, III Extraordinary General Assembly of the Synod of Bishops
- 2014: Member, Council for the Economy, Council of Cardinals for the Study of Organizational and Economic Affairs of the Holy See
- 2015: President delegate, XIV Ordinary General Assembly of the Synod of Bishops
- 2019-present: Chair, Department of Finance, South African Catholic Bishops' Conference

Membership

- Congregation for the Evangelization of Peoples
- Congregation for Institutes of Consecrated Life and Societies of Apostolic Life
- Council for the Economy
- Council of Cardinals for the Study of Organizational and Economic Affairs of the Holy See

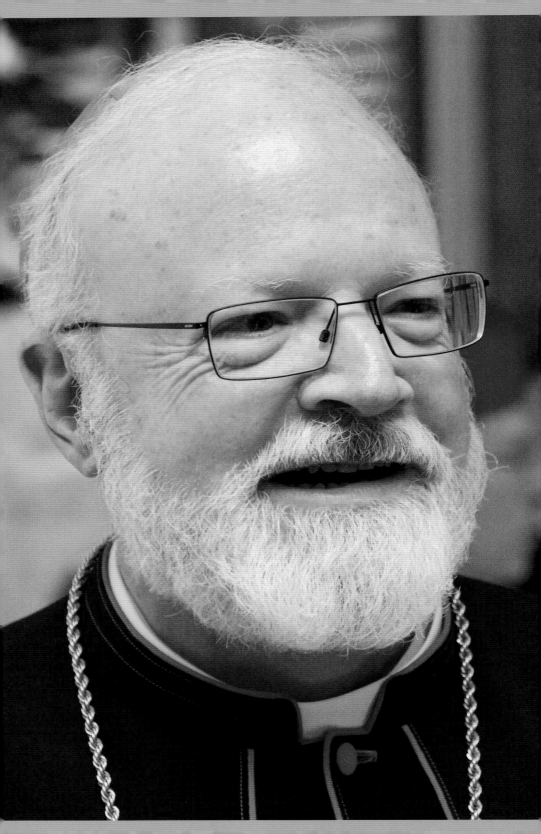

SEÁN PATRICK CARDINAL O'MALLEY, O.F.M. CAP.

"Do Whatever He Tells You"

Born: 29 June 1944
Lakewood, Ohio, USA
Nationality: American
Title: Archbishop of Boston

BIOGRAPHY

One of three children, Seán O'Malley grew up in a devout Irish family in Pennsylvania, United States. He recalls learning to serve Mass at six o'clock in the morning at the local Irish parish, even before he made his First Communion.[893] At the age of twelve, he entered a Franciscan minor

---

[893] Antonio Enrique, "Cardinal O'Malley Speaks on Significance of Elevation, Challenges of the Church," *Boston Pilot*, 31 March 2006, https://www.thebostonpilot.com/article.asp?ID=2981.

seminary and boarding school. He then attended Capuchin College in Washington, D.C., and the Catholic University of America, eventually professing vows as a Capuchin friar in 1965. After ordination as a priest in 1970, he earned a Ph.D. in Spanish and Portuguese literature, which he put to use as a professor at Catholic University and as a chaplain to Latinos in the Washington, D.C., area for many years.

In 1984, John Paul II appointed O'Malley bishop, and he served the Virgin Islands in the episcopal capacity until 1992. O'Malley subsequently served in the sees of Fall River, Palm Beach, and eventually Boston. Created a cardinal in 2006 by Benedict XVI, O'Malley has been very active on apostolic fronts, including serving as apostolic visitor for many seminaries in Central America and the Caribbean, working to clean up dioceses harmed in the sexual abuse crisis, and being an active blogger. On April 13, 2013, Pope Francis made him a member of the Council of Cardinals to advise him on reforms of universal Church governance. On February 17, 2018, O'Malley was reappointed by the pope to a second term as head of the Pontifical Commission for the Protection of Minors. He was on a number of shortlists at the last conclave, finding unexpected favor from Italians. Cardinal O'Malley's bishop's ring is inscribed with Mary's words at the wedding feast in Cana: "Do whatever He tells you."

SANCTIFYING OFFICE

Importance of Sunday Mass

Seán Cardinal O'Malley published a pastoral letter in 2011 on the Solemnity of Christ the King that captures his teaching on the significance and role of Sunday Mass in the lives of believers.

The timing of his letter may have been due in part to the new English translation of the Roman Missal that came out around that time, and in part to the Catholics Come Home initiative that had been launched on Ash Wednesday that year.

In the pastoral letter, O'Malley elaborates on both "Jesus' eager desire ... to celebrate this thanksgiving meal with every one of us" and on the two-thousand-year history of Christians' risking their lives to participate in Sunday Mass.[894] He reiterates the ancient symbolism of sharing a family thanksgiving meal, a *Eucharistic* meal, with fellow Catholics, and compares Christian discipleship to a lifelong family pilgrimage. In this way, he points out the dangers of an unhealthy individualism that would keep believers from joining the feast.[895]

The cardinal expresses sadness that so many Catholics "choose to be absent from Mass." He recounts examples of oppressed Catholics in other countries who appreciate "that the Mass is so precious," and then calls on the faithful to "never take for granted the wonder that is the encounter we have with God each Sunday that we celebrate the Eucharist together."[896]

O'Malley extensively quotes Pope Benedict's description of what happens at Mass: "Here now is the central act of transformation that alone can truly renew the world. The Body and Blood of Christ are given to us so that we ourselves will be transformed in our turn. We are to become the Body of Christ."[897] O'Malley describes the very real efficacy of Mass participation. "The graces and transformative insights God provides in each celebration of Mass help us move toward a happier, holier life." Quoting St. John Paul II, O'Malley adds that the "Eucharist is a ... foretaste of the fullness of joy promised by Christ; it is in some way the anticipation of heaven."[898]

---

[894] Cardinal Seán P. O'Malley, O.F.M. Cap., "Jesus' Eager Desire: Our Participation in the Sunday Mass," Archdiocese of Boston, 20 November 2011, https://www.bostoncatholic.org/cardinal-sean-patrick-omalley-ofm-cap/importance-sunday-mass.

[895] Ibid.

[896] Ibid.

[897] Ibid., quoting Benedict's Homily on the Occasion of the XX World Youth Day, Cologne-Marienfeld, Sunday, 21 August 2005.

[898] Ibid., quoting John Paul II's 2004 Encyclical on the Eucharist, *Ecclesia de Eucharistia* (cf. John 15:11).

The cardinal reveals a pastor's heart in the section of the pastoral letter titled "Particular Messages." The first is addressed to Catholics who have been away from Sunday Mass. Here O'Malley speaks to Catholics who feel unwelcome at Mass because of "some irregularity or moral struggle." He reaffirms God's love and the welcome that the Catholic community desires to give to such persons. The cardinal acknowledges the various reasons why people are not in the pews and then develops two thoughts. First, he speaks plainly of God's ever-present love for each person, but then he asserts that Church teaching does not change because people disagree with it or have questions about it. He plainly teaches that "an inability to fulfill all aspects of Christian worship or to receive Communion should not keep you from Mass. In fact, the habit of being faithful to the Sunday obligation can provide the actual grace, if you cooperate with it, to give you the strength to overcome current obstacles and find paths of reconciliation. We stand ready to help you."[899] Here the cardinal charitably yet firmly acknowledges that the reception of the Eucharist is not a "come one, come all" event.

Cardinal O'Malley called on various groups in the Church to take concrete, practical steps to increase Mass attendance. Speaking to priests, he encourages "an emphasis on sacred music" and calls on priests and deacons to carry out their roles "with a deep sense of reverence for the mysteries" they celebrate.[900] He gives thanks and direction to parish councils and staff, Catholic school and religious-education teachers. He asks parents, and fathers in particular, to take an active role in the catechetical formation of their children and to live Sunday as the Lord's Day. Young people who witness to the joy and richness of the Faith are especially needed.

Priest as First Responder
In 2013, the Archdiocese of Boston sponsored a campaign to raise funds for the Clergy Health and Retirement Trust. A video was created to highlight

---

[899] Ibid.
[900] Ibid.

several priests serving in various capacities. In his thank-you letter for the $1.4 million raised, and with a nod to the video feature of a priest who serves as a police chaplain, the cardinal explained "that every priest, regardless of his role, serves as a first responder in fulfilling the sacramental and spiritual needs of the body of Christ."[901] The cardinal did, however, comply with directives to Catholic parishes to cancel all Masses during the coronavirus pandemic.[902]

At the Mass during which he ordained nine men to the priesthood in 2014, the cardinal preached on the Good Shepherd. Referencing the Holy Father's Chrism Mass homily of that year, he reminded his priests that Christ has anointed them with the oil of gladness and called on them to live with a spirit of missionary joy and to be energetic evangelizers.[903]

O'Malley said of the priest's role as confessor: "One of the greatest joys of a priest is to bring those words of comfort — Go in peace, your sins are forgiven." He encouraged his priests to "use the sacrament of God's mercy" to deepen their *own* conversion. "The confessional is the emergency room of the field hospital that is the church. Learn to be a man of compassion and mercy so as to help your people experience God's healing mercy."[904] The cardinal shows his willingness to utilize the images of the Church that Pope Francis has used, even when such linguistic choices are unusual or particularly striking.

---

[901] Seán Cardinal O'Malley, Homily at the Fifth Anniversary Celebration of the Priesthood Dinner, Archdiocese of Boston, 23 September 2013, https://www.bostoncatholic.org/press-release/2013/09/september-23-2013-fifth-anniversary-celebration-priesthood-dinner.

[902] Lisa Kashinsky, "Cardinal O'Malley Temporarily Suspends Mass in Response to Coronavirus," *Boston Herald*, 13 March 2020, https://www.bostonherald.com/2020/03/13/cardinal-omalley-temporarily-suspends-mass-in-response-to-coronavirus/.

[903] Seán Cardinal O'Malley, Cardinal's Homily for the 2014 Ordination, Archdiocese of Boston, 24 May 2014, https://www.bostoncatholic.org/press-release/2014/05/may-24-2014-cardinals-homily-2014-ordination.

[904] Ibid.

Continuing his emphasis on the Good Shepherd, O'Malley explained: "Too often we lack the courage that shepherding requires.... We will find that courage to lead God's people, only through our prayer life and the support of priestly fraternity. Without Him we can do nothing. Without each other, we can do little." In conclusion, His Eminence blessed the ordinands thus: "May your ministry abound with the missionary joy, born of giving your life for God's people and seeking out those who have stormed off, dozed off, or just drifted away. Put them lovingly on your shoulders and rejoice with the Good Shepherd."[905]

In his pastoral letter on mercy for the Year of Mercy (2016), Cardinal O'Malley urged Catholics to come to the sacrament of Reconciliation. The letter, titled "God's Mercy Runs to Meet Us," was published on Divine Mercy Sunday. In it O'Malley explained: "Each confession is an encounter with the merciful Lord, who, like the loving father in the Parable of the Prodigal Son, runs out to meet us and rejoices when we return to him.... If we have been away for a long time, like the younger son in the parable, it is now time to 'come to our senses' and to realize that we will be better off to be with our Father who loves us."[906] As he encourages his flock to make a more frequent habit of confessing their sins, the cardinal quotes his dad: "When it's time to get a haircut, it's time to go to confession."[907]

Cardinal O'Malley appears not to be averse to the Extraordinary Form of the Roman Rite, and there is record of his administering the sacrament of Confirmation in the *Vetus Ordo* in Boston in 2011.[908]

---

[905] Ibid.

[906] Cardinal Seán P. O'Malley, "God's Mercy Runs to Meet Us," *Boston Pilot*, 2 April 2016, https://www.thebostonpilot.com/opinion/article.asp?ID=176149.

[907] Ibid.

[908] Augustinus, "Cardinal O'Malley of Boston to Confirm According to the Traditional Rite in His Cathedral," *Rorate Caeli*, 30 May 2011, https://rorate-caeli.blogspot.com/2011/05/cardinal-omalley-of-boston-to-confirm.html.

GOVERNING OFFICE

Archbishop of Boston

Since Seán O'Malley became archbishop of Boston in 2003, the number of Catholics in the archdiocese decreased from almost 53 percent of the population to 47 percent in 2015.[909] The number of diocesan priests decreased from 867 to 685. The number of parishes decreased from 360 to 289.[910] These statistics track the general decline in numbers of professed Catholics and perhaps, in this diocese, especially because of the fallout from the sexual abuse crisis in the American Catholic Church. The number of permanent deacons, on the other hand, has increased from 246 in 2003 to an all-time high of 280 in 2015. This represents solid growth, especially from the low of 234 deacons in 2006.[911] The diaconate program is ordaining a new class every year.[912] In May of 2018, moreover, seven men were ordained to the priesthood; in 2019 the largest number of new priests in more than twenty years was ordained—thirteen. The cardinal opined on his blog that this was probably the largest ordination class of 2019 in the United States.[913] This is a sign of hope, of course, and of trust in O'Malley as the shepherd of his flock.

Considered a moderate, conservative-leaning Catholic, O'Malley has long been a consistent advocate for the unborn and for refugees and

---

[909] "Archdiocese of Boston," Catholic Hierarchy, www.catholic-hierarchy. org/diocese/dbost.html#stats.

[910] Ibid.

[911] Ibid. To illustrate the recent health of the program, thirteen men were ordained to the diaconate in September 2014, seven in 2017. Cf. Seán Cardinal O'Malley, "Reflecting on the Synod," *Cardinal Seán's Blog*, 25 October 2019, http://cardinalseansblog.org/2019/10/25/reflecting-on-the-synod/.

[912] Seán Cardinal O'Malley, "Ordaining Our New Permanent Deacons," *Cardinal Seán's Blog*, 6 October 2017, www.cardinalseansblog.org/2017/10/06/ ordaining-our-new-permanent-deacons-2/.

[913] Seán Cardinal O'Malley, "13 New Priests for Boston," *Cardinal Seán's Blog*, 24 May 2019, http://www.cardinalseansblog.org/2019/05/24/.

immigrants. On the eve of his appointment as archbishop of Boston, the *Boston Globe* described the prelate in these words:

> But O'Malley clearly met one key Vatican requirement for the Boston appointment: He has a lengthy and generally admired record for cleaning up dioceses sullied by sex abuse scandals. In 1992, he was appointed to head the Fall River Diocese, which was reeling from disclosure of abuse by the Rev. James R. Porter, and last year, O'Malley was appointed to the Palm Beach Diocese after two bishops in five years resigned after being accused of molesting boys....
>
> According to people who know him, O'Malley is an intelligent, spiritual man who speaks many languages. He wears a full beard and the habit of his order: a floor-length brown robe, a long pointed hood (the "capuchin"), sandals, and a white cord with three knots to remind him of his three vows, poverty, chastity, and obedience.[914]

Cardinal Blogger

O'Malley was among the first (if not the first) ordinaries to launch his own blog, which he did shortly after arriving in Boston. He was certainly the first cardinal in the world to launch a personal blog when he did so in 2006.[915] The entries clearly required thought and care on the prelate's part. Photos, videos, texts of sermons, and talks are accessible there. The blog posts reveal a priest who cares for and instructs the priests, seminarians, members of religious orders, immigrants, parishioners, and employees of his diocese.

Even in the reporting of small matters, the cardinal's blog posts reveal much about his governing initiatives. When he served as bishop of Saint Thomas, for example, Seán O'Malley started a Catholic television station in the Caribbean. Mother Angelica went there to help him. Years later, after she died in 2016, he celebrated a Memorial Mass for Mother Angelica on the

---

[914] Ibid.
[915] "About Cardinal Seán," Archdiocese of Boston, https://www.bostoncatholic.org/.

feast of Corpus Christi.[916] Elsewhere, the cardinal mentions in his posts the work of Fellowship of Catholic University Students (FOCUS) missionaries in campus ministry[917] as well as the ministry and work of Opus Dei members.[918]

Parish Closings

In 2004, during his first year in Boston, then-Archbishop O'Malley followed through on Bishop Richard G. Lennon's recommendations to close many parishes. Bishop Lennon served as archdiocesan administrator after Cardinal Law resigned in late 2002, and during his tenure, he oversaw the selection process for parish closings. As a result of O'Malley's actions, sixty-five parishes were closed, five merged with other parishes, and five more were to be kept open for Sunday Mass only.[919] A large number (120) of affiliated buildings were slated to be closed and sold, as were close to a dozen more in Lawrence and Lowell. O'Malley said at the time that money from the closings would not go toward the $85 million settlement reached by the diocese, home to more than five hundred victims of sexual abuse.[920] He did, however, decide "to sell millions of dollars' worth of archdiocesan property, including the archbishop's mansion, to settle clergy abuse claims."[921]

---

[916] Cardinal Seán O'Malley, "Pastoral Letter on Mercy," *Cardinal Seán's Blog,* 1 April 2016, http://www.cardinalseansblog.org/2016/04/01/.

[917] Cardinal Seán O'Malley, "Walking with Mary," *Cardinal Seán's Blog,* 8 April 2016, http://www.cardinalseansblog.org/2016/04/08/.

[918] Cardinal Seán O'Malley, "A Disappointing Decision by the Supreme Court," *Cardinal Seán's Blog,* 26 June 2015, http://www.cardinalseans-blog.org/2015/06/26/; "Cardinal O'Malley's Homily for Feast of Saint Josemaria," *Opus Dei,* 23 June 2015, https://opusdei.org/en-us/article/cardinal-omalleys-homily/.

[919] Pam Belluck, "Archdiocese in Boston Plans to Close 65 Catholic Parishes by the End of the Year," *New York Times,* 26 May 2004, https://www.nytimes.com/2004/05/26/us/archdiocese-in-boston-plans-to-close-65-catholic-parishes-by-the-end-of-the-year.html.

[920] Ibid.

[921] "Cardinal Seán's Profile," *Cardinal Seán's Blog,* http://www.cardinalseans-blog.org/cardinal-seans-profile/.

Pontifical Commission for the Protection of Minors

Cardinal O'Malley has headed the Pontifical Commission for the Protection of Minors since it was set up by Pope Francis in 2014 in response to victims who questioned whether the Church understood the full extent of the problem. The cardinal has been the public face of the commission, but the day-to-day running of it is left to its secretary, Bostonian priest Msgr. Robert Oliver. Frequently the commission is mistaken as an investigative body of abuse crimes, whereas it is primarily preventative and does not deal with individual cases. In its early years, the commission had on its panel, along with experts in child protection, abuse survivors Peter Saunders and Marie Collins. Both were critical of how the Vatican was responding to victims' concerns, and voluntarily left their associations with the body. The commission has also not had an easy ride fitting in and winning cooperation with other Vatican bodies, and its relationship with the Congregation for the Doctrine of the Faith, which handles individual cases, is unclear.[922] Furthermore, its most significant proposal—to create an in-house Vatican tribunal to judge cases of bishops who are accused of failing to protect victims—was initially approved by Pope Francis but has since stalled, though not, it seems, because of any fault of the commission or O'Malley's leadership.

Despite O'Malley's track record and prominence in the field of dealing with clergy sexual abuse, Pope Francis overlooked him as the American representative on a four-member preparation committee ahead of the Vatican's 2019 global summit of bishops on child protection. The pope chose Cardinal Blase Cupich of Chicago instead, although O'Malley was relatively prominent during the meeting itself. He co-chaired a press conference with Cupich during the event and stressed the importance of "transparency" in the United States and the Vatican when it comes to confronting sexual abuse. He was speaking in the context of high-profile

---

[922] Phil Lawler, "Vatican Reform on Sexual Abuse Has Stalled," Catholic Culture, 22 March 2017, https://www.catholicculture.org/commentary/vatican-reform-on-sexual-abuse-has-stalled/.

abusers such as Theodore McCarrick.[923] The reasons for Francis' decision not to include O'Malley in the preparation committee are unknown.[924]

Handling of Two Letters on Abuse

In April 2015, Marie Collins and three other members of the Pontifical Commission for the Protection of Minors personally handed a letter to O'Malley written by an abuse victim detailing abuse that Chilean Fr. Fernando Karadima had inflicted, and claiming the abuse was witnessed by other clergy members (photographs made public show Collins handing the letter to O'Malley). O'Malley assured Collins he had delivered the letter to the pope, contradicting Pope Francis' own claims made on a trip to Chile that victims who accused one of those clergy members, Bishop Juan Barros, of knowing about Karadima's abuse were spreading calumny against him.[925] O'Malley never denied giving the letter. He declined to comment publicly, preferring instead to direct all inquiries to the Vatican.

Another letter, also written in 2015, regards New York priest Fr. Boniface Ramsey, who had detailed accusations against former cardinal and priest Theodore McCarrick and sent them to O'Malley because of his role as head of the child protection commission. In 2018, O'Malley apologized for not seeing the letter.[926] The incident caused some surprise

---

[923] Inés San Martín, "O'Malley Wants Vatican Report on Who Knew What about McCarrick," *Crux*, 22 February 2019, https://cruxnow.com/february-abuse-summit/2019/02/omalley-wants-vatican-report-on-who-knew-what-about-mccarrick/.

[924] John L. Allen Jr., "How to Read Overlooking O'Malley to Plan Rome Abuse Summit," *Crux*, 24 November 2018, https://cruxnow.com/news-analysis/2018/11/how-to-read-overlooking-omalley-to-plan-rome-abuse-summit/.

[925] Meghna Chakrabarti and Lily Tyson, "2015 Letter Contradicts Claim That Pope Did Not Know About Chilean Sexual Abuse," Radio Boston, 6 February 2018, https://www.wbur.org/radioboston/2018/02/06/letter-pope-chile.

[926] "Cardinal O'Malley Apologizes for Missed Letter on McCarrick Allegations," Catholic News Agency, 21 August 2018, https://www.catholicnewsagency.com/news/cardinal-omalley-apologizes-for-missed-letter-on-mccarrick-allegations-14053.

in view of O'Malley's reputation for advocating "zero tolerance" when it comes to clergy sexual abuse (see more on this in the later section: "Clergy Sexual Abuse: Cleaning Up the Mess").[927]

Hope in Crisis

In March 2019, Cardinal O'Malley gave a talk to seminarians and young religious in which he was asked to speak about causes for hope in the Church today. Speaking to an audience of hundreds at Catholic University of America, where he is a member of the board of directors, he said:

> In this terrible time of crisis, it is only holiness that is going to help the Church move forward. If we are faithful to our formation and faithful in taking care of people, and if our words and actions are paired with the values of the Gospel and what we profess in our faith, only then will we be able to bring healing to our Church and all those who have been wronged by it.[928]

Funeral of Edward Kennedy

Cardinal O'Malley drew controversy in 2009 when he attended the funeral of Edward M. Kennedy. The senator had been a lifelong supporter of abortion. O'Malley defended his decision by appealing for greater civility among Catholics when discussing divisive issues and warned against "harsh judgments" and attributing "the worst motives" to people with whom Catholics have disagreements. Such attitudes, he wrote on his blog, "do irreparable damage to the communion of the Church." He added: "If any

---

[927] Ed Condon, "Will Cardinal O'Malley's Response to McCarrick Allegations Be Enough?," *Catholic News Agency*, 26 July 2018, https://www.catholicnewsagency.com/news/will-cardinal-omalleys-response-to-mccarrick-allegations-be-enough-47597.

[928] Seán Cardinal O'Malley, "Meeting with Priests, Seminarians and Religious," *Cardinal Seán's Blog*, 22 March 2019, www.cardinalseansblog.org/2019/03/22/.

cause is motivated by judgment, anger or vindictiveness, it will be doomed to marginalization and failure."[929]

TEACHING OFFICE

New Evangelization

In an interview with the *Boston Pilot* shortly after his elevation to the cardinalate, O'Malley spoke of the importance of the New Evangelization. The task of evangelization is vital and is "directed not just to the mission '*ad gentes*,' the foreign mission, but to our own supposedly Christian societies where many people have received the sacraments and yet are not truly on fire with their faith. They don't understand their faith or live their faith so we need to once again reach out to those who at least are nominally Catholics and invite them to be a part of the community and help them to understand the Church's teachings."[930] The cardinal lamented the "privatization of religion" which has seen it become "very sentimental, very personal."[931] But, O'Malley warned, "Jesus did not come so we can have the 'warm fuzzies.' He came to establish a Church, a people, and to give us a mission ... to recapture that sense of who we are, that we do have a personal vocation."[932]

In seeking to revitalize a sense of personal vocation through his own work of evangelization, O'Malley is conscious that witness is more powerful than words. "The best way of evangelization is the witness of holiness in the Church where Catholics live a life of discipleship and take the Gospel in all of its radical nature seriously and do that joyfully and lovingly. Because if we are trying to convince people by arguing sort of

---

[929] Michael Paulson, "O'Malley Defends Role at Kennedy Rites," *Boston.com*, http://archive.boston.com/news/local/massachusetts/articles/2009/09/03/omalley_defends_kennedy_funeral_role/.

[930] Enrique, "Significance of Elevation, Challenges."

[931] Ibid.

[932] Ibid.

the peripheral, ethical issues out there, we'll never convince them."[933] Evangelization must bring people to know and encounter Christ on a personal level. Personal witness, the cardinal argues, is the most effective means of bringing about that encounter. At the same time, O'Malley takes his role as a teacher seriously and has written and spoken on a wide-ranging array of pressing issues facing the Church.

Right-to-Life Defender

O'Malley issued a strong statement upholding the right to life in response to the enactment of a permissive abortion law in New York and the governor of New York's comments in support of the law. The governor of New York argued that pro-life Catholics should not try to impose their religion on the country and reflect their views in law. O'Malley, in a statement released on February 9, 2019, countered that "opposition to abortion is not a 'Catholic issue.' ... Abortion, like racism, anti-Semitism, and human trafficking are violations of human rights. Innocent human life should be protected by civil laws."[934] Defending innocent human life, he added, "is the obligation of all governments and all people whatever their religious affiliation might be or not be."[935]

"The eroding of the sacredness of human life is a slippery slope that begins with abortion, moves to euthanasia and then the elimination of the weak, feeble, and the 'undesirable' whose lives are not as important and are inconvenient," O'Malley has argued. "Cheapening human life is to devaluate all life."[936] The cardinal has, in this instance and many others, witnessed to the truth of Church teaching on the inviolability of human life, even in the face of public opposition and in contradiction to the politics

---

[933] Ibid.

[934] Seán Cardinal O'Malley, "Statement of Cardinal O'Malley," Archdiocese of Boston, 9 February 2019, https://www.bostoncatholic.org/press-release/2019/02/february-9-2019-statement-cardinal-omalley.

[935] Ibid. O'Malley further explained that abortion is a "matter of public morality and the defense of human rights."

[936] Ibid.

of the day. In the spring of 2019, O'Malley criticized legislative proposals to make abortion access more permissive in the state of Massachusetts. In opposing the legislation, O'Malley emphasized that he does not "seek to impose the Catholic Church's teachings on a diverse society but wish[es] to help build a society which protects human life from its inception to natural death."[937]

In 2013, O'Malley spoke with the *Catholic Herald* to urge Irish Catholics to oppose the abortion lobby seeking to liberalize abortion laws in Ireland. He stated plainly, "Abortion is the taking of an innocent human life; everyone should resist abortion."[938]

O'Malley's public witness in defense of human life demonstrates his commitment to the Church's teaching that there are without-exception negative moral norms (such as "do not kill the innocent") that bind all people in all places, even those wielding public authority. The cardinal has been a vocal opponent of legislative measures in the United States seeking to legalize physician-assisted suicide and has expressed strong support of Church teaching condemning that practice and euthanasia. In an interview with the *National Catholic Register* in 2012, O'Malley explained that proposals to legalize physician-assisted suicide (at that time pending in the state of Massachusetts) represent "an encroachment of the culture of death," a culture that preaches that "the autonomous self needs to be in control of every moment of our lives, and if we aren't in control, the quality of life is such that we would be better off dead."[939] He lamented

---

[937] Laura Crimaldi, "Cardinal O'Malley Opposes Abortion Proposal Pending at State House," *Boston Globe*, 6 April 2019, https://www.bostonglobe.com/metro/2019/04/06/cardinal-malley-opposes-abortion-proposals-pending-state-house/e39SRcXrlYVNneStk3zwjN/story.html.

[938] Staff Reporter, "Cardinal O'Malley Urges Ireland to Stand up to Abortion Lobby," *Catholic Herald*, 10 May 2013, https://catholicherald.co.uk/cardinal-omalley-urges-ireland-to-stand-up-to-abortion-lobby/.

[939] Joan Frawley Desmond, "Cardinal O'Malley: We Can Win the Fight Against Euthanasia," *National Catholic Register*, 21 September 2012, http://www.ncregister.com/daily-news/cardinal-omalley-we-can-win-the-fight-against-euthanasia.

that so-called Death with Dignity movements treat some lives as dispensable and not worth living. This approach "strikes at the heart of the kind of compassion and mercy that the Church is supposed to be about. The sacredness of human life is cheapened by this kind of behavior."[940]

The cardinal especially lamented that most proposed legislation in this area does not contain any provision calling for psychiatric or psychological evaluations of patients prior to authorization of physician-assisted suicide, despite the fact that studies "indicate that about half of the people dying of cancer become clinically depressed and depression can lead to suicide."[941] The central moral wrong with physician-assisted suicide (and all the more so with euthanasia), O'Malley explained (quoting John Paul II), is that "to concur with the intention of another person to commit suicide and to help in carrying it out through so-called 'assisted suicide' means to cooperate in, and at times to be the actual perpetrator of, an injustice *which can never be excused*, even if it is requested."[942]

In dealing with issues related to assisted suicide and euthanasia O'Malley is careful to note that the Church's teaching "does not say that you must keep people alive by any means; we don't believe in keeping people alive when they really are dying. But assisted suicide is quite different: This person is dying, so give them poison."[943] The cardinal also argues that assisted suicide and euthanasia should be prohibited in civil law because permitting them sends pernicious messages to certain vulnerable communities, especially the elderly, the disabled, and the terminally ill. "Once you legalize this choice, it puts pressure on the terminally ill to make that choice. They begin to think, *I'm a burden on my family,*

---

[940] Ibid.

[941] Ibid.

[942] Seán Cardinal O'Malley, "Cardinal Sean O'Malley's Remarks on the Defeated Massachusetts Ballot Initiative on Physician Assisted Suicide," USCCB, http://www.usccb.org/about/leadership/usccb-general-assembly/2012-november-meeting/cardinal-omalley-ballot-initiative-on-physician-assisted-suicide.cfm (emphasis added).

[943] Desmond, "Fight Against Euthanasia."

and I'm using up their resources; so if this is permitted, I should end my life and save my family this grief."[944] The effect of this sort of thinking on the culture is degrading. The widespread mentality of "complete autonomy," O'Malley argues, is mistaken. "The truth is that we are very dependent on each other, at the beginning and the end of life in particular. We need other human beings to take care of us. And at different points in our life, we are called upon to be the caretaker. That interdependence is part of being a human being. This whole notion of complete autonomy reflects the extreme individualism of our culture."[945]

Defense of Teaching on Contraception

O'Malley has defended the Church's teaching against the use of contraception and opposed practices such as in vitro fertilization (IVF). O'Malley issued a strong condemnation of the Obama administration's Department of Health and Human Services (HHS) mandate, which required employers of a certain size, including many Catholic employers and institutions, to offer their employees health insurance coverage that included sterilization, abortion-inducing drugs, and contraception. O'Malley condemned this action for "cast[ing] aside the First Amendment to the Constitution of the United States" and "denying to Catholics our Nation's first and most fundamental freedom, that of religious liberty."[946] The cardinal notes that complying with the law would cause Catholics to "violate [their] consciences" and that Catholics "cannot simply accept this unjust law now proposed at the federal level."[947]

In a 2001 pastoral letter, O'Malley noted that "marriage is the only morally acceptable framework for human reproduction."[948] Human life is a gift, and "in the act of procreation the spouses are called to cooperate

---

[944] Ibid.

[945] Ibid.

[946] Cardinal Seán O'Malley, "Important Issues," *Cardinal Seán's Blog*, 3 February 2012, http://www.cardinalseansblog.org/2012/02/03/important-issues/.

[947] Ibid.

[948] Seán P. O'Malley, O.F.M. Cap., "In Vitro Fertilization: Ethical Implications and Alternatives: A Pastoral Letter," Corazones, 9 November 2011, https://www.corazones.org/moral/invitro_fert_omalleyeng.htm.

with God; therefore, the Church teaches that a child's coming-to-be should be sought only as a fruit of the spouses' personal loving union in the marital act."[949] The marital act, the Church has always taught, entails both unitive and procreative significance. In vitro fertilization does away with the unitive meaning of the marital act, while contraception suppresses the procreative meaning of the conjugal act.[950] In this same pastoral letter, O'Malley repeatedly emphasized the "constant and very clear" teaching of the Church on the respect that must be accorded to human embryos, no less than to all other human life.[951]

Opposition to Same-Sex "Marriage"

O'Malley opposed the legalization of same-sex "marriage" in the United States and has defended the institution of marriage as an indissoluble union of one man and one woman. In response to the Supreme Court's decision in *Obergefell v. Hodges* in 2015, O'Malley released a statement that he was "saddened" by the decision, both as a citizen of the United States and as a Catholic bishop.[952] The institution of marriage is a fundamental building block in any society, the cardinal notes, and its protection is a shared responsibility of all people. "Certainly every citizen of this land, regardless of their sexual orientation, deserves to be respected in their personal and civic life," O'Malley noted. "But enshrining same sex marriage in our constitutional system of governance has dangers that may become fully evident only over time."[953] A decade earlier, in response to developments in Massachusetts threatening to require adoption and foster agencies to place children with same-sex couples, O'Malley said that Catholic Charities

---

[949] Ibid.

[950] Ibid.

[951] Ibid.

[952] "Cardinal O'Malley Issues Statement on Supreme Court's Marriage Decision," Massachusetts Catholic Conference, https://www.macatholic. org/news-article/cardinal-omalley-issues-statement-supreme-courts-marriage-decision.

[953] Ibid.

in Boston would stop all adoption-related work rather than comply with such a law.[954]

Unclear on Communion for "Remarried" Divorcees

O'Malley was asked in a 2014 interview with the *National Catholic Register* about proposals within the Church to modify Church teaching on the indissolubility of marriage to permit Catholics who are divorced and "remarried" to receive Holy Communion. O'Malley said in response, "The Church will not change her teaching on the indissolubility of marriage."[955] It is unclear whether he has offered a definitive statement about admitting divorced-and-"remarried" Catholics to Communion. He acknowledged that Pope Francis was anxious to discuss such issues and predicted that there would be "an effort to help those people who have had a failed marriage and try to sift through ways [to consider what] can be done." The cardinal suggested that simplifying the annulment process "would be a wonderful first step for addressing a very crucial pastoral problem for the Church."[956]

Opposition to Cohabitation

In other remarks about the importance of marriage and the family as a building block of society, O'Malley has lamented that a "cohabitation mentality" is undermining a strong marital ethic in the United States. He also cites the increase in out-of-wedlock births, student debt (leading to delayed marriages), and poor marriage-preparation programs as other

---

[954] Ian Urbina, "Church May Cut Charity if D.C. Passes Gay Marriage Bill," *Chicago Tribune*, 15 November 2009, https://www.chicagotribune.com/news/ct-xpm-2009-11-15-0911140253-story.html.

[955] Joan Frawley Desmond, "Cardinal O'Malley: 'The Church Will Not Change Her Teaching on Marriage,'" *National Catholic Register*, 20 March 2014, http://www.ncregister.com/daily-news/cardinal-omalley-the-church-will-not-change-her-teaching-on-the-indissolubi.

[956] Ibid.

issues harming the marriage culture.[957] Shortly after being elevated to the cardinalate, O'Malley elaborated on this theme. "People are postponing marriage or substituting it for cohabitation or they think that marriage is only about adults. So they get married without the idea of having children, or they justify, then, same-sex 'marriage' because it is an arrangement of friendship between adults rather than a family that is to generate life, to bring children into the world, to nurture them to prepare them to be good citizens of this world, and citizens of heaven."[958]

Priestly Celibacy

Regarding a proposal to relax the discipline of mandatory clerical celibacy in the Latin Rite, O'Malley said in 2006 that married clergy were "not an impossibility because we have Eastern rite clergy and we also have married deacons." But he added: "In the mainline churches that have married clergy, they are having the same shortage of clergy in the same secularized countries."[959] So, he noted, married clergy is not the silver bullet to the problems that have appeared in recent years, and departing from the discipline of celibacy would "bring a whole set of other problems" including practical, not just theological, ones. O'Malley explained that celibacy is "not just seen for its practical value—and it does have a practical value, it makes people much more available to go wherever, to be able to serve God's people—but it's done more for the spiritual reasons behind it. In imitation of Jesus's celibate life, [celibacy is] an invitation to renunciation, to follow Him."[960] Priestly celibacy is "a sign of the Church's faith in the resurrection."[961] The cardinal sees significant practical and theological value in the charism of priestly celibacy and

[957] Adelaide Mena, "Cardinal O'Malley: Cohabitation, Student Debt Threaten Marriage," Catholic News Agency, 20 November 2013, https://www.catholicnewsagency.com/news/cardinal-omalley-cohabitation-student-debt-threaten-marriage.

[958] Enrique, "Significance of Elevation, Challenges."

[959] Ibid.

[960] Ibid.

[961] Ibid.

has been vocal in calling for serious consequences for violations of the priestly vow of celibacy.[962]

At the 2019 Amazon synod, which discussed extensively the possibility of married clergy to deal with the priest shortage in the region, O'Malley said one reason for the shortage was the lack of resources for indigenous seminaries, adding that it was important to "make sacrifices" so people can "promote vocations and accompany and train seminarians in their own milieu and their own languages." Pope Francis praised the cardinal for the remark, saying: "I thank Cardinal O'Malley for his courage in this because he put his finger on the sore in something that is a real social injustice, which is, in fact, the Indians are not allowed to go on the seminarian path and on the path of the priesthood.[963]

Women Priests

The cardinal garnered attention when in a 2014 interview on the television program *60 Minutes* he said that, were he starting a church, he would "love to have women priests."[964] While his remark was headline grabbing, he did not in the interview advocate a change of Church teaching on the priesthood. The interviewer asked O'Malley whether excluding women from the Church hierarchy was immoral, to which he responded: "Christ would never ask us to do something immoral. It's a matter of vocation and what God has given to us."[965] After noting that the laity have important roles

[962] Michael Warren Davis, "Cardinal O'Malley Condemns McCarrick's Morally Unacceptable Alleged Behaviour," *Catholic Herald*, 25 July 2018, https://catholicherald.co.uk/cardinal-omalley-condemns-mccarricks-morally-unacceptable-alleged-behaviour/.

[963] Emily Sweeney, "Pope Francis Gives Shout-Out to Cardinal O'Malley During Meeting on the Amazon Priest Shortage," *Boston Globe*, 28 October 2019, https://www.bostonglobe.com/metro/2019/10/28/pope-francis-gives-shout-out-cardinal-malley-during-meeting-amazon-priest-shortage/i6LnN6SQbvAntzoU7JN6PI/story.html.

[964] "O'Malley: If I were founding a Church I'd Love to Have Women Priests," *Catholic Herald*, 17 November 2014, https://catholicherald.co.uk/omalley-if-i-were-founding-a-church-id-love-to-have-women-priests/.

[965] Ibid.

to play and that it is not just priests who are called to be holy, O'Malley then said: "The tradition in the Church is that we ordain men. If I were founding a church, I'd love to have women priests. But Christ founded it, and what he has given us is something different."[966] The cardinal has therefore not advocated a change in Church teaching and has defended the tradition of a male priesthood, though his views on the possibility of ordaining women to the diaconate are unclear. It is likely that he would not support changes in Church teaching on such topics, regardless of his personal preferences "were [he] founding a church."

Migration Concerns

Cardinal O'Malley has been an influential spokesman for the Church on issues relating to immigration in America. O'Malley seems to treat a nation's immigration policies as calling for a Good Samaritan, tying it to the principle of Catholic social teaching commonly called the "preferential option for the poor." "By and large, our immigrants [in America] were very poor people and even the words of the Statue of Liberty remember that there was a preferential option for the poor and the unwanted from the beginning of our country."[967] He argues that Catholics in America should denounce divisive language in the immigration debate and be empathetic to the plight of immigrants. "We have to recall that we are an immigrant Church. The immigrants who have come to our country have made an incredible contribution to the life of the country, as well as the life of our Church," he said.[968] He sees the spirit of anti-immigration in America today as an "aberration" in America's history, one that is neither American nor Catholic. "If we become an unwelcoming, closed country, we're going to suffer the consequences of our selfishness."[969]

---

[966] Ibid.

[967] Christopher White, "Cardinal O'Malley: America Has Always Had Preferential Option for the Poor," *Crux*, 22 January 2018, https://cruxnow.com/church-in-the-usa/2018/01/22/cardinal-omalley-america-always-preferential-option-poor/.

[968] Ibid.

[969] Ibid.

In a 2017 letter to his diocese, O'Malley acknowledged that "many Americans are frustrated by a broken immigration system and others are fearful of the threat of terrorism," but he believes "that most people in [America] recognize that we are a nation of immigrants and that we have an established history of assimilating people of different languages, religions, ethnicities into the magnificent mosaic that is America."[970] He continued: "The Catholic Church in the United States has always stood with people who have come to this country from other lands and found in the Church a community and spiritual home."[971] He assured his diocese that the American bishops were committed to working for comprehensive immigration reform and "for a welcoming policy towards those who are fleeing persecution and violence."[972]

O'Malley has strongly criticized certain immigration-related policies implemented by the Trump administration, such as limits on the numbers of refugees and immigrants permitted into the country from certain areas and policies entailing separation of children from parents. In June 2018, O'Malley deplored that "children are now being used as a deterrent against immigrants who are appealing to us for asylum in order to protect themselves and their families," reflecting the "misguided moral logic of the policy." The cardinal acknowledges that "developing sound immigration policy that respects the needs of a nation and those of the international community is a complex and challenging process," one that involves reconciling domestic priorities with global demands.[973] "Immigration policy is a moral question that cannot be separated from decisions of what is right

---

[970] Seán P. Cardinal O'Malley, O.F.M. Cap., "Letter on Immigration of February 3, 2017," http://www.documentcloud.org/documents/3454729-Cardinal-Sean-O-Malley-letter-on-immigration.html.

[971] Ibid.

[972] Ibid.

[973] Seán Cardinal O'Malley, "Border Immigration Statement," Archdiocese of Boston, 13 June 2018, https://www.bostoncatholic.org/press-release/2018/06/june-13-2018-cardinal-sean-p-omalley-border-immigration-statement.

and wrong, of justice and injustice. It is about respecting and reverencing the dignity of the human person."[974]

In the context of Trump administration policies limiting the number of immigrants to America from certain Muslim countries, O'Malley acknowledged that Americans "cannot afford to be sloppy about security" but at the same time "must guard against letting the darkness of hatred and prejudice poison [their] own hearts."[975] He noted that many Americans likely lack Muslim friends and might be unaware that "American Muslims are much less apt to be radicalized than their European counterparts." American Muslims are "economically better off, better educated and much better integrated into the mainstream."[976] Fewer than 250 Americans have attempted to join the Islamic State, O'Malley added, of whom it is estimated only two dozen succeeded. Peace in the Middle East and at home — an end to terrorism — "can be achieved only if people of goodwill actively seek ways to strengthen community and overcome divisions and prejudices."[977]

Islam

O'Malley recognizes the prevalence of Islam in the world today as an important challenge facing the Church but is optimistic about points of commonality between Muslims and Christians. "There are historical reasons for tensions and rivalry [between Christians and Muslims,]" O'Malley noted in 2006, "and yet there are also points of convergence: the way [Muslims] look at life and issues like abortion, and marriage and things like this. There would be greater understanding among believers and people who practice the Muslim faith."[978]

---

[974] Ibid.

[975] Cardinal Seán P. O'Malley, "Walking in the Path of the Good Samaritan," *Boston Pilot*, 17 December 2015, https://www.thebostonpilot.com/opinion/article.asp?ID=175449.

[976] Ibid.

[977] Ibid.

[978] Enrique, "Significance of Elevation, Challenges."

Mission

The cardinal emphasizes in his pastoral ministry the importance of the New Evangelization and the vocation of all members of the Church to witness to the gospel by their lives and words. We can pass on only what we have and receive, so Catholics must constantly undergo their own conversion and reconversion to love of Christ in order to share that love with others, O'Malley explains. As we each learn and come to live more fully our own faith, we are better able to "share that teaching with others and realize that having the faith is a responsibility and a mission."[979] In America especially, the Catholic Church, which has seen so many of its own drift away from the Faith over recent decades, must move "from a maintenance mode to a missionary one."[980] In a 2011 pastoral letter, the cardinal explained that Catholics today share in the same Great Commission that the first disciples received two thousand years ago.[981] Catholics and non-Catholics alike are called to ongoing conversion. For Catholics, the call is to growth in the Faith. For those who have fallen away from the Church, the call is to reconciliation. For non-Catholic Christians, it is to know the fullness of the gospel message. And for those who do not have faith, the call is an invitation to know Jesus and to experience a change to new life in His Church.[982] O'Malley prizes the work of evangelization and sees in it an urgent priority for the Church in modern times, noting that it "must be the first focus of our Church."[983]

Research has not indicated that O'Malley has articulated in-depth views on the proper mode of biblical interpretation and the historicity of the

---

[979] Elise Harris, "Evangelization Blocked by Our Own 'Hesitancy' to Convert," Catholic News Agency, 7 August 2013, https://www.catholicnewsagency.com/news/evangelization-blocked-by-our-own-hesitancy-to-convert.

[980] Ibid.

[981] Cardinal Seán P. O'Malley, "A New Pentecost: Inviting All to Follow Jesus," Archdiocese of Boston, 12 June 2011, https://www.bostoncatholic.org/cardinal-sean-patrick-omalley-ofm-cap/new-pentecost-inviting-all-follow-jesus.

[982] See ibid.

[983] Ibid.

Gospels, nor of the role of Mary as a model for women in family life. It is unclear if he has spoken to the issue of universalism—the view that all will eventually be saved—but he did note in an interview that while he hopes everyone will be welcomed into heaven, he is not in a position to judge whether that state of affairs will, ultimately, obtain.[984]

CLERGY SEXUAL ABUSE: CLEANING UP THE MESS

Seán O'Malley has emerged as a leader of the American Church's response to the clergy sex abuse scandal. For much of his ministry he has served as the "Catholic Church's public face of repentance and reform" in the wake of the crisis.[985] The troubles snowballed in the early 2000s, when the *Boston Globe*'s Spotlight investigation revealed the shocking scope of clergy sex abuse and related cover-ups in the Boston area.[986] Certainly the situation in Boston when O'Malley took over was dire. By nearly every account he has done an outstanding job cleaning up the mess.

O'Malley was chosen in July of 2003 by John Paul II to lead the Boston Archdiocese after serving only nine months as leader of the Palm Beach Diocese. He already had a proven track record "for cleaning up dioceses sullied by sex abuse scandals."[987] O'Malley's second assignment as a bishop was to Fall River, Massachusetts, where he was tasked with cleaning up

---

[984] "The Latest: Cardinal Law's Successor Dodges Heaven Question," AP News, 20 December 2017, https://apnews.com/8f58ee12d2044f90bb546 db9e82a82f8.

[985] Emma Green, "Why Does the Catholic Church Keep Failing on Sexual Abuse?," *Atlantic*, 14 February 2019, https://www.theatlantic.com/politics/ archive/2019/02/sean-omalley-pope-francis-catholic-church-sex-abuse/ 582658/.

[986] Ibid.

[987] Michael Paulson, "Florida Bishop O'Malley Seen Choice to Lead Boston Diocese," *Boston Globe*, 1 July 2003, archive.boston.com/globe/spotlight/ abuse/stories4/070103_bishop.htm.

the fallout from clergy sex abuse. His time in Fall River gave him his first experience "settling lawsuits and translating tragedy into child-protection policies."[988] A few years later, O'Malley was moved to Palm Beach, Florida, to address a situation in which the two preceding bishops had both been accused of abusing children. O'Malley's time there was short lived, as he was moved to Boston in 2003 to address the crisis there, having by this time earned a reputation as one of the few American bishops with experience handling these issues.

In Boston, O'Malley pushed "for meaningful accountability not just for the crime but the cover-up of sexual abuse for decades."[989] In August 2018, he published a statement in which he referred to activities in the seminary "which are directly contrary to the moral standards and requirements of formation for the Catholic priesthood."[990] After two months of study and reflection, the cardinal announced (in October 2018) an expanded review of St. John's Seminary and two other seminaries by an outside firm.[991] "Every time we thought we were rounding a corner," O'Malley told the *Atlantic* in 2019, "there will be another explosion."[992] He was here referring to the shockwaves that went through the Catholic (and non-Catholic) world when in 2018 former cardinal Theodore McCarrick was exposed publicly as a serial abuser.

"The focus on the victims, the survivors, is the way out [of this problem] for the Church," O'Malley told the *Atlantic*[993] — to understand "the depth of the pain and the seriousness of our responsibility to address sexual abuse, and to do everything to eradicate it, and to establish the very safest environments for our own people."[994] O'Malley has even gone so far

---

[988] Ibid.
[989] Allen, "How to Read Overlooking O'Malley."
[990] Jim Fair, "Cardinal O'Malley Issues Statement on Seminary Review in Boston," Zenit, 12 October 2018, https://Zenit.org/articles/cardinal-omalley-issues-statement-on-seminary-review-in-boston.
[991] Ibid.
[992] Ibid.
[993] Green, "Why Does the Church Keep Failing?"
[994] Ibid.

as to correct Pope Francis publicly for comments suggesting that Chilean survivors of abuse were guilty of "slander" in accusing a bishop of covering up the crimes of their abuser.[995]

O'Malley believes that the Church in America has the right tools in place to solve the problem. He is a defender of the 2002 Dallas Charter, believing that it made a "huge difference" in the way the Church responds to sexual abuse.[996] Before Pope Francis promulgated his plan for dealing with (among other issues) delinquent bishops (*Vos Estis Lux Mundi*), O'Malley had called for three specific actions to help address this problem. "First, a fair and rapid adjudication of these accusations; second, an assessment of the adequacy of our standards and policies in the Church at every level, and especially in the case of bishops; and third, communicating more clearly to the Catholic faithful and to all victims the process for reporting allegations against bishops and cardinals."[997]

After news broke about former cardinal McCarrick's misconduct, many American bishops called for the Holy See to release all documents relating to the affair. The USCCB was split over a proposal that would have asked the Vatican to release the information. "That failed resolution, to me, was a mystery," O'Malley said after the fact. "I think to express the urgency of doing it now, rather than later, would have been appropriate, and I'm sorry that they didn't."[998] O'Malley himself was caught up in the McCarrick allegations insofar as Fr. Boniface Ramsey claimed to have sent O'Malley (via the Pontifical Commission for the Protection of Minors) a letter in June 2015 detailing McCarrick's predations.[999] O'Malley claimed not to

---

[995] Ibid.

[996] Ibid.; Inés San Martín, "O'Malley Wants Vatican Report."

[997] Joan Frawley Desmond, "Cardinal O'Malley Says 'More Than Apologies' Needed in Cardinal McCarrick Scandal," *National Catholic Register*, 24 July 2018, http://www.ncregister.com/blog/joan-desmond/cardinal-omalley-says-more-than-apologies-needed-in-cardinal-mccarrick-scan.

[998] Green, "Why Does the Church Keep Failing?"

[999] Christine Niles, "Cardinal O'Malley Launches Inquiry into Gay Misconduct at Seminary," Church Militant, 10 August 2018, https://

have received the letter personally, noting that the letter was handled by a staff member who reviewed it and sent Ramsey a reply explaining that the matter did not fall under the purview of the commission.[1000] The cardinal, like many others, has called for a report from the Vatican detailing who knew what and when about McCarrick's misconduct.[1001] O'Malley has called for the establishment of "clear and transparent systems of accountability and consequence for Church leadership whose failures have allowed these crimes [of sexual abuse] to occur."[1002] Though the crisis facing the Church is "a product of clerical sins and clerical failures," it can only fruitfully be addressed by the "involvement and leadership of lay men and women in our Church, individuals who can bring their competence, experience and skills to the task we face."[1003]

SUMMARY

Combining interpersonal skills with administrative capabilities, O'Malley has extensive pastoral experience. He hews close to papal guidance, having extensively quoted Benedict XVI during his papacy, and then Francis under his. Francis both likes and has confidence in the cardinal.

Seen as trustworthy to handle sensitive tasks, he is rightly praised for his work in correcting wrongs from sexual abuse in the Dioceses of Palm Beach and Boston and in many parts of the world. A center-right conservative, O'Malley has publicly opposed abortion and euthanasia as well as the use of contraception and in vitro fertilization.

---

www.churchmilitant.com/news/article/cdl.-omalley-launches-inquiry-into-gay-misconduct-at-seminary1.

[1000] Desmond, "More Than Apologies."

[1001] San Martín, "O'Malley Wants Vatican Report."

[1002] Sr. Bernadette Mary Reis, F.S.P., "Cardinal O'Malley Calls for Consequences for Church Leadership," Vatican News, 21 August 2018, https://www.vaticannews.va/en/church/news/2018-08/sean-omalley-video-message-clerical-sexual-abuse-grand-jury.html.

[1003] Ibid.

Defending the Catholic view of marriage and family life, O'Malley decided to cease Catholic adoption activities in his diocese rather than complying with state-mandated same-sex "marriage" and placing children in the homes of same-sex couples.

While supporting the male priesthood, and calling for serious consequences to violations of celibacy, O'Malley has also said, "I'd love to have women priests" if not for the decision of Christ. He has criticized the American immigration system and emphasizes the positive qualities of Islam and its overlap with some Catholic values.

For O'Malley, the New Evangelization is a chief pastoral concern, which, for him, seems to mean preaching the gospel with gentleness and under the directives of the pope. He has urged the faithful to refrain from being harsh and judgmental when discussing divisive topics. He rarely enters into the fray when it comes to controversial matters or shares his views about serious topical issues.

As a member of Francis' inner circle of advisers, O'Malley has shown himself willing to correct the pope publicly when it seemed that the pontiff dismissed the plights of abuse victims in Chile, although O'Malley has generally supported Francis' policies and gestures.

SERVICE TO THE CHURCH

Ordination to the Priesthood: 29 August 1970
Ordination to the Episcopate: 2 August 1984
Elevation to the College of Cardinals: 24 March 2006

Education
(degrees conferred in the 1970s; precise
dates could not be found)

- Catholic University of America; Religious education (master's)
- Catholic University of America; Spanish and Portuguese Literature (Ph.D.)

Assignments

- 1969-1973: Professor, Catholic University of America
- 1970-1984: Priest, Order of Friars Minor Capuchin
- 1973-1978: Executive director of Centro Catolico Hispano, Archdiocese of Washington
- 1978-1984: Executive director, Office of Social Ministry, Archdiocese of Washington
- 1984-1985: Coadjutor bishop, Diocese of Saint Thomas, Virgin Islands
- 1985-1992: Bishop, Diocese of Saint Thomas, Virgin Islands
- 1992-2002: Bishop, Diocese of Fall River, Massachusetts
- 2002-2003: Bishop, Diocese of Palm Beach, Florida
- 2003-present: Archbishop, Archdiocese of Boston, Massachusetts
- 2006-present: Cardinal-priest of Santa Maria della Vittoria
- 2013-present: Member, Council of Cardinal Advisers to Pope Francis

Roman Curia

- 2006-present: Congregation for the Clergy
- 2006-present: Congregation for Institutes of Consecrated Life and Societies of Apostolic Life
- 2014-present: President, Pontifical Commission for the Protection of Minors
- 2017-present: Congregation for the Doctrine of the Faith

UT UNUM SINT

MARC CARDINAL OUELLET

"That They May Be One"

Born: 8 June 1944
La Motte, Quebec
Nationality: Canadian
Title: Prefect of the Congregation for Bishops

BIOGRAPHY

Raised in a practicing but not devout Catholic family in Quebec, one of eight children of a farmer, Marc Ouellet grew closer to the Catholic Faith as a teenager. Having attended college at the University of Laval, he entered the Grand Séminaire in Montreal and received a license in theology at the University of Montreal. Ordained priest in 1968, and having served in Canada for two years, he taught for two years in Spanish at Bogotá, Colombia, where he entered the Sulpicians in 1972. He was then sent to Rome, where he earned a license in philosophy from the University of St. Thomas Aquinas (the Angelicum) in 1974 while studying German at Innsbruck, Austria. After some time serving at a seminary in Canada, he returned to Rome and completed a degree in dogmatic theology at the Gregorian University in 1982. For the next twelve years, he taught in seminaries and served as rector in Colombia and Montreal until he came to teach theology at the John Paul II Institute for Studies on Marriage and the Family in Rome (1996-2002).

In 2001, John Paul II consecrated Ouellet a bishop and in the following year appointed him to be archbishop of Quebec and primate of Canada. In 2003, Ouellet was created a cardinal and since 2010 has been the prefect of the Congregation for Bishops as well as the president of the Pontifical Commission for Latin America. More recently, in 2018, Pope Francis elevated Ouellet to the order of cardinal-bishops, equating him in all respects to the cardinals who were given the title of a suburbicarian church.

SANCTIFYING OFFICE

The Eucharist

"The Eucharist belongs not simply to the *bene esse* but to the *esse* of the Church. The whole life, word and structure of the Church is eucharistic in its very essence,"[1004] Cardinal Marc Ouellet said in 2012.

In Ouellet's view, "the Church's Eucharistic tradition is so rich that it cannot be reduced to the celebration of the Eucharist alone. We need all the Church's Eucharistic culture in order to keep all of its aspects in balance."[1005] For example, the cardinal believes that adoration of the Blessed Sacrament "is a form of spiritual communion, which prolongs sacramental

---

[1004] Marc Cardinal Ouellet, "Cardinal Ouellet at International Theology Symposium: The Ecclesiology of Communion, 50 Years after the Opening of Vatican Council II," Zenit, 7 June 2012, https://zenit.org/articles/cardinal-ouellet-at-international-theology-symposium/.

[1005] Ibid.

communion or replaces it when an obstacle hinders the reception of the sacrament."

In addition to linking devotions to the Eucharist, the cardinal calls for a reexamination of the "pastoral practice of Christian initiation and a [reaffirmation of] the link between confirmation and the Eucharist ... not only because of the limits of current pastoral practice, but out of fidelity to the profound significance of the sequence of the sacraments of initiation."[1006]

The Priesthood

Ouellet thinks that both priest and people play an essential role in the Mass. He resists "the widespread tendency to relativize the role of the ordained minister in order to affirm the conscious and active participation of the assembly in Christ's sacrificial offering."[1007] More broadly, he thinks it essential to understand "the Trinitarian foundation both of the essential difference and of the existential correlation between the two modes of participation" in Christ's priesthood:[1008]

> On the one hand, the common priesthood of the baptized expresses their participation in Christ's divine sonship, which as such includes his mediation of the Spirit.... On the other hand, the ministerial or hierarchical priesthood expresses Christ's mediation insofar as he represents the Father. In virtue of this representation of the Father, Christ pours out the Spirit whom he receives from the Father in response to his, Christ's, own sacrificial and Eucharistic offering. This is why he institutes the ministerial priesthood and the Eucharist simultaneously at the Last Supper.

[1006] Ibid.

[1007] Ibid.

[1008] Marc Cardinal Ouellet, "Towards a Renewal of the Priesthood for Our Time," St. Mary's Seminary and University, 15 November 2016, http://www.stmarys.edu/seminary/welcome-to-st-marys/cardinal-ouellet-towards-a-renewal-of-the-priesthood-for-our-time/.

Approach to the Liturgy

Cardinal Ouellet celebrates a liturgy solemnly. According to Fr. Gilles Routhier, a Canadian theologian specializing in Vatican II, Ouellet "emphasized liturgical form, devoting considerable resources to preparing celebrations that [were] beautiful and well executed. Nothing [was] improvised or left to spontaneity. The missal [was] always used, even for the opening Sign of the Cross."[1009] His choice of sacred music and singing included Latin chant and other classical forms.[1010] He did, however, celebrate Mass in New Brunswick with dancing altar girls.[1011]

Ouellet's homilies are "short, carefully—even painstakingly—worked out, and often notable for their deep and rich content," Routhier says.[1012] The cardinal has tended to give a spiritual commentary on the Word of God that was proclaimed, although he was not known for wholly avoiding mention of politics[1013] or world events, calling in 2008, for example, for a government and United Nations response to a looming world food crisis.[1014] In general, Ouellet was "in line with the understanding of the liturgy put forth by Pope Benedict: not the assembly celebrating itself, but the assembly celebrating God."[1015]

Attitude toward the Extraordinary Form

As archbishop of Quebec, Cardinal Ouellet supported Pope Benedict XVI's *Summorum Pontificum*, encouraging the celebration of the Extraordinary

---

[1009] Gilles Routhier, "Liturgical Views of the Papabili: Cardinal Marc Ouellet," *Pray Tell* (blog), 10 March 2013, http://www.praytellblog.com/index.php/2013/03/10/liturgical-views-of-the-papabili-cardinal-marc-ouellet/.

[1010] Ibid.

[1011] Michael W. Higgins, "Who Is Marc Ouellet?," *Commonweal*, 22 July 2010, https://www.commonwealmagazine.org/who-marc-ouellet.

[1012] Routhier, "Liturgical Views."

[1013] Ibid.

[1014] "The International Eucharistic Congress in Quebec City: a Flood of Graces!," *Michael Journal*, no. 350 (July-August 2008): 3, https://www.michaeljournal.org/julyaugust2008full.pdf.

[1015] Routhier, "Liturgical Views."

Form of the Mass. Fr. Routhier reports that, "unable to find a priest in the diocese who wanted to celebrate Mass according to the extraordinary rite, and without any real demand for it, [the Cardinal] brought in a French priest of the Fraternity of Saint Peter."[1016] The fraternity, to whom Ouellet later entrusted a parish, provided "Eucharistic celebrations following the Extraordinary Rite," "catechetical instruction that involved the use of the Catechism of the Council of Trent," and efforts "to create a demand for the Extraordinary rite and to interest other dioceses in it."[1017] In the cardinal's eyes, these actions properly responded to the "need of the population" and to the Holy Father's intention in issuing his *Motu Proprio* on the Tridentine Mass.

Suspension of Collective Absolution

Beyond the Mass, the cardinal gave attention to other sacraments and devotions while in Quebec. He suspended the practice of collective absolution in the Archdiocese of Quebec in the face of painful pushback, including rebellion from his own priests that ultimately brought him to tears. He insisted on individual confession of sins as better realizing "communion with the Church, the truth of the sacrament, a sign of the Covenant, and personal encounter with Christ."[1018] Also, Ouellet restored the "consecration of the diocese to the Holy Virgin at the Mass of the Immaculate Conception and processed through the streets with the Blessed Sacrament."[1019]

Before and after moving to Rome in 2010, Ouellet served as a member of the Congregation for Divine Worship and the Discipline of the Sacraments. Pope Francis did not renew his term in 2016.

[1016] Ibid.

[1017] Ibid.

[1018] Marc Cardinal Ouellet, "Québec: Promoting the Personal Dimension of the Sacrament of Reconciliation," Zenit, 15 February 2005, https://fr.zenit.org/articles/quebec-promouvoir-la-dimension-personnelle-du-sacrement-de-la-reconciliation/ (translated from French).

[1019] Routhier, "Liturgical Views."

GOVERNING OFFICE

Archbishop of Quebec

Among the governing offices Cardinal Ouellet has exercised, two have been central. First, he was archbishop of Quebec from 2002 to 2010. Since 2010 he has held the position of prefect for the Congregation for Bishops—one of the most important and influential positions in the Roman Curia, primarily responsible for the appointment of bishops. In both positions, he has made widely noticed decisions.

In 2002, one year after Ouellet's episcopal ordination and six years after he came to Rome to teach and to serve in curial positions, Pope John Paul II named him archbishop of Quebec City and, therefore, primate of Canada. At that time, although 96 percent of the diocesan population was Catholic, Mass attendance was not much above 15 percent.[1020]

Cardinal Ouellet had grown up in Quebec before the Quiet Revolution, which rejected Catholicism,[1021] and he spent the first half of the 1970s (as well as much of the 1980s) in Colombia.[1022] Later, he spent six or seven

---

[1020] Fifteen percent was the reported rate of Mass attendance in the province in 2007. See Reginald W. Bibby, "Religion à la Carte in Quebec: A Problem of Demand, Supply, or Both?," *Globe*, July 2007, http://www.reginaldbibby. com/images/Quebec_Paper_July07.pdf. There seems to be little reason to think that the rate in the Archdiocese of Quebec was much higher in 2002. By comparison, Mass attendance in France was said to be under 10 percent, but in Greece and Spain around 20 percent and in Ireland, Italy, and Poland above 30 percent.

[1021] In the 1960s and '70s, after centuries of Church dominance in Quebecois social and political life, dramatic changes ensued: "schools, hospitals, and social services were rigorously secularized; priestly vocations evaporated; Mass attendance plummeted; [and] the churches were emptied." See Preston Jones, "Quebec after Catholicism," *First Things* (June 1999), https:// www.firstthings.com/article/1999/06/quebec-after-catholicism. Nationalism is said to have taken the place of religion for many.

[1022] Ouellet reports that while in the seminary, he had a desire to do some missionary work. See EWTN, "Marc Cardinal Ouellet: An Interview with the Archbishop of Quebec — *The Journey Home*," YouTube video,

years in Rome. Ouellet spent sixteen years, spread across four decades, in Quebec as it was becoming increasingly secularized, and afterward a few more years in Alberta. Thus, he was not entirely unfamiliar with his home province when he returned as archbishop in 2002.

Early in his tenure, Ouellet showed himself to be a sign of contradiction, rejected by the world and the mainstream media but beloved by faithful Catholics.

He began to criticize Quebec's newly mandated Ethics and Religious Culture program for relativizing religion.[1023] He pushed for schools to keep catechetical education, claiming that Quebecois children were "grossly ignorant" of religion.[1024] "Kids ask who's that guy hanging from the cross," he said. "It's clear that one hour a week of religious instruction in school isn't enough to get the message across."[1025] By pushing back against the curriculum change, Cardinal Ouellet distinguished himself from his brother bishops in Quebec,[1026] many of whom did not come around to his less accommodating position.[1027] That said, even the cardinal seemed to suggest

---

53:58, posted 27 December 2004 by EWTN, https://www.youtube.com/watch?v=gU-W0sLiN1I. At first, he was inclined to go to Asia, but after he was ordained as a Sulpician, he went to Colombia. He taught for six years there, at two seminaries. Later, he would return to Colombia for five more years as rector of one of those seminaries. See "Biography of Cardinal Marc Ouellet, p.s.s.," Society of the Priests of Saint-Sulpice, Province of Canada, 25 November 2010, http://www.sulpc.org/evsulpc_ouellet_en.php.

[1023] Deborah Gyapong, "Cardinal Ouellet Celebrates 50 Years of Priesthood," *Catholic Register*, 29 May 2018, https://www.catholicregister.org/item/27460-cardinal-ouellet-celebrates-50-years-of-priesthood.

[1024] Joseph Brean, "Beyond the Self-Effacing Facade, Canadian Cardinal Marc Ouellet Is a Cardboard Cutout of Benedict XVI," *National Post*, 15 February 2013, https://nationalpost.com/news/canada/cardinal-marc-ouellet-is-cardboard-cutout-of-benedict-xvi.

[1025] Ibid.

[1026] Gyapong, "50 Years of Priesthood."

[1027] Jean-Claude Leclerc, "Religion in Schools — Bishops Say No to Cardinal Ouellet," *Le Devoir*, 20 October 2008, https://www.ledevoir.com/opinion/chroniques/211458/la-religion-dans-les-ecoles-les-eveques-disent-non-au-cardinal-ouellet (translated from French).

that the decision was, ultimately, one for politicians and the people, not the Church, to decide.[1028] The curriculum is in place today, although some slight exemptions are permitted.[1029]

Defense of Marriage

In 2005, Cardinal Ouellet took a leading role in opposing the redefinition of civil marriage. In testimony before the Canadian senate, he described same-sex unions as "pseudo-marriage, a fiction."[1030] Later, he testified that "the Church would refuse to baptize children of same-sex couples if both parents insisted on signing as co-fathers or co-mothers."[1031] His Eminence also supported the "removal of MP Joe Comartin from some church activities—including altar serving and marriage-preparation courses—because of [Comartin's] vote for same-sex 'marriage.'" On the other hand, he did not block then-prime minister Paul Martin from receiving Communion. "We are a community of sinners," the cardinal explained.[1032] Later, after comments relating to the Church's role in Quebec met public backlash, Ouellet published an open letter apologizing for "errors [that] were committed" before 1960, including "anti-Semitism,

---

[1028] "Maintenant la parole est aux politiciens et la population décidera." "Religious Freedom at School," *Inquisition*, https://www.inquisition.ca/fr/serm/liberte_religieuse.htm (translated from French).

[1029] Loyola High School v. Quebec (Attorney General), 2015 SCC 12, [2015] 1 S.C.R. 613, https://scc-csc.lexum.com/scc-csc/scc-csc/en/item/14703/index.do.

[1030] Allan Woods, "Marc Ouellet: Canadian Pope Prospect Who Says Top Job Would Be a 'Nightmare,'" *Guardian*, 15 February 2015, https://www.theguardian.com/world/2013/feb/15/marc-ouellet-pope-prospect.

[1031] Brean, "Beyond the Self-Effacing Facade."

[1032] Ibid. Calgary Bishop Frederick Henry, although he seems not to have addressed the Communion question directly, seems to have been blunter than the cardinal in his criticism of Martin. See Robson Fletcher, "Calgary Bishop Fred Henry, Who Drew Fire for Stances on Gay Marriage and Abortion, Resigns after 19 Years," *CBC News,* 4 January 2017, https://www.cbc.ca/news/canada/calgary/bishop-fred-henry-resigns-calgary-catholic-diocese-1.3920594.

racism, indifference to First Nations and discrimination against women and homosexuals."[1033] The cardinal's letter received some praise[1034] but was not warmly received by those claiming to represent some groups whom the letter mentioned.[1035] In Canada today, same-sex unions are recognized as civil marriages.

As mentioned in the previous section, around the same time that Ouellet was opposing the redefinition of civil marriage, he also sought to rein in the common practice of collective absolution. On February 9, 2005, he published a pastoral letter "confirming the orientation given before by [his] decision to suspend the practice of collective absolution in the diocese."[1036] Data about the practice in 2010 or today is not readily available.

Handling Dissent, Secularism

Two months after his pastoral letter regarding collective absolution, Cardinal Ouellet issued another pastoral letter, this one calling on the Army of Mary to cease its activities.[1037] The Army of Mary was an association of Catholic believers founded by Marie-Paule Giguère in Quebec in 1971.[1038] The association was at first formally approved, but the archbishop of Quebec revoked that approval in 1987 after theologians investigated the group's writings.[1039] In 2000, Cardinal Ratzinger identified "gravely

---

[1033] "Quebecers Reluctantly Accept Archbishop's Apology," *CBC News*, 21 November 2007, https://www.cbc.ca/news/canada/montreal/quebecers-reluctantly-accept-archbishop-s-apology-1.689424.

[1034] Deborah Gyapong, "Cardinal Ouellet's Apology Greeted with Praise and Suspicion," *Canadian Catholic News*, 2007, https://canadianchristianity.com/nationalupdates/2007/071129cardinal.html.

[1035] Ibid.; Brean, "Beyond the Self-Effacing Facade."

[1036] Ouellet, "Quebec: Promoting the Personal Dimension."

[1037] Marc Ouellet, "Pastoral Message on the Army of Mary," Catholic Planet, 4 April 2005, http://www.catholicplanet.com/apparitions/05-04-04_army_of_mary.pdf.

[1038] Malea Hargett, "What Is the Army of Mary? What Do They Believe?," Catholic News Service, 6 October 2007, https://www.arkansas-catholic.org/news/article/1010/What-is-the-Army-of-Mary-What-do-they-believe.

[1039] Ibid.

erroneous" content in Army of Mary publications, including a false claim about the reincarnation of Mary, the mother of Jesus, in the person of Marie-Paule Giguère.[1040] Warnings notwithstanding, the Army of Mary did not retract its claims and instead sought to ordain new priests. In March 2007, Cardinal Ouellet issued a second warning to the group, and later that year, the pope approved a declaration of excommunication against the Army.[1041]

In 2009, Ouellet was asked whether the Church is persecuted in Quebecois society. "Of course, absolutely," he answered and put the cause down to the Church's telling "the truth that She received from God."[1042] Indeed, Quebecois (and other) political and social leaders were outraged in 2010 when Cardinal Ouellet reasserted that abortion is a "moral crime," not even justified by rape.[1043] In those same remarks, the cardinal called for greater support for pregnant women in crisis,[1044] but the abortion comments drew the focus and condemnation. A federal cabinet minister, for example, called His Eminence's remarks "unacceptable."[1045]

Ouellet's tenure as archbishop of Quebec ended in 2010. In his seven years in office, the share of the population identifying as Catholic had declined by 8 percent.[1046] Mass attendance across the various dioceses of

---

[1040] Ibid.

[1041] JD Flynn, "Army of Mary Excommunicated by the Vatican," Catholic News Agency, 14 September 2007, https://www.catholicnewsagency.com/news/army_of_mary_excommunicated_by_the_vatican.

[1042] "Québec: 'The Church Is Persecuted Because It Speaks the Truth Received from God,'" Eucharistie Sacrement de la Miséricorde, 13 April 2009, http://eucharistiemisericor.free.fr/index.php?page=1304093_card_ouellet.

[1043] "Cardinal's abortion remarks anger politicians," CBC News, 17 May 2010, https://www.cbc.ca/news/canada/montreal/cardinal-s-abortion-remarks-anger-politicians-1.890873.

[1044] Brean, "Beyond the Self-Effacing Facade."

[1045] Ibid.

[1046] "Archdiocese of Québec," Catholic Hierarchy, http://www.catholic-hierarchy.org/diocese/dqueb.html.

the province of Quebec is lower than in 2003.[1047] Similarly, monthly Mass attendance declined across the province between 2003 and 2010, albeit more slowly than before.[1048]

2008 International Eucharistic Congress

The following year, Cardinal Ouellet participated in the 2008 International Eucharistic Congress. The event brought more than twenty thousand pilgrims to Quebec City and featured among its speakers Jorge Cardinal Bergoglio.[1049] The future Pope Francis spoke on "The Eucharist, Gift of God for the Life of the World."[1050] The congress took place during the four hundredth anniversary of the founding of Quebec City, and Cardinal Ouellet, perhaps optimistically, deemed it a "turning point" for the archdiocese.[1051]

Prefect of the Congregation for Bishops

The work of Congregation for Bishops noticeably changed when Cardinal Ouellet arrived. According to the former Canadian ambassador to the Holy See, Anne Leahy, Ouellet was "known as a very hard worker" and "a lot of people noticed when he took on the job" that "a slower rhythm of decisions

---

[1047] M. D. and Erasmus, "Why Francophone Canada Is So Post-Catholic a Place," *Economist*, 23 September 2016, https://www.economist.com/erasmus/2016/09/23/why-francophone-canada-is-so-post-catholic-a-place (claiming a weekly Mass attendance rate of 11 percent in 2016).

[1048] *Canada's Changing Religious Landscape*, Pew Research Center, 27 June 2013, http://www.pewforum.org/2013/06/27/canadas-changing-religious-landscape/.

[1049] Gyapong, "50 Years of Priesthood."

[1050] Jorge Mario Cardinal Bergoglio, "The Eucharist, Gift of God for the Life of the World," Vatican, 18 June 2008, http://www.vatican.va/roman_curia/pont_committees/eucharist-congr/documents/rc_committ_euchar_doc_20080618_mistero-alleanza_en.html.

[1051] "2008 Eucharistic Congress," *Michael Journal* (15-22 June 2008), https://www.michaeljournal.org/articles/roman-catholic-church/category/2008-eucharistic-congress.

on bishops" had been the norm. "When he came in, he cleared up a lot of the backlog. Decisions were made and things were done," she said.[1052]

In 2012, Cardinal Ouellet described his view of what the Church needs in its bishops:

> Today, especially in the context of our secularized societies, we need bishops who are the first evangelizers, and not mere administrators of dioceses, who are capable of proclaiming the Gospel, who are not only theologically faithful to the magisterium and the pope but are also capable of expounding and, if need be, of defending the faith publicly.[1053]

After the election of Pope Francis, bishop appointments slowed.[1054] In May 2013, controversy arose over Roberto Octavio González Nieves, archbishop of San Juan, Puerto Rico. Following reports that the archbishop had supported same-sex civil-union legislation and protected pedophile priests in his diocese, Cardinal Ouellet urged him to resign and take another position in the Church.[1055] The archbishop firmly denied the reports, claiming

---

[1052] Woods, "Canadian Pope Prospect." Appointments made between Cardinal Ouellet's elevation to prefect and the election of Pope Francis include Ricardo Andrello (archbishop of Concepción to archbishop of Santiago, Chile), Michel Aupetit (priest to auxiliary bishop of Paris), Charles Chaput (archbishop of Denver to archbishop of Philadelphia), Blase Cupich (bishop of Rapid City to bishop of Spokane), William Lori (bishop of Bridgeport to archbishop of Baltimore), Charles Morerod (priest to bishop of Lausanne, Geneva, and Fribourg), Peter Ebere Okpaleke (priest to bishop of Ahiara, Nigeria), Angelo Scola (patriarch of Venice to archbishop of Milan), and Luis Antonio Tagle (bishop of Imus to archbishop of Manila).

[1053] Sandro Magister, "Theologians, Apologists. What the New Bishops Have to Be," chiesa.espressonline.it, 1 December 2011 http://chiesa.espresso. repubblica.it/articolo/1350096bdc4.html?eng=y

[1054] Edward Pentin, "Concerns Rising over Slow Appointments of Bishops," *National Catholic Register*, 13 July 2013, http://www.ncregister.com/blog/ edward-pentin/concerns-rising-over-slow-appointments-of-bishops.

[1055] Santiago Wills, "Pope Francis' First Crisis? Defiant Archbishop Refuses to Quit," ABC News, 8 May 2013, https://abcnews.go.com/ABC_Univision/ News/popes-crisis-rebel-archbishop-quit/story?id=19132392.

that they were politically motivated, and refused to resign in a letter leaked to the press.[1056] He remains archbishop of San Juan.

In October 2013, the pope took the highly unusual and unorthodox step of elevating Ilson de Jesus Montanari, apparently a friend of the pope's personal secretary, from a lower position in the congregation to the office of secretary. As early as 2014, there were reports that Pope Francis was not consulting the Congregation for Bishops regarding various important episcopal appointments, such as that of Bishop Cupich as archbishop of Chicago.[1057] Similar stories surfaced in 2016 from an authoritative Quebecois journalist.[1058] Cardinal Ouellet reports, however, that he continues to "have long meetings with Pope Francis every week to discuss the appointment of bishops and the problems that affect their governance."[1059] He continues to offer thoughts about the bishop selection process.

Bishops and the Sexual Abuse Crisis
In light of the sexual abuse crisis, he has said:

> I think something more needs to be done within the Church, and with the formation of priests and certainly more prudence in the choice of bishops.... On the question on vigilance, as you know, there is the *motu proprio* of Pope Francis "As a Loving Mother." So, we need to address the issue of bad governance of bishops on these

[1056] "Metropolitan Archbishop of San Juan of Puerto Rico, Letter to Marc Cardinal Ouellet of February 20, 2013," LifeSite News, 20 February 2013, https://www.lifesitenews.com/images/pdfs/Letter_of_Gonzalez_Nieves_to_Cardinal_Ouellet-1.pdf.

[1057] Sandro Magister, "Behind the Scenes of the Chicago Appointment," chiesa.espressonline.it, 30 September 2014, http://chiesa.espresso.repubblica.it/articolo/1350881bdc4.html?eng=y.

[1058] Hugo Duchaine, "Le Cardinal Ouellet Perd un Poste au Vatican," *Le Journal de Montréal*, 4 November 2016, https://www.journaldemontreal.com/2016/11/04/le-cardinal-ouellet-perd-un-poste-au-vatican.

[1059] Edward Pentin, "Cardinal Ouellet Writes Open Letter to Archbishop Viganò," *National Catholic Register*, 7 October 2018, http://www.ncregister.com/blog/edward-pentin/cardinal-ouellet-writes-open-letter-to-archbishop-vigano.

questions. This is already something that is implemented, so we are [at] the beginning of this implementation. We need to do some sort of criteria. We also need to coordinate among the various dicasteries of the Holy See to make sure that we ... work in the same direction with the same parameters, to apply this and be effective. But I think we will accelerate now, with the recent events, we will accelerate and we hope to develop something more effective.[1060]

Two months after these comments, Cardinal Ouellet controversially issued a directive to prevent U.S. bishops from voting on proposals to address the sexual abuse crisis. The United States Conference of Catholic Bishops' (USCCB) leaders had met with the pope about this issue in September, at which time the pope suggested that they replace a highly anticipated annual meeting with a spiritual retreat.[1061] USCCB leaders met the pope again in October, reportedly about general matters.[1062] Apparently, canon law did not require the USCCB to submit to the Vatican proposals to be considered at its meeting, but it did so on October 30.[1063] On November 6, Cardinal Ouellet indicated opposition to voting on the proposals.[1064] In a letter dated November 11, the day before the USCCB meeting, the

---

[1060] Deborah Castellano Lubov, "INTERVIEW: Cardinal Ouellet: Dicasteries of the Holy See Must Communicate Better among Themselves and Women Need to Have Greater Role in Priestly Formation," Zenit, 17 September 2018, https://zenit.org/articles/interview-cardinal-ouellet-dicasteries-of-the-holy-see-must-communicate-better-among-themselves-women-need-to-have-greater-role-in-priestly-formation/.

[1061] Cindy Wooden, "Pope Francis to U.S. Bishops on Retreat: Abuse Crisis Requires Conversion and Humility," America, 3 January 2019, https://www.americamagazine.org/faith/2019/01/03/pope-francis-us-bishops-retreat-abuse-crisis-requires-conversion-and-humility.

[1062] Christopher White and Inés San Martín, "Confirmed: Pope to Meet USCCB Leaders on Monday," Crux, 7 October 2018, https://cruxnow.com/vatican/2018/10/07/confirmed-pope-to-meet-usccb-leaders-on-monday/.

[1063] Nicole Winfield, "Vatican Letter Undermines US Cardinal on Abuse," AP News, 1 January 2019, https://www.apnews.com/bc645408ad404df3bc9797c26cfde6d2.

[1064] Ibid.

cardinal directed the USCCB not to vote on the proposals because the ideas needed to "properly mature."[1065] The Vatican, he said in the letter, was not given enough time to study the proposals and potential conflicts with Church law.[1066]

Responding to Archbishop Viganò

A key moment of Cardinal Ouellet's tenure as prefect for the Congregation for Bishops was his response to open letters published in the fall of 2018 by Archbishop Carlo Maria Viganò.

In a stinging critique of Viganò's letters, Ouellet did not contest that Benedict XVI had responded to abuse allegations against Theodore McCarrick. Instead he qualified his response by saying they were not "sanctions." He made no comment about the central discussions between Viganò and Pope Francis that Viganò said occurred during private meetings on June 23 and October 10, 2013. He also expressed doubt that Pope Francis would have remembered what any particular nuncio said on June 21, 2013, when Viganò met the pope in Rome, along with all the Church's nuncios. Finally, Cardinal Ouellet did not deny that Cardinal McCarrick had any influence in the Vatican but suggested that the former cardinal had less influence on Pope Francis than either McCarrick or Viganò supposed.[1067]

[1065] "Ouellet Letter: US Bishops' Vote on Abuse Reform Measures Was Blocked to Allow More Discussion," Catholic News Agency, 1 January 2019, https://www.catholicnewsagency.com/news/ouellet-letter-us-bishops-vote-on-abuse-reform-measures-was-blocked-to-allow-more-discussion-60649.

[1066] Cindy Wooden, "Details Published on Vatican Delaying USCCB Vote on Abuse Provisions," *Crux*, 2 January 2019, https://cruxnow.com/vatican/2019/01/details-published-on-vatican-delaying-usccb-vote-on-abuse-provisions/.

[1067] "Open Letter by Card. Marc Ouellet on Recent Accusations against the Holy See," Vatican News, 7 October 2018, https://www.vaticannews.va/en/vatican-city/news/2018-10/letter-ouellet-vigano-mccarrick-sexual-abuse-united-states.html; Edward Pentin, "Ex-Nuncio Accuses Pope Francis of Failing to Act on McCarrick's Abuse," *National Catholic Register*, 25 August 2018, http://www.ncregister.com/daily-news/ex-nuncio-accuses-pope-francis-of-failing-to-act-on-mccarricks-abuse; Archbishop

Whereas some were taken aback by the vehemence of Ouellet's letter to a prelate whom many saw as courageously criticizing a grave injustice at the highest levels of the Church, friends of Ouellet said the episode showed Ouellet's deep loyalty to the pope and his instinct to hold a position on a team. His episcopal motto *Ut Unum Sint* (That They May Be One) signifies that unity and communion mean a great deal to him and that, according to his friends, he has a "horror" of anything tending toward schism or division in the Church—hence his disdain for Viganò's testimonies, or at least the perceived effect they might have. Those who know Ouellet say he would have seen them as an act of disloyalty to Francis, or what Ouellet himself called an "open and scandalous rebellion" which is why it angered him, even though Viganò saw his criticisms of the pope as services to the truth, and ultimately acts of charity and loyalty to the Petrine Office. For Ouellet, his loyalty to the pope is the *sine qua non* of being Catholic, but it is a principled loyalty, driven not by personality worship but by reverence for the office.

Approach to the Pachamama Statues

During the Amazon synod in October 2019, Ouellet allowed indigenous groups to use his titular church of Santa Maria in Traspontina, where various questionable ceremonies took place and where fertility symbols, or pagan Pachamama statues, were present. He made no public expression of disapproval of the use of the church in this way. Instead, he said the veneration of these symbols during various synod activities "did not bother me," adding that he did not know the Amazonian culture "sufficiently well to say what is the meaning of those symbols." In spite of people prostrating themselves in front of the statues, he said that to say such actions were akin to "adoration of idols is an exaggeration."[1068]

Carlo Viganò, "Sept. 29, 2018 letter of Archbishop Carlo Vigano," 29 September 2018, https://www.scribd.com/document/389623829/Vigano-Scio-Cui-Credidi.

[1068] Martin M Barillas, "Cardinal Ouellet: Pachamama Statues 'Did Not Bother Me,' 'Exaggeration' to Speak of Idolatry," LifeSite News, 11 December 2019,

TEACHING OFFICE

Priestly Celibacy

Cardinal Ouellet once praised Pope Benedict for shifting the focus from "ecclesiastical questions or moral questions to fundamental questions."[1069] The cardinal holds that the Eucharist is central to Catholic life and that priests are necessary for the celebration of the Mass. Here it is worth adding that Ouellet has emphasized the importance of priestly celibacy for Latin-Rite priests. According to Ouellet:

> The Church tradition of celibacy and abstinence of the cleric did not arise just at the beginning of the 4th century as something new, but rather, was—both in the East and the West—the confirmation of a tradition that goes back to the apostles.... It is important to understand that this need ... was for both celibacy and the ban against marriage as well as also the perfect abstinence for those who were already married.[1070]

Cardinal Ouellet acknowledges priestly celibacy as "not a dogma but a rule of life," and said that it is "conceivable for the Latin Church" to "associate another form of life, marriage, to the pastoral ministry."[1071] Still, he considers sacerdotal celibacy "a gift for the Church" that is founded "in

---

https://www.lifesitenews.com/news/cdl-ouellet-pachamama-statues-did-not-bother-me-exaggeration-to-speak-of-idolatry.

[1069] CBC News: The National, "Cardinal Marc Ouellet, Pt. 2," YouTube video, 10:52, posted 5 March 2013, https://www.youtube.com/watch?v=OKgAUJg1s3Y.

[1070] Giuseppe Nardi, "Priestly Celibacy 'in the Example of Christ'—Cardinal Secretary: 'One Can Talk about It, but without Haste,'" *The Eponymous Flower* (blog), 10 February 2016, http://eponymousflower.blogspot.com/2016/02/priestly-celibacy-in-example-of-christ.html.

[1071] Domenico Agasso, Andrea Tornielli, and Isabelle Cousturié, "Priesthood Celibacy: No Reform in the Air," *Aleteia*, 9 February 2016, https://fr.aleteia.org/2016/02/09/celibat-des-pretres-pas-de-reforme-dans-lair/ (translated from French).

the person of Christ," and he notes "the supreme authority of the Church, which has preferred until now, for serious reasons, to maintain the validity of the law on obligatory ecclesiastic celibacy."[1072]

Shortly before the Amazon synod in October 2019, Ouellet published a book arguing that in the face of challenges, the Church should not seek quick solutions but, rather, should deepen its understanding of the tradition of priestly celibacy in the Latin Rite. In the introduction, he had some harsh words about synod politics, and he had joined other cardinals in fighting to prevent the concept of *viri probati*—the ordination of married men of proven virtue—from going forward.[1073]

Homosexuality in the Seminary

Asked in 2008 whether "homosexuals" are to be admitted to seminary, His Eminence called the question "delicate" and pointed to Pope Benedict's 2005 document prohibiting men with deep-seated homosexual tendencies to enter the seminary, apparently affirming it.[1074]

The public record of the cardinal's teaching on the ordination of women is similar. In 2008, Ouellet cited John Paul II as having reached a "definitive" conclusion on the question.[1075] Just before the election of Pope Francis, he repeated that "ordained ministry" is not to consist of women,[1076] and in October 2018, he reaffirmed that position, opposing the "pretension" on behalf or on the part of women "to that which is for ministers in the sacerdotal sense."[1077]

[1072] Ibid.; Michel Arseneault, "The Msgr. Ouellet Mystery," *L'Actualité*, 5 June 2008, https://lactualite.com/societe/2008/06/05/le-mystere-mgr-ouellet/ (translated from French).

[1073] "Cardinal Ouellet Defends Priestly Celibacy ahead of Amazon Synod," Catholic News Agency, 2 October 2019, https://www.catholicnewsagency.com/news/cardinal-ouellet-defends-priestly-celibacy-ahead-of-amazon-synod-27576.

[1074] Arsenault, "The Msgr. Ouellet Mystery."

[1075] Ibid.

[1076] CBC News: The National, "Cardinal Marc Ouellet, Pt. 2."

[1077] Manuella Affejee, "At the Synod, Cardinal Ouellet Evokes the Place of Women in the Church," Vatican News, 18 October 2018, https://www.vaticannews.

The Role of Women

Cardinal Ouellet has been relatively outspoken in his support of greater roles for women in the Church. In 2013, referring to "what is already done in the life of the Church," he said if one visits "many dioceses," what one sees is "a majority of women working . . . in key positions." He added that this "is open to further development."[1078] In 2018, he called for further integration of women into the Church, "accelerating the processes of struggle against the 'machista' culture and clericalism, to develop respect for women and the recognition of their charisms as well as their equal integration in the life of society and the Church."[1079] In particular, he has suggested that the Church needs to involve more women in the formation of priests.[1080] He repeated his call in April 2020, saying that "the experience of collaborating with women on an equal level helps the candidate [for priesthood] to envisage his future ministry and how he will respect and collaborate with

---

va/fr/vatican/news/2018-10/au-synode-le-cardinal-ouellet-evoque-la-place-des-femmes.html (translated from French).

[1078] CBC News: The National, "Cardinal Marc Ouellet, Pt. 2."

[1079] Junno Arocho Esteves, "Women's Voice Needed to Fight Clericalism, 'Macho' Culture, Cardinal Ouellet Says," *National Catholic Reporter*, 18 October 2018, https://www.ncronline.org/news/vatican/womens-voice-needed-fight-clericalism-macho-culture-cardinal-says.

[1080] Lubov, "INTERVIEW: Cardinal Ouellet." His Eminence seems not to have remarked publicly and directly on the specific role of women in forming their children. He has, however, held up the Holy Family as "a living ideal." See "Cardinal Ouellet Defends the Family as a Child's First Teacher of Love and Life," Catholic News Agency, 26 January 2010, https://www.catholicnewsagency.com/news/cardinal_ouellet_defends_the_family_as_a_childs_first_teacher_of_love_and_life. He has promoted the family as the most precious inheritance of the Christian tradition (ibid.) and has extolled Our Lady of Guadalupe's example of bearing a child in the womb: "Mary is reminding us that the word of God took flesh in the womb of a woman." See Carl Bunderson and Alan Holdren, "Cardinal Ouellet: Cultural Renewal in Americas Requires Mary's Message," Catholic News Agency, 12 December 2012, https://www.catholicnewsagency.com/news/cardinal-ouellet-cultural-renewal-in-americas-requires-marys-message.

them." He said such collaboration would also help prevent the risk of a priest's living his relationship with women "in a clerical way."[1081]

Another activity that the cardinal would ask of women—and men, too—is evangelization:

> To bear witness to Jesus Christ ... to announce the Paschal mystery of Jesus Christ ... which is bringing salvation to the whole world, even to those who do not know ... (they are included in what he did for the whole humanity), ... we are called to announce that.... It is the good news, and people have the right to know, you know, and to rejoice about that, and to embrace this mystery of faith and salvation.... To the extent that we are aware of the gift, we are committed to give it to others ... to communicate what has been received. Otherwise, we ... really risk losing the gift, if we do not share it.[1082]

Ouellet cheers "old and new communities of consecrated life, ecclesial movements, the lay apostolate, and everything St. Paul describes in his non-exhaustive list of charisms."[1083] In youth outreach, His Eminence would first "express the trust of the Church in young people" and second, reflect on education "because the young people need models, witnesses, [of] encouragement, but also of parameters, of correction, to go ahead."[1084] Furthermore, he said "if we want young people to make the choice of following Jesus, they must learn who Jesus is: the beloved who comes to meet us to make us discover the Father through him, in the communion of the Holy Spirit."[1085]

[1081] Hannah Brockhaus, "Vatican Cardinal: Involve More Women in Seminary Formation," *National Catholic Register/CNA*, 24 April 2020, https://www.ncregister.com/daily-news/vatican-cardinal-involve-more-women-in-seminary-formation.

[1082] EWTN, "An Interview with the Archbishop of Quebec."

[1083] Marc Cardinal Ouellet, "Ouellet at International Theology Symposium."

[1084] Lubov, "INTERVIEW: Cardinal Ouellet."

[1085] CBC News: The National, "Cardinal Marc Ouellet, Pt. 2."

Holy Scripture

To make known the trinitarian God, Ouellet turns to Holy Scripture. In the cardinal's eyes, "it is indispensable for the Church to hold to the real facts and events."[1086] He praised Pope Benedict for clarifying "the historical foundation of Christianity," deepening our "understanding of the events of the Last Supper, the meaning of the prayer of Gethsemane, the chronology of the Passion and, in particular, the historical traces of the Resurrection."[1087] For the cardinal, "Scripture is a historical assertion and a canonical reference that are necessary for prayer, the life and the doctrine of the Church."[1088] Indeed, it is "thanks to the Bible [that] humanity knows it has been called upon by God; the Spirit helps it to listen and welcome the Word of God, thus becoming the 'Ecclesia,' the community assembled by the Word."[1089]

Islam

Notwithstanding the cardinal's affirmation of Tradition and emphasis on the trinitarian nature of God,[1090] he holds that the Muslim faithful are "rooted in the Biblical tradition" and "believers in the one God."[1091] Ouellet holds that "we cannot stereotype Islam as a religion of terrorism,

---

[1086] Zenit Staff, "Pope Addresses 5 Disputed Questions in New Book," Zenit, 11 March 2011, https://zenit.org/articles/pope-addresses-5-disputed-questions-in-new-book/.

[1087] Ibid. The cardinal applauded the pope, for example, for "exclud[ing] ... absurd theories" that "declare as compatible the proclamation of the resurrection of Christ and his corpse's remaining in the sepulcher."

[1088] "Church Must Bring People to a 'Vivid Encounter' with God, Cardinal Ouellet Says," Catholic News Agency, 6 October 2008, https://www.catholicnewsagency.com/news/church_must_bring_people_to_a_vivid_encounter_with_god_cardinal_ouellet_says.

[1089] Ibid.

[1090] "According to the Revelation of Holy Scripture (1 Jn 4:16), the divine nature is nothing other than the divine Love subsisting in three absolutely correlative Persons." Ouellet, "Towards a Renewal of the Priesthood."

[1091] "Church Must Bring People to a 'Vivid Encounter.'"

for example. We must move toward a climate of fraternity."[1092] On the other hand, the cardinal does not always shy away from distinctions about groups claiming to be religions. For example, in 2010, he called for Quebec to distinguish "sects" such as Scientology from "historic religions" such as Christianity and, presumably, Judaism and Islam, among others.[1093] In Cardinal Ouellet's eyes, historic religions should stand together as "allies in the defense of human life and in the assertion of the social importance of religion" in the face of secularism.[1094]

Effects of Secularism

Secularism is dominant in Quebec. Responding to it, Cardinal Ouellet defended the Church's right to remain present in areas from which society sought to exclude it, especially, although not exclusively, in education. For example, in 2010, the cardinal "sadly" noted that the "total rejection of our Catholic identity leads more and more to a total mess in education." In his view, "the byproducts are well known: fragile couples, broken families, massive abortions, soon euthanasia, suicides at alarming rates, evident school dropouts, work seven days out of seven, etc., etc. Long live a Quebec free from religion!"[1095]

Right-to-Life Issues

The cardinal has stated plainly that euthanasia, abortion, and breaking a marriage are wrong. He asserted, for example, "the honor or the misfortune

[1092] Carol Glatz, "Life in Latin America, Quebec, Rome Gives Cardinal Unique World View," *Catholic Sun*, 28 February 2013, http://www.catholicsun.org/2013/02/28/life-in-latin-america-quebec-rome-gives-cardinal-unique-world-view/.

[1093] Yves Therrien, "Scientologie: le cardinal Ouellet sert une mise en garde," Le Soleil, 4 February 2010, https://www.lesoleil.com/actualite/scientologie-le-cardinal-ouellet-sert-une-mise-en-garde-4b6d1642cad876eaf64aaa79c230a86d (translated from French).

[1094] "Church Must Bring People to a 'Vivid Encounter.'"

[1095] Patrick B. Craine, "Cardinal Ouellet: Quebec Must 'Return to God,'" LifeSite News, 29 March 2010, https://www.lifesitenews.com/news/cardinal-ouellet-quebec-must-return-to-god.

of defending the dignity of the human person unconditionally and without compromise" during Canada's debate over euthanasia[1096] and when he opposed abortion, also of a child conceived through rape. ("The child is not responsible for how he was conceived, it is the aggressor who is responsible," he told reporters. "We can see him (the child) as another victim."[1097]) In Ouellet's view, "human dignity is not in the least diminished when a person is not yet born, is ill, handicapped, or dying."[1098] From these and other public comments, it seems that Ouellet recognizes that the indispensable foundations of political society include human rights grounded, at least in their essence, in absolute moral norms.

During the 2008 International Eucharistic Congress, Cardinal Ouellet praised *Humanae Vitae*. He noted the connection between the Eucharist and respect for human life. "The consequences of the culture of contraception," he said, "are visible in the culture with abortion and with the question of marriage."[1099] Again in 2018, while interpreting *Amoris Laetitia*, he sounded the same theme, connecting the use of contraception, abortion, euthanasia, divorce, and "the pseudo-marriage of same-sex couples" as part of what St. John Paul II called "the culture of death."[1100]

These issues are not the only questions of justice that Ouellet addresses. For example, he has preached on "migrants and refugees to whom we do not remain indifferent despite the temptation to ignore or repress them so

---

[1096] "Cardinal Ouellet Appointed Prefect of the Congregation for Bishops," FSSPX News, 12 July 2010, https://fsspx.news/en/news-events/news/cardinal-ouellet-appointed-prefect-congregation-bishops-22068.

[1097] Patrick B. Craine, "Cardinal Ouellet 'Buoyant' amidst Attacks over Abortion Comments," LifeSite News, 25 May 2010, https://www.lifesitenews.com/news/cardinal-ouellet-buoyant-amidst-attacks-over-abortion-comments.

[1098] "Ouellet Appointed Prefect."

[1099] John-Henry Westen, "Cardinal Ouellet Praises Humanae Vitae—Abortion the Consequence of the 'Culture of Contraception,'" LifeSite News, 19 June 2008, https://www.lifesitenews.com/news/cardinal-ouellet-praises-humanae-vitae-abortion-the-consequence-of-the-cult.

[1100] Card. Marc Ouellet, "Let Us Understand 'Amoris Laetitia,'" Abouna, 9 November 2017, http://en.abouna.org/en/print/11810.

as not to be disturbed in our peace or comfort."[1101] Indeed, as archbishop of Quebec, His Eminence went so far as to give $20,000 of his own money, plus $20,000 from the archdiocese, to start the Cardinal Marc Ouellet Foundation to integrate immigrants and refugees into Quebecois society.[1102]

MARRIAGE, COMMUNION, AND AMORIS LAETITIA

Cardinal Ouellet's most complicated exercise of the teaching office has been his public comments on marriage and admittance to Holy Communion.

[1101] Philippe Vaillancourt, "Cardinal Ouellet Reminds Canada to Be Mindful of Migrants, Refugees," *Crux*, 27 July 2018, https://cruxnow.com/global-church/2018/07/27/cardinal-ouellet-reminds-canada-to-be-mindful-of-migrants-refugees/. His Eminence distinguishes between the terms "migrant" and "refugee," but it is not clear that he thinks any distinction in policy is permissible or desirable.

[1102] "Cardinal Launches Foundation to Assist Immigrants, Refugees," Catholic News Agency, 6 March 2006, https://www.catholicnewsagency.com/news/cardinal_launches_foundation_to_assist_immigrants_refugees. The cardinal seems particularly fond of Catholic immigrants from Haiti and Latin America who "help us to remember our own roots." See "Cardinal Marc Ouellet on the State of Quebec," Catholic Online, 11 December 2003, https://www.catholic.org/featured/headline.php?ID=563. "When they come to Canada or the U.S., they help to restore or save a Christian culture ... they must bring and keep their religious identity, and enrich us with their faith." Bunderson and Holdren, "Cultural Renewal." "There will not be a radiant and missionary Church in America without a solidarity that is more concrete and creative between the North and the South of the continent." Kevin J. Jones, "Cardinal Encourages Creative Catholic Unity across Americas," Catholic News Agency, 10 December 2012, https://www.catholicnewsagency.com/news/cardinal-calls-for-creative-catholic-unity-across-americas. The status of the Cardinal Marc Ouellet Foundation after 2008, when it had a $312,000 endowment, is not readily available. "The Eucharist Is Also Service," *Catholic Register*, 21 June 2008, https://www.catholicregister.org/item/8277-the-eucharist-is-also-service.

Prior to the 2014 Extraordinary Synod on the Family, His Eminence published an article in opposition to the distribution of Holy Communion to those who were divorced and civilly "remarried." In 2015, the cardinal continued to be critical of this practice but after the publication of *Amoris Laetitia*, he tried to reconcile the document with the Church's traditional teaching on the indissolubility of marriage.

Cardinal Ouellet's 2014 article in *Communio* begins with the nature of a sacrament. He holds that a sacrament is both a "means of salvation" and also a "sign and mystery of communion."[1103] In other words, sacraments are not only "responses to anthropological needs," but also "organic articulations of a body."[1104] In this latter sense, the Church's performance of a sacrament is a missionary sign to the world of what the Church is. Furthermore, sacraments are "articulations" of the "nuptial relationship between Christ and the Church."[1105]

The cardinal applies his general discussion of sacraments to the particular nature of sacramental marriage. Marriage between the baptized is "an authentic participation of the spouses in the very love of Christ for the Church."[1106] It realizes not only "the natural ends" of marriage—"the unity of the spouses" and "the procreation and education of children"—but is also a visible manifestation of the "invisible reality of divine Love, committed in a covenant relationship with the humanity in Jesus Christ."[1107] In this sense, a sacramental marriage is truly a "domestic church"—a visible expression of Christ's union with the Church.[1108] Furthermore, because Christ's love abides in a sacramental marriage, and this love is "indestructible and victorious over every fault," a sacramental marriage cannot be broken.

[1103] Marc Cardinal Ouellet, "Marriage and the Family within the Church," *Communio* 41 (Summer 2014): 229, 230, http://www.communio-icr.com/files/ouellet41-2.pdf.

[1104] Ibid., 230.

[1105] Ibid.

[1106] Ibid., 231.

[1107] Ibid., 232.

[1108] Ibid., 232-33.

"Such a possibility would directly contradict the irreversible commitment of Christ the Bridegroom in the first union."[1109]

In this light, Ouellet thought in 2014, "the Church has always maintained a limit with regard to divorced-and-'remarried' Catholics, without excluding them from the community, from participation in the eucharistic assembly or from community activities."[1110] That is, even if divorced-and-"remarried" persons have had "an authentic conversion," have "repented of their faults," and have "obtained forgiveness," if they "are incapable of abandoning their new union," the Church "does not authorize sacramental absolution and Eucharistic Communion,"[1111] for the "sacramental reason"[1112] that the Church dare not "betray the truth that is the foundation of the indissolubility of marriage."[1113] That said, "the core of sacramental

---

[1109] Ibid., 236.

[1110] Ibid.

[1111] In the cardinal's view, "Maintaining such a limit is not equivalent to declaring that these couples live in mortal sin or that they are denied Holy Communion for this moral reason." He does not give further detail, but he likely means that, by refusing to authorize Communion, the Church does not speak to the subjective imputability of the gravely sinful act of divorce and civil remarriage. From the language quoted in this footnote and in the accompanying body text, one might think that the cardinal would exclude from Communion even divorced-and-"remarried" couples who are abstaining from sexual acts (see Marc Cardinal Ouellet, *Mystery and Sacrament of Love: A Theology of Marriage and the Family for the New Evangelization* [Grand Rapids: Wm. B. Eerdmans Publishing, 2015], 169-70). Nothing in the text alone would preclude that reading, but it would be surprising because the cardinal has carefully studied *Familiaris Consortio*, which seems to allow such an exception, albeit only if there are serious reasons not to satisfy the obligation to separate (*FC* 84). Possibly, Ouellet cuts out that exception to strengthen the clarity of his expression of opposition to making further exceptions to the sacramental discipline.

[1112] See Ouellet, "Marriage and the Family," 238. According to Ouellet, "the reason for this limit is not first moral; it is sacramental." By this, he seems to mean that something other than the moral character of the specific divorced-and-"remarried" individuals determines the wrongful character of distribution of Communion to them.

[1113] Ibid.

grace can be communicated to these couples in the form of 'spiritual communion,' which is not a pale substitute for sacramental Communion, but rather a dimension of the latter."[1114]

In 2014, His Eminence noted only one type of "exceptional case" in past Church teaching on this matter. That is, if the "juridical path for a recognition of nullity is impossible but pastoral conviction of such nullity exists," it may be possible for such persons, although apparently divorced and "remarried," to receive "absolution and sacramental Communion."[1115] Ouellet avoided giving specific examples of such exceptional cases because "much work would have to be done to give examples, specify the criteria and procedures, and determine the conditions and responsibilities for the pastoral decisions these imply."[1116] He was keen, however, to distinguish this approach from "shifting the resolution of such cases into the 'private forum.'"[1117]

Thus stood Cardinal Ouellet's teaching about marriage and Eucharistic Communion in 2014. In 2015, the cardinal republished in English a 2007 book chapter critiquing Cardinal Kasper's penitential path for those who were married and then divorced and "remarried."[1118] Then, in 2016, Pope Francis published *Amoris Laetitia*, which Cardinal Ouellet has interpreted

---

[1114] Ibid., 238-39.

[1115] Ibid., 239.

[1116] Ibid.

[1117] Ibid. In a 1998 article republished in 2011, Cardinal Ratzinger had asserted a similar position (Benedict XVI, "The Pastoral Approach to Marriage Must Be Founded on Truth," *L'Osservatore Romano*, 30 November 2011, https://www.ewtn.com/catholicism/library/pastoral-approach-to-marriage-must-be-founded-on-truth-5021) and in 2017, Cardinal Müller reasserted this view and interpreted *Amoris Laetitia* to accord with this position (Sandro Magister, "The 'Dubia' Are More Alive Than Ever. And Cardinal Müller Is Adding Another All His Own," chiesa.espressonline.it, 6 November 2017, http://magister.blogautore.espresso.repubblica.it/2017/11/06/the-dubia-are-more-alive-than-ever-and-cardinal-muller-is-adding-another-all-his-own/).

[1118] See, e.g., Ouellet, *Mystery and Sacrament of Love*.

in at least two speeches[1119] and one article.[1120] The cardinal reads *Amoris Laetitia* not to contradict previous Church teaching or the positions he advanced in 2014 and 2015.

According to Ouellet, *Amoris Laetitia* accords with previous Church teaching. The document "does not distance itself from [*Veritatis Splendor*] with respect to the question of determining the objective morality of human acts and of the fundamental role of conscience as a 'witness' to the divine law inscribed in the sacred depths of each person."[1121] Rather, *Amoris Laetitia* complements *Veritatis Splendor* by "noting the way this conscience can be clouded by factors that influence one's knowledge of moral norms and one's will to follow them, thus, according to Church doctrine, affecting the subjective imputability of wrong acts."[1122] Similarly, Ouellet reads *Amoris Laetitia* not to contradict, but rather to "extend the openings initiated by His Holiness John Paul II's Apostolic Exhortation *Familiaris Consortio*."[1123] According to the cardinal, the "novelty" of *Amoris Laetitia* is not contrary to past Church teaching.

Nor does it seem that Ouellet judges *Amoris Laetitia* contrary to his own interpretation of Church teaching in 2014 and 2015, when he deemed episcopal conviction of nullity the sole legitimate exception to the rule that persons who are divorced and civilly "remarried" not receive Eucharistic Communion. In the cardinal's view, although *Amoris Laetitia* allows that " 'in certain cases' divorced-and-'remarried' persons might receive the help

---

[1119] "Cardinal Ouellet's Talk to the Knight's Supreme Convention," *Foolishness to the World* (blog), 4 August 2016, https://foolishnesstotheworld. wordpress.com/2016/08/04/cardinal-ouellets-talk-to-the-knights-supreme-convention/; "Verbatim of Cardinal Marc Ouellet's Conference with Canadian Bishops," *Présence*, 25 September 2017, http://presence-info.ca/article/verbatim-de-la-conference-du-cardinal-marc-ouellet-aux-eveques-canadiens (translated from French).

[1120] Marc Cardinal Ouellet, "Accompanying, Discerning, Integrating Weakness," *L'Osservatore Romano*, 21 November 2017, http://www.osservatoreromano.va/en/news/accompanying-discerning-integrating-weakness.

[1121] Ibid.

[1122] Ibid. His Eminence cites the *Catechism* in holding that subjective imputability may be "nonexistent" (ibid.).

[1123] Ibid.

of the sacraments," still, *Amoris Laetitia* "does not give a clear and precise answer to [which cases], other than to maintain the traditional discipline in a way that is open to exceptional cases."[1124] Particularly, *Amoris Laetitia* "does not settle" whether those who express to a pastor a conscientious judgment that they are not in a state of mortal sin, "in certain cases," might be allowed to receive Eucharistic Communion or "might be left to their conscience the freedom to choose."[1125] At no point does Cardinal Ouellet hold necessary under *Amoris Laetitia* that new exceptions to the sacramental discipline against Eucharistic Communion for persons who are divorced and civilly "remarried" be recognized.

That said, the cardinal reads *Amoris Laetitia* to "broaden [the] cases" in which "a collaborative decision between a pastor and a couple in the internal forum, overseen in some fashion by the bishop of the place, might provide access in certain cases to the help of the sacraments of Penance and Eucharist."[1126] Furthermore, he thinks

> it may well be that such help [of the sacraments] might be granted for a period where individuals discern that this help is necessary for them in conscience. The same individuals may then give these up later in their journey, not out of rigorism but as a free choice, by virtue of the fact that, with competent and respectful help, they have arrived at a better understanding that the help of the sacraments for their growth in grace does not resolve the contradiction between their public state of life and the sacramental meaning of Eucharistic communion.[1127]

If Cardinal Ouellet still thought that the help of Eucharistic Communion may be provided only in cases of moral, but not juridical, certainty of the first marriage's nullity, it seems unlikely that something would change such that "the same individuals may then give [Communion] up."[1128] In contrast is the

---

1124 Ibid.
1125 Ibid.
1126 Ibid.
1127 Ibid.
1128 Ibid.

case of those who have "subjectively repented and may desire deeply to make a change that is compatible with the truth of the sacrament, for example by making the decision to live as 'brother and sister' "—but to whom "this does not seem possible."[1129] Such persons would, in Ouellet's eyes, have reason to give up the sacrament of Eucharistic Communion. Thus, such persons may be those whom the cardinal now thinks, under *Amoris Laetitia*, may be granted Communion "for a period." Indeed, although he is "personally hesitant about this approach," he explicitly allows that "such openness may be discerned in certain cases in the internal forum."[1130]

This seems quite different than Cardinal Ouellet's view in 2014:

> It seems to me of capital importance that exceptional cases involve only the sphere of a conviction of nullity, and exclude that of a real conversion after the failure of a first, sacramental marriage. There is no conversion that can change the primary effect of the sacrament, the conjugal bond, which is indissoluble because it is linked to the witness of Christ himself. To act otherwise would mean to profess the indissolubility of marriage in word and to deny it in practice, thereby sowing confusion in the People of God, especially in those persons who have sacrificed opportunities to rebuild their life out of fidelity to Christ.[1131]

His Eminence appears now to be "personally hesitant" about what he previously thought "of capital importance" not to be done, lest the witness of Christ Himself be contradicted.

SUMMARY

A strong contender for the papacy during the last conclave, Cardinal Marc Ouellet is widely seen as papal material even if he modestly remarked in 2013: "I don't see myself at that level, not at all."

[1129] Ibid.
[1130] Ibid.
[1131] Ouellet, "Marriage and the Family."

A conservative-leaning prelate but with a somewhat modern, post-conciliar and non-traditionalist outlook in the mold of Pope St. John Paul II and Pope Benedict XVI, his episcopacy was formed through the challenging secular environment of Quebec, where he fearlessly resisted vociferous opposition to his steadfast adherence to Church teaching, especially on life issues.

A strong defender of priestly celibacy in the Latin Rite, he is firmly against women's ordination but favors giving women a greater role in the Church. He opposes same-sex "marriage" and the redefinition of civil marriage, has praised *Humanae Vitae*, and has concretely supported migrants in difficulty. His views on Islam are moderate.

The cardinal has a detailed knowledge of Latin America, having spent the first half of the 1970s as well as much of the 1980s in Colombia—a background that helped him to forge good relations with Pope Francis, whom he knew before his election as pope.

Unity and communion (his episcopal motto is *Ut Unum Sint*—"That They May Be One") are central to Ouellet, as is the Eucharist, which he sees as not only a celebration but also a "culture" needed to keep matters in balance. He is regarded as a world-class theologian but has appeared inconsistent on the issue of admitting Catholics living in irregular unions to Holy Communion.

As a personally principled, prayerful, yet sensitive man, sometimes given to emotion and with concern for unity, he is reluctant to criticize in public and instead takes a diplomatic and low-key approach both to the papacy and his important role as prefect of the Congregation for Bishops. He is known to be a man of holiness, transparency, and humility, with a passion for life. He rarely gives interviews.

Ouellet has a preference for solemn liturgies and wishes them to be about celebrating God, not people. He supported *Summorum Pontificum* and appears open and accepting of the Extraordinary Form of the Roman Rite. He has a devotion to Our Lady and is widely known to be a deeply spiritual prelate with a great sense of loyalty and a commitment to honor a position held—an attribute thought to be partly formed by an early love of sports, particularly hockey.

Although someone with a deep love for the Church's teaching, he is not considered doctrinaire and has a personal warmth and affability that those who know him say single him out as a true pastor.

SERVICE TO THE CHURCH

Ordination to the Priesthood: 25 May 1968
Ordination to the Episcopate: 19 March 2001
Elevation to the College of Cardinals: 21 October 2003

Education
- 1959-1964: École Normale of Amos; Philosophy
- 1964: Laval University; Bachelor of Pedagogy
- 1964-1968: Major Seminary, University of Montreal; License in theology
- 1976: Pontifical University of St. Thomas Aquinas; License in philosophy
- 1982: Pontifical Gregorian University; Doctorate in dogmatic theology

Assignments
- 1968-1970: Curate, Saint-Sauveur Parish of Val d'Or, Canada
- 1970-1972: Professor of philosophy, Major Seminary of Bogotá, Colombia
- 1974-1976: Professor and formator, Major Seminary of Manizales, Colombia
- 1976-1978: Professor, Major Seminary of Montreal, Canada
- 1982-1983: Professor and formator, Major Seminary of Cali, Colombia
- 1983-1988: Rector, Major Seminary of Manizales, Colombia
- 1988-1994: First consultor, Canadian Provincial Council of Sulpicians

- 1988-1994: Rector, Major Seminary of Montreal, Canada
- 1994-1996: Rector, St. Joseph's Seminary, Edmonton, Canada
- 1995-2000: Consultor, Congregation for the Clergy
- 1996-1997: Professor, Newman Theological College, Edmonton, Canada
- 1996-1997: Lecturer, John Paul II Institute, Rome, Italy
- 1997-2001: Professor of dogmatic theology, John Paul II Institute, Rome, Italy
- 2001-2002: Titular archbishop of Acropolis
- 2001-2003: Secretary, Pontifical Council for Promoting Christian Unity
- 2001-2009: Consultor, Congregation for the Doctrine of the Faith
- 2001-2016: Consultor, Congregation for Divine Worship and the Discipline of the Sacraments
- 2002-2010: Metropolitan archbishop of Quebec
- 2008: Relator general, XII Ordinary Synod of Bishops, "The Word of God"
- 2010-present: Prefect of the Congregation for Bishops
- 2010-present: President of the Pontifical Commission for Latin America

Membership

- Congregation for Bishops
- Congregation for the Clergy
- Congregation for Catholic Education
- Congregation for the Oriental Churches
- Congregation for Institutes of Consecrated Life and Societies of Apostolic Life
- Secretariat of State, Second Section—Relations with States
- Pontifical Council for Culture
- Pontifical Council for Promoting the New Evangelization
- Pontifical Council for Legislative Texts
- Pontifical Committee for International Eucharistic Congresses

PIETRO CARDINAL PAROLIN

"What Will Separate Us from the Love of Christ?"

Born: 17 January 1955
Schiavon, Italy
Nationality: Italian
Title: Vatican Secretary of State

BIOGRAPHY

Pietro Parolin was born in Schiavon, in the province and Diocese of Vicenza in Northern Italy, to a hardware-store manager and an elementary school teacher, both practicing Catholics. When Pietro was only ten years old, his father was killed in an automobile accident, and it destabilized him for a time.[1132] He sensed a call to the priesthood at a very early age and entered

---

[1132] Francesca Tenerelli, "'My Brother Don Piero': Di Lugagnano the Sister of the Vatican Secretary of State," *Il Baco da Seta*, 11 February 2014, https://www.

the seminary in Vicenza when he was fourteen. After his ordination to the priesthood in 1980, at the age of twenty-five, his superiors sent him to study canon law at the Gregorian University in Rome. During that time, he began training for the Vatican's diplomatic service. Having completed a thesis on the Synod of Bishops, he began his formal work as a diplomat in 1986.

After a three-year stint in Nigeria, he worked in the nunciature of Mexico and there helped to reestablish diplomatic ties between that country and the Holy See. In 1992, he was recalled to Rome and there began to work in the "Second Section" of the Secretariat of State under Cardinal Angelo Sodano, then Vatican secretary of state. Parolin was placed in charge of diplomatic relations for Spain, Andorra, Italy, and San Marino. Fluent in Italian, French, and Spanish, he is also proficient in English. From 2002 to 2009, Parolin was undersecretary of state for Relations with States, an influential yet low-key position, in which he directed relations with Vietnam, North Korea, Israel, and China. In 2009, he was ordained a bishop by Benedict XVI and nominated nuncio to Caracas, Venezuela. Pope Francis appointed Parolin secretary of state in 2013 and, in 2014, appointed him to his inner-circle "Council of Cardinals," who advise him on Church reform.

SANCTIFYING OFFICE

On the Liturgy
Cardinal Pietro Parolin believes the Church's liturgy can be "transformative"—that a better understanding of its meaning and symbolic language, especially the Mass, can help Catholics "encounter the Lord and grow in holiness."[1133]

---

ilbacodaseta.org/mio-fratello-don-piero-di-lugagnano-la-sorella-del-segretario-di-stato-vaticano-2/ (translated from Italian).

[1133] Hannah Brockhaus, "Understanding the Liturgy Can Be Transformative, Cardinal Parolin Says," Catholic News Agency, 26 August 2019, https://www.catholicnewsagency.com/news/understanding-the-liturgy-can-be-transformative-cardinal-parolin-says-77155.

In a letter for Italy's National Liturgical Week in 2019, he said that in a "practical sense" the liturgy helps "communities to internalize better the prayer of the Church, to love it as an experience of encounter with the Lord and with brothers, and in the light of this, to rediscover its content observe its rites."[1134]

He continued: "The liturgy will be authentic, that is, able to form and transform those who participate in it, if the latter, pastors and laypeople, learn increasingly well to grasp its meaning and symbolic language, including art, hymns and music at the service of the mystery celebrated, also including silence. *Mystagogy* is shown to be the most suitable way of entering in this path, in which one learns to welcome with wonder the new life received through the Sacraments and to renew it continually with joy," he wrote in the letter that drew heavily on Pope Francis' reflections on the liturgy.

Parolin sees the liturgy as indispensable for growth in holiness, and that the liturgy "calls us" to greater sanctity.[1135]

In 2014, during a homily coinciding with a Rome conference on *Sacrosanctum Concilium*, the Second Vatican Council's Constitution on the Liturgy, then-Archbishop Parolin noted how the "simplicity" of liturgical signs and symbols is disproportionate to the "superhuman extent" of their effects, realized in the "ordinariness of daily life." It is "almost as though the Lord wants to meet, heal and renew in the context of disarming normality, wants to reach and transform us in the daily routine of our existence," he said. The Lord, therefore, "does not seek a show," he continued. "The accomplished good has its own unstoppable internal dynamism of growth and diffusion, a powerful, constant, delicate, silent dynamism."

[1134] "Letter of the Cardinal Secretary of State for the 70th National Liturgical Week on the Theme: 'Liturgy: A Call for All to Baptismal Sanctity', 26.08.2019," http://press.vatican.va/content/salastampa/en/bollettino/pubblico/2019/08/26/190826a.html.

[1135] Pietro Parolin, "Parolin: 'Giussani, Peter and the Effectiveness of Christ's Pedagogy,'" *Communion and Liberation*, 24 February 2020, https://english.clonline.org/news/church/2020/02/24/parolin-giussani-peter-and-the-effectiveness-of-christ-s-pedagogy.

The important task of the liturgy, he believes, is to preserve and make present the gift of grace:

> The mystery of the Church's life is realized in the life of the Church through the action of the Spirit, and the liturgy is the main channel, always open, in which flows the pure water that emanates from the paschal mystery of Christ. The liturgy preserves and opens the door of grace and must, therefore, in turn, be cultivated and preserved in its truth and its authentic purpose.[1136]

Cardinal Parolin's views on more traditional forms of liturgy, such as the Mass in the Extraordinary Form, are less clear. In 2014, soon after taking up his role as secretary of state, he conveyed a message from Pope Francis in which the pope gave his "most cordial welcome" to a Rome pilgrimage of traditional Catholics and hoped that their visit to the tombs of the apostles would help them "comply more closely with Our Lord as celebrated at Mass."[1137] He does not appear to have spoken publicly about the Extraordinary Form since that time.

Determined by Diplomacy

Evidence indicates that Parolin's diplomatic career, begun early in his priesthood, has had a bearing on his role to sanctify the Church and the world. The majority of his public Masses and homilies appear to be extensions of his diplomatic work.

In 2013, in response to questions about the reform of the Curia that Francis tasked him with, Parolin stated, "I really hope there will be a real

---

[1136] Michelangelo Nasca, "Parolin sulla Liturgia 'Non dev'essere spettacolarizzazione, ma sobria. Si riscopra il dinamismo silenzioso,'" *Messainlatino*, 21 February 2014, http://blog.messainlatino.it/2014/02/parolin-sulla-liturgia-non-devessere.html.

[1137] Alberto Carosa, "Francis and Traditionalist Catholics," *Catholic World Report*, 12 March 2014, https://www.catholicworldreport.com/2014/03/12/francis-and-traditionalist-catholics/.

reform of the spirit." He continued, "The important thing is for all of us to renew ourselves in order to be in a continual conversion."[1138]

During an official state visit to the Republic of Bulgaria in 2016, at the conclusion of a Mass, Parolin stated: "We find ourselves in a church, intended as a structure in which the faithful gather together to pray and celebrate the liturgy. The community gathered here is not isolated but connected to all the other Christian communities in the world. We are therefore called to turn our eyes to the Church in its catholicity, that is, in its universality. When we are united in church, dear brothers and sisters, we can sense our belonging to this great Christian family which lives, works, and prays in the entire world."[1139]

Francis Focus

Nearly all of Parolin's homilies include a quotation from Pope Francis, and his esteem for the current pontiff was shown in November 2017, when the cardinal delivered remarks at the Catholic University of America. His speech, delivered in Italian, was titled "The Council: A Prophecy That Continues with Pope Francis." In his speech, the cardinal said that among the chief fruits of the Second Vatican Council was the introduction of the liturgy into local languages.[1140] At a Mass celebrating the Church's social

---

[1138] Joshua J. McElwee, "New Vatican Secretary of State Says Change Will Come to His Office," *National Catholic Reporter*, 4 December 2013, https://www.ncronline.org/news/people/new-vatican-secretary-state-says-change-will-come-his-office.

[1139] "Card. Parolin Consecrates New Cathedral of Bulgarian Catholic Exarchate of Sofia," Vatican Radio, 21 March 2016, http://www.archivioradiovaticana.va/storico/2016/03/21/card_parolin_consecrates_new_cathedral_of_bulgarian_catholic/en-1216933.

[1140] "Parolin: Vatican II Continues to Shape Church Life, Pope Francis' Papacy," Catholic News Service / U.S. Conference of Catholic Bishops, 2017, https://www.archbalt.org/parolin-vatican-ii-continues-shape-church-life-pope-francis-papacy/?print=print; "Holy See's Secretary of State Discusses the Legacy of Vatican II," Catholic University of America, 16 November 2017, https://communications.catholic.edu/news/2017/11/cardinal-parolin-address.html.

doctrine, Parolin stated, "The believer who lives in union with Christ, the Incarnate Word, head of a people who walks toward a new heaven and earth, is solicitous to take account of the social dimension of his faith, as Pope Francis has shown in his Apostolic Exhortation *Evangelii Gaudium*."[1141]

In a homily delivered during a Mass in 2018 celebrating the 750th anniversary of the dedication of the Sicilian Cathedral of Monreale, Parolin praised the beauty of the cathedral, spoke of the "daily miracle" that is Transubstantiation, and named as a "fundamental pillar" of "every truly ecclesial community" the worshipping community's participation in the Eucharist, which he called the "source and centre of the community," recalling the familiar words of *Sacrosanctum Concilium*.[1142]

GOVERNING OFFICE

Meteoric Diplomatic Rise

Pietro Parolin has been an influential force in the Church for almost twenty years, known for his diplomatic expertise and pragmatism, which have catapulted him to the second-highest position in the Church.

After training at the Pontifical Ecclesiastical Academy and entering the Holy See's diplomatic service in 1986, he served in Nigeria and Mexico, took a degree in canon law, and worked on matters related to the Lateran Pacts before Cardinal Sodano secured Parolin's first major diplomatic

---

[1141] Roberto Piermarini, "Card. Parolin: il credente non può ignorare impegno missionario," Vatican News, 27 November 2017, https://www.vaticannews. va/it/vaticano/news/2017-11/card-parolin-il-credente-non-puo-ignorare-impegno-missionario.html.

[1142] "Eucharistic Celebration Presided at by Cardinal Secretary of State Pietro Parolin for the 750th Anniversary of the Dedication of the Cathedral of Monreale," Holy See Press Office, 27 April 2018, https://press.vatican.va/content/salastampa/en/bollettino/pubblico/2018/04/27/180427e.html.

appointment in 2002 as undersecretary of the Holy See's Relations with States—effectively its deputy foreign minister.[1143]

During the end of John Paul II's pontificate and the beginning of Benedict XVI's, Parolin was the Holy See's chief negotiator with Israel, Vietnam, and China. In 2006, *Inside the Vatican* magazine named Parolin one of its "Top Ten" people of the year, citing his work on nuclear disarmament, dialogue with Iran and North Korea, and the fight against human trafficking.[1144]

As undersecretary, Parolin was at the forefront of Vatican efforts to conclude a long-standing impasse with Israel over its 1993 agreement establishing diplomatic ties with the Holy See, but as of 2020, seemingly intractable issues concerning tax and property rights for the Holy See continue to be unresolved.

Parolin had more success in helping to approve and implement the Nuclear Nonproliferation Treaty and in trying to find a diplomatic solution to Iran's nuclear program. By raising the Holy See's profile and good offices to be an effective "soft-power" mediator, he forged close relations not only with Iranian diplomats in Rome but also with United States officials who would often rely on him as one of the most accessible, informed, and straightforward contacts within the Holy See.[1145]

His accessibility was especially valued at a time when, during Benedict XVI's pontificate, efficiency of communications between the Holy See and foreign diplomats in Rome had reached a low ebb. Confidential files published by WikiLeaks showed him appearing far more often in diplomatic

---

[1143] Francesco Antonio Grana, "Holy See, the Era of Tarcisio Bertone Ends; Pietro Parolin Arrives at the State Secretariat," *Il Fatto Quotidiano*, 15 October 2013, https://www.ilfattoquotidiano.it/2013/10/15/santa-sede-finisce-lera-di-tarcisio-bertone-arriva-pietro-parolin/743961/ (translated from Italian).

[1144] John L. Allen Jr., "Francis Reboots Vatican System with New Secretary of State," *National Catholic Reporter*, 31 August 2013, https://www.ncronline.org/blogs/ncr-today/francis-reboots-vatican-system-new-secretary-state.

[1145] Stefania Maurizi, "Parolin? Un uomo degli USA," *L'Espresso*, 12 September 2013, https://espresso.repubblica.it/palazzo/2013/09/12/news/parolin-un-uomo-degli-usa-1.58878?refresh_ce.

cables during the first four years of Benedict's pontificate than even the Vatican secretary of state at the time, Cardinal Tarcisio Bertone (who did not speak English and was deemed too powerful to be easily accessible), and Archbishop Dominique Mamberti, the Holy See's foreign minister. An unnamed U.S. diplomatic source described Parolin in 2002 as an "open-minded" Vatican diplomat, "someone who has been trained to be able to take on more responsible positions."[1146]

As undersecretary, he also helped pave the way for the establishment of diplomatic ties between the Holy See and Vietnam and made several trips to North Korea in a bid to improve relations with the rogue communist state.

Venezuela

Benedict appointed Parolin to his first senior diplomatic post as apostolic nuncio to Venezuela in 2009. During that time, Archbishop Parolin had to guide the Church carefully through the tumultuous last years of President Hugo Chavez and his hostility to the Church. Chavez died shortly before Parolin came to Rome as secretary of state in 2014. Cardinal Jorge Urosa Savino, the archbishop emeritus of Caracas, said Parolin "played an important role in the process of rapprochement between the Church and the government, between different sectors of society and the authorities."[1147]

Secretary of State, Foreign Relations

On his appointment as secretary of state at the age of fifty-eight—the youngest since Cardinal Eugenio Pacelli, who later became Pope Pius XII—*L'Espresso* magazine wrote of Parolin: "From Syria to Lebanon to Iran, from the Middle East to Cuba, from China to East Timor and Venezuela, there is no chessboard on which Monsignor Parolin does not demonstrate his ability to move and know how to handle great situations."[1148] On

---

[1146] Ibid.

[1147] Gianni Cardinale, "Biografia di Pietro Parolin. Da Roma al Venezuela e ritorno," *Avvenire*, 8 February 2014, https://www.avvenire.it/chiesa/pagine/biografia-parolin-segretario-di-stato-vaticano.

[1148] Ibid.

receiving news of his appointment, Parolin said in 2014 he was "surprised and even a bit troubled at the idea of being called to such an important responsibility."[1149]

Many of Rome's state diplomats who had had dealings with him over the years lauded his appointment. According to Honduran cardinal Oscar Rodríguez Maradiaga, Pope Francis took only four days after his election in 2013 to choose Parolin to replace Cardinal Tarcisio Bertone as secretary of state, and Parolin had still to be made a cardinal.[1150]

Early on in his tenure as secretary of state, Cardinal Parolin was called on again to use his arbitration skills in Venezuela when, in 2014, Chavez's successor, President Nicolás Maduro, invited him to mediate talks between his government and the opposition as violence killed dozens in the worst unrest in the country in decades.[1151] Vatican-backed talks in 2017 failed after Venezuela's opposition walked away,[1152] and the protests and political crisis continue to this day.

In December 2014, Parolin and U.S. Secretary of State John Kerry agreed to find an "adequate humanitarian solution" for prisoners in the Guantanamo Bay detention camp.[1153] The number of detainees was significantly reduced, but despite the Vatican's wishes, the camp remains open. Cardinal Parolin had more success, at Pope Francis' instigation, in allowing the Holy See to play a major role in reestablishing U.S.-Cuba diplomatic

---

[1149] Salt and Light Media, "Witness—Cardinal Pietro Parolin," YouTube video, 28:21, posted 5 December 2014, https://www.youtube.com/watch?v=p_GgMMMAupg.

[1150] Grana, "Era of Tarcisio Bertone Ends."

[1151] Andrew Cawthorne, "Venezuela Reaches Out to Vatican No. 2 to Mediate Crisis," Reuters, 9 April 2014, https://www.reuters.com/article/us-venezuela-protests/venezuela-reaches-out-to-vatican-no-2-to-mediate-crisis-idUSB-REA381VW20140409.

[1152] "Venezuela's Opposition Walks Away from Vatican-Backed Talks," *Deutsche Welle*, 18 April 2017, https://www.dw.com/en/venezuelas-opposition-walks-away-from-vatican-backed-talks/a-36672319.

[1153] "US Asks for Vatican's Support to Shut Guantanamo Down," *La Stampa*, 15 December 2014, https://www.lastampa.it/vatican-insider/en/2014/12/15/news/us-asks-for-vatican-s-support-to-shut-guantanamo-down-1.35581480.

relations in 2014.[1154] He reportedly played a key role in those talks, partly helped by having built up a "very good relationship" with Kerry.[1155]

"Dialogue" and "encounter" are two of Parolin's main objectives for Vatican diplomatic policy.[1156] For him, "the reason why the Holy See has a diplomatic corps is in order to strive for peace.... Vatican diplomacy is concerned with the common good of humanity."[1157] Furthermore, he believes "diplomacy should have the good of humanity as its aim."[1158] He has frequently stressed that the Church's diplomacy is a "diplomacy of peace" and that it does not have "power interests, neither political, economic, nor ideological." For this reason, he says, it has "greater freedom to represent the reasoning of one side to the other side, and make both aware of the risks that a self-referential vision can entail for all."[1159]

In June 2018, Cardinal Parolin controversially spoke at the secretive Bilderberg Meeting, noted for its globalist agenda and what some say are aspirations for a one-world government. A Vatican official said the cardinal decided to attend after persistent invitations from its organizers and

[1154] John Hooper, "Renewed US-Cuba Relations Biggest Success in Vatican Diplomacy in Decades," *Guardian*, 17 December 2014, https://www.the-guardian.com/world/2014/dec/17/pope-us-cuba-vatican-diplomacy.

[1155] Edward Pentin, "Cardinal Parolin Played Key Role in U.S.-Cuba Negotiations," Edward Pentin, 30 December 2014, https://edwardpentin.co.uk/cardinal-parolin-played-key-role-in-u-s-cuba-negotiations/.

[1156] "Vatican, Parolin: 'My Mission in the Footsteps of Casaroli,'" *Libertà*, 22 November 2014, http://www.liberta.it/foto-gallery/2014/11/22/il-segre-tario-di-stato-vaticano-parolincostruiamo-ponti-non-muri/ (translated from Italian).

[1157] "Archbishop Pietro Parolin Is the New Vatican Secretary of State," *Inside the Vatican*, 1 October 2013, https://insidethevatican.com/news/archbishop-pietro-parolin-new-vatican-secretary-state.

[1158] Ibid.

[1159] Gianfranco Brunelli, "Interview with Cardinal Pietro Parolin, Vatican's Top Diplomat: Moscow and Beijing Are the New Interlocutors, Waiting for Europe," *Il Sole 24 Ore*, 27 July 2017, https://www.ilsole24ore.com/art/interview-with-cardinal-pietro-parolin-vatican-s-top-diplomat-moscow-and-beijing-are-the-new-interlocutors-waiting-for-europe-AEDGuK4B?refresh_ce=1.

because he wished, after giving it much thought, to take the teaching of the Church to a group who would not otherwise hear it.[1160]

PROPONENT OF OSTPOLITIK

The Italian cardinal's view of Vatican diplomacy matches most closely that of the Vatican secretary of state under the early part of John Paul II's pontificate, Cardinal Agostino Casaroli—as Parolin himself emphasized in a conference dedicated to the hundredth anniversary of Casaroli's birth.[1161]

Under Pope St. Paul VI, but less so under John Paul II, Casaroli reversed Pius XII's confrontational strategy with communism and other anti-Catholic forces, instead employing the strategy of *Ostpolitik,* that is, pragmatic collaboration through compromise and conciliation. Cardinal Parolin has clearly adopted the strategy in his relations with China's Communist Party (see "Diplomacy with China," below).

Benedict XVI's assessment of Casaroli is remarkably distinct from Parolin's. Benedict has said:

> It was clear that Casaroli's politics, although well-intentioned, had basically failed.... Of course, one could not hope that this [dictatorial] regime would soon collapse. But it was clear that, rather than trying to be reconciled with it through conciliatory compromises, one must strongly confront it. That was John Paul II's basic insight, which I shared.[1162]

[1160] Edward Pentin, "Vatican Official Explains Why Cardinal Parolin Attended Bilderberg Meeting," *National Catholic Register,* 15 June 2018, https://www.ncregister.com/blog/edward-pentin/spokesman-explains-why-cardinal-parolin-attended-bilderberg-meeting.

[1161] "Footsteps of Casaroli."

[1162] Pope Benedict XVI and Peter Seewald, *Last Testament: In His Own Words* (London: Bloomsbury, 2017), 170.

Curial Reform, Third Section

Parolin has had a low public profile when it comes to reform of the Roman Curia, one of Pope Francis' mandated tasks on being elected pope, but the appearance has been deceptive, and in fact, Francis has relied on him. According to Italian Vaticanist Andrea Gagliarducci, Parolin helped the Secretariat of State to regain its position as guiding and coordinating the Roman Curia, and it now also acts as a kind of "regulator" of Pope Francis' reforms, with Parolin issuing papal decrees (rescripts) in the pope's name—a change aimed at enabling reforms to be more quickly enacted. Under Parolin's watch, the Secretariat of State also exercises more diplomatic influence than before, delineating pastoral initiatives from diplomatic ones and placing a premium on diplomatic pragmatism. This contrasts with Benedict XVI's approach, which was to ensure Vatican diplomacy was, first and foremost, grounded in truth.[1163]

In 2017, Pope Francis reorganized the Secretariat of State by establishing a "Third Section." This new section is meant to manifest the "attention and closeness" of the pope with respect to diplomatic personnel.[1164,1165] The creation of the Third Section reportedly extends Parolin's influence, for it enables him to exercise oversight and control more directly all persons

---

[1163] Andrea Gagliarducci, "Pope Francis, a Double-Faceted Government?," *MondayVatican*, 18 January 2016, http://www.mondayvatican.com/vatican/pope-francis-a-double-faceted-government.

[1164] "Communiqué of the Secretariat of State," Holy See Press Office, 21 November 2017, https://press.vatican.va/content/salastampa/en/bollettino/pubblico/2017/11/21/171121c.html.

[1165] Vaticanist Marco Tosatti has written that Parolin is a "progressive nuncio with ties to Silvestrini's faction," a reference to the late liberal cardinal Achille Silvestrini and the so-called Saint Gallen Group of diplomats and Vatican insiders who banded together to promote the cause of a progressive pope originally for the conclave following the death of John Paul II and then again in 2013. Significantly, shortly before the 2013 conclave, Bergoglio began meeting with diplomats from the Spanish section of the Vatican's Secretariat of State, which included Parolin. Marco Tosatti, "The Pope's Power," *First Things* (29 June 2017), https://www.firstthings.com/web-exclusives/2017/06/the-popes-power.

who work for the Secretariat of State.[1166] In the midst of Francis' curial changes, Parolin has "gradually achieved an ever more central role." Contrary to initial predictions, the "bureaucratic" Secretariat of State is the only office whose structure has been reinforced and even strengthened in its powerful work.[1167]

In 2015, Parolin suggested that an "office for pontifical mediation" be established within the ranks of the Secretariat of State, in order to function as a link between the on-the-ground commitment of papal diplomacy and its commitment within international institutions. It is not clear if that office has yet been created.[1168]

In 2014, Parolin sent a letter to all Vatican department heads, notifying them of an immediate end to new hires, wage increases, and overtime in an urgent effort to cut costs and offset budget shortfalls. He has helped to oversee a number of cost-cutting initiatives that have been welcomed by some in terms of increased efficiency and lower costs but have also led to loss of morale among Vatican staff who have complained of these internal reforms being poorly executed.[1169]

Vatican Finances

In 2019, it emerged that the Secretariat of State had become embroiled in a dubious financial deal in the 2010s largely associated with Cardinal

---

[1166] Ibid.

[1167] Andrea Gagliarducci, "Why a Third Section of the Secretariat of State?," *MondayVatican*, 27 November 2017, http://www.mondayvatican.com/vatican/why-a-third-section-of-the-secretariat-of-state; John L. Allen Jr., "More and More, Parolin's the Face of Authority in Francis's Vatican," *Crux*, 10 August 2017, https://cruxnow.com/analysis/2017/08/10/parolins-face-authority-franciss-vatican/.

[1168] Andrea Gagliarducci, "Curia Reform May Include an Office for Negotiations in the Secretariat of State," Catholic News Agency, 11 March 2015, https://www.catholicnewsagency.com/news/curia-reform-may-include-an-office-for-negotiations-in-the-secretariat-of-state-13513.

[1169] Edward Pentin, "Vatican Staff Nervous about Possible Layoffs," Edward Pentin, 23 March 2014, https://edwardpentin.co.uk/vatican-staff-nervous-about-possible-layoffs/.

Parolin's deputy at the time, Archbishop (now Cardinal) Angelo Becciu. Cardinal Parolin appeared to have little knowledge of the deal, saying the fund in question appeared to be "well managed" but the transaction was "rather opaque" and his office was "trying to clear it up." The deal involved a controversial speculative purchase of a London property development that led to a Vatican police raid on the offices of the Secretariat of State. Some reports claimed that the transaction involved the use of Holy See funds meant for the poor and was financed using loans, although Becciu denied the accusations, saying such property investments were "accepted practice for the Holy See."[1170]

More problematic is what appears to have been Cardinal Parolin's involvement in two areas. The first regards Vatican financial reforms. In 2016, Archbishop Becciu instructed PricewaterhouseCoopers that its major external audit of the Vatican—the first to ever be carried out on Vatican departments—was not to include the Secretariat of State. This rendered the audit useless, causing it to end abruptly just four months after it had begun in December 2015.[1171] The finance reforms had already faced obstructions, and by 2016, whatever progress had been made since Francis' election was rolled back by an "old guard" resistant to change and exposure of malpractice.[1172] Some reports say that Parolin gave Becciu the instruction not to audit the Secretariat of State. Overall it is unclear how much of a role, if any, Cardinal Parolin played in these obstructions, but they appear to have had the intention of regaining for the Secretariat of State some of the powers it had lost to the Secretariat for the Economy, established by Francis in 2014 to bring Vatican finances

[1170] See Ed Condon, "Vatican's $200 Million London Property Deal Financed with Borrowed Money, Sources Say," *Catholic World Report*, 4 November 2019, https://www.catholicworldreport.com/2019/11/04/vaticans-200-million-london-property-deal-financed-with-borrowed-money-sources-say/.

[1171] Marcantonio Colonna (Henry Sire), *The Dictator Pope: The Inside Story of the Francis Papacy* (Washington, D.C.: Regnery, 2018).

[1172] Edward Pentin, "Pope Francis and Reform: Financial Problems Persist," *National Catholic Register*, 12 March 2018, https://www.ncregister.com/daily-news/pope-francis-and-reform-financial-problems-persist.

to order. At the very least, despite holding the second-highest-ranking position in the Vatican, Cardinal Parolin was in a position to prevent these obstructions and see to it that finance reform continued along the path being mapped out by Cardinal George Pell, the Vatican treasurer, but the evidence suggests he either did not do so or was ineffective in whatever action he did take.

The second area regarding governance of Vatican finances concerns Parolin's role in allowing funds belonging to a Vatican children's hospital to be used to keep afloat a bankrupt Italian hospital, despite warnings from the Vatican treasurer not to go ahead with the transaction.[1173]

Fifty million euro from the children's hospital in Rome, the Bambino Gesù, was reportedly used in 2014 by Vatican officials to guarantee a loan to the Istituto Dermopatico dell'Immacolata hospital, also in Rome. The loan was firmly opposed by Cardinal George Pell, then prefect of the Vatican Secretariat for the Economy, who, according to an informed source, advised Cardinal Parolin and Pope Francis not to proceed with it because he considered it "immoral to condemn the children's hospital to losing money that it needed to treat needy children."

But Parolin and the pope went ahead with the loan guarantee on the strength of a dubious feasibility study carried out by accountancy firm KPMG that appeared to show how the loan could and would be repaid, but which the firm refused to sign or endorse.

Although the loan was primarily arranged by lower officials who received large payments for their work, Cardinal Parolin said he was responsible for arranging the controversial loan guarantee.[1174]

[1173] Edward Pentin, "Tangled Web of Transactions Utilized to Fund Bankrupt Italian Hospital," *National Catholic Register*, 10 December 2019, https://www.ncregister.com/daily-news/tangled-web-of-transactions-utilized-to-fund-bankrupt-italian-hospital.

[1174] JD Flynn and Ed Condon, "Cardinal Parolin says he arranged controversial hospital loan, Papal Foundation Grant," Catholic News Agency, 20 November 2019, https://www.catholicnewsagency.com/news/cardinal-parolin-says-he-arranged-controversial-hospital-loan-papal-foundation-grant-99539.

Order of Malta Controversy

Cardinal Parolin played a significant role in a controversy that came to a head in 2016-2017 involving the Holy See and the Sovereign Military Order of Malta (hereafter the Order). The Knights of the Order, founded by a papal bull in the twelfth century during the First Crusade, have traditionally been defenders and teachers of the Faith and enjoy the status of a sovereign state, but today primarily serve as humanitarian actors.

The controversy, which Parolin himself called an "unprecedented crisis," was complex and primarily involved two warring factions within the Order: on the one side, professed religious of a more traditionalist and conservative disposition who wished to preserve the Order's traditions as much as possible; on the other, the Order's modernizing members who wished to bring the Order "up to date," both in terms of some traditions and approach to Church teaching. To the latter, the traditional wing of the Order was a hindrance to such reform, whereas to the former, the modernists were dissenters whose designs on the Order would ultimately secularize and destroy it.[1175]

Many nevertheless agreed that the Order needed some kind of reform, and Pope Francis instructed the patron of the Order, Cardinal Raymond Burke, to help achieve this, including explicitly asking him to clear the Order of Freemasonry. Parolin was friends with Albrecht Freiherr von Boeselager, the Order's Grand Chancellor and *de facto* leader of the modernist reformers. The two had struck up a rapport when, from 1989 to 2014, Boeselager was Grand Hospitaller, responsible for the Order's international humanitarian work and often in contact with Parolin on the diplomatic circuit.

On December 6, 2016, the Order's Grand Master, Fra' Matthew Festing, dismissed Boeselager for insubordination after he resisted a disciplinary instruction taken against him for being ultimately responsible for

---

[1175] Steve Skojec, "Malta Besieged: An Ancient and Sovereign Order Toppled by Rome," *One Peter Five*, 28 January 2017, https://onepeterfive.com/malta-besieged-an-ancient-and-sovereign-order-toppled/.

distributing hundreds of thousands of contraceptives in the developing world when he served as Grand Hospitaller. Boeselager contested the accusation, which Festing made on the basis of an investigation carried out by a three-person commission the year before. Cardinal Burke, who was present at the December 6 meeting, helped exert pressure on Boeselager but always denied that Francis had asked him to demand Boeselager's resignation (see more on this in the Cardinal Burke profile). Boeselager then appealed to Cardinal Parolin, who, believing that Cardinal Burke had conveyed the dismissal from Francis, wrote to Festing, stressing that the pope had asked for dialogue to resolve problems and not to expel anyone. Due to a "perceived irregularity" of the dismissal procedure, which had "deeply divided the Order," Parolin decided to establish a five-person commission, all its members generally supportive of liberal reforms, to investigate the distribution of contraceptives and the grounds for Boeselager's dismissal. Three members of the commission, along with Boeselager, had some involvement in a $118 million bequest to the Order held in a Swiss trust whose true origins the Grand Master suspected. Parolin had reportedly been aware of the bequest since 2014.[1176] The consultancy firm Promontory carried out a "due diligence" study of the trust in 2017 and found no wrongdoing, but the precise details of the funds and exactly how the total amount has been, and is being, spent by the Order remains unknown.

Within one month of its formation, Parolin's commission declared Boeselager innocent of all wrongdoing.[1177] In January 2017, Festing was

---

[1176] Ibid.

[1177] While Boeselager claimed that the findings of the commission established by Festing were inaccurate, when challenged by Burke at the December 6, 2016, meeting to explain why he, Boeselager, had not requested corrections to the document throughout 2016 or provided materials to disprove its investigative conclusions, Boeselager had no response. This, Burke is reported to have said, did not surprise him, for had heard Boeselager himself vocalize a justification for precisely the dubious questions in practice—a justification that the commission also asserts was invoked by MI personnel in defense of the dubious practice. See also: Maike Hickson, "Leaked

invited to a private audience with Pope Francis. According to reports, Francis asked Festing to resign on the spot, and together they formulated a resignation letter. The pope subsequently ordered Boeselager reinstated, stripped Cardinal Burke of all prerogatives and duties with respect to the Order, announced the appointment of a new papal delegate to the Order, and declared that the Holy See would oversee a review of the ancient sovereign entity and guide its reorientation. It remains unclear why, perhaps acting on instructions, Parolin interfered in the internal affairs of the autonomous Order, especially in setting up a commission to examine its internal affairs (something Festing denounced as "unacceptable"), thereby compromising the Order's sovereign status. Although a 1953 ruling decreed that the Congregation for Religious had some jurisdiction over the Order, the Secretariat of State did not have such rights, leading to charges that Parolin had flouted that law.

Sant'Egidio

Cardinal Parolin is close to the Sant'Egidio community, a worldwide Catholic lay group founded in Rome that helps the poor, the needy, and the vulnerable and is allied to Italy's political center-left (see more detailed information on the organization under the profile of Cardinal Matteo Zuppi). Cardinal Parolin has attended a number of its events over the years. In 2018, he gave the homily at the organization's fiftieth anniversary and again at its fifty-second anniversary in 2020.[1178] In 2019, Parolin wrote the preface to a book summarizing the value of the 2018 controversial provisional agreement between China and the Holy See (see more on Parolin's diplomacy with China below). The book's launch was moderated by Sant'Egidio president

---

Report of Cardinal Burke Audience Reveals Background on Malta Crisis," *One Peter Five*, 28 April 2017, https://onepeterfive.com/leaked-report-of-cardinal-burke-audience-reveals-background-on-malta-crisis/.

[1178] Roberto Zuccolini, "Parolin: Sant'Egidio, People of 'Salt and Light,'" Vatican News, 10 February 2020, https://www.vaticannews.va/it/vaticano/news/2020-02/parolin-52-anni-comunita-santegidio-laterano.html.

Marco Impagliazzo and attended by the community's founder, Andrea Riccardi.[1179] Cardinal Joseph Zen Ze-kiun, a longtime critic of the Vatican's approach to China, criticized the Sant'Egidio community in 2012 for its history of submissiveness to the Chinese communist regime.[1180]

Handling Church Division, Episcopal Governance

Immersed in the world of politics, Parolin has tried to apply his long-honed skills of arbitration to defusing internal Church tensions and healing divisions. He firmly believes, however, that the Church is unlike other institutions in which politics often takes center stage. "Enough with seeing the Vatican and the Catholic Church as a party divided by political currents, as a place of factions that confront and sometimes clash," he said in 2020, adding that sin also exists in the Church and conversion is necessary, but "reducing the Church to these [political] categories seems to me to be deadly for the ecclesiastical world." Such a reading for Parolin "does not account for what the Church is," and he invites the faithful "to go a little beyond these criteria and these categories and see instead what is good and positive that is being done in the Church, despite the difficulties that exist in every human relationship."[1181]

He takes a different stance to Benedict XVI when it comes to bishops' conferences. Whereas Benedict saw them merely as bureaucratic structures, Parolin insists they are "episcopal" in the full sense of the authority of a bishop, which includes the power to define doctrine.[1182] He is

---

[1179] Alessandro Gisotti, "The Holy See and China: the Door Is Open," Vatican News, 27 September 2019, https://www.vaticannews.va/en/vatican-city/news/2019-09/vatican-china-holy-see-gisotti.html.

[1180] Sandro Magister, "China: Cardinal Zen against Saint Egidio," chiesa.espressonline.it, 9 February 2012, http://chiesa.espresso.repubblica.it/articolo/1350164bdc4.html?eng=y.

[1181] "Parolin replica ai veleni anti-Bergoglio: 'Il Papa è uno solo, chi non è più Papa non ha l'autorità,'" *Globalist*, 6 February 2020, https://www.globalist.it/life/2020/02/06/parolin-replica-ai-veleni-anti-bergoglio-il-papa-e-uno-solo-chi-non-e-piu-papa-non-ha-l-autorita-2052635.html.

[1182] Edward Pentin, "'Evangelii Gaudium'—A Key to Understanding Francis' Papacy," *National Catholic Register*, 28 February 2018, https://www.ncregister.

naturally a supporter of Pope Francis' vision for greater decentralization and "synodality," including on matters of doctrine, ostensibly to allow local churches to deal better pastorally with the complexities of their local circumstances.[1183]

Villa Nazareth

In March 2020, Cardinal Parolin was appointed president of Villa Nazareth, a small university college based in Rome, governed by a foundation under the supervision of the Secretariat of State.[1184] Parolin was once also a director of the institution. Founded in 1946 by Cardinal Domenico Tardini, secretary of state under Pope St. John XXIII, to welcome poor and orphaned children, for many years Villa Nazareth was run by Cardinal Achille Silvestrini, who turned it into an elite training school largely managed by Holy See diplomats. According to *Il Foglio*, Silvestrini was the "powerful leader" of the "left wing of the Catholic Church" during the John Paul II era who helped turn the institution into a kind of headquarters for progressivism.[1185] Archbishop Claudio Maria Celli, a papal diplomat who has had many dealings with China and Vietnam and played a significant role in current Holy See–China relations, is a former head of the university and remains a member of the institution's board. Among

---

com/daily-news/evangelii-gaudium-a-key-to-understanding-francis-papacy.

[1183] Ibid.

[1184] "Il cardinale Pietro Parolin presidente di Villa Nazareth," Villa Nazareth, 4 March 2020, https://villanazareth.org/il-card-parolin-presidente-di-villa-nazareth/.

[1185] Matteo Matzuzzi, "Il Conte di Villa Nazareth," *Il Foglio*, 27 August 2019, https://www.ilfoglio.it/chiesa/2019/08/27/news/il-conte-di-villa-nazareth-270997/. This was reportedly witnessed during the election of Benedict XVI in 2005, when a group of cardinals, including Godfried Danneels, Carlo Maria Martini, and Cormac Murphy-O'Connor, met with Silvestrini to try to prevent Cardinal Joseph Ratzinger from being elected. Edward Pentin, "Still Controversial: Cardinal Danneels and the Conclave of 2005," *National Catholic Register*, 5 November 2015, https://www.ncregister.com/daily-news/still-controversial-cardinal-danneels-and-the-conclave-of-2005.

Villa Nazareth's alumni is Giuseppe Conte, the current prime minister of Italy. It has also had other close connections with prominent figures in Italian politics.

Clergy Sexual Abuse, Theodore McCarrick

Cardinal Parolin has said relatively little publicly about clergy sexual abuse. He believes it is "devastating" and that the Church's "first duty" is to take care of the victims, then recognize and repent for the crimes, and find ways to prevent them in the future.[1186] He has given relatively frequent updates on the progress of an eagerly awaited Vatican commission of investigation, announced in 2018, to determine "all the relevant facts of the case" of Theodore McCarrick, the laicized former cardinal found guilty of abusing seminarians.[1187] In May 2019, Parolin said the results of the study would be in the form of a declaration but gave no timeline of its release;[1188] in February 2020, he said the report would "come out soon" but could not say "exactly when." The work "that is done is done," he said, "but the pope must give the final word."[1189] As of May 2020, the report had yet to be published.

[1186] "Sex Abuse 'Devastating,' Says Parolin," *ANSA*, 22 August 2018, https://www.ansa.it/english/news/2018/08/22/sex-abuse-devastating-says-parolin_ea6bf947-2962-428b-be46-70b5940a7b90.html.

[1187] Edward Pentin, "Pope Francis Orders New, 'Thorough Study' of Archbishop McCarrick," *National Catholic Register*, 6 October 2018, https://www.ncregister.com/blog/edward-pentin/pope-francis-orders-new-thorough-study-of-archbishop-mccarrick.

[1188] Courtney Mares, "Cardinal Parolin Says Vatican Will Issue Declaration on McCarrick Investigation," Catholic News Agency, 30 May 2019, https://www.catholicnewsagency.com/news/cardinal-parolin-says-vatican-will-issue-declaration-on-mccarrick-investigation-16052.

[1189] Hannah Brockhaus, "Parolin: On McCarrick Report Release, Pope Francis Has 'Final Word,'" Catholic News Agency, 6 February 2020, https://www.catholic-newsagency.com/news/pope-francis-has-final-word-on-mccarrick-reports-release-parolin-says-99372.

Coronavirus

During the coronavirus outbreak in 2020, Cardinal Parolin said it "would be nice," in order to counter the loneliness of the lockdowns, "if all churches rang their bells for a minute," calling everyone to "pray together, even if physically apart."[1190]

TEACHING OFFICE

On Priestly Celibacy

On September 8, 2013, Parolin said that priestly celibacy is "not a church dogma and it can be discussed because it is a church tradition.... We can talk, reflect, and deepen on these subjects that are not definite, and we can think of some modifications, but always with consideration of unity, and all according to the will of God.... as well as to the opening to the spirit of the times."[1191] In 2016, in prepared remarks, Parolin recalled that the requirement of celibacy is a disciplinary one that has never been imposed on all clerics:

> If the problematic ["vocations crisis"] does not appear irrelevant, it is nevertheless necessary not to take rushed decisions, or decisions based solely on the basis of present need.... It remains true now as ever that the exigencies of evangelization, together with the history and multiform tradition of the Church, leave open the possibility for legitimate debate, if these are motivated by the [imperative of] Gospel proclamation and conducted in a constructive way, [and]

[1190] Andrea Tornielli, "Pandemia, Parolin: nonostante la paura, non chiudiamoci in noi stessi," *Vatican News*, 2 April 2020, https://www.vaticannews.va/it/vaticano/news/2020-04/coronavirus-pandemia-segretario-stato-vaticano-parolin-chiesa.html.

[1191] John L. Allen Jr., "New Secretary of State Parolin on celibacy, democracy," *National Catholic Reporter*, 11 September 2013, https://www.ncronline.org/blogs/ncr-today/new-secretary-state-parolin-celibacy-democracy.

safeguarding the beauty and high dignity of the choice for celibate life.[1192]

He noted a "sacramental emergency" in some areas suffering from priest shortages, but pointed out that celibacy was not required by the "very nature of the priesthood" but had special advantages, such as the "freedom to serve" and the ability for priests to "travel light."[1193]

Female Cardinals

Speaking about the role of women in the hierarchy of the Church, Parolin said, "A woman could become Secretary of State, in the sense that the role of the Secretary of State is evidently not bound to the sacraments or the priesthood.... In any case, I repeat, let's look at the path that has been travelled, and the Lord will tell us how far we can go."[1194] Canon law stipulates that although the pope may choose to elevate to the College of Cardinals a man who has not yet been ordained a bishop, that candidate must already have received Holy Orders and must then immediately be ordained a bishop in order to become a cardinal. Only males, therefore, may be made cardinals. Parolin seems to be arguing that the Vatican secretary of state need not be a cardinal or one who has received Holy Orders. The secretary of state has been a cardinal at least since the middle of the seventeenth century.

Parolin was personally present at the redesign launch of a monthly women's publication published under the auspices of *L'Osservatore Romano*. The publication is edited and produced by an all-female staff. The

---

[1192] "Card. Parolin Addresses Gregorian Conference on Celibacy," Vatican Radio, 2 June 2016, http://www.archivioradiovaticana.va/storico/2016/02/06/card_parolin_addresses_gregorian_conference_on_celibacy/en-1206478.

[1193] Christopher Lamb, "INTERVIEW: Ordaining Married Men a Possibility Due to Global Shortage of Priests, Says Pope Francis," *Tablet*, 9 March 2017, https://www.thetablet.co.uk/news/6828/interview-ordaining-married-men-a-possibility-due-to-global-shortage-of-priests-says-pope-francis.

[1194] Inés San Martín, "Trusted Papal Aide Says Woman Could Be Vatican's 'Prime Minister,'" *Crux*, 4 May 2016, https://cruxnow.com/church/2016/05/04/trusted-papal-aide-says-woman-could-be-vaticans-prime-minister/.

editor of the magazine described Parolin's presence at the launch event as "more than beautiful, [it] is auspicious."[1195] Parolin spoke on that occasion of the need to cultivate a habit within the Church of "listening to women, looking at the many things they have to say and to the many initiatives they undertake, implementing the male and female synergy that so often has been invoked in official documents but not always put into practice." Later that day, Parolin said although women could not be ordained priests, since "the Church has taken its stance on this matter," they could assume many other leadership roles within the Church. "I believe that women don't want the 'pink quota,' but they want to move forward through their merit and their capabilities, without having institutionally reserved spaces," he said.[1196]

Populism, Migration

Parolin has said the Holy See is "concerned" about the emergence of populism around the world and regards the "inability to welcome and integrate" as "dangerous." [1197] He believes history "teaches us this, and we hope that in this sense it will not be repeated."[1198]

In 2020 he warned against a drift toward nationalism and isolationism, which he said are "fundamentally infantile reactions to a globalised world that seems invasive" while *Romanità* (Roman ethos) means "true universality, fraternity, openness to others and peace." His comments, made to the Sant'Egidio lay community, were reported as implicit criticism of a Rome conference on national conservatism on the theme "God, Honor, Country" that had taken place just days before, and whose speakers included Hungarian prime minister Viktor Orbán.[1199]

[1195] Ibid.

[1196] Ibid.

[1197] "Cardinal Parolin: Holy See 'Concerned' about Populism," Vatican Radio, 15 February 2017, http://en.radiovaticana.va/news/2017/02/15/cardinal_parolin_holy_see_concerned_about_populism/1292655.

[1198] Ibid.

[1199] Céline Hoyeau, "Cardinal Parolin warns against nationalism, urges integration," *La Croix*, 10 February 2020, https://international.la-croix.com/news/cardinal-parolin-warns-against-nationalism-urges-integration/11783.

In December 2018, world leaders met in Morocco to sign and announce an accord informally known as the Global Compact on Migration.[1200] The compact outlined best practices regarding immigration, refugee, and asylum policies—in short, "migration governance." The compact was not binding, but fifteen nations pulled out of the meeting, including Italy and the United States, mainly on the grounds that it could potentially compromise national sovereignty.

Parolin pressed ahead for the Holy See to take part, saying the Church was "convinced that the enormous challenges" posed by migration are "better addressed through multilateral processes" than "isolationist" ones.[1201] He also hoped better migration governance would "stem the wave of racism and xenophobia."[1202]

He argued that "a dignified response to migration must be reasonable, with governments prudently determining their actual capacity for meaningful integration."[1203] But he also spoke of Holy See "reservations" to the compact concerning "ideological interpretations of human rights" that do not "recognize the inherent value and dignity of human life at every stage of its beginning, development, and end."[1204]

In further remarks, Parolin stated that nations must respect the "fundamental right" for a person to practice his religion "freely, without fear of persecution or discrimination."[1205] Religious freedom, he said, is a "necessary prerogative," one that states should respect and support and that the

---

[1200] "Global Compact for Safe, Orderly and Regular Migration," Global Compact for Migration, 13 July 2018, https://refugeesmigrants.un.org/sites/default/files/180713_agreed_outcome_global_compact_for_migration.pdf.

[1201] Iacopo Scaramuzzi, "Global Compact, Parolin: 'No State Can Manage Migration on Its Own,'" *La Stampa*, 14 October 2019, https://www.lastampa.it/vatican-insider/en/2018/12/11/news/global-compact-parolin-no-state-can-manage-migration-on-its-own-1.34066523.

[1202] Ibid.

[1203] Parolin, "Speeches by the Secretary of State," http://press.vatican.va/content/salastampa/it/bollettino/pubblico/2018/12/11/0924/02005.html.

[1204] Ibid.

[1205] Ibid.

Secretariat of State takes into account when discussing potential concordats with states.[1206]

A few days after telling the delegates in Morocco that it was "essential to adopt an inclusive approach in addressing migrants' needs," Parolin came under fire for saying the Vatican would not be helping Asia Bibi, a Pakistani Catholic woman who had been on death row for many years on account of blasphemy charges, to obtain asylum.[1207] "It's an issue inside Pakistan," he said. "I hope it can be resolved in the best way."

Islam, Interreligious Dialogue

Parolin is a supporter of Pope Francis' prioritization of dialogue with the Islamic world and sees it as a vital means of achieving peace in the face of Islamism. On the eve of Pope Francis' historic 2019 visit to Abu Dhabi, he told Vatican News that people of different religions are "all brothers, we all have the same dignity, we share the same rights and the same duties, we are children of the same Father in heaven." He said it was therefore important to "rediscover the root of our fraternity, which is belonging to a shared humanity."[1208]

He later praised the Document on Human Fraternity for World Peace and Living Together, signed in Abu Dhabi by Pope Francis and Sheikh Ahmad Al-Tayyeb of Al-Azhar University in Cairo, as "a significant text that deserves to be counted among the creative efforts to safeguard peace."[1209]

[1206] Claire Giangravè, "Vatican's Deals with States Reflect Its Drive to Project 'Soft Power,'" *Crux*, 1 March 2019, https://cruxnow.com/church-in-europe/2019/03/01/vaticans-deals-with-states-reflect-its-drive-to-project-soft-power/.

[1207] David Nussman, "Vatican Refuses to Offer Asylum to Asia Bibi," Church Militant, 17 December 2018, https://www.churchmilitant.com/news/article/vatican-refuses-to-offer-asylum-to-asia-bibi.

[1208] Roberto Piermarini, "Papa negli Emirati. Parolin: nuova pagina di fraternità tra le religioni," Vatican News, 2 February 2019, https://www.vaticannews.va/it/vaticano/news/2019-02/papa-francesco-abu-dhabi-intervista-card-parolin.html#play.

[1209] Pietro Parolin, "Being Mediterranean: Brothers and Citizens of the 'Mare Nostro,'" *La Civiltà Cattolica*, 15 February 2020, https://www.laciviltacattolica.

Parolin sees the document as part of a "journey" that began with *Nostra Aetate*, the Second Vatican Council's declaration that taught that all religions have elements of truth in them.[1210]

Observers praised the Human Fraternity document as an effort to push back against a drift toward a "clash of civilizations," but some scholars have argued that the document is heretical because it states that the "diversity of religions" is "willed by God."[1211] Parolin has not addressed this controversy, but has instead praised the document for its "common language and perspective" which he believes allow "Christians, Jews, and Muslims to seek a common understanding of problems."

Parolin rarely speaks explicitly of Christ as essential to peace and as the solution to violent religious extremism, but rather promotes more general, sociopolitical remedies such as "fraternity," a sense of "humanity," and equal "citizenship."[1212]

Second Vatican Council

Cardinal Parolin believes the Second Vatican Council, when rightly understood, "can be, and become more and more, a great force for the ever-necessary renewal of the Church." He welcomes particular "consequences" of the Council, such as use of the vernacular in the liturgy, and the "emergence of a 'local' Church"—something he believes is creating a "'new' Church consciousness."[1213] He also sees as a permanent and important aspect of the Council the irreversible introduction of the Church as a

---

it/articolo/essere-mediterranei-il-discorso-del-card-parolin/ (translated from Italian).

[1210] Ibid.

[1211] Edward Pentin, "Does the New Catholic-Muslim Declaration Deviate from Catholic Teaching?," *National Catholic Register*, 15 February 2019, https://www.ncregister.com/daily-news/does-the-new-catholic-muslim-declaration-deviate-from-catholic-teaching.

[1212] Parolin, "Being Mediterranean."

[1213] "For Cardinal Parolin, Vatican II Still Benefits the Church," Catholic News Agency, 17 November 2017, https://www.catholicnewsagency.com/news/for-cardinal-parolin-vatican-ii-still-benefits-the-church-87918.

"world Church." The Council, he believes, introduced a "new style" that grew from "new seeds, drawn from the source of Tradition, especially biblical and patristic." He criticizes those who blame Vatican II for "all the calamities of the Church."[1214]

THE NATURAL LAW AND HUMAN RIGHTS

In remarks delivered in May 2018, Parolin said the following, indicating his affirmation of the existence of moral norms proscribing certain kinds of actions:

> The proliferation of ever more extreme images of violence and pornography profoundly affects the psychology and even the neurological functioning of children. Cyberbullying, sexting and sextortion corrupt interpersonal and social relationships. Forms of sexual grooming on the internet, the live viewing of acts of rape and violence, organized prostitution online, human trafficking and incitement to violence and terrorism: all these are clear examples of horrendous crimes that can in no way be tolerated.[1215]

Parolin has also stressed the universal character of human rights grounded in natural law and knowable by natural reason.[1216] In remarks delivered in Rome in 2018, he said that firm and unwavering respect for human rights, knowable by reason and by revelation, is the cornerstone

---

[1214] Ibid.

[1215] Pietro Parolin, "Message of the Cardinal Secretary of State to the Participants in the Annual Meeting of the Commission on Crime Prevention and Criminal Justice (CCPCJ)," Holy See Press Office, 15 May 2018, https://press.vatican.va/content/salastampa/en/bollettino/pubblico/2018/05/15/180515a.html.

[1216] Virginia Forrester, "Cardinal Parolin: Fundamental Rights and the Conflicts between Rights," Zenit, 20 November 2018, https://zenit.org/articles/cardinal-parolin-fundamental-rights-and-the-conflicts-between-rights/.

of humane societies, noting that "the Church approaches human rights from their universality, rationality, and objectivity."[1217]

But he has also warned against "the modern temptation" to "accentuate the word 'rights' and leave aside the most important one: 'human.'" He believes that "every human being is linked to a social context, in which his rights and duties are connected to those of others and to the common good of society itself."[1218]

Euthanasia

Parolin contributed remarks to a February 2018 international congress on palliative care sponsored by the Pontifical Academy for Life. While endorsing the distinction drawn by Pius XII between intentional end-of-life killing and the acceptance of a shortening of life resulting from a choice to administer drugs to relieve pain, Parolin praised palliative care but added that, as medicine and medical research have an enduring commitment to discovering new cures and defeating illness, palliative care shows an awareness that, when everything medical has been attempted, limits must be "recognized and accepted."[1219]

Homosexuality

When Ireland voted to legalize same-sex "marriage" in 2015, Parolin said: "I was deeply saddened by the result. Of course, as the Archbishop of Dublin has said, the Church must take account of this reality, but it should" serve to "strengthen all" in their commitment to "make an effort to evangelize

---

[1217] Ibid.

[1218] "Intervento di S.E. Card. Pietro Parolin Segretario di Stato all'VIII Simposio della Fondazione Ratzinger / Benedetto XVI," 16 November 2018.

[1219] Pietro Parolin, "Letter of the Cardinal Secretary of State to the President of the Pontifical Academy for Life on the Occasion of the Congress on Palliative Care Organized by the PAL," Holy See Press Office, 28 February 2018, https://press.vatican.va/content/salastampa/en/bollettino/pubblico/2018/02/28/180228a.html.

our culture." He added that the ballot result was not just "a defeat for Christian principles, but of a defeat for humanity."[1220]

In April 2019, Parolin received in the Vatican a group of about fifty activists, lawyers, and other professionals working on behalf of efforts to decriminalize consenting homosexual conduct. According to a Vatican press release, Parolin listened to those gathered, accepted a compilation of their research concerning criminalization of such conduct, stated the Catholic Church's teachings on the dignity of all human persons, and assured those gathered that he would inform Pope Francis of their concerns and perspectives.[1221]

Synods on the Family and Amoris Laetitia

On October 16, 2014, Parolin supported Cardinal George Pell and others in requesting that the contents of the Extraordinary Synod be made public after the general secretary, alongside the pope, gave notice that the reports of the ten groups would not be made public.[1222] In 2015, during the Ordinary Synod on the Family, Parolin characterized the divisions among the bishops over the pastoral and sacramental-disciplinary implications of the indissolubility of marriage this way: "It is true that Pastors can sometimes have differing opinions on single pastoral issues, but this really shows that the Church is a living institution."[1223] He said it would be good for the

---

[1220] Stefania Falasca, "Referendum on Gay Marriage: Ireland, Parolin: 'Defeat for Humanity,'" *Avvenire*, 26 May 2015, https://www.avvenire.it/chiesa/pagine/irlanda-nozze-gay-parolin-sconfitta-per-umanit%C3%A0 (translated from Italian).

[1221] Zenit Staff, "Cardinal Parolin Meets with Opponents of Criminalizing Homosexuality," Zenit, 5 April 2019, https://zenit.org/articles/cardinal-parolin-meets-with-opponents-of-criminalizing-homosexuality/.

[1222] "The True Story of This Synod: Director, Performers, Aid," chiesa.espressonline.it, 17 October 2014, http://chiesa.espresso.repubblica.it/articolo/1350897.html (translated from Italian).

[1223] Staff Reporter, "Cardinal Parolin: All Attending Synod Agree on 'Christian Doctrine of Marriage,'" *Catholic Herald,* 9 September 2015, https://catholicherald.co.uk/all-attending-synod-agree-on-christian-doctrine-of-marriage/.

Church to try to "tend to the wounds of those who have made mistakes and are suffering."

Parolin has given an enthusiastic endorsement of *Amoris Laetitia* and in general gives the sense that his theology is directed largely by diplomatic exigencies.[1224]

Following the 2014 and 2015 synods, he said that we must "look at *Amoris Laetitia* as a great gift."[1225] The new pastoral approach, according to Parolin, must "also take into consideration the present conditions in which [a] family is living: a family marked by the original sin as is all humankind." He continued, "*Amoris Laetitia* has given great impulse to the pastoral ministry of the family and has produced fruits of renewal, hope, and accompaniment for those in fragile family situations."[1226] On criticism of *Amoris Laetitia*, he said: "There have always been critical voices in the Church! It is not the first time it happens. I believe that, as the Pope himself says, they [should] be 'sincere and constructive, and willing to find a way to make progress together and a better way of putting God's will to work'!"[1227] Parolin has also said of *Amoris Laetitia* that it "arose from a new paradigm" of accompanying and listening, a paradigm that Pope Francis is trying to embody and proliferate. He said that the document was "a change in paradigm" embodying a "new spirit" and a "new approach" but he has been unclear precisely what that new spirit and approach are.[1228]

[1224] Germain Grisez and John Finnis, "An Open Letter to Pope Francis," The Way of the Lord Jesus, 21 November 2016, http://twotlj.org/AmorisLaetitia.html.

[1225] Andrea Tornielli, "It Is Not the Functional Criteria That Should Guide the Reform," *La Stampa*, 13 March 2017, https://www.lastampa.it/vatican-insider/en/2017/03/13/news/it-is-not-the-functional-criteria-that-should-guide-the-reform-1.34634470.

[1226] Ibid.

[1227] Ibid.

[1228] Alessandro Gisotti, "Card. Parolin: The 2018 of Francis in the Name of Youth and Family," Vatican News, 11 January 2018, https://www.vaticannews.va/it/vaticano/news/2018-01/card-parolin-il-2018-di-francesco-allinsegna-di-giovani-e-fami.html#play (translated from Italian).

Views on Contraception

Parolin's stated views on contraception are unclear and largely noncommittal, although in a 2014 meeting, Parolin and Secretary of State John Kerry discussed — alongside geopolitical issues — the Obama administration's mandate requiring nearly all religious organizations to include contraceptives (some inducing early-stage abortion) in their insurance coverage. By bringing up the issue at such a meeting, he left little doubt about the Vatican's support for U.S. bishops' opposition to the mandate.[1229]

In an October 2018 conference organized by the Congregation for the Doctrine of the Faith in Rome, Parolin spoke on a book drawing on classified Secretariat of State documents relating to the commission that Paul VI consulted in advance of promulgating his Encyclical *Humanae Vitae*. The book, *La nascita di un'enciclica* (The birth of an encyclical) by Fr. Gilfredo Marengo, attempted to situate *Humanae Vitae* in the context not only of the commission's work and advice but also in contemporary culture and society. Catholics opposed to *Humanae Vitae*'s central teaching hailed Marengo's work as a "milestone" that relativizes the encyclical;[1230] other Catholic scholars called Marengo a "bitter critic" of the encyclical's doctrinal core.[1231] In his prepared remarks, Parolin emphasized that Paul VI had no doubt about the relevant doctrinal propositions — a statement observers believe Marengo would disagree with. Parolin said what could be seen as the "delay" in the encyclical's publication was due to the fact that Paul VI had wanted to study the issues patiently and consult experts.[1232] But Parolin's comments on the

---

[1229] Francis X. Rocca, "On Abortion and Contraception, Vatican Puts Words in Context," *National Catholic Reporter*, 14 January 2014, https://www.ncronline.org/news/vatican/abortion-and-contraception-vatican-puts-words-context.

[1230] Massimo Faggioli, "'Humanae Vitae' Was a Rewrite," *Commonweal*, 12 July 2018, https://www.commonwealmagazine.org/humanae-vitae-was-rewrite.

[1231] E. Christian Brugger, "A New Assault on 'Humanae Vitae' Begins," *National Catholic Register*, 27 February 2018, http://www.ncregister.com/blog/guest-blogger/a-new-assault-on-humanae-vitae-begins.

[1232] Andrea Gagliarducci, "Cardinal Parolin: For Paul VI, 'Humanae Vitae' Had to Be Pastoral," Catholic News Agency, 22 October 2018, https://

occasion of the book launch were not a ringing endorsement of the encyclical's position on contraception. Rather his support of the book, by way of his presence, together with the absence of any critical comments about the book's problematic reconstruction of the history behind the encyclical, and the book's problematic presentation of Paul VI's moral teaching, permits a plurality of interpretations.

During the 2016-2017 Order of Malta affair, Parolin made no comment in support of Fra' Matthew Festing or Cardinal Raymond Burke and their strong positions against the distribution of large numbers of contraceptives by the Order's humanitarian branch in parts of Asia.

Religious Freedom

Cardinal Parolin embraces religious pluralism. He has asserted that the state should promote religious conduct and practice in general: "I would like also to stress the importance of the religions. Religions cannot be left only on the private ground; it is not only the expression of the personal feelings of the person, but religions have something to say also in a public arena."[1233] For Parolin, liberal democratic regimes need not provide any privilege or special recognition for the Catholic Church: "Of course in dialogue with all the faiths, we are not asking nor requesting any privilege for the Catholic Church.... We know that now we live in a pluralistic society where there are so many expressions of religious belief and religious faith; but I think that it is important that the authorities, the government, recognize the public role that religions could give to the public life."[1234]

Speaking on the fiftieth anniversary of *Nostra Aetate* about religious pluralism, Parolin cited John Paul II's 1986 address to the Curia, saying: "The differences [among religions] are a less important element in relation

---

www.catholicnewsagency.com/news/cardinal-parolin-for-paul-vi-humanae-vitae-had-to-be-pastoral-30944.

[1233] "Davos 2017—An Insight, an Idea with Cardinal Pietro Parolin," interview by Philipp Rösler, YouTube video, 32:15, posted 19 January 2017 by World Economic Forum, https://youtu.be/iF1rWoSglEM?t=21m11s.

[1234] Ibid.

to unity that, on the contrary, is radical, fundamental and determinant."[1235] Parolin also said, "The acceptance of diversity is fundamental in education to mutual respect and in the freedom to express one's ideas and one's religious convictions. This constructive attitude finds its natural *humus* in selfless dialogue (cf. *Evangelii Gaudium*, n. 42), which in the common search for peace and justice becomes 'an ethical commitment that creates new social conditions' (*ibid.*, n. 250)."[1236] For Parolin, the interreligious gatherings at Assisi, in 1986 and subsequently, allowed "men and women to witness an authentic experience of God in the heart of their religions."[1237]

On the Right to Life

During his September 22, 2016, address in New York at the General Debate of the seventy-first session of the UN General Assembly, Parolin said: "As Pope Francis said here last year, 'The pillars of integral human development have a common foundation, which is the right to life,' which presumes that 'we recognize a moral law written into human nature itself, one that includes the natural difference between man and woman (cf. *Laudato Si'*, 155), and absolute respect for life in all its stages and dimensions.' "[1238] Parolin has praised Mother Teresa for her opposition to abortion: "This led her to identify the children not yet born and threatened in their existence as '*the poorest among the poor.*' In fact each one depends, more than any other human being, on the love and care of a mother and on society's protection.... Therefore, she defended courageously nascent life, with that

---

[1235] Zenit Staff, "Cardinal Parolin's Address to 'Nostra Aetate' Conference," Zenit, 30 October 2015, https://zenit.org/articles/cardinal-parolin-s-address-to-nostra-aetate-conference/.

[1236] Ibid.

[1237] "Synod: Parolin Confirms: 'The Pope Will Write an Apostolic Exhortation,' " Zenit, 29 October 2015, https://it.zenit.org/articles/sinodo-parolin-conferma-il-papa-scrivera-un-esortazione-apostolica/ (translated from Italian).

[1238] His Eminence Cardinal Pietro Parolin, "Cardinal Parolin Address at the General Debate of the 71st Session of the GA," The Permanent Observer Mission of the Holy See to the United Nations, 22 September 2016, https://holyseemission.org/contents//statements/57e42347c0069.php.

frankness of word and line of action that is the most luminous sign of the presence of the Prophets and of the Saints, who do not bow to anyone except to the Almighty."[1239] In a similar vein, Parolin said the teaching of Pope St. Pius X—with his insistence on the "sanctity of life," as "an indispensable condition for the credibility of the sacred ministry"—is of "utmost urgency for the Church today."[1240]

Additionally, at the U.S. bishops' meeting in Baltimore in 2018 on the occasion of the conference's hundredth anniversary, he praised the ordinaries for their defense of the unborn.[1241] He has also asserted that the right to life is the foundation of all human rights.[1242]

DIPLOMACY WITH CHINA

Pietro Parolin has been a leading figure in Vatican diplomacy with the People's Republic of China, which has had troubled relations with Rome since it broke diplomatic ties with the Holy See in the early 1950s.

For decades, two separate Catholic communities have existed in China, the first being an "underground" Church led by about thirty bishops recognized by Rome and comprising Catholics unwilling to submit their religious practice to the approval of the communist state. The second is

[1239] Zenit Staff, "Text of Cardinal Parolin's Homily in Thanksgiving for Canonization of Mother Teresa," Zenit, 6 September 2016, https://zenit.org/articles/text-of-cardinal-parolins-homily-in-thanksgiving-for-canonization-of-mother-teresa/.

[1240] Hilary White, "Church 'Urgently Needs' the Teaching of Anti-Modernist Pope Pius X: Cardinal Parolin," LifeSite News, 26 August 2014, https://www.lifesitenews.com/news/church-urgently-needs-the-teaching-of-anti-modernist-pope-pius-x-cardinal-p.

[1241] "Card. Parolin Urges US Bishops to Work for a More Just and Inclusive Society," Vatican News, 14 November 2017, https://www.vaticannews.va/en/vatican-city/news/2017-11/card--parolin-urges-us-bishops-to-work-for-a-more-just-and-inclu.html.

[1242] Forrester, "Fundamental Rights."

a state-run "official" Catholic Church, the Chinese Patriotic Catholic Association (CPCA), led by seventy bishops, several of whom had not, until late 2018, been recognized by Rome and a few of whom were publicly excommunicated by Pope Benedict XVI in 2011 for receiving episcopal ordination without a pontifical mandate.

Initiating Contact

In 2005, with Parolin's significant assistance, the Holy See made direct diplomatic contact with China. That contact later bore fruit in a historic 2007 letter[1243] sent by Benedict XVI to the Catholics in China, encouraging them to endure in faith amid state-imposed religious persecution. Cardinal Joseph Zen Ze-kiun, bishop of Hong Kong from 2002 to 2009, participated in the letter's drafting.

Under Pope Francis, Parolin has made overtures to China's communist government aimed at uniting the Catholic community in the country, but they have been severely criticized by Cardinal Zen. In 2015, Zen wrote that Parolin had called those who refused to accede to the control of the government "systematic opponents" of the government and "gladiators" who enjoy displaying themselves in the public square.[1244] Such an attitude, Zen said, "does little to allay the fears" and help the confidence of persecuted Catholics who want to remain faithful to the Holy See and who support the Church's independence from state control.

[1243] "Letter of the Holy Father Pope Benedict XVI to the Bishops, Priests, Consecrated Persons and Lay Faithful of the Catholic Church in the People's Republic of China," Vatican, 2007, http://w2.vatican.va/content/benedict-xvi/en/letters/2007/documents/hf_ben-xvi_let_20070527_china.html; Daniel Blackman, "Cardinal Zen: I Fear the Vatican's Ostpolitik with Communist China," *National Catholic Register*, 17 February 2017, http://www.ncregister.com/daily-news/cardinal-zen-i-fear-the-vaticans-ostpolitik-with-communist-china.

[1244] Card. Joseph Zen Ze-kiun, "It Looks Like Someone Is Trying to Shout Us Down," *AsiaNews*, 17 February 2015, http://www.asianews.it/news-en/It-looks-like-someone-is-trying-to-shout-us-down-33489.html.

Cardinal Zen's Warnings

Cardinal Zen and others in the Chinese underground have persistently warned that an arrangement between the Vatican and the Communist Party without proper safeguards would be a betrayal of faithful persecuted Catholics. Cardinal Parolin, on the other hand, has stated that the claim that "two different Churches" exist in China "does not correspond to historical reality or to the life of faith of Chinese Catholics."[1245] He has also stated that good relations between the Holy See and China are not merely a political ambition but are something "of the Church, which belongs to God."[1246]

In 2017, Parolin's designs on the Church in China began to come into focus when it was reported that he had likely authorized a Vatican delegation of diplomats to travel to China in order to encourage underground bishops to yield their sees to CPCA-recognized bishops who had been illicitly ordained.[1247]

But as far back as May 2005, his aspirations for the Church in China and his stance on the vexed question of episcopal appointments became known through a Vatican communiqué that was later leaked:[1248]

> Parolin was confident that if Beijing had the will, the two sides could work something out. "It's not a major problem," he said, noting that the Holy See had reached a *modus vivendi* with Vietnam regarding bishops. The Vatican simply presents its episcopal candidates to the government of Vietnam, and Hanoi says yes or no. "It's not ideal,"

[1245] Gianni Valente, "Reconciliation among China's Catholics Is Close to Pope's Heart," *La Stampa*, 24 August 2016.

[1246] Sandro Magister, "Parolin to the Nuncios: No Concession with China," chiesa.espressonline.it, 26 September 2016, http://chiesa.espresso.repubblica.it/articolo/1351379bdc4.html?eng=y.

[1247] Michael Warren Davis, "Vatican and China: Cardinal Zen's Intervention Raises Some Very Uncomfortable Questions," *Catholic Herald*, 30 January 2018, https://catholicherald.co.uk/vatican-and-china-cardinal-zens-intervention-raises-some-very-uncomfortable-questions/.

[1248] "Pope Reaches Out to China," WikiLeaks, 19 May 2005, https://search.wikileaks.org/plusd/cables/05VATICAN477_a.html.

Parolin admitted, "but it's a way to take a step forward and increase our engagement."

Cardinal Zen, writing in *AsiaNews* in 2018, noted that from 1989 to 1996, while he was teaching in seminaries run by the CPCA, he had had "direct experience of the slavery and humiliation to which those our brother bishops are subjected." He also pointed out that the government had, as of early 2018, begun ratcheting up religious persecution, including enforcing laws that had hitherto been inert—for example, attendance by the faithful at "underground" Masses would no longer be tolerated.[1249]

"So, do I think that the Vatican is selling out the Catholic Church in China?" Zen wrote. "Yes, definitely."[1250]

Provisional Agreement

Tensions between Cardinal Parolin and Cardinal Zen further increased when on September 22, 2018, the Vatican and Beijing jointly announced a landmark provisional accord, signed by diplomatic personnel from both Beijing and the Vatican, concerning the appointment of bishops in China.

The specific content of the accord has never been made public and is subject to "periodic review," but it is thought to stipulate that the power to appoint new bishops rests no longer only with the Holy See but with the Chinese authorities. The pope, however, can veto their choices, though not unlimitedly.

Also part of the accord was the lifting of the excommunications of eight CPCA bishops (one deceased) who had not been in full communion with Rome principally because the official, state-backed church had appointed them without papal permission. The Vatican said Pope Francis hoped that

---

[1249] Cardinal Joseph Zen, "Card. Zen on the Bishops of Shantou and Mindong," *AsiaNews*, 29 January 2018, http://www.asianews.it/news-en/Card.-Zen-on-the-bishops-of-Shantou-and-Mindong-42951.html.

[1250] Cardinal Zen, "Dear Friends in the Media," *It's Up to Him to Land Safely* (blog), 29 January 2018, https://oldyosef.hkdavc.com/?p=967 (translated from Chinese).

"with these decisions, a new process may begin that will allow the wounds of the past to be overcome, leading to the full communion of all Chinese Catholics."[1251]

Parolin said that through the agreement, "for the first time all the Bishops in China are in communion with the Bishop of Rome, with the Successor of Peter."[1252] In an in-flight press conference three days after the signing, Pope Francis singled out Parolin for praise along with others who had helped with the agreement, saying:

> Cardinal Parolin, who is a very devoted man [has] a particular attachment to the magnifying glass: he studies every document down to the period, comma, accent mark.... And this gives me a great deal of certitude.[1253]

Francis also said episcopates of the world, the Patriotic church, and the "traditional Chinese Catholic Church" had written to him to say the agreement bore the signature of the faithful of both churches and this was therefore a "sign of God." He then insisted it is "a dialogue about eventual candidates. The matter is carried out through dialogue. But the appointment is by Rome; the appointment is by the Pope."[1254]

Reaction to Agreement

Supporters of the provisional accord believe it favors rapprochement, including the possible reestablishment of Sino-Vatican diplomatic ties after

---

[1251] "Briefing Note about the Catholic Church in China, 22.09.2018," Holy See Press Office, https://press.vatican.va/content/salastampa/en/bollettino/pubblico/2018/09/22/180922g.html.

[1252] "Pope Entrusts Commitment to Reconciliation to Chinese Catholics," Vatican News, 22 September 2018, https://www.vaticannews.va/en/vatican-city/news/2018-09/pope-commitment-reconciliation-chinese-catholics.html.

[1253] "Press Conference on the Return Flight from Tallinn (Estonia) to Rome," Holy See Press Office, 25 September 2018, http://www.vatican.va/content/francesco/en/speeches/2018/september/documents/papa-francesco_20180925_voloritorno-estonia.html.

[1254] Ibid.

a break of over half a century.[1255] And yet state repression of Catholics, and other religious followers, considerably worsened in the months and years that followed the agreement, including the bulldozing of churches and Marian shrines.

In an October 2018 *New York Times* op-ed,[1256] Cardinal Zen blasted the accord as "a major step toward the annihilation of the real Church in China." "I was among those who applauded Francis' decision to appoint Pietro Parolin as secretary of state in 2013," Zen wrote. "But I now think that Cardinal Parolin cares less about the Church than about diplomatic success. His ultimate goal is the restoration of formal relations between the Vatican and Beijing."

Others, too, have roundly criticized the Vatican for the agreement, including the last governor of Hong Kong, Christopher Patten, who said the Vatican had "got it very badly wrong about China," given its human-rights record.[1257] Stephen Mosher, China expert and president of the Population Research Institute, said the deal was a "terrible mistake" and that the increase in religious persecution should come as "no surprise" to the Vatican, as Mosher said he had "warned Cardinal Parolin" of the dangers in March 2018. He said he passed on these warnings because the Chinese Communist

---

[1255] "Gianni Valente, a journalist close to Pope Francis, believed an orchestrated 'global media campaign' had sought to sabotage the agreement, portraying it in a false and poor light." Edward Pentin, "This Year's Vatican-China Agreement Causes Widespread Consternation," *National Catholic Register*, 21 December 2018, https://www.ncregister.com/blog/edward-pentin/this-years-vatican-china-agreement-causes-widespread-consternation.

[1256] Joseph Zen Ze-Kiun, "The Pope Doesn't Understand China," *New York Times*, 24 October 2018, https://www.nytimes.com/2018/10/24/opinion/pope-china-vatican-church-catholics-bishops.html.

[1257] Lord Patten, a well-known British Catholic who usually takes liberal positions and who spent many years negotiating with Beijing before handing Hong Kong over to the Chinese in 1999, said in February 2020 that he felt it was an "extraordinary time" to be dealing with China in this way, which has "gone back on human rights." Sarah Mac Donald, "Vatican 'Got It Wrong' about China, Says Patten," *Tablet*, 28 February 2020, https://www.thetablet.co.uk/news/12538/vatican-got-it-wrong-about-china-says-patten.

Party's United Front Department had just "ominously assumed" direct control of religious affairs, meaning that Vatican officials would be dealing with "atheistic" party officials "determined to stamp out Catholicism."[1258] A group of thirty-one British Catholics wrote a letter to the *Catholic Herald* in March 2020 calling for the provisional agreement to be "torn up" on the grounds that China is continuing to commit human-rights violations, including organ harvesting and the persecution of Catholics.[1259]

Fr. Bernardo Cervellera, director of *AsiaNews*, said in March 2020 that the underground Catholic community now feels "abandoned by the Vatican because the Vatican doesn't stress at all the freedom of religion."[1260] He urged Parolin and Zen to meet and talk. To date, they have not done so.

Pastoral Guidelines

Cardinal Zen believes that even worse than the still-secret accord and the lifting of the excommunications are pastoral guidelines the Vatican issued in 2019 encouraging Chinese clergy to join the country's state-run church. In comments to the *National Catholic Register* in March 2020, he said the guidelines were part of a move to "push everybody" into joining the independent official church and that he and others believed it would force clergy into apostasy. "It's terrible," he said, "the most evil thing."[1261]

Zen also believes it was chiefly Parolin who had Cardinal Giovanni Battista Re write a letter to all the Church's cardinals, criticizing Zen in

---

[1258] Stephen Mosher, "'Terrible Mistake': US Govt. Religious Freedom Watchdog Slams Vatican's Deal with China," LifeSite News, 27 May 2019, https://www.lifesitenews.com/blogs/terrible-mistake-us-govt-religious-freedom-watchdog-slams-vaticans-deal-with-china.

[1259] "Letters: China's Latest Atrocity; Communion and the Coronavirus," *Catholic Herald*, 12 March 2020, https://catholicherald.co.uk/letters-chinas-latest-atrocity-communion-and-the-coronavirus/.

[1260] Edward Pentin, "Cardinal Zen: 'Terrible' Vatican-China Deal Sending Catholics 'to Catacombs,'" *National Catholic Register*, 26 March 2020, https://www.ncregister.com/daily-news/cardinal-zen-terrible-vatican-china-deal-sending-catholics-to-catacombs.

[1261] Ibid.

February 2020 for his position on China relations, and alleging that he, Re, had seen a document proving that Benedict XVI had approved a draft of the provisional agreement. "It seems incredible," Zen said. "I'm 100% sure they can't prove it to me. It doesn't fit."[1262]

Cardinal Zen believes that Vatican officials are ignorant of the issues in China but reserves most of his ire for Cardinal Parolin. In 2018, just before the announcement of the agreement, he fired further broadsides, accusing Parolin of despising heroes of faith and calling on him to resign.[1263] He said in 2020 that he believed Parolin had let himself be cheated.[1264] Asked if he or Cardinal Parolin had tried to dialogue with each other, Zen replied: "No, no, absolutely no."

Cardinal Parolin Responds

In comments to the *National Catholic Register* in March 2020, Cardinal Parolin said he did not wish to "release interviews on this matter, since any statement about it can cause intense controversy, which is of benefit to nobody." He added: "We have seen this occur recently, not only in relation to opinions, but also to facts," and said he had already "addressed the questions" being put to him.

In April 2019, Cardinal Parolin urged patience over Sino-Vatican relations and advised not to judge rashly the provisional agreement that is meant to protect religious freedom. "History was not built in one day; history is a long process," he said. "I think we have to put ourselves in this

---

[1262] Ibid.

[1263] James Pomfret, Anne Marie Roantree, "Leading Asian Cardinal Calls for Vatican Foreign Minister to Resign over China Dealings," Reuters, 20 September 2018, https://www.reuters.com/article/us-china-vatican-zen/leading-asian-cardinal-calls-for-vatican-foreign-minister-to-resign-over-china-dealings-idUSKCN1M025C.

[1264] Catholic News Agency, "Cardinal Zen: 'Cardinal Parolin Manipulates the Pope,'" *National Catholic Register*, 21 March 2020 https://www.ncregister.com/daily-news/cardinal-zen-parolin-manipulates-the-pope-and-vaticans-china-policy-is-immo.

perspective."[1265] Parolin insists that the Holy See "deeply understands" the sufferings of the Church in China and its "heroic witnesses."[1266]

SUMMARY

Pietro Parolin has long been highly regarded by secular diplomats as a reliable and trusted papal representative on the world stage, someone who seems to be on a similar papal trajectory to that of former diplomat Pope St. Paul VI.

A protégé of the late cardinal Achille Silvestrini, also a papal nuncio and member of the notorious Saint Gallen Group, which tried to thwart Pope Benedict XVI's election in 2005, between 2002 and 2009 then-Msgr. Parolin used his diplomatic skills and ever-growing network of contacts in a wide variety of areas, notably nuclear disarmament, outreach to communist countries, and even mediation activities. But perhaps most significant has been his role in reestablishing direct contact between the Holy See and Beijing in 2005 — a lauded achievement at the time but a diplomatic overture that could now prove to be his Achilles' heel.

His single-minded approach to Sino-Vatican relations culminated in 2018 in a controversial secret provisional agreement on the appointment of bishops. It attracted widespread criticism, not only from Cardinal Joseph Zen Ze-kiun, bishop emeritus of Hong Kong, and ordinary Chinese Catholics faithful to Rome, but also from prominent Catholics in Europe and the United States who accused the Church of selling out to Communist

---

[1265] Junno Arocho Esteves, "Cardinal Parolin Defends Vatican-China Agreement amid Criticism," *America*, 4 April 2019, https://www.americamagazine. org/politics-society/2019/04/04/cardinal-parolin-defends-vatican-china-agreement-amid-criticism.

[1266] Fr. Paul Han Qingping, "The Interview of Cardinal Parolin and the Threat of a Return to 'Novatianism' and 'Donatism,'" *La Stampa*, 4 July 2019, https://www.lastampa.it/vatican-insider/en/2018/02/08/news/the-interview-of-cardinal-parolin-and-the-threat-of-a-return-to-novatianism-and-donatism-1.33976989.

China at the wrong time and with devastating consequences. Undeterred, Parolin has typically avoided succumbing to public rancor over the issue.

In 2016-2017, he was attacked for his handling of another crisis at the Order of Malta and the forced resignation of its Grand Master, Fra' Matthew Festing, in 2017. His interference, and that of the pope, reportedly violated laws protecting the Order's sovereignty and may have been connected with a mysterious bequest to the Order, but Parolin's propensity for discretion has meant few know the real motives for his involvement in the affair. Similarly opaque is his handling of certain aspects of Vatican finances—namely, his roles in hindering, or at least failing to promote, financial reform and in allowing a bankrupt Rome hospital to be propped up using millions of dollars of funds from a Vatican-run children's hospital as a loan guarantee. Further questions persist over his position on contraception.

To Cardinal Parolin's critics, he is a pragmatist who places ideology above truth and the Faith, a master of the discredited *Ostpolitik* of the 1960s, especially when dealing with China. To his supporters, Cardinal Parolin is a courageous idealist, a master of discretion and arbitration who wants no more than to carve out a future for the Church in the twenty-first century.

Still relatively young, he suffered a serious health scare in 2014 but is understood to have fully recovered.

As someone close to the poor and with an ecclesial and political outlook similar to Francis', he is seen as a natural successor to the current pope, someone expected to continue many, if not all, of Francis' reforms but in a quieter, subtler, and more diplomatic manner.

SERVICE TO THE CHURCH

Ordination to the Priesthood: 27 April 1980
Ordination to the Episcopate: 12 September 2009
Elevation to the College of Cardinals: 22 February 2014

Education
- 1986: Pontifical Gregorian University (S.T.L.)
- Pontifical Ecclesiastical Academy; Diplomatic sciences

Assignments
- 1980-1982: Assistant pastor, Holy Trinity Parish, Schio, Italy
- 1983-1986: Student of canon law, Pontifical Gregorian University
- 1986: Entered the diplomatic service of the Holy See
- 1986-1989: Worked in the diplomatic mission in Nigeria
- 1989-1992: Worked in the diplomatic mission in Mexico
- 1993-2002: Worked in the Section for Relations with States of the Secretariat of State
- 2002-2009: Undersecretary of the Section of the Secretariat of State for Relations with States
- 2009-2013: Apostolic nuncio to Venezuela
- 2009-2014: Titular archbishop of Aquipendium
- 2013-present: Secretary of state
- 2014-present: Cardinal-priest of Santi Simone e Giuda Taddeo a Torre Angela

Membership
- Council of Cardinals
- Congregation for the Doctrine of the Faith
- Congregation for the Oriental Churches
- Congregation for the Evangelization of Peoples
- Congregation for Bishops
- Congregation for Divine Worship and the Discipline of the Sacraments
- Cardinal Commission for the Supervision of the Institute for the Works of Religion (IOR)

MAURO CARDINAL PIACENZA

"One Rest in the Truth"

Born: 15 September 1944
Genoa, Italy
Nationality: Italian
Title: Major Penitentiary of the Apostolic Penitentiary

BIOGRAPHY

Mauro Piacenza is an only child whose father was an official in the *Marina Mercantile* (Merchant Marines).[1267] Mauro's early studies were in classics, and then political science, until he entered Genoa's major seminary in 1964. He was ordained priest in 1969 by Cardinal Giuseppe Siri. During

---

[1267] "Vatican in Genoese Sauce, from Bagnasco to Piacenza under Bertone's Reign," *SFERA*, https://www.teneraerbetta.it/component/content/article/9-bazzecole/notizie-e-articoli/1650-vaticano-in-salsa-genovese-da-bagnasco-a-piacenza-sotto-il-regno-di-bertone.html.

the 1970s, Piacenza simultaneously exercised a number of roles: from 1970 to 1975, he was parochial vicar; from 1973 to 1978, he was a spiritual director in the seminary; and from 1975 to 1976, he studied at the Lateran University in Rome, earning a license in canon law *summa cum laude*.[1268] Similarly, from 1970 to 1990, he was a judge for the diocesan tribunal. From 1978 to 1990, he taught canon law at a university, and also taught in his alma mater secondary school, Cristoforo Colombo. During this period, he offered weekly catechetical programs on the local television network and was an official visitor for many religious communities, while preaching numerous spiritual exercises for clergy, seminarians, male and female religious, and laity. His numerous writings have focused on spiritual formation, especially for clergy.

In 1990, Piacenza was called to Rome to serve as an official at the Congregation for the Clergy. He was appointed Secretary in 2000, and in 2003, Pope John Paul II appointed Piacenza to be president of the Pontifical Commission for the Cultural Heritage of the Church (*Beni Culturali*). In the same year, Piacenza was consecrated bishop by Cardinal Tarcisio Bertone (then archbishop of Genoa), with Cardinal Darío Castrillón Hoyos, then prefect of the Congregation for the Clergy and president of the Pontifical Commission *Ecclesia Dei*, as a co-consecrator. In 2004, John Paul appointed Piacenza president of the Pontifical Commission for Sacred Archaeology. Benedict XVI selected Piacenza to lead the Congregation for the Clergy in 2010 and, in the same year, elevated him to the cardinalate. Since 2011, Cardinal Piacenza has served as president of Aid to the Church in Need, a pontifical foundation that helps persecuted Christians. In 2013, Pope Francis replaced him as prefect of the Congregation for the Clergy with the diplomat Cardinal Beniamino Stella, previously nuncio in Cuba and Colombia, and promoted Piacenza to major penitentiary, the head of the Apostolic Penitentiary, the Church's highest tribunal responsible for issues related to the forgiveness of sins.

[1268] "Piacenza Card. Mauro," Vatican, http://press.vatican.va/content/sala-stampa/it/documentation/cardinali_biografie/cardinali_bio_piacenza_m.html.

SANCTIFYING OFFICE

In 2006—when Cardinal Piacenza was president of both the Pontifical Commission for the Cultural Heritage of the Church and the Pontifical Commission for Sacred Archaeology—Fides News Agency published two of his lectures, titled "Planning and Building God's House" and "The Stones, Sounds and Colours of the House of God."[1269] In them Piacenza explained the history and reasoning behind the layout, interior, and symbolism of church buildings.

He emphasized that "the building of a church is an ecclesial event since it symbolizes the Christian community as it celebrates the divine mysteries."[1270] "Each single element [architecture, decoration, painting, sculpture, windows, furniture, sacred objects, vestments, lighting, and sound] becomes an integrant part of the one 'installation' which has the altar as its focal point."[1271] The cardinal added that the "altar is the heart

---

[1269] "'Stones, Sounds, Colours of the House of God': Inspiring Principles for the Building of Churches and Places for the Celebration and Adoration of the Eucharist (3) by Bishop Mauro Piacenza," Agenzia Fides, 31 October 2006, http://www.fides.org/en/news/8332-VATICAN_STONES_SOUNDS_CO-LOURS_OF_THE_HOUSE_OF_GOD_Inspiring_Principles_for_the_building_of_churches_and_places_for_the_celebration_and_adoration_of_the_Eucharist_3_by_Bishop_Mauro_Piacenza.

[1270] "'Stones, Sounds, Colours of the House of God': Inspiring Principles for the Building of Churches and Places for the Celebration and Adoration of the Eucharist (1) by Bishop Mauro Piacenza," Agenzia Fides, 17 October 2006, http://www.fides.org/en/news/8264-VATICAN_STONES_SOUNDS_CO-LOURS_OF_THE_HOUSE_OF_GOD_Inspiring_Principles_for_the_building_of_churches_and_places_for_the_celebration_and_the_adoration_of_the_Eucharist_I_by_Bishop_Mauro_Piacenza.

[1271] "'Stones, Sounds, Colours of the House of God': Inspiring Principles for the Building of Churches and Places for the Celebration and Adoration of the Eucharist (2) by Bishop Mauro Piacenza," Agenzia Fides, 24 October 2006, http://www.fides.org/en/news/8286-VATICAN_STONES_SOUNDS_CO-LOURS_OF_THE_HOUSE_OF_GOD_Inspiring_Principles_for_the_building_of_churches_and_places_for_the_celebration_and_the_adoration_of_the_Eucharist_2_by_Bishop_Mauro_Piacenza.

of the whole church plan, since on it the holy sacrifice is celebrated. It is the altar on which Christ offers Himself as sacrificed victim and as high priest. It is the table to which Christ invites His disciples for the holy supper in its aspect of memory and memorial; it is the tomb which recalls the death and resurrection of Christ."[1272]

For Piacenza, the "ecclesiology of Vatican II describes the Church as an assembly born from listening to the Word of God and built up by the Holy Spirit who confirms believers in Christ through the sacraments, an assembly which allows communion, is nourished in prayer and presents itself to the world as a sign of the salvation brought by Christ."[1273] He said that church-building must be shaped by these principles. "Since the liturgy is an action of the whole people of God, the arrangement of space should foster participation, so people may come and go, see and hear."[1274] The interior design of a church should be conducive to the active participation of the faithful.[1275] "In this perspective also images present in church, on the walls or on furniture are not only of decorative value, they have a liturgical function. Therefore we can speak of mystagogic images for the presbyterium, which synthetically present the mystery of Christ (incarnation, passion, resurrection and second coming); didactical images for the hall of biblical subject and lastly devotional images (the Stations of the Cross, images of Christ, the Blessed Virgin Mary and the saints)."[1276]

[1272] "Stones, Sounds, Colours (3)."

[1273] " 'Planning and Building God's House': Contribution by Bishop Mauro Piacenza, President of the Pontifical Commission for the Cultural Heritage of the Church: 'A Place for Liturgy,' " Agenzia Fides, 15 March 2006, http://www.fides.org/en/news/6948-VATICAN_Planning_and_building_God_s_house_Contribution_by_Bishop_Mauro_Piacenza_President_of_the_Pontifical_Commission_for_the_Cultural_Heritage_of_the_Church_A_place_for_liturgy.

[1274] Ibid.

[1275] "Stones, Sounds, Colours (2)."

[1276] "Planning and Building."

Christocentric Approach

Cardinal Piacenza has consistently preached in his ministry the importance of keeping Christ at the center of life: "May you set your eyes and your heart on God. May this highest and fullest act of your mission establish the order and the hierarchy of your whole life. Daily prayer, especially before the Blessed Sacrament, will help you rise higher day by day, purifying your eyes and your heart, so that you may see the world with the eyes of God and to love the brothers with His very heart."[1277] In a 2009 homily, Piacenza called on all who nourish themselves on the Bread of the Eucharist to be concerned for the needs of others, to notice the suffering of others, and to offer themselves as a gift for others. "Love of neighbor must never be simply proclaimed. It must be practiced."[1278]

In a message to the rectors of Catholic shrines throughout the world, Piacenza observed that, in a climate of widespread secularism, shrines continue to be privileged places in which the loving and saving presence of God can be experienced.[1279] A shrine is a place away from daily distractions, a place where one can recollect oneself, gather one's thoughts, and reacquire the spiritual health to reembark upon the journey of faith with greater ardor. "It is there, too, that he can find space to seek, find and love Christ in his ordinary life, in the midst of the world."[1280] At the same time, Piacenza urged that shrines be more than this. He would point pilgrims to Jesus. "The Eucharistic celebration constitutes the heart of the sacramental life of the Shrine. In it the Lord gives himself to us. Pilgrims who come to the Shrines ought to be made aware that, if they trustingly welcome the

---

[1277] Mauro Cardinal Piacenza, "The Deaconate of the Word, the Eucharist and the Poor," Agenzia Fides, 1 July 2009, www.fides.org/en/news/24584-EUROPE_ITALY_The_deaconate_of_the_Word_the_Eucharist_and_the_Poor_homily_of_Archbishop_Mauro_Piacenza_at_the_ordination_of_38_deacons_Legionaries_of_Christ.

[1278] Ibid.

[1279] Mauro Cardinal Piacenza, message to the rectors of Catholic shrines, Congregation for the Clergy, 15 August 2011, http://www.clerus.org/clerus/dati/2011-10/11-13/EN_Santuari.pdf.

[1280] Ibid.

Eucharistic Christ in their most intimate being, He offers them the possibility of a real transformation of their entire existence."[1281]

Sacrament of Reconciliation

In 2011—when he was still the prefect of the Congregation for the Clergy—Piacenza explained that our celebration of the Eucharist is not the only time when we celebrate the joy of the Resurrection. We embody the joy of the Resurrection in our celebration of the sacrament of Reconciliation as well. He called for a growth in knowledge about the spiritual fruits that flow from the remission of sins, because the sacrament of Penance brings about a true spiritual resurrection, a restoration of the dignity of the life of the children of God.[1282] As the current major penitentiary of the Apostolic Penitentiary, Piacenza has continuously called for a rediscovery of the sacrament of Penance,[1283] reiterating that "Confession and Holy Communion always have an extraordinary value capable of renewing man."[1284]

In a 2018 interview with the *National Catholic Register* in which he discussed his new book *The Feast of Forgiveness with Pope Francis: An Aid*

[1281] Ibid.

[1282] Ibid.

[1283] "An Advent Gift: God's Mercy in the Confessional, Cardinal Says," Catholic News Agency, 17 December 2014, www.catholicnewsagency.com/news/an-advent-gift-gods-mercy-in-the-confessional-cardinal-says-43310; Angela Ambrogetti, "Cardinal Piacenza Explains Why Abortion Needs a Particular Acquittal," ACI Stampa, 4 September 2015, www.acistampa.com/story/il-cardinale-piacenza-spiega-perche-laborto-ha-bisogno-di-una-assoluzione-particolare-1361; "Cardinale Mauro Piacenza. Tanti Sono Tornati A Confessarsi," *Famiglia Cristiana*, 24 November 2016, www.famigliacristiana.it/articolo/cardinale-mauro-piacenza-tanti-sono-tornati-a-confessarsi.aspx; Salvatore Cernuzio, "Mercy: The 'Supreme Law' of the Church, without Deceiving the Faithful," Zenit, 18 April 2014, https://zenit.org/articles/mercy-the-supreme-law-of-the-church-without-deceiving-the-faithful/.

[1284] Federico Cenci, "Interview: Cardinal Piacenza: 'Confession and Communion at Easter Assume Exorcistic Value,'" Zenit, 23 March 2017, https://zenit.org/articles/interview-cardinal-piacenza-confession-and-communion-at-easter-assume-exorcistic-value/.

for Confession and Indulgences, Cardinal Piacenza said forgiveness "is the most evident demonstration of the omnipotence and love of the Father, which Jesus revealed in his whole earthly life." Of all the sacraments, he said, Reconciliation is the one that "effectively highlights the merciful gaze of God." He praised Pope Francis for placing Confession at the center of his pontificate and said the book aimed to help readers see Confession "as a liberating and rich meeting of humanity" and to leave the confessional "with happiness in the heart, with the radiant face of hope, even if sometimes it is wet by the tears of conversion and the joy that derives from it."[1285]

Devotion to Our Lady

Piacenza has manifested a fervent and authentic devotion to the Blessed Virgin. In 2012, the Committee for the Preparation of the Year of Faith, of which Piacenza was a member, drew up a note inviting the faithful to turn with particular devotion to Mary, model of the Church, who "shines forth to the whole community of the elect as the model of virtues." The committee encouraged all initiatives that help the faithful to recognize the special role of Mary in the mystery of salvation, love her, and follow her as a model of faith and virtue.[1286] In 2013, Piacenza penned a remarkable letter to "All the Mothers of Priests and Seminarians" of the world. He encouraged these women, who gave their sons to the Church, to exercise a "spiritual motherhood," like that of Mary, for all the faithful to whom their sons would minister.[1287]

[1285] Edward Pentin, "Pope Francis' Feast of Forgiveness—Confession," *National Catholic Register,* 19 February 2018, https://www.ncregister.com/daily-news/pope-francis-feast-of-forgiveness-confession.

[1286] Congregation for the Doctrine of the Faith, "Note with Pastoral Recommendations for the *Year of Faith,*" Vatican, 6 January 2012, www.vatican.va/roman_curia/congregations/cfaith/documents/rc_con_cfaith_doc_20120106_nota-anno-fede_en.html#_ftnref16.

[1287] Cardinale Mauro Piacenza, "*Causa nostrae Letitiae:* Lettera del cardinale Mauro Piacenza nella Solennità di Maria Santissima Madre di Dio," Zenit, 1 January 2013, https://it.zenit.org/articles/causa-nostrae-letitiae-causa-della-nostra-gioia/.

When the jubilee Year of Mercy (2015-2016) began on the Solemnity of the Immaculate Conception, Piacenza explained in an interview why dedication to Mary matters and also what the dogma of the Immaculate Conception can still teach us today. "Every word and every choice of Christ, who is God made man, is for us simply an inexorable necessity. If He divinely chose not to do without Mary of Nazareth to become man and save us, we cannot, nor do we certainly want to, pretend to do without her. Moreover, in Mary the whole Christian Revelation finds, we can say, its 'foundation,' its 'method' and its continuous 'protection.' "[1288]

Cardinal Piacenza values reverence for the Eucharist, which underlines the "mystery of the permanence of the Real Presence" and "creates the conditions for its Adoration," but his precise views on the liturgy are less well known.[1289] He does, however, very much adhere to the teachings of the Second Vatican Council and the Ordinary Form of the Mass. He is not known to have celebrated Mass in the Extraordinary Form but respects it, along with Benedict XVI's norms liberalizing it; would not oppose it; and views the *Vetus Ordo* as in continuity with the Church's Magisterium and previous councils.

GOVERNING OFFICE

Mauro Piacenza worked as a priest in the Diocese of Genoa for over twenty years. He has been a member of the Roman Curia since 1990 and during this time has mainly served the Congregation for the Clergy (as staff member, undersecretary, secretary, and prefect). In addition, he has been a member of numerous other congregations, committees, and pontifical councils and has served as president of the Pontifical Commission for

---

[1288] Antonio Gaspari, "Interview: The Immaculate: She Is Mother of Mercy," Zenit, 9 December 2015, https://zenit.org/articles/interview-the-immaculate-she-is-mother-of-mercy/.

[1289] Mauro Piacenza, "The Casing of the Eucharist," *30 Days* (June 2005), http://www.30giorni.it/articoli_id_9045_13.htm.

the Cultural Heritage of the Church and the Pontifical Commission for Sacred Archaeology.[1290] Currently, Piacenza is the major penitentiary of the Apostolic Penitentiary and the president of the pontifical foundation Aid to the Church in Need.

Congregation for the Clergy

Piacenza's signal contribution as a pastor has been his attention to the reform of the clergy. In a 2011 interview with Catholic News Agency, Piacenza discussed his role as prefect of the Congregation for the Clergy, a position whose primary responsibility is promoting the proper formation of diocesan priests and deacons.[1291]

In response to a question about the sexual abuse crisis within the Church, he noted that "the horrible sins of a few do not delegitimize the good actions of many, nor do they change the nature of the Church."[1292] He spoke of Benedict XVI's emphasis on reforming the clergy: "Obedience, chastity in celibacy, total dedication to the ministry without limits of time or days," which, he stressed, "are not seen as constrictions if one is truly in love, but rather as the demands of the love that one cannot help but give."[1293] The cardinal noted he has been calling for "reform of the clergy" since his time as a seminarian and a young priest. Thus, his aims and those of Benedict XVI are aligned. They have sought "a clergy that is truly and humbly proud of its identity and completely absorbed with the gift of grace it has received, and that consequently sees a clear distinction between the 'Kingdom of God' and the world."[1294]

Mercy is a recurring theme in many of Piacenza's writings, and pertains to his service as the major penitentiary of the Apostolic Penitentiary. He

---

[1290] "Piacenza Card. Mauro."

[1291] "Cardinal Piacenza Explains 'Crisis' of Catholic Priesthood," Catholic News Agency, 11 October 2011, https://www.catholicnewsagency.com/news/cardinal-piacenza-explains-crisis-of-catholic-priesthood.

[1292] Ibid.

[1293] Ibid.

[1294] Ibid.

has also emphasized the need for frequent Confession and the possibility of obtaining indulgences not only for oneself but also for deceased loved ones.[1295] He calls the sacrament of Confession the "unique ecology of the soul," in which man's true good is fostered.[1296]

During the coronavirus outbreak of 2020, the cardinal issued two decrees, the first granting special indulgences to the faithful during the pandemic and the second granting bishops the faculty of allowing priests to offer general absolution in cases of "grave necessity."[1297]

Pastoral Administrator

Cardinal Piacenza has held an impressive number of Church governing positions, from being a parish priest to serving as an ecclesiastical judge, from teaching at schools and universities to running influential and prestigious bodies of the Roman Curia. He has served for nine years as president of the Church charity Aid to the Church in Need. As secretary at the Congregation for the Clergy under prefect Cardinal Cláudio Hummes during the pontificate of Benedict XVI, he wielded considerable influence. As head of the Apostolic Penitentiary, he has been responsible for the first tribunal of the Church, considered in spiritual terms more important since it deals primarily with the afterlife.

Toward the end of his tenure as prefect at the Congregation for the Clergy, he devised a "Directory for the Ministry and the Life of Priests"—a well-received manual for clergy.

[1295] Antonio Gaspari, "All Saints and All Souls Day: A Time of Mercy, Forgiveness and Reflection (Part 1)," Zenit, 30 October 2014, https://zenit.org/articles/all-saints-and-all-souls-day-a-time-of-mercy-forgiveness-and-reflection-part-i/.

[1296] Alessandro Di Bussolo, "Card. Piacenza: Confession Is the Only 'Ecology of the Soul,'" Vatican News, 25 March 2019, https://www.vaticannews.va/it/vaticano/news/2019-03/penitenzieria-corso-confessori-cardinale-piacenza-peccato-errore.html (translated from Italian).

[1297] Edward Pentin, "Coronavirus Update from Rome," National Catholic Register, 20 March 2020, https://www.ncregister.com/blog/edward-pentin/coronavirus-latest-italys-bishops-call-for-all-churches-to-be-closed.

ON SEXUAL ABUSE

In a rare interview given in 2011, Cardinal Piacenza said he rejected using the sexual abuse crisis as an opportunity to change the priestly celibacy rule in the Latin Rite. Such a change, he said, would be an "unprecedented break" and added that "suggested cures would make the disease even worse" and "turn the Gospel on its head." He questions the argument that loneliness is the problem. "Why? Is Christ a ghost? Is the Church dead or alive? Were the holy priests of centuries past abnormal men? Is holiness a utopia, a matter for a predestined few, or a universal vocation, as the Second Vatican Council reminded us?" He said he wishes for a Catholic reform of the priesthood, not a worldly one (see more on Cardinal Piacenza's views on celibacy in the final section of this profile).[1298]

TEACHING OFFICE

Given the focal points of his presidential postings in the Curia,[1299] it is scarcely surprising that a good part of Piacenza's teachings revolves around history, symbolism, and art. One might expect from a person with this pedigree many long-winded, theoretical studies on such topics. But Piacenza surprises his readers with concise writings (some of which are discussed earlier in the section of this essay addressing the cardinal's sanctifying office), applying history, symbolism, and art to the Faith.

In discussing the liturgy, Piacenza explains that the norms of the liturgical books (the rubrics) all have an underlying theological meaning.

[1298] "Cardinal Piacenza Explains 'Crisis' of Catholic Priesthood," Catholic News Agency, 11 October 2011, https://www.catholicnewsagency.com/news/cardinal-piacenza-explains-crisis-of-catholic-priesthood.

[1299] Namely, president of the Pontifical Commission for the Cultural Heritage of the Church and president of the Pontifical Commission for Sacred Archaeology.

Any "style of celebrating that introduces arbitrary liturgical innovations [in addition to] generating confusion and division amongst the faithful, harms the venerable Tradition and the very authority of the Church, as it does also ecclesial unity."[1300]

Given that he has been a member of the Congregation for the Clergy for most of his time in Rome, Piacenza's teachings primarily concern matters of the priesthood.[1301]

Views on Vocations Crisis

In a 2011 interview with Zenit, the cardinal answered a question regarding the possible growth in the number of priestly vocations were celibacy to be abolished. Piacenza turned to the problem of secularization:

> The crisis from which, in reality, we are slowly emerging, is linked, fundamentally, to the crisis of faith in the West. It is in making faith grow that we must be engaged. This is the point. In the same spheres the sanctification of the feast is in crisis, confession is in crisis, marriage is in crisis.... Secularization and the consequent loss of the sense of the sacred, of faith and its practice have brought about and continue to bring about a diminution in the number of candidates to the priesthood. Along with these distinctively theological and ecclesial causes, there are also some of a sociological character ... [the] evident decline in births, with the consequent diminution in the number of young men and, thus, also of priestly vocations. This too is a factor that cannot be ignored. Everything is connected. Sometimes the premises are laid down and then one does not want to accept the consequences, but these are inevitable.[1302]

[1300] Ibid.

[1301] See "Helping Priests Live Their Vocation," below.

[1302] Antonio Gaspari, "Cardinal Piacenza on Women Priests, Celibacy, and the Power of Rome," Catholic Culture, https://www.catholicculture.org/culture/library/view.cfm?recnum=9743.

Pro-Life Positions

Abortion and contraception are directly linked to the decline in number of births, Piacenza believes. As major penitentiary of the Apostolic Penitentiary, he was asked in a 2015 interview with Catholic News Agency about special absolution for the sin of abortion. Piacenza explained that in cases where the mother is the victim of severe pressure by other people, she may be the only one who does not fall under the excommunication penalty, precisely because she is "forced." Piacenza underlined, however, that in every case, from the first moment of a baby's unborn existence, this innocent and defenseless human being must be recognized to have the same basic rights as every person, among which is the inviolable right to life.[1303]

When asked about politicians who propose and approve abortion laws and how they ought to be held accountable, Piacenza said such politicians "do not fall under the penalty of excommunication as they do not directly and materially commit the crime," but they "certainly have very serious moral responsibility, they sin and, therefore, are in need of confession."[1304]

Piacenza calls priests to be faithful to the authoritative teachings of the Magisterium on marriage: "Priests ... should ... carry out this special ministry by adhering with fidelity to the authentic teaching of the Church.... In the matrimonial area too let them respect what the ecclesial Magisterium teaches authoritatively."[1305] Piacenza endorsed[1306] English bishop Patrick

---

[1303] Ambrogetti, "Piacenza Explains Why Abortion Needs a Particular Acquittal."
[1304] Ibid.
[1305] Mauro Cardinal Piacenza and Archbishop Celso Morga Iruzubieta, "Shrines: A Tool for Evangelization," Catholic Culture, 15 August 2011, www.catholic-culture.org/culture/library/view.cfm?recnum=9686.
[1306] "Roman Dicastery Lauds Bishop O'Donoghue for His Courageous Action," *The Hermeneutic of Continuity* (blog), 23 September 2008, https://the-hermeneutic-of-continuity.blogspot.com/2008/09/bishop-odonoghue-of-lancaster-has.html?m=0.

O'Donoghue's[1307] document *Fit for Mission? Church*,[1308] which focuses on the strength of the Church's doctrine on the inseparability of sexual love and procreation and calls for both clergy and parents to study and teach the theology of the body.

During the 2015 Synod of Bishops, Piacenza spoke of the need to affirm that the Church has a positive view of sexuality, as it is an expression of the "symphonic tension between *eros* and *agape*."[1309] In a 2015 interview, when asked for examples of "new sins," Piacenza explicitly referred to "the practices of abortion and contraception," along with "the many evils linked to artificial fertilization such as the 'rent uterus' and the destruction of embryos."[1310] Piacenza underlined that through these practices of abortion, contraception, and artificial fertilization, "the alleged dominion of man on the mystery of life, one's own and others', is manifested along with the consequent commodification of the human person, who sees himself denied his own irreducible dignity."[1311]

Social Justice

Piacenza has often emphasized the existence and universal binding quality of nonnegotiable moral norms, such as those against abortion. But he has not explicitly addressed the challenge that Pope John Paul II laid down in *Veritatis Splendor* concerning the essential connection between those norms and social justice. Piacenza has stressed, though, how social structures "are simply impossible to convert if you do not start from the conversion of the heart."

[1307] Bishop emeritus of Lancaster, United Kingdom.

[1308] *Fit for Mission? Church*, Diocese of Lancaster—England, May 2015, www.lancasterdiocese.org.uk/wp-content/uploads/2015/05/Missions1-1.pdf.

[1309] Zenit Staff, "Small Groups Give Reports on Their Discussions of Part 1 of *Instrumentum Laboris*," Zenit, 9 October 2015, https://zenit.org/articles/small-groups-give-reports-on-their-discussions-of-part-1-of-instrumentum-laboris/.

[1310] Saverio Gaeta, "Sins and Forgiveness: Indulgence, What It Is and How It Is Obtained," *Famiglia Cristiana*, 10 December 2015, www.famigliacristiana.it/articolo/peccati-e-perdono-come-ottenere-l-indulgenza.aspx (translated from Italian).

[1311] Ibid.

"To have fair social structures, it is necessary to live in a culture that recognizes justice and, above all, recognizes the Just, the Lord of time and history," he continued. "And for there to be a culture, which recognizes Christ as Lord, an Advent culture that waits for Him who is known as the Beloved, it is necessary that everyone is open to an ever-renewed conversion."

Cardinal Piacenza believes the condition for changing the structures of society "cannot be determined by the imposition of an external power, not even by the democratically legitimized power of the States, but it is always the free and conscious response of each person to the call to conversion that the Lord leads us."[1312]

Loss of Sense of Sin

During the Extraordinary Jubilee of Mercy, Piacenza spoke of how a sense of sin is being lost in today's society. "Fundamentally [sin] is putting oneself in the place of God.... If I refer to God, with reason I can understand and share a very broad vision with others. If I replace God with myself, I have no reason to talk. We fall into an exasperated subjectivism, and we open the door to all dictatorships."[1313] Without the law of God and reason, one cannot see how one's personal sin damages the other and damages society.[1314]

[1312] Pontifical Council for the Pastoral Care of Migrants and Itinerant People, *People on the Move: III World Congress on the Pastoral Care of International Students*, suppl. no. 116 (Rome: Pontifical Council for the Pastoral Care of Migrants and Itinerant People, 2012), www.humandevelopment.va/content/dam/sviluppoumano/pubblicazioni-documenti/archivio/mobilita-umana/rivista-people-on-the-move/POTM%20116%20suppl.pdf.

[1313] Angela Ambrogetti, "Jubilee: Faith and Reason in Dialogue," ACI Stampa, 26 January 2016, www.acistampa.com/story/fede-e-ragione-e-il-rapporto-con-le-altre-religioni-il-cardinale-piacenza-ci-accompagna-n-2491 (translated from Italian).

[1314] Ibid.; Angela Ambrogetti, "Piacenza: Do You Want to Be Modern Priests and Ecologists? Stay More in the Confessional," ACI Stampa, 25 March 2019, www.acistampa.com/story/piacenza-volete-essere-preti-moderni-ed-ecologisti-state-di-piu-in-confessionale-10998 (translated from Italian).

Sin causes genuine damage. But the mercy poured out in the sacrament of Reconciliation brings healing. Piacenza explained that "in Christianity, mercy and truth are co-inherent, inseparable, so much so as to be not properly distinguishable." Mercy and truth, he said, "are united without confusion, and are distinct without separation.... A mercy without truth is not Christian, and at the same time truth without mercy is not Christian."[1315] In response to pressure for changes in the Church's discipline regarding the distribution of Communion, Piacenza refuted the notion that Catholic moral teachings must be ignored in order for the Church to dispense "mercy."[1316]

Approach to Islam, Interreligious Dialogue

Piacenza has not publicly identified himself with the view that Islam's conception of the relationship between reason and faith is incompatible with Christian civilization. He has spoken of the need for mercy in the dialogue between Catholicism and Islam. "For the Christian, the act of faith is an act that must be absolutely free. No one can force a person to believe in a certain way and no one can force him to disbelieve as he thinks he believes. You can bring so many arguments of reason to confront, to speak, but then you must keep in mind that the act of faith is a free act."[1317]

Furthermore, Piacenza emphasized that it "is always necessary to bear in mind that the starting point is not essentially interreligious dialogue, but intercultural dialogue. Inter-religious dialogue, in the strict sense, is only possible between revealed religions such as Judaism and Christianity. With Islam, a great and fruitful *cultural* dialogue can be deepened, since many human values can be shared."[1318] In such dialogue, however, we should avoid any temptation to colonization. Only openness to transcendence and

---

[1315] Hilary White, "There Can Never Be Opposition between 'Pastoral Action and Doctrine': Cardinal Piacenza Refutes Kasper," LifeSite News, 18 February 2015, www.lifesitenews.com/news/we-can-never-oppose-pastoral-action-and-doctrine-cardinal-piacenza-refutes.

[1316] Ibid.

[1317] Ambrogetti, "Jubilee: Faith and Reason."

[1318] Angela Ambrogetti, "Catholicism, Islam, Modernity: Dialogue in the Words of Cardinal Piacenza," ACI Stampa, 5 August 2016, www.acistampa.com/

to the values of the Spirit will encourage this attempt at authentic dialogue and can lead to a fruitful encounter with Islamic traditions, he said.

In a 2016 interview with ACI Stampa, the cardinal said:

> The Spirit can also act outside the boundaries of the Catholic Church and, therefore, it can guide consciences to an ever-greater recognition of the truth and, in it, of the dignity of the human person. The power of prayer is absolutely and urgently to be rediscovered. In every Diocese, in every parish, in every community, association, movement and aggregation, in every Christian family, it is necessary to start praying for peace. It is essential for Christians to discover how Eucharistic Adoration, meditated and prayed reading of the Holy Scriptures, the prayer of the Holy Rosary, entrustment to Mary, who is the compassionate Mother of all peoples, are all indispensable elements for maturing in themselves the awareness of the drama of the moment and to humbly implore the supernatural help in order to be able to live this grave moment in the most Christian way possible.[1319]

Piacenza also underlined the necessity of "rediscover[ing] the strength and clarity of one's own [cultural and religious] identity," denoting this as an indispensable element for every hypothesis of integration.[1320] "To integrate, it is essential to have an identity in which to integrate, know and recognize the roots of culture, in which the other is called to integrate, and overcome any sense of guilt and any inferiority complex determined by bad, or partial or preconceived reading of history. A Europe that hates itself has no future and will not be able to integrate any[one]," he said.[1321]

---

story/cattolicesimo-islam-modernita-il-dialogo-nelle-parole-del-cardinale-piacenza-3935 (translated from Italian; emphasis added).

[1319] Ibid.

[1320] "Piacenza Explains 'Crisis.'"

[1321] Nina Fabrizio, "Islam and the Church, the Cardinal: 'Integrating? An Identity Is Needed First,'" *Quotidiano.net*, 2 August 2016, www.quotidiano.net/cronaca/islam-chiesa-1.2395788 (translated from Italian).

Migration Position

Though a member of the Pontifical Council for the Pastoral Care of Migrants and Itinerant People, Piacenza has not spoken much on migration and refugees, other than noting his concern (together with the other Italian bishops) regarding the migratory phenomenon, which affects many families fleeing from war and poverty, and increasingly involves other families and the Church.[1322] In a 2016 interview, Piacenza called governments to act with caution in deciding which migrants to accept:

> Only a rediscovery of one's own cultural and religious identity will allow an adequate response, capable, on the one hand, of not renouncing one's identity and, on the other, not letting oneself be annihilated. Legitimate defense, as the *Catechism of the Catholic Church* teaches, is always lawful when immediate and proportionate and it is a duty, when the weakest is to be affected. In this sense, states and governments cannot fail in their duty to defend citizens, even in a secular manner, even beyond what the Christian type of sectarian inspiration could indicate.[1323]

Persecuted Christians and Religious Freedom

Piacenza's more pressing "call to action" relates to speaking out against anti-Christian persecution. "In many countries of the world, even not very far from us, a real persecution is underway but, one could say, 'in white gloves,' almost a 'systematic purge' of all that is Christian; persecution that, where it has not yet assumed the tone of physical violence, is no less aggressive from an ideological point of view, in that systematic attempt, which is made in cultural and legislative venues," he told Aid to the Church in Need.[1324]

[1322] Zenit Staff, "Small Groups Give Reports."

[1323] Fabrizio, "Islam and Church."

[1324] "Cardinal Piacenza: Red Wednesday Praise Initiative: 'Countless Christians Suffer for the Name of Jesus, Expand Our Pusillanimous Indifference,'" ACS Italia, 21 November, https://acs-italia.org/acs-notizie-dal-mondo/cardinale-piacenza-redwednesday-lodevole-iniziativa-innumerevoli-cristiani-

He has also said that the "real challenge" in the coming decades "will be anthropological; it will be the one between those who want to build a world without God, in which man becomes an object, and [those] who recognize God as the Author of the cosmos and of history."[1325]

We have times, before us, in which it will be increasingly necessary to defend religious freedom, including freedom of thought which is the mother of every other freedom! In this regard, there are disturbing signs throughout the West of a stubborn desire to reduce the space of freedom of men.... We must ... always educate our young people about freedom ... the freedom we see in St. Luigi ... the one that springs from belonging to Christ, from the awareness that every man is born free because he is wanted, created and loved by God.[1326]

As president of the pontifical foundation Aid to the Church in Need, Piacenza has underlined that hands-on support for refugees as part of the missionary task of the Church goes hand in hand with the topic of "new evangelization."[1327]

True versus False Mercy

"Mercy isn't blind tolerance, it isn't justification of sin and, above all, it isn't a right."[1328] Piacenza thereby teaches us that although, because of God's

soffrono-nome-gesu-espiano-la-nostra-indifferenza-pusillanime/ (translated from Italian).

[1325] Niccolò Mochi-Poltri, "Immigration: The Short Circuit for Catholics between the Words of Ravasi on Reception, the Rules and the Boundaries," *Sovrano Militare Ordine Del Tempio*, 22 March, www.smodelt.org/author/andrea-guenna/page/11/?lang=en (translated from Italian).

[1326] Domenico Agasso, "Chiesa esci dalla mediocrità, sii capace di piegarti su ogni uomo," *Sovrano Militare Ordine Del Tempio*, 22 March, www.smodelt.org/chiesa-esci-dalla-mediocrita-sii-capace-di-piegarti-su-ogni-uomo/.

[1327] *Because Faith Gives Hope: Activity Report 2017*, Aid to the Church in Need, October 2018, www.millionkidspraying.org/wp-content/uploads/2018/10/ACN-English.pdf.

[1328] Antonio Gaspari, "Interview: Cardinal Mauro Piacenza Explains Jubilee of Mercy," *Zenit*, 26 October 2015, https://zenit.org/articles/interview-

infinite mercy, it is possible for all of mankind eventually to be with God in heaven, we should not be presumptuous. Piacenza warns of manifestations that "have a spiritualistic and even satanic origin and, therefore, by feeding them and not correcting them, youth can unwittingly become stokers of the 'smoke of Satan', which already intoxicates the world too much. We must all be very careful not to breathe the toxic fumes; sometimes that happens inadvertently."[1329]

Responding to Secularism

Piacenza has noted the differences between the secularized and relativist West and other parts of the world where the sense of the sacred is still strong and has spoken out about the fact that even the priestly ministry experiences certain temptations. As an example, Piacenza named

> the temptation to activism, experienced by no few priests, who, might appear to be heroic in their total dedication, yet they frequently actually endanger their vocation and the effectiveness of their apostolate, if they are not stable in that vital relationship with Christ which is nourished with silence, prayer, *Lectio Divina* and above all daily celebration of Mass, Eucharistic adoration and the Holy Rosary. The Holy Father himself, has reminded priests that "no one proclaims himself in the first person, but within and through his own humanity every priest must be well aware that he is bringing to the world Another, God himself. God is the only treasure which ultimately people desire to find in a priest."[1330]

---

cardinal-mauro-piacenza-explains-jubilee-of-mercy/.

[1329] Antonio Gaspari, "All Saints and All Souls Day: A Time of Mercy, Forgiveness and Reflection (Part II)," Zenit, 31 October 2014, https://zenit. org/articles/all-saints-and-all-souls-day-a-time-of-mercy-forgiveness-and-reflection-part-ii/.

[1330] "The Year of Priesthood: 'Faithful to Christ, Faithful to the Priesthood,'" Agenzia Fides, 18 June 2009, www.fides.org/en/news/24492-Dossier_The_Year_of_Priesthood_Faithful_to_Christ_faithful_to_the_priesthood.

Our secular world requires a new evangelization, Piacenza argues, which, in turn, requires "new" priests. "Not Priests in the superficial sense, like every passing fashion, but in the sense of a heart profoundly renewed by every Holy Mass, renewed by the love of the Sacred Heart of Jesus, Priest and Good Shepherd."[1331] Piacenza urges priests to draw strength from silence—to move "from the anxious need 'to do' to the desire to 'remain' with Jesus participating ever more consciously with His being. Every pastoral action must always be an echo and expansion of what the Priest is!"[1332] He further underlined the importance of living out and announcing "the same doctrine, the same tradition, the same history of holy men and therefore the same Church."[1333]

Relationship to Pope Francis

Cardinal Piacenza is the epitome of discretion and someone who almost never gives interviews. His public views on Pope Francis and this pontificate, including such controversies as Francis' Post-Synodal Apostolic Exhortation *Amoris Laetitia* and the *dubia* are therefore largely unknown.

HELPING PRIESTS LIVE THEIR VOCATION

Having served the Congregation for the Clergy for a total of nearly twenty years,[1334] Piacenza is well known for his writings on the vocation to the priesthood and all that such a vocation entails. His major works include the books *Il Sigillo, Cristo fonte dell'identità del prete* (The seal: Christ the font of the priest's identity; Siena: Cantagalli, 2010), translated into Spanish and French; and *Il Vescovo animatore della comunione* (The bishop, animator of communion; Rome: Libreria Editrice Vaticana, 2016).

[1331] Ibid.

[1332] Ibid.

[1333] Ibid.

[1334] First as a staff member for ten years, followed by undersecretary for three years and later secretary for three years, concluded by prefect for three years.

"The most important virtue for a priest is pastoral charity," Piacenza has often said. This consists in "being completely true to oneself ... not [as] a [bureaucrat], not an employee of the church" but in making "Jesus Christ present among the people ... to embody the person of Christ in the world."[1335]

Year of the Priesthood

During Piacenza's time as secretary of the Congregation for the Clergy, Pope Benedict XVI instituted the Year of the Priesthood in 2009. The goal of the year was to focus on the importance and the indispensability of the priestly ministry in the Church for the salvation of the world. Piacenza gave numerous conferences during this time, encouraging his brother priests and working to build up vocations.

He kept a supernatural view of the priesthood, arguing that the Church does not want priests who are "showmen." This is because

> the Church does not invent its doctrine [on the priesthood] but has received it from the Lord Jesus.... The priest plays a decisive and irreplaceable role in the liturgy. He is not just an organizer of prayers and celebrations, as he is sometimes thought to be! In the liturgy, the priest stands for Christ Himself. In his offering to God, he repeats Christ's words and gestures with effectiveness. The thing which the priest really needs in the celebration of the liturgy is prayer.... If we all think of ourselves as being in the presence of the Lord, the liturgy will look quite different to us, along with our faith.[1336]

[1335] "Secretary of Congregation for Clergy speaks about a priest's identity," Priestly Society of the Holy Cross, 10 October 2009, https://opusdei.org/en/video/secretary-of-congregation-for-clergy-speaks-about/ (translated from Italian).

[1336] "The Vocation to Be a Priest Relies on a Daily Dialogue with Jesus, Living with the Church," *Communio* (blog), 7 June 2013, http://communio.stblogs.org/index.php/tag/mauro-piacenza/.

In a 2011 letter to priests, Piacenza (then prefect of the Congregation for the Clergy) reiterated this point by saying:

The [priestly] identity, welcomed and received sacramentally in our wounded humanity, demands the progressive confirmation of our hearts, our minds, our behaviors to everything that we are in the image of Christ the Good Shepherd that has been sacramentally imprinted in us. We must enter into the Mysteries that we celebrate, especially in the most Holy Eucharist, and to allow ourselves to be formed by them. It is in the Eucharist that the Priest rediscovers his true identity! It is in the celebration of the Divine Mysteries that one can catch sight of "how" to be a shepherd and "what" is necessary to truly serve each other.... We must convert ourselves to the daily participation of the Sacrifice of Christ on the Cross. Christ made possible and efficacious our Salvation with His perfect vicarious substitution. In the same way, every Priest, *alter Christus*, is called, as were the great saints, to live firsthand the mystery of their substitution for the service of all especially in the faithful celebration of the Sacrament of Reconciliation.[1337]

Piacenza reiterated that adhering to the authentic teaching of the Church calls for knowledge.

Priests, in dispensing divine mercy, should conscientiously carry out this special ministry by adhering with fidelity to the authentic teaching of the Church. Let them be well formed in doctrine and let them not neglect to bring themselves up to date every so often concerning those questions that pertain especially to the sphere of morals and bioethics (cf. CCC, n. 1466). In the matrimonial area too let them respect what the ecclesial Magisterium teaches authoritatively. Let them avoid setting out private doctrines in the

---

[1337] "Cardinal Piacenza's Letter to Priests," Zenit, 9 March 2011, https://zenit.org/articles/cardinal-piacenza-s-letter-to-priests/.

sacramental seat—personal opinions and arbitrary estimations that do not conform to that which the Church believes and teaches.[1338]

In this regard, Piacenza has called—both for priests and religious as well as laypeople—for a renewed knowledge and spreading of the teachings contained in Holy Scripture.[1339]

In a 2008 interview with Fides, the Holy See's news agency for missions, Piacenza noted that "In a secularized context, where everything appears to conspire 'to be silent about Christ', or to set him in the pantheon of vague imaginary, ironicized and relativized 'values', men who become priests bear witness with conviction and joy, with the eloquence of their life of total dedication, to the Truth and to Beauty and above all to the Presence of the Mystery in the world."[1340]

Views on Priestly Celibacy

In the same interview, Piacenza emphasized that being a priest is indivisibly connected with celibacy. "The Church selects for Holy Orders, those who have received from God the charisma of celibacy, since virginity, understood as total giving of self, is the greatest testimony a Christian can ever render to the Lord in this earthly life. Only martyrdom is greater than virginity! For this reason, much greater and far loftier than mere disciplinary or pastoral opportuneness—which is simply the logical consequence of greater premises—the very effectiveness of priestly witness is inseparably connected with holy celibacy."[1341]

In a 2009 homily, Piacenza added that

[1338] Piacenza and Iruzubieta, "Shrines."

[1339] "Church and Modernity: An Open Debate," InternEtica, 10 November 2012, www.internetica.it/Piacenza-Chiesaemodernit%C3%A0.htm.

[1340] Fides Dossier, "The Congregation for the Clergy, Interview with Archbishop Mauro Piacenza, Secretary of the Congregation for the Clergy," Catholic Culture, 26 July 2008, www.catholicculture.org/culture/library/view.cfm?recnum=8401#7.

[1341] Ibid.

a person called by [Our Lord Jesus Christ] cannot fail to give an answer which involves the whole of his being: soul, body, mind, heart, present and future. Everything is forever. A person who has recognized in Christ, the center, the reason and the meaning of his life cannot fail to love Him with the greatest love of which the human heart is capable.... Celibacy does not mean renouncing love. It means generous and magnanimous readiness to heed every beat of the heart and offer them to the family of the Church, to dispose of as she wishes, exclusively for the service of the brothers and sisters.[1342]

In a 2011 address, Piacenza once more stressed the Church's firm will to maintain the law that demands perpetual and freely chosen celibacy for present and future candidates for priestly ordination in the Latin Rite. He added that celibacy should be presented and explained "in the fullness of its biblical, theological and spiritual richness, as a precious gift given by God to his Church and as a sign of the kingdom which is not of this world—a sign of God's love for this world and of the undivided love of the priest for God and for God's people."[1343]

Piacenza further emphasized that celibacy is a question of evangelical radicalism and that poverty, chastity, and obedience are not reserved exclusively for religious, but are, rather, virtues to be lived with intense missionary ardor. He warned against lowering the level of formation—lightening the load of priestly formation and expectations—as a response to the declining number of priests. "The number decreases when the temperature of the faith is lowered, since vocations are a divine 'affair' and not a human one, and they follow the Divine logic, which is foolishness from a human point of view. Faith is called for!"[1344]

[1342] Piacenza, "The Deaconate of the Word."

[1343] "Conclusion of Cardinal Piacenza's Address to Priestly Celibacy Congress," Zenit, 27 January 2011, https://zenit.org/articles/conclusion-of-cardinal-piacenza-s-address-to-priestly-celibacy-congress/.

[1344] Ibid.

Women's Ordination, Homosexuality

With respect to who can be admitted to the sacrament of Holy Orders, Piacenza is known to support the "Instruction Concerning the Criteria for the Discernment of Vocations with Regard to Persons with Homosexual Tendencies in View of Their Admission to the Seminary and to Holy Orders," published by the Congregation for Catholic Education, which states that (while profoundly respecting the persons in question) those who practice homosexuality, present deep-seated homosexual tendencies, or support the so-called gay culture cannot be admitted to the seminary or to Holy Orders.[1345]

Regarding female ordinations, Piacenza has said "apostolic tradition" on the matter has been "unequivocally clear" and "has always recognized that the Church has not received the power from Christ to confer ordination on women."[1346] He has also clearly stated that for all the offices and tasks that are not connected with Holy Orders, "the feminine genius could make a specific contribution."[1347]

He has emphasized that "the Church is not a political government in which it is right to demand adequate representation. The Church is something quite different; the Church is the Body of Christ and, in her, each one is a part according to what Christ established. Moreover, in the Church it is not a question of masculine and feminine roles but rather of roles that by divine will do or do not entail ordination. Whatever a layman can do, so can a laywoman. What is important is having the specific and proper formation, then being a man or a woman does not matter."[1348]

[1345] Congregation for Catholic Education, "Instruction Concerning the Criteria for the Discernment of Vocations with Regard to Persons with Homosexual Tendencies in View of Their Admission to the Seminary and to Holy Orders," Vatican, 31 August 2005, www.vatican.va/roman_curia/congregations/ccatheduc/documents/rc_con_ccatheduc_doc_20051104_istruzione_en.html; Mauro Cardinal Piacenza and Archbishop Celso Morga Iruzubieta, *The Priest, Minister of Divine Mercy*, Catholic Culture, 9 March 2011, www.catholicculture.org/culture/library/view.cfm?recnum=9658.

[1346] "Piacenza Explains 'Crisis.'"

[1347] Gaspari, "Cardinal Piacenza on Women Priests."

[1348] Ibid.

He continued:

Priestly ordination... is reserved to men, and this is not discrimination against women, but rather a consequence of the unsurpassed historicity of the act of the Incarnation and of the Pauline theology on the mystical body, in which each one has his own role and is sanctified and produces fruit consistent with his own place. If this is seen in terms of power, then we are totally off base, because in the Church only the Blessed Virgin Mary is "suppliant omnipotence" like none other, and thus she is more powerful in that sense than St. Peter. But Peter and the Virgin Mary have distinct roles that are both essential. I have heard this in not a few circles of the Anglican Communion as well.[1349]

SUMMARY

Keeping the salvation of souls in mind above all, Mauro Piacenza has extensive experience as a teacher and spiritual guide. His devotion to the Eucharist and the Blessed Virgin Mary has helped in a particular way in his work for priests in the Congregation for the Clergy, where he labored for more than twenty years, eventually becoming prefect. He was an obvious choice to lead the congregation, being what some might call "a priest's priest," someone sought after to give retreats who works effectively and discreetly also when it comes to defending orthodoxy against errors within the Church.

His work in Genoa and then in Rome in caring for the cultural treasures of the Church is a manifestation of his commitment to maintain Catholic traditions and make them accessible to new generations. He holds fast to all doctrines of the Church on moral matters, clearly stating magisterial teachings on issues such as abortion, surrogate motherhood, and the need to evangelize non-Christian cultures. For him, there is no question that the priesthood in the Latin Church should remain for celibate males

---

[1349] "Piacenza Explains 'Crisis.'"

alone, with no room for "homosexual culture" in the seminary or rectory, or for women's ordination. He discreetly battles revolutionary ideas while affirming right principles and has a reputation for being a good judge of character, placing faithful people in the right posts.

Correcting a false sense of mercy, Cardinal Piacenza has frequently recalled the beauty and efficacy of the sacrament of Confession as a remedy for many evils faced by individuals today. The gospel is for migrants as well, he says, such that all care for refugees must include a spiritual component to ensure that they have the opportunity to meet Christ when they also seek material welfare. He also has a special concern for the persecuted.

A man of great discretion, Cardinal Piacenza has proven experience in academia, administration, and pastoral work. He shows piety and reverence in worship, handles difficult situations with sensitivity, and possesses a detailed knowledge of, and respect for, religious vocations.

Given his proven administrative abilities and profound spiritual sensibilities, Cardinal Piacenza has shown himself to have qualities that would surely suit a pastor not only in Italy but in a broader capacity.

SERVICE TO THE CHURCH

Ordination to the Priesthood: 21 December 1969
Ordination to the Episcopate: 15 November 2003
Elevation to the College of Cardinals: 20 November 2010

Education
- 1969: Major Archiepiscopal Seminary of Genoa
- 1976: Pontifical Lateran University, Rome; Canon Law (J.C.D.)

Assignments
- 1969-2003: Priest, Archdiocese of Genoa
- Chaplain, University of Genoa
- Lecturer in canon law, Theological Faculty of Northern Italy

- Professor of Contemporary Culture and History of Atheism, Ligurian Higher Institute of Religious Studies
- Professor of Dogmatic Theology, Institute of Theology for the Laity, Genoa
- 1986-1990: Canon, Genoa Cathedral

Roman Curia
- 1990-2000: Staff, Congregation for the Clergy
- 2000-2003: Undersecretary, Congregation for the Clergy
- 2003-2007: President, Pontifical Commission for the Cultural Heritage of the Church
- 2004-2007: President, Pontifical Commission for Sacred Archaeology
- 2007-2010: Secretary, Congregation for the Clergy
- 2007-2010: Vice president, International Council for Catechesis
- 2010-2013: Prefect, Congregation for the Clergy
- 2013-present: Major penitentiary, Apostolic Penitentiary

Membership
- 2010-present: Member, Congregation for Divine Worship and the Discipline of the Sacraments
- 2010-present: Member, Congregation for Catholic Education
- 2010-2013: President, International Council for Catechesis
- 2010-2016: Member, Pontifical Council for Social Communications
- 2011-present: President, Aid to the Church in Need
- 2011-2013: Member, Committee for the Preparation of the Year of Faith
- 2013: President, Interdicasterial Commission for Candidates to Sacred Order
- 2014-present: Member, Congregation for the Causes of Saints

PATABENDIGE DON ALBERT MALCOLM CARDINAL RANJITH

"The Word Was Made Flesh"

Born: 15 November 1947
Polgahawela, Sri Lanka
Nationality: Sri Lankan
Title: Archbishop of Colombo

BIOGRAPHY

Albert Malcolm Ranjith Patabendige Don—usually known simply as Malcolm Ranjith—was born in Polgahawela, fifty miles northeast of the Sri Lankan capital, Colombo. The eldest of four, Ranjith is the son of devout parents. His father was a railway station master whose work often took him from home, and Ranjith says his mother was the "great influence" in his life. Young Malcolm grew up in a village of strong, militant Catholics, proud of their traditions and feasts, and loyal to the Church and their priests. He became familiar with politics as a child, taking part in protests at age twelve after the socialist government decided to nationalize Catholic schools.

Educated by Lasallian Brothers, he entered St. Aloysius Seminary in Borella at eighteen after being impressed by the witness of a French missionary. A year later, he transferred to the national seminary in Kandy to study theology and philosophy. He was soon sent by Archbishop Thomas Cooray to Rome, where he graduated with a bachelor's degree in theology from the Pontifical Urbaniana University. Pope St. Paul VI ordained him priest in 1975 in St. Peter's Square. From 1975 to 1978, Fr. Ranjith pursued postgraduate studies at the Pontifical Biblical Institute in Rome, where he obtained a licentiate in Sacred Scripture. While there, he studied under Carlo Maria Martini and Albert Vanhoye (both later cardinals) and attended the Hebrew University of Jerusalem. On returning to Sri Lanka, he was quickly immersed in pastoral life in Pamunugama, where he helped poor fishermen in a village lacking running water, electricity, or adequate housing. He says the experience rooted his priestly ministry in the realism of life.

Appointed auxiliary bishop of Colombo in 1991, he took the episcopal motto *Verbum Caro Factum Est* in the firm belief that priestly life should be about witnessing to the Incarnation of the love of God. Four years later, Pope John Paul II appointed him bishop of Ratnapura, and, in 2001, Ranjith returned to Rome as adjunct secretary of the Congregation for the Evangelization of Peoples (Propaganda Fide) and president of the Pontifical Missionary Aid Societies. In 2004, despite having no diplomatic training, he was appointed apostolic nuncio to Indonesia and East Timor and raised to archbishop. In December 2005, Pope Benedict XVI appointed him secretary of the Congregation for Divine Worship and the Discipline of the Sacraments, where he promoted a liturgy more in keeping with the Second Vatican Council's Constitution *Sacrosanctum Concilium*. Benedict appointed him archbishop of Colombo in 2009 and elevated him to cardinal in 2010. In 2010, he was elected president of the Sri Lankan bishops' conference. He remains a member of the Congregations for Divine Worship and the Discipline of the Sacraments, and for the Evangelization of Peoples. He is fluent in ten languages: Italian, German, French, Hebrew, Greek, Latin, Spanish, English, Sinhalese, and Tamil.

SANCTIFYING OFFICE

Liturgy and the Poor

"Love for the liturgy and love for the poor, two true and proper treasures of the Church, one might say, have been the compass of my life."[1350] Cardinal Ranjith most clearly exhibited and developed his devotion to the liturgy both as the second-ranking official on the Congregation for Divine Worship and the Discipline of the Sacraments and as the archbishop of Colombo.

In Cardinal Ranjith's view, the heart of the liturgy is Christ, and any abuses usurping such a truth must be resisted, because "the protagonist of the Mass is Christ."[1351] For Ranjith, other conceptions of the Mass are therefore ordered by this principle. "Others explain the Eucharist in a way that places the accent on its banquet/meal dimension, linking it to 'communion,'" he has said. "This too is an important consideration, but we should remember that it is not so much a communion created by those taking part in the Eucharist as much as by the Lord Himself."[1352]

Traditional Guidelines

One of his first actions as archbishop of Colombo was to bring back altar rails and to issue guidelines reinstituting reception of Holy Communion

---

[1350] Gianni Cardinale, "Liturgy and the Poor, the Treasures of the Church," *30 Days* (September 2006), http://www.30giorni.it/articoli_id_11335_13.htm.

[1351] "Ranjith Speaks: Episcopal 'Rebellion' Going On; 'Bishops and Cardinals' Must Obey the Pope," *Rorate Caeli*, 5 November 2007, https://rorate-caeli.blogspot.com/2007/11/ranjith-speaks-episcopal-rebellion.html.

[1352] "Cardinal Malcolm Ranjith on the Liturgy and Its Abuses," *Ephesians-511* (blog), 22 March 2015, https://ephesians511blog.com/2015/03/22/cardinal-malcolm-ranjith-on-the-liturgy-and-its-abuses/.

on the tongue and while kneeling. But he did not impose such changes on parishes; rather, many had asked for them, and he says it was reception of Holy Communion in the hand while standing up that had been the imposition. Ranjith also prefers celebration of the Mass *ad orientem* but believes such directives should be left to bishops. Like others, such as Cardinal Raymond Burke and the former head of the Vatican's liturgical office, Cardinal Antonio Cañizares,[1353] Cardinal Ranjith also has strong reservations about concelebration, a novelty promoted since the Second Vatican Council, largely because he believes it deters priests from celebrating daily Mass themselves.

One implication Cardinal Ranjith draws from the centrality of the Eucharist is that Sunday Mass should not be "easily replaced by Liturgies of the Word [with distributions of Holy Communion], or worse still by so-called ecumenical prayer services." Rather, "the Eucharist . . . makes the Church,"[1354] and it should be celebrated if at all possible.

If the Eucharist were "celebrated under various guises along with the Protestant pastors," it would be "totally unacceptable and [constitute] *graviora delicta*."[1355] For Ranjith, the celebration of the Eucharist must be carried out in the appropriate manner. Priests should wear proper vestments, a discipline Cardinal Ranjith has enforced in the Archdiocese of Colombo.[1356] Proper vestments symbolize that the priest is putting on Christ,

[1353] David Kerr, "Cardinal Burke Cautions Against Over-Use of Concelebration," Catholic News Agency, 10 July 2012, https://www.catholicnewsagency.com/news/cardinal-burke-cautions-against-over-use-of-concelebration.

[1354] Ibid.

[1355] Ibid. A *graviora delicta*—a "more serious crime"—is an "external violation against faith and morals, or in the celebration of the sacraments. The Church considers such violations so serious that there is a special process to handle them." Cardinal William Levada, "Considerations on the Delicta Graviora," Vatican, 13 November 2011, http://www.vatican.va/roman_curia/congregations/cfaith/documents/rc_con_cfaith_doc_20111123_levada-belo-horizonte_en.html.

[1356] "Cardinal Ranjith to His Clergy: Communion on the Tongue Only and While Kneeling Is Mandatory," *Rorate Caeli*, 3 April 2004, https://rorate-caeli.blogspot.com/2012/04/cardinal-ranjith-to-his-clergy.html.

whose centrality in the Mass should not be marginalized by, for example, an excessively long homily. Instead, in the cardinal's view, homilies should be "10 minutes, 15 at most."[1357]

Boundaries for the Laity

The laity, too, should be careful not to obscure the presence of Christ in the Mass. Thus, according to Cardinal Ranjith, laypersons should not engage in "dances and applause in the middle of the Masses, which are not a circus or a stadium." Nor should they "arrogate to [themselves] tasks that are reserved for the priests," such as "preach[ing] the homily instead of the priest, even when he is present, or ... distribut[ing] Holy Communion, leaving the priest to sit idle at the altar."[1358]

Cardinal Ranjith favors traditional Roman influence on the liturgy, and, although not opposed to the Ordinary Form of the Roman Rite, he regrets that it has often been reduced to a "humanistic, man-centered festival" or a "Protestant Bible-service."[1359] He laments the existence in the Church of "a certain anti-Roman 'feeling'" and "a sense of misunderstanding of the true nature, content and meaning of the Roman rite and its norms and rubrics, which [has] led to an attitude of free experimentation."[1360] He also identifies "the quasi total abandonment of the Latin language, tradition and chant" as a negative development since Vatican II.[1361]

Inculturation

This is not to say that Cardinal Ranjith opposes all inculturation of the liturgy. For example, he has praised "the use of vernacular languages in the liturgy, which helped to lead the faithful to better understand the

---

[1357] "Ranjith Speaks."

[1358] "Liturgy and Its Abuses."

[1359] Forthcoming book interview with Roman Catholic Books Publishers (2021).

[1360] Luc Perrin, "A Broad Liturgical Program for the Hermeneutic of Continuity?," *Rorate Caeli*, 29 April 2007, https://rorate-caeli.blogspot.com/2007/04/is-ranjith-presenting-broad-liturgical.html.

[1361] Ibid.

Word of God."[1362] In his view, certain Roman or traditional elements of the Faith may aid inculturation efforts. "Learning the simplicity and beauty of [the] great body of chant," for instance, would "help musically talented priests and seminarians in Asia to be inspired by it and be able to compose dignified and prayerful chant forms that can harmonize better with the local culture."[1363] Also, wearing "cassocks or religious garb" is important because "in Asian culture, persons dedicated to God or religion are always visible in his or her own garb, like the Buddhist monk or the Hindu sannyasi (holy man)."[1364] Finally, the cardinal thinks that receiving Holy Communion while kneeling is important in conveying the Divine Presence in a culture where prostration before God is normal.[1365] To oppose such measures is, in Cardinal Ranjith's view, to favor "de-culturation," not inculturation[1366]—and "to project our faith as an appendix of a secular and globalizing culture that endorses secular values and seeks to represent these in Asia."[1367]

Ranjith nonetheless opposes "a far too facile interpretation of what could be absorbed from local cultures into the liturgy."[1368] In explanation of this concern, he has said, "I once was listening to a radio talk given by a Buddhist monk in Sri Lanka who ridiculed Christians for allowing local drum beating in their churches without knowing that those beats in fact were chants of praise for the Buddha."[1369]

Cardinal Ranjith would have the liturgy draw people not to Buddha but to Christ—whatever the circumstances. During a recent epidemic, for example, His Eminence recommended "special prayers at the Holy Mass during the week and the possible celebration of a triduum on Friday,

---

[1362] Ibid.
[1363] Ibid.
[1364] Ibid.
[1365] Ibid.
[1366] Ibid.
[1367] Ibid.
[1368] Ibid.
[1369] Ibid.

Saturday and Sunday."[1370] More generally, the cardinal thinks the liturgy is essential to "convinc[ing] the faithful to make sacrifices in their ethical and moral options," for "in the liturgy, we should experience the closeness of God to our heart so intensely that we in turn begin to believe fervently and are compelled to act justly."[1371]

GOVERNING OFFICE

Early Governance

From the start of his priestly ministry, Malcolm Ranjith was active in Church governance, founding the Colombo Archdiocese's social service arm, which "focused on helping the poor and marginalized."[1372] As a priest in 1988, he revitalized Sri Lanka's Holy Childhood Society, an organization that aims to foster a missionary spirit among children aged six to fourteen. Ranjith has a great love for leading children in the Faith and is known by locals as the "Children's Bishop."

Tissa Balasuriya

In 1994, he was named auxiliary bishop of Colombo. In that same year, he led "a commission that denounced the theological work of Sri Lankan theologian Tissa Balasuriya, charging that he had questioned original sin and the divinity of Christ, as well as supporting women's ordination."[1373]

[1370] "What Saint Sebastian and Saint Anthony of Padua Looked Like Before the Bombing," *The Eponymous Flower* (blog), 23 April 2019, http://eponymousflower.blogspot.com/search/label/Cardinal%20Ranjith.

[1371] "Liturgy and Its Abuses."

[1372] Krishan Francis, "Sri Lankan Cardinal Ranjith Holds Tight to Tradition in Papal Stakes," *Windsor Star*, 10 March 2013, http://www.windsorstar.com/business/lankan+cardinal+ranjith+holds+tight+tradition+papal+stakes/8076229/story.html.

[1373] John L. Allen Jr., "Papabile of the Day: The Men Who Could Be Pope," *National Catholic Reporter*, 28 February 2013, https://www.ncronline.org/blogs/ncr-today/papabile-day-men-who-could-be-pope-9.

The move was controversial, but Pope John Paul II encouraged the denunciation, telling Ranjith that Balasuriya's work was "neopelagianism." Then-Cardinal Joseph Ratzinger, prefect of the Congregation for the Doctrine of the Faith, was also fully supportive.

In 1995, Ranjith was named bishop of the new diocese of Ratnapura, Sri Lanka. He was active in the Catholic Bishops' Conference of Sri Lanka and led the National Commission for Justice, Peace and Human Development. He played a key role in helping to organize the beatification of St. Joseph Vaz, known as the "Apostle of Ceylon," in 1995.

Propaganda Fide

Called to Rome in 2001, Ranjith began work as adjunct secretary at the Congregation for the Evangelization of Peoples (Propaganda Fide), where his resistance to corrupt practices led him to be forced out by his superiors. He was then sent back to Southeast Asia, where, despite not having any formal training to be a papal diplomat, he was appointed apostolic nuncio to Indonesia and East Timor. The appointment has been a highlight of his episcopal career. He already knew many of Indonesia's bishops and, through his connections, was effective in helping bring aid to the country through the Church's humanitarian arm, Caritas.

Congregation for Divine Worship

The appointment was short, and the following year he was recalled to Rome to serve as the second-ranking official on the Congregation for Divine Worship and the Discipline of the Sacraments. During that tenure, Pope Benedict XVI authorized wider use of the Tridentine Mass in his 2007 *Motu Proprio Summorum Pontificum*. Then-Bishop Ranjith strongly supported the measure and criticized its slow implementation by some bishops as "rebellion towards the Pope."[1374]

While in Rome, Ranjith expressed some goodwill toward the Society of Saint Pius X (SSPX). In particular, he affirmed that "sometimes" what

---

[1374] "Ranjith Speaks."

they say about the liturgy "they say for good reason."[1375] Later, according to an SSPX priest, the cardinal said he would entrust his archdiocesan seminarians to the SSPX, if they were reconciled with the Church.[1376] On the other hand, Cardinal Ranjith has also declared himself "not a fan of the Lefebvrians" because "they still haven't re-entered into full communion with the Holy See."[1377] He seems to have made no public comment on Pope Francis' recent initiatives aimed at reconciliation with the SSPX.

Archbishop of Colombo

In 2009, Ranjith was named archbishop of Colombo and issued his famous liturgical guidelines, mentioned above.[1378] In 2010, then-Archbishop Ranjith was elevated to cardinal. The cardinal's directives to priests did not appear to deter vocations to the priesthood. On the contrary, the archdiocese added as many diocesan priests from 2013 to 2016 as it had in the preceding seven years.[1379] By contrast, the number of men in religious life in the archdiocese fell during that whole period.[1380] Like the number of diocesan priests, however, the numbers of women in religious life,[1381] of Catholics in general,[1382] and of parishes[1383] all increased.

[1375] Cardinale, "Liturgy and the Poor."

[1376] "Card. Ranjith Reported to Be Open to the SSPX Running His Seminary," Catholic News Live, 16 May 2012, https://catholicnewslive.com/story/26118. See also "FSSPX Superior of Belgium Comments on the News," Gloria.tv, 12:30, 14 May 2012, https://gloria.tv/language/ypC7nuVcYwSj66r2P3eNDSo8U/video/XwkfgyfaatzG4g7CGTcFDpVzR.

[1377] Cardinale, "Liturgy and the Poor."

[1378] Francis, "Holds Tight to Tradition."

[1379] The archdiocese had 341 diocesan priests, up from 298 in 2013 and 255 in 2006. "Archdiocese of Colombo," Catholic Hierarchy, http://www.catholic-hierarchy.org/diocese/dcolk.html.

[1380] Ibid.

[1381] Ibid. The number of women religious reached its most recent peak in 2013.

[1382] Ibid. Although the number of Catholics in the country peaked in 2013, it was up in 2016 relative to 2006.

[1383] Ibid. The number of parishes increased from 123 in 2006 to 127 in 2013 and 130 in 2016.

Guidance to Priests

In the midst of establishing new parishes, Cardinal Ranjith explained his understanding of the role of the priest. Citing *Pastores Dabo Vobis*, the cardinal characterizes the priest as a shepherd called to the "care of his people" so that they "never need to fear nor be dismayed."[1384] Furthermore, "in the image of Jesus, the priest gives his capacity to love, to all those to whom he is sent especially to the weak, the sinful, the stubborn, the poor and the unloved ones, those sick or distraught and those who have lost all hope."[1385] In Ranjith's view, the priest must "give himself totally to the Church or the community to which he is sent," such that "the Church and souls become his first interest, and with this concrete spirituality he becomes capable of loving the Universal Church and that part of it entrusted to him with a deep love of a husband for his wife."[1386] Cardinal Ranjith understands priestly celibacy, as well as poverty and obedience, in this light—a way of loving the community "in the total and exclusive manner in which Jesus Christ her head and spouse loved."[1387]

Lay Missionaries and Benedict XVI Cultural Institute

This is not to say that Cardinal Ranjith sees no role for the laity in spreading the gospel and manifesting the love of Christ. On the contrary, in the same speech, he announced the establishment of a Lay Missionaries Institute under the direction of a "competent priest director."[1388] The institute would "call for volunteers and after having trained those selected, give them the mission cross at a solemn ceremony to be held at the Cathedral and send them in groups to work in far flung outstations, especially in

---

[1384] Malcolm Cardinal Ranjith, "Presbyteral Meeting 2012 Address by His Eminence Malcolm Cardinal Ranjith, Archbishop of Colombo," 19 March 2012, https://megalodon.jp/2014-0909-1641-16/www.archdioceseofcolombo.com/inner.php?news_id=37.

[1385] Ibid.

[1386] Ibid.

[1387] Ibid.

[1388] Ibid.

the missionary region."[1389] The missionaries would remain lay but would "consecrate themselves to live a life of chastity, poverty and obedience as well as an intense prayer life and service to the remotest communities and will take temporary promises or permanent promises."[1390] Their work would be subject to periodic evaluation.[1391] Information about the current status of this project is not readily available, but the proposal alone indicates that Ranjith sees an important role for the laity in executing the Church's mission.

In 2015, Cardinal Angelo Bagnasco opened the Benedict XVI Cultural Institute in Negombo that Cardinal Ranjith had helped to found. The idea for the institute for tertiary education was born out of Ranjith's discussions with Benedict XVI and their mutual concerns about syncretism regarding interreligious dialogue and theological experimentation in Asia.

2019 Islamist Bombings

The attacks on Easter Sunday 2019, which killed more than 250 people and seriously maimed hundreds of others, presented arguably Cardinal Ranjith's greatest governing challenge to date. The cold-blooded bombings affected him deeply, and he was intensely moved by the suffering of the Sri Lankan faithful. Ranjith has frequently called for justice since the attacks, urging an inquiry and expressing frustration both at the lack of prevention prior to the attacks and an absence of investigative rigor after the atrocity. Responding to the concerns of his flock, he initially closed all churches in Sri Lanka for two weeks and then reopened them when the faithful asked for public Masses again. He was particularly concerned about the wounded and those left destitute on account of the attacks, especially 476 children who lost one or both parents.[1392]

[1389] Ibid.

[1390] Ibid.

[1391] Ibid.

[1392] Edward Pentin, "Cardinal Ranjith Calls for Accountability for Easter Bombings' Victims," *National Catholic Register*, 2 July 2019, https://www.

Cardinal Ranjith's governing style is never to decide anything unilaterally but only after consultation with experts. In leadership, he says, it is important to have dreams and "help others to feel it's their dream, too" but "never try to impose your will on others."[1393]

TEACHING OFFICE

Religion versus Human-Rights Ideology

Cardinal Ranjith exercises the teaching office vigorously, not least in teaching that human-rights ideology should not take the place of religion.[1394] In his view, "with regard to the essentially non-religious nature of the state, human rights as a common platform has its own role to play."[1395] If, however, "religion is truly practiced, it could take us to achieve levels of justice, going even beyond the expectations of human rights and thus need not be such an issue for our Catholic community."[1396] Thus, the Catholic

---

ncregister.com/daily-news/cardinal-ranjith-calls-for-accountability-for-easter-bombings-victims.

[1393] Forthcoming book interview with Roman Catholic Books Publishers.

[1394] The cardinal may have in mind, *inter alia*, an issue that he raised in 2012: "As we all know abortion is always a crime—it is murder and murder of a voiceless, defenseless human person even if that person is still in the fetal stage or appears deformed.... The *Catechism of the Catholic Church* is categorical on this.... The Catholic Bishops' Conference will shortly come out in the open against any relaxation of the laws in Sri Lanka. When contacted the President did inform me that he will not allow any relaxation of the rules on this matter. But instigated and pushed by the United Nations Population Programme and other international agencies, some local women's groups are agitating for this on the pretext of the enhancement of women's rights. Western Nations in their greed to continue to possess over 75% of the world's resources are telling us that there is not enough food to feed everyone—so we need to bring down our birth rates." Ibid.

[1395] "Sri Lanka: A Land Like No Other," *Daily FT*, 29 September 2018, http://www.ft.lk/opinion/Sri-Lanka-A-land-like-no-other/14-663693.

[1396] Ibid.; see also Sudath Pubudu Keerthi, "People Shaped by Buddhist Civilization Don't Violate HR: Cardinal," *Daily Mirror Online*, 28 September

faithful should "practice their faith truthfully, avoiding turning religious values into something that is ephemeral."[1397]

Holy Scripture

On the inerrancy of Scripture, Cardinal Ranjith observes that one threat to practicing the Faith truthfully is "the [Industrial Revolution-era] ascendance of biblical criticism (relativizing, to a certain extent, the Holy Scriptures), which in turn had negative influences on theology, generating a questioning attitude about the objectivity of established truth and the usefulness of defending ecclesial traditions and institutions."[1398] The cardinal believes that the Second Vatican Council was called to respond to this threat, as well as "the emergence of Marxism and positivism."[1399] He has praised the Council for producing such beautiful theological and pastoral reflections as *Lumen Gentium, Dei Verbum, Gaudium et Spes*, and *Sacrosanctum Concilium*."[1400] By contrast, Cardinal Ranjith blames "tendencies ... not necessarily connected to the orientations or recommendations of the documents of Vatican II" for "shak[ing] the foundations of ecclesial teaching and faith to a surprising extent."[1401] He sees Vatican II as part of a continual process of necessary dialogue with the world in relation to "changing social patterns and life options that people make."[1402]

2018, http://www.dailymirror.lk/article/People-shaped-by-Buddhist-civilization-don-t-violate-HR-Cardinal-156097.html; Ada Derana, "No Space for Human Rights if a Society Lacks Faith in Religion—Cardinal Ranjith," YouTube video, 1:38, posted 26 July 2016, https://www.youtube.com/watch?v=D5oKTCHpPyk. The cardinal has not been more specific regarding this claim. For example, he has not discussed how, if at all, either human rights or religion would guide immigration policy.

[1397] "Sri Lanka."

[1398] Archbishop Malcolm Ranjith, "True Development of the Liturgy," *First Things* (May 2009), https://www.firstthings.com/article/2009/05/true-development-of-the-liturgy.

[1399] Ibid.

[1400] Ibid.

[1401] Ibid.

[1402] Forthcoming book interview with Roman Catholic Books Publishers.

Educating Youth

Cardinal Ranjith strongly values the importance of teaching religion to children, and not just with regard to Catholicism. "Children should be given time to participate in [Buddhist] Dhamma schools and Sunday schools, or else there will be no enhancement in their spiritual traits."[1403] Indeed, in the cardinal's view, government should ban even private tutoring on Sunday mornings and Poya days (Buddhist/public holidays).[1404] On the other hand, government should not "allow politicians to interfere in school administration" but rather "ensure the independence of all education institutions" so that "such institutes [may] create a just and disciplined society."[1405]

According to Cardinal Ranjith, parents have primary responsibility to instill good values in children, and he thinks that mothers are central, if not primary, in doing so. He laments that, more and more in Sri Lanka, "women go to work, leaving their children with others. They have to work because the cost of living is high. However, if one brings children into this world, they should be looked after and should be brought up in a proper manner."[1406] He attributes the trend toward women working outside the home, at least in part, to parents not welcoming children as a blessing and people not valuing the work that women do in raising children. To address the latter problem, at least, Cardinal Ranjith thinks (citing St. John Paul II) that "a salary should be paid to non-working mothers who

---

[1403] Amali Mallawaarachchi, "Ensure Independence of All Education Institutes," *Daily News*, 4 November 2017, http://www.dailynews.lk/2017/11/04/local/133439/ensure-independence-all-education-institutes-archbishop; see also Charunya Rajakaruna, "Religious Discipline in School Has Declined," Ada Derana, 1 July 2018, http://www.adaderana.lk/news/48388/religious-discipline-in-school-has-declined-cardinal-malcolm-ranjith.

[1404] Ibid.

[1405] Ibid.

[1406] "Open Economy Destroyed Lankan Values: Cardinal," Onlanka, 18 August 2018, https://www.onlanka.com/news/open-economy-destroyed-lankan-values-cardinal.html.

stay at home to look after their children."[1407] Perhaps relatedly, in 2016, he preached to three thousand people about the gift of Mother Mary on the occasion celebrating the centennial of the first church dedicated to Our Lady of Lourdes in the country. Ranjith noted that Jesus "realized he had to give his Mother to us to protect this church, guide the faithful and make us strong, because Jesus knew that Mother Mary did the same for him."[1408]

Right-to-Life Issues

Among the primary values that should be practiced and taught to children is the value of human life. Cardinal Ranjith has said that "all children are born according to God's will and no one is born outside his will."[1409] Indeed, "even those who are differently-abled keep their parents together and play a role in ensuring well-being of their families."[1410] The cardinal firmly denies abortion as a human right,[1411] affirming instead that "abortion is murder."[1412]

He is naturally opposed to population control and rejects it as a solution to environmental challenges because it allows people to increase selfishness. "Exploitation of nature will continue," he believes. Ranjith is also

---

[1407] Ibid.

[1408] Melani Manel Perera, "For Card Ranjith, the Greatest Gift Received Is the Blessed Mother of Lourdes," *AsiaNews*, 2 February 2016, http://www.asianews.it/news-en/For-Card-Ranjith,-the-greatest-gift-received-is-the-blessed-Mother-of-Lourdes-(video)-36756.html.

[1409] "Abortion Is Not a Human Right," *Daily Mirror Online*, 30 August 2017, http://www.dailymirror.lk/135608/Abortion-is-not-a-human-right-Cardinal.

[1410] Ibid. It seems that Cardinal Ranjith has not addressed euthanasia explicitly, but his stand in favor of the dignity of the "differently-abled" may suggest his opposition to the practice.

[1411] Ibid.

[1412] See Sharanya Sekaram, "Where Are We Now in the Abortion Debate: The Sri Lankan Spectrum (Part I)," Bakamoono, 3 May 2018, http://www.bakamoono.lk/en/article/2759/where-are-we-now-on-abortion-debate-the-sri-lankan-spectrum-part-i.

opposed to advocates of population control and contraception, such as economist Jeffrey Sachs, being invited to the Vatican.[1413] He is vehemently against "ideological colonization," which he sees as largely perpetrated by nongovernmental organizations and the European Union.

Death Penalty

Cardinal Ranjith has taught generally that "human life is a precious thing," and "we can never agree to kill someone."[1414] Nevertheless, in July 2018, he supported "a limited application of the death penalty to certain types of prisoners."[1415] That is, "if there are prisoners who engage in drug importation and distribution or in the perpetration of violence through the underworld causing death to others, one needs to reconsider that practice and implement whatever punishment has been received by them through the Courts of Law."[1416] He argued that, if "credible witnesses and solid facts" establish that people in prison are organizing "gruesome crimes," then they "could be considered as having forfeited their own right to life," for "such activities cause death to other people."[1417]

Cardinal Ranjith's remarks on the death penalty immediately preceded Pope Francis' August 2018 change in the *Catechism* regarding capital punishment, but followed public comments by the pope criticizing the

---

[1413] Forthcoming book interview with Roman Catholic Books Publishers.

[1414] "Archbishop of Colombo Clarifies Position on Death Penalty," *Daily News*, 20 July 2018, http://www.dailynews.lk/2018/07/20/local/157454/archbishop-colombo-clarifies-position-death-penalty.

[1415] Ibid.

[1416] Ibid.

[1417] Ibid. "The cardinal added that if he had been warned that Catholic Churches could be bombed on Easter Sunday, he would have cancelled Sunday Masses, 'because, for me, the most important thing is human life. Human beings, they are our treasure.' 'I would have cancelled even the holy week itself,' Ranjith told Radio Canada." See "Sri Lanka's Ranjith: 'I Would Have Cancelled' Easter Mass if Bomb Warnings Were Passed On," *Catholic Herald*, 25 April 2019, https://catholicherald.co.uk/sri-lankas-ranjith-i-would-have-cancelled-easter-mass-if-bomb-warnings-were-passed-on/.

death penalty. Ranjith acknowledged, "The Holy Father Pope Francis has, in fact, not accepted the death penalty, which is also my own position invariably. I am not for a generalized return of capital punishment. It should be the last option, if at all."[1418] The cardinal cited the 1997 *Catechism*, paragraph 2267, as support for his position.[1419] As of October 2018, he had not addressed how he interprets the pope's change to the *Catechism* or how that change affects his view on executing certain types of prisoners.

Amoris Laetitia

Cardinal Ranjith has sought to read *Amoris Laetitia* with an orthodox interpretation. Prior to *Amoris Laetitia*, the cardinal held that, according to the "religious teachings and beliefs of the Catholic Church, marriage is a relationship between a man and a woman. God's Word says that man and woman shall unite in marriage and procreate, which is also the natural order."[1420] Moreover, the cardinal affirmed, "in that light, lesbian and homosexual unions cannot be allowed. These people could be defective and cannot overcome this problem due to shortcomings in their conduct and upbringing. While we must treat people facing this problem with empathy, we cannot allow them to be married."[1421] The cardinal had made no public comment on divorce or reception of Holy Communion by those living contrary to Church teaching on marriage and sexuality.

[1418] Ibid.

[1419] Ibid.

[1420] "Cardinal Malcolm Ranjith, Homosexuality Is Not a Human Defect. Equal Rights Not Sympathy!," Change.org, https://www.change.org/p/cardinal-malcolm-ranjith-cardinal-malcolm-ranjith-homosexuality-is-not-a-human-defect-equal-rights-not-sympathy; see also Allen Jr., "Papabile of the Day," 28 February 2013.

[1421] Ibid. The cardinal seems not to have spoken directly on whether men who experience same-sex attraction should be allowed in the seminary. Cultural opposition to homosexual acts in Sri Lanka may make this question less salient there.

In an interview about *Amoris Laetitia*, Cardinal Ranjith maintained that

> marriage is, continues to be, indissoluble. That is what Jesus said, and the ethics of Jesus Christ are very strict, even though he was a very compassionate man, a very compassionate God, who loved the sinner, who went looking for the sinner.... He had ... very strict rules on family life, marriage, love.... And so this is something that we have to preserve, but that doesn't mean that there cannot be certain questions on which the Holy Father can express views that may open a dialogue and a discussion in order to ascertain what is the procedure or what steps we can take....
>
> Necessarily all these things have to be understood in the light of the teaching of Jesus Christ and in the light of the tradition of the Church, which teaches very strongly about the indissolubility of marriage and about various cases of annulments and other things. The documents of the Church pinpoint what those cases are, and then we can find out various strategies to face this challenge without having to whittle down the basic doctrine of the Church on the indissolubility of marriage. That's what we should do, instead of rousing up a hornet's nest and falling into a trap of the modern world to divide us.[1422]

Specifically about *Amoris Laetitia*, Cardinal Ranjith thinks, "you can't say that ... everything is not good; neither can you say that everything is perfect."[1423] More broadly, regarding Church and papal teaching, Cardinal Ranjith has emphasized that "not all [documents and statements] have the same value. In the Church, there is a hierarchy of values for these documents and these statements."[1424] In response to papal statements, "while we remain strongly loyal to the Holy Father, we can open up a discussion,

---

[1422] Edward Pentin, "Cardinal Ranjith Discusses *Amoris Laetitia* Controversy," YouTube video, 17:36, posted 5 December 2017, https://www.youtube.com/watch?v=LeQaonhD4ks.

[1423] Ibid.

[1424] Ibid.

and there's nothing wrong with opening up a discussion or a study."[1425] On the other hand, in the cardinal's view, the pope may form a commission, take the minority position, and still end up making a statement which becomes "a kind of *ex cathedra* [statement]."[1426] As an example of the latter, Ranjith mentioned Pope Paul VI's "not accept[ing] contraception" in *Humanae Vitae*.[1427]

The cardinal believes that the *dubia* cardinals "had a point" in their attempt to elicit clarification from Pope Francis on this contentious part of *Amoris Laetitia*, but he would have preferred it if confrontation had been avoided and they had sat down together and discussed and studied the matter.[1428] The cardinal also does not think that appealing to the natural law is enough when it comes to defending marriage; rather, he stresses the importance of speaking about the beauty and spirituality of married life.[1429]

Pope Francis

Regarding Pope Francis, Cardinal Ranjith is strongly supportive of his outreach to the poor and to those on the periphery.[1430] More generally, he has said it is "correct that we defend him and we stand with him — in spite of his human weaknesses. Everybody is weak. All of us are weak. In fact, Simon Peter himself was weak.... Always I believe that God gives us the successor of Peter that is most suitable for the time in which he is given and by circumstances that we cannot explain always."[1431] These views are consistent with the cardinal's response to a perceived "rebellion" against Pope Benedict XVI's authorization of the Tridentine Rite in 2007. He said: "I invite all, particularly the Shepherds, to obey the

---

[1425] Ibid.

[1426] Ibid.

[1427] Ibid.

[1428] Forthcoming book interview with Roman Catholic Books Publishers.

[1429] Ibid.

[1430] Ibid.

[1431] Pentin, "Cardinal Ranjith Discusses *Amoris Laetitia*."

Pope, who is the Successor of Peter. The Bishops, in particular, have sworn fidelity to the Pontiff: may they be coherent and faithful to their commitment."[1432]

Cardinal Ranjith's loyalty to the pope does not appear to be driven by any sense of personal ambition. After he advocated execution of certain prisoners in 2018, it was put to him whether his position had ruined his chances to become "the Third World's first South Asian Pope." [1433] His Eminence replied: "I only have to state that I am hardly anyone worthy of such responsibilities for which God will choose in His own time someone far better than me."[1434] He has had a good rapport with Pope Francis, who values Ranjith's frankness, and they have known each other since Ranjith's time at Propaganda Fide.

Islam

Speaking in November 2017, eighteen months before the church bombings on Easter Sunday 2019, Cardinal Ranjith put Islamist extremism down to two main reasons: first, it was a "reaction to Western secularism and its turning away from God" and second, a "lack of resolution of the Palestinian problem."[1435] One month after the attacks, he said he had not changed his position, saying secularism "seeks to marginalize" those with religious beliefs "and that is not acceptable, especially to the Muslims. Therefore, the Muslims get radicalized more and more, the more that secularism tends to marginalize religion."[1436] On the one-year anniversary of the attacks, Cardinal Ranjith offered forgiveness to the six jihadist youths, calling them

---

[1432] "Ranjith Speaks."

[1433] Malcolm Cardinal Ranjith, "Death Penalty: Cardinal's Clarification on Sunday Punch Remarks," *Sunday Times*, 22 July 2018, http://www.sundaytimes. lk/180722/sunday-times-2/death-penalty-cardinals-clarification-on-sunday-punch-remarks-303389.html.

[1434] Ibid.

[1435] Forthcoming book interview with Roman Catholic Books Publishers.

[1436] Edward Pentin, "Cardinal Ranjith's Anguish: 'Justice Should Be Done,'" *National Catholic Register*, 1 May 2019, https://www.ncregister.com/daily-news/cardinal-ranjiths-anguish-justice-should-be-done.

"misguided" and saying "we meditated on Christ's teachings and loved them, forgave them and had pity on them. We did not hate them and return them the violence."[1437]

Coronavirus

In comments about the coronavirus in March 2020, Cardinal Ranjith said he was inclined to believe the conspiracy theory that COVID-19 was a man-made virus concocted in a laboratory rather than originating from animal-human contact. He urged the United Nations to open an investigation and bring the "perpetrators to trial for genocide."[1438]

ROLE IN SRI LANKAN POLITICS

Malcolm Ranjith has been a national figure in Sri Lanka since 2009. At the time of his elevation to cardinal in 2010, some criticized Ranjith for being too close to the government.[1439] He would face a similar charge in 2014, when President Rajapaksa, in the midst of a hard reelection campaign, appointed Cardinal Ranjith's niece to a position in the Sri Lankan embassy in Paris, allegedly without her having the typical qualifications.[1440] There was no allegation that the cardinal had lobbied for her appointment.

[1437] Frances Martel, "Sri Lanka Celebrates First Easter Since Jihadist Bombings in Quarantine," *Breitbart*, 13 April 2020, https://www.breitbart.com/asia/2020/04/13/sri-lanka-celebrates-first-easter-since-jihadist-bombings-in-quarantine/.

[1438] Franca Giansoldati, "Coronavirus, cardinale accusa: 'Creato in laboratorio da una nazione ricca e potente,'" *Il Messaggero*, 18 March 2020, https://www.ilmessaggero.it/vaticano/papa_francesco_coronavirus_vaticano_cardinale_complotto-5118291.html#.

[1439] Melani Manel Perera, "Sri Lankans Welcome Mgr Malcolm Ranjith as a New Cardinal," *AsiaNews*, 20 October 2010, http://www.asianews.it/news-en/Sri-Lankans-welcome-Mgr-Malcolm-Ranjith-as-a-new-cardinal-19778.html

[1440] "Archbishop Malcolm Ranjith Bought Over by DPL Post to Niece," *Colombo Telegraph*, 25 December 2014, https://www.colombotelegraph.com/index.php/archbishop-malcolm-ranjith-bought-over-by-dpl-post-to-niece/.

At the time of Ranjith's return to Sri Lanka to serve as Colombo's archbishop, Mahinda Rajapaksa was the democratically elected president of a country composed of Buddhists (70 percent), Hindus (12 percent), Muslims (10 percent), Catholics (6 percent), non-Catholic Christians (1 percent), and other religious minorities.[1441] A few months before Cardinal Ranjith arrived, Rajapaksa declared a total military victory over Tamil Hindu rebels who had been fighting a civil war for twenty-five years.[1442] Both sides had been accused of human-rights violations.[1443]

The cardinal "urged the government to quickly resettle civilians held in military-run camps" and "appeared before the country's Reconciliation Commission with suggestions to promote harmony between the Sinhalese and minority Tamil communities."[1444] According to a WikiLeaks cable, the cardinal told the U.S. ambassador that these positions earned him criticism and death threats from the Buddhist Right.[1445] The cardinal also reportedly said that Rajapaksa was a good man who should not be pressed too hard for alleged human-rights violations, lest that pressure induce destabilized democracy, a revolution, or a coup.[1446] Cardinal Ranjith has denied the accuracy of the WikiLeaks cable.[1447]

However close the cardinal was to the Rajapaksa government (which lost power from 2015 until 2019, when Rajapaksa's brother Gotabaya became president, and Mahinda was appointed prime minister), he sometimes

---

[1441] Central Intelligence Agency, "Sri Lanka," *World Factbook*, https://www.cia.gov/library/publications/the-world-factbook/geos/ce.html.

[1442] Matthew Weaver and Gethin Chamberlain, "Sri Lanka Declares End to War with Tamil Tigers," *Guardian*, 19 May 2009, https://www.theguardian.com/world/2009/may/18/tamil-tigers-killed-sri-lanka.

[1443] Ibid.

[1444] Francis, "Holds Tight to Tradition."

[1445] "Archbishop's Office Slams US Cable – Response to Colombo Telegraph Revelation Based on Wikileaks," *Colombo Telegraph*, 24 September 2011, https://www.colombotelegraph.com/index.php/archbishops-office-slams-us-cable-respond-to-colombo-telegraph-revelation-based-on-wikileaks/.

[1446] Ibid.

[1447] Ibid.

publicly challenged that government. First, he boycotted government functions in protest of the arrest of a Missionary of Charity sister for alleged child trafficking.[1448] The sister was released two weeks later.[1449] Second, in 2012, Cardinal Ranjith joined other religious leaders in condemning the impeachment of Sri Lanka's chief justice as a threat to the rule of law.[1450] Reportedly, the cardinal's involvement in this criticism surprised the Rajapaksa government;[1451] however, the chief justice was not reinstated until the next administration.[1452] Finally, in 2013, His Eminence warned the government and the Tamil National Alliance that foreign intervention would result if they did not find a way to address rights abuses and achieve reconciliation.[1453]

Cardinal Ranjith has rarely publicly opposed the new presidential administration. In a prominent and controversial move, the cardinal supported the government's plans to implement death sentences against drug offenders.[1454] His Eminence clarified that his support for the government's

---

[1448] "Church 'to Boycott' Govt Functions," BBC Sinhala, 3 December 2011, https://www.bbc.com/sinhala/news/story/2011/12/111203_cardinal_nun_boycott.shtml.

[1449] "Lankan Court Drops Child-Trafficking Charge against Indian Nun," Rediff.com, 15 December 2011, http://www.rediff.com/news/report/lankan-court-drops-child-trafficking-charge-against-indian-nun/20111215.htm.

[1450] "Move to Impeach the CJ Is Another Instance of the Breakdown of Law and Order—Congress of Religions Writes to Rajapaksa," *Colombo Telegraph*, 14 December 2012, https://www.colombotelegraph.com/index.php/move-to-impeach-the-cj-is-another-instance-of-the-breakdown-of-law-and-order-congress-of-religions-writes-to-rajapaksa/.

[1451] Dharisha Bastians, "All Frosts, No Thaws in Impeachment Imbroglio," *Colombo Telegraph*, 19 December 2012, https://www.colombotelegraph.com/index.php/midweek-politics-all-frosts-no-thaws-in-impeachment-imbroglio/.

[1452] "Sri Lanka Reinstates Chief Justice Shirani Bandaranayake," BBC, 28 January 2015, https://www.bbc.com/news/world-asia-31021540.

[1453] "Red Flag about War Crimes Inquiry from Archbishop of Colombo," *Colombo Telegraph*, 12 December 2013, https://www.colombotelegraph.com/index.php/red-flag-about-war-crimes-inquiry-from-archbishop-of-colombo/.

[1454] Ray Downs, "Sri Lanka to Bring Back Death Penalty for Drug Dealers," *UPI*, 16 July 2018, https://www.upi.com/Sri-Lanka-to-bring-back-death-penalty-for-drug-dealers/2811531706802/.

action was dependent on a certain understanding of the action as limited in a way that is consistent, in his view, with Catholic teaching.

As detailed above, he has been forthright in calling the government to account over the 2019 Easter Sunday terrorist attacks on churches. In March 2020, he pledged to lead public protests if the current government failed to produce a credible report on the bombings, saying questions about the previous government's inaction ahead of the attacks remained unanswered.[1455]

Cardinal Ranjith has also privately criticized the present government. According to the *Colombo Telegraph* (which tends toward a secular-internationalist view), he rebuked the current Christian Affairs minister, a Catholic, for not preventing an international summit of Jehovah's Witnesses from taking place in Sri Lanka.[1456] The minister denied the story—"no such incident took place and the entire report is a figment of the imagination of the author"—but the paper stood by its claim, citing affirmation by confidential sources.[1457]

During both the former and current administrations, Cardinal Ranjith has taken notable stands on religious liberty questions. In 2006, while serving in Rome, he responded carefully to an anti-conversion law under consideration in Sri Lanka, not condemning it, but rather calling it "a question debated at a national level" and emphasizing that "we have no desire to subvert the religious and cultural traditions to which the majority

---

[1455] "'We Will Take to the Streets': Cardinal Demands Answers over 2019 Easter Bombings," Catholic News Agency, 10 March 2020, https://www.catholicnewsagency.com/news/we-will-take-to-the-streets-cardinal-demands-answers-over-2019-easter-bombings-90329.

[1456] "Cardinal Berates John Amaratunga Over Jehovah's Witnesses Colombo Convention," *Colombo Telegraph*, 16 July 2018, https://www.colombotelegraph.com/index.php/cardinal-berates-john-amaratunga-over-jehovahs-witnesses-colombo-convention/.

[1457] "John Responds to 'Cardinal Story': CT Stands by Report," *Colombo Telegraph*, 16 July 2018, https://www.colombotelegraph.com/index.php/john-responds-to-cardinal-story-ct-stands-by-report/.

of the people of Sri Lanka belong."[1458] In 2007, he spoke generally against state attempts in Asia to control the Catholic Church, either by state-sponsored churches or by "restrictions and controls indirectly placed on the Catholic Church."[1459] As archbishop of Colombo, however, Cardinal Ranjith has made common cause with the Buddhist majority against what seem to be "massive and well-funded proselytism campaigns enacted in Sri Lanka by evangelical groups connected to the global Pentecostal networks" (not the cardinal's words).[1460] In 2011, he proposed a government-backed interreligious committee to monitor and sanction aggressive evangelical efforts—especially those involving financial incentives—and to reconcile religious communities.[1461] In 2017, the cardinal advocated a state ban on forcible conversions.[1462]

In 2016, Cardinal Ranjith supported preservation of the constitutional priority of Buddhism in Sri Lanka. Some Sri Lankan Catholics opposed this position.[1463] The cardinal, for his part, thought the effort to remove the constitutional provision was a move toward the atheistic secularization of Sri Lanka.[1464] On another occasion, Cardinal Ranjith has supported a

---

[1458] Cardinale, "Liturgy and the Poor."

[1459] "Liturgy and Its Abuses."

[1460] "Sri Lanka's Cardinal and the Buddhist-Catholic Axis," *La Stampa*, 2 June 2013, http://www.lastampa.it/2011/11/11/vaticaninsider/sri-lankas-cardinal-and-the-buddhistcatholic-axis-Ppn3wTAoMeMgaNHpe5dMHJ/pagina.html.

[1461] Ibid.

[1462] Ajith Alahakoon, "Cardinal Calls for New Laws to Ban Forcible Conversion," *Island*, 29 March 2017, http://www.island.lk/index.php?page_cat=article-details&page=article-details&code_title=162777.

[1463] P. K. Balachandran, "Does Vatican Disapprove of Cardinal's Nod to Give Buddhism 'Foremost Place' in Sri Lanka?," *New Indian Express*, 8 August 2016, http://www.newindianexpress.com/world/2016/aug/08/Does-Vatican-disapprove-of-Cardinals-nod-to-give-Buddhism-foremost-place-in-Sri-Lanka-1507022.html.

[1464] "9th Clause of the Constitution Should Remain Unchanged," Ada Derana, 11 September 2016, http://www.adaderana.lk/news/36895/9th-clause-of-the-constitution-should-remain-unchanged-cardinal-ranjith.

different sort of secularization. In that case, he opposed "racial and religious ideologies" and advocated banning political parties that promote such ideologies.[1465]

After the Easter Sunday 2019 church bombings, Cardinal Ranjith met with ambassadors of Islamic countries, who expressed their condolences over the deadly suicide bombings and assured him, he said, that there was "no connection to Islam." The cardinal said after the meeting, "We are very happy and thankful to the ambassadors of the Islamic countries for having coming [sic] here to express their solidarity with us."[1466] He also called on Sri Lanka's government to punish "mercilessly" those responsible "because only animals can behave like that."[1467] He later said it was an "initial reaction," that he did not "intend to hurt animals or animal lovers"

[1465] "S. Lanka President, Cardinal Stress Role of Religion in Building National Unity," Vatican Radio, 22 January 2016, http://www.archivioradiovaticana.va/storico/2016/01/22/s_lanka_president,_cardinal_stress_role_of_religion_in_building/en-1203034. See also "Cardinal Ranjith's Address Giving Thanks to Pope Francis," Zenit, 14 January 2015, https://zenit.org/articles/cardinal-ranjith-s-address-giving-thanks-to-pope-francis/: "Holy Father, our nation blessed by the teachings of the great world religions, Buddhism, Hinduism, Islam and Christianity does possess the moral and spiritual strength and nobility needed to generate such peace but we will all need to make that leap towards each other with a genuine spirit of reconciliation, trust and a sense of reciprocity." It seems that the cardinal has not moved beyond this claim regarding the conditions for temporal peace (a pressing matter in the wake of the long civil war in Sri Lanka) to address explicitly in English whether all human persons will reach heaven or all religions can guide persons to heaven. To that question, however, it may be telling that he continues to promote missionary work.

[1466] Patrick Goodenough, "Sri Lanka Cardinal Says Muslim Envoys Assured Him Bombings Had 'No Connection to Islam,'" CNS News, 25 April 2019, https://www.cnsnews.com/news/article/patrick-goodenough/sri-lanka-cardinal-says-muslim-envoys-assured-him-bombings-had-no.

[1467] "Easter Sunday Blasts Kill at Least 207 in Sri Lanka," Religion News Service, 21 April 2019, https://religionnews.com/2019/04/21/easter-sunday-blasts-kill-at-least-207-in-sri-lanka/.

but that he still hoped the perpetrators would be dealt with seriously and that justice would be served.[1468]

Finally, when he was asked if he agrees with a comment made by a Tamil National Alliance MP that the tragedy was a result of minority rights' being suppressed, Cardinal Ranjith said, "I don't think this incident was because of any suppression of minority rights. These politicians should not try to bring their political views to the fore using this incident. This atrocity was unleashed by a group of misguided youth who were manipulated by an international terror organization."[1469]

A critic of the cardinal called him "a realist," a "true Christian" who "renders unto Caesar what is Caesar's."[1470] In the realm of things that are Caesar's, he has emphasized that "the ownership of the country is with the people"; those in political power are, in his view, "caretakers."[1471]

Ranjith takes a particularly negative view of Sri Lanka's colonial history, referring to the former British rulers of then-Ceylon as "occupiers." He blames the British for favoring minority ethnic groups against the majority because the majority refused to cooperate with the "British occupying force."

SUMMARY

Cardinal Malcolm Ranjith is the consummate all-rounder, a conservative and a polyglot with a deeply pastoral vision who has extensive governing

---

[1468] Pentin, "Cardinal Ranjith's Anguish."

[1469] "Stop Violence against Muslims—Malcolm Cardinal Ranjith," MSN.com, 16 May 2019, https://www.msn.com/en-xl/asia/srilanka/stop-violence-against-muslims-malcolm-cardinal-ranjith/ar-AABnYq9.

[1470] Sarath de Alwis, "A Doddering Prophet Battles a Fallen God," *Colombo Telegraph*, 31 August 2016, https://www.colombotelegraph.com/index.php/a-doddering-prophet-battles-a-fallen-god/.

[1471] "There Are No Trustworthy Politicians," *News 1st*, 3 September 2018, https://www.newsfirst.lk/2018/09/03/there-are-no-trustworthy-politicians-cardinal/.

experience. Having relished serving poor fishermen as a young parish priest, he has governed numerous dioceses as bishop, represented the pope as a papal diplomat in the world's most populous Muslim country, overseen liturgical practices and served missionary dioceses as a high-ranking curial official, and governed a major metropolitan archdiocese as cardinal-archbishop in challenging times. He has lectured on Sacred Scripture and catechetics, set up institutes and commissions, and revitalized Church societies.

The fruits of his work have included attracting a greater number of priestly vocations in his archdiocese, bringing many children to the Faith through his love of catechizing the young (he is fondly known as the "Children's Bishop"), and spreading greater reverence for the liturgy across Sri Lanka. As the country has a more traditional society, he is less engaged with issues such as same-sex "marriage," euthanasia, and life issues generally, but he takes an uncompromising view on each of them, firmly believing in the importance of protecting all human life and condemning ideological colonization.

Due to his upbringing and formation, he is deeply loyal to the papacy and the hierarchy and has had a frank and relaxed relationship with Pope Francis, with whom he shares a fervent concern for the poor. He has nevertheless been willing to depart slightly from Francis; for instance, Ranjith would allow the death penalty in certain cases, he clearly favors ethical capitalism, and he rejects socialism. Although he prefers the Novus Ordo celebrated reverently and is partial to the Traditional Latin Mass, he is a firm proponent of the Second Vatican Council reforms and sees the post-conciliar Church as an imperfect yet necessary development of a process of dialogue with the world. Cardinal Ranjith also takes a pronounced post-conciliar view of religious liberty, willing to support the nation's constitution in giving preference to Sri Lanka's Buddhist majority as a vital bulwark against secularization.

Cardinal Ranjith is generally politically astute, has many contacts in government, and is close to the ruling party, but he is prepared to criticize the authorities at times, especially when it comes to truth and justice. He can be outspoken and sometimes impulsive but is recognized for being upstanding and willing to confront corruption.

Few cardinals have the breadth of experience Ranjith has gained over the years, making him a preferred candidate for those seeking a reliable, traditional, conservative pope more in continuity with Benedict than with Francis, but someone with a proven track record in governance and orthodoxy from the global south—this time from Asia, an area where the Church is growing relatively rapidly.

SERVICE TO THE CHURCH

Ordination to the Priesthood: 29 June 1975
Ordination to the Episcopate: 17 June 1991
Elevation to the College of Cardinals: 20 November 2010

Education
- 1965-1966: St. Aloysius Seminary, Borella, Colombo, Sri Lanka; Theology and philosophy
- 1966-1970: National Seminary, Ampitiya, Kandy, Sri Lanka; Theology and philosophy
- 1970-1974: Pontifical Urbaniana University, Rome; Theology (B.Th.)
- 1975-1978: Pontifical Biblical Institute, Rome; Sacred Scripture (S.S.L.)
- 1976: Hebrew University of Jerusalem; Biblical studies (D.C.B.S.)

Assignments
- 1975-1991: Priest, Archdiocese of Colombo, Sri Lanka
- 1980-1983: Spiritual director and staff, Daham Sevana Seminary, Kalutara, Sri Lanka

- 1983-1984: Professor in Sacred Scripture, Sinhala Theology Faculty, Colombo, Sri Lanka
- 1983-1993: National director, Pontifical Mission Societies
- 1984-1991: Coordinator for human development, Archdiocese of Colombo
- 1984-1991: Director, Caritas Colombo—Seth Sarana, Archdiocese of Colombo
- 1985-1991: Chaplain to St. Vincent de Paul Society, Archdiocese of Colombo
- 1991-1995: Auxiliary bishop, Archdiocese of Colombo, Sri Lanka
- 1991-1995: Titular bishop of Cabarsussi, Tunisia
- 1995-2001: Bishop, Diocese of Ratnapura, Sri Lanka
- 1995-2001: Secretary-general, Catholic Bishops' Conference, Sri Lanka
- 1995-2001: Chairman, National Commission for Justice, Peace and Human Development
- 2001-2004: President, Pontifical Mission Societies, International
- 2001-2004: Official, Congregation for the Evangelization of Peoples
- 2002-2009: Member, Pontifical Committee for International Eucharistic Congresses
- 2004-2005: Apostolic nuncio to Indonesia and East Timor
- 2004-2009: Titular archbishop of Umbriatico
- 2005-2009: Secretary, Congregation for Divine Worship and the Discipline of the Sacraments
- 2009-present: Archbishop, Archdiocese of Colombo, Sri Lanka
- 2010-present: Cardinal-priest of San Lorenzo in Lucina
- 2010: President, Catholic Bishops' Conference, Sri Lanka
- 2010: Chairman, Catholic National Commission for Priests, Religious, Seminaries, and Secular Institutes, Sri Lanka

Membership
- Congregation for Divine Worship and the Discipline of the Sacraments
- Congregation for the Evangelization of Peoples

State Appointments
- Justice of the Peace, Sri Lanka
- Member, University Council of Sabaragamuwa State University, Sri Lanka

GIANFRANCO CARDINAL RAVASI

"Preach the Word"

Born: 18 October 1942
Merate, Lecco, Italy
Nationality: Italian
Title: President of the Pontifical Council for Culture

BIOGRAPHY

Gianfranco Ravasi was born in the midst of the Second World War and has two younger sisters. He acknowledges that his childhood was deeply marked by alienation from his parents. During the war, his father, from whom he received an interest in art, was sent from Northern Italy to Sicily. His father deserted the army and arrived home eighteen months later, and little Gianfranco neither recognized him nor wanted him in the home.[1472] Gianfranco was very close to his mother, but was separated from her to live with his aunt, where he took up studies in Greek and Latin. Then his mother died, an event he described as "a severe blow."[1473] At a young age, he entered seminary and was ordained with a special exception when only twenty-three years old, in 1966.[1474] Jesuits supplied the bulk of his higher education, as he earned a degree at the Pontifical Gregorian University in Rome and a license in Sacred Scripture at the Pontifical Biblical Institute in Rome (the Biblicum). He later studied archaeology at the Hebrew University in Jerusalem. He taught Old Testament in Northern Italy for some time and served as prefect of the Ambrosian Library in Milan from 1989 to 2007.

In 2007, Ravasi was appointed titular archbishop of Villamagna di Proconsolare by Benedict XVI and simultaneously made president of the Pontifical Council for Culture, the Pontifical Commission for the Cultural Heritage of the Church, and the Pontifical Commission for Sacred Archaeology. In 2010, Benedict created Ravasi a cardinal-deacon. A prolific writer, Ravasi has over 150 books to his name as author or collaborator, and he worked in a journalistic capacity for *Avvenire*, the daily of the Italian Episcopal Conference; *L'Osservatore Romano*, the Vatican daily; *Il Sole 24 Ore*; the weekly *Famiglia Cristiana*; and the monthly *Jesus*. He has been the recipient of many honorary doctorates, awards, and medals. In 2014, Pope Francis confirmed Ravasi as president of the Pontifical Council for Culture. About himself, Ravasi has said he is "motivated not by Mediterranean optimism but Northern pessimism." He explains: "My search has always been for something permanent, for what is behind the transitory,

---

[1472] Desmond O'Grady, "The Vatican's Culture Maven," *National Catholic Reporter*, 16 May 2008, https://web.archive.org/web/20120213105849/http://ncronline.org/node/1016.

[1473] Ibid.

[1474] "Ravasi Card. Gianfranco," Vatican, http://press.vatican.va/content/salastampa/en/documentation/cardinali_biografie/cardinali_bio_ravasi_g.htm.

the contingent. I'm fighting loss and death, which probably relates to the absence of my father in my first years."[1475]

SANCTIFYING OFFICE

Cardinal Ravasi's approach to the liturgy has been shaped by his broader approach to Catholic culture and what he sees as modern needs.

According to one observer, Ravasi is a strong supporter of the liturgy that emerged following the Second Vatican Council and has no interest in the pre-conciliar form of the Latin Rite.[1476] He holds that the liturgy is "continuously looking upward, toward the transcendence of God and Christ, to His Word; but on the other hand, it also directs its gaze to the gathered community."[1477]

Liturgical Preferences

At the same time, Ravasi eschews what he calls "rigidity" in the liturgy, and argues that "active participation" is not guaranteed by an "essentialist" liturgy that is reduced to "obedience to all the rubrics."[1478] In 2012, Pope Benedict XVI established the Pontifical Academy for Latin with the goal of fostering deeper knowledge and a more competent use of Latin in both the ecclesiastical context and in the wider world.[1479] While speaking about the new academy in an interview with *La Stampa*, Ravasi commented on "traditionalists" who want the Mass to be celebrated in Latin, noting that

---

[1475] O'Grady, "Vatican's Culture Maven."

[1476] Andrea Grillo, "Liturgical Views of the Papabili: Cardinal Gianfranco Ravasi," *Pray Tell* (blog), 6 March 2013, http://www.praytellblog.com/index. php/2013/03/06/liturgical-views-of-the-papabili-cardinal-gianfranco-ravasi/.

[1477] Ibid.

[1478] Ibid.

[1479] "Ravasi: Traditionalists Should Go Over Their Latin," *La Stampa*, 26 November 2012, https://www.lastampa.it/2012/11/26/vaticaninsider/ravasi-traditionalists-should-go-over-their-latin-PYUvPtG5IDfON2Vs98qUBN/pagina.html.

while these people desire the Latin Mass, "it is likely they do not know the language that well."[1480] He added, "I myself have witnessed cases in which some of them did celebrate the rite of Mass or the liturgy in Latin with great strength but were unable to work out certain specific aspects of the language."[1481] Nevertheless, Ravasi explained that the new academy could help those who celebrate the Traditional Latin Mass.[1482]

Cardinal Ravasi believes that beauty is an important element of Catholic worship. He has criticized modern trends in church architecture, noting that the lack of integration between architects and the faith communities for which they design worship spaces has sometimes been negative.[1483] In 2013, for example, Ravasi noted that "the problem is that in Catholicism, unlike Protestantism, things like the altar, the images, are essential, while architects tend instead to focus on space, lines, light and sound."[1484] In the same interview, Ravasi lamented that more discussion about how the worship space could build up, or impede, liturgical life is warranted up front in building projects. He noted that the Vatican hoped to help heal the fracture between religion and art by commissioning modern liturgical art and building up dialogue with artists prior to commissions.[1485] The goal must be to produce churches that resemble not museums but places of prayer.

Attention to Preaching

Ravasi has called upon priests to improve their preaching so that the faithful are gripped by the power of God's Word and participate more fully in

---

[1480] Ibid.

[1481] Ibid.

[1482] Ibid.

[1483] Tom Kington, "Modern Catholic Churches Resemble Museums, Says Vatican," *Telegraph*, 2 June 2013, https://www.telegraph.co.uk/news/worldnews/europe/vaticancityandholysee/10094337/Modern-Catholic-churches-resemble-museums-says-Vatican.html.

[1484] Ibid.

[1485] See ibid.

the liturgy.[1486] He has said modern homilies risk becoming irrelevant to worshippers who are accustomed to the thrill and excitement of modern technology, and the "advent of televised and computerized information requires us to be compelling and trenchant, to cut to the heart of the matter, resort to narratives and color."[1487] The theological language employed by priests in their homilies, Ravasi argued, is "grey, dull and flavorless," and he urged priests to resort to the graphic and dramatic imagery of the Bible to bring their sermons to life.[1488] Biblical imagery and stories are well suited to grabbing the attention of the "children of television and the internet" who grace church pews, he added.[1489] The cardinal also encouraged priests to utilize social media to communicate God's Word: "We need to remember that communicating the faith does not just take place through sermons. It can be achieved through the 140 characters of a Twitter message."[1490] Ravasi has often called on the Church to find new language to evangelize more effectively.

The cardinal is known for his homilies, especially for his scriptural exegesis. In 2013, Pope Benedict XVI chose Ravasi to preach the Curia's Lenten retreat, which took place just prior to the pope's formal resignation.[1491] Ravasi's meditations during the course of the retreat provide a glimpse of his learning and ability to weave themes and thinkers together. In one thirty-eight-minute reflection, Ravasi not only repeatedly cited Scripture but also drew on diverse sources such as Etty Hillesum, Søren Kierkegaard, Yves Congar, Novalis, Aristotle, Blaise Pascal, Heidegger, and a hadith regarding

---

[1486] Madeleine Teahan, "Vatican Cardinal Urges Priests to Spice Up 'Dull, Irrelevant' Sermons," *Catholic Herald*, 10 November 2011, https://catholicherald. co.uk/vatican-cardinal-urges-priests-to-spice-up-%e2%80%98dull-irrelevant %e2%80%99-sermons/.

[1487] Ibid.

[1488] Ibid.

[1489] Ibid.

[1490] Ibid.

[1491] Estefania Aguirre, "Pope's Retreat Focuses on Faces of God and Man," Catholic News Agency, 18 February 2013, https://www.catholicnewsagency. com/news/popes-retreat-focuses-on-faces-of-god-and-man.

Muhammad.[1492] During this talk, he provocatively claimed, "even a blasphemous cry, as we might judge it on the outside, may be heard by God with
more attention than so many prayers offered up on Sunday morning."[1493]

Church Aesthetics and Pagan Worship?

The cardinal initiated a project to study how priests and other ministers
in the Church might be better trained in aesthetics and the history of art
through the Pontifical Council for Culture.[1494] Ravasi explained that beautiful art can be a path that leads to contemplation, which is at the heart of
faith.[1495] "Imagine a church," he said, "that is built in a refined manner, that
expresses a profound beauty. And to find inside this space the possibility of
silence, and contemplation, that is, it is the eyes that see. Because faith is
made, most of all, of contemplation."[1496] Beauty is an important aspect of
the liturgy because worship is a physical, and not just spiritual, act. Sacred
spaces must foster the ability to praise in a luminous way. "This church
that, for example, has bad acoustics, does not fulfill its mission because
listening is as important as contemplation," Ravasi explained.[1497] Faith
and art are "like sisters, because they both have as their main task to try
not only to represent what can be seen, or the surface of things, but also
to find the more profound sense."[1498]

Shortly before the beginning of the Amazon synod in October 2019, a
ceremony took place in the Vatican Gardens during which people prostrated

---

[1492] John L. Allen Jr., "Ravasi: Sometimes God Listens More to Blasphemy,"
National Catholic Reporter, 18 February 2013, https://www.ncronline.org/
blogs/ncr-today/ravasi-sometimes-god-listens-more-blasphemy.

[1493] Ibid.

[1494] Hannah Brockhaus, "Why the Vatican Thinks Priests Should Learn about
Art, Beauty," Catholic News Agency, 29 January 2017, https://www.catholic-
newsagency.com/news/why-the-vatican-thinks-priests-should-learn-about-
art-beauty-72534.

[1495] Ibid.

[1496] Ibid.

[1497] Ibid.

[1498] Ibid.

themselves in front of a fertility-symbol statue, or what Pope Francis later referred to as a Pachamama. The event caused scandal in the Catholic world. Cardinal Ravasi may have laid the groundwork for this event, since in 2015 he actively participated in a similar event for the Courtyard of the Gentiles project (more on this below). During that event in Argentina, caught on video, Ravasi followed a shaman and other worshippers as they circled a blanket that held religious symbols, while they prayed to "Mother Earth" and "Father Sun, Tata Inti."[1499] These symbols included food, as well as talismans, herbs, and, if the pagan practices were similar to those in La Paz, Argentina, llama fetuses and little fetish dolls. At the time, this event was televised on Argentinian stations, but it surfaced in the wider world after the Pachamama cult emerged during the Amazonian synod.

Pop Culture and Freemasonry

Provocation and praise for immoral, anti-Catholic artists and thinkers are not foreign to Ravasi, who has frequently made the words of such figures his own. Praised for his vast cultural knowledge, Ravasi draws upon it to tweet affirmations from individuals such as Giordano Bruno, a friar excommunicated and burned at the stake for occult practices (January 15, 2016), and Buddha (January 4, 2015). He has tweeted such messages as "Sadness is the world's greatest evil (J. Langer)" (September 29, 2015) and praised homosexual rocker Lou Reed (October 29, 2013)[1500] and gender-bending

---

[1499] Editorial, "El cardenal participa en un culto idolátrico pero sobre todo hace el imbécil," *La Cigüeña de la Torre*, 17 July 2015, https://web.archive.org/web/20150720222547/http://infovaticana.com/blog/cigona/el-cardenal-participa-en-un-culto-idolatrico-pero-sobre-todo-hace-el-imbecil/; Dorothy Cummings McLean, "Video of Vatican Cardinal at Pachamama, 'Father Sun' Ceremony Surfaces," LifeSite News, 19 November 2019, https://www.lifesitenews.com/news/video-of-vatican-cardinal-at-pachamama-father-sun-ceremony-surfaces.

[1500] Miguel Cullen, "Cardinal Tweets Tribute to Lou Reed," *Catholic Herald*, 29 October 2013, https://web.archive.org/web/20191221055748/https://catholicherald.co.uk/news/2013/10/29/cardinal-tweets-tribute-to-lou-reed/. Ravasi changed his tune somewhat when he received criticism

David Bowie (January 11, 2016), making headlines across the world: "Vatican Praises David Bowie."[1501] Under Ravasi's watch, the controversial pop singer Katy Perry, known for her demonic videos and large young following, was invited to speak on transcendental meditation for children at a conference on biotechnology in the Synod Hall (April 2018). Perry was given the pope's chair to deliver her talk at the conference, co-sponsored by the Pontifical Council for Culture.[1502]

Freemasonry and atheist and esoteric thinkers have also found shelter under Ravasi's wings. In 1990, the Italian book *Dossier Templari 1118-1990* included a list of names under the title "Testimony of industriousness of the Grand Prefecture for Italy of the 'Supreme Military Order of Templars of Jerusalem' in the social, cultural, artistic field for peace, faith, and universal fraternity," among whom was Gianfranco Ravasi.[1503] A 2000 article in the Italian Bishops' Conference's newspaper, *Avvenire*, titled, "Hermes, come sei Cristiano" (Hermes, how Christian you are), ambiguously praised the figure Hermes Trismegistus, often referenced by modern occultists.[1504] In 2008, Ravasi published a book titled *Le parole e i giorni. Nuovo breviario*

for supporting Lou Reed: Eric J. Lyman, "Vatican's Pop Culture Guru Gianfranco Ravasi Backpedals His Tribute to Rocker Lou Reed," *National Catholic Reporter*, 30 October 2013, https://www.ncronline.org/news/media/vaticans-pop-culture-guru-gianfranco-ravasi-backpedals-his-tribute-rocker-lou-reed.

[1501] E.g., Thomas D. Williams, "Vatican Pays Extraordinary Tribute to David Bowie, in His Own Words," Breitbart, 12 January 2016, https://www.breitbart.com/national-security/2016/01/12/vatican-pays-extraordinary-tribute-to-david-bowie-in-his-own-words/.

[1502] Diane Montagna, "Vatican Invites Katy Perry to Talk about Transcendental Meditation," LifeSite News, 2 May 2018, https://www.lifesitenews.com/news/vatican-invites-katy-perry-to-speak-on-meditation.

[1503] Maria Lo Mastro, *Dossier Templari 1118-1990* (Rome: Edizioni Templari, 1991), 484.

[1504] Gianfranco Ravasi, "Hermes, come sei Cristiano," *Avvenire*, 7 October 2000, https://web.archive.org/web/20060708184119/http://www.swif.uniba.it/lei/rassegna/001007b.htm.

laico (Words and days: a new lay breviary), which was supposedly a book of prayers adapted for laypeople—"laity" for him embraces "areligious, agnostics, and even atheists"—that includes reflections from atheists.[1505] Finally, in 2016, Ravasi published an article with the title "Dear Masonic Brothers." In it, he clearly states the various authoritative Catholic reasons for the "incompatibility" between being a member of the Church and a member of the Masons, while also saying that dialogue between the two groups should be encouraged and one should oppose "that stance from certain Catholic integralist spheres" that apodictically accuses opponents of Freemasonry.[1506] Masons around the world praised the work as a recognition of their deep unity with Ravasi's version of Catholicism.[1507] In response, concerned Catholics wrote him, asking if Ravasi was referring to Freemasons much as some Catholics call Protestants "separated brethren," or if Ravasi was implying that he belonged to the Masons. The prelate replied that the newspaper's staff created the headline and that the document speaks for itself.[1508]

[1505] Gianfranco Ravasi, *Le parole e i giorni. Nuovo breviario laico* (Milan: Mondadori, 2008). See the book review in Ravasi, "Scorte di saggezza per la vita quotidiana," in *L'Osservatore Romano*, 5 February 2009, 4.

[1506] Javier Lozano, "¿Sigue siendo la masonería la gran enemiga de la Iglesia Católica?" *Actuall*, 23 February 2016, https://www.actuall.com/laicismo/20804/; English translation of Ravasi's document on the official site of the Italian Freemasonic "Grand Orient": http://www.grandeoriente.it/wp-content/uploads/2016/02/Dear-Brethren-Masons-by-Cardinal-Ravasi.pdf.

[1507] Ravasi, "Cari fratelli massoni," *Il Sole 24 Ore*, 14 February 2016, https://www.grandeoriente.it/la-chiesa-la-loggia-il-cardinale-ravasi-sul-sole-24-ore-cari-fratelli-massoni-il-dialogo-ce/.

[1508] Editor, "'DEAR BROTHER MASONS' - Full Article on Catholic-Masonic Dialogue by Cardinal Ravasi ~ And, exclusive, an answer by Card. Ravasi," *Rorate Caeli*, 21 February 2016, https://rorate-caeli.blogspot.com/2016/02/dear-brother-masons-full-article-on.html.

GOVERNING OFFICE

Cardinal Ravasi's main administrative roles in a scholarly capacity have been his oversight of the Ambrosian Library in Milan and his curial responsibilities most central to his presidency of the Pontifical Council for Culture. In Milan, Ravasi played a large role in revitalizing the storied Ambrosian Library during his eighteen years directing it.[1509] He computerized the library and opened it up in a more effectual way to the modern world. He has not served as the administrator of a diocese or run his own parish.[1510]

Ravasi has transformed the workings of the Council for Culture since taking the reins in 2007.[1511] He assigned a department to each council official, making each individually responsible for the council's endeavors and bolstering accountability and transparency in the process.[1512] His mission in leading the council has been to continue its good work of using culture as a bridge between people of other faiths, in the hope that culture and religion should interact not as in a duel but as in a duet, "when two voices remain different, but harmonious."[1513] Part of his efforts at reinvigorating the council's work involved revamping its website.[1514]

[1509] John L. Allen Jr., "Interview with Ambassador Glendon; A possible papabile," *National Catholic Reporter*, 2 May 2008, https://www.ncronline.org/blogs/all-things-catholic/interview-ambassador-glendon-possible-papabile.

[1510] Paolo Gambi, "The Men Who Could Be Pope: Cardinal Gianfranco Ravasi," *Catholic Herald*, 5 March 2013, https://catholicherald.co.uk/the-men-who-could-be-pope-cardinal-gianfranco-ravasi/.

[1511] Carol Glatz, "Cardinal Ravasi, Bible scholar, uses culture as bridge to unite people," Catholic News Service, 25 February 2013, http://www.catholicnews.com/services/englishnews/2013/cardinal-ravasi-bible-scholar-uses-culture-as-bridge-to-unite-people.cfm.

[1512] Ibid.

[1513] Ibid.

[1514] Ibid.

Ravasi has led initiatives to engage with the broader culture and especially with young people. In 2013, Ravasi hosted a meeting on youth culture to solicit from young people what they were thinking and feeling. He appealed to the young people by featuring a concert by an Italian rock band.[1515] Another well-known initiative Ravasi leads at the council is the Courtyard of the Gentiles project that began during Benedict XVI's pontificate and aims to promote dialogue among agnostics, atheists, and people of the Catholic Faith.[1516] The project is one of encounter and dialogue and provides "a space of expression for those who do not believe, and for those who are asking questions about their faith, a window open to the world, to contemporary culture and to the voices that resonate."[1517] Operating under its own webpage, the project sponsors events and publishes blogs that seek to achieve the aforementioned goals.[1518] The project has sponsored high-profile events in cities such as Bologna, Paris, Bucharest, and Stockholm.[1519] Another example of Ravasi's engagement with modern culture was his decision to have the Council for Culture host its own pavilion at the 2013 Venice arts festival known as the Biennale. The

---

[1515] Ibid.

[1516] Ibid. For a criticism of Ravasi's work on the Courtyard of the Gentiles project, see George Weigel, "Craving Approval Isn't Evangelization," *First Things* (6 June 2018), https://www.firstthings.com/web-exclusives/2018/06/craving-approval-isnt-evangelization (explaining that the project frequently featured the media-savvy philosopher Julia Kristeva, who appears not always to have been the champion of freedom she claimed to be, based on her apparent involvement as an informer to the Bulgarian secret intelligence service during the Cold War and her tendency to provide intellectual cover to some of the twentieth century's worst regimes).

[1517] "What Is the Courtyard of the Gentiles?," Pontifical Council for Culture, http://www.cultura.va/content/cultura/en/dipartimenti/ateismo-e-non-credenza/che-cos-e-il-cortile-dei-gentili-.html.

[1518] Cortile dei Gentili Foundation, https://www.cortiledeigentili.com/.

[1519] John L. Allen Jr., "Is Ravasi 'the Most Interesting Man in the Church'?," *National Catholic Reporter*, 11 September 2012, https://www.ncronline.org/blogs/ncr-today/ravasi-most-interesting-man-church.

council used the space to host artists whose work reflects themes from the book of Genesis.[1520]

Against Fundamentalism

Ravasi argues that "fundamentalist" ideas about faith cause problems in dialogue with nonbelievers, as "oftentimes this fear (of dialogue) stems from the fact that the person doesn't feel capable of defending or justifying his own reasons, hence he doesn't want to listen to the other."[1521] In this way, he psychologizes reasons for avoiding dialogue. Christians must strengthen the roots of their own faith if they hope to coexist peacefully and dialogue constructively with the growing Muslim population in Europe, Ravasi believes.[1522]

In response to some efforts across Europe to remove Christian symbols from public places (e.g., crucifixes displayed in public classrooms and other public places in Italy), Ravasi has argued that removing such symbols risks erasing the identity of Europe.[1523] "Having white walls leads to a void, to cultural fragility. You may need to explain what a religious symbol means, but it isn't right to have to take down your symbols simply to avoid offending someone," Ravasi said.[1524]

Met Gala Scandal

One very ill-advised initiative of the Council for Culture under Ravasi was its role in coordinating a display of Vatican items at New York's Metropolitan Museum of Art in 2018, in an exhibit called "Heavenly Bodies—Fashion and the Catholic Imagination."[1525] Ravasi wanted to engage with the relationship between fashion, art, and faith; he agreed

---

[1520] Ibid.
[1521] Glatz, "Cardinal Ravasi, Bible Scholar."
[1522] Ibid.
[1523] Ibid.
[1524] Ibid.
[1525] Weigel, "Craving Approval Isn't Evangelization."

to collaborate with an exhibit at the Met because of its cultural significance and potential global reach.[1526] Vatican officials (including Ravasi) were allegedly unaware that the Met Gala, a curtain-raising event for the exhibit, which ran all summer, would be what it was—an occasion at which some celebrities dressed in ways that sacrilegiously mocked the Church.[1527] Indeed, prominent critics, including George Weigel, called into question the judgment of Ravasi and other Vatican officials: "Was the cardinal really surprised that the opening of an exhibit devoted to the impact of liturgical vestments and Catholic art on contemporary fashion turned into an exercise in louche camp and vulgarity that bordered on the blasphemous? If not, what precisely does Cardinal Ravasi know about contemporary culture, presumably the remit of his Vatican office?"[1528] Criticism also extended to the world of entertainment with British Catholic and talk-show host Piers Morgan saying the gala "crossed a line and was openly, brazenly disrespectful."[1529]

The Vatican's involvement in the Met Gala serves as a cautionary tale about the limits of evangelization and engagement with mainstream culture. The decision to participate was rooted in a desire to exploit the potential reach that such a venue could provide for widespread appreciation of the beauty of sacred and liturgical objects. "Our remit is to engage the world," said one Vatican official, noting that the Met is "one of the most significant cultural institutions in the world."[1530] But the Church's official presence at the Gala (most notably, the presence of Cardinal Timothy Dolan of New York City) created scandal, due to the disrespect for the sacred at the event with celebrities dressing in provocative ways while utilizing liturgical-style garments and themes. The support of the local

---

[1526] Edward Pentin, "How the Vatican Became Enmeshed in the Met Gala," *National Catholic Register*, 9 May 2018, http://www.ncregister.com/blog/edward-pentin/how-the-vatican-got-involved-in-the-met-gala.

[1527] Ibid.

[1528] Weigel, "Craving Approval."

[1529] Pentin, "Enmeshed in the Met Gala."

[1530] Ibid.

Church (and especially the support of Cardinal Dolan) eased the Vatican's concerns about affiliating itself with such an event, but because Ravasi was the person chiefly responsible for the Vatican's involvement, his judgment was called into question.

Vetoed for Assisi

According to Vaticanist Sandro Magister, in 2005 Ravasi was seriously considered a contender for archbishop of Assisi but was vetoed by Cardinal Carlo Maria Martini, the progressive archbishop emeritus of Milan (whom Ravasi admired), and Cardinal Atillio Nicora, a conservative prelate who had known Ravasi since seminary. Ravasi's reference to Jesus, that "He did not rise, he arose," led him to be rejected by the Congregation for Bishops, Magister wrote. He also said Ravasi had already been placed under suspicion in Rome for an exegesis believed to owe too much to the demythologizing theories of the Protestant exegete Rudolf Bultmann.[1531]

TEACHING OFFICE

Cardinal Ravasi's cultural influence has been greater than that of many scholars. Before assuming curial responsibilities in 2007, when he was granted the titular archbishopric of Villamagna, Ravasi spent many years teaching Old Testament exegesis at the Theological Faculty of Northern Italy.[1532] Over the course of his career, he has published alone or as a collaborator some 150 volumes on mostly biblical topics.[1533] From 1988 to

---

[1531] Sandro Magister, "Vatican Diary / Cardinal Ravasi's Comeback," chiesa. espressonline.it, 12 October 2012, http://chiesa.espresso.repubblica.it/ articolo/1350345bdc4.html?eng=y.

[1532] "The President, His Eminence Cardinal Gianfranco Ravasi," Pontifical Council for Culture, http://www.cultura.va/content/cultura/en/organico/ cardinale-presidente.html.

[1533] Ibid.

2017, Ravasi served as the host and public face of a television program, *Le frontiere dello Spirito* (Frontiers of the Spirit), that ran on mainstream Italian media every Sunday morning. The program included a Gospel reading followed by commentary by Ravasi.[1534] The cardinal is very active on Twitter and has relatively large followings on accounts that tweet in Spanish, Italian, and English.[1535] Ravasi regularly and often very prominently engages secular culture and has addressed a variety of important issues bearing on Catholic teaching, not only in his scholarly works but in interactions with and publications in the popular media as well. In 2007, Benedict XVI called upon Ravasi to write the texts of the meditations for the papal Via Crucis on Good Friday at the Colosseum.

Women in the Church

Pope Francis established the Study Commission on the Women's Diaconate, in August 2016, to consider the possibility of allowing women to serve as deacons in the Roman Catholic Church. In an interview in February 2017, Ravasi explained that he thought it was a possibility that women could be ordained to the diaconate.[1536] "I think a diaconate for women would be possible. But of course it has to be discussed, the historical tradition is very complex," Ravasi said.[1537] The cardinal thus has not affirmatively backed the idea of a female diaconate but has not rejected the possibility either.

In the same interview, Ravasi described his own extensive efforts to promote the role of women in the Church. He observed that the current fixation on women's ordination is overly clerical, and argued that our time

---

[1534] Ibid.

[1535] Glatz, "Cardinal Ravasi, Bible Scholar."

[1536] Christa Pongratz-Lippitt, "Cardinal Ravasi: Women Deacons 'A Possibility,' Fixation on Women's Ordination 'Clerical,'" *National Catholic Reporter*, 28 February 2017, https://www.ncronline.org/news/world/cardinal-ravasi-women-deacons-possibility-fixation-womens-ordination-clerical.

[1537] Stefanie Stahlhofen, "Ravasi: Women's Diaconate Would Be Possible," *Katholisch.de*, 24 February 2017, https://www.katholisch.de/aktuelles/aktuelle-artikel/ravasi-diakonat-der-frau-ware-moglich (translated from German).

might be better spent "talking about other important church functions that women could take on like the structural administration of parishes, church finances or architectural planning."[1538] The cardinal himself has acted on that last point: in 2015, his dicastery—the Council for Culture—set up a group of female consultants (now numbering thirty-seven)[1539] who critically assess the work of the council from their point of view. Ravasi's council was the first Vatican dicastery to do so. His female consultant group includes two Muslims, a Jewess, and nonbelievers.[1540] "Women see many things differently from men," Ravasi explained. "Our women advisors help prepare our general assembly and take part in it."[1541] The cardinal noted that "good advice is sometimes feminine," and lamented that in the Vatican "that is a new discovery."[1542]

When thinking about the role and importance of women in the Church, Ravasi refers to Mary. In an interview in 2012, Ravasi referred with approval to Pope Benedict XVI's remarks during the Angelus on the feast of the Immaculate Conception in 2006, when, asking himself *why* God chose Mary of Nazareth, among all women, to be the Mother of God, Benedict quoted the prayer of St. Bernard to the Virgin Mary.[1543] "The answer [to the question]," Benedict said, "is hidden in the unfathomable mystery of the divine will. However there's a reason that the Gospel evidences: [Mary's] humility."[1544] Benedict then cited the great poet Dante (Ravasi recalled with approval), noting that the Florentine "clearly emphasizes this in the last canto of *Paradiso*: 'Virgin Mother, daughter

---

[1538] Pongratz-Lippitt, "Women Deacons 'a Possibility.'"

[1539] Inés San Martín, "In the Vatican's Department for Culture, Women Get Their Say," *Crux*, 7 March 2017, https://cruxnow.com/vatican/2017/03/07/vaticans-department-culture-women-get-say/.

[1540] Stahlhofen, "Ravasi: Women's Diaconate."

[1541] Pongratz-Lippitt, "Women Deacons 'a Possibility.'"

[1542] Ibid.

[1543] Paolo Mattei, "The Cardinal in the House of the Poet," *30 Days* (February/March 2012), http://www.30giorni.it/articoli_id_78389_l3.htm.

[1544] Ibid.

of thy Son,/ humble and exalted more than any creature/ fixed term of eternal counsel.'"[1545]

Returning to Ravasi's decision to set up a council of female advisers in his dicastery, he is not unaware that doing so runs certain risks. He said, "For example, if one of the female counselors said that she was for the women's priesthood—and I think it would be legitimate to express her opinion—this would probably be the headline afterwards: Cardinal Ravasi has suggested women's priesthood. This ambiguity in communication and the media is currently a very big problem."[1546] Ravasi's statement here indicates that he does not think it would be problematic to install women in positions of influence at the Vatican who then publicly advocate for female priesthood.

Religious Liberty

In light of developments in culture, Ravasi emphasizes that "religious liberty is not a luxury of which we can avail ourselves or discard according to our whims and fancies, but an imperative imposed on modern society for congenial living and progress."[1547] According to him, the Second Vatican Council's Declaration on Religious Freedom *Dignitatis Humanae* includes the right of the individual to liberty of conscience as well as the right of groups to liberty of corporate worship, "with the necessary elements of fellowship, association and organization needed for maintaining the cult, teaching, preaching and evangelization."[1548] Ravasi laments that in many areas of the world, religious liberty is suppressed; in some places, the rights of religion are openly trampled upon and believers are persecuted, and in others (modern democratic countries), there are more "subtle" methods for impinging on religious liberty. Ravasi argues that all these "restrictions on

[1545] Ibid.
[1546] Stahlhofen, "Ravasi: Women's Diaconate."
[1547] Zenit Staff, "Cardinal Ravasi's Speech to TED Conference," Zenit, 19 April 2013, https://zenit.org/articles/cardinal-ravasi-s-speech-to-ted-conference/.
[1548] Ibid.

religious liberty are not simply legal or political issues but a direct outrage on the human dignity of persons."[1549] Governments should not be indifferent to the value of religion, and should "protect individuals and religious communities from those who would coerce them in religious matters on the basis of theological objections to their beliefs and practices."[1550] Ravasi's defense of religious liberty does not seem to distinguish between the Catholic right to worship the one true God from the freedom of coercion that ought to be accorded to everyone.

In a 2001 article in *L'Osservatore Romano*, Ravasi reflected on Pope John Paul II's emphasis on evangelization and the Word of God.[1551] Ravasi notes that the Word of God will "stand forever," as the prophet Isaiah foretold, and that it is the root of evangelization—a root that was reinvigorated at the Second Vatican Council, "when the Bible penetrated more intensely the daily life of the ecclesial community."[1552] Evangelization requires fidelity to the message, to the Word of God, but fidelity entails a delicate balancing act: "on the one hand, it must preserve the aspect of radical, unadulterated fidelity to the word, but on the other, it must also address the aspect of 'inculturation' and patient, gradual progress."[1553] Knowledge of biblical texts is of course necessary. Ravasi, however, cautioned that knowledge is not enough, and the Word must flourish in an acceptance of faith and love. Ravasi concluded, following Kierkegaard, that the Bible should be read as a young man reads a letter from the girl he loves: as if it were written precisely for him.[1554]

[1549] Ibid.

[1550] Ibid.

[1551] Archbishop Gianfranco Ravasi, "Spiritual Power of the Word of God," Catholic Culture, 23 May 2001, https://www.catholicculture.org/culture/library/view.cfm?recnum=3928.

[1552] Ibid.

[1553] Ibid.

[1554] Ibid.

Immigration

Ravasi reduces the question of government immigration policy to the virtue of hospitality. In June 2018, for example, the Italian government denied entry of a boat of migrants to one of its ports (the boat was named *Aquarius* and belonged to a French organization). Criticizing the government's decision to turn away the 629 migrants on board, Ravasi tweeted, "I was a stranger and you did not welcome me (Mt 25:43) #Aquarius."[1555] In an interview discussing his book *The Spiritual Significance of Eating*, Ravasi was asked to expand on the theme of hospitality. The interviewer noted that in the book, Ravasi quotes Jesus' words in the Gospel of Matthew, that "he who offers hospitality, offers hospitality to Jesus. He who offers hospitality to Jesus also offers it to whoever sent him."[1556] In response to a question about Pope Francis' statement that every European country should divide fairly the responsibility of hospitality to immigrants fleeing war and famine, Ravasi lamented that it was unlikely that European countries would respond to the pope's call.[1557] "Fear is difficult to eradicate. Love your neighbor as you love yourself is utopian, because you start to love yourself and stop there. Fear allows you to see others only negatively, as different and therefore threatening, to be eliminated."[1558] Ravasi agreed with Pope Francis on the need to welcome immigrants but was pessimistic that countries would respond to the call, noting that some European countries were Christian by tradition but not in lifestyle.[1559]

[1555] Grégory Roth, "Migrants: Armed with Cardinal Ravasi and Minister of the Interior Matteo Salvini," Cath.ch, 12 June 2018, https://www.cath.ch/newsf/migrants-passe-darmes-entre-le-cardinal-ravasi-et-le-ministre-de-linterieur-matteo-salvini/.

[1556] "Giancarlo Cardinal Ravasi," *Inside the Vatican*, 30 May 2015, https://insidethevatican.com/magazine/culture/books/giancarlo-cardinal-ravasi/.

[1557] Ibid.

[1558] Ibid.

[1559] Ibid.

Artificial Intelligence

In 2017, the Pontifical Council for Culture hosted a plenary assembly on the theme "The Future of Humanity: New Challenges to Anthropology."[1560] Panelists discussed the state of scientific research and potential applications of new developments in genetics, neuroscience, and artificial intelligence. Cardinal Ravasi delivered the closing address of the meeting and explained, Socratically, that the unexamined life is not worth living—and that this is as true for scientists as it is for the rest of us.[1561] Ravasi noted the almost science-fiction-like quality of some recent developments, such as gene editing and neuronal interventions, and warned that these advances present "fundamental, urgent questions from the cultural, theological and pastoral angles."[1562] Ravasi mostly expressed a desire that the Church engage with these developments at a deeper level so as not to be left out of the conversation, but he did note, with respect to gene editing, that "there is a risk of manipulations aimed at creating a new enhanced genotype to the extent of envisaging a new human phenotype," a problem that obviously raises important anthropological and moral concerns.[1563]

In the same vein, Ravasi expressed concern over the "overproduction of technological gadgets," and complained of "an era of bulimia in the means, and atrophy in the ends."[1564] His concerns strike at the core of a scientism that asks only whether it *can* do something and fails to pause to consider whether it *should* do that thing. Ravasi expressed wariness

---

[1560] Giovanna Pasqualin Traversa, "#FutureOfHumanity: Cardinal Ravasi: 'May Culture and Science Walk Together in Equilibrium along the Rope of Life,'" SIR, 21 November 2017, https://www.agensir.it/chiesa/2017/11/21/futureofhumanity-cardinal-ravasi-may-culture-and-science-walk-together-in-equilibrium-along-the-rope-of-life/.

[1561] Ibid.

[1562] Ibid.

[1563] Ibid.

[1564] Charles Collins, "Vatican Cardinal on a Quest for the Soul Inside the Machine," Crux, 28 June 2017, https://cruxnow.com/vatican/2017/06/28/vatican-cardinal-quest-soul-inside-machine/.

about biotechnology changing the role of humanity from being a "guardian of nature" into being a "kind of creator."[1565] All of these biotechnological innovations "have ethical and cultural implications that need to be considered."[1566] Ravasi's comments at the conclusion of this summit show that he is interested in the potential of new scientific advances, but concerned about their coherence with Church teaching and susceptibility for abuse. He stops short of offering a full account of principles that can be used to reason about these moral issues and is content with flagging the need for ethical consideration.

Pro-Life Issues

In 2013, Ravasi's Council for Culture hosted a meeting on regenerative medicine focused on adult stem cell research. The conference was intended to show the Church's support for moral forms of scientific inquiry into regenerative medicine and fight against stereotypes that the Church's role is always to say no to science. One of Ravasi's officials who helped organize the conference noted that it was also intended as a "preventative" step "against euthanasia."[1567] Vatican commentator Sandro Magister claimed that on the "crucial topics of abortion, euthanasia, unborn life, when ultimate principles are at stake, [Ravasi] is cutting as a sword. He preaches absolute respect for the life of every person, at every moment, 'for the same reason why respect is due even to the sinful man.' "[1568] In 2007, he upheld the Church's teaching on embryology, saying: "For the Bible, the purpose of the embryo is clear: it is an inseparable unity, a unitary and coherent

---

[1565] Ibid.

[1566] Ibid.

[1567] Edward Pentin, "Vatican Conference to Look at Cultural Impact of Adult Stem Cell Research," *National Catholic Register*, 10 April 2013, http://www. ncregister.com/blog/edward-pentin/vatican-conference-to-look-at-cultural-impact-of-adult-stem-cell-research.

[1568] Sandro Magister, "An Air of Appointments in the Curia—With a Gust of New Culture," Catholic Culture, 9 August 2007, https://www.catholic-culture.org/culture/library/view.cfm?recnum=7738.

process, compact and harmonious with the goal to be achieved, that of the human person."[1569]

Ravasi attended the October 2014 Synod of Bishops on the Family and presided over the commission that produced the meeting's final message. A month before the synod, Ravasi noted during a press conference at the Vatican that the debate over the indissolubility of marriage is nothing new and has been around in the Church since its origins.[1570] He said that the Gospel of Matthew includes an exception to the general ban on divorce for cases of "porneia," a Greek word often translated as "fornication" but which could have other meanings as well. "We don't know exactly what it was, but we know that the primitive Christian community recognized an exception to the ban on divorce, without questioning Jesus' message over the indissolubility of the sacrament," Ravasi said.[1571]

Ravasi's clarity on a variety of positions is mixed, and he remains ambiguous on such important questions as whether the discipline of celibacy should be alleviated for Latin-Rite priests, whether use of contraceptives is sometimes licit, and whether same-sex "marriage" is a matter of civil law.

Coronavirus Reaction

Cardinal Ravasi responded to the crisis with a series of reflections and interviews posted on the Courtyard of the Gentiles website. In one, he said the pandemic has taught many things to both believers and nonbelievers, revealing the "greatness of science but also its limits." It has "rewritten the scale of values that does not have money or power at its top" and brought back "being at home together, fathers and children, young and old, the labors and joys of not only virtual relationships." The pandemic has also

---

[1569] "Aborto: Mons. Ravasi, per bibbia embrione e' persona," 15 November 2007, *AdnAgenzia*, http://www1.adnkronos.com/Archivio/AdnAgenzia/2007/11/15/Cronaca/ABORTO-MONS-RAVASI-PER-BIBBIA-EMBRIONE-E-PERSONA_180759.php.

[1570] Associated Press, "Cardinals Publicly Battling over Divorce," *Crux*, 18 September 2014, https://cruxnow.com/church/2014/09/18/walter-kasper-cardinals-debate-marriage-ahead-of-crucial-meeting/.

[1571] Ibid.

"simplified the superfluous and taught us the essentials," he wrote. "It has forced us to fasten in the eyes of our loved ones our own death," and he recalled the book of Job, saying we have "the right to even protest with God, to raise our questions and complaints to Him." But he also pointed out that in the Bible, the words "Do not be afraid" appear 365 times, almost like a "good morning" that God "repeats at every sunrise" and "in these days of terror."[1572]

RELIGIOUS PLURALISM AND DIALOGUE WITH NONBELIEVERS

Dialogue is a key value for Ravasi. He holds that such encounters sharpen minds and lead to greater mutual understanding. Under his watch and Benedict XVI's direction, in 2009 he had the Pontifical Council for Culture sponsor the Courtyard of the Gentiles project, mentioned above, which aims to promote dialogue among agnostics, atheists, and people of the Catholic Faith.

Ravasi said of the initiative: "I want really fundamental questions to be asked—questions of anthropology, then good and evil, life and afterlife, love, suffering, the meaning of evil—questions that are substantially at the basis of human existence."[1573] The project initially made waves in the news but has since disappeared from public view.[1574]

Catholics should have a greater willingness to listen to the opinions of those who disagree with the Church, Ravasi believes. He thinks fear of such

---

[1572] Cardinal Gianfranco Ravasi, "La passione nei giorni del Coronavirus," Cortile dei Gentili, https://www.cortiledeigentili.com/la-passione-nei-giorni-del-coronavirus/.

[1573] Zenit Staff, "Cardinal Ravasi Urges Dialogue with Nonbelievers," Zenit, 13 February 2011, https://zenit.org/articles/cardinal-ravasi-urges-dialogue-with-nonbelievers/.

[1574] Sandro Magister, "Notice of Renovation in the 'Courtyard of the Gentiles,'" chiesa.espressonline.it, 30 November 2012, http://chiesa.espresso.repubblica.it/articolo/1350375bdc4.html?eng=y.

exchanges often occurs when people do not "feel capable of defending or justifying [their] own reasons."[1575] On the other hand, willingness to enter such a dialogue depends on both parties having an "identity that's serious and well-formed, not just fundamentalist."[1576]

Islam

Ravasi presents Islam's conception of the relationship between faith and reason as if it were compatible with Christian civilization. He maintains that there are cornerstones of a real general anthropology to Islam "with which it would be interesting to dialogue, far from the brutal reactions of obtuse fundamentalism that has nothing to do with this vision of authentic Muslim thought."[1577] Ravasi noted that diverse paths can lead to understanding, citing a verse of the Quran to the effect that: "To each of you God has assigned a ritual and a way. If God had wanted, he would have made you a single community. If he has not done so, it is to test yourself in what he has given you. Compete, therefore, in good works, for you will all return to God, and then he will inform you of those things for which you are now in dispute."[1578]

All Might Be Saved

On the question of universalism, Ravasi seems to hold that all might be saved. He has emphasized the significance "that the Second Vatican Council recognized that in obeying the injunctions of his conscience, even the non-believer can participate in Christ's Resurrection which 'holds true not for Christians only but also for all men of good will in whose

---

[1575] John L. Allen Jr., "Vatican Academy Mulls How Pro-Life Is Pro-Life Enough," *National Catholic Reporter*, 30 May 2012, https://www.ncronline.org/news/vatican/vatican-academy-mulls-how-pro-life-pro-life-enough.

[1576] Ibid.

[1577] Gianfranco Ravasi, "Dialogue with Islam," Cortile Dei Gentili, 11 March 2018, https://www.cortiledeigentili.com/dialogo-con-lislam-gianfranco-ravasi/ (translated from Italian).

[1578] Ibid.

hearts grace is active invisibly. For since Christ died for all, and since all men are in fact called to one and the same destiny, which is divine, we must hold that the Holy Spirit offers to all the possibility of being made partners, in a way known to God, in the paschal mystery' (*Gaudium et Spes*, n. 22)."[1579]

SUMMARY

Gianfranco Ravasi's engagement with culture presents Christ as a small part of a much larger mosaic composed of atheist, pagan, and non-Catholic thinkers. In favor of beauty in architecture and the liturgy almost as an abstraction, Ravasi has been a critic of the Extraordinary Form of the Mass. His homilies display a desire to invigorate listeners, to find the new language to engage the people of the current time, and he encourages priests to delve into Scripture more deeply for this purpose. Most of his public speeches are littered with literary or cultural references from across the socioreligious and political spectrum, demonstrating his breadth of knowledge and insatiable appetite for books and culture.

But many of his endeavors have shown questionable judgment at best —from actively participating in a pagan Pachamama ceremony in Argentina; to praising figures such as Martin Luther, Buddha, and deviant rock stars; to compiling a "prayer book" with atheist reflections and calling for fraternity with Freemasons. Many of his gestures are at the very least ambiguous. His notorious quote that Jesus "did not rise, he arose" led to suspicions in Rome.

The Courtyard of the Gentiles initiative demonstrated his ability to make news with events intended to reach non-Catholics. Some events, however, have been unquestionably harmful, as in the support given to the

---

[1579] "Gianfranco Ravasi: An Ethical Position Shared by 'Atheists' Like Zinoviev Should Serve as a Model for Emulation for True Christians," Zinoviev, 16 March 2017, http://zinoviev.info/wps/archives/3010.

blasphemous New York Met Gala in 2018, and other controversial events for which he was primarily responsible. Undoubtedly a public Catholic figure, his presence in journals, newspapers, books, and television has been almost unparalleled by other prelates.

But many of Ravasi's doctrinal and moral positions have more in common with the Protestants he praises than with Catholic tradition, such as his openness to women deacons, his vague notion of religious liberty, and his seeming unwillingness to speak clearly about unpopular moral norms. Indeed, notwithstanding his immense output of scholarly writings, there is little evidence that he has made definitive statements about the relationship of nonnegotiable moral norms, human rights, and public policy.

SERVICE TO THE CHURCH

Ordination to the Priesthood: 28 June 1966
Ordination to the Episcopate: 29 September 2007
Elevation to the College of Cardinals: 20 November 2010

Education
- Pontifical Gregorian University, Italy; Sacred Scripture (licentiate)
- Pontifical Biblical Institute, Italy; Doctorate

Assignments
- 1966-2007: Priest, Archdiocese of Milan, Italy
- 1989-2007: Prefect, Ambrosian Library, Milan
- 2007-2010: Titular archbishop, Villamagna di Proconsolare, Italy
- 2010-present: Cardinal-deacon of San Giorgio in Velabro

Roman Curia

- 2007-present: President, Pontifical Council for Culture
- 2007-present: President, Pontifical Commission for Sacred Archaeology
- 2010-present: Member, Congregation for Catholic Education
- 2010-present: Member, Pontifical Council for Interreligious Dialogue
- 2010-present: Member, Pontifical Council for Promoting the New Evangelization
- 2016-present: Member, Congregation for Divine Worship and the Discipline of the Sacraments

SUFFICIT TIBI GRATIA MEA

ROBERT CARDINAL SARAH

"My Grace Is Sufficient for You"

Born: 15 June 1945
Ourous, Youkounkoun, Guinea
Nationality: Guinean
Title: Prefect, Congregation for Divine Worship
and the Discipline of the Sacraments

BIOGRAPHY

Widely seen as a leading contender to be the first African pope since Pope Gelasius I in the fifth century, Cardinal Robert Sarah was born on June 15, 1945, in Ourous, Guinea, to parents who were converts to Christianity from animism. After middle school, he was obliged to leave home in order to continue his studies at the minor seminary in Bingerville, Ivory Coast. Following Guinea's independence in 1958, he returned home, completed his studies, and was ordained priest on July 20, 1969, in Conakry. After his ordination, he earned a licentiate in theology at the Pontifical Gregorian University in Rome and a licentiate in Scripture at the Studium Biblicum Franciscanum in Jerusalem. Upon completion of his studies, he was nominated rector of the minor seminary of Kindia, and served as parish priest in Boké, Katace, Koundara, and Ourous. In 1979, he was appointed archbishop of Conakry at the age of thirty-four, making him the youngest bishop in the world and earning him the nickname the "baby bishop" from John Paul II. As archbishop, he lived under the Marxist dictatorship of Ahmed Sékou Touré, who put Sarah on a hit list.

In October 2001, John Paul II appointed Sarah secretary of the Congregation for the Evangelization of Peoples, a post he held for nearly a decade. On leaving Guinea to take up the post, he was awarded the country's highest honor by Guinea's leader, General Lansana Conté, but the decoration did not prevent Sarah from publicly criticizing the regime's corruption and poor administration.[1580] Benedict XVI appointed Sarah president of the Pontifical Council *Cor Unum* in 2010 and elevated him to cardinal the same year. He took part in the 2013 conclave that elected Pope Francis. In 2014, Francis nominated Sarah prefect of the Congregation for Divine Worship and the Discipline of the Sacraments and allowed him to continue beyond his five-year mandate, which expired in November 2019. Sarah is a member of the Congregations for the Evangelization of Peoples and for the Causes of Saints and a member of the Pontifical Committee for International Eucharistic Congresses. As cardinal, Sarah has written a number of highly acclaimed books, most notably his three-volume series: *God or Nothing: A Conversation on Faith* (2015); *The Power of Silence: Against the Dictatorship of Noise* (2017); and *The Day Is Now Far Spent* (2019). He speaks Italian, French, and English fluently.

[1580] Cardinal Robert Sarah and Nicolas Diat, *God or Nothing* (San Francisco: Ignatius Press, 2015).

SANCTIFYING OFFICE

Approach to the Liturgy

Robert Cardinal Sarah possesses great admiration for the piety and liturgical devotion of the Holy Ghost Missionaries, who evangelized his village in Guinea.[1581] He maintains this deep gratitude for the missionary work that converted many of his people alongside his profound love for traditional virtues present in his culture. Sarah writes: "As an African I certainly inherited our joyful fear of everything sacred."[1582] Sarah displays a characteristically subtle attitude toward the pagan traditions of his forefathers, for he appreciates some genuine human religious insights in those traditions[1583] even as he condemns surviving superstitious practices.[1584] In relation to interreligious dialogue, he asserts that "there is only one truth that must be sought, attained and proclaimed: it is Jesus Christ."[1585]

Sarah says that the spirit of this age is to be peculiarly inimical to a true liturgical sense. "The best example of this is when we create new liturgies, the result of more or less artistic experiments, that do not allow any encounter with God."[1586] In answer to the question "Some people are alarmed about a crisis of the liturgy in the Church. Are they right?" Sarah replied, "Alas I think they are right to be worried and to fear the worst."[1587]

In 2017, on the tenth anniversary of *Summorum Pontificum*, Benedict XVI's decree that fully liberalized the Traditional Latin Mass, Sarah gave arguably his most outspoken critique of liturgical practice in the Church today. He criticized the "superficial spirit" of modern liturgies and the

---

[1581] Ibid.
[1582] Ibid., 51.
[1583] Ibid., 226.
[1584] Ibid., 21.
[1585] Ibid., 139.
[1586] Ibid., 125.
[1587] Ibid., 275.

"disaster, the devastation and the schism that modern promoters of a living liturgy caused by remodeling the Church's liturgy according to their ideas." He added that "the serious crisis of faith" had "made us incapable of understanding the Eucharistic liturgy as a sacrifice," and he lambasted a "sacrilegious tendency to reduce the Holy Mass to a simple convivial meal." He criticized a "significant number of Church leaders" for underestimating the "serious crisis" in the Church, characterized by "relativism in doctrinal, moral and disciplinary teaching, grave abuses, the desacralization and trivialization of the Sacred Liturgy, a merely social and horizontal view of the Church's mission." Rather than a "true springtime" since Vatican II, he said, a "growing number of Church leaders see this 'springtime' as a rejection, a renunciation of her centuries-old heritage, or even as a radical questioning of her past and Tradition." He lamented that "many refuse to face up to the Church's work of self-destruction through the deliberate demolition of her doctrinal, liturgical, moral and pastoral foundations." And he singled out increasing numbers of "high-ranking prelates" who "stubbornly affirm obvious doctrinal, moral and liturgical errors that have been condemned a hundred times and work to demolish the little faith remaining in the people of God, while the bark of the Church furrows the stormy sea of this decadent world and the waves crash down on the ship, so that it is already filling with water."[1588]

Sarah desires a unifying synthesis in the Roman Liturgy[1589] and believes a return to the text of the Second Vatican Council on the liturgy would resolve present disputes.[1590] Sarah's general approach is captured in his

[1588] Christopher Ferrara and Brian Kelly, "Cardinal Sarah Unloads Barrage of Criticism of Liturgical Abuses in Address," *Catholicism.org*, 6 April 2017, https://catholicism.org/cardinal-sarah-unloads-barage-criticism-novus-ordo-address.html.

[1589] Cardinal Robert Sarah, "Cardinal Sarah's Address on the 10th Anniversary of 'Summorum Pontificum,'" *Catholic World Report*, 21 March 2017, http://www.catholicworldreport.com/2017/03/31/cardinal-sarahs-address-on-the-10th-anniversary-of-summorum-pontificum/.

[1590] Cardinal Robert Sarah, *The Power of Silence: Against the Dictatorship of Noise* (San Francisco: Ignatius Press, 2017), 131.

professed allegiance to the "reform of the reform,"[1591] although he has been officially criticized for using the phrase.[1592]

In 2016, the cardinal gave a talk on authentically implementing *Sacrosanctum Concilium*, the Second Vatican Council's Constitution on the Sacred Liturgy; in the talk, he reasserted that God, not man, is the center of the liturgy. He said the *usus antiquior*—the Extraordinary Form of the Mass—should be "an important part" of liturgical formation and that the Council never intended that the Roman Rite be "exclusively celebrated in the vernacular" but did call for greater uses of the readings. He said adoration must be at the heart of liturgical celebrations and that "kneeling at the consecration (unless I am sick) is essential." He also reminded those attending that for a priest not to permit a member to kneel to receive Holy Communion is a "grave violation" of a basic Christian right. In short, Cardinal Sarah was keen to promote "the right way of celebrating the liturgy inwardly and outwardly" and in ways that he said were "utterly consistent with … the Second Vatican Council."[1593]

Ad Orientem

The cardinal maintains that the celebration of the Mass *ad orientem*, as the apostolic practice,[1594] is preferable, licit, and in conformity with the spirit and the letter of the decrees of the Second Vatican Council.[1595] He has stated

---

[1591] Sarah and Diat, *God or Nothing*, 125; Sarah, *Power of Silence*, 134.

[1592] Christopher Lamb, "Cardinal Sarah Wants 'Liturgical Reconciliation' between Old and New Forms of Mass," *Tablet*, 13 July 2017, http://www.thetablet.co.uk/news/7466/0/cardinal-sarah-wants-liturgical-reconciliation-between-old-and-new-forms-of-mass.

[1593] Address of His Eminence, Robert Cardinal Sarah, Prefect of the Congregation for Divine Worship and the Discipline of the Sacraments to the Conference "Sacra Liturgia UK 2016," London, England, 5 July 2016, https://drive.google.com/file/d/0B8CZzED2HiWJNzdaOE9ycVI4ekU/view.

[1594] Sarah, *Power of Silence*, 133.

[1595] The east has significance as the place where the sun rises, symbolizing the Resurrection of Christ and His Second Coming, and Masses used to be celebrated only in this way before the reforms of the Second Vatican Council.

that "as soon as we reach the moment when one addresses God—from the Offertory onwards—it is essential that the priest and faithful look together towards the East. This corresponds exactly to what the Council Fathers wanted."[1596] Sarah has made such statements repeatedly.[1597] At the 2016 liturgy conference in London, he invited all priests to celebrate Mass *ad orientem* on the first Sunday of Advent that year, thereby ensuring that "in our celebrations, the Lord is truly at the center." Sarah also held that, "contrary to what has sometimes been maintained, and quite in keeping with the conciliar Constitution, it is altogether appropriate, during the penitential rite, the singing of the Gloria, the orations and the Eucharistic prayer, that everyone, priest and faithful, turn together toward the East, so as to express their intention to participate in the work of worship and redemption accomplished by Christ."[1598]

His appeal was met with a swift rebuttal from the Vatican that claimed that the cardinal's words had been "misinterpreted," that Pope Francis had made clear that facing east did not have to apply to the Ordinary Form of the Mass, and that "no new liturgical directives" had been foreseen for Advent.[1599] At the end of 2016, the membership of the Congregation for

---

[1596] Staff Reporter, "Vatican Liturgy Chief Urges Priests to Celebrate Mass Facing East," *Catholic Herald*, 26 May 2016, https://catholicherald.co.uk/vatican-liturgy-chief-urges-priests-to-celebrate-mass-facing-east/.

[1597] Dan Hitchens, "Cardinal Sarah Asks Priests to Start Celebrating Mass Facing East This Advent," *Catholic Herald*, 5 July 2016, https://catholicherald.co.uk/cardinal-sarah-asks-priests-to-start-celebrating-mass-facing-east-this-advent/; Aymeric Pourbaix, "Cardinal Sarah: How to Put God Back at the Heart of the Liturgy," *Famille Chrétienne*, 23 May 2016, http://www.famillechretienne.fr/vie-chretienne/liturgie/cardinal-sarah-comment-remettre-dieu-au-caeur-de-la-liturgie-194987#.VObFpURrE2U.twitter (translated from French).

[1598] CWR Staff, "Silent Action of the Heart," *Catholic World Report*, 15 June 2015, http://www.catholicworldreport.com/2015/06/15/silent-action-of-the-heart/.

[1599] Edward Pentin, "Father Lombardi: Cardinal Sarah's Ad Orientem Suggestion 'Misinterpreted,'" *National Catholic Register*, 11 July 2016, https://www.ncregister.com/blog/edward-pentin/father-lombardi-cardinal-sarahs-

Divine Worship and the Discipline of the Sacraments (hereafter, "the Congregation") was also significantly overhauled in a move widely perceived as a purge of those sympathetic to Cardinal Sarah's perspective.[1600]

After issuing his appeal, the cardinal was pressured by at least one bishop to cancel a speaking engagement in the bishop's diocese. He has also been occasionally deterred from speaking in other dioceses. He has never wished to make a spectacle of such restrictions, however, preferring instead to respect the bishops' wishes and make no public statements.

Communion in the Hand

Cardinal Sarah has been outspoken in his criticisms of receiving Holy Communion in the hand, calling it a "diabolical attack" that is "trying to extinguish faith in the Eucharist by sowing errors and fostering an unsuitable way of receiving it."[1601] In a preface to a book on the subject, he wrote that "truly the war between Michael and his Angels on one side, and Lucifer on the other, continues in the hearts of the faithful" and that Satan's target "is the Sacrifice of the Mass and the Real Presence of Jesus in the consecrated Host."[1602]

---

ad-orientem-suggestion-misinterpreted; Diane Montagna, "Vatican: Cardinal Sarah's Ad Orientem Invitation 'Misinterpreted,'" *Aleteia*, 11 July 2016, https://aleteia.org/2016/07/11/vatican-cardinal-sarahs-ad-orientem-invitation-misinterpreted/.

[1600] Jan Bentz, "Pope Francis Again Elevates Church Progressives in Complete Overhaul of Vatican Liturgy Office," LifeSite News, 2 November 2016, https://www.lifesitenews.com/news/vatican-steers-congregation-for-divine-worship-to-the-left-with-new-appoint.

[1601] Raymond Arroyo, "Communion in the Hand: A 'Diabolical Attack' on Eucharist—Cardinal Robert Sarah," *The World Over*, YouTube video, 0:53, posted 2 March 2018 by Reverence Restoration, https://www.youtube.com/watch?v=6q9RLXui8IA.

[1602] Diane Montagna, "Cardinal Sarah: Widespread Communion in the Hand Is Part of Satan's Attack on the Eucharist," LifeSite News, 22 February 2018, https://www.lifesitenews.com/news/cardinal-sarah-we-need-to-rethink-the-way-communion-is-distributed.

In 2017, Cardinal Sarah sought to limit the impact of new regulations from Pope Francis' redirecting power of liturgical translations to bishops' conferences by insisting that the 2001 document *Liturgiam Authenticam*[1603] remains in force. For this he was publicly rebuked by the pope.[1604]

Power of Silence

Sarah's highly acclaimed book, *The Power of Silence: Against the Dictatorship of Noise*, is a profound reflection from a man who lives a deeply prayerful life. Pope Emeritus Benedict XVI wrote an afterword to the work, describing Cardinal Sarah as a "great spiritual teacher." Because he is "a master of silence and of interior prayer, the liturgy is in good hands," he wrote.[1605] Sarah's attraction to monastic life, silence, and contemplation pervades his three-volume series.[1606] He writes that for a long time, "I thought about entering a Benedictine monastery."[1607] When he became an ordinary, he went to some trouble to establish monasticism in his diocese.

Connected to his love of silence and contemplation is his disdain for some modern technology, particularly smartphones. "If our 'interior cell phone' is always busy because we are 'having a conversation' with other creatures, how can the Creator reach us, how can he 'call us'?" he wrote in *The Power of Silence*. And while he appreciates the convenience of a cell

---

[1603] Congregation for Divine Worship and the Discipline of the Sacraments, Fifth Instruction "For the Right Implementation of the Constitution on the Sacred Liturgy of the Second Vatican Council," Vatican, http://www.vatican.va/roman_curia/congregations/ccdds/documents/rc_con_ccdds_doc_20010507_liturgiam-authenticam_en.html.

[1604] Marco Tosatti, "The War against Cardinal Sarah," *First Things* (23 October 2017), https://www.firstthings.com/web-exclusives/2017/10/the-war-against-cardinal-sarah.

[1605] Benedict XVI, "With Cardinal Sarah, the Liturgy Is in Good Hands," *First Things* (17 May 2017), https://www.firstthings.com/web-exclusives/2017/05/with-cardinal-sarah-the-liturgy-is-in-good-hands.

[1606] Sarah and Diat, *God or Nothing*, 51, 108, 209, 251, 261-62; Sarah, *Power of Silence*, passim.

[1607] Sarah and Diat, *God or Nothing*, 53.

phone to read the Divine Office, he believes it is "not worthy" of the task as it "desacralizes prayer." Such devices, he said, "are not instruments consecrated and reserved to God, but we use them for God and also for profane things! Electronic devices must be turned off, or better still they can be left behind at home when we come to worship God."[1608]

Women and Intercommunion

Sarah has stated that the ordination of women is "an insurmountable obstacle" to "real progress"[1609] with the Anglicans. He has ruled out female deacons, calling them an impossibility.[1610] He has sought to avoid placing priests who do not accept the washing of women's feet on Holy Thursday in conscientious difficulties. The Congregation, with his eventual approval, issued a decree on Pope Francis' instruction allowing pastors to select for the washing of feet a small group that may (but not must) be made up of both men and women.[1611]

The cardinal rejects an ecumenism that ignores the importance of faith: "Intercommunion is not permitted between Catholics and non-Catholics. You must confess the Catholic Faith. A non-Catholic cannot receive Communion. That is very, very clear. It's not a matter of following

[1608] Christopher Lamb, "Mass Should Transport People away from the 'Cacophony of Consumerism,' says Cardinal Sarah," *Tablet*, 15 September 2017, https://www.thetablet.co.uk/news/7772/mass-should-transport-people-away-from-the-cacophony-of-consumerism-says-cardinal-sarah-.

[1609] Sarah and Diat, *God or Nothing*, 136.

[1610] "New book by Pope Benedict, Cdl Sarah rules out female deacons," LifeSite News, 13 January 2020, https://www.lifesitenews.com/blogs/new-book-by-pope-benedict-cdl-sarah-rules-out-female-deacons.

[1611] Diane Montagna, "Cardinal Sarah: Priests Don't Have to Wash Women's Feet on Holy Thursday," *Aleteia*, 15 March 2016, https://aleteia.org/2016/03/15/cardinal-sarah-catholic-priests-dont-have-to-wash-womens-feet-on-holy-thursday/; Robert Card. Sarah, "In Missa in Cena Domini," Vatican, http://www.vatican.va/roman_curia/congregations/ccdds/documents/rc_con_ccdds_doc_20160106_decreto-lavanda-piedi_en.html.

your conscience."[1612] He disapproves of the excesses of "enculturated" African liturgies: "God is horrified by forms of ritualism in which man satisfies himself."[1613]

As to his own personal sanctification, Cardinal Sarah has said that he prepares for spiritual battle by prayer and fasting—a discipline he learned when facing challenges as archbishop in Guinea. He decided at that time that every two months he would make a spiritual retreat in an isolated place and fast from food and water for three days. He would take with him only a Bible, a Mass kit, and a book of spiritual reading. The practice, he said, helped him to "recharge and return to the battle."[1614]

GOVERNING OFFICE

As a Priest

Robert Sarah has recalled that when he was still a young priest, he was asked to run the minor seminary in Conakry. There he found that discipline had seriously broken down. He imposed a strict new regime that provoked hostility in the "almost a hundred" seminarians. An unknown arsonist set fire to the chapel. When the culprit did not come forward and was not identified by the other seminarians, Fr. Sarah closed down the seminary. He refused to reverse this decision despite the government's insistence that he do so.[1615]

[1612] Diane Montagna, "Cardinal Sarah, Bishop Schneider Respond to Pope's Comment on Intercommunion," *Aleteia*, 30 November 2015, https://aleteia.org/2015/11/30/cardinal-sarah-and-bishop-schneider-respond-to-pope-francis-comments-on-intercommunion/.

[1613] Sarah and Diat, *God or Nothing*, 126.

[1614] Jack Carrigan, "Meet the Cardinal Who 'Recharges for Battle' by Fasting from Food and Water," *Catholic Herald*, 4 February 2016, https://catholicherald.co.uk/meet-the-cardinal-who-recharges-for-battle-by-fasting-from-food-and-water/.

[1615] Sarah and Diat, *God or Nothing*, 56-57.

As a Young Bishop

When he was made a bishop at the age of thirty-four, Sarah became the youngest bishop in the world. Cardinal Sarah emphasizes his feeling of inadequacy. He took as his motto *Sufficit tibi gratia mea,* "My grace is sufficient for you" (2 Cor. 12:9). He states that he sought to avoid elevation to the episcopate and nearly resigned his see.[1616] His twenty years as ordinary in Conakry, Guinea, nevertheless provided him extensive experience as a pastor of a vibrant local church.

Sarah manifests pride in his African identity and confidence in the future of African Catholicism: "How can anyone forget that Africa welcomed and saved the infant Jesus from the hands of Herod who wanted to kill him? How can we forget that the man who helped Christ to carry his Cross to Golgotha was an African, Simon of Cyrene?"[1617] He notes: "In Africa, the sacred is something quite obvious for the Christian people, but also for believers of all religions. Many Westerners look down on the sacred as something infantile and superstitious, but this disdain results from the self-importance of spoiled children."[1618] While expressing confidence about the expansion of the Church in Asia and Africa, he cautions that "the beauty of the Church does not lie in the numbers of her faithful but in their holiness."[1619]

Cor Unum

Sarah worked tirelessly in his later capacity as president of the Pontifical Council *Cor Unum* to promote practical charity and to care for the needy throughout the world. It was under this aegis that he assisted Benedict XVI in writing the *Motu Proprio De Caritate Ministranda,* "On the Service of Charity." This legislation governs the Church's charitable

[1616] Ibid., 70.
[1617] Sarah and Diat, *God or Nothing,* 91.
[1618] Sarah, *Power of Silence,* 120.
[1619] Sarah and Diat, *God or Nothing,* 75.

activities.[1620] Many consider the chief assertion in the document to be the following: "The service of charity is a constitutive element of the Church's mission and an indispensable expression of her very being."[1621] In continuity with this view, Sarah openly laments the growing institutional substitution of secularized philanthropy for authentic Christian charity: "Some Catholic organizations are ashamed and refuse to manifest their faith."[1622] Accordingly, the 2012 rule change stipulated that *Cor Unum* should monitor the activity of Caritas Internationalis, effectively putting Sarah in charge of the Catholic charitable activity then governed by Honduras' Cardinal Oscar Rodríguez Maradiaga.[1623]

The position also gave a platform to criticize institutions pursuing ungodly agendas under the guise of humanitarianism. In 2012, then-UN Secretary-General Ban Ki-moon told African nations to stop discrimination on account of sexual orientation or gender identity, even though such issues are taboo on most of the continent. In response, Cardinal Sarah described Ban's comments as "stupid." African bishops "must react" to such a move, he said, as "this is not our culture; it's against our faith."[1624]

[1620] John L. Allen Jr., "Pope Demands Stronger Catholic Identity for Charities," *National Catholic Reporter*, 18 December 2012, https://www.ncronline.org/news/vatican/pope-demands-stronger-catholic-identity-charities.

[1621] "Apostolic Letter Issued 'Motu Proprio' of the Supreme Pontiff Benedict XVI on the Service of Charity," Vatican, 11 November 2012, http://w2.vatican.va/content/benedict-xvi/en/motu_proprio/documents/hf_ben-xvi_motu-proprio_20121111_caritas.html.

[1622] Sarah and Diat, *God or Nothing*, 80.

[1623] John L. Allen Jr., "Papabile of the Day: The Men Who Could Be Pope," *National Catholic Reporter*, 1 March 2013, https://www.ncronline.org/blogs/ncr-today/papabile-day-men-who-could-be-pope-10.

[1624] Edward Pentin, "Cardinal Responds to U.N.'s Criticism of Africa's Social Policies," *National Catholic Register*, 21 February 2012, https://www.ncregister.com/daily-news/cardinals-responds-to-u.n.s-criticism-of-africas-social-policies.

Living Under a Marxist Dictatorship

Cardinal Sarah seems to have been powerfully affected by the difficulty of living and exercising great spiritual authority under a cruel dictator. For six "terrible years," Sarah served as bishop of Conakry during the regime of the communist-inspired Ahmed Sékou Touré. Under Touré's direction, all the Church's social works were confiscated and nationalized—schools, medical dispensaries, youth movements, goods of the Church. At the same time, all European missionaries were expelled from Guinea.[1625] Sarah is thus keenly aware of how to combat dictatorial regimes and when to maintain a prudent silence while saying enough to avoid complicity with them; indeed, the choice of his book's title, *The Power of Silence*, seems to be influenced by a history of the Catholic Church in Guinea under the regime of Touré.[1626]

At the same time, Sarah has not been afraid to condemn systems and policies contrary to Christ's teaching. John Allen reports:

When Pope John Paul II visited Guinea in 1992, Sarah publicly asked the pope to push African leaders to clean up their act. "Tell the African governments that reforms will be meaningless if they are tainted in blood, provoking considerable human and economic catastrophes," Sarah told the pope.[1627]

When leaving Guinea in 2001 to take up his new position as secretary for the Congregation for the Evangelization of Peoples in Rome, Sarah used the opportunity to decry the government of dictator Lansana Conté. In his prophetic address, Sarah said that Conté's administration "built on the oppression of the insignificant by the powerful, on contempt for the

---

[1625] Gérard Vieira, *L'Église catholique en Guinée à l'épreuve de Sékou Touré, 1958-1984*, History of the Catholic Church in Guinea, vol. 3 (Paris: Editions Karthala, 1984), 4.

[1626] See the chapter about the Diocese of Conakry under the dictatorial regime of Ahmed Sékou Touré, "L'Église du Silence (1970-1984)," in Vieira, *L'Église catholique en Guinée*; see also Sarah and Diat, *God or Nothing*, 66-68.

[1627] Allen, "Papabile of the Day," 1 March 2013.

poor and the weak, on the cleverness of poor stewards of the public good, on the bribery and corruption of the administration and the institutions of the republic."[1628]

Cardinal Sarah has also expressed strong hostility to "egalitarian" ideologies: "The humility of the [missionary] faith was the strongest defense against the egalitarian aberrations of the revolutionary Marxist ideology of the State Party in Guinea."[1629] At the 2015 Synod on the Family, Cardinal Sarah compared radical Islam and gender ideology to "two apocalyptic beasts," saying "we are not contending against creatures of flesh and blood" and observing that "what Nazi-Fascism and Communism were in the 20th century, Western homosexual and abortion Ideologies and Islamic Fanaticism are today."[1630] The cardinal has also criticized "the great drift,"[1631] which began when "Catholic intellectuals began to write or say 'green light for abortion' and 'green light for euthanasia.'"[1632] Both abortion and euthanasia have led to the "destruction of the natural institutions of marriage and the family."[1633]

Indeed, Sarah describes these evils in nearly apocalyptic terms. He sees much of this harmful activity as the latest iteration of colonialism. It is not mere indigenous decadence. It is "a dictatorship of horror, a programmed Genocide of which the Western powers are guilty."[1634] In light of evils perpetuated by forces in the West, Sarah states, "I think that the immense

---

[1628] Sarah and Diat, *God or Nothing*, 73.

[1629] Ibid., 37.

[1630] Edward Pentin, "Cardinal Sarah: ISIS and Gender Ideology Are Like 'Apocalyptic Beasts,'" *National Catholic Register*, 12 October 2015, http://www. ncregister.com/blog/edward-pentin/cardinal-sarahs-intervention-isis-and-gender-ideology-are-like-apocalyptic-.

[1631] Tom Heneghan, "Prelates Dilute Christian Teaching, Warns Sarah," *Tablet*, 1 March 2018, https://www.thetablet.co.uk/news/8659/prelates-dilute-christian-teaching-warns-sarah.

[1632] Ibid. During the same speech in Belgium, the cardinal criticized the widespread acceptance and legalization of euthanasia.

[1633] Ibid.

[1634] Sarah and Diat, *God or Nothing*, 161.

economic, military, technological, and media influence of a godless West could be a disaster for the world. If the West does not convert to Christ, it could end up making the whole world pagan."[1635]

While serving as bishop of Conakry, Robert Sarah participated in the great assemblies of African religious and bishops, helping guide them as president of the Guinean bishops' conference as well as of the Episcopal Conference of West Africa. Through these positions, he came to work with German Catholic donors who wanted to assist the Church in Africa.[1636] Having in this instance witnessed the faith of Christian Europe firsthand, Sarah denounced the European Union as having turned away from the source of authentic rights in God and in the gospel in favor of secular abstractions.

General Governance Abilities

Cardinal Sarah is widely seen as a potential occupant of the See of Rome, someone who would symbolically express the phenomenal growth and dynamism of Catholicism outside the West.[1637] From a variety of sources, a picture emerges of Cardinal Sarah as a prelate with a deep prayer life. He is known to spend several hours a day in his private chapel and also prays a great deal at night. Both a contemplative and an ascetic, Cardinal Sarah is known never to make a single decision without praying about it for a long time. His attitude toward work and life in general is very much *ora et labora*—prayer and work: he has great admiration for the contemplative life but loves the apostolic life, too, and wishes to be very much a contemplative living in the world. He keeps up to date with current affairs and likes to read newspapers.

Cardinal Sarah's governance of the Congregation is based on an implicit trust in his colleagues. Questions have been raised about his administrative skills and the fact that he is often absent, spending much time traveling

---

[1635] Ibid.

[1636] See, for example, Vieira, *L'Église catholique en Guinée*, 419.

[1637] Allen, "Papabile of the Day," 1 March 2013.

or writing. But even if tending to other tasks, he has a reputation for taking his work at the Congregation and liturgical matters seriously. He does not like to make decisions alone and will consult others, listening closely to the advice he is given. He also has no problem delegating tasks. He is honest and expects others to be so as well, and he treats everyone the same, whether laborers, students, poor persons, or heads of state.

Some criticize him for being naïve or at least appearing to be so, and this has led some to believe that he is a poor judge of character. But his supporters say this owes itself to a personal guilelessness and the simple fact that he does not understand meanness, cowardice, and betrayal. He simply cannot understand how they originate, despite having faced such a cruel dictatorship in Guinea. Much of this was learned when he took many risks to defend his people, and yet on a daily basis he is always surprised when he has to face a wicked situation. This is not naïveté, say some who know him, but rather due to a personal innate goodness that makes him a stranger to evil.

Some argue that, especially when it comes to putting his head above the parapet, criticizing or taking a stand against dubious actions of this pontificate, he can be too cautious and circumspect; others believe it to be wise and strategic.

TEACHING OFFICE

Biblical Studies

Cardinal Sarah's intellectual formation reached its highest development in biblical studies. His doctoral thesis in biblical exegesis focused on proposing a "new critical examination of certain textual difficulties in the Masoretic text of the Book of Isaiah"[1638] that emphasized that copyists of the Hebrew text were completely faithful to the original text. For Cardinal Sarah, one is required to show fidelity to the biblical text "so as not to

---

[1638] Sarah and Diat, *God or Nothing*, 37.

manipulate it to fit historical, political or ideological circumstances, for the purpose of pleasing men and acquiring a reputation as a scholar or avant-garde theologian."[1639] He expresses carefully phrased admiration for certain academics whom he encountered in the course of his studies at the Gregorian University in Rome, as well as at the Pontifical Institute for Biblical Studies—scholars such as Ignace de la Potterie, Stanislas Lyonnet, Etienne Vogt, and Albert Vanhoye.[1640]

Evangelization

For Cardinal Sarah, the proper approach to evangelization is a love of the truth of Christ: "God is truth; through his Son, he intends to draw us towards his truth. Attachment to and love of the truth are the most authentic, the most righteous, and the noblest attitude that a man could ever want on this earth."[1641] Consequently, absolutely key to the reevangelization of the neo-pagan West, which is an urgent task for the cardinal, is the *Catechism of the Catholic Church.* "The entire doctrine of the Church is found in this document." Behind it are the sources of the Faith: "the ancient tradition, [the] teaching and faith of the Catholic Church, which was revealed by the Lord, proclaimed by the apostles, and guarded by the Fathers. For upon this faith the Church is built, and if anyone were to lapse from it, he would no longer be Christian either in fact or name. But the faith is strengthened by way of the heart, through a personal encounter with the experience of Jesus. Every day we must once again choose Christ as our guide, our light and our hope."[1642] Because of Muslim rejection of Christ, he asserts that "with Islam there can be no theological dialogue,"[1643] although a *modus vivendi* has been and is occasionally possible in some contexts (such as his own Guinea).

[1639] Ibid., 37. This statement provides evidence that Sarah recognizes the inerrancy of Scripture and the historicity of the Gospels.

[1640] Sarah and Diat, *God or Nothing,* 49.

[1641] Ibid., 244.

[1642] Ibid., 147.

[1643] Ibid., 137.

Sarah critiques the "prevailing narrative" that comes from Protestant-ism and the Enlightenment, which "constantly seeks to present the idea of an outmoded, mediaeval church."[1644] Because of the secular narrative, he states, "I think it is necessary to acquire the ability to come to terms with oneself as 'intolerant', in other words, to have the courage to tell someone else that what he does is bad or wrong. Then we will be able to take some-one else's criticism when it is meant to open our eyes to the truth."[1645] His guiding lights for an integration between pagan and Christian thought are St. Augustine, St. Thomas Aquinas, and others who received Greek philosophy and baptized it with Christian revelation.[1646] He also expresses his hope that Benedict XVI will one day be canonized and proclaimed a Doctor of the Church.[1647]

Sexuality and Marriage

Regarding matters of sexuality and marriage, Sarah holds firmly to tra-ditional Catholic practices and those of Africa in accord with natural law. He states, "African philosophy declares: 'Man is nothing without woman, woman is nothing without man, and the two are nothing with-out a third element which is the child.' Fundamentally, the African view of man is trinitarian. In each of us there is something divine; the Triune God dwells within us and imbues our whole being."[1648] According to the bishop of Antwerp, Cardinal Sarah blocked all discussion of new solutions for the "pastoral care of gay Catholics" in his group at the 2015 synod.[1649] Sarah has described attempts to separate doctrine from pastoral practice regarding marriage and the family as "a form of heresy" and "a dangerous,

---

[1644] Ibid., 157, 167.

[1645] Ibid., 133.

[1646] Ibid., 177.

[1647] Ibid., 99.

[1648] Ibid., 163.

[1649] Elena Curti, "Cardinal Sarah Blocked Discussion of Gays, Says Bishop," *Tab-let*, 24 October 2015, http://www.thetablet.co.uk/news/2785/cardinal-sarah-blocked-discussion-of-gays-says-bishop-.

schizophrenic pathology."[1650] He espouses the intellectual equality and marital freedom of women, and therefore, citing the prevalent objectification of women's bodies and the growth of prostitution, he strongly rejects modern Western feminism: "the West falsely claims to champion and defend women's rights."[1651] He has also encouraged motherhood by stating that "it is important that women should be able to have a job that is compatible with motherhood."[1652] In a 2018 homily to the Girl Guides of Europe, Cardinal Sarah championed Our Lady as the model for contemporary womanhood. Sarah stated that "in the hierarchy of holiness, it is precisely a woman, the Most Blessed Virgin Mary, who is at the top. She precedes you on the path of holiness."[1653] He encouraged the Girl Guides to "listen to her; learn from her: in her lies the fully realized woman, in her lies the secret of true joy and peace."[1654]

Humanae Vitae *and Contraception*

On *Humanae Vitae*, the cardinal observes that the "successor of Peter knew that he was faithful to the truth," and, "this document was prophetic."[1655] In a recent address on *Humanae Vitae*, the cardinal described contraception as inherently evil because it destroys the truth of love and the human relationship.[1656]

[1650] "Cardinal Sarah: Efforts to 'Soften' Christ's Teaching Ignore the Good News of Mercy," Catholic News Agency, 23 September 2015, https://www.catholicnewsagency.com/news/cardinal-sarah-efforts-to-soften-christs-teaching-ignore-the-good-news-of-mercy-41570.

[1651] Sarah and Diat, *God or Nothing*, 117.

[1652] Ibid., 158.

[1653] Equipe Communication Uigse-Fse, "Homily of Cardinal Sarah to the Guides of Europe in Paray-Le-Monial," Fédération du Scoutisme Européen, 12 November 2018

[1654] Ibid.

[1655] Sarah and Diat, *God or Nothing*, 89, 157.

[1656] Cardinal Sarah, "Contraception Is Inherently Evil, That Is, It Destroys the Truth of Love and the Human Relationship," *Jeunes Pour la Vie*, 27 August 2018, http://www.jeunespourlavie.org/accueil/cardinal-sarah-la-

On the question of Communion for the divorced and "remarried," he cites paragraph 1650 of the *Catechism* and goes on to state, "*Familiaris Consortio* definitively sealed the teaching and discipline of the Church that are founded on Sacred Scripture. Today, I think we should stop discussing this question like disrespectful intellectuals, giving the impression of disputing the teaching of Jesus Christ and the Church."[1657] He wryly observes, "Many expect as something normal that God should pour out his mercy upon them while they remain in sin."[1658] Sarah thus declares that he will "untiringly denounce" clerics who "consider God's thinking about conjugal life to be an 'evangelical ideal'. Marriage is no longer a requirement willed by God, modelled and manifested in the nuptial bond between Christ and the Church."[1659]

Gender Ideology

Sarah calls gender ideology "a crude lie"[1660] and "nightmarish totalitarianism."[1661] He insists: "A man will never become a woman, and she will never become a man, no matter what mutilations one or the other agrees to undergo."[1662] The Catholic alternative view of gender and sexuality is found in St. John Paul II's moral teachings, including his *Theology of the Body*.[1663] Regarding "gay marriage," Sarah states, "we are departing from the moral history of mankind."[1664] "The chief enemies of homosexual persons are the LGBT lobbies. It is a serious error to reduce an individual to his behavior, especially sexual behavior. Nature always ends up having

---

contraception-est-intrinsequement-un-mal-cest-a-dire-quelle-detruit-la-verite-de-lamour-et-du-couple-humain (translated from French).

[1657] Sarah and Diat, *God or Nothing*, 249.

[1658] Ibid., 173.

[1659] Sarah, *Power of Silence*, 38.

[1660] Sarah and Diat, *God or Nothing*, 130.

[1661] Ibid., 164.

[1662] Ibid.

[1663] Ibid., 157, 156.

[1664] Ibid., 149. From these comments, it is clear that Sarah would oppose legalization of civil same-sex "marriage."

its revenge."[1665] The French popular movement against "gay marriage," *Manif pour tous*, "offers an example of the necessary initiatives.... It was a manifestation of the spirit of Christianity."[1666] Furthermore, "the battle to preserve the roots of mankind is perhaps the greatest challenge that our world has faced since its origins."[1667] He notes that "Western colonialism continues today in Africa and Asia, more vigorously and perversely through the imposition of a false morality and deceitful values."[1668] Accordingly, "in some African countries, ministries dedicated to gender theory have been created in exchange for economic aid!"[1669] Sarah therefore unequivocally condemns attempts by politicians "to make homosexuality the cornerstone of a new global ethic."[1670]

Priestly Celibacy

Regarding the sacrament of Holy Orders, the cardinal strongly opposes the relaxation of the discipline of priestly celibacy:

> To detach celibacy from the priesthood by conferring the sacrament of the Order on married men ... would have serious consequences, in fact, to definitively break with the Apostolic Tradition. We would to manufacture a priesthood according to our human dimension, but without perpetuating, without extending the priesthood of Christ, obedient, poor and chaste.[1671]

[1665] Sarah and Diat, *God or Nothing*, 160.

[1666] Ibid., 149.

[1667] Ibid., 166.

[1668] Ibid., 158.

[1669] Ibid., 159.

[1670] Ibid., 164.

[1671] James Roberts, "Cardinal Sarah Warns That the West Is Like a 'Drunken Boat,'" *Tablet*, 23 May 2018, https://www.thetablet.co.uk/news/9132/cardinal-sarah-warns-that-the-west-is-like-a-drunken-boat-. Although the cardinal has not expressly addressed the question of restricting same-sex-attracted men from entering the ministerial priesthood, his comments on priestly celibacy seem to point to his support of preventing same-sex-attracted men from entering the priesthood.

In January 2020, Cardinal Sarah wrote a book with Pope Emeritus Benedict XVI, *From the Depths of Our Hearts: Priesthood, Celibacy and the Crisis of the Catholic Church*, which upheld priestly celibacy and addressed the crisis in the priesthood. The timing of the book caused controversy, published just ahead of Pope Francis' apostolic exhortation on the Amazon synod, *Querida Amazonia*, which was expected to relax mandatory priestly celibacy in the Latin Rite in the Amazon region as a means of coping with priest shortages there. Many were concerned that the change, which was not later explicitly made in the document, would undermine priestly celibacy worldwide.

A controversy ensued, leading Benedict's secretary, Archbishop Georg Gänswein, to claim that Benedict had been involved in the book on false pretenses. Cardinal Sarah stressed that there was no misunderstanding but rather "sordid machinations" enacted by "opponents of the priesthood," intent on diverting attention from the "content of the book." He argued that the faithful did not want an end to celibacy, that he was "in no way in opposition to Pope Francis" and those who claimed he was wanted to "divide the Church."[1672]

Cardinal Sarah said in an interview shortly before the publication of *Querida Amazonia* that the priesthood was in "mortal danger" and called for better formation. He said the Church has been "overwhelmed by lukewarmness and mediocrity" and that "we must aspire to holiness." The West, he said, is "out of breath" and "waits for priests who are radically saints."[1673]

Furthermore, he stated, "The idea of a woman cardinal is as ridiculous as the idea of a priest who wanted to become a nun!"[1674] and "I understand

---

[1672] Edward Pentin, "Cardinal Sarah: The Priesthood Today 'Is in Mortal Danger,'" *National Catholic Register*, 8 February 2020, https://www.ncregister.com/daily-news/cardinal-sarah-the-priesthood-today-is-in-mortal-danger.

[1673] Ibid.

[1674] Sarah and Diat, *God or Nothing*, 118-19.

what a big trap it would be to entrust a dicastery of the Roman government to a woman just because she is a woman."[1675]

Decentralization of Doctrine

Cardinal Sarah strongly condemns the movement toward decentralizing the doctrinal authority of the Church. In the present situation, he says, "we would commit a grave sin against the unity of the Body of Christ and the doctrine of the Church by giving episcopal conferences any authority of decision-making ability concerning doctrinal, disciplinary, or moral questions."[1676] Cardinal Sarah is also concerned at an academicization of the Faith. He says that "some have intellectualized and complicated the Christian message so much that a great number of people are no longer touched by or interested in the teaching of the Church."[1677] Elsewhere: "The Gospel is not a theoretical path; it must not become a sort of school reserved for the elite. The Church is a plainly evident path to the risen Lord."[1678]

Of Pope Francis, he writes, "For my part, I do not believe that the pope means to endanger the integrity of the Magisterium. Indeed, no one, not even the pope, can destroy or change Christ's teaching. No one, not even the pope, can set pastoral ministry in opposition to doctrine. That would be to rebel against Jesus Christ and his teaching."[1679]

Migration

At a conference in Poland in 2017, Cardinal Sarah distinguished between genuine refugees and economic migrants and emphasized the right of Poland and countries like it to do the same despite the attempts of external

---

[1675] Ibid.
[1676] Ibid., 111.
[1677] Ibid., 114.
[1678] Ibid., 145.
[1679] Ibid., 246.

forces to impose an indiscriminate policy upon them.[1680] His solution is to turn to Christ: "Christians will never succeed in overcoming the challenges of the world by appealing to political tools, human rights, or respect for religious liberty."[1681]

View on Coronavirus

During the COVID-19 pandemic, Cardinal Sarah said in an interview that the virus had dispelled the illusion of human self-sufficiency and an "all-powerful man" and that he hoped it would allow people to turn back to essentials, and rediscover God and prayer.

> This virus acted as a warning. In a matter of weeks, the great illusion of a material world that thought itself all-powerful seems to have collapsed. A few days ago, politicians were talking about growth, pensions, reducing unemployment. They were sure of themselves. And now a virus, a microscopic virus, has brought this world to its knees, a world that looks at itself, that pleases itself, drunk with self-satisfaction because it thought it was invulnerable.... I believe this epidemic has dispelled the smoke of illusion. The so-called all-powerful man appears in his raw reality. There he is naked. His weakness and vulnerability are glaring. Being confined to our homes will hopefully allow us to turn our attention back to the essentials, to rediscover the importance of our relationship with God, and thus the centrality of prayer in human existence. And, in the awareness of our fragility, to entrust ourselves to God and to his paternal mercy.[1682]

[1680] Bogdan Gancarz, "Card. Sarah: You Can't Challenge the Right to Distinguish a Refugee from an Economic Immigrant," *GOSC.PL*, 22 October 2017, http://gosc.pl/doc/4266054.Kardynal-Sarah-Nie-mozna-podwazac-prawa-do-rozroznienia (translated from Polish).

[1681] Sarah and Diat, *God or Nothing*, 194.

[1682] Edward Pentin, "Coronavirus Latest from Rome," *National Catholic Register*, 9 April 2020, https://www.ncregister.com/blog/edward-pentin/coronavirus-latest-italys-bishops-call-for-all-churches-to-be-closed.

In May 2020, Cardinal Sarah strongly criticized what he called "bizarre proposals" implemented in Germany and under consideration in Italy and elsewhere for "do-it-yourself" Communion, whereby consecrated hosts would be packaged in plastic bags so the faithful could take them away in order to avoid contagion. He said such a practice was "absolutely not possible," and argued that the Eucharist "must be treated with faith." God, he said, "deserves respect; you can't put him in a bag."

In the face of some parishes and dioceses in which both Communion and Confession had been suspended, Cardinal Sarah said "nobody has the right to stop" a priest from celebrating the sacraments, a duty that "must be respected." The cardinal added that even if it is not possible to attend Masses, "the faithful can ask to be confessed and receive Communion."

He also criticized a German bishop for not allowing Eucharistic assemblies, only the liturgy of the Word, saying it is "Protestantism."[1683]

In May 2020, Cardinal Sarah was initially listed as one of over eighty signatories, including prelates, physicians, lawyers, and journalists, who put their name to an appeal expressing concern about global measures being implemented to stem the coronavirus pandemic, and calling for "inalienable rights of citizens and their fundamental freedoms" to be respected. He withdrew his name from the initiative on receiving advice that it was not appropriate for a senior curial official to sign such an appeal.[1684]

[1683] Riccardo Cascioli, "Sarah: Profanities Have to Stop, The Eucharist Isn't Negotiable," *New Daily Compass*, 2 May 2020, https://newdailycompass.com/en/sarah-profanities-have-to-stop-the-eucharist-isnt-negotiable.

[1684] Edward Pentin, "Cardinals, Bishops Sign Appeal Against Coronavirus Restrictions," *National Catholic Register*, 7 May 2020, https://www.ncregister.com/blog/edward-pentin/four-cardinals-several-bishops-sign-appeal-against-coronavirus-restrictions.

CONGREGATION FOR DIVINE WORSHIP AND THE DISCIPLINE OF THE SACRAMENTS

Sarah is the prefect of the Congregation for Divine Worship and the Discipline of the Sacraments. He has a profound liturgical sensibility which he attributes, in part, to his African heritage, from which he derived "a joyful fear of everything sacred."[1685] During seminary, Sarah came to understand that "the greatest way to be with the Son of God made man was still the liturgy."[1686] Sarah's deep piety and love for the liturgy can be summed up in the following quote: "The Mass is the most important thing in our lives." [1687]

Cardinal Sarah has acknowledged the sad reality of "ideological pitched battles"[1688] over the liturgy and explained that "the lack of understanding between different ways of thinking about the liturgy can be explained by legitimate cultural factors, but nothing can justify its transformation into anathemas hurled by either side."[1689] Sarah praised the good work and the fruits of the communities dedicated to the pre-conciliar forms of worship. "They're not nostalgic or oppressed by the ecclesiastical battles of recent decades, they're full of joy to live life with Christ amid the challenges of the modern world." He also observed that the pre-conciliar missal was "never abrogated"[1690] and that it had been the Mass of "innumerable saints."[1691]

[1685] Sarah and Diat, *God or Nothing*, 51.

[1686] Ibid.

[1687] Ibid.

[1688] Ibid., 125.

[1689] Ibid.

[1690] Ibid.

[1691] John L. Allen Jr., "Despite Wing-Clipping, Sarah Not Going Quiet in Defense of Tradition," *Crux*, 15 September 2017, https://cruxnow.com/news-analysis/2017/09/15/despite-wing-clipping-sarah-not-going-quiet-defense-tradition/.

At the same time, he seems to see a danger of Pharisaism in some liturgical traditionalism. For the cardinal, "if a person respects the ancient rite of the Church but is not in love, that individual is perishing.... Strict, almost fundamentalist ritualism or the modernist-type deconstruction of the rite can cut people off from a true search for the love of God."[1692] Although he respects the pre–Vatican II liturgy, he dislikes the term "traditionalist" and told a conference held at the Angelicum to celebrate the tenth anniversary of *Summorum Pontificum*, "You do not belong in a box on the shelf or in a museum of curiosities. You are not traditionalists: you are Catholics of the Roman rite as am I and as is the Holy Father. You are not second-class or somehow peculiar members of the Catholic Church because of your life of worship and your spiritual practices."[1693]

In regard to the concrete implementation of the liturgical reforms associated with the Second Vatican Council, particularly in his own diocese, Cardinal Sarah is overtly condemnatory of "the botched preparation for the liturgical reform,"[1694] which, he says, "had devastating effects on the Catholic population."[1695] The cardinal wonders how "such a strange movement [could] produce in the life of the Church anything but great confusion among the people."[1696] He states:

> Certainly, the Second Vatican Council wished to promote greater active participation by the people of God and to bring about progress day by day in the Christian life of the faithful (see *Sacrosanctum Concilium*, n. 1). Certainly, some fine initiatives were taken along these lines. However we cannot close our eyes to the disaster, the

---

[1692] Sarah and Diat, *God or Nothing*, 125.

[1693] Gregory Dipippo, "'Silence and the Primacy of God in the Sacred Liturgy': Address by His Eminence Card. Sarah," New Liturgical Movement, 14 September 2017, http://www.newliturgicalmovement.org/2017/09/silence-and-primacy-of-god-in-sacred.html#.WiB8T0yZMcg.

[1694] Sarah and Diat, *God or Nothing*, 84-85.

[1695] Ibid.

[1696] Ibid.

devastation and the schism that the modern promoters of a living liturgy caused by remodelling the Church's liturgy according to their ideas.[1697]

Some have observed that despite Cardinal Sarah's frequent pleas for a more reverent liturgy and an end to abuses, little has changed in that regard during his time as prefect of the Congregation. His effectiveness is said to have less to do with his governing abilities and more to do with serving a pontificate with a considerably different vision.

SUMMARY

At the 2013 conclave, Cardinal Sarah hardly figured on papabile lists, serving at the time as president of the Pontifical Council *Cor Unum*, in which he was quietly helping Benedict XVI to instill greater fidelity to Catholic teaching among Catholic charities. But even then, he demonstrated a certain fearlessness and measured outspokenness in defending the Faith, particularly when it came to sensitive elements of the Church's moral teaching that many of his Western brother cardinals noticeably lacked. He went on to speak with greater authority after Pope Francis appointed him prefect of the Congregation for Divine Worship and the Discipline of the Sacraments, in which he could draw attention to one of his great concerns: the loss of the sacred and the need to defend it from the spirit of the age that had rejected it—but which remains central to Christians in Africa.[1698]

[1697] Sarah, "Address on the 10th Anniversary."

[1698] Edward Pentin, "Cardinal Sarah's Cri de Coeur: The Catholic Church Has Lost Its Sense of the Sacred," *National Catholic Register*, 23 September 2019, https://www.ncregister.com/daily-news/cardinal-sarahs-cri-de-coeur-the-catholic-church-has-lost-its-sense-of-the.

He has favored "reform of the reform" when it comes to the liturgy, a return to what the Second Vatican Council taught about the liturgy rather than what came later. He has placed particular importance on promoting the Mass *ad orientem*, spoken strongly in favor of Communion on the tongue, and argued against intercommunion between Catholics and non-Catholics. He has also warned against the danger of Pharisaism in some traditional liturgical circles.

His experience in resisting a Marxist dictatorship is credited for the cardinal's sensitivity in knowing when to speak out and when to keep quiet, as well as his fearlessness in defending truths of the Faith. Usually he has kept silent in the face of some deep concerns about Francis' pontificate, staying out of the *dubia* controversy and debates over papal pronouncements and instead offering oblique warnings.

His three best-selling books further burnished his image as a Church leader with depth, insight, and even a gift of prophecy that has resonated with those who have felt starved of hearing the truths of the Faith firmly rooted in the Church's Tradition. He has spoken almost apocalyptically about the contemporary evils of abortion, the same-sex agenda, and Islamism. His most recent book *From the Depths of Our Hearts* with Benedict XVI on the crisis of the priesthood and defense of priestly celibacy, controversially released just ahead of Pope Francis' apostolic exhortation on the Amazon synod, further cemented his image as a faithful and orthodox Church leader. Although his effectiveness in fulfilling his aims as prefect has been limited, he has shown himself to be driven to help the Church facing the crisis of relativism and secularism, to revitalize the Church in a spirit of true evangelization, and to resist further succumbing to the spirit of the age.

SERVICE TO THE CHURCH

Ordination to the Priesthood: 20 July 1969
Ordination to the Episcopate: 8 December 1979
Elevation to the College of Cardinals: 20 November 2010

Education
- 1971: Studium Biblicum Franciscanum, Jerusalem (S.S.L.)
- 1974: Pontifical Gregorian University, Rome (S.T.L.)

Assignments
- 1974-1976: Parish priest, Boké, Guinea
- 1976-1979: Professor then director, Archdiocesan Seminary of Conakry, Guinea
- 1979-2001: Metropolitan archbishop, Archdiocese of Conakry, Guinea

Roman Curia
- 2001-2010: Secretary of the Congregation for the Evangelization of Peoples
- 2010-2014: President of the Pontifical Council *Cor Unum*
- 2011-present: Cardinal-deacon of S. Giovanni Bosco in via Tuscolana
- 2011-present: Member, Congregation for the Evangelization of Peoples
- 2011-present: Member, Pontifical Council for the Laity
- 2011-present: Member, Pontifical Council for Justice and Peace

- 2014: Synod Father, Third Extraordinary General Assembly of the Synod of Bishops
- 2014-present: Member, Congregation for the Causes of Saints
- 2014-present: Prefect of the Congregation for Divine Worship and the Discipline of the Sacraments
- 2015-present: Member, Pontifical Committee for International Eucharistic Congresses
- 2015: Synod Father, Fourteenth Ordinary General Assembly of the Synod of Bishops

VOS AUTEM DIXI AMICOS

CHRISTOPH CARDINAL SCHÖNBORN

"I Have Called You Friends"

Born: 22 January 1945
Skalsko (now Czech Republic)
Nationality: Austrian
Title: Archbishop of Vienna

BIOGRAPHY

Born in the ancestral castle of his noble family, with two brothers and a sister, he was given the name of Christoph Maria Michael Hugo Damian Peter Adalbert Schönborn. Months after his birth, his family was forced to flee to Austria, where he was raised. When he was fourteen, his parents divorced—an event that affected him deeply. When he was eighteen, Christoph entered the Order of Preachers, initially saddening his mother,

Eleonore (who turned one hundred in April 2020), as he had been a "great help in all life situations."[1699] He studied at the Dominican house of studies in Walberberg, Bonn, Germany, and earned a doctorate at Le Saulchoir, studying also at La Sorbonne university, and the Institut Catholique, all in Paris, as well as in Vienna for some time. In 1970, he was ordained a priest, after which he served as a university chaplain from 1973 to 1975 and then as a faculty member at the University of Fribourg from 1976 to 1991. During his tenure as professor in Switzerland, he became acquainted with Joseph Ratzinger and served as secretary of the commission of the Congregation for the Doctrine of the Faith to edit the new *Catechism of the Catholic Church* (1987-1992).

Schönborn was consecrated a bishop in 1991 by Cardinal Hans Hermann Groër, O.S.B., archbishop of Vienna. Since 1995, he has been metropolitan archbishop of Vienna. Pope John Paul II created Schönborn a cardinal-priest in 1998. In that same year, he was elected chairman of the Austrian Bishops' Conference. Schönborn has served in various curial positions. He is known to be a popular homilist and a prolific writer and giver of conferences, and his books have been translated into many languages. He is fluent in German, French, and Czech and speaks English and Italian.

SANCTIFYING OFFICE

Liturgy as Divine Service

For Cardinal Schönborn, the Church is both "*end* and *means*, the *final goal* of the plan of creation and at the same time 'a kind of sacrament or *sign*

[1699] "Eleonore Schönborn: 'Heute ist alles viel schlimmer,'" *News.at*, 8 April 2020, https://www.news.at/a/mutter-kardinal-schoenborn-eleonore-schoenborn-11435898.

and instrument of intimate union with God and of the unity of the whole human race' (LG 1)."[1700]

Cardinal Schönborn described his views on the liturgy in a 2005 interview.[1701] When asked about Hans Hermann Groër, and customized Masses—those in which prayers and other elements are changed—the cardinal replied: "The faithful are entitled to participate in a celebration of the liturgy that is valid in the community of the Church Universal."

He said the "deepest reason for this liturgical order is the fact that this is a Divine Service, i.e. in the Christian service it is God himself turning to mankind first, Christ himself is the celebrant."[1702] When asked which elements of the Holy Mass are changeable, he replied: "Quite some places ... allow for creativity" but that the Church "holds unambiguously to the fact that the Eucharistic Prayer, which is the core of the Eucharist, is not at disposal for private compositions."

He noted frequent complaints that the participation of the faithful in the Eucharistic Prayer is missing. "This can only be due to a misunderstanding," he said. "It is the prayer of the Church spoken by the priest [and him alone] for the whole Church."[1703]

In the excerpt "What Is Liturgy?" from his book *Living the Catechism of the Catholic Church*,[1704] Schönborn writes about the subject fully in continuity with the Church's discipline and tradition:

[1700] Christoph Cardinal Schönborn, "The Church Is the Goal of All Things," Ignatius Insight, http://www.ignatiusinsight.com/features2005/schonborn_church_oct05.asp (internal citations omitted).

[1701] Christoph Cardinal Schönborn, "The Eucharist Is More Thrilling Than Any Show," *Kath.net*, 5 March 2005, http://www.kath.net/news/9891.

[1702] Ibid.

[1703] Ibid.

[1704] Christoph Cardinal Schönborn, "What Is Liturgy?," in *Living the Catechism of the Catholic Church: A Brief Commentary on the Catechism for Every Week of the Year*, vol. 2, *The Sacraments* (San Francisco: Ignatius Press, 2000), posted at Catholic Way, http://sites.silaspartners.com/partner/Article_Display_Page/0,,PTID5339_CHID26_CIID151650,00.html.

The liturgy...is "the summit towards which all the Church's activity is directed." No ordinary event in the Church's life, the liturgy is the commemoration, initiated and indeed celebrated by Christ himself, of his saving death and resurrection. As the "work of God," liturgy effects our salvation, leading us to the Father as we respond to him in love and praise.... The liturgy is like a fountain in which the living wellspring, that is Christ, is contained and given to us to drink.[1705]

Lack of Liturgical Discipline

And yet despite these sublime reflections upon the Mass, Cardinal Schönborn has often exhibited a lack of liturgical discipline. For example, at a Mass he celebrated at the Church of St. Florian in the Archdiocese of Vienna on October 9, 2005, for the opening of the first "Youth Church" in the archdiocese, he consecrated a pita-bread-type of host.[1706] On November 16, 2008, Cardinal Schönborn presided at a "Youth Mass" in Wolfsthal near Vienna. Balloons, a rock band, smoke machines, a projection screen, and a light show were used during Mass, and Cardinal Schönborn again consecrated pita bread, which was distributed to those present in the hand. Congregants could be seen consuming the host a bite at a time. After international criticism of the consecration of pita bread, the Archdiocese of Vienna issued a press release, in which it stated that the "Youth Mass" had "in no way violated the liturgical regulations of the Catholic Church" because "the Eucharistic bread was unleavened."[1707]

[1705] Ibid.

[1706] "Stay True to This Experiment," *Kreuz.net*, 11 October 2005, https://web.archive.org/web/20051013054922/http://www.kreuz.net/article.2017.html.

[1707] "Bad News from Vienna—Update: With the Icebreaker to Liturgical Nirvana," *Motu Proprio: Summorum Pontificum*, 20 November 2008, http://www.summorum-pontificum.de/meinung/jugendmesse.shtml (translated from German).

Under his watch, "Youth Masses" in the Archdiocese of Vienna ran from 2003 to 2011. Highlights from these Masses, which were held in churches throughout the diocese, were compiled into an official twenty-minute video. Throughout the video of these Masses, Cardinal Schönborn is seen sending text messages during Mass. Priests are wearing psychedelic vestments; there are crowd surfing, heavy-metal rock music, lasers and strobe lights, artificial smoke, flame throwers, and balloons. Superstitious "care dolls" make an appearance, as does a graphic pornographic magazine (held up by a priest during a homily).[1708]

Further blasphemy was promoted by him when, in the summer of 2010, an American West–themed Mass was celebrated in Austria. Cardinal Schönborn gave explicit approval for this event and sent his personal greeting and blessing to those present. The Mass featured an integrated barbecue with people eating, drinking, and smoking at picnic tables. The Mass took place in the context of the *Donauinselfest*, a festival organized by the Viennese socialists on the Danube island. "All baptized Christians" were invited to receive Holy Communion.[1709] In 2011, in response to international protests against the "Western Mass," Cardinal Schönborn canceled the Holy Mass two days before it was scheduled to take place.[1710]

In 2018, Schönborn faced criticism for attending a pro-LGBT event in the Vienna cathedral featuring a shirtless pro-homosexual actor standing on the altar rail as well as loud rock and electronic music, and actors dressed

---

[1708] KJWien, "Eight Years in Fast Motion," YouTube video, 19:49, posted 26 June 2011, https://youtu.be/CWY7Pw6TjII.

[1709] "Mit dem Segen des Kardinals," Gloria.tv, 30 June 2010, https://www.gloria.tv/video/3MTZ9hmPaYzz439TAVki4TAiT. Recordings of the Western Mass 2010, including the reading of "Cardinal Schönborn's Greetings: With the Cardinal's Blessing." See also Tito Edwards, "Unholy Mass in Austria with Explicit Approval of Cardinal Schönborn," *American Catholic*, 5 July 2010, https://www.the-american-catholic.com/2010/07/05/unholy-mass-in-austria-with-explicit-approval-of-cardinal-schonborn/.

[1710] See "Food, Drink and Smoke Fair Is Canceled," *Kreuz.net*, 17 June 2011, http://web.archive.org/web/20111211131424/http://www.kreuz.net/article.13381.html (translated from German).

as demons. "The *Jedermann* (Everyman) play depicted a wealthy man in his last hours of life who realizes that neither his friends nor his money follow him in death. He then converts to Christianity."[1711] The event, sponsored by the Order of Malta, Austria and organized by a homosexual activist, was in aid of AIDS sufferers. Cardinal Schönborn was not deterred by the criticism, and the following year, he allowed the same benefit concert to take place in the Vienna cathedral, this time featuring the Austrian drag queen Conchita Wurst. It was the third year running in which Schönborn had allowed such a benefit concert in the cathedral. Archbishop Carlo Maria Viganò denounced the event as sacrilegious and blasphemous and implored, through Mary's intercession, the Lord's forgiveness.[1712]

Open to Women Deacons

Women already preside over funeral rituals in the Archdiocese of Vienna, by express decree of Cardinal Schönborn. He brought this up as a pertinent fact to illustrate the sorts of new ministries envisioned for the Church in the Amazon synod, saying, "They do so in a traditional Austrian Catholic environment and they are well accepted."[1713] Schönborn has expressed an openness to the female diaconate. He told an Austrian news site that "there were deaconesses in the first centuries, which could be reintroduced."[1714]

[1711] Maike Hickson, "Charity Concert at Cdl Schönborn's Cathedral Features Shirtless Actor Dancing on Communion Rail," LifeSite News, 4 December 2018, https://www.lifesitenews.com/blogs/charity-concert-at-cdl.-schoenborns-cathedral-features-shirtless-actor-danc.

[1712] Edward Pentin, "Archbishop Viganò Condemns Vienna Cathedral Pro-LGBT Concert as 'Blasphemous,'" Edward Pentin, 1 December 2019, https://edwardpentin.co.uk/archbishop-vigano-condemns-vienna-cathedral-pro-lgbt-concert-as-blasphemous/.

[1713] Linda Bordoni, "Amazon Synod: Cardinal Schönborn on 'Viri Probati' and Permanent Deacons," Vatican News, 19 October 2019, https://www.vaticannews.va/en/vatican-city/news/2019-10/synod-amazonia-schonborn-presence-pastors-pentecostals-women.html.

[1714] "Cardinal Schönborn: Women Priests 'Too Profound a Change' for the Church," *Catholic Herald*, 20 June 2018, https://catholicherald.co.uk/cardinal-schonborn-women-priests-too-profound-a-change-for-the-church/.

Although he will sing the Mass in Latin, the cardinal is not known to be a friend of the Extraordinary Form of the Roman Rite. Most Austrian bishops believe the form is not to be encouraged, but it is not prohibited, and several Extraordinary Form Masses can be found in the Vienna Archdiocese.

GOVERNING OFFICE

Diplomacy and Dialogue

Since his installation as Vienna's archbishop in 1995, Cardinal Schönborn has "weathered several major storms with his patient pastoral approach," Catholic News Service reported in 2013.[1715] The news agency, run by the U.S. bishops, also praised Schönborn's "diplomatic and administrative abilities" to "create an atmosphere of openness and dialogue,"[1716] no matter the issue, whether it be "clergy dissenting over Church teachings, massive parish closings or the scandal of clerical sex abuse."[1717] "Nothing can replace the personal meeting, contact and witness—listening and witnessing; we have to look at how Jesus did it. He is the master of evangelization," Schönborn told Canada's Salt and Light TV during the Synod of Bishops on the New Evangelization.[1718]

When the Vienna Archdiocese announced plans in 2018 to reduce its parishes by more than 75 percent over the next ten years, Cardinal Schönborn accentuated the positive. He said the reorganization, prompted by falling numbers of clergy and laity, would help pool resources, reduce administration, and "leave more time for evangelization."[1719] "We have to free ourselves of the traditional image that the Church is present only

---

[1715] "Austrian Cardinal-Theologian Known for Patient Pastoral Approach," *Catholic Sun*, 24 February 2013, https://www.catholicsun.org/2013/02/24/austrian-cardinal-theologian-known-for-patient-pastoral-approach/.

[1716] Ibid.

[1717] Ibid.

[1718] Ibid.

[1719] Ibid.

where there's a priest and stress the common priesthood of all baptized."[1720] Schönborn denied he was suggesting "priestless eucharistic liturgies" (as a group of Austrian priests were requesting). He said that he was aiming for a reinvigoration of the sense of mission, where the baptized give true witness to their faith at work, at home, in society, and in small Christian communities.[1721]

Handling Sexual Abuse

The cardinal dealt with the reality of sexual abuse by clergy at the start of his tenure as archbishop. Named coadjutor archbishop in the spring of 1995, Schönborn replaced the archbishop, Cardinal Hans Hermann Groër, just five months later, after the late cardinal was forced to step down amid allegations by former students that he had sexually abused them in the 1970s.[1722]

Cardinal Schönborn was initially defensive of Groër but gained respect by later more fully confronting the extent of the crisis. He has spoken frankly about sexual abuse, describing it in 2019 as a "massive reality" in both the family and the Church.[1723] He appears to agree with Benedict XVI that the sexual revolution that began around 1968 led to such abuses, but he also blames the crisis on the "closed nature of the system" in the Church before the Second Vatican Council and the "exaggerated authority" of the priest that existed then.[1724] Schönborn believes the new spiritual movements have also been particularly susceptible and refers to "guru behaviour" of people such as Cardinal Groër and movement founders such as Marcial Maciel, founder of the Legionaries of Christ, and former fellow Dominican Marie-Dominique Philippe, all of whom were found to have carried out abuse.[1725]

[1720] Ibid.

[1721] Ibid.

[1722] Ibid.

[1723] "Schönborn: Abuse in the Church a 'Massive Reality,'" Vatican News, 12 November 2019, https://www.vaticannews.va/de/kirche/news/2019-11/schoenborn-kirche-missbrauch-groer-oesterreich-kardinal-taeter.html (translated from German).

[1724] Ibid.

[1725] Ibid.

In 2010 Schönborn made headlines when he publicly criticized Cardinal Angelo Sodano, then retired Vatican secretary of state, for dismissing the abuse crisis as "petty gossip" at a Mass on Easter Sunday in St. Peter's Square.[1726] Speaking to Austrian Catholic media, he accused Sodano of covering up the Groër scandal by using Vatican diplomacy to block the investigation. He said Sodano's "petty gossip" comment caused "massive harm." The public spat led to Benedict's summoning Schönborn to the apostolic palace and the Vatican's issuing an unusual critical statement, reminding the faithful that "in the Church, only the Pope has the authority to accuse a cardinal."[1727]

Handling Dissent

Although his views on women's ordination appear confused (see the next section), Schönborn has been seen publicly to act decisively against such dissenting positions. In 2011, a dissident group of Austrian priests called *Pfarrer-Initiative* (Priests' Initiative) made a push for the ordination of women as well as optional clerical celibacy, and the granting of Holy Communion to Catholics in irregular unions and to non-Catholic Christians. The initiative was called *Aufruf zum Ungehorsam.*[1728] Cardinal Schönborn met with the members of the *Pfarrer-Initiative* and publicly reaffirmed the Church's position on the issues raised by the group. Cardinal Schönborn further directed on June 26, 2012, that no priest supporting the *Aufruf zum Ungehorsam* may be appointed to the office of dean in the Archdiocese of Vienna.[1729] Schönborn "backed celibacy for priests, limiting ordination to

---

[1726] Nick Pisa, "Vatican Cardinal Attacks Fellow Cardinal for 'Covering Up' Abuse Case," *Telegraph*, 10 May 2010, https://www.telegraph.co.uk/news/worldnews/europe/vaticancityandholysee/7703232/Vatican-cardinal-attacks-fellow-cardinal-for-covering-up-abuse-case.html.

[1727] Philip Pullella, "Pope Rebukes Austrian Cardinal Who Accused Peer," Reuters, 28 June 2010, https://www.reuters.com/article/us-pope-abuse/pope-rebukes-austrian-cardinal-who-accused-peer-idUSTRE65R33T20100628.

[1728] "Call for Disobedience," *Pfarrer-Initiative*, 19 June 2011, http://www.pfarrer-initiative.at/site/de/wir/article/187.html.

[1729] The position of Christoph Cardinal Schönborn regarding the *Aufruf zum Ungehorsam* of 26 June 2012 is published on the archdiocesan website.

men and preserving marriage as a life-long commitment"[1730] and reiterated a warning to the dissident clergy that they faced serious consequences if they continued to advocate disobedience to the Vatican.[1731]

But the cardinal has also acted less decisively. On March 18, 2012, the parish of Stützenhofen, in the Archdiocese of Vienna, elected Florian Stangl, a twenty-six-year-old man who was living in a homosexual civil union, to be a member of the parish council. The pastor, Fr. Gerhard Swierzek, refused to accept Stangl's election because of his civil union. Schönborn initially supported Swierzek's decision, saying the election "is actually not possible" and that "members of the parish council have to follow the teachings of the Church and the discipline of the Church." He said that would be consistent with established bylaws of parish councils and that he "agree[d] with the pastor."[1732] Later, however, Cardinal Schönborn wrote that "in the personal conversation I had with Mr. Stangl, I was very impressed by his faith, his humility and his desire to serve."[1733] He then decided to support Stangl, explaining, "I know that, from the perspective of the rules, it is problematic, but I will support him."[1734]

Christoph Cardinal Schönborn, "Deans Are Responsible for the Unity of the Church," Erzdioezes Wien, 26 June 2012, https://www.erzdioezese-wien.at/pages/inst/14428675/text/stellungnahmen/article/31007.html (translated from German).

[1730] "Cardinal Schönborn: I Am Shaken by the Open Call for Disobedience," Kath.net, 7 July 2011, http://www.kath.net/news/32234 (translated from German).

[1731] Michael Shields, "Vienna Cardinal Takes Tough Line on Priest Revolt," Reuters, 17 September 2011, http://uk.reuters.com/article/uk-austria-church-idUKTRE78G1F220110917.

[1732] "Das geht eigentlich nicht. Das ist nicht Kompatibel. Pfarrgemeinderäte haben sich an die Lehre der Kirche und die displine der Kirche zu halten.... Das ist in der Pfarrgemeinderatsordnung festgeschrieben.... Ich habe den Pfarrer eigentlich auch recht gegeben."

[1733] "Bei dem persönlichen Gespräch, das ich mit Herrn Stangl führen konnte, war ich von seiner gläubigen Haltung, seiner Bescheidenheit und seiner gelebten Dienstbereitschaft sehr beeindruckt." "Schönborn to Stangl."

[1734] "Ich weiss, von der Regel her gesehen, ist das Problematisch, aber ich stell mich hinter ihn." "Schönborn to Stangl," at 2:45-2:47.

Medjugorje Visit

In 2009, Schönborn made a private pilgrimage to the Marian shrine of Medjugorje without taking the customary action of first informing the local bishop, Ratko Perić. Like the Vatican, Perić was skeptical about the Medjugorje apparitions and wrote an open letter expressing his displeasure at Schönborn's visit. Schönborn faxed a letter of apology to the bishop, saying it was not his intention that his visit be "a disservice to peace."[1735]

International Start-Ups

Cardinal Schönborn has been crucial in the establishment of two organizations that have received international acclaim. In the 1990s, the Holy See appointed him the founding Grand Chancellor of the International Theological Institute near Vienna, which has become respected for its sound theological teaching. The cardinal remains Grand Chancellor to this day. In 2010, the cardinal cofounded the International Catholic Legislators Network with the British Catholic peer Lord Alton of Liverpool. A nonpartisan organization, the network aims to bring together practicing Catholics and other Christians in elected office on a regular basis for faith formation, education, and fellowship.

TEACHING OFFICE

Drafting the Catechism

From 1987 to 1992, Cardinal Schönborn served as secretary of the commission responsible for drafting the *Catechism of the Catholic Church* (CCC).[1736] Together with Joseph Cardinal Ratzinger, he wrote *Introduction to the Catechism of the Catholic Church* (Ignatius Press, 1994). Cardinal

---

[1735] "Cardinal Schönborn Issues Apology to Bishop of Medjugorje," Catholic News Agency, 18 January 2010, https://www.catholicnewsagency.com/news/cardinal_schnborn_issues_apology_to_bishop_of_medjugorje.

[1736] "Schönborn Card. Christoph, O.P.," Vatican, https://press.vatican.va/content/salastampa/en/documentation/cardinali_biografie/cardinali_bio_schonborn_c.html.

Schönborn was also the editor of *YouCat: Youth Catechism of the Catholic Church* (2011). In a press conference in the context of the Synod on the Family, in October 2015, the cardinal stated that the teaching in the CCC on homosexuality should be changed.[1737] He responded: "We can and we must respect the decision to form a union with a person of the same sex, [and] to seek means under civil law to protect their living together with laws to ensure such protection."[1738]

Pope Benedict XVI provided the foreword to the English edition of *YouCat*, in which he commended the publication and recommended it to youth.[1739] But *YouCat* remains controversial. Some consider it unfaithful to the *Catechism* and unclear about important moral teachings, whereas others consider it to be a faithful explanation of the teachings of the *Catechism*.

Same-Sex "Marriage" and Unions

Schönborn insists that civil laws that authorize same-sex "marriage" ought to be respected:

> We can and we must respect the decision to form a union with a person of the same sex, to seek means under civil law to protect their living together with laws to ensure such protection. But if we are asked, if it is demanded of the Church to say that this is a marriage, well, we have to say: *non possumus* [we cannot]. It is not a discrimination of persons: to distinguish does not mean to discriminate. This absolutely does not prevent having great respect, friendship, or collaboration with couples living in this kind of union, and above

---

[1737] See Antonio Spadaro, S.J., "Marriage and Pastoral Conversion: Interview with Cardinal Christoph Schönborn," *La Civiltà Cattolica*, 25 September 2016, https://web.archive.org/web/20151013202235/http://www.laciviltacattolica.it/it/quaderni/articolo/3667/matrimonio-e-conversione-pastorale-intervista-al-cardinale-christoph-sch%C3%B6nborn/ (translated from Italian).

[1738] Ibid.

[1739] Pope Benedict XVI, foreword to *YouCat* (San Francisco: Ignatius Press, 2011), 10. (He encouraged them with the following words: "I invite you: study this Catechism! That is my heartfelt desire.")

all we mustn't look down on them. No one is obliged to accept this doctrine, but one can't pretend that the Church does not teach it.[1740]

Cardinal Schönborn has also said that he has "no objection" to the introduction of homosexual civil unions. "We have—also as Church—if you remember, not protested against this Austrian law for civil partnerships."[1741] During a lecture given at the National Gallery in London on April 8, 2013, Schönborn again emphasized the importance of the civil recognition of homosexual unions, saying that "there can be same-sex partnerships and they need respect, and even civil law protection."[1742] On April 20, 2013, Cardinal Schönborn's spokesman Michael Prüller clarified the cardinal's remarks: "The state may choose to respect certain choices made by its citizens, it may as a consequence legislate upon them, but it must never equate marriage with non-marriage. This cannot be seen as an endorsement of same-sex civil unions, neither in a legal sense, nor in a moral sense."[1743]

Right-to-Life Issues

Abortion is morally impermissible, according to Schönborn, although his moral principles are always subject to what he considers "pastoral" concerns.

One such example occurred when Auxiliary Bishop Andreas Laun of Austria stated that a mall owner, Richard Lugner, who rented space to an abortion clinic, had automatically excommunicated himself because of his "material cooperation" with evil. Cardinal Schönborn's spokesman Erich Leitenberger appeared to distance the cardinal from Bishop Laun's comment:

[1740] Irene Niravalambana, "Schönborn: The Door Is Never Closed," *Eyebeleave* (blog), 11 September 2015, http://eyebeleave.blogspot.com/2015/09/schonborn-door-is-never-closed.html (translation of much of the Spadaro-Schönborn interview).

[1741] "Schönborn to Stangl," 6:07-6:12.

[1742] Patrick Craine, "Vienna Cardinal: Same-Sex Relationships Need 'Civil Law Protection,'" LifeSite News, 12 April 2013, https://www.lifesitenews.com/news/vienna-cardinal-same-sex-couples-need-civil-law-protection.

[1743] Deacon Nick Donnelly, "The Tablet Is Accused of 'Gross Misinterpretation' of Cardinal Schönborn's Comments on Gay Civil Partnerships," *Protect the Faith* (blog), 21 April 2013, http://protectthepope.com/?p=7137.

"Academic discussions about excommunication will not help to save the right to life of even one child." Cardinal Schönborn himself said: "The destruction of life must not be made banal and viewed like a shopping trip. It must not be that a society is viewed as a way out. Everything you need to know about abortion is to be found in the Fifth Commandment."[1744] Schönborn said that he had asked Lugner not to sign a contract with the abortion clinic, but he apparently did not listen to him. Cardinal Schönborn has endorsed Priests for Life and initiated the creation of a Priests for Life chapter in Austria.[1745]

In 2016, and in advance of an Austrian presidential election, Cardinal Schönborn criticized Bishop Laun, who discouraged votes for a pro-abortion presidential candidate, Alexander Van der Bellen (Laun referenced the candidate's public statements and his party's platform in making his critique). Schönborn said in a statement that "a good decision in the election cannot base itself just on the core issues of the Catholic Church like the defense of human life, but must also take into consideration many other components like the attitude of the candidates toward the weakest members of society, among them, immigrants."[1746]

He also discouraged attendance at a pro-life counterrally.[1747] Michael Häupl, the mayor of Vienna, planned to host a celebration marking the thirtieth anniversary of a "busy" abortion clinic.[1748] But Schönborn discouraged pro-life activists from staging a counterdemonstration at city hall

[1744] John L. Allen Jr., "Austrian Bishop Says Mall Owner Excommunicated for Abortion Clinic," *National Catholic Reporter*, 7 February 2007, https://www.ncronline.org/news/austrian-bishop-says-mall-owner-excommunicated-abortion-clinic.

[1745] "History of Priests for Life," Priests for Life, https://www.priestsforlife.org/generalpfl/pflhist.html.

[1746] Michael Kant, "Cardinal Schönborn Criticizes Bishop Who Discouraged Votes for Pro-Abortion Presidential Candidate," LifeSite News, 30 May 2016, https://www.lifesitenews.com/opinion/cardinal-schoenborn-criticizes-bishop-who-discouraged-votes-for-pro-abortio.

[1747] "Vienna's Cardinal Schönborn Discourages Attendance at Pro-Life Rally," Catholic Culture, 18 September 2009, https://www.catholicculture.org/news/headlines/index.cfm?storyid=4072.

[1748] Ibid.

to protest that event. Bishop Laun "revealed that he stayed away from the protest at the cardinal's specific request."[1749]

The cardinal, in advance of Pope Benedict's visit to Austria in September 2007, called the lack of respect for life a "great wound" and said that it "exists in many European countries, but above all in ours, in Austria, where the 'yes' to life—whether to its beginning or its natural end—is more and more up for discussion." He went on to say, "The Church is very active in this sphere, whether it is to help women in difficulty welcome their own child, or to favor the alternative to euthanasia, that is, the network of houses in which there is a human and Christian accompaniment of the dying." He concluded by saying, "All of these initiatives are closely linked to the Church and produce a positive effect on society."[1750]

In a published interview, Schönborn contradicted the chairman of the Council of the Evangelical Church in Germany, Nikolaus Schneider, who had spoken in favor of euthanasia, saying, "There can be no debate about the absolute 'no' to euthanasia."[1751]

Record on Contraception

Schönborn's record on contraception is not so straightforward. One commentator has observed that "the official website of the Austrian bishops under Cardinal Christoph Schönborn's watch, as well as his own diocesan website, has published a series of articles in light of the 50th anniversary of the promulgation of Pope Paul VI's encyclical *Humanae Vitae*. These articles present a major undermining of essential Church teachings as they were laid out in *Humanae Vitae*, even putting into doubt the abiding unlawfulness of contraception."[1752]

[1749] Ibid.
[1750] Zenit Staff, "Cardinal: Pope Will Call Austrians to Respect Life," Zenit, 19 August 2007, https://zenit.org/articles/cardinal-pope-will-call-austrians-to-respect-life/.
[1751] Giuseppe Nardi, "Cardinal Schönborn: There Will Be 'Signs and Wonders' from the Pope—'Frightening': Governments Equip Themselves against Their Own People," *The Eponymous Flower* (blog), 14 August 2014, http://eponymousflower.blogspot.com/2014/08/cardinal-schonborn-there-will-be-signs.html.
[1752] Maike Hickson, "In Austria, Official Websites under Cdl. Schönborn Undermining Humanae Vitae," *One Peter Five*, 18 July 2018, https://onepeterfive.

There was also considerable confusion over the issue in 2011 with the Italian translation of *YouCat*. Question 420 of the Italian edition read: "Can a Christian couple turn to contraceptive methods?" The answer read: "Yes, a Christian couple can and must be responsible about their capacity of being able to give life." The answer in Italian goes on to explain—in line with Church teaching—that the Church does not accept artificial means of contraception but does allow regulation of fertility through natural methods. The corrected question now reads in Italian, "Can a Christian couple turn to methods that regulate fertility?"[1753] The English version of the question reads: "May a Christian married couple regulate the number of children they have?" And the answer reads: "Yes, a Christian married couple may and should be responsible in using the gift and privilege of transmitting life."[1754]

Holy Scripture

Cardinal Schönborn appears to endorse the historicity of the Gospels in a way that conforms to the teaching of *Dei Verbum*, although his views on the sources of Christian doctrine appear problematic. Schönborn cites *Dei Verbum* in support of truths about Sacred Scripture and Tradition. In an excerpt[1755] from his 2010 book, he writes of "three pillars" that together "support Christology: Scripture, tradition, and experience." He

---

com/schonborn-undermining-humanae-vitae/: "Cardinal Schönborn is the 'media bishop' of the Austrian Bishops' Conference and, as such, officially the editor of Kathpress, the news website of the bishops' conference. He is also responsible, as the archbishop of Vienna, for what his diocesan website publishes." Ibid.

1753 Carol Glatz, "Vatican to Organize Corrections to Be Made to New Youth Catechism," Catholic News Service, 13 April 2011, https://www.catholic-news.com/services/englishnews/2011/vatican-to-organize-corrections-to-be-made-to-new-youth-catechism.cfm.

1754 *YouCat: Youth Catechism of the Catholic Church* (San Francisco: Ignatius Press, 2015).

1755 Christoph Cardinal Schönborn, "The Three Pillars of Christology: Scripture-Tradition-Experience," Ignatius Insight, http://www.ignatiusinsight.com/features2010/cschonborn_threepillarsgshs_nov2010.asp.

goes on to say, "The soundness of these three determines the soundness of Christology."[1756] It is unclear whether he places experience on equal footing with divine revelation and Apostolic Tradition.

On Communion for "Remarried" Divorcees

Schönborn affirms the possibility of Communion for the divorced and "remarried." After *Amoris Laetitia* was released, Pope Francis asked Cardinal Schönborn if he thought the encyclical was "orthodox." To which he replied, "Holy Father, it is fully orthodox."[1757] Pope Francis chose Schönborn to be one of *Amoris Laetitia*'s interpreters.[1758] Schönborn gave an extremely lengthy interview to *America* magazine after *Amoris Laetitia*'s release.[1759] The interviewer, the close Jesuit papal aide Fr. Antonio Spadaro, asked:

> The Pope states that "in some cases," when a person is in an objective situation of sin—but without being subjectively guilty . . .—it is possible to . . . receiv[e] for this purpose the help of the Church, including the sacraments, and even the Eucharist. . . . Is there a rupture here with what was affirmed in the past?[1760]

[1756] Christoph Cardinal Schönborn, *The Three Pillars of Christology: Scripture-Tradition-Experience* (San Francisco: Ignatius Press, 2010).

[1757] Austen Ivereigh, "Cardinal Schönborn: Moral Theology Needs Both Principles and Prudence," *Crux*, 15 July 2017, https://cruxnow.com/commentary/2017/07/cardinal-schonborn-moral-theology-needs-principles-prudence/.

[1758] John-Henry Westen, "Pope Says Schönborn Interpretation on Communion for Remarried Is the Final Word," LifeSite News, 16 April 2016, https://www.lifesitenews.com/news/pope-says-Schönborn-interpretation-on-communion-for-remarried-is-the-final; Steve Skojec, "What Does the Choice of Exhortation Presenters Tell Us?," *One Peter Five*, 31 March 2016, https://onepeterfive.com/what-does-the-choice-of-exhortation-presenters-tell-us/.

[1759] Antonio Spadaro, S.J., "Cardinal Schönborn on 'The Joy of Love': The Full Conversation," *America*, 9 August 2016, https://www.americamagazine.org/issue/richness-love.

[1760] Ibid.

To which Cardinal Schönborn, after referencing St. Paul's famous exhortation to Christians not to receive the Eucharist unworthily (1 Cor. 11:29), replied:

> It is possible, in certain cases, that the one who is in an objective situation of sin can receive the help of the sacraments.... One cannot pass from the general rule to "some cases" merely by looking at formal situations.... In some cases, one who is in an objective situation of sin can receive the help of the sacraments.[1761]

When Spadaro asked, "What does 'in some cases' mean? [Why can we] not get a kind of inventory to explain what this means?,"[1762] Cardinal Schönborn explained: "We would risk creating, even by means of a norm that spoke of exceptions, a right to receive the Eucharist in an objective situation of sin."[1763] Spadaro intuited that "After this exhortation ... it is no longer meaningful to ask whether, in general, all divorced and 'remarried' persons can or cannot receive the sacraments."[1764] Cardinal Schönborn responded in the affirmative:

> [Amoris Laetitia] is located on the very concrete level of each person's life. There is an evolution, clearly expressed by Pope Francis, in the Church's perception of the elements that condition and that mitigate, elements that are specific to our own epoch:
>> The Church possesses a solid body of reflection concerning mitigating factors and situations. Hence it can no longer simply be said that all those in any "irregular" situation are living in a state of mortal sin and are deprived of sanctifying grace. More is involved here than mere ignorance of the rule. A subject may know the rule full well yet have great difficulty in understanding "its inherent values," or may be

[1761] Spadaro, "Joy of Love."
[1762] Ibid.
[1763] Ibid.
[1764] Ibid.

in a concrete situation which does not allow him or her to act differently and decide otherwise without further sin.[1765]

Immigration

Cardinal Schönborn was generally supportive of immigration, until he came to "rethink" his position because of the "unbelievable number" of migrants that flooded into Germany because of Chancellor Merkel's 2015 "open doors" refugee and immigration policy.[1766] That rethinking came at the end of 2016. In 2018, in an interview with the Austrian daily *Österreich*, the cardinal said, against the backdrop of a stricter Austrian immigration policy since 2015, that "it is clear to everyone that a correction [of the 2015 open-frontiers policy] was necessary." Asylum, for Schönborn, is a "sacred" right and must not become a term of abuse.[1767]

"What worries me is that Austria might be seen internationally as a particularly nasty country. The danger lies in the language that is used. Linguistic sensitivity is called for. The use of violent language is the first step to violent actions. We must remain vigilant."[1768]

Female Ordination

Schönborn's views on female priests are confused. He thinks ordaining women to the priesthood is not impossible in principle but that it should not be done at this time because it would be too radical a shift in the Church's *praxis*: "[Female priests] would be too profound an encroachment

---

[1765] Ibid.

[1766] Jon Rogers, " 'Europe's Christian Legacy in Danger' Archbishop of Vienna in Warning about Migrant Crisis," *Express*, 25 December 2016, https://www.express.co.uk/news/world/747224/Archbishop-Vienna-Cardinal-Schönborn-migrant-crisis-Austria; see also Christa Pongratz-Lippitt, "Austrian Cardinal Schönborn Addresses Europe's Refugee Crisis," *National Catholic Reporter*, 23 March 2016, https://www.ncronline.org/blogs/ncr-today/austrian-cardinal-Schönborn-addresses-europes-refugee-crisis.

[1767] Christa Pongratz-Lippitt, "Schönborn: All Religions Must Respect Rule of Law," *Tablet*, 18 June 2018, https://www.thetablet.co.uk/news/9261/sch-nborn-all-religions-must-respect-rule-of-law.

[1768] Ibid.

on the 2,000-year tradition, and even Pope Francis said: 'that is not fore-seen.' "[1769] Cardinal Schönborn had previously caused controversy after saying that a pope "cannot decide" by himself whether the ordination of women is permitted. "Ordination [of women] is a question that surely can only be settled by a Council," he told *Die Presse*.[1770] It is unclear how this fits with John Paul II's definitive declaration that the Church does not have the power to ordain women.[1771] In 2020, Schönborn reaffirmed on Austrian television his desire to see women ordained deacons and even expressed "disappointment" that Pope Francis had not sufficiently advanced this cause. He insisted the issue was "still on the table" despite Francis' clearly not including it in *Querida Amazonia*, his post-synodal summary of the Amazon synod.[1772]

Priestly Celibacy

Schönborn has questioned the Latin-Rite discipline of priestly celibacy. The *Australian* reported that in Rome in 2009, Cardinal Schönborn "presented a petition signed by leading Austrian lay Catholics calling for the abolition of the requirement for priestly celibacy."[1773] He has also raised the possibility that priestly celibacy might be a cause of the sex abuse crisis; in 2010,

---

[1769] "Women Priests 'Too Profound a Change.'"

[1770] Ibid.

[1771] "Wherefore, in order that all doubt may be removed regarding a matter of great importance, a matter which pertains to the Church's divine constitution itself, in virtue of my ministry of confirming the brethren (cf. Lk 22:32) I declare that the Church has no authority whatsoever to confer priestly ordination on women and that this judgment is to be definitively held by all the Church's faithful." St. John Paul II, Apostolic Letter *Ordinatio Sacerdotalis* (22 May 1994), Vatican, http://w2.vatican.va/content/john-paul-ii/en/apost_letters/1994/documents/hf_jp-ii_apl_19940522_ordinatio-sacerdotalis.html.

[1772] "Vienna Cardinal 'Disappointed' about Francis," Gloria.tv, 31 March, https://gloria.tv/post/WhDKfEsxtpBN13fnkqWmz9YQn.

[1773] Richard Owen, "Cardinal Christoph Schönborn Questions Priest Celibacy," *Australian*, 12 March 2010, https://www.theaustralian.com.au/news/world/cardinal-christoph-Schönborn-questions-priest-celibacy/news-story/4bd5354f9a0fd82fce26f47ce6628a1e.

Schönborn said that there needed to be an "unflinching examination" of the causes of the scandal and that the causes include "the issue of priests' training, as well as the question of what happened in the so-called sexual revolution of the generation of 1968 [as well as] the question of priest celibacy and the question of personality development."[1774] He concluded by saying that to confront and solve the scandal "requires a great deal of honesty, both on the part of the Church and of society."[1775]

Islam

Cardinal Schönborn wants Islam to reform itself; he wants Europe to retain its Christian heritage, and he is cautious about the Islamization of Europe. In 2016, he gave a homily in the cathedral of Vienna and said, "On this day, 333 years ago, Vienna was saved. Will there now be a third attempt at an Islamic conquest of Europe?" He continued: "Many Muslims think so and long for it."[1776] Schönborn tried to make it clear that he was not championing a sort of defensive battle, defending Christian values against Islam. He offered the official newspaper of the Archdiocese of Vienna, *Der Sonntag*, the following clarification: "Europe's Christian legacy is in danger, because we Europeans have squandered it. That has absolutely nothing to do with Islam nor with the refugees. It is clear that many Islamists would like to take advantage of our weakness, but they are not responsible for it. We are." The cardinal further clarified: "One must not take my homily to be a call to defend ourselves against the refugees, this was not at all my intention. The opportunity for a Christian renewal of Europe lies in our hands: if we look at and come to Christ, spread his

---

[1774] Richard Owen, "Cardinal Schönborn Says Celibacy Partly to Blame for Clerical Sex Abuse," BishopAccountability.org, 11 March 2010, http://www.bishop-accountability.org/news2010/03_04/2010_03_11_Owen_CardinalSchonborn.htm.

[1775] Ibid.

[1776] He also clarified these remarks here: Christoph Cardinal Schönborn, "Renewal of Christian Legacy," Erzdioezese Wien, https://www.erzdioezese-wien.at/pages/inst/14428675/text/stellungnahmen/article/52187.html (translated from German).

gospel and deal with our fellow men, strangers included, as he has taught us, in love and responsibility."

Schönborn also stated:

> The Enlightenment was a salutary, cleansing challenge for Christianity. It had to go through a long and painful regeneration process which was not resolved until the founding of the ecumenical movement in the twentieth century.... Why shouldn't there be similar regeneration powers in Islam which will lead to genuine spiritual renewal and a strict "no" to the use of violence? I personally very much hope so.[1777]

Schönborn stated in response to the expulsion of sixty imams and the closings of seven mosques in Austria in June 2018, that religious freedom must prevail in Austria but also that "that means that the state is obliged to exercise a supervisory role and see to it that religious communities do not abuse the freedom of religion. They must abide by the rule of law and the government can intervene should they not do so."[1778]

Universalism

It appears Cardinal Schönborn implicitly embraces universalism; his comments recorded in the following excerpt suggest that, in fact, no one might ever reside in hell. The 2008 Divine Mercy congress

> was marked by a respectful theological disagreement between the Russian Orthodox Bishop Hilarion of Vienna and Cardinal Schönborn. The Orthodox prelate, in his presentation, argued that God's mercy is so great that He does not condemn sinners to everlasting punishment. The Orthodox understanding of hell, Bishop Hilarion said, corresponds roughly to the Catholic notion

---

[1777] Christa Pongratz-Lippitt, "Cardinal Schönborn: Islam Must Reform Itself," *Tablet*, 3 January 2017, https://www.thetablet.co.uk/news/6557/cardinal-sch-nborn-islam-must-reform-itself-.

[1778] Pongratz-Lippitt, "All Religions Must Respect."

of purgatory. Cardinal Schönborn politely disagreed, noting that the idea expressed by Bishop Hilarion "is not a doctrine of the Church." While hell is a reality, he said, it is God's will for all men to be saved, and all Christians should pray "that no one will be lost."[1779]

Schönborn spoke on November 19, 2015, at the International Dialogue Centre (KAICIID) about the potential of interreligious dialogue for peace. He said: "I think that we will not be judged about our religion but about the question: What did you do for justice in the world? For the hungry? For the refugees? For the poor, the needy? What have you done for the ecological needs of our planet? This is a common responsibility ... about [which] ... we have to work together."[1780]

What Cardinal Schönborn thinks about evangelization of non-Catholics and the nature of the political common good is unclear. His thoughts on Islam seem to indicate that, regarding proselytization, he values a conversion-and-shining-example approach to converting non-Catholics, at least with respect to Muslims, over an explicit approach to helping them convert. But that is because the Faith in Europe is dying, so the conversion of the lukewarm must precede the conversion of non-Catholics; if the Faith in Europe were more vibrant, it is possible he might think that proselytization would be effective and so should be done.

[1779] "Divine Mercy Congress Ends—Spiced by Theological Disagreement," *Catholic Culture,* 7 April 2008, https://www.catholicculture.org/news/features/index.cfm?recnum=57674. On July 10, 2004, Cardinal Schönborn presided at the funeral Mass for Austrian president Thomas Klestil (1932-2004). President Klestil died while living in an irregular union. At the funeral Mass, Cardinal Schönborn declared: "We firmly believe that you are home, at home with God," where "there is no greater happiness." Cf. Cardinal Christoph Schönborn, *Happiness, God and Man* (San Francisco: Ignatius Press, 2011), 104.

[1780] " 'Religion Is Not Imaginable without Responsibility,' Cardinal Schönborn at KAICIID," KAICIID, 20 November 2015, http://www.kaiciid.org/news-events/news/%E2%80%9Creligion-not-imaginable-without-responsibili-ty%E2%80%9D-cardinal-sch%C3%B6nborn-kaiciid.

THE NEW EVANGELIZATION

Schönborn has spoken about the "New Evangelization." When it was put to him that several people at the 2012 Synod on the New Evangelization were impressed with what he had said about such gatherings "being a chance for bishops to talk to each other about their pastoral challenges," the cardinal replied:

> As successors of the apostles, we are called to be the first evangelizers.... We all asked ourselves, "Do I really evangelize?" I preach a lot, I'm in the parishes, I write pastoral letters, and so on, but what's meant by the "New Evangelization" is not only the daily pastoral work, which obviously we have to do and we do it with joy, but what Pope Benedict repeatedly says to us, encourages us to do, is to reach out to those who no longer have, or never have had, any direct contact with the gospel. This is the real challenge of the New Evangelization. I was very moved by some examples in the synod of real shared experiences of our work of evangelization. Of course, we also have to talk about all the questions of secular society, of globalization, of the social dimension, and all these subjects.[1781]

On the coronavirus, Schönborn avoided linking it to a punishment from God but wondered if it was connected to the "ecological question" and speculated that God might be trying to tell humanity something. "Do we really need to have 200,000 airplanes in the air every day?" he asked in an interview with Austrian television. "Does He perhaps want to remind us that He has entrusted creation to us, and not given it to us to devastate it?"[1782]

[1781] John L. Allen Jr., "Interview with Cardinal Christoph Schönborn," *National Catholic Reporter*, 25 October 2012, https://www.ncronline.org/blogs/ncr-today/interview-cardinal-christoph-sch-nborn.

[1782] Martin Bürger, "Cdl Schönborn Uses Coronavirus Pandemic to Push 'Ecological' Questions," LifeSite News, 1 April 2020, https://www.lifesitenews.com/news/cdl-schoenborn-uses-coronavirus-pandemic-to-push-ecological-questions.

APPROACH TO MORAL THEOLOGY

Schönborn's understanding of the foundations of moral theology, and of the moral life, is troubling.

In a talk in Vienna in July 2017 on *Amoris Laetitia*, Schönborn explained that moral theology must "stand on two feet: Principles, and then the prudential steps to apply them to reality."[1783] It is true, of course, that moral principles must be applied to concrete situations by the acting person in order to arrive at a decision, here and now, about what to do. But it is scarcely accurate or helpful to describe these both as foundations ("the two feet") of moral theology. Application is essential, but it is downstream, contingent, and secondary to the great moral truths that serve as the anchors and the architecture of morality.

Cardinal Schönborn has declared that "*Amoris laetitia* is the great document of moral theology that we have been waiting for since the time of Vatican II and that develops the choices already made by the CCC and by [John Paul II's] *Veritatis splendor*."[1784] Schönborn recognizes the obvious tension between *Amoris Laetitia* and *Veritatis Splendor*'s teaching on exceptionless moral norms. But he doubles down on the equality of "principles" and "prudence." According to him, the two documents represent an intrinsically unstable setting:

> The great preceding document *Veritatis splendor* of John Paul II showed one side of reality, so to speak, but did not have the other side in view. John Paul II's concern was establishing the existence of objective norms. And that is absolutely necessary. It's not like I put together my own norms. There are objective norms. But this expresses only one half of the matter. And the second half Francis has added with *Amoris laetitia*. In that document one can sense where his existential background lies. Those countless extremely

---

[1783] Ivereigh, "Moral Theology Needs Both Principles and Prudence."

[1784] Massimo Faggioli, "A Non-Synodal Reception for a Post-Synodal Exhortation," *Commonweal*, 12 July 2016, https://www.commonwealmagazine.org/non-synodal-reception-post-synodal-exhortation.

poor families he experienced in Latin America. You can't just come along with the objective norm! You have to take a look at what realization of humaneness, at times even heroic, and what realization of mutual help people manage to engender under such living conditions. This concrete attentiveness to that reality has helped the Church tremendously.... Pope Francis says: neither laxism nor rigorism, but discerning, looking, verifying. Of course this is to be done also when listening to what the Church says. But above all in looking at the real situation and the judgment of my conscience.... Pope Francis' challenge is the difficult way of discernment.[1785]

Here we see unmistakably how, for Schönborn, "discernment," "application," and "prudence" cannot peacefully live on terms of equality with objective moral truths. Their alleged parity as two foundational pillars cannot persist. So Schönborn ends up implicitly concluding that objective moral norms can sometimes—in the concrete situation—undermine "humaneness," and that the "heroic" moral choice can sometimes be contrary to "objective" moral norms. This denies precisely what St. John Paul II taught in *Veritatis Splendor,* which is that the basic moral norms are *truths* invariably constitutive of human flourishing ("humaneness"), and that no one *ever, anywhere* does right or pleases God by, for example, choosing to commit adultery or to have an abortion.

Schönborn tried to justify the contentious passages in *Amoris Laetitia* by claiming that they represented a "classic case" of an "organic development of doctrine" along the lines envisaged by St. John Henry Newman and "not a rupture" with past papal teaching.[1786]

[1785] "'Cardinal' Schönborn: Amoris Laetitia Adds What Is Missing from One-Sided Veritatis Splendor," *Novus Ordo Watch,* 11 January 2018, https://novusordowatch.org/2018/01/schonborn-amoris-laetitia-veritatis-splendor/ (internal brackets omitted).

[1786] Gerard O'Connell, "Amoris Laetitia Represents an Organic Development of Doctrine, Not a Rupture," *America,* 8 April 2016, https://www.americamagazine.org/faith/2016/04/08/amoris-laetitia-represents-organic-development-doctrine-not-rupture.

But Schönborn's other comments suggest that there is indeed a rupture with previous Church teaching, and his positions undermine the indissoluble nature of marriage. In an interview with Spadaro, given on August 26, 2015, and published in *La Civiltà Cattolica*, he concurred with what appears to be Pope Francis' understanding—namely, that marriage is a composite and not a moral unity. In other words, both he and Pope Francis seem to hold that a "true" or "real" marriage is a life together that exhibits a maximum number of admirable qualities (mutual care, emotional closeness, sex, children, long- [longer-, longest-] term commitment, psychological satisfaction, community orientation, etc.), so that persons—such as those in homosexual "civil unions" or cohabiting adulterers—for whom marriage is morally impossible could, in reality, be just as "married" as most heterosexual couples who have exchanged marital vows to form a sacramental union.

Schönborn said Matrimony is "realized *fully* where justly there is a sacrament between a man and a woman living in faith etc. *But, that does not prevent that, outside of this full realization of the Sacrament of Matrimony, there are elements of matrimony that are signals of expectation, positive elements.*"[1787] He added that one can "know to view and to discern in a couple, in a *de facto* union, in cohabitants, the elements of true heroism, of true love, of a true mutual gift. Even if we must say: 'There is not yet a full reality of the sacrament.' But, who are we to judge that in them elements of truth and sanctification do not exist?"[1788] For example, he said, a civil marriage is better than simply living together, because it signifies a couple has made a

---

[1787] "Il sacramento del matrimonio si realizza pienamente là dove giustamente c'è il sacramento tra un uomo e una donna che vivono nella fede ecc. Ma ciò non impedisce che, al di fuori di questa realizzazione piena del sacramento del matrimonio, ci siano elementi del matrimonio che sono segnali di attesa, elementi positivi." Christoph Cardinal Schönborn, interview with Father Antonio Spadaro, S.J., "Matrimonio e conversione pastorale. Intervista al Cardinale Christoph Schönborn," *La Civiltà Cattolica* 3, no. 3966 (2015): 494-510, https://www.laciviltacattolica.it/articolo/matrimonio-e-conversione-pastorale-intervista-al-cardinale-christoph-schonborn/ (emphasis added).

[1788] "Sanno guardare e discernere in una coppia, in un'unione di fatto, in dei conviventi, gli elementi di vero eroismo, di vera carità, di vero dono reciproco. Anche se dobbiamo dire: 'Non è ancora una piena realtà del sacramento'.

formal, public commitment to each other. "It's an improvement," he said. They share "a life, they share their joys and sufferings, they help one another. It must be recognized that this person took an important step for his own good and the good of others, even though it certainly is not a situation the Church can consider 'regular.' "[1789] The Church's negative "judgment about homosexual acts is necessary," he said, "but the Church should not look in the bedroom first, but in the dining room! It must accompany people."[1790]

With regard to irregular unions, Schönborn said the Church "cannot transform an irregular situation into a regular one, but there do exist paths for healing, for learning, for moving gradually closer to a situation in compliance with Church teaching."[1791]

In October 2011, Schönborn reportedly wrote in the preface to *Thema Kirche*, the magazine for the staff of the Archdiocese of Vienna, that the readers should focus on the subject of failed relationships.[1792] A pastoral

Ma chi siamo noi per giudicare e dire che non esistono in loro elementi di verità e di santificazione?" Ibid.

[1789] "Invece di dire tutto ciò che manca, ci si può anche avvicinare a tali realtà, notando ciò che di positivo esiste in questo amore che si stabilizza." Cardinal Schönborn spoke in the interview about someone he knows who, after many temporary relationships, entered a stable homosexual relationship. He commented: "Ora ha trovato una relazione stabile. È un miglioramento, se non altro sul piano umano, il non passare più da un rapporto all'altro, ma stabilizzarsi in una relazione che non è basata solo sulla sessualità. Si condivide una vita, si condividono gioie e sofferenze, ci si aiuta a vicenda. Bisogna riconoscere che questa persona ha fatto un passo importante per il proprio bene e per il bene degli altri, anche se, certamente, non è una situazione che la Chiesa possa considerare regolare." Ibid.

[1790] "Il giudizio sugli atti omosessuali come tali è necessario, ma la Chiesa non deve guardare prima nella camera da letto, ma nella sala da pranzo! Occorre accompagnare." Ibid.

[1791] "Non si può trasformare una situazione irregolare in una regolare, ma esistono anche cammini di guarigione, di approfondimento, cammini in cui la legge è vissuta passo dopo passo." Ibid.

[1792] Wolfgang Bergmann, "Kardinal Schönborns Coming-Out," *Der Standard*, 31 October 2011, http://derstandard.at/1319181642732/ChurchWatch-Kardinal-Schoenborns-Coming-out.

service of the Archdiocese of Vienna to assist those who are divorced and "remarried," WIGE "Plattform für geschiedene und Wiederverheiratete in der Kirche,"[1793] maintained in its brochure that "it is certain that proper sacramental marriage is indissoluble. It has the *highest* value before God."[1794] But the brochure went on to state that "for those people whose first marriage is broken, a 'second vow' should be possible. In this way, the new relationship receives appropriate value and is raised above the mere civil union. Such a vow is not to be equated with an ecclesial marriage!"[1795]

What of issues relating to the nature of marriage and homosexuality? Cardinal Schönborn has said, "The 'marriage-for-all' [position] poses for us as Church some challenges for which we do not have sure formulas. We have to find careful answers to these questions which keep the dignity and the salvation of the souls of the concerned in view."[1796] When asked by Fr. Spadaro of *La Civiltà Cattolica* just before the October 2015 Synod on the Family whether he had ever "come across circumstances in the lives of homosexuals" that had spoken to or resonated with him in a particularly positive way, Schönborn replied:

> I know a homosexual person who has lived [promiscuously for years but has now] found a stable relationship. It is an improvement, if nothing else then [sic] on a human level, this ... being in a stable relationship that is not based only on sexuality. One shares one's life, one shares

---

[1793] *Aufmerksamkeiten*, Erzdioezese Wien, https://www.erzdioezese-wien.at/dl/ptOuJKJLLLLNJqx4KJK/wige_broschuere_aufmerksamkeiten.pdf.

[1794] "Fest steht, dass die aufrechte sakramentale Ehe unauflöslich ist. Sie hat vor Gott die höchste Würde." Ibid., 12 (emphasis added).

[1795] "Für Menschen, deren erste Ehe zerbrochen ist, soll ein 'zweites Gelöbnis' möglich sein. Dadurch erhält diese neue Verbindung eine entsprechende Würde und hebt sich von einer nur standesamtlich geschlossenen Zivilehe ab. Dieses ist nicht mit einer kirchlich geschlossenen Ehe gleichzusetzen!" Ibid.

[1796] Maike Hickson, "Cardinal Schönborn Outraged at Bishop's Critique of Blessings for Homosexual Unions," LifeSite News, 14 February 2018, https://www.lifesitenews.com/news/cardinal-schoenborn-outraged-at-bishops-critique-of-blessings-for-homosexua.

the joys and sufferings, one helps one another. We must recognize that this person has made an important step for his own good and for the good of others, even though, of course, this is not a situation that the Church can consider regular. The judgment on homosexual acts as such is necessary, but the Church … must accompany.[1797]

For Schönborn, the moral norm that Holy Communion may be offered only to those who live in a state in conformity with the gospel may be superseded by circumstances. He has stated that the "general norm is very clear, and it is equally clear that it cannot cover all the cases exhaustively. On the level of principle, the doctrine of marriage and the sacraments is clear. Pope Francis has newly expressed it with great clarity. On the level of discipline, the Pope takes account of the endless variety of concrete situations. He has affirmed that one should not expect a new general set of norms in the manner of canon law that would be applicable to every case."[1798]

Schönborn has been intensely loyal to Pope Francis and ever willing to defend him over theological controversies, even adding his Dominican weight to tenuous attempts to justify contentious passages of *Amoris Laetitia* by asserting they were Thomistic.[1799] He privately criticized heated public criticism of the pope over the apostolic exhortation, viewing such criticism as distasteful and un-Catholic.

SUMMARY

Christoph Schönborn is a paradoxical figure, with elements to his views that are difficult to reconcile. He has been called a "spiritual son" of Benedict XVI and worked with Joseph Ratzinger on the *Catechism of the Catholic Church*, with highest honor received from John Paul II, which would seemingly give him

[1797] Niravalambana, "Door Is Never Closed."
[1798] Antonio Spadaro, S.J., "Cardinal Schönborn on the Demands and Joys of Love," *America*, 21 July 2016, https://www.americamagazine.org/issue/demands-love.
[1799] O'Connell, "Organic Development."

impeccable doctrinal credentials.[1800] And yet he displays an openness to positions that John Paul II and Benedict XVI would repudiate, such as accepting the possibility of ordaining women deacons, openness to same-sex "marriages" in society, and lack of clarity regarding contraception. Eager to please, he appears intent on trying to appease critics of some but not all of the Church's moral teaching, both within the Church and in secular society, by finding paths of compromise that many find unacceptable. This tendency appears to originate not from ill will but rather an openness to, and compassion for, people's problems, needs, and concerns, and a priestly willingness to shepherd the faithful in their brokenness, however misplaced his remedies may be.

His dogmatic theology is often expressed in a beautiful way, and he displays an understanding and appreciation for Catholic teaching, and yet he has been the celebrant at blasphemous celebrations of the Mass, and his cathedral in Vienna periodically is the home of morally problematic art shows. His rejection of "norms" regarding who may or may not receive Communion leans toward a rejection of universal moral norms, but he also condemns priestly unchastity. Initially defensive, he has been consistent and firm in trying to eradicate clerical sexual abuse and its cover-up by the hierarchy.

As of April 2020, he was to undergo surgery for prostate cancer. Doctors expected him to make a complete recovery.[1801]

With his long pastoral and professorial experience, his warm personality, and his administrative capability, it is undoubtable that Christoph Schönborn has had much to offer the Church, even while holding positions that seem to be at odds with each other. Perhaps he is, as one commentator has suggested, "a dialogue-ready pragmatist."[1802]

[1800] Editorial, "C. Schönborn, the 'Spiritual Son' of Benedict XVI," *La Revue Internationale*, 27 February 2013, https://www.revue-internationale.com/2013/02/c-schonborn-le-fils-spirituel-de-benoit-xvi/.

[1801] "Austrian Cardinal Schönborn Has Prostate Cancer, to Undergo Surgery," *La Croix International*, 25 March 2019, https://international.la-croix.com/news/austrian-cardinal-schnborn-has-prostate-cancer-to-undergo-surgery/9744.

[1802] "Christoph Schönborn Is Considered a Candidate for Pope," *WeltHeute.at*, 11 February 2013, https://web.archive.org/web/20130215024253/https://www.heute.at/news/welt/art23661,850765 (translated from German).

SERVICE TO THE CHURCH

Ordination to the Priesthood: 27 December 1970
Ordination to the Episcopate: 29 September 1991
Elevation to the College of Cardinals: 21 February 1998

Education

- Philosophisch-theologische Hochschule, Walberberg; Theology and philosophy
- University of Vienna; Philosophy and psychology
- Institut Catholique, Paris; Theology
- 1972-1973: University of Regensburg; Philosophy and theology (member of the "student group" of Joseph Ratzinger)[1803]
- École Pratique des Hautes Études, Sorbonne: Byzantine Christianity and Slavic studies

Assignments

- 1963: Entered the Dominican Order
- 1973-1975: Chaplain for students at the University of Graz
- 1975-1991: Professor of Dogmatic Theology and the Christian East, Catholic Theological Faculty, Fribourg, Switzerland
- 1980-1987: Member of the Swiss Commission for Dialogue between Orthodox and Roman Catholics

---

[1803] Throughout Pope Benedict's pontificate, Schönborn was an active member of Ratzinger Schülerkreis, a group of the pope's former students who meet annually with the Holy Father to discuss theological issues. In a 2012 article, the Catholic News Agency described Schönborn's relationship with Pope Benedict as a "lifelong friendship." David Kerr, "Cardinal Schönborn: A Faithful Catholic Minority Can Re-Convert Europe," Catholic News Agency, 26 May 2012, http://www.catholicnewsagency.com/news/cardinal-Schönborn-a-faithful-catholic-minority-can-re-convert-europe/.

- 1980-1991: Member of the Theological Commission of the Swiss Bishops' Conference
- 1980-present: Member of the International Commission of Theologians
- 1984-present: Member of the Foundation *Pro Oriente*
- 1987-1992: Editing secretary of the *Catechism of the Catholic Church*
- 1991: Titular bishop of Sutri and auxiliary bishop of the Archdiocese of Vienna
- 1995: Coadjutor archbishop of Vienna
- 1995-present: Archbishop of Vienna
- 1996: Preacher of the Lenten Spiritual Exercises for Pope John Paul II and the Roman Curia
- 1995-present: Grand Chancellor, International Theological Institute, Trumau, Austria
- 2010: Cofounder, International Catholic Legislators Network

Membership
- Congregation for the Doctrine of the Faith
- 2014: Congregation for the Oriental Churches
- 2013: Congregation for Catholic Education
- Pontifical Council for Culture
- Pontifical Commission for the Cultural Heritage of the Church
- 2014: Pontifical Council for the Laity
- 2011: Pontifical Council for Promoting the New Evangelization

ANGELO CARDINAL SCOLA

"Your Grace Is Sufficient"

Born: 7 November 1941
Malgrate, Lombardy, Italy
Nationality: Italian
Title: Archbishop Emeritus of Milan

BIOGRAPHY

Angelo Scola was born to a communist truck-driver father and a devout, practicing Catholic mother.[1804] His hometown was Malgrate, a village close to Milan, and he grew up in a small apartment on a farm on the edge of

---

[1804] Desmond O'Grady, "Cardinal Scola: the Man Who Was Nearly Pope," *Catholic Herald*, 3 January 2019, catholicherald.co.uk/magazine/cardinal-scola-the-man-who-was-nearly-pope.

some woods. Scola was the younger of two sons.[1805] After studying engineering for two years at a university in Milan, Scola began studying philosophy at the Catholic University of Milan, earning a doctorate in 1967.[1806] During this time, he became closely acquainted with Communion and Liberation and its founder, Don Luigi Giussani, who had a great influence on the rest of his life. Ordained a priest in 1970, Scola earned another doctorate at the University of Fribourg in collaboration with the Dominicans there. In the 1970s, he was involved in student movements, continued to participate in Communion and Liberation, and, coming into contact with Joseph Ratzinger, served as editor of the conservative theological journal *Communio*, while conducting book-length interviews with Henri de Lubac and Hans Urs von Balthasar. In 1982, Scola began teaching at the Pontifical Lateran University and the John Paul II Institute for Studies on Marriage and the Family. From 1986 to 1991, he served a consultor to the Congregation for the Doctrine of the Faith.

In 1991, Scola was consecrated a bishop and John Paul II appointed him overseer of the Diocese of Grosseto. For the next four years, he worked to encourage Catholic education in Grosseto, reopening the seminary there and publishing a book for young people. He also established a diocesan mission to Santa Cruz, Bolivia. In 1995, Scola vacated the Diocese of Grosseto in order to serve as full-time rector of the Lateran University and as president of the John Paul II Institute. In 2002, he was appointed patriarch of Venice and elected president of the bishops' conference of the Triveneta region in Northern Italy. John Paul II made Scola a cardinal the following year. In 2011, Scola was elected president of the Episcopal Conference of Lombardy, and Benedict XVI appointed him archbishop of Milan. Scola was the bookies' favorite at the 2013 conclave and reportedly Benedict

---

[1805] Catholic News Service, "Scholarly Venice cardinal intent on raising Church's profile," *American Catholic*, tinyurl.com/y52jyxbr.

[1806] Andrea Tornielli, "Scola: the Reason Why He Left the Seminary in Milan," *La Stampa*, 6 September 2011, www.lastampa.it/2011/09/06/vaticaninsider/scola-the-reason-why-he-left-the-seminary-in-milan-TbvTqdd74LmN-JWgzULRWZK/pagina.html.

XVI's anointed successor, but not enough Italian cardinals could unite around him.[1807] He served in Milan until his resignation was accepted on account of age by Pope Francis in 2017. He is the author of many books and more than 120 scholarly articles.

SANCTIFYING OFFICE

Eucharistic Theology

Angelo Scola has conspicuously underlined the importance of Eucharistic theology in his writings. In his *relatio* delivered at the 2005 Synod of Bishops, organized to discuss the Eucharist in the life of the Church (and which bore fruit in Benedict XVI's *Sacramentum Caritatis*, the post-synodal apostolic exhortation on the Eucharist as the source and summit of Christian life), Scola emphasized that the Eucharist is the locus of the revelation of God's love for humanity.[1808] In the Eucharist, he added, the believer is allowed access to the living and personal Truth who saves. Similarly, in 2008, Scola gave a conference to the Italian Federation of Spiritual Exercises titled, "Christian Spirituality in Light of the Post-Synodal Exhortation *Sacramentum Caritatis*." He explained, "Spirituality is not to take oneself away from life. At its root, there is the Holy Spirit, the Spirit of the Son Incarnate, who died and rose again." Hence, spiritual exercises cannot but have the Eucharist as their center, such that life itself should have a "eucharistic shape."[1809]

[1807] Edward Pentin, "Italian Cardinal Scola Once Again Emerging as Papal Favorite," Edward Pentin, 12 March 2013, https://edwardpentin.co.uk/italian-cardinal-scola-once-again-emerging-as-papal-favorite/.

[1808] "Eleventh Ordinary General Assembly of the Synod of Bishops: The Eucharist: Source and Summit of the Life and Mission of the Church," General Secretariat for Synod of Bishops, October 2005, http://www.synod.va/content/synod/en/synodal_assemblies/2005-eleventh-ordinary-general-assembly~the-eucharist~source-a.html.

[1809] Mimmo Muolo, "Gli esercizi spirituali sono un'esperienza," Vatican Radio, 2 September 2008, http://www.archivioradiovaticana.va/storico/2008/02/09/

Liturgy

Although liturgy has not been a focus of Scola's thought, he was one of the few Italian bishops supportive of Benedict XVI's 2007 *Motu Proprio Summorum Pontificum*, which granted greater license to priests and bishops to celebrate the Mass and other liturgies and sacramental rites in the forms used prior to the Second Vatican Council. Scola defended the document, saying that the "Latin Mass is not in contradiction with the liturgical reform of the [Second Vatican] Council," and that certain parishes in Venice were dedicated to the Extraordinary Form without any tension thereby in the diocese.[1810] He even placed a chapel under the care of the Fraternal Society of Saint Peter (FSSP), formally inaugurating their care by personally assisting at a Mass in the Extraordinary Form as bishop in 2010 in Venice.[1811] In Milan, he allowed for a community to have a chapel in which the traditional Ambrosian Rite would be offered weekly.[1812] Himself not given to celebrate the Extraordinary Form, he was known to celebrate the Novus Ordo in Latin from time to time.[1813]

---

gli_esercizi_spirituali_sono_unesperienza_che_favorisce_lincontro/it1-185553 (translated from Italian).

[1810] Editorial, "Sacramentum Caritatis: Card. Scola, the Latin Mass Is Not in Contrast with the Liturgical Reform of the Council," *toscanaoggi.it*, 13 March 2007, https://www.toscanaoggi.it/Vita-Chiesa/SACRAMENTUM-CARITATIS-CARD.-SCOLA-LA-MESSA-IN-LATINO-NON-E-IN-CON-TRASTO-CON-LA-RIFORMA-LITURGICA-DEL-CONCILIO (translated from Italian).

[1811] Editorial, "Santa Messa tridentina a Venezia con il Cardinal Scola," *Messainlatino*, 25 January 2010, http://blog.messainlatino.it/2010/01/santa-messa-venezia-con-il-cardinale.html.

[1812] Marco, "A Milano messa in latino nell'antica tradizione Ambrosiana," *Milano Today*, 11 May 2018, http://www.milanotoday.it/eventi/a-milano-messa-in-latino.html.

[1813] Desirée Spreafico, "Festival Zelioli. Duemila fedeli in Basilica per la messa in latino con il Cardinal Scola," lecconotizie.com, 8 July 2018, https://lecconotizie.com/attualita/festival-zelioli-duemila-fedeli-in-basilica-per-la-messa-con-il-cardinal-scola/.

Importance of Prayer

Prayer has been an important focus for Angelo Scola throughout his life. In his early days, his commitment to prayer was manifested in how he joined young people for sessions of encounter with Communion and Liberation. As a sign of his confidence in prayer, when Scola was about to enter Milan as its new archbishop, he wrote the people: "I need you, all of you, your help.... I ask in particular for the prayer of children, of the aged, of the sick, of the poor and marginalized."[1814] In his latter days, he led many spiritual exercises for diverse groups, including, for example, the Association of Friends of the Seminary of Milan, in which he described the importance of being rooted in the life of Christ.[1815]

Another example of Scola's spiritual sense is how he led the Rosary in the Duomo of Milan to encourage the diocese to dedicate the month of May to the Blessed Virgin Mary. On that occasion he said, "We feel the desire and the charm of gathering together in prayer under the Madonna. The Virgin Mary, who rushed into heaven to enter into glory, persuades us to raise our eyes, to reinvigorate our hope, to confirm us in the belief that, if we do all that Jesus tells us, we will once again see joy flow through the streets of this troubled and wounded metropolis, the center of the world and the existential periphery that invokes [her] consolation."[1816] Mary, the mother of the Lord, is the archetype of every human being[1817] and the archetype of women, according to Scola.[1818] He cites affirmatively certain passages from John Paul II's 1987 Encyclical *Redemptoris Mater*, in

---

[1814] Andrea Tornielli, *Il futuro e la speranza: vita e magistero del cardinale Angelo Scola* (Milan: Edizioni Piemme, 2011), 16.

[1815] "Spiritual Exercises Friends of the Seminary," Seminario di Milano, 2 September 2015, https://www.seminario.milano.it/news_seminario/esercizi-spirituali-amici-del-seminario-10072.html (translated from Italian).

[1816] "Rosary Prayer in the Duomo, Presided Over by Cardinal Angelo Scola," Parish of the Divine Worker Jesus – Milan, 27 May 2014, http://www.gesudivinlavoratoremilano.it/index.php?option=com_icagenda&view=list&layout=event&id=11&Itemid=129.

[1817] Tornielli, *Il futuro e la speranza*, 54.

[1818] Ibid., 55.

which John Paul says that Mary is the model for women of the "self-offering totality of love" (no. 46).

Vocations

Encouraging vocations of all kinds, Scola wrote the people of the Diocese of Milan in 2015 a pastoral letter titled, "Educate Yourself in the Thought of Christ."[1819] In this synthesis of his personalism and pastoral commitment to Catholic teaching, Scola wrote, "In the Church through communion, at the school of Scripture, Tradition and the Magisterium, we make Christ's thoughts and feelings our own, which grow progressively in us by generating a mentality. The encounter with Jesus for the believer is the source of a new way of thinking about affections, work, rest and celebration, education, pain, life and death, evil and justice." He insists that Christian spirituality is not a generic religious sense, or some mere practical outcome, but "is rooted in the Incarnation of the Son of God and therefore in the inhabitation of the Spirit in us as the Generator of communion."[1820]

GOVERNING OFFICE

Grosseto

Angelo Scola's first pastoral assignment was to the Diocese of Grosseto, situated on Italy's western coast between Florence and Rome. Scola's chief concerns there included the education of children and youth, vocations and clergy formation, pastoral care for laborers whose job security was threatened due to the dismantling of mines in Grosseto, and family culture. During this time, Scola wrote and published a book addressed to young people and focused on the subject of the Church's educational mission,

---

[1819] "Pastoral letter from Cardinal Angelo Scola: 'Educate Yourself in the Thought of Christ,'" *Avvenire*, 8 September 2015, https://www.avvenire.it/chiesa/ pagine/lettera-pastorale-scola-sintesi-diocesi (translated from Italian).

[1820] Angelo Scola, "Spirituality and Care," Angelo Scola, 20 January 2020, https://angeloscola.it/spiritualita-e-cura/.

titled *And Who Am I? A Bishop Speaks to the Young*. His first pastoral letter,[1821] "You Will Be Truly Free," was published in 1992 not long after he was ordained a bishop. In it, Scola focused on the connection between beauty and hope.[1822] Scola founded a choir, "Gaudete," during his years in Grosseto.[1823] When he had arrived, diocesan schools were in poor shape: only a few nursery schools and one grammar school were operational.[1824] As a result of his efforts, the Mother of Grace middle school opened its doors in 1994.

Italian journalist Andrea Tornielli devoted a chapter in his 2011 book *The Future and Hope: The Life and Teaching of Cardinal Angelo Scola*[1825] to Scola's pastoral ministry in Grosseto. In that chapter Tornielli notes that Scola's name was unknown to the people of Grosseto when he was announced on July 20, 1991, as the successor to Adelmo Tacconi. Scola quickly won his new flock over by his attentiveness to the youth, for whom he regularly celebrated special Masses, whom he accompanied on pilgrimages, and whom he encouraged in their discernment of priestly or religious vocations. His encouragement of vocational discernment found institutional footing in the creation of the *Gruppo di verifica,* a supportive community for young men and women discerning calls to religious and consecrated life.

Tornielli also recounts how Scola reopened the diocesan seminary —which had been closed for twenty-three years—in response to a group of young men from the *Gruppo di verifica* who said that they wanted to become priests. Scola also started a theology school in the diocese so that seminarians would not have to travel to take their studies. He oversaw the creation of a Christian radio station, Toscana Oggi. A diocesan priest in

---

[1821] "A Grosseto la prima esperienza pastorale," Chiesa di Milano, 12 September 2011, www.chiesadimilano.it/news/chiesa-diocesi/a-grosseto-la-prima-esperienza-pastorale-71862.html.

[1822] "Cardinal Scola Opens the Beauty Week," *Il Tirreno*, 22 October 2017, iltirreno.gelocal.it/grosseto/cronaca/2017/10/21/news/il-cardinale-scola-apre-la-settimana-della-bellezza-1.16021379 (translated from Italian).

[1823] Ibid.

[1824] Tornielli, *Il futuro e la speranza*, tinyurl.com/y2bzr7n9.

[1825] Tornielli, *Il futuro e la speranza*, 83-97.

Grosseto with whom Scola collaborated closely in the course of energetically pursuing his vision for a renewed local church stated that, even after Scola was recalled to Rome by John Paul II, he always replied quickly and helpfully to requests for counsel and advice.

When Pope John Paul II in 1995 wanted Scola to take up academic positions in Rome, he resisted. Scola wanted to continue his pastoral work at Grosseto, where he had served for fewer than four years.[1826]

Patriarch of Venice

Scola's next pastoral assignment was announced in 2002: he would be the next patriarch of Venice, a see that three twentieth-century popes had occupied prior to their election. The announcement surprised Scola. In his 2018 autobiography, *Ho scommesso sulla libertà* (I bet on liberty),[1827] he relates that John Paul II had personally assured him earlier that year that Scola would not be nominated for the See of Venice because John Paul II thought it more important that he remain the rector of the Lateran. When the pope invited Scola to dinner and informed him of his looming appointment, Scola immediately said yes.[1828]

In 2004, Scola founded an integrated educational system that spanned from primary school to university, the Fondazione Studium Generale Marcianum. The Marcianum comprised a theology faculty, a canon-law faculty, university courses, and primary and secondary schools. Its curriculum was interdisciplinary, spanning bioethics, religion, and cultural-heritage courses.[1829] Scola asserts that his primary reason for founding the Marcianum was to effect the "unity of the subject."[1830] The fragmentation and specialization of disciplines in contemporary education, he said, entailed the fragmentation of the knowing subject who learns and appropriates what

---

[1826] See Angelo Cardinal Scola, with Luigi Geninazzi, *Ho scommesso sulla libertà* (Milan: Solferino, 2018), 141. Quotations in the text are translated from Italian.

[1827] Scola, *Ho scommesso sulla libertà*.

[1828] Ibid., 163.

[1829] See ibid., 178-79.

[1830] Ibid., 176.

he is taught. The Marcianum, which was free of cost and open to Christian and non-Christian students alike, was an effort to restore the original vision of the university: to bring all knowledge into a harmonious whole, a single "subject" in the learning of which the thinking "subject" (the pupil) can achieve intellectual integration.[1831] Scola's successor, Cardinal Francesco Moraglia, downsized the foundation, but its canon-law faculty, created by Scola and currently the only one in Northern Italy, survives.[1832] Scola believes that his major mistake in administrating the Marcianum was in not identifying someone with stable roots in Venice who could administer the Marcianum once he, Scola, was no longer patriarch.[1833]

Oasis: *Christian-Muslim Dialogue*

In 2004 then-Archbishop Scola founded *Oasis*, an international journal published in English, French, Italian, Arabic, and Urdu, devoted to Christian-Muslim dialogue and to strengthening the bonds of understanding and support between Christians in the East and the West. Scola says that he began thinking of a project like *Oasis* in the aftermath of a meeting, organized by the Vatican nuncio in May of 2000, with seven representatives from diverse Eastern Catholic rites. At this meeting, Scola, who was then still at the Lateran, came under fire from members of the Eastern churches for doing nothing to help them in their plight, for failing to understand their churches, and for being completely ignorant of Islam. If it were not for this experience, Scola reports, he would not have thought to found *Oasis*, a primary objective of which is to overcome what Scola calls the "abysmal" reciprocal ignorance between Christians and Muslims.[1834] Ninety percent of Christians, if asked to explain what Islam is, could not do so, Scola surmised—and vice versa.[1835] "*Oasis* was founded," Scola wrote in

---

[1831] See ibid.

[1832] O'Grady, "Man Who Was Nearly Pope."

[1833] See Scola, *Ho scommesso sulla libertà*, 181.

[1834] See ibid., 182-83.

[1835] Gerard O'Connell, Scola: "A Certain Faith Paves the Way to Open Dialogue," *La Stampa*, 30 June 2011, www.lastampa.it/2011/06/30/vaticaninsider/eng/

2013, "because we realized there was a substantial mutual ignorance in terms of the two faiths. Ignorance causes fear to grow and hinders people from being able to interpret the processes that take place throughout history. We cannot stop these [phenomena from occurring], but we can try to influence their direction."[1836] Scola remains the president for life of the *Oasis* foundation.

Scola describes Venice as "the city of religions."[1837] It is home to one of only two European sees for Latin Church patriarchs. It has a small but vibrant Jewish community, and its rabbi and Scola maintained good terms while Scola was patriarch. In Scola's view, moreover, Venice generally exhibited the kind of interreligious public relationships that undergird and make possible a healthy democratic life.[1838] Interreligious dialogue, Scola says, is "not something additional to the act of faith but is a constitutive element of it."[1839]

Parish and Cultural Outreach, Evangelization

In 2005, Scola began a tour during which he visited every one of the 128 parishes in the diocese. This undertaking took him a full six years. He traveled every weekend except for some in the summer and during certain liturgical seasons.[1840] Scola said of this prolonged pastoral experience that it made him appreciate more deeply the importance of living the Faith in community. He also founded a "school of the method of Christian life," a community educational program that, in two cycles, gave three hundred

---

news/scola-a-certain-faith-paves-the-way-to-open-dialogue-NGcQrDfMu4L-nI7M0j1aPiJ/pagina.html.

[1836] "Scola Warns against European Decline as Church and Society Grow Old and Tired," *La Stampa*, 15 July 2019, https://www.lastampa.it/vatican-insider/en/2013/06/16/news/scola-warns-against-european-decline-as-church-and-society-grow-old-and-tired-1.36085037.

[1837] Scola, *Ho scommesso sulla libertà*, 171.

[1838] Ibid., 172.

[1839] Ibid., 146.

[1840] Ibid., 167.

groups within the diocese the opportunity to work through texts on themes of Christian community, faith, and culture.[1841]

While in Venice, Scola fostered close practical relationships with political and cultural leaders, especially with Venice's mayor, Massimo Cacciari. He teamed up with them to address the problems that can beset any large, popular city and that beset Venice in a particular way as a hugely popular tourist site.[1842] On one occasion, Scola took the initiative to gather thirty or so leading political figures for an informal colloquy in which everyone was invited to speak freely and everyone was forbidden from publicizing anything that was said during the weekend-long gathering.[1843]

Scola has been credited with the idea for creating the Pontifical Council for Promoting the New Evangelization, which was founded by Pope Benedict in 2010.[1844] The author of dozens of books and many dozens of academic articles, Scola is also generally reputed to have raised the academic profile of the Lateran University while acting as its rector.[1845]

YouCat Controversy

During his time in Venice, Scola was publicly criticized by Christoph Cardinal Schönborn of Vienna about the Italian translation (from the German original) of *YouCat*—a youth catechism that distilled the 1997 *editio typica* of the *Catechism of the Catholic Church*. Schönborn cited deviations from doctrinal orthodoxy. The Italian manuscript included errors, such as the provision of an affirmative answer to the question of whether married couples can licitly practice contraception under some

---

[1841] Ibid., 169.

[1842] See ibid., 173-74.

[1843] See ibid., 174.

[1844] Edward Pentin, "Pontifical Council for the New Evangelization?," *National Catholic Register*, 26 April 2010, https://www.ncregister.com/blog/edward-pentin/pontifical_council_for_the_new_evangelization.

[1845] O'Connell, Scola: "A Certain Faith."

circumstances.[1846] It does not appear Cardinal Scola publicly responded to the rebuke.

Archbishop of Milan: Pastoral Letters

In 2011, Scola was appointed archbishop of Milan, Italy's most important financial and cultural center. With more than one thousand parishes and five million baptized Catholics, it is one of the world's largest dioceses. Scola quickly published a short pastoral letter in anticipation of 2012's seventh World Meeting of Families, focusing on the theme "Family, Work, and Celebration." (The meeting would include a visit by Pope Benedict XVI to Milan in the late summer.) In this pastoral letter[1847] Scola praises Pope Benedict's ministry, recalls the importance of the Petrine ministry in and for the Church, underscores the importance and role of family in society, and encourages the faithful of his new archdiocese to participate with open hearts in the meeting, especially by showing hospitality and renewing the education of children in the context of the home.

Scola's second pastoral letter[1848] was published in 2012, during the Year of Faith proclaimed by Pope Benedict. In it, Scola invited the faithful to renew their commitment to Christ and to rediscover the richness of faith, flowing forth from an encounter with the Christ who saves. He urged them also to root themselves in community with the Church of today, and also with the Tradition that transmits the Faith through generations.

[1846] "Vatican Embarrassed by Error-Filled Catechism Book," *Fox News*, 12 April 2011, www.foxnews.com/world/vatican-embarrassed-by-error-filled-catechism-book.

[1847] Angelo Cardinal Scola, "Il bene della famiglia. Per confermare la nostra fede (Anno 2011)," Chiesa di Milano, www.chiesadimilano.it/cms/documenti-del-vescovo/scola/as-lettere-pastorali/il-bene-della-famiglia-per-confermare-la-nostra-fede-anno-2011-14099.html.

[1848] Angelo Cardinal Scola, "Alla scoperta del Dio vicino (Anno 2012)," Chiesa di Milano, www.chiesadimilano.it/cms/documenti-del-vescovo/scola/as-lettere-pastorali/alla-scoperta-del-dio-vicino-anno-2012-14100.html.

Scola's third and by far the longest pastoral letter[1849] of his time in Milan, "The Field Is the World," is a reflection on the parable of the sower from Matthew 13. The entire world is the field—in Italian, the *campo*—of God, who, like the sower in the parable, initiates the entire drama of human freedom with His loving invitation to communion. God's Word calls forth our freedom, not only presenting us with but necessitating a choice to open ourselves to, or close ourselves off from, His love. Scola also reflects on the transition from Benedict to Francis in the midst of the Year of Faith, calling Benedict's resignation *un gesto umile di profonda fede*, "a humble gesture of profound faith."

Communion and Liberation

In Milan, Scola has sought to distance himself from the Communion and Liberation movement and was applauded for not bringing in friends from the movement to serve in Milan's curia, instead filling positions with members of Catholic Action, another Church movement—but one that has had public disputes with Communion and Liberation. The way he managed the diocesan curia was taken as proof that he could govern, according to his supporters. Being an Italian but outside the Roman Curia, Scola is believed to be in an ideal position to cleanse it of malpractice and corruption.

From 2015 to 2017, Scola undertook a pastoral visit program that involved all the deaneries (canonically sanctioned organizational combinations of parishes) of Milan in a series of visits and discussions between Scola and members of the deanery parishes.[1850] The heart of his message, Scola said of the preaching and teaching he would dispense during these visits, was the necessity for the faithful to place themselves into intimate contact with the life and history of Jesus Christ and the necessity of testifying boldly that

---

[1849] Angelo Cardinal Scola, "Il campo è il mondo. Vie da percorrere incontro all'umano (2013)," Chiesa di Milano, 2013, https://www.chiesadimilano.it/cms/documenti-del-vescovo/scola/as-lettere-pastorali/il-campo-e-il-mondo-vie-da-percorrere-incontro-allumano-2013-14098.html.

[1850] See Scola, *Ho scommesso sulla libertà*, 240.

Christianity is the most captivating way to live a properly human life.[1851] While acknowledging the lasting fruits of this pastoral visitation program, Scola rued the failure of his discourses on the fundamentals of the Faith really to take root in the Milanese faithful.[1852]

Carlo Acutis

Scola also presided over the close of the diocesan phase of the canonization process of Carlo Acutis, a Milanese boy who died of leukemia at age fifteen but who had practiced a deep devotion to the Eucharist and inspired many Catholics in Milan to grow in their faith. Scola spoke warmly of Carlo's influence on the diocese and on him.[1853] In February 2020, the Vatican announced that Carlo would be beatified.[1854]

TEACHING OFFICE

On Sexual Identity

Sexual difference for Scola is a fundamental datum of human existence. In an article he published in anticipation of the controversial 2014 Extraordinary Synod on the Family,[1855] he asserted that "every human being is situated as an individual within the difference between the sexes. We

---

[1851] See ibid.

[1852] See ibid., 241.

[1853] Federico Cenci, "INTERVIEW: Cardinal Scola: 'Carlo Acutis Points Out Highest Ideal to Young People: Jesus Christ,'" Zenit, 10 January 2017, zenit.org/articles/interview-cardinal-scola-carlo-acutis-points-out-highest-ideals-to-young-people/.

[1854] Courtney Mares, "Computer Programming Teen Carlo Acutis to Be Beatified," Catholic News Agency, 22 February 2020, https://www.catholicnewsagency.com/news/computer-programming-teen-venerable-carlo-acutis-to-be-beatified-19861.

[1855] Angelo Cardinal Scola, "Marriage and the Family between Anthropology and the Eucharist: Comments in View of the Extraordinary Assembly of the Synods of Bishops on the Family," Communio 41 (Summer 2014): 208-25.

must recognize that this can never be overcome."[1856] Scola helpfully explains that *difference* is not *diversity*. Diversity, he says, is when two autonomous subjects choose different paths while remaining in their autonomy. Diversity is interpersonal. Difference, however, is intrapersonal.[1857] "Every individual finds himself inscribed within this difference [between the sexes] and is always confronted with this other way of being a person, which is inaccessible to him."[1858] Scola speaks of the "insuperable" and "primordial" character of the difference between the sexes[1859] and says: "The original character of sexual difference indelibly marks every person in his or her singularity."[1860]

As such, Scola rejects the claim that the human person can exist as both male and female, simultaneously or alternately, or that one can decide what sexual identity one has or will have: "Man exists always and only as a masculine or feminine being.... He always has before himself the other way of being human, which is to him inaccessible."[1861] In his book *The Nuptial Mystery*,[1862] Scola asserts: "The [human] body (as sacrament of the whole person) is defined all the way through by its insuperable sexual difference."[1863] This remark is made in the context of a section on "androgyny," by which Scola means the claim that man is " 'capable' of both sexes"—in other words, capable of asserting himself as either male or female, depending on his psychological self-understanding.

The elimination of sexual difference from human relationships is a violation of the nature of the human person. Scola thinks that a culture that does not accept the revelation of the trinitarian God makes itself incapable of

---

[1856] Ibid., 211.

[1857] Ibid., 212.

[1858] Ibid.

[1859] Ibid.

[1860] Ibid., 215.

[1861] Angelo Cardinal Scola, "The Dignity and Mission of Women: The Anthropological and Theological Foundations," *Communio* 25 (Spring 1998): 46.

[1862] Angelo Scola, *The Nuptial Mystery*, trans. Michelle K. Boras (Grand Rapids, Mich.: Eerdmans, 2005). This edition combines what, in the Italian, had been two volumes.

[1863] Ibid., 374.

understanding sexual difference in a positive sense. Hence, Scola comments that "not for nothing does the open acceptance of homosexuality belong both to classical paganism and to the paganism of the present day."[1864] He stated in a 2013 interview, "I am convinced that a family based on marriage between a man and a woman and open to life is good for society." Asked about the growing civil recognition of same-sex unions, Scola said: "To guarantee individual rights to everyone is one thing. To attack the family either directly or indirectly is quite another."[1865]

The Nuptial Mystery, Women's Ordination, and Life Issues

Scola's fullest treatment of the nuptial mystery is in his book of the same name, published in English in 2005. In the book, Scola broaches several controversial moral issues and gives his "nuptial mystery" perspective on them. This book thus furnishes a very helpful insight into his thought.

Appendix 1[1866] of the book is a brief treatment of recent magisterial teaching, by Paul VI, John Paul II, and the Congregation for the Doctrine of the Faith (CDF), concerning the male priesthood. Here Scola makes very clear that he completely affirms the Church's teaching concerning the inadmissibility of women to the ministerial priesthood. He characterizes John Paul II's teaching in the 1994 Apostolic Letter Ordinatio Sacerdotalis thus: "the Catholic Church in no way possesses the faculty of conferring priestly ordination on women"; the Church has made "a definitive pronouncement on the impossibility of the admission of women to the ministerial priesthood." He affirms the CDF's classification of this teaching as "infallibly proposed by the ordinary and universal magisterium." He agrees with the argument of one Catholic scholar who avers that by restricting his appointments to the college of apostles to males, Jesus "expresses his positive intention to reserve the ministerial priesthood only to men." Scola says that the Church does "not have the power to make [women priests], if she wishes to remain faithful to herself." Finally, he affirms that "the

---

[1864] Scola, "Dignity and Mission of Women," 52.

[1865] "Scola Warns against European Decline."

[1866] All citations in this paragraph are from Scola, The Nuptial Mystery, 307-13.

definitive character of the magisterial pronouncement on the question of the inadmissibility of women to the ministerial priesthood is based, in its turn, on the proper nature of freedom and power in the church."

In the same book, Scola says of abortion: "When human life is no longer a sacred and inviolable right, but a consumer good which can be appraised in terms of usefulness or pleasure, a 'culture of death' [citation to *Evangelium Vitae*, no. 95] develops, threatening both man and his civilization."[1867] He also states that artificial fertilization "transforms the child into the object of a process of production."[1868]

Appendix 3 of the book touches upon the 1987 CDF instruction *Donum Vitae*, the "Instruction on Respect for Human Life in Its Origin and on the Dignity of Procreation." Scola defends the document, accepts its teachings, and seeks to explicate the anthropological-theological underpinnings of its two central norms, which are, first, "from the moral point of view, procreation is deprived of its proper perfection when it is not willed as the fruit of the conjugal act"; and second, "the procreation of a human being must be pursued as the fruit of a specific conjugal act of love between spouses."[1869]

Appendix 5 is on *Humanae Vitae*, which Scola calls "profoundly coherent with the tradition of the Church";[1870] there can be no doubt, he says, that "the doctrine of *Humanae Vitae* belongs to the ordinary universal Magisterium of the Church [note omitted]."[1871] Its essence Scola summarizes and affirms thus: "The life of a new human being," he says, "is willed and sought after rightly when it is awaited and welcomed as a 'gift from a gift,' when medical intervention aids but does not substitute the physical and spiritual gift that the spouses make of themselves in the conjugal act."[1872] Scola pins a host of problems on a scientific mentality fostered by the advent

---

[1867] Ibid., 169.
[1868] Ibid., 170.
[1869] Ibid., 331.
[1870] Ibid., 357.
[1871] Ibid., 361.
[1872] Ibid., 359.

of technical methods for manipulation of conception. "It [the scientific mentality according to which practices such as contraception, nonmarital sex, artificial reproductive technologies *should* be engaged in since they *can* be engaged in] is the idolatrous expression of a utopian madness, to which, particularly in the popular understanding, the achievements of science and technology remain exposed."[1873] Elsewhere in the book he writes that "a human being must always be conceived in an act of love-gift constituted by the conjugal union of a man and a woman."[1874]

On Communion for "Remarried" Divorcees

Scola has been unflinching in his defense of the teaching of John Paul II and Benedict XVI that persons party to a sacramental marriage who divorce and then civilly remarry may not be admitted to the Eucharist unless they obtain a decree of nullity for their first marriage. He affirms the indissolubility of marriage, grounding it in the nature of the sacrament's relationship to the Eucharist, which is the bond that unites Christ indefectibly to His Church; again, Ephesians 5 surfaces often in Scola's treatments of marriage and indissolubility.

For example, Scola has written: "Indissolubility is ultimately what makes Christian marriage a sacrament.... In fact, only by its being indissoluble does marriage participate in the nuptial sacrifice that the Word Incarnate makes of himself on the Cross to his Immaculate Bride."[1875] And in his statements leading up to 2014's Extraordinary Synod of Bishops,[1876] Scola

---

[1873] Angelo Cardinal Scola, "The Nuptial Mystery: A Perspective for Systematic Theology?," *Communio* 30 (Summer 2003): 217.

[1874] Scola, *The Nuptial Mystery*, 135. Scola speaks of the "objective inadequacy of every act of human procreation which is not the fruit of the love expressed in the conjugal union of man and woman." Ibid., 137.

[1875] Angelo Cardinal Scola, "The Nuptial Mystery at the Heart of the Church," *Communio* (Winter 1998), https://www.communio-icr.com/articles/view/the-nuptial-mystery-at-the-heart-of-the-church.

[1876] Vatican insider Sandro Magister notes that Scola's opposition to the Kasper Proposal was known at the time of the synods. See Sandro Magister, "Figments. If Instead of Bergoglio They Had Elected Cardinal Scola Pope," *L'Espresso*, 6 September 2018, magister.blogautore.espresso.repubblica.

unequivocally affirmed the indissolubility of sacramental marriage.[1877] He states that the state or condition of persons who have entered a second bond while the first is still valid is what makes it "impossible" for those persons to receive the Eucharist worthily. "This condition [of the second 'marriage'] is one that needs to be changed in order to correspond to what is effected in these two sacraments [marriage and the Eucharist]."[1878] Scola points out that the Eucharist is not a sacrament of healing. It is not, contrary to what some Catholics assert, just there for those "who need grace."[1879] What the Eucharist effects and signifies is of its nature such that those who *inter alia* persist in second "marriages" that are objectively adulterous are not in a state to receive it worthily.

Scola testifies that in his pastoral ministry he has come to know couples in "second marriages" who, with the grace of God, have come to live as brother and sister in complete continence. As such, he affirms the possibility of this "solution" to the problem of the divorced and "remarried," affirms John Paul II's commendation of it, and encourages Christians to attempt it.[1880] Scola also suggests a new canonical model for handling annulment cases. He proposes that a bishop or his delegates, instead of a tribunal, could exercise authority, following the example of canonical administrative procedures currently governing the process of dissolving nonconsummated marriages (CIC 1697-1706) or dissolving consummated marriages for reasons of faith (CIC 1143-1150).[1881]

Scola reaffirmed his view on divorce, remarriage, and the Eucharist in *Ho scommesso sulla libertà*, alleging that he also expressed this view of his

---

it/2018/09/06/figments-if-instead-of-bergoglio-they-had-elected-cardinal-scola-pope/?refresh_ce.

[1877] See Scola, "Marriage and the Family," 210, 216, 217, 222. See also Scola, "Dignity and Mission of Women," 52: "Indissolubility constitutes the destiny and the very core of the relation of man and woman in marriage."

[1878] Scola, "Marriage and the Family," 219.

[1879] Ibid., 220.

[1880] Ibid., 221.

[1881] Ibid., 223.

privately to Pope Francis.[1882] In sum, Scola's sexual ethics are remarkably consistent with those of John Paul II and Benedict XVI.

Scola affirms that the Magisterium is competent to teach authoritatively on matters of morality and natural law. Scola states that "the Encyclical *Veritatis Splendor*, in the doctrinal core of its teaching, affirms 'the universality and immutability of the moral commandments, especially those which prohibit always and without exception intrinsically evil acts' (n. 115)."[1883] Here he also cites favorably on the subject of moral absolutes the work of the American moral theologian William E. May, who, together with the Australian legal philosopher John Finnis, was the first layperson ever appointed to the International Theological Commission, for the 1986 quinquennium (five-year appointment term). "It belongs to the nature of the Magisterium," Scola has written, "to enunciate Christian doctrine by affirming its contents and marking its parameters."[1884]

Priestly Celibacy

As mentioned above, Scola is a staunch defender of the all-male priesthood, but he also defends the Roman Catholic Church's discipline of mandatory celibacy for those who receive Holy Orders. In a 2010 speech at the end of a large Mass in St. Mark's Basilica in Venice, responding to recently surfaced allegations of pedophilia among priests and consecrated persons, Scola told the congregation: "It is misleading and unacceptable to question, from cases of pedophilia in the ecclesiastical environment, the holy celibacy that the Latin Church asks for, in full liberty, of the candidates to the priesthood in the light of a very long tradition."[1885]

[1882] Dan Hitchens, "Cardinal Scola: Communion for the remarried contradicts Church teaching," *Catholic Herald*, 6 September 2018, catholicherald. co.uk/news/2018/09/06/cardinal-scola-communion-for-the-remarried-contradicts-church-teaching/.

[1883] Scola, "The Nuptial Mystery," 360. On page 361, Scola again affirms that the Magisterium is competent to offer authentic interpretation of the moral law.

[1884] Scola, "Dignity and Mission of Women," 45.

[1885] Angelo Cardinal Scola, "Condemning Pedophilia, Cardinal Angelo Scola Explains the Beauty and Value of Celibacy for Priests," *Oasis*, 28 March

Universalism

Human freedom is a leading theme of Scola's work. To his mind, the encounter with Christ is what elicits human freedom and sets it off on its path. Scola would then presumably countenance the prospect of eternal damnation for those who grossly abuse their freedom. But Scola does not often preach or write about damnation, let alone as a reality (not merely a possibility that may well go unrealized). He is also a fervent disciple of Hans Urs von Balthasar, who strenuously argued in his later years that the hope that nobody will be lost is theologically well founded.

Scola has praised the Second Vatican Council's 1965 Dogmatic Constitution on Divine Revelation *Dei Verbum* for stressing the "event" nature of revelation, which is not merely the transmission of information (propositions) but a personal self-disclosure appropriated only by a personal assent, the yes that initiates one into the relationship being held out as an invitation. Scola was very favorable toward *Verbum Domini*, the Post-Synodal Apostolic Exhortation on the Word of God in the Life and Mission of the Church promulgated in 2010 by Pope Benedict, which cites many passages from *Dei Verbum*, though not those most central to its treatment of the Gospels' historicity. Scola commends *Verbum Domini*'s clarity and precision in dealing with thorny questions of Scripture and revelation, praising its accessibility even to non-theologians.[1886]

Migrants and Refugees

The meeting in Damascus organized by the Vatican nuncio between Scola and representatives of Eastern Catholic rites in the year 2000 left a mark on Scola's thinking and led him to found *Oasis*. In his 2018 autobiography, Scola is asked several questions about his work with *Oasis*. These questions

---

2018, www.oasiscenter.eu/en/cardinal-scola-addresses-sexual-abuse-crisis.

[1886] Angelo Cardinal Scola, " 'La Parola di Dio ci chiama e ci coinvolge'. Il Patriarca su 'Verbum Domini,' " Angelo Scola, 2 March 2011, https://angeloscola.it/la-parola-di-dio-ci-chiama-e-ci-coinvolge-il-patriarca-su-verbum-domini-2/.

touch upon immigration policy, religious freedom, and the compatibility of Islam with Christian civilization.

Scola believes that it is incumbent upon political institutions to direct and govern mass migration. But he believes European governments have not done a good job of this. Citing a 2017 report indicating that more than 250 million persons had left their country of origin that year—Scola points out that this is about 50 percent higher than the number from the year 2000—he speaks of a "gross naiveté" of which the West is guilty—namely, the mass media's presenting Western life as being so wonderful that it has attracted many migrants who seek those places where the world is "better" than where they are.[1887] "We have been blind and deaf for many years," Scola says, to the plight of the immigrant and to the conditions that foster it.

Scola rejects the relevance of a distinction between refugees and economic immigrants for purposes of immigration policy.[1888] "How can one think of welcoming only the former while rejecting the latter?" he asks.[1889] Such thinking, he states, lends itself toward a caste-system mentality proper to the Middle Ages.[1890]

Islam

Scola acknowledges that Islam needs to initiate a transformation with respect to its doctrines on liberty of conscience. Recalling a meeting in Amman, Jordan, sponsored by *Oasis*, Scola notes that while his interlocutors—members of an Islamic institution noted and respected for its openness to dialogue and led by Prince Ghazi bin Muhammad bin Talal—were "in principle favorable" to liberty of conscience, they nevertheless would not consent to subscribe to a clear recognition of freedom of conversion.[1891]

Asked directly whether Islam needs to accept the principle of the laicity, the secular status, of the state, Scola replies: "In principle it is correct

---

[1887] See Scola, *Ho scommesso sulla libertà*, 185-86.
[1888] See ibid., 186.
[1889] Ibid.
[1890] Ibid.
[1891] See ibid., 191.

to recall the distinction between the religious and civil spheres, but in the concrete doing so risks becoming an abstract discourse that does not make contact with how Islam was originated and how it has developed."[1892] Scola points out that laicization efforts by Turkey's president Recep Erdoğan had an "inverted result" from what Westerners would want from Islamic state laicization, and he points to France as an instance of a country in which the separation of religion and state has been implemented in an extreme way. Scola also accuses Westerners of being disingenuous when, on the one hand, they exhort Muslims to submit to the "purifying bath of secularism" while, on the other, they bemoan the negative effects of the advanced secularism in the West on Christianity and society.[1893]

Scola asserts that Muslim countries should make real the respect for the liberty of every believer living in their jurisdictions. He acknowledges that "it is undeniable that the expansion of Islam by way of Muhammad's activities happened by use of violent force," and states clearly that "Islam must also do this [recognize freedom of conscience]": "The fact remains that the Muslim world is called to reflect in a new way on the theme of liberty."[1894] Similarly, Scola said in 2011 that "it is necessary to foster an evolution in Islam so as to arrive at a distinction between the religious dimension and the civil dimension."[1895] In a 2010 interview, Scola stated that suicide bombing is "intrinsically an evil."[1896] And he has written: "There exists a violence that is perpetrated in the name of God. Religions must remove all legitimacy from these criminal acts."[1897]

[1892] Ibid.

[1893] See ibid., 192.

[1894] See ibid., 193-94.

[1895] O'Connell, "Certain Faith Paves the Way."

[1896] Angelo Cardinal Scola, "Europe Must Act in a More Clear-Cut Way for the Respect of Fundamental Rights," *Oasis*, 10 January 2011, https://www.oasiscenter.eu/en/europe-must-act-in-a-more-clear-cut-way-for-the-respect-of-fundamental-rights.

[1897] Ibid.

Religious Freedom

In a December 2012 speech given shortly before the seventeen hundredth anniversary of the Edict of Milan, Scola noted that because bedrock anthropological institutions and experiences such as marriage, childbirth, and death have been shorn of their Christian religious significance in Western liberal democracies, religious freedom has become an increasingly important and vexed topic.[1898] Referring to the U.S. bishops' resistance to the Obama administration's health-care mandate that required religious employers, including hospitals and schools, to provide free contraceptives, abortifacients, and sterilization services to those employees whose health care these institutions covered, Scola noted that unless religious freedom is considered to be the first and most important of human rights, the whole edifice of human rights will crumble. He reflected that when religious freedom is construed as indifference on the part of the state to religious phenomena—he adduced the French model of laicity as an example—what happens is that the state adopts a "neutrality" toward religion *simpliciter* that is, practically, an enshrining of one controversial worldview, secularism, over others (religious worldviews). In that situation, religious worldviews are *de facto* evacuated from the public domain and relegated to the realm of the private, mythological, and folkloric. Alleged "religious neutrality" often results in the official promotion of an atheistic culture.

Scola on Being a Papal Contender

Notwithstanding his long and deep friendship with Joseph Ratzinger and the widely held view that he was Benedict's anointed successor (when Benedict presented him with the pallium in a separate ceremony after Scola's appointment to Milan, it was taken as a clear sign), Scola states that he, like everyone else, was "absolutely surprised" by Benedict XVI's announcement on February 11, 2013, that he was resigning.[1899] Scola was

---

[1898] Much of Scola's speech was recorded in the Italian-language edition of *L'Osservatore Romano*, a copy of which was furnished to the author by a source in Rome.

[1899] Scola, *Ho scommesso sulla libertà*, 259.

a leading "favorite" papabile for the ensuing conclave. The Italian Bishops' Conference even erroneously published a communiqué when white smoke was spotted at the Sistine Chapel, congratulating Scola on his election as the new pope. It is said that Scola garnered the highest tally of votes during the initial round of voting in that conclave.[1900] Despite the media's consistent presentation, before, during, and subsequent to the conclave, that he was the favorite, Scola claims never to have believed it: "I never believed in the possibility of becoming pope," he writes in his 2018 autobiography.[1901] Scola confesses to having felt "marginalized" by the media's presentation of him as the "loser" of the "contest" with Bergoglio, who was depicted as representing the "Church of the future" in contrast to Scola's more traditional and thus, in the eyes of some, backward-looking outlook on Church life.[1902]

Coronavirus Reflection

During the 2020 coronavirus pandemic, Cardinal Scola advocated a dual attitude: to remain united by following the government's instructions, even when it involves some sacrifice, and to reflect on the meaning of life. He said the suspension of the Mass was an opportunity to develop more of a hunger for the Eucharist and the Word of God. He disagreed with those who said the virus was divine punishment. "God wants the good," he said. "The idea of divine punishment, especially with a dramatic situation like the one we are experiencing, is not part of the Christian view." The proper Christian view, he said, is one that does not involve God's having "recourse to the practice of punishment in order to convert."[1903]

[1900] Magister, "Figments."

[1901] Scola, *Ho scommesso sulla libertà*, 262.

[1902] See ibid.

[1903] Fabio Colagrande, "Cardinal Scola, Coronavirus: An Opportunity to Ask Ourselves about the Meaning of Life," Vatican News, 6 March 2020, https://www.vaticannews.va/it/chiesa/news/2020-03/cardinale-angelo-scola-milano-messa-coronavirus-italia.html (translated from Italian).

COMMUNIO *THEOLOGY*

Tracey Rowland is a member of the ninth and current quinquennium of the Vatican's International Theological Commission (ITC). The ITC consists of leading theologians worldwide tasked with publishing documents on topics of contemporary import to the Church. In her book *Catholic Theology*,[1904] Rowland describes the school of thought sharing the name of the international journal founded by "conservative" theologians not long after Vatican II ended in 1965. One characteristic of this *Communio* school is fidelity to the Magisterium and an emphasis on a philosophical personalism utilized to interpret Scripture.

Having described the *Communio* school, Rowland writes:

> The leading proponent of the *Communio* approach to theology in contemporary times is Cardinal Angelo Scola, the Archbishop of Milan and the alleged runner-up in the last papal conclave, described by *The Tablet* as the Crown Prince under the papacies of John Paul II and Benedict XVI.... He developed John Paul II's ideas contained in his *Catechesis on Human Love* in conjunction with Balthasar's ideas on Trinitarian theology, and the combination of the two produced his [Scola's] proposal for a Nuptial Mystery perspective for systematic theology.[1905]

Here some background is necessary. Following the close of Vatican II in December 1965, a group of theologians, many of whom had been very influential at the Council, founded an academic journal, *Concilium*, devoted to continued exploration of the "spirit" of Vatican II's *aggiornamento* reforms. These theologians included Yves Congar, Hans Küng, Johann Baptist Metz, Karl Rahner, Henri de Lubac, Hans Urs von Balthasar, Joseph Ratzinger, and Edward Schillebeeckx. But de Lubac, Balthasar, and Ratzinger resigned before long from *Concilium*'s board and, in 1972, founded an alternative

---

[1904] Tracey Rowland, *Catholic Theology* (London: Bloomsbury, 2017).
[1905] Ibid., 129-30.

and, as it is commonly thought, rival theological journal, *Communio*, whose editors and contributors were less keen on instigating "Vatican III" and who interpreted the Council through its texts, not its "spirit."

Communio, meaning "communion," was chosen as the title by its founders because, whereas a council (the meaning of the Latin *concilium*) is an act within the life of the Church—an occasion on which the Church pauses and deliberates about particular issues—communion is what the Church *is*: a communion of persons in the one Lord Jesus Christ. As such, the founding editors of *Communio* believed that the enduring bond of persons united in communion in Christ—in the Trinity, in the communion of saints, through the Eucharist, through the nuptial mystery of marriage, and so forth—was the proper locus for basic theological reflection.

Scola was and is an admirer of Balthasar, Ratzinger, and de Lubac. He published a book-length interview with Balthasar (published in English in 1989) and constantly cites him in his writings. Scola's thought takes its decisive orientations from Balthasar's work. Rowland's identification of him as the quintessence of the *Communio* school is well founded.

In a 2011 interview, Scola stated that the most important question confronting the Church today is whether we are living in a postmodern world.[1906] A year earlier,[1907] Scola had defined what he meant by "postmodern" in reference to three characteristics. First, there is widespread advanced secularization, which Scola defined in reference to the third of the three meanings of "secularization" that Canadian philosopher Charles Taylor furnishes in his 2007 study *A Secular Age*: namely, faith in God is but one valid option among other valid options. Relatedly, Scola states in the same interview that the problem besetting the modern world is the divorce between life and faith. The Faith seems irrelevant; its practice does not

---

[1906] O'Connell, "Certain Faith Paves the Way."

[1907] Angelo Cardinal Scola, "'God's Plan for Man and Woman in the Sacrament of Marriage': The Nuptial Mystery and Contemporary Culture," Dicastery for the Laity, the Family and Life, 29 April 2010, http://www.laityfamily-life.va/content/dam/laityfamilylife/Documenti/donna/teologia/english/nuptial-mistery-contemporary-culture.pdf.

seem to have purchase or import for life in the modern world, especially for the young. Second, freedom of choice is now construed as unbounded by any objective standard of right decision. Third and finally, truth is now reduced to the technically feasible: if you can do something, you must.

In the same interview Scola suggests that the crisis for the Church in the third millennium is the question "Who is man?" This is a question of anthropology. And it is in the context of theological anthropology that Scola has developed and defended the "nuptial mystery" perspective of which Rowland writes.

The nuptial-mystery perspective on systematic theology, Scola once wrote, places the themes of marriage and family at the heart of the knowledge of the Faith.[1908] For Scola, the nuptial mystery is located at the intersection of sexual difference, love, and procreation.[1909] It is the perfect identity in difference, the unity-in-duality, that finds its paradigm in the one-flesh communion between man and wife but which also expresses the relationship between the Father, Son, and Spirit; Scola often has recourse to Balthasar's thought that the relationship between husband, wife, and the child who is the fruit of their love is the most apt natural analogue for the trinitarian relations[1910] and for Christ and His Church. "The mystery of the Trinity ... is the ultimate foundation of dual unity," he writes.[1911] For Scola, who here follows Balthasar, the loving procession of Father and Son generating the Spirit is the ontological basis for the possibility of the Incarnation, in which divine and human natures in Christ are "married." The Incarnation is in turn the basis for the Church poured forth from Christ's side, making Christians brides to the Bridegroom. This mystical union, in turn, grounds Christian marriage as the human paradigm of (but not exhaustive of!) the nuptial mystery; Ephesians 5, wherein Paul, in verses 21 through 32, compares the union of man and wife to the union of Christ with the Church, is a leitmotif threading through all of Scola's writings.

[1908] Scola, "The Nuptial Mystery: A Perspective for Systematic Theology?"
[1909] Scola, "The Nuptial Mystery at the Heart of the Church," 630-62.
[1910] Ibid., 655.
[1911] Scola, "Dignity and Mission of Women," 51 and cf. generally 42-56.

By "nuptial mystery" Scola means, first of all, "the concrete experience of the man-woman relationship that lies at the very origin of the phenomenon of nuptiality in all its various types, and thus forms its constitutive nucleus."[1912] Nuptiality manifests an asymmetrical reciprocity between the "I" and the "other."[1913] There is another modality, another irreducible way, of being human than the way I experience: if I am a man, that other way is existing as human as female (and vice versa). She is identical in her being *qua* person possessed of a human nature, but different in her being *qua* sexed.

Thus, the nuptial mystery and *communio* are connected insofar as both are about man's creation in God's image and likeness, a characteristic in virtue of which man is called to communion: "*Communio* as an essential dimension of man is part of his being in the image of God."[1914]

SUMMARY

Angelo Scola's life has been marked by his fidelity to a personalistic vision of Catholic life and thought. His friendship with Don Luigi Giussani and Communion and Liberation is one example. Another was his close collaboration with John Paul II, especially the pontiff's teachings about sexual morality and the human person. Still another is Scola's rootedness in the *Communio* school and his friendship with Joseph Ratzinger, later Benedict XVI.

He has significant experience both as a professor and scholar, as well as pastorally as archbishops of Venice and Milan, both traditionally "papabile" sees. His role in founding the Pontifical Council for Promoting the New Evangelization indicates the importance he places on helping non-Christians convert to the Catholic Faith.

Given Scola's significant intellect, his writings and speeches can be dense and, in keeping with the work of Communion and Liberation, overly intellectual and sometimes inaccessible to the common man. During

[1912] Scola, "The Nuptial Mystery at the Heart of the Church," 639.
[1913] Ibid., 643.
[1914] Scola, "Dignity and Mission of Women."

Benedict's pontificate, he took an optimistic view of the Church's travails and was skeptical of descriptions of a "Church in crisis." He also disdains the expression "crisis of the family" and believes there still is a big zest for family life; "we are just living through the period of big choices." The problem, according to Scola, is not that today's men and women do not consider families important, but that they do not know how to preserve them. He has nevertheless shown sound orthodoxy regarding controversial matters, such as the inadmissibility of women to the ministerial priesthood and his opposition to the "culture of death" in all its forms.

A critic of secularization, Scola nevertheless has praised an authentic "laicity," which ought to foster holiness among the laity in their proper sphere, which is the world. His various comments on the importance of bringing sound ethical and anthropological judgments to bear on civil life bespeak a recognition that true morality, which the Church proclaims in its teaching, is essential for the common good. He has been near the top of the list of *papabili* for the last two conclaves, and with administrative, pastoral, and spiritual characteristics such as he possesses, it is no surprise.

SERVICE TO THE CHURCH

Ordination to the Priesthood: 18 July 1970
Ordination to the Episcopate: 21 September 1991
Elevation to the College of Cardinals: 21 October 2003

Education
- Catholic University, Milan; Doctorate in philosophy
- Fribourg, Switzerland; Doctorate in theology

Assignments
- 1965-1967: High school teacher[1915]

[1915] Tornielli, "Scola: The Reason Why He Left."

- 1979-1982: Assistant Professor of Fundamental Moral Theology, University of Fribourg
- 1982-1991: Professor of Theological Anthropology, John Paul II Institute for Studies on Marriage and the Family
- 1982-1991: Professor of Contemporary Christology, Pontifical Lateran University
- 1991-1995: Bishop of Grosseto, Italy
- 1995-2002: Rector of the Pontifical Lateran University
- 1995-2002: Dean of the John Paul II Institute for Studies on Marriage and the Family
- 2002-2011: Patriarch of Venice
- 2003-2017: Cardinal-priest of Santi XII Apostoli
- 2011-2017: Archbishop of Milan
- 2017: Retired

Membership
- Congregation for the Doctrine of the Faith
- Congregation for the Clergy
- Congregation for Divine Worship and the Discipline of the Sacraments
- Congregation for the Oriental Churches
- Pontifical Council for the Family
- Pontifical Council for Culture
- Pontifical Council for Promoting the New Evangelization
- Council of Cardinals for the Study of Organizational and Economic Affairs of the Holy See[1916]

[1916] "Scola Card. Angelo," Vatican, http://press.vatican.va/content/salastampa/en/documentation/cardinali_biografie/cardinali_bio_scola_a.html.

LUIS ANTONIO GOKIM CARDINAL TAGLE

"It Is the Lord"

Born: 21 June 1957
Manila, Philippines
Nationality: Filipino
Title: Archbishop of Manila

BIOGRAPHY

Luis Antonio Gokim Tagle's paternal grandfather was from an upper-class Filipino family, and his maternal grandmother was from a well-off Chinese family that immigrated to the Philippines. One of two children, he often goes by his nickname, "Chito." Originally preparing to become a physician, Chito was somewhat "tricked" into considering seminary, which later led him to laugh about how the "jokes" of God and others can influence one's life.[1917] Jesuits have played an important role in his formation, having taught him in the San José Seminary and then at the Ateneo de Manila University, where he earned a bachelor's degree in 1977 and then a master of arts. Leaving the Jesuits, he was ordained a priest for the Archdiocese of Manila in 1982. Immediately, he became the spiritual director and professor at the local seminary, and then its rector from 1983 to 1985. Sent to the United States by his bishop, he earned a license in theology in 1987 and then a doctorate in 1991 on the topic of episcopal collegiality in the praxis and doctrine of Paul VI, under the theologian Joseph Komonchak. This opened the door for Tagle to become a prominent proponent of the "Bologna School" of ecclesiology and historiography, which views the Second Vatican Council as a rupture from the pre-conciliar period. For fifteen subsequent years, he sat on the editorial board of the History of Vatican II historical research project, overseen by Giuseppe Alberigo.

Returning to the Philippines, Tagle served as Episcopal Vicar for Religious from 1993 to 1995 and as pastor of the cathedral parish in Imus from 1998 to 2001. In 2001, John Paul II appointed Tagle bishop of the Imus Diocese, where he served until Benedict nominated him archbishop of Manila in 2011. His theological apostolate has included serving as a member of the International Theological Commission from 1997 until 2003. He has also participated in the Federation of Asian Episcopal Conferences. Benedict XVI created Tagle a cardinal in 2012, after which time he has served on many councils and in many congregations. Having participated in recent Synods of Bishops in Rome (on the New Evangelization in 2012, on the family in 2014 and 2015, on youth in 2018, and on the Amazon in 2019), since 2015 Tagle has been president of Caritas Internationalis, reelected for another four-year term in 2019. More recently, Pope Francis called Tagle to reside in Rome as prefect of the prestigious Congregation

---

[1917] Shalom World, "Special Interviews from Asia: Cardinal Luis Antonio Tagle," YouTube video, 20:26, posted 29 June 2018, https://www.youtube.com/watch?v=q2YqAVHgJa8.

for the Evangelization of Peoples. In 2020, the Pope also elevated Tagle to the rank of cardinal-bishop, possibly signifying the Filipino cardinal as a favored successor.

SANCTIFYING OFFICE

Humanitarian and Pastoral Work

Ranked among the youngest cardinals in the Catholic Church, Tagle heads the Archdiocese of Manila, one of the most densely populated cities in the world, and capital of the Philippines.[1918] His country is unique for many reasons: it is Asia's only predominantly Christian country, where abortion is illegal, divorce and same-sex "marriage" are not permitted under the law, and the Church is still fighting the government's plan to distribute free contraceptives to the poor. Cardinal Tagle has been appointed to leadership roles for various charitable and humanitarian works, including president of Caritas Internationalis and the prefect of the Congregation for the Evangelization of Peoples.[1919]

Tagle is a consistent supporter of Pope Francis' approach to governing the Church and to Church teaching. "[Francis'] first year in a way articulated many of the things that I believed in and probably could not or have not been able to articulate verbally or even pastorally in terms of action," Tagle explains.[1920] The American journalist John Allen described Tagle as the "Asian Pope Francis."[1921] Fr. Joseph Komonchak, Tagle's doctoral dis-

---

[1918] Ibid.

[1919] Salvador Miranda, *The Cardinals of the Holy Roman Church*, https://webdept. fiu.edu/~mirandas/bios2012-ii.htm#Tagle.

[1920] Quoted in Cindy Wooden, *Luis Antonio Tagle: Leading by Listening* (Collegeville, Minn.: Liturgical Press, 2015), 59.

[1921] John L. Allen Jr., "Meet the Philippine Pope Francis," *Boston Globe*, 16 March 2014, http://www.bostonglobe.com/news/world/2014/03/15/ conversation-with-asian-pope-francis/tYuecMO8hOG2gW8mZE5rOO/story. html.

sertation director, agrees: "He was, in many respects by the way he exercised his ministry, a Pope Francis before Pope Francis."[1922]

Cardinal Tagle has been the president of Caritas Internationalis since 2015. In August of 2015, just a few months after he became the new president, Cardinal Tagle encouraged Indonesia's Catholic community to be active in interfaith working groups to spread the message of Pope Francis' Encyclical Letter *Laudato Si'*.[1923] Tagle's message to Caritas encouraged members to be less wasteful and, instead, to be sacrificial and share with others in a form of "active love." In the presidential role, Tagle focuses on helping those who are in need, spiritually or physically, by responding to humanitarian needs, which is a reflection of Tagle's involvement in helping the poor in the Philippines.

As part of World Youth Day in January 2019, Tagle accepted a prophetic manifesto on behalf of the Church. Young activists created the manifesto, "calling for everyone, ourselves first, to urgently act to protect our planet and the poorest and most vulnerable people."[1924] Cardinal Tagle has been celebrated for his work with youth in Manila and other parts of the world. In one case, Tagle led the Baptism of more than four hundred children from some of Manila's poor districts.[1925]

[1922] Quoted in Wooden, *Luis Antonio Tagle*.

[1923] "Card. Tagle Urges Indonesian Bishops to Engage Other Faiths to Care for Creation," Vatican Radio, 20 August 2015, http://en.radiovaticana. va/news/2015/08/20/card_tagle_urges_other_faiths_to_join_in_care_for_creation/1166381.

[1924] "Top 10 Highlights 2019," *Global Catholic Climate Movement*, 17 December 2019, https://catholicclimatemovement.global/top-10-highlights-2019/#1; "Youth Manifesto," Laudato Si' Generation, https://laudatosigeneration. org/2019/04/04/youth-manifesto/.

[1925] "Cardinal Tagle Leads Baptism of 400 Children from Manila Slums," *UCA News*, 16 January 2017, https://www.ucanews.com/news/cardinal-tagle-leads-baptism-of-400-children-from-manila-slums/78099.

Media Presence

Cardinal Tagle has a strong media presence, including on social networking sites. Tagle has collaborated with Jesuit Communications in the Philippines for various television and radio productions, including *The Word Exposed*, *Prayer over Coffee*, and *Light Talk*.[1926] He has utilized each production to share his thoughts and reflections about the gospel, as well as evangelize those living in the Philippines and abroad. Tagle's messages during the various broadcasts may not be theologically complex but are admired by his audiences. Tagle is seen in many cases dressed in a simple clerical shirt and has regularly worn lay clothing in his public appearances, talks, and meetings. *The Word Exposed* continues to be produced and streamed live on Facebook from Rome every Sunday.[1927] Tagle has emphasized the importance of building relationships through virtual platforms and encountering others in more social gatherings, encouraging others to share personal stories and learn from one another.

Dancing Liturgies

During Tagle's installation as archbishop of Manila, his parents danced the Caracol, a traditional dance of the Cavite natives.[1928] Cardinal Tagle concelebrated the installation Mass of Msgr. Reynaldo Evangelista as the new bishop of Imus in 2013.[1929] During the offertory, Bishop Evangelista

---

[1926] "Cardinal Tagle: Evangelization through the Media," Jesuits, 28 January 2020, https://jesuits.global/en/stories/743-cardinal-tagle-evangelization-through-the-media.

[1927] Christina Hermoso, "Cardinal Tagle to Continue TV Program from Rome," *Manila Bulletin*, 8 March 2020, https://news.mb.com.ph/2020/03/08/cardinal-tagle-to-continue-tv-program-from-rome/.

[1928] Josephine Darang, "Colorful 'Caracol' Leads Tagle to Manila Cathedral Throne," *Philippine Daily Inquirer*, 18 December 2011, http://lifestyle.inquirer.net/27787/colorful-%E2%80%98caracol%E2%80%99-leads-tagle-to-manila-cathedral-throne/.

[1929] "The Bishop as the Chief Liturgical Dancer of His Diocese," *Rorate Caeli*, 25 June 2013, https://rorate-caeli.blogspot.com/2013/06/the-bishop-as-chief-liturgical-dancer_25.html; "Evangelista to Be Installed Bishop of Imus,"

and several priests began dancing the Caracol. The cardinal has also danced in front of an altar during youth gatherings.[1930] In January 2015, Cardinal Tagle opened the Philippine Conference on New Evangelization by celebrating the Misa ng Bayang Pilipino on a round platform with a round altar in the center. During the opening of the Mass, a line of men, women, and children danced four times around the stage with the altar on it. Following the procession of dancers, moving to the beat of a clapping audience, four men stood at the four corners of the stage (or the four points of the compass), blowing bullhorn trumpets.[1931] The Mass included colored lights and laser light projections.[1932]

In January 2015, Pope Francis visited Manila and celebrated a massive outdoor Mass arranged by Cardinal Tagle. According to reports, nearly six million Catholics attended the Mass.[1933] One of the reasons the Mass was so large was because Cardinal Tagle canceled all of the Sunday Masses in every church in the diocese for that day, forcing every Catholic wishing to fulfill his Sunday obligation to attend the outdoor papal Mass.[1934]

CBCP News, 3 June 2013, https://web.archive.org/web/20130711065510/http://cbcpnews.net/blog/2013/06/03/evangelista-to-be-installed-bishop-of-imus-on-june-5/.

[1930] Radyo Veritas, PH (@RadyoVeritasPH), "Cardinal Tagle doing the #Dab #Dabshot at the @ThePCNE #PCNE3 #Awa2016 #MayMercySaPCNE3 Have a blessed Sunday," Twitter, 16 July 2016, 10:11 p.m., https://twitter.com/Veritasph/status/754498623921065984.

[1931] Rev. Fr. Jessie G. Somosierra Jr., "Philippine Conference on New Evangelization 2," YouTube video, 6:34, posted 23 October 2013, https://youtu.be/me7ha9fOjIM.

[1932] Rev. Fr. Jessie G. Somosierra Jr., "Philippine Conference on New Evangelization 49," YouTube video, 14:59, posted 19 November 2013, https://youtu.be/emKhziQQ8Zc.

[1933] "Pope Francis in Manila: Six Million Attend Outdoor Mass," BBC News, 18 January 2015, http://www.bbc.com/news/world-asia-30869019.

[1934] Philippine News Agency, "Tagle Cancels Afternoon Masses on Sunday in All Churches under the Archdiocese of Manila in Connection with the Papal Mass at the Luneta," Manila Bulletin, 17 January 2015, https://web.archive.org/web/20151017123236/http://www.mb.com.ph/tagle-cancels-afternoon-

Liturgical Feasts, Pachamama

Tagle's approach to governing his local Church reflects his strong desire to reconcile or mesh Catholic life with local culture. On Ash Wednesday 2015, for example, Cardinal Tagle granted a dispensation from the canonically imposed fasting and abstinence from meat that mark the first day of Lent.[1935] Tagle said that this dispensation was made "in view of the celebration of the Chinese Lunar New Year, its cultural and spiritual importance and the traditional practices associated with it."[1936]

On October 4, 2019, Cardinal Tagle attended an event hosted at the Vatican Gardens which purported to celebrate the feast of St. Francis.[1937] During the event, a tree from Assisi was planted by Pope Francis and Amazonian leaders from Brazil, "as a symbol of integral ecology, to consecrate the Synod on Amazonia to Saint Francis, shortly before the fortieth anniversary of the papal proclamation of the Poverello of Assisi as the patron of ecologists."[1938] At the same time, the indigenous participants, with Tagle looking on, bowed down in a circle to what many said were Pachamama idols. The Vatican called them life and fertility symbols.

---

masses-on-sunday-in-all-churches-under-the-archdiocese-of-manila-in-connection-with-the-papal-mass-at-the-luneta/.

[1935] Deacon Greg Kandra, "Manila's Cardinal Tagle Grants Dispensation for Fasting, Abstinence on Ash Wednesday," Patheos, 18 February 2015, http://www.patheos.com/blogs/deaconsbench/2015/02/manilas-cardinal-tagle-grants-dispensation-for-fasting-abstinence-on-ash-wednesday/.

[1936] Ibid.

[1937] Vatican News, "Pope Francis-Feast of Saint Francis 2019-10-04," YouTube video, 1:13:00, posted 4 October 2019, https://www.youtube.com/watch?v=1wioisaIU2I.

[1938] "Feast of Saint Francis in the Vatican Gardens," Holy See Press Office, 4 October 2019, http://press.vatican.va/content/salastampa/en/bollettino/pubblico/2019/10/04/191004e.html.

GOVERNING OFFICE

Church and State

The Philippines is host to rich jurisprudence regarding the relationship of the church and the state,[1939] resulting in a constant media following on statements issued by the cardinal on matters of public life, not only on doctrinal ones but even on political matters. As a Church leader in the Philippines, Tagle has dealt with illegal-drug issues and the policies of Philippine president Rodrigo Duterte.[1940] Tagle has also been cast into the public spotlight due to President Duterte's extremely aggressive, violent campaigns against organized crime and rebel groups.

In a homily given at the Manila cathedral on the day of the 2016 elections, Tagle called on the candidates to make it clear to themselves what human dignity and human rights mean to them. To the voters, he said that the Catholic bishops of the country do not ask them to vote for any particular candidate, only that they be guided by the common good.[1941]

Tagle urged the faithful not to vote for candidates who have declared indifference to the Church's moral teachings.[1942] The voters were asked to make sure that the candidate they voted for, as well as being a great leader, a capable administrator of government affairs, and a person with a plan for the country and people, was a person of strong moral character.[1943]

[1939] The most notable recent case being *Re: Letter of Tony Q. Valenciano, Holding of Religious Rituals at the Hall of Justice Building in Quezon City* (2017), which challenged the constitutionality of Catholic Masses being held at the Quezon City Hall of Justice. The Supreme Court held that such does not offend the principle of separation of church and state.

[1940] "Philippines Drug Campaign Condemned by Senior Catholics," BBC News, 20 August 2017, https://www.bbc.com/news/world-asia-40992618.

[1941] "Human Dignity, Human Rights, Morality In The Election," *Tempo*, 8 May 2016, https://www.pressreader.com/philippines/tempo-9gc1/20160508/281651074315866.

[1942] Ibid.

[1943] Ibid.

In the face of President Duterte's controversial tirades against God,[1944] Tagle told his priests to stay calm and urged them not to be distracted from other pressing concerns. "While these questions are extremely important for the dialogue between faith and current concerns, let us not be distracted from addressing other pressing concerns with the fervor of faith and love," Tagle said. In a letter to the priests of the Archdiocese of Manila, he reminded them of issues such as rising prices of goods, job security, the plight of overseas Filipino workers, and violence in communities, even as they deal with questions about God.[1945]

"We cannot address these problems just by blaming someone. Those who believe in God must work faithfully and joyfully for the Lord. Those who do not believe in God must serve out of human decency, generosity, and concern for neighbors," he added.[1946]

Drug Crime

On September 8, 2017, the feast of the Birth of the Blessed Virgin Mary, Cardinal Tagle published a written statement against the radical drug-related killings in the Philippines. Tagle noted that he had met with families of victims, as well as individuals from the Philippine National Police Academy. He not only encouraged pastors and leaders of parishes to support any grieving families in their parish communities, but also asked that beginning on September 14, 2017, the feast of the Exaltation of the Cross, "there be a 5-minute tolling or ringing of church bells at 8:00 in the evening to call on everyone to remember the dead and pray for them."[1947] In previous statements, Tagle also requested "all the parishes in the Archdiocese of Manila

---

[1944] Pia Ranada, "Duterte Blasts Bible Creation Story: 'Who is This Stupid God?'" *Rappler,* 23 June 2018, https://www.rappler.com/nation/205572-duterte-stupid-god-bible-story.

[1945] Paterno Esmaquel II, "Cardinal Tagle on Duterte's Rant vs. God: Don't Be Distracted," *Rappler,* 28 June 2018, https://www.rappler.com/nation/205897-cardinal-tagle-statement-duterte-stupid-god.

[1946] Ibid.

[1947] Luis Antonio G. Cardinal Tagle, "Day of Prayer, Fasting and Action for Truth and the Common Good," Roman Catholic Archdiocese of

to mark the nine days from August 21 (memorial of Pope St. Pius X) to August 29 (Beheading of St. John the Baptist) as time to offer prayers at all Masses for the repose of those who have died in this war, for the strength of their families, for the perseverance of those recovering from addiction and the conversion of killers."[1948]

China Connections

Cardinal Tagle's family ties with China, his generally good and close Sino-Philippine relations, and his recent appointment as prefect of the Congregation for the Evangelization of Peoples are seen as placing him in a strategically important position for furthering Sino-Vatican ties at a time when those relations are most sensitive. They would also naturally be useful if he were ever to be elected pope. Tagle, however, is not expected to bring any moral hawkishness to the negotiating table but rather to continue with his current dovish stance.[1949]

Cardinal-Bishop

In May 2020, Pope Francis elevated Tagle to the rank of cardinal-bishop, making him one of the highest-ranking prelates in the Church and the most senior Filipino bishop in the history of Christianity in the Philippines. The pope had to break with tradition to make the promotion, which observers read as a sign that he has Francis' stamp of approval.[1950]

Manila, 13 May 2018, https://rcam.org/index.php/archbishop/pastoral-statements.

[1948] Santosh Digal, "Card. Tagle against Duterte's War on Drugs: 'Stop the Waste of Human Life,'" *AsiaNews*, 21 August 2017, http://www.asianews.it/news-en/Card.-Tagle-Against-Dutertes-War-on-Drugs:-Stop-the-Waste-of-Human-Life-41569.html.

[1949] John L. Allen Jr., "New Vatican missionary chief could be pivotal player on China," *Angelus News*, 13 December 2019, https://angelusnews.com/voices/new-vatican-missionary-chief-could-be-pivotal-player-on-china/.

[1950] Paterno Esmaquel II, "Pope Broke Tradition Again to Make Tagle 'Cardinal-Bishop,'" *Rappler*, 2 May 2020, https://www.rappler.com/nation/259750-pope-francis-broke-tradition-tagle-cardinal-bishop.

TEACHING OFFICE

Theological Influences

When asked to name which writers have made the biggest impression on him during his theological studies, Tagle said, "The French Dominican Yves Congar, the German Jesuit Karl Rahner, Cardinal Joseph Ratzinger.... Among South Americans I read a lot of Leonardo Boff, Gustavo Gutiérrez, and Segundo Galilea. Among the women, I read Professors Elizabeth Johnson, Elisabeth Schüssler Fiorenza, and Rosemary Ruether.... Among Italians I read many lectures by Cardinal Carlo Martini."[1951]

Educated at the Jesuit-run Ateneo de Manila and the Loyola School of Theology, Tagle wrote his doctorate at the Catholic University of America on "Episcopal Collegiality in the Teaching and Practice of Paul VI." Tagle's director was Fr. Joseph A. Komonchak, S.J., who helped his student become a member of the editorial board of the so-called Bologna School's monumental five-volume *History of Vatican II*, co-edited by Komonchak and Giuseppe Alberigo.[1952] In many other speeches and writings, Tagle has praised Paul VI's furtherance of the "collegial process," especially his institution of the Synod of Bishops. Tagle has argued that Vatican II was a "transitional council" and "the institutional reforms initiated by the council and Paul VI were also transitional in character," for the Council requires "acceptance of the breakdown of the logic that gave coherent form to 'Roman Catholicism,'" an acceptance that takes time and changes in ecclesial praxis, institutions, and laws.[1953]

[1951] Luis Antonio Tagle, *I Have Learned from the Least: My Life, My Hopes* (Maryknoll, N.Y.: Orbis Books, 2017), chap. 4, "Theology, a Second Love," ebook ed.

[1952] Wooden, *Luis Antonio Tagle*, 65.

[1953] Luis Antonio G. Tagle, "Episcopal Collegiality and the Ecclesiological Project of Vatican II," *Landas* 7 (1993): 149-60 at 158.

During his tenure as a professor, Tagle did not publish any works on theology.[1954] He has been praised for mastering "The Art of Theological Narrative—in the Philippines and Asia."[1955]

Tradition for New Situations

On the eve of Pope Paul VI's beatification, Tagle, who was attending the Extraordinary Synod of Bishops on the Pastoral Challenges to the Family, spoke with Fr. Thomas Rosica, C.S.B., of Salt and Light Media about Paul VI's contribution to the development of a modern Catholic Church. "What I learned from Paul VI is the ability to listen. . . . [It's] very clear that we received a patrimony—something that we do not invent—the Word of God, the tradition," Tagle declared. He continued:

> But [we should be] convinced that it is a living tradition . . . and that the Word is still in the hands of God. How do we listen to the Word and discover in the tradition things we have forgotten, or things we have not seen yet? Because the tradition is very rich! No single person, no single country, no single local Church, or even the greatest saint could have captured the totality of that tradition. So if it is a living tradition, there is also a living mode of rediscovering it and the changing times could really push us. Some might say we are succumbing to pressures of the world, but in my studies of Vatican II and Paul VI, it was not their intention to change doctrine but to go into the wealth of Christian tradition and discover what will the Christian tradition say about these new situations.[1956]

In an interview with Catholic News Agency, Cardinal Tagle described his general approach to pastoral care when that care comes in close contact

---

[1954] Ibid.

[1955] Victor R. Salanga, review of *"It Is the Lord!": Occasional Lectures at Loyola School of Theology*, by Luis Antonio Tagle, *Landas* 17, no. 2 (2003): 315-16 at 316.

[1956] Salt and Light Media, "Witness—Cardinal Luis Antonio Tagle," YouTube video, 4:59, posted 17 October 2014, https://www.youtube.com/watch?v=uOS1LzwdrX8.

with objective moral norms. He was asked, "How do we open the doors of those [with unique situations] in a compassionate way without compromising the Church's teaching?" To this, the cardinal replied,

> I think it's a matter also of pastoral approach.... An appreciation again of the beauty of the teachings of the Church, presented calmly, without any judgment, and then: how do we help those who are not in harmony with the Church? Sometimes, the situation has to be remedied. But, sometimes, the situation cannot be remedied any more.[1957]

Moral Ambiguities

In most interviews and press statements, Tagle has been very careful with his language, particularly on controversial moral questions. True to his pastoral style, he uses various arguments in promoting the Church's position on different issues. When he was once confronted with leading questions citing statistics that may present a strong case for contraception and against natural family planning,[1958] he quipped: "There are studies showing that natural planning is scientific.... The trend now is natural. With food, people want organic. How come when it comes to size of families, they want it artificial? The world must decide."[1959]

During a news conference held during Pope Francis' apostolic visit to the Philippines in 2015, Tagle spoke alongside Vatican spokesman Federico Lombardi about same-sex "marriage" after it had been discussed in the Extraordinary Synod. Lombardi laid the groundwork for the conference that "it is well known that the perspective of the Church on the family is that the family is based on the union of a man and the woman and the

---

[1957] "'Rock Star' Cardinal Talks Big Cities, Small Gestures," Catholic News Agency, 8 February 2015, https://www.catholicnewsagency.com/news/rock-star-cardinal-talks-big-cities-small-gestures-11752.

[1958] BBC journalist Stephen Sackur mentioned UN statistics of 100,000 children on the streets of Manila. See "Tagle Urges Indonesian Bishops to Engage Other Faiths."

[1959] Shalom World, "Cardinal Luis Antonio Tagle."

children that come from this union." Tagle, who was seated beside him, augmented the discussion by sharing some sentiments by bishops and lay-people during the Extraordinary Synod that foreign aid extended to them oftentimes is linked to some measures that the receiving country is forced to accept. Some of those conditions of the aid seem to be an acceptance of views regarding marriage or sexuality that could be foreign to the bishop of the receiving country.[1960] It is thus difficult to say confidently whether Tagle opposes same-sex civil "marriages."

At the 2018 youth synod, it was noted at a Vatican press conference attended by Tagle that moral issues were hardly discussed except in a negative sense related to moralism, despite the importance of morality in young people's formation. Cardinal Tagle would only say "it was discussed" in his English-language group but offered no further details. None of the others on the panel responded. Observers found the response inadequate and showing unease about discussing the Church's moral teaching.[1961]

Contraception

Tagle seems to affirm Church teaching on the immorality of contraception. In an interview with the BBC, he was asked if he regretted the very strong stand he and the Catholic Church took against the "Reproductive Health" bill passed by the Filipino government in 2011, guaranteeing universal access to contraception and promoting population control. To this, he replied, "I think the Church . . . cannot reinvent a teaching [about contraception]. . . . We are duty bound to proclaim again and again the teaching that we have received."[1962] But he said although this is Church

---

[1960] AP Archive, "Papal Spokesman Comments on Gay Marriage," YouTube video, 2:15, posted 3 August 2015, https://www.youtube.com/watch?v=1zibPJBaZhQ.

[1961] Catholic Sat (@CatholicSat), "At #Synod2018 Presser; @EdwardPentin raises the point that the Church's Moral teaching is almost completely absent from the reports of the small language groups," Twitter, 23 October 2018, 6:25 a.m., https://twitter.com/CatholicSat/status/1054725442068996096?s=20.

[1962] "Cardinal Tagle's Interview with the BBC Hard Talk," Catholica, 9 May 2015, http://www.catholica.com.au/forum/index.php?mode=thread&id=171216.

teaching, "we have to be sensitive, pastorally, to the difficulties that persons and families face."[1963] In the same interview, he was asked his opinion on a strong statement made by one of the bishops on the issue, who characterized contraception as corruption. Tagle answered, "That was only a statement of a bishop.... The Church has a common stand but each bishop has their own language." When asked if he considered the statement a mistake, Tagle replied, "I would probably have used a different language."[1964]

In an interview with Catholic News Agency, Tagle was asked whether the strong statements of the popes made any impact on those pushing for contraception legislation. Tagle replied:

> I think those who support the law knew from the very start the position of the Church. So I don't think they were surprised that the Holy Father would reiterate the teaching of the Church.... He is not at liberty to just invent his own teaching.
>
> So, we see his affirmation of the teaching of Pope Paul VI in *Humanae Vitae*. The Holy Father also alerted us to another aspect of the teaching of Paul VI, which is this: particular cases must be addressed individually, and they must be brought to the confessors, and the confessors must bring with them hearts of compassion and understanding as they evaluate particular situations and cases. There he was able to blend fidelity to teaching, and at the same time, seeing how individual cases are unique.[1965]

It is unclear what, if any, action Cardinal Tagle has taken as president of Caritas Internationalis, the umbrella organization for all Catholic humanitarian agencies, with regard to some prominent Caritas members receiving considerable funding from organizations promoting contraception and

---

[1963] Ian O'Reilly, "BBC Hardtalk on Location in Manila—Cardinal Luis Antonio Tagle," YouTube video, 24:43, posted 5 October 2016, https://www.youtube.com/watch?v=xbqB3dKZgHM.

[1964] Ibid.

[1965] Shalom World, "Cardinal Luis Antonio Tagle."

abortion. One such organization is Catholic Relief Services (CRS), the U.S. bishops' relief agency. Since Tagle was first elected Caritas president in 2015, CRS has not only received millions of dollars from such organizations as the pro-contraception Bill and Melinda Gates Foundation (nearly $4 million in 2019)[1966] but has also been complicit in working with contraception and abortion providers.[1967] Cardinal Tagle has yet to make any public comment about the issue.

Under Tagle's leadership, Caritas has also given strong and uncritical support for the United Nations' Sustainable Development Goals,[1968] despite goal number three, which promotes "sexual and reproductive health" (code for abortion and contraception) for the world's poorest.[1969]

Against Liberal and Conservative Labels

On several occasions, Cardinal Tagle has implored the media to stop using labels when it comes to a person's stand on issues involving the Church. During a press briefing with Philippine media on issues discussed during the 2014 Extraordinary Synod of Bishops with the theme "Pastoral Challenges to the Family in the Context of Evangelization," the reporters chose to highlight the outcome of the discussions on same-sex "marriage" and divorce as indicative of a "divide" between progressives or liberals and

[1966] "Awarded Grants," Bill and Melinda Gates Foundation, https://www.gates-foundation.org/how-we-work/quick-links/grants-database#q/k=Catholic%20relief%20services.

[1967] "Catholic Relief Services," Lepanto Institute, 2011-2020, https://www.lepantoin.org/crs/.

[1968] "Caritas Updates on Sustainable Development Goals," Caritas, https://www.caritas.org/what-we-do/development/sustainable-development-goals/; "2030 Agenda and the Sustainable Development Goals," Position Paper, Caritas Europa, 13 March 2018, https://www.caritas.eu/wordpress/wp-content/uploads/2018/10/180103_agenda_2030_sdg_position_paper.pdf.

[1969] UNFPA, "Decade of Action," https://www.unfpa.org/sdg.

conservatives or traditionalists within the Catholic Church.[1970] To this, Tagle replied:

> Let me address the journalists. I don't think it is helpful to label people. Labelling people as progressive, as conservative, as tradition-alists, may hinder a full listening to them. If we have decided already in our minds, "this person is traditionalist," whatever the person says, you or we, will always say, "Ah, traditionalist." Or if a person says something that does not sound traditionalist, we change the label—"Ah, he's not a traditionalist, he's a progressive."
>
> A person will always be deeper than any label. And no person especially talking about deep, deep mysteries—love, marriage, rela-tionship—could be labelled. It is not helpful to the public.... It is not helpful to us. It is not helpful to you to think of persons based on names. Let us listen, listen, to the totality. Try to understand, and from that understanding we will get a better picture of the event.[1971]

From these and other public comments, it is unclear how Tagle's desire for no "labels" accords with the Church's teaching that some situations are objectively contrary to nonnegotiable moral norms, such as living in a conjugal manner with someone who is not one's sacramental spouse.

Right-to-Life Issues

On the matter of abortion, the cardinal stated in an interview with Church-run radio station Radio Veritas that "many of us are worried about the extra-judicial killings, but why are there only a few who raise their misgivings about abortion? We have to be more vocal against abortion because that is a form of murder too."[1972]

[1970] Angela Casauay, "Cardinal Tagle to Media: Avoid Using Labels," *Rappler*, 30 October 2014, https://www.rappler.com/nation/73574-cardinal-tagle-media.

[1971] Ibid.

[1972] Katrina Domingo, "Tagle Slams Killings, Says Gov't Must Give People a Chance," ABS-CBN News, 29 August 2016, https://news.abs-cbn.com/news/08/29/16/tagle-slams-killings-says-govt-must-give-people-a-chance.

Tagle emphasizes the need for consistency in protecting life. He stresses that human life, which is sacred, must be respected and protected at every stage and in every condition, but the moral outcry in the name of life is nothing without consistency. "[Be] consistent in defending the sacredness of life," the cardinal said.[1973] Tagle called for strong condemnation of all forms of murder, from summary executions of alleged criminals to aborting babies.

The cardinal has also spoken clearly about his view on the impermissibility of euthanasia in law. At a time when pro–death penalty lawmakers pushed for the supposed benefits of capital punishment, Cardinal Tagle reiterated the Church's stance regarding legislation that threatens life, emphasizing the fact that man was created in the image and likeness of God. "This is the reason why an ethic of life, a culture of life, is inconsistent with abortion, euthanasia, human trafficking, mutilation, and violence against innocent and vulnerable persons. Before God the source of life, we are humble. We cannot pretend to be gods."[1974]

During a visit to Canada, where doctor-assisted suicide had recently been legalized, Tagle stated in an interview that priests in the Philippines do not come across such situations because of the strong support system within the Church and their families.[1975] "In the moral tradition of the church, we have a process of discernment," he said. "When a sick person employs what we call extraordinary means to be alive and then there is really almost no chance of recovery. Then the Church with pastoral accompaniment helps either the patient or the family to see whether maybe this is already the moment of natural death."

[1973] Ibid.

[1974] "Cardinal Tagle on Death Penalty: 'We Cannot Pretend to Be Gods,'" ABS-CBN News, 2 February 2017, https://news.abs-cbn.com/focus/02/02/17/cardinal-tagle-on-death-penalty-we-cannot-pretend-to-be-gods.

[1975] Cecile Docto, "Cardinal Luis Antonio Tagle on Family Values, Doctor-Assisted Suicide, Philippine Divorce Bill," Balitang America, 21 March 2018, https://balitangamerica.tv/cardinal-luis-antonio-tagle-on-family-values-doctor-assisted-suicide-philippine-divorce-bill/.

Priestly Celibacy, Women's Diaconate, Homosexual Priests

Priestly celibacy, a women's diaconate, homosexuals in Holy Orders, and Communion for divorced-and-civilly-"remarried" Catholics: these are all issues about which the cardinal admits he does not yet have definitive answers. For example, Tagle believes that the discipline of priestly celibacy deserves further discernment.[1976] In an article written by Tagle for the United States Conference of Catholic Bishops,[1977] he suggested that priestly celibacy requires a "fuller and more just understanding" in order to "situate it within the Church's rich spiritual, pastoral and canonical tradition."[1978]

Attempting to make sense of possible correlation between the sexual abuse crisis in the Church and priestly celibacy, the cardinal suggests:

> The crisis has impelled us to understand again the promise to remain celibate and to lead a chaste life. This approach will resonate with the traditions of the ancient religions in Asia. We need, especially in formation, theology, canon law and moral theology a serious evaluation of this issue and the varying opinions on it. Many people think that celibacy is simply a rule that the conservative Church has to observe for the sake of tradition. Some make it the culprit for all types of sexual misconduct. Others defend it but in a narrowly legalistic way that proves ineffectual. We need a serene but comprehensive consideration of the matter.[1979]

Another contentious issue is who may be admitted to Holy Orders. At a press briefing during the Vatican youth synod held in October 2018, Cardinal Tagle was asked about the possible admission of homosexuals to

---

[1976] Cardinal Luis Antonio G. Tagle, "Clergy Sexual Misconduct: Some Reflections from Asia," United States Conference of Catholic Bishops, http://www.usccb.org/issues-and-action/child-and-youth-protection/resources/upload/Reflections-from-Asia-Tagle.pdf.

[1977] Ibid.

[1978] Ibid.

[1979] Ibid.

seminaries and to Holy Orders.[1980] His reply was noncommittal. Cardinal Tagle said that while the discussions during the synod focused on "the humane regard of the Church to people, whatever their sexual orientation may be ... it was also very clear that, while the constant attitude is that of respect for human dignity and the human person, we also recognize that in different states of life, especially in the Church, there are some demands or some requisites or some requirements that we have to look at, for the proper exercise of a charism or a ministry."[1981]

It is unclear whether Tagle has made any public pronouncement concerning the ordination of women to the diaconate. As a member of the International Theological Commission, however, he was part of a subcommittee that unanimously adopted the document *From the Diakonia of Christ to the Diakonia of the Apostles*, which at the very least recognized that "the present historical overview shows that a ministry of deaconesses did indeed exist, and that this developed unevenly in the different parts of the Church. It seems clear that this ministry was not perceived as simply the feminine equivalent of the masculine diaconate. At the very least it was an ecclesial function, exercised by women, sometimes mentioned together with that of sub-deacon in the lists of Church ministries."[1982]

While the cardinal has not spoken of women in the diaconate, he has alluded to the role of women in discussions on issues directly concerning the universal Church, its doctrine, and its administration. During the 2018 youth synod, Tagle said it had been a different synod as the feminine voice

---

[1980] Diane Montagna, "Prominent Cardinal, I Have a 'Hunch' that 'LGBT' Will Be in Youth Synod Final Document," LifeSite News, 23 October 2018, https://www.lifesitenews.com/news/cardinal-tagle-i-have-a-hunch-that-lgbt-will-be-present-in-the-synods-final.

[1981] Ibid.

[1982] International Theological Commission, "From the Diakonia of Christ to the Diakonia of the Apostles," 2002, http://www.vatican.va/roman_curia/congregations/cfaith/cti_documents/rc_con_cfaith_pro_05072004_diaconate_en.html.

certainly had been a focal point.[1983] He said that it was suggested often that female figures in Scripture should be used as interpretative lights for young people today[1984] and that the testimony of the young women at the synod provided a much-needed expansion of horizons. The cardinal said that when the Church talks about diversity it is not just about cultures but also the experience of women, which is unique.[1985]

Tagle holds that there is no all-encompassing answer to the question of Communion for the divorced and "remarried."

> Every situation for those who are divorced and "remarried" is quite unique. To have a general rule might be counterproductive in the end. My position at the moment is to ask, "Can we take every case seriously and is there, in the tradition of the Church, paths towards addressing each case individually?" This is one issue that I hope people will appreciate is not easy to say "no" or to say "yes" to. We cannot give one formula for all.[1986]

Islam

Tagle has often addressed difficult questions about Islam. His general attitude is probably best captured in his comment that "Vatican II stressed that we Catholics should respect non-Catholics and their religions. We

---

[1983] Russell Pollitt, S.J., "Synod of Bishops: Young people Are Used-Less, Not Useless," Vatican News, 2018, https://www.vaticannews.va/en/church/news/2018-10/synod-youth-2018-press-briefing10.html.

[1984] This is one of the rare times the cardinal has highlighted Mary as a model for women in particular. He has given a myriad of statements, however, on why Mary is a role model for people in general.

[1985] Carol Glatz, "Iraqi Patriarch: Fast Track for Christian Refugees Will Fuel Tensions," Catholic News Service, 30 January 2017, http://www.catholic-news.com/services/englishnews/2017/iraqi-patriarch-fast-track-for-christian-refugees-will-fuel-tensions.cfm.

[1986] Rachel Obordo, "Cardinal Tagle: There Is No 'Formula for All' on Communion for the Divorced and Re-Married," *Catholic Herald*, 17 March 2015, https://catholicherald.co.uk/cardinal-tagle-there-is-no-formula-for-all-on-communion-for-the-divorced-and-re-married/.

also respect those who do not believe in God. All people should strive to respect those who differ from their beliefs. Religions are not to be used for conflicts but for mutual understanding and peace."[1987]

Tagle has spoken up to address issues relating to the relationship between Catholic and Islamic faith communities. In January 2017, Cardinal Tagle denounced the preferential option for Christians in refugee resettlement programs.[1988] Speaking to Catholic News Service, Tagle said that any policy that gave priority to Christians "might revive some of these animosities and might even pit Christians against Muslims, and that (also) might generate contrary action from the Muslims against Christians. This is a time when we don't want to add to the prejudice, the biases and even discriminatory attitudes evolving in the world."[1989]

Several months later, Tagle suggested that radical Islamist terrorists were to blame for the widespread perception of religiously motivated conflict. Promoting unity and understanding, he called for Muslims and Christians to "remove the wall that separates us ... because we belong to one human family." "Whoever plans to divide Muslims and Christians will not triumph,"[1990] the cardinal warned.

Regarding the Charlie Hebdo attacks in January 2015, Cardinal Tagle told CNN's Christiane Amanpour: "We also do not want to jump to the conclusion that these acts are always associated with the religion called Islam." He went on to say that, in the Philippines, "We have many friends of the Islamic religion and they are the first ones to say, 'Acts of terror are

[1987] Esmaquel, "Tagle on Duterte's Rant."

[1988] Carol Glatz, "Iraqi Patriarch: Fast Track for Christian Refugees Will Fuel Tensions," Catholic News Service, 30 January 2017, http://www.catholic-news.com/services/englishnews/2017/iraqi-patriarch-fast-track-for-christian-refugees-will-fuel-tensions.cfm.

[1989] Ibid.

[1990] "Cardinal Tagle urges Muslim-Christian unity amid Marawi conflict," Vatican Radio, 5 July 2017, http://en.radiovaticana.va/news/2017/07/05/cardinal_tagle_urges_muslim-christian_unity_in_conflict_/1323379.

not part of our religion.' And I believe them. We have a lot of peace-loving people and they cry also when their religion is in a way misused."[1991]

In 2017, Tagle once again issued statements on the matter amid armed conflict in the Mindanao island of the Philippines involving a radical Islamist group. Some three hundred thousand people, mostly Muslims, had languished in evacuation centers around Marawi since May 23 of that year, when terrorists attacked the city, burning the city's Catholic cathedral and Protestant church properties.[1992] While stating that those who plan division will not triumph, he highlighted "stories of hope" that continued to emerge from the conflict zone and underlined that all belong to one family. Tagle said he had heard of stories about Muslims taking care of Christians whose lives were in danger and Christians help-ing suffering Muslims.[1993]

Migrants and Refugees

Tagle's views on migration are also complex, but they almost invariably tend to regard views that he considers too nationalistic, deriving from the emotional motives of those who hold such positions. At an interfaith conference on migrants and refugees at the United Nations, co-hosted by the Permanent Mission of the Holy See to the UN and Caritas Internatio-nalis, Tagle shared religious beliefs that inspire faith-based organizations to champion the rights of migrants and encourage good behavior toward displaced people and the communities that host them.[1994] The experiences of Abraham, Moses, Jesus, and the prophet Muhammad were highlighted

---

[1991] Ayee Macaraig, "Tagle on Charlie Hebdo: Respect both diversity and life," *Rappler*, 15 January 2015, https://www.rappler.com/nation/80908-tagle-charlie-hebdo-respect-both-diversity-and-life.

[1992] "Cardinal Tagle Urges Muslim-Christian Unity."

[1993] Ibid.

[1994] Beth Griffin, "Faith Groups Care for Refugees in Ways Governments Can't, Group Tells U.N.," *Crux*, 5 May 2018, https://cruxnow.com/global-church/2018/05/05/faith-groups-care-for-refugees-in-ways-governments-cant-group-tells-u-n/.

as examples of forced migration. "Migration is about human persons," the cardinal said. "I have observed that some people who are afraid of migrants or refugees have had very little personal encounter with them. They do not even know the people they fear. By meeting them, touching their wounds, listening to their stories and dreams, we might see ourselves in them. They are not strangers. They could be me, my parents, my brothers and sisters, my friend."[1995]

Describing how his Chinese grandfather migrated to the Philippines as a child, Cardinal Tagle said, "I have migrant DNA. I am sure you do, too."[1996]

A few months later, right before governments around the world were to discuss in the United Nations, for the first time, a global framework to provide an orientation to states on how to govern migration and how to respond to migrants,[1997] Cardinal Tagle wrote:

> To the governments who have withdrawn support from the compact on migration, I appeal that they reconsider their decision. In an interconnected world, global issues such as climate change, poverty and the persecution of ethnic and religious minorities call on us to work together. They will not go away if we ignore them or put up walls. When governments look beyond their immediate needs and electoral demands, they begin to protect and promote the common good, which is at the heart of any flourishing society.[1998]

[1995] Ibid.

[1996] Ibid.

[1997] "Global Compact for Safe, Orderly and Regular Migration," International Organization for Migration, 19 September 2016, https://www.iom.int/global-compact-migration.

[1998] Cardinal Luis Antonio Gokim Tagle, "Cardinal Tagle: We need to create a global vision for migration," *America*, 4 December 2018, https://www.americamagazine.org/politics-society/2018/12/04/cardinal-tagle-we-need-create-global-vision-migration.

Coronavirus Reaction

Cardinal Tagle urged the faithful to look beyond themselves and see the needs of others. "A pandemic spread of a virus must produce a pandemic 'contagion' of charity," he said in a message. "History will judge our generation by the power of self-less love that this common emergency will have generated and spread or will have failed to do so. We thank the heroic people whose love and courage have already been a source of healing and hope these past weeks."[1999]

He said people should wash their hands as advised, "but not the way Pilate did. We cannot wash our hands of our responsibility towards the poor, the elderly, the unemployed, the refugees, the homeless, the health providers, indeed all people, creation and future generations."[2000]

SUMMARY

Touted as the "Asian Francis," Cardinal Tagle possesses not only attributes similar to Jorge Bergoglio and extensive pastoral and administrative experience but also significant theological and historical training.

Unafraid to share his emotions and sentimentality in public, even seemingly eager to do so, he often displays a playful side, as when dancing with youth or celebrating Mass in a folksy and casual manner.[2001] Nevertheless, Tagle is known as a shrewd negotiator, and he employs political tactics with sophistication. His tutelage under the Jesuits in the Philippines and his graduate studies in the United States, subsequent fifteen years of work

---

[1999] Luis Antonio G. Cardinal Tagle, "Emergencies and Charity: A Reflection by Cardinal Tagle," Vatican News, 26 March 2020, https://www.vatican-news.va/en/vatican-city/news/2020-03/emergency-charity-cardinal-tagle-coronavirus-covid.html.

[2000] Ibid.

[2001] Roy Lagarde, "Emotional Cardinal Tagle: 'Thy Will Be Done,'" Zenit, 9 December 2019, https://zenit.org/articles/emotional-cardinal-tagle-thy-will-be-done/.

with Joseph Komonchak and Giuseppe Alberigo, and connections with the "Bologna School," firmly root him more in the camp of those with a progressive ecclesiological vision—or, as someone who prefers to eschew such labels, perhaps just a different one.

Tagle often uses the pulpit to respond to issues of social justice, but his positions on moral matters appear somewhat incoherent. On the one hand, he railed against a Filipino "Reproductive Health" bill, albeit less strongly than some of his fellow bishops, that introduced anti-family and antilife policies, and he has spoken strongly against abortion and euthanasia. On the other hand, he holds that some situations exist where universal moral principles do not apply, as in the case of Communion for couples who live together conjugally but without sacramental marriage and issues relating to homosexuality. He opposes use of "harsh" or "severe" language when describing certain sins and believes the Church needs to "learn over" its teaching of mercy due in part to the "shifts in cultural and social sensibilities." In short, he downplays the gravity of such sins and the public scandal that they give.[2002]

But when it comes to popular causes, Cardinal Tagle has shown himself to be a clear and vocal advocate. This is especially true of issues such as ecology, seen most recently in his active participation in the Pachamama ritual in the Vatican Gardens. Along with his ambiguous statements about the goodness of all religions, these factors raise questions about what Tagle believes to be the essence of the gospel.

His appointment as prefect of the Congregation for the Evangelization of Peoples and elevation to the rank of cardinal-bishop nevertheless place Tagle in a leading position for the papacy if voting cardinals desire continuity with Francis' pontificate.

[2002] "Two Cardinals, Two Visions of the Church," Society of Saint Pius X, 30 March 2015, https://www.sspx.ca/en/news-events/news/two-cardinals-two-visions-church.

SERVICE TO THE CHURCH

Ordination to the Priesthood: 27 February 1982
Ordination to the Episcopate: 12 December 2001
Elevation to the College of Cardinals: 24 November 2012

Education

- 1973: Ateneo de Manila University and San Jose Seminary; Philosophy (B.A.)
- 1982: Loyola School of Theology and San Jose Seminary; Theology (M.A.)
- 1987: Catholic University of America, Washington, D.C.; Sacred theology (licentiate)
- 1991: Catholic University of America, Washington, D.C.; Sacred theology (doctorate)

Assignments in the Diocese of Imus[2003]

- 1982-1983: Spiritual director, Diocesan Seminary of Imus, Tahanan ng Mabuting Pastol, Tagaytay City
- 1982-1984: Associate pastor, Mendez, Cavite
- 1983-1984: Acting rector, Diocesan Seminary of Imus, Tahanan ng Mabuting Pastol, Tagaytay City
- 1984-1985; 1992-2011: Rector, Diocesan Seminary of Imus, Tahanan ng Mabuting Pastol, Tagaytay City
- 1993-2000: Member, Board of Consultors and Presbyteral Council of the Diocese of Imus
- 1993-2000: Episcopal Vicar for Religious
- 1998-2001: Parish priest, Imus, Cavite

[2003] For biographical information, see the biography provided on the website of the Archdiocese of Manila: "His Eminence Luis Antonio Gokim Cardinal Tagle Archbishop of Manila," Roman Catholic Archdiocese of Manila, 2017, https://www.rcam.org/index.php/archbishop/biography.

- 2002-2011: Rector, Our Lady of the Pillar Seminary, Imus, Cavite

Other Ministries
- 1982-1985, 1992-2011: Instructor of Theology, San Carlos Seminary, Manila; Loyola School of Theology, Quezon City; Divine Word Seminary, Tagaytay
- 1995-2001: Consultant, Catholic Bishops' Conference of the Philippines; Commission on the Doctrine of the Faith; Commission on Seminaries
- 1997-2002: Member, International Theological Commission, Vatican City
- 2003-present: Chair, Catholic Bishops' Conference of the Philippines; Episcopal Commission on the Doctrine of the Faith
- 2005-2008: Elected member of the Council of the Synod of Bishops, Vatican
- 2007: Elected chair of the Federation of Asian Bishops' Conferences, Office of Theological Concerns
- 2011-present: Archbishop of Manila
- 2012: Appointed member of the XIII General Assembly of the Synod of Bishops on the New Evangelization, Vatican (October)
- 2015: Elected president of Caritas Internationalis

Membership
- 2008-present: Permanent Council of the Synod of Bishops
- 2012-present: Congregation for Catholic Education
- 2013-present: Pontifical Council for the Family
- 2013-present: Pontifical Council for the Pastoral Care of Migrants and Itinerant People
- 2014-present: Pontifical Council for the Laity

- 2014-present: Congregation for Institutes of Consecrated Life and Societies of Apostolic Life
- 2014-present: Congregation for the Evangelization of Peoples
- 2015-present: Pontifical Council *Cor Unum*
- 2015-present: President of the Catholic Biblical Federation
- 2015-present: President of Caritas Internationalis

PETER KODWO APPIAH CARDINAL TURKSON

"To Live Is Christ"

Born: 11 October 1948
Nsuta-Wassaw, Ghana
Nationality: Ghanaian
Title: Prefect, Dicastery for Promoting
Integral Human Development

BIOGRAPHY

Peter Turkson has indicated that he is well acquainted with the need for "coexisting" with people from diverse backgrounds, as he was born into a family of ten children of a Catholic father and a mother who was a convert from a Methodist sect. He also had a Muslim paternal uncle.[2004] At the age of fourteen, he entered a minor seminary in Ghana. He continued in a regional seminary from 1969 to 1971. From 1971 to 1974, he studied at a seminary run by Franciscans in New York State, before being ordained in Ghana in 1975.[2005] After a brief stint teaching in a minor seminary, he was sent to Rome, where, after four years, he earned a license at the Pontifical Biblical Institute (Biblicum) in 1980. For the next six years, he taught in a seminary while also assisting in a parish. In 1987, Turkson's bishop sent him back to Rome, this time to earn a doctorate. However, John Paul II asked Turkson to become a bishop in 1992, and the doctorate was never completed.

In 1993, Turkson was consecrated a bishop and took up his role as archbishop of Cape Coast, Ghana. Having been elected president of the Ghana Bishops' Conference, Turkson served in that position from 1997 to 2005. During this period, in 2003, John Paul II created Turkson a cardinal-priest at the relatively young age of fifty-five. From 2006 to 2010, he served as the chairman of the Ghanaian National Peace Council (NPC), established with the help of the United Nations Development Programme (UNDP). In that capacity, he helped the country peacefully elect a president in 2008, despite countrywide tensions.[2006] He sees Archbishop Oscar Romero of El Salvador as a model.[2007] A year later, in 2009, in view of Turkson's background in social justice and affiliations with the UN, Benedict XVI appointed him president

[2004] Gianni Cardinale, "Celibacy? It's Not Foreign to African Culture," *30 Days*, no. 10 (2005), http://www.30giorni.it/articoli_id_9604_13.htm?id=9604; Gerard O'Connell, "Cardinal Turkson: 'For Me to Attack Islam Would Be to Attack My Own Family,'" *La Stampa*, 25 October 2012, https://web.archive.org/web/20180612185340/http://www.lastampa.it/2012/10/21/vaticaninsider/cardinal-turkson-for-me-to-attack-islam-would-be-to-attack-my-own-family-JM29sJssgZJ2DBi8mWeKkO/pagina.html.

[2005] Robert Mickens, "The Rising Star of Justice and Peace," *Tablet*, 31 October 2009, https://web.archive.org/web/20110627120323/https://www.thetablet.co.uk/article/13830.

[2006] Cardinal Peter Turkson, "Archbishop Romero as Preacher and Teacher" (lecture delivered at Notre Dame University, Indiana), *Independent Catholic News*, 25 March 2011, https://www.indcatholicnews.com/news/17969.

[2007] Ibid.

of the Pontifical Council for Justice and Peace. Pope Francis confirmed him in that position in 2013. In 2017, Turkson became the prefect of the new "super dicastery" for Promoting Integral Human Development, the Pontifical Council for Justice and Peace having been juridically dissolved. In 2020, Pope Francis appointed Turkson coordinator of a five-group Vatican task force to respond to the socioeconomic fallout from the coronavirus.

SANCTIFYING OFFICE

Speaking of the spiritual state of the Catholic Church in Africa, Turkson explained that "most of us came to the Church after the Second Vatican Council, so we do not look back at a well-established Church that now has to adopt and implement the Second Vatican Council. Instead, we feel part of the Council."[2008] The cardinal clearly embraces the changes brought about by Vatican II but has remained silent as to whether the changes it caused in the liturgy have been misdirected in some cases. He has, however, noted the differences between African and European styles of worship:

> For African priests serving in parishes in the United States, it is difficult to understand the stringent impositions on worship. Sermons can't be longer than five minutes, or the whole Mass has to be done in 25 minutes. They will do what they are asked to do, but deep down they think, how can this be?[2009]

[2008] Ann Rodgers, "Cardinal Peter Turkson Discusses Vatican II at Duquesne," *Pittsburgh Post-Gazette*, 30 September 2012, https://www.post-gazette.com/life/lifestyle/2012/09/30/Cardinal-Peter-Turkson-discusses-Vatican-II-at-Duquesne/stories/201209300229.

[2009] A U.S. Catholic Interview, "We Are the World: An interview with Cardinal Peter Turkson," *U.S. Catholic*, August 2010, https://www.uscatholic.org/culture/social-justice/2010/07/we-are-world-interview-cardinal-peter-turkson. In a 2005 interview, when asked about inculturation of the liturgy in Africa, the cardinal stated that "the use of the tom-tom, our concepts, our way of representation, our chants, our dances are our gifts with which we want to adore the Lord. The Holy See doesn't impose vetoes on us but does invite

Care for Creation

For the cardinal, participating in the liturgy helps us to reflect on who we are as human beings and our mission to the world as Christians. As part of this, Turkson connects the liturgy to care for creation, which is integrally linked to the flourishing of the human person and fundamental human relationships. In a recent catechesis on the Eucharist and care for creation, the cardinal said:

> Having a wide-angle lens on as much of life as possible is true to Catholic principle of sacramentality. Part of the challenge which celebrating sacramental liturgy can offer is to help us reflect back on the world in which we live and to ponder our care for it as well as our concern for those who dwell on it. This means taking seriously our obligation of being in communion with and caring for our common home.[2010]

Because of the centrality of the sacraments to Catholic life, Cardinal Turkson has called for a more thorough catechesis on the sacraments. During the Second Special Assembly for Africa of the Synod of Bishops in 2009 (the "Second African Synod"), the cardinal warned that "the Eucharist has not yet penetrated the daily life and activity of many of the faithful."[2011] Turkson has asked for "greater attention and vigilance on the

---

us to take care that these modes of inculturation don't get perceived as a pagan cult or a simple spectacle. It is the task of us African bishops to watch that it doesn't happen." Cardinale, "Celibacy?"

[2010] Cardinal Peter K. A. Turkson, "The Eucharist and the Care for Creation," *Pontificium Consilium De Iustitia Et Pace*, 27 January 2016, http://www.iustitiaetpax.va/content/dam/giustiziaepace/presidenteinterventi/2016/2016.01.27%20Turkson-Ledesma_IEC_ENG.pdf.

[2011] Card. Peter Kodwo Appiah Turkson, "The Church in Africa at the Service of Reconciliation, Justice and Peace," *Synodus Episcoporum*, http://www.vatican.va/roman_curia/synod/documents/rc_synod_doc_20091013_rel-post-disceptationem_en.html.

part of bishops and priest to guarantee prayerful liturgical celebrations,"[2012] which must be based on "solid liturgical theology."[2013]

Cardinal Turkson's understanding of the liturgy as relational also extends to his understanding of those who serve in the liturgy: deacons. Turkson described the deacon's ministry as "humble service at the altar and in all of life as a consequence of what occurs at the altar table."[2014]

Women in the Church

The cardinal has clearly stated that limiting priestly ordination to men does not discriminate against women. When asked directly in an interview with CNN in 2013 about the role of women in the Church and the ordination of women priests, the cardinal affirmed the reservation of priestly ordination to men. He stated that limiting ordination to the priesthood to men "is not a discrimination against one's sex or gender"[2015] nor a "denial of rights";[2016] rather, "it is how the Church understood this order of ministry to be."[2017]

Although he understands that priestly ordination is reserved to men, Turkson affirms the important role that women play in the Church. In an interview in 2010, Cardinal Turkson stated that "apart from the question of ordination,"[2018] he did not "see why we should exclude women from positions of responsibility in the Church."[2019] During his tenure as president of the Pontifical Council for Justice and Peace, the council had

---

[2012] Cardinal Peter K. A. Turkson, foreword to *Understanding the Mass: Historical, Biblical, Theological, and Liturgical Perspectives*, by Bishop Joseph Osei-Bonsu (New York: Paulist Press, 2017).

[2013] Ibid.

[2014] Turkson, "Eucharist and Care for Creation."

[2015] "Cardinal Peter Turkson, Contender to Be the First Black Pope?," CNN, 12 February 2013, https://www.cnn.com/videos/international/2013/02/12/exp-peter-turkson-amanpour.cnn.

[2016] Ibid.

[2017] Ibid.

[2018] "We Are the World."

[2019] Ibid.

a female undersecretary. In addition, Turkson asserted that Ghana has "many women catechists, which is a very important position,"[2020] and as "many communities do not have a priest to lead them in worship every Sunday ... it is this woman catechist who leads the worship."[2021] Although the cardinal has not commented on the role of Our Lady as a model for women in family life, he has predicted that more women will "take up leadership positions in the church and the Roman Curia."[2022]

Priestly Celibacy

In terms of *viri probati* (ordination of married men of proven virtue), the cardinal has framed removing the requirements of clerical celibacy as one of many solutions to the shortage of priestly vocations.[2023] At the end of the 2019 Amazon synod, he said the issue would "likely be the subject of further study" for the universal Church.[2024] He does not, however, believe that the celibate priesthood presents a particular problem for the Church in Africa.[2025]

GOVERNING OFFICE

The Catholic Church in Cape Coast grew from 13 percent of the population in the mid-1990s to over 17 percent of the population in 2006 during the

---

[2020] Ibid.

[2021] Ibid.

[2022] Ibid.

[2023] Edward Pentin, "Will Pan-Amazonian Synod Result in End to Clerical Celibacy?," *National Catholic Register*, 8 March 2018, http://www.ncregister.com/blog/edward-pentin/will-pan-amazonian-synod-result-in-end-to-clerical-celibacy.

[2024] Courtney Mares, "Cardinal Turkson Says Ordination of Married Men May Get Further Study," Catholic News Agency, 22 October 2019, https://www.catholicnewsagency.com/news/cardinal-turkson-says-ordination-of-married-men-may-be-subject-of-further-study-22245.

[2025] Ibid.

leadership of Cardinal Turkson.[2026] The high number of priestly vocations in his diocese enabled the cardinal not only to staff his own ministries, but to send his priests to other parts of the world.[2027]

Seminary Formation

During the Second African Synod, Turkson spoke of the importance of forming seminarians in his region. For the cardinal, "the formation of seminarians ought to be taken care of,"[2028] and "a good blending of philosophy and theology will ensure an adequate response to the questions posed by the world."[2029] Taking the obligation to form seminarians seriously, Turkson believes that "it is necessary to create a *ratio nationalis institutionis sacerdotalis*, to help favor discernment and spiritual and affective formation, adapted to circumstances and persons."[2030] The results of this "rigorous discernment and a spiritual, affective formation adapted to situations"[2031] will help priests to be "persons firmly rooted in their cultures and faithful to the teaching of the Church."[2032]

Finding "competent and well-trained formators"[2033] for seminarians has been a priority. During his tenure as the archbishop of Cape Coast, the cardinal collaborated with Renewal Ministries,[2034] a U.S. Catholic charismatic

---

[2026] "Archdiocese of Cape Coast," Catholic Hierarchy, http://www.catholic-hierarchy.org/diocese/dcaco.html#stats.

[2027] George P. Matysek, "Cardinal Turkson Says African Catholics Have Numbers, But Faith Must Mature," Archdiocese of Baltimore, 26 May 2005, https://www.archbalt.org/cardinal-turkson-says-african-catholics-have-numbers-but-faith-must-mature/.

[2028] Turkson, "The Church in Africa at the Service of Reconciliation."

[2029] Ibid.

[2030] Ibid.

[2031] Ibid.

[2032] Ibid.

[2033] Ibid.

[2034] Renewal Ministries, April 2007, https://www.renewalministries.net/?module=Page&event=Download&docID=46; "Mission to Ghana," Renewal Ministries, 2015, https://www.renewalministries.net/?module=Missions&missionID=16.

movement, to form priests and seminarians in his archdiocese. Part of this formation also included the provision of scholarships by Renewal Ministries for priests from Ghana who were interested in attending evangelization and formation programs at the Sacred Heart Seminary in Detroit.[2035]

Divorce and Remarriage

In addition to addressing the need for good formation of African priests, Turkson has tackled more difficult issues facing the Church in Africa. In an interview with the *Boston Globe* in 2014, the cardinal was ambiguous on the issue of relaxing the ban on divorced-and-civilly-"remarried" couples from receiving Communion. In responding to a question about whether relaxing the ban would negatively affect the Church's prohibition on polygamy, the cardinal said, "I don't think giving consideration to the divorced and remarried would create any problem for the ministry of marriage in Africa."[2036]

Although the cardinal favors interreligious dialogue, he affirms nonetheless the unicity of salvation through Jesus Christ and that the fullness of truth resides in the Catholic Church. During the 2004 Eucharistic Congress, Turkson stated that "God desires everyone to come to the knowledge of the truth, namely, *'there is one God; there is also one mediator between God and humankind, Christ Jesus . . . who gave himself as ransom for all'* (1 Tim. 2:5)."[2037] For Cardinal Turkson, the Church is the "household of God and a pillar of truth ... [and] sound teaching nourishes the Church (1 Tim. 4:6)."[2038] As part of this understanding, the cardinal has endorsed

---

[2035] Ibid.

[2036] John L. Allen, "Catholicism Growing in Heart of Muslim World," *Boston Globe*, 8 March 2014, https://www.bostonglobe.com/news/world/2014/03/08/catholicism-growing-heart-muslim-world/LxIiUYwSlro7Zl6ugvVQJM/story.html.

[2037] Card. Peter Turkson, "The Eucharist, Mystery of Communion and Mission," 48th International Eucharistic Congress, http://www.vatican.va/roman_curia/pont_committees/eucharist-congr/documents/rc_committ_euchar_doc_20041010_turkson-catechisis-youth_en.html.

[2038] Ibid.

a book that criticizes a form of practical universalism about salvation for non-Catholics and non-Christians.[2039] In addition, during a Bible Summit in 2012, Turkson praised *Dei Verbum*, saying that it "led to a surging vitality in the life of the Church."[2040] Turkson remarked that Pope Benedict XVI affirmed *Dei Verbum* and stated that "nothing that the Church does is not rooted in Scripture."[2041]

Merging of Dicasteries

Turkson oversaw the merging of the Pontifical Councils for Justice and Peace, for the Pastoral Care of Migrants and Itinerant People, and for Health Care Workers into the "super dicastery" for the Promotion of Integral Human Development, completed in 2017. However, as with each of these reforms of the Roman Curia, efficiency has increased in some areas and declined in others. Throughout his time at the Vatican, Turkson has been closely assisted by Cardinal Michael Czerny, S.J., who served as his principal aide before Czerny's appointment to head the migrant section of the new dicastery and his subsequent elevation to the College of Cardinals.

Coronavirus

In April 2020, Pope Francis asked Cardinal Turkson, as head of the Dicastery for Promoting Integral Human Development, to create and coordinate

---

[2039] Michael Potemra, "Hell: A Populous Place?," *National Review*, 8 October 2012, https://www.nationalreview.com/corner/hell-populous-place-michael-potemra/; Father C. John McCloskey, "Who Will Be Saved, How Many and How?," *National Catholic Register*, 28 September 2013, http://www.ncregister.com/daily-news/who-will-be-saved-how-many-and-how; John L. Allen Jr., "Synod Notebook: Salvation, the Movements, and the Poor," *National Catholic Reporter*, 13 October 2012, https://www.ncronline.org/blogs/ncr-today/synod-notebook-salvation-movements-and-poor.

[2040] Beth Griffin, "Vatican Cardinal Affirms Church's Scriptural Roots at Bible Summit," *Catholic New York*, 27 June 2012, http://cny.org/stories/vatican-cardinal-affirms-churchs-scriptural-roots-at-bible-summit,7729.

[2041] Ibid. These comments show Turkson's support for *Dei Verbum*, the historicity of the Gospels, and the inerrancy of Scripture.

a new commission of five working groups to express "the Church's concern and love for the entire human family in the face of the COVID-19 pandemic." The so-called task force primarily has a socioeconomic and scientific focus to deal with the fallout from the virus outbreak. Similarly, in interviews,[2042] Turkson focused on the "concrete" help the dicastery was to offer in terms of support, consisting of assisting local churches to help save lives, to help the poorest, and to deal with the economic crisis and social consequences to follow. Observers pointed out that he made no mention of the sacraments or their deprivation after several weeks of public Mass cancellations.

TEACHING OFFICE

In 2009, Pope Benedict XVI appointed Turkson president of the Pontifical Council for Justice and Peace (hereafter the "council") and Francis appointed him head of the new Dicastery for Promoting Integral Human Development (hereafter the "dicastery") in 2017. The dicastery situates human development firmly within a personalist framework, which focuses on the dignity of the human person as the center and root of economic, social, and cultural development.

Rooting Out Church Corruption

In addition to concerns regarding technology and ecology, Turkson has devoted significant efforts to weeding out corruption in the ecclesial and secular spheres. In 2011, echoing the contents of Benedict XVI's 2009 social encyclical *Caritas in Veritate*, he called for a "global public authority" and a "central world bank" to be established with the task of ruling local

---

[2042] Massimiliano Menichetti, "Five Working Groups Formed," Zenit, 15 April 2020, https://zenit.org/articles/vatican-news-interview-with-cardinal-turkson-on-coronavirus-initiatives/.

financial institutions;[2043] and in 2017 he published a book titled *Corrosione. Combattere la corruzione nella Chiesa e nella società* (Rome: Rizzoli), which included a laudatory preface by Pope Francis. The book has also been translated into Spanish.

Cardinal Turkson has spoken widely on the topic of human dignity and its core meaning. His view of human rights "stem[s] from the deepest foundation stone"[2044] of human dignity, the *imago Dei.*[2045] In an address to the United Nations on human rights,[2046] the cardinal articulated certain natural human rights that flow from authentic human dignity, including the right to health care and religious liberty. He distinguished from these natural rights those rights that have proliferated through political discourse and are unconnected to the true dignity of the human person, including such *faux rights* as those to same-sex "marriage" and homosexual behavior.[2047] Advocating for integral human development has led Turkson to address other human-rights issues in the public square. In 2018, Cardinal Turkson spoke about the problem of antibiotic overuse,[2048] the problem

[2043] Pontifical Council for Justice and Peace, "Towards Reforming the International Financial and Monetary Systems in the Context of Global Public Authority," 24 October 2011, http://www.vatican.va/roman_curia/pontifical_councils/justpeace/documents/rc_pc_justpeace_doc_20111024_nota_en.html.

[2044] Cardinal Peter K. A. Turkson, "The Catholic Church and Human Rights, Slovak Bishops Conference," *Tablet,* 4 March 2014, https://www.thetablet.co.uk/UserFiles/Files/2014.03.04_Catholic_Church__Human_Rights_Bratislava.PDF.

[2045] Ibid.

[2046] Zenit Staff, "Cardinal Turkson on Human Rights," Zenit, 5 March 2014, https://zenit.org/articles/cardinal-turkson-on-human-rights/.

[2047] Julie Minda, "Cardinal Turkson Asserts Health Care Is a Human Right, Not a Privilege," Catholic Health Association of the United States, 1 June 2017, https://www.chausa.org/publications/catholic-health-world/article/june-1-2017/cardinal-turkson-asserts-health-care-is-a-human-right-not-a-privilege; Zenit Staff, "Cardinal Turkson on Human Rights."

[2048] Anne Condodina, "Cardinal Makes 'Urgent Call' to Combat Antibiotic Overuse, Misuse," *Crux,* 20 November 2018, https://cruxnow.com/vatican/2018/11/20/cardinal-makes-urgent-call-to-combat-antibiotic-overuse-misuse/.

of prostitution and human trafficking,[2049] and the current human-rights abuses in the fishing industry.[2050]

Human Rights

Turkson has spoken openly about many of the social issues affecting the African continent, including the imposition of certain Westernized understandings of health care onto the African people. In 2017, Cardinal Turkson described health care as a "human right" for every human person, not just the privileged population. He stated that the practice of abortion was part of an antilife mentality in health care rather than women's legitimate health care.[2051]

Turkson has distinguished what he calls "healthy realism" from relativism in the human-rights discourse, which, he says, "removes these rights from their proper context because it implies that rights are not based on the natural law inscribed on our hearts and thus not present in all cultures and civilizations."[2052] The cardinal's approach to human rights is informed by the truths of the Catholic Faith. For the cardinal, "respect for orthodoxy and the teaching of the true faith seems to have been very crucial in the maintenance of unity among the communities (Acts 2:42)."[2053]

Reproductive-Rights Opposition

Cardinal Turkson's pro-life lens colors his approach to defining human rights. He has condemned using the term "reproductive rights" to encompass

---

[2049] Joanna Bogle, "A Cardinal from Africa Goes to London," *National Catholic Register*, 20 November 2018, http://www.ncregister.com/blog/joannabogle/a-cardinal-from-africa-goes-to-london.

[2050] "Let Us Stop Human Trafficking and Forced Labour at Sea: Cardinal Turkson Urges All in a World Fisheries Day Message," Knights and Ladies of Marshall, 21 November 2018, http://marshallan.org/let-us-stop-human-trafficking-and-forced-labour-at-sea-cardinal-turkson-urges-all-in-a-world-fisheries-day-message/.

[2051] Minda, "Cardinal Turkson Asserts Health Care."

[2052] Turkson, "Catholic Church and Human Rights."

[2053] Turkson, "The Eucharist."

abortion rights. As an African, Cardinal Turkson has spoken against the imposition of Western norms about abortion and contraception on the developing world. "It's not for people sitting here (in the West) to decide [that] the issues for people in the developing world are abortion and contraception. These are not health issues."[2054] Cardinal Turkson rejects the proliferation of new human rights that are unconnected to the flourishing of the human person and human communities, explaining that "the Church has a serious concern when the ideology of a particular group of individuals can somehow create a new human right."[2055] Turkson clearly indicated a view that abortion is never morally permissible when he condemned "the attempt on the part of some to legitimize the killing of an unborn child through the promotion of so called 'reproductive rights', 'reproductive services', and other loaded terms which mask the tragedy of abortion."[2056]

Life Issues

In 2017, Cardinal Turkson stated that euthanasia is part of an antilife mentality in health care.[2057] To those who would offer assistance to suicide,[2058] Turkson called for people to respect the fullness and dignity of every life.[2059] The cardinal linked the Church's teaching on the prohibition on euthanasia to the relationality of the human person. "No individual is an island,"[2060] the cardinal stated. "Relationship is fundamental to being human. End-of-life provisions must not neglect this point."[2061]

[2054] Deborah Gyapong, "Abortion Pushed on Third World May Have Racist Agenda, Says Cardinal Turkson," *Catholic Register*, 1 October 2012, https://www.catholicregister.org/item/15162-abortion-pushed-on-third-world-may-have-racist-agenda-says-cardinal-turkson.

[2055] Zenit Staff, "Cardinal Turkson on Human Rights."

[2056] Ibid.

[2057] Minda, "Cardinal Turkson Asserts Health Care."

[2058] Michael Swan, "Progress Is Not Always a Good Thing, Says Cardinal," *Catholic Register*, 23 March 2016, https://www.catholicregister.org/item/21992-progress-is-not-always-a-good-thing-says-cardinal.

[2059] Ibid.

[2060] Ibid.

[2061] Ibid.

Turkson has made a clear distinction between pain management and intentional killing. During the 2016 John M. Kelly Lecture at the University of St. Michael's College, Toronto, he stated that "compassion is misplaced when it intentionally hastens death."[2062] Rather, euthanasia is "the ultimate form of exclusion, marginalization and throwing away."[2063] Turkson taught clearly that "the Church has long taught that physicians may manage the pain and suffering of the dying so that they can live their final period as richly as possible, in relationship with others and with God, even if that period becomes shorter as a side-effect of the pain management measures."[2064] The cardinal has also defended conscientious objection for Catholic physicians and hospitals.

In addition, the cardinal has spoken frequently about the problems of HIV and poverty in Africa. When asked what specific challenges the Catholic health-care ministry was facing in 2017, the cardinal talked generally about the cultural "antilife" mentality that runs contrary to the gospel of life.[2065] He described this mentality as "touch[ing] on all stages of human life, from its initial stages to its natural end: procreation, living and death,"[2066] which manifests itself as "artificial means of fertility control, contraceptives and abortion, genetic manipulation, euthanasia, [and] assisted suicide."[2067] Cardinal Turkson urged the Church to counter the growing antilife mentality[2068] and encouraged a commitment to the "absolute respect for human life and its sacredness."[2069]

Turkson has stressed the urgency of nations meeting the UN's Sustainable Development Goals, which he praised wholeheartedly. To date, he has neither mentioned nor warned against goal number three, which sets

---

[2062] Ibid.

[2063] Ibid.

[2064] "Cardinal Turkson Gives Laudato Si Lecture in Canada," Vatican Radio, 22 March 2016, http://www.archivioradiovaticana.va/storico/2016/03/22/cardinal_turkson_gives_laudato_si_lecture_in_canada/en-1217138.

[2065] Minda, "Cardinal Turkson Asserts Health Care."

[2066] Ibid.

[2067] Ibid.

[2068] Ibid.

[2069] Ibid.

targets for promoting "sexual and reproductive health" (code for abortion and contraception) for the world's poorest by 2030.[2070]

Contraception and HIV and AIDS

Turkson's views on contraception are unclear, and on the use of condoms to prevent the transmission of AIDS, they are permissive. In an interview with the BBC in 2015 to discuss climate change, he made a statement that suggested a lower population could be a climate-change solution, which sparked controversy. His full response was as follows:

> This has been talked about, and the Holy Father on his trip back from the Philippines also invited people to some form of birth control, because the church has never been against birth control and people spacing out births and all of that. So yes, it can offer a solution.... The amount of population that is critical for the realisation of this is still something we need to discover, yet the Holy Father has also called for a certain amount of control of birth.[2071]

Following the BBC interview, Turkson clarified that in using the term "control of birth," he was referring to the spacing of children.[2072] Cardinal Turkson explained that "you don't deal with one good with another evil: The Church wants people to be fed, so let's do what the Church feels is not right? That is a kind of sophistry that the church would not go for."[2073]

[2070] "Press Conference to Present the International Conference 'Religions and the Sustainable Development Goals (SDGs): Listening to the Cry of the Earth and of the Poor', 05.03.2019," Vatican, http://press.vatican.va/content/salastampa/en/bollettino/pubblico/2019/03/05/190305a.html.

[2071] Matt McGrath, "COP21: Cardinal Says Birth Control May Offer Climate 'Solution,'" BBC News, 9 December 2015, https://www.bbc.com/news/science-environment-35040477.

[2072] Ibid.; Diane Montagna, "Exclusive: Cardinal Turkson Clarifies Birth Control, Climate Change Comments," *Aleteia*, 10 December 2015, https://aleteia.org/2015/12/10/cardinal-turkson-clarifies-birth-control-climate-change-comments/.

[2073] McGrath, "Birth Control May Offer Climate 'Solution.'"

Cardinal Turkson has signaled openness to the separate argument that condoms might be appropriate for couples where one partner is HIV-positive to prevent the disease from spreading. In a Vatican news conference in 2009 the cardinal answered a question on the problem of HIV and AIDS, saying, "In Africa there are so very, very many various scenarios involving the HIV/AIDS question. There is a situation in Southern Africa which is tragic, which is very pressing and that's where most of the references about the [treatment] of HIV refer." He noted the discovery now antiretrovirus drugs, adding: "It is either the antiretrovirus or it is the use of condom to stop the spread of HIV/AIDS, unless we go with the abstinence, you know, and fidelity to partners and things like that.[2074]

Examining a survey of Catholic hospitals in Ghana, Turkson said that "when even people propose" the "use of condoms, it becomes only effective in families where they resolve also to be faithful.... But still our primary concern and our priority are such that what we will talk first about will probably be this: the abstinence and loyalty and fidelity and you refrain from sex when it is not the case."[2075]

Cardinal Turkson articulated his own view on the matter, which emphasized the role of pastoral accompaniment and case-by-case decision-making:

> If anybody came to me ever with HIV/AIDS and wanted my view, I know that in all situations of pastoral counselling the pastor never decides what a candidate must do. It's the same in psychological counselling situations: you just expose the issues, discuss the issues with the candidate and allow the person to decide, take his own decision.... And when that is the case, I would not undervalue the possibility that somebody who has AIDS, recognizing his own Christian commitment, would simply just decide to refrain from sex.... Some would, in such a situation,

---

[2074] John L. Allen Jr., "African Cardinal on Condoms and AIDS," *National Catholic Reporter*, 5 October 2009, https://www.ncronline.org/blogs/ncr-today/african-cardinal-condoms-and-aids.
[2075] Ibid.

have advised the use of a condom by the partner who has HIV/AIDS so it doesn't spread.[2076]

His final view on the matter was to prioritize funding of antiretroviral drugs instead of investing in the production of condoms because "the use of condoms is sometimes risky: risky in the sense that will we have cases of condoms that have burst during sex."[2077] However, the cardinal's main argument seems to be that condoms give Africans "a false sense of security,"[2078] because of improper use. Cardinal Turkson stated that "people think that using condoms will prevent the spreading of AIDS but it is actually helping the disease spread."[2079] It is not clear if Turkson was limiting this discussion to married couples with discordant AIDS or HIV status who used condoms to combat disease or if he was speaking of condom use more generally. However, he subsequently stated that "the position of the church on condoms is pretty clear."[2080]

Homosexuality

Turkson appears to maintain that homosexual behavior is immoral and calls same-sex-attracted persons to chastity.[2081] He has described homosexuality as an "alternative lifestyle"[2082] and once criticized the previous Secretary-General of the United Nations for conflating mere desires with human rights. The cardinal stated:

[2076] Ibid.

[2077] Ibid.

[2078] Rod McCullom, "An African Pope Won't Change the Vatican's Views on Condoms and AIDS," *Atlantic*, 26 February 2013, https://www.theatlantic.com/sexes/archive/2013/02/an-african-pope-wont-change-the-vaticans-views-on-condoms-and-aids/273535/.

[2079] Ibid.

[2080] "We Are the World."

[2081] Zenit Staff, "Cardinal Turkson on Human Rights."

[2082] Edward Pentin, "Cardinal Responds to U.N.'s Criticism of Africa's Social Policies," *National Catholic Register*, 21 February 2012, http://www.ncregister.com/daily-news/cardinals-responds-to-u.n.s-criticism-of-africas-social-policies.

We [the Church] push for the rights of prisoners, the rights of others; and the last thing we want to do is infringe upon the rights of anyone. But when you're talking about what's called "an alternative lifestyle," are those human rights?... He [Ban Ki-moon] needs to recognize there's a subtle distinction between morality and human rights, and that's what needs to be clarified. [2083]

Cardinal Turkson has commented on the connection between gender fluidity and homosexuality in the human-rights context and rejected the inclusion of both as genuine human-rights issues:

Another example is the use of the term "gender" to suggest that sex is not biologically grounded as male and female but is simply a social construct or produced by what individuals think or feel they are. Moreover, attempts to recognize those engaging in homosexual behaviour as a specific group to be accorded human rights go beyond the protection to be guaranteed to all people under the Universal Declaration of Human Rights. [2084]

Respect and compassion for homosexual persons also mark Turkson's approach, and he has made it clear that all persons "must be accepted with respect, compassion and sensitivity" [2085] and that "every sign of unjust discrimination in their regard should be avoided." [2086] This posture of respect and compassion does not, however, take away from the cardinal's view that "the Church regrets the discordance between homosexual behavior as such and what we understand as the norm for God-given human nature." [2087] Instead, Turkson asks that we emulate compassion and respect for all people and "see our Lord's reaction when the townspeople wished

[2083] Ibid.
[2084] Turkson, "The Catholic Church and Human Rights."
[2085] Ibid.
[2086] Ibid.
[2087] Ibid.

to stone a woman to death for adultery: He managed to preserve her life and bodily security (John 8:1-11)."[2088]

Indeed, in his role as relator for the Second African Synod, Turkson spoke about the many attacks on the traditional family in Africa.[2089] The cardinal described the "ferocious onslaught on the family and the related fundamental institution of marriage from outside Africa"[2090] which comes from "ideological (gender ideology, a new global sexual ethic, genetic engineering) and clinical (contraception: Planned Parenthood and Reproductive Health Education, sterilization), and emerging 'alternative' life styles (same-sex marriages, sexual unions)."[2091] During the Second African Synod, Turkson, along with the synod fathers, "vigorously denounced the ideology and international programs which are imposed on African countries under false pretexts or as conditions for development assistance."[2092]

During his tenure as president of the Pontifical Council for Justice and Peace, Turkson described the criminal sanctions imposed on homosexuals in Africa as an "exaggeration"[2093] and publicly criticized laws criminalizing homosexual behavior in Uganda.[2094] The cardinal linked the draconian nature of criminal sanctions for homosexuals as "probably commensurate with tradition."[2095] The tradition referred to here is the cultural stigmatization of homosexuality in Africa. Turkson stated that one should understand the reasons for stigmatization because "just as there's a sense of a call for rights, there's also a call to respect culture, of all kinds of people," he said.

[2088] Ibid.
[2089] Turkson, "The Church in Africa at the Service of Reconciliation."
[2090] Ibid.
[2091] Ibid.
[2092] Ibid.
[2093] Pentin, "Cardinal Responds to U.N.'s Criticism."
[2094] Staff Reporter, "Cardinal Turkson Criticises Uganda's Anti-Gay Law," *Catholic Herald*, 4 March 2014, https://catholicherald.co.uk/cardinal-turkson-criticises-ugandas-anti-gay-law/.
[2095] Pentin, "Cardinal Responds to U.N.'s Criticism."

"So, if it's being stigmatized, in fairness, it's probably right to find out why it is being stigmatized."[2096]

In an interview with CNN in 2013,[2097] when asked about whether he was worried that the sex abuse scandal in the Catholic Church would spread to Africa, Turkson stated that the stigmatization of homosexuality would probably prevent this. In his own words:

> African traditional systems kind of protect or have protected its population against this tendency ... because in several communities, in several cultures in Africa homosexuality or for that matter any affair between two sexes of the same kind are not countenanced in our society. [2098]

For Cardinal Turkson, marriage, by nature, is between one man and one woman and cannot be redefined by the Church or the state. He believes same-sex "marriage" is not permissible as a matter of civil law. In an address to the Slovak Bishops' Conference in 2014, the cardinal clearly articulated this point:

> Related to this is the suggestion that marriage could somehow be redefined, despite the fact that marriage is, by nature, between one man and one woman for their mutual love and increase of the human family, as affirmed in international law. Such positions distort reality because they attempt to rewrite human nature, which *de natura* cannot be rewritten.... Marriage comes to us from nature. Christ sanctifies marriage as a sacrament for the baptized, giving it significance beyond its natural reality; the State protects marriage because it is essential to family and to the common good of society.

[2096] Ibid.

[2097] Samuel Burke, "Meet the Man Who Could Be the First Black Pope," CNN, 12 February 2013, http://amanpour.blogs.cnn.com/2013/02/12/meet-the-man-who-could-be-the-first-black-pope/.

[2098] Ibid.

But neither Church nor State invented marriage, and neither can change its nature.[2099]

But his views on homosexuality in general considerably loosened a year later when he told a homosexual advocacy group "we are all growing" with regard to criminalization of homosexual acts. Moreover, he told reporters later the same day that homosexuality is no longer considered a taboo in Africa "because it has been spoken of in an open way.... If you think it is taboo, you should go to Russia." Homosexuality, he added, was considered an "abnormality" in the United States in the 1970s, but "now it has changed." He said countries that "do not accept [homosexuality] need further education" and that although a "lot of countries have learned ... we need to let them grow and improve."

Polygamy and the Dubia

Cardinal Turkson has spoken of the complexity of providing pastoral care to polygamous families, a common problem in parts of Africa.[2100] Taking a nuanced approach to the issue, the cardinal is in favor of pastoral discretion when directing and dealing with polygamous families. For example, at the 2005 Synod of Bishops in the Vatican, Turkson said:

> You can't just say to a man, let the other [wives] go and stay with the first wife.... There's a question of justice. You can ask the man to provide for her ongoing security, setting up a small business for her, for example.... There's also [the wives'] need for a sexual partner.... You can't just say to everyone they should be celibate.... You don't want to expose them to prostitution and so on.[2101]

[2099] Turkson, "The Catholic Church and Human Rights."

[2100] Zenit Staff, "Cardinal Turkson on Human Rights."

[2101] John L. Allen Jr., "Surprise! One of the Church's Family Issues Is Polygamy," *Crux*, 11 September 2014, https://cruxnow.com/church/2014/09/11/surprise-one-of-the-churchs-family-issues-is-polygamy/.

Turkson called for an open dialogue between Pope Francis and the cardinals[2102] who wrote the *dubia* on the Post-Synodal Apostolic Exhortation *Amoris Laetitia*, saying all parties involved should debate the controversy on a stage. The cardinal expressed perplexity at Pope Francis' silence in response to the *dubia*.[2103]

Immigration

Although the dicastery that Turkson heads is tasked with attention to immigration, it is Pope Francis who officially oversees the section that deals with refugee and migrant matters.[2104] Cardinal Turkson has a nuanced understanding of the issue and acknowledges that the solution to immigration at a policy level is not straightforward. In a 2016 interview, the cardinal stated that "the causes of it are not the same,"[2105] and he identified four separate causes of movement among peoples:

> From Latin America to the U.S., a motivation that's economic essentially, from sub-Saharan Africa to Europe; the motivation essentially is economic, apart from a few random cases like Boko Haram and security and conflict in Nigeria. Then there's a movement from Syria, Iraq, Afghanistan and the Middle East towards Europe. They're clearly [issues of] security and conflict. Then, from South East Asia

---

[2102] Edward Pentin, "Church Leaders Respond to the 'Dubia,'" *National Catholic Register*, 6 December 2016, http://www.ncregister.com/daily-news/church-leaders-respond-to-the-dubia.

[2103] Claire Chretien, "Cardinal Turkson Calls for Open Debate on Amoris Laetitia amid Attacks on Four Cardinals," LifeSite News, 7 December 2016, https://www.lifesitenews.com/news/prominent-cardinals-decline-to-comment-on-dubia-cardinal-turkson-suggests-d.

[2104] Pope Francis, "Statutes of the Dicastery for Promoting Integral Human Development," Vatican, 17 August 2016, http://w2.vatican.va/content/francesco/en/motu_proprio/documents/papa-francesco_20160817_statuto-dicastero-servizio-sviluppo-umano-integrale.html.

[2105] Edward Pentin, "Cardinal Turkson Discusses His New Role," *National Catholic Register*, 23 December 2016, http://www.ncregister.com/daily-news/cardinal-turkson-discusses-his-new-role.

towards Australia and Singapore, there are two things: religious persecution, Buddhist elements and the economic thing. So for these various reasons, people are on the move now.[2106]

Turkson has not advocated for an immigration policy that requires wealthy countries to grant permanent residence to migrants seeking to escape poverty. Rather, the cardinal has identified two conflicting values that should be addressed. In 2017, he responded to a question about current U.S. immigration by stating:

> These are two core values that may be in conflict: You provide safety for your people, yes, but would ensuring the safety of the U.S. alone lead to general safety for the world? Is there also a global value that needs to be looked at, instead of a simple national value?[2107]

Islam and Interreligious Dialogue

In discussing the role of the dicastery, the cardinal has identified the problem that Islam poses to the growth of the Catholic Church. He stated that "the first challenge comes from Islamic countries"[2108] because "they have a lot of resources, building mosques everywhere, encouraging and paying for conversions."[2109] Turkson identified the incompatibility of Islam with human freedom in situations of forced Islamic conversions where groups provide material goods as an incentive.

During the 2012 Synod of Bishops, Cardinal Turkson screened a controversial and inflammatory video about Europe's growing Muslim population.[2110] Shortly after the video screening, the cardinal said he regretted

---

[2106] Ibid.

[2107] John L. Allen Jr., "Vatican's Top African Challenges Trump to Think Globally," *Crux*, 26 March 2017, https://cruxnow.com/africaund/2017/03/26/vaticans-top-african-challenges-trump-think-globally/.

[2108] Pentin, "Turkson Discusses His New Role."

[2109] Ibid.

[2110] John L. Allen Jr., "Synod Notebook: Video on Islam Rocks the House," *National Catholic Reporter*, 15 October 2012, https://www.ncronline.org/blogs/ncr-today/synod-notebook-video-islam-rocks-house.

showing the film and clarified that the "point was not to be anti-Islam," but rather, to "highlight the demographic situation as a result of the antilife tendency and culture in the Western world."[2111] Ghana has a large Islamic population, and Turkson seems to have a relatively good understanding of the Muslim community because his paternal uncle was a Muslim.[2112] In discussing the high population of Muslims in Ghana, the cardinal differentiated between moderate Muslims and "the movement of purifying Islam."[2113] Turkson has expressed concern that this movement is making Ghana "less tolerant of non-Islamic elements in society."[2114]

As part of his advocacy of interreligious dialogue, Turkson has signaled his openness to dialogue with Muslims of goodwill. In 2009, the cardinal invited the African bishops "to overcome their fears and past burdens (relationships between the Arab world and black Africa), and to establish partnerships with Muslims of good will, so as to reduce tensions."[2115] For the cardinal "in the pursuit of the common good and other social/humanitarian values with non-Christians, praiseworthy approaches inspired by Christian values help win esteem and respect for one's religion."[2116]

Politics and Finance

The cardinal argues that education is integral to a greater understanding of the purpose of politics as serving the common good. Turkson understands that individual Christian formation for politicians will enable them to carry out their role of serving the common good effectively. Cardinal Turkson has called for the training of "men and women politicians,"[2117] which includes:

[2111] O'Connell, "For Me to Attack Islam."

[2112] Ibid.

[2113] James Kelly, "Cardinal Turkson Discusses the Turmoil in North Africa," *National Catholic Register*, 23 March 2011, http://www.ncregister.com/daily-news/cardinal-turkson-discusses-the-turmoil-in-north-africa.

[2114] Ibid.

[2115] Turkson, *Relatio Post Disceptationem*.

[2116] Turkson, "The Eucharist."

[2117] Turkson, *Relatio Post Disceptationem*.

A solid Christian formation (the Bible, moral theology, the social teachings of the Church, Church History …) and with juridical tools that will enable them to defend Christian values (especially the family) and thus contribute positively to the formulation of legislative texts which respect Christian moral values.[2118]

In a note, "Towards Reforming the International Financial and Monetary Systems in the Context of Global Public Authority," written by the dicastery, urging reform of the international financial system in 2011, Turkson highlighted the importance of submitting secondary political goals to the service of the global common good. He stated that:

Every individual and every community shares in promoting and preserving the common good. To be faithful to their ethical and religious vocation, communities of believers should take the lead in asking whether the human family has adequate means at its disposal to achieve the global common good.[2119]

In the same note, Turkson advocated for an international public authority to oversee the financial system.[2120] In a talk on the subject in 2019, Turkson stated that "local and global economics must be viewed not only in terms of production and distribution, but also in terms of their effect on the environment, the dignity of people and the way it ensures their well-being."[2121]

Cardinal Turkson has brushed off criticism that the modern Church has lost its Christocentric focus and become too man-centered and horizontal. "We've heard that, too, but for me, it's not either/or," he said in 2016.

[2118] Ibid.

[2119] Pontifical Council for Justice and Peace, "Towards Reforming the International Financial and Monetary Systems."

[2120] Ibid.

[2121] Heidi Schlumpf, "Vatican Official Challenges Ethics of Markets at University of Chicago Event," *National Catholic Reporter*, 1 April 2019, https://www.ncronline.org/news/justice/vatican-official-challenges-ethics-markets-university-chicago-event.

"The separation has never been this or that, that we've been horizontal and now we're vertical. The Church by its character can never be purely horizontal or purely vertical."[2122]

LAUDATO SI'

Care for creation has been a central theme of Cardinal Turkson's episcopate. The Pontifical Council for Justice and Peace took part in the drafting of the Encyclical *Laudato Si'*. Pope Francis has commented that Cardinal Turkson and his team prepared the first draft of the encyclical letter.[2123] Since its publication in 2015, Cardinal Turkson has traveled to a range of forums to speak about the main themes of the encyclical. He has made a number of statements regarding the direct connection between care for the environment and respect for human dignity.

Cardinal Turkson has advocated for a human-rights-based approach to environmental policy. The cardinal views environmental issues through the lens of what he has called "integral ecology,"[2124] which acts "as a paradigm able to articulate the fundamental relationships of the person with God, with him/herself, with other human beings, with creation."[2125] Turkson's broad approach to human and ecological development was summarized well in his address on *Laudato Si'* to a "High Level Event on Climate Change" in 2015:

[2122] Pentin, "Turkson Discusses His New Role."

[2123] "Press Conference of His Holiness Pope Francis Onboard the Flight from Colombo to Manila," Vatican Press, 15 January 2015, http://w2.vatican.va/content/francesco/en/speeches/2015/january/documents/papa-francesco_20150115_srilanka-filippine-incontro-giornalisti.html.

[2124] Cardinal Peter K. A. Turkson, "*Laudato Si'*: Presentation in the ECOSOC Chamber," Vatican, 30 June 2015, http://www.vatican.va/roman_curia/pontifical_councils/justpeace/documents/rc_pc_justpeace_doc_20150630_laudato-si-ecosoc_en.html.

[2125] Ibid.

Laudato Si' insists that the plight of the poor and the fragility of the planet are intimately related, and so encourages the world's governments to embrace integral ecology as the necessary approach to such development, inclusive of all and protective of the earth.... Overcoming poverty and reducing environmental degradation will require the human community seriously to review the dominant model of development, production, commerce and consumption.... The political dimension needs to re-establish democratic control over the economy and finance, that is, over the basic choices made by human societies.[2126]

In describing the "broad vision" of *Laudato Si'*, the cardinal stated that "humanity is not separate from the environment in which we live; rather humanity and the natural environment are one."[2127] He has also spoken about the harmful effect of certain human activities on the environment, particularly the climate. For Turkson, "the accelerating change in climate is undeniable, catastrophic, worsened by human activities, but also amenable to human intervention."[2128] This anthropocentric problem has an anthropocentric solution for Turkson, who stated that "we must address the ethical nature of our crisis, both through dialogue, and by recovering our fundamental spiritual dimension."[2129]

Cardinal Turkson's emphasis on environmentalism is inseparable from the pro-life cause[2130] and integrally connected to it. Again, this perspective is

---

[2126] Cardinal Peter K. A. Turkson, "High Level Event on Climate Change," Vatican, 29 June 2015, http://www.vatican.va/roman_curia/pontifical_councils/justpeace/documents/rc_pc_justpeace_doc_20150629_climate-change_en.html.

[2127] Cardinal Peter K. A. Turkson, "Remarks on Laudato si' to Child-Focused Agencies," Vatican, 30 June 2015, http://www.vatican.va/roman_curia/pontifical_councils/justpeace/documents/rc_pc_justpeace_doc_20150630_insights-laudato-si_en.html.

[2128] Ibid.

[2129] Ibid.

[2130] Inés San Martín, "Turkson: Pro-life Cause and Concern for Environment Are 'Inseparable,'" *Crux*, 1 September 2017, https://cruxnow.com/

embedded in the viewpoint of integral ecology illustrated by the cardinal's statement "When we abuse one relationship or one justice, we trample on everything."[2131] In discussing care for the environment vis-à-vis life issues, Cardinal Turkson indicated that while care for the environment is a policy consideration that can be realized in many ways, abortion and the death penalty take precedence and are different in kind.[2132]

Turkson understands the common good as considering the good of future generations. For the cardinal, care for the environment is closely connected to care for human life, for the vulnerable, and for future generations. In his address to child-focused agencies in 2015, Turkson spoke about the requirements of justice in the following terms:

> Thinking about the needs and the world of children now and yet to be born is also an index of justice. The common good is not just horizontal (the good of everyone now) but vertical (the good of future generations).[2133]

Although he has advocated for environmental policy change in line with this view of integral ecology, the cardinal has warned that "it is imperative that practical proposals not be developed in an ideological, superficial or reductionist way."[2134] In his presentation in the ECO-SOC Chamber in 2015, Turkson made it clear that "there are certain

---

interviews/2017/09/01/turkson-pro-life-cause-concern-environment-inseparable/.

[2131] Joshua J. McElwee, "Cardinal Turkson: 'We Do Not Stop War by Starting Another War,'" *National Catholic Reporter,* 20 September 2016, https://www.ncronline.org/news/people/cardinal-turkson-we-do-not-stop-war-starting-another-war.

[2132] Cardinal Turkson states that opposition to abortion and the death penalty are part of "our religion." Suzanne Goldenberg, "Abortion and Death Penalty Come before Climate Change for Church, Vatican Official Says," *Guardian,* 25 September 2015, https://www.theguardian.com/world/2015/sep/25/abortion-and-death-penalty-come-before-climate-change-for-church-vatican-official-says.

[2133] Turkson, "Remarks on Laudato si'."

[2134] Turkson, "*Laudato Si*': Presentation in the ECOSOC Chamber."

environmental issues where it is not easy to achieve a broad consensus"[2135] and that "the Church does not presume to settle scientific questions or to replace politics."[2136]

SUMMARY

A fully modern cardinal who for many years has been the darling of Western liberals wanting to see a malleable African pope, Cardinal Peter Turkson appreciates the influence of the Second Vatican Council in the Church and the world at large. He came to the Vatican with some surprise and trepidation but soon embraced the role and ended up overseeing one of the first major curial reforms under Pope Francis: the merger of his pontifical council with two others into a "super dicastery" headed by him.

With pastoral and curial experience under his belt, Turkson has committed himself to addressing some of the most prominent issues of the day, including human rights, ecology, and corruption. Given his curial role, he has focused almost exclusively on socioeconomic issues and sees no excessive emphasis on the temporal at the expense of the spiritual.

As a bishop, he was especially active in Ghana and the African continent, while his work as a cardinal has established a global platform for his apostolic activity. Ready to engage with non-Catholics, Turkson has generally not shied away from affirming the Church's traditional positions on the priesthood, marriage between a man and a woman, and homosexuality—although his views on the latter significantly loosened during Francis' pontificate.

While condemning abortion and euthanasia, he is permissive regarding the use of contraceptives in certain circumstances. And despite his close interaction with United Nations officials and affiliations over the years, he has generally steered clear of publicly warning against "reproductive

---

[2135] Ibid.
[2136] Ibid.

health" policies—that is, abortion and contraception, which the UN fiercely promotes.

Given that some of his family is Muslim, he denounces Islamophobia while not turning a blind eye to the dangers that Islam poses to human freedom in Africa as well as in the West, especially to migrants. Turkson's enthusiastic support for Pope Francis' Encyclical *Laudato Si'* and ecological conservation is contextualized by his recognition that "human ecology," especially the protection of human life, takes precedence.

A cardinal with significant pastoral and international experience whose approach resonates with globalists and the environmentally conscious on the world stage, Cardinal Turkson would doubtless continue the trajectory begun by Pope Francis while representing a continent where the Faith is growing the fastest.

SERVICE TO THE CHURCH

Ordination to the Priesthood: 20 July 1975
Ordination to the Episcopate: 27 March 1993
Elevation to the College of Cardinals: 21 October 2003

Education
- 1962-1969: St. Teresa's Seminary, Amisano
- 1969-1971: St. Peter's Regional Seminary, Pedu
- St. Anthony-on-Hudson Seminary, New York; Master of theology and master of divinity
- 1976-1980: Pontifical Biblical Institute, Rome; Licentiate in Sacred Scripture
- 1987-1992: Pontifical Biblical Institute, Rome; Doctorate (not yet complete)

Assignments

- 1975: Priest, Archdiocese of Cape Coast, Ghana
- 1983-1986: Visiting lecturer, Catholic Major Seminary, Anyama, Ivory Coast
- 1984-1986: Chaplain and lecturer, University of Cape Coast
- 1992-2009: Archbishop, Cape Coast
- 1997-2004: President, Ghana Catholic Bishops' Conference
- 2003-present: Titular cardinal-priest, San Liborio
- 2003-present: Chancellor, Catholic University College, Ghana
- 2007-2009: Treasurer, Symposium of Episcopal Conferences of Africa and Madagascar
- 2007-2009: Vice president, Association of Episcopal Conferences of Anglophone West Africa
- 2007-2009: President, Regional Episcopal Conference of West Africa
- 2009: Relator, Special Assembly for Africa of the Synod of Bishops
- 2009-2017: President, Pontifical Council for Justice and Peace
- 2017-present: Prefect, Dicastery for Promoting Integral Human Development

Membership

- Congregation for the Doctrine of the Faith
- Congregation for Divine Worship and the Discipline of the Sacraments
- Congregation for the Evangelization of Peoples
- Congregation for Catholic Education
- Pontifical Council for Promoting Christian Unity
- Pre-Synodal Council of the Special Assembly of the Synod of Bishops for the Pan-Amazon Region

MATTEO MARIA CARDINAL ZUPPI

"The Joy of the Lord Is Your Strength"

Born: 11 October 1955
Rome, Italy
Nationality: Italian
Title: Archbishop of Bologna

BIOGRAPHY

Matteo Maria Zuppi was born and raised in Rome. He has close family connections to the Vatican and lifelong ties to the Sant'Egidio lay community. His father, Enrico, was a journalist and a photographer whom the then–deputy secretary of state, Giovanni Battista Montini (the future Paul VI), appointed editor of *L'Osservatore della Domenica,* a weekly illustrated edition of *L'Osservatore Romano.* Matteo's mother, Carla Fumagalli, was the niece of Cardinal Carlo Confalonieri, who served as secretary to Pope

Pius XI, then as prefect of the Congregation for Bishops and as dean of the College of Cardinals at the funerals of Popes Paul VI and John Paul I.[2137]

The fifth of six children, young Matteo went to secondary school in Rome's historic center[2138] and there met Andrea Riccardi, founder of the Sant'Egidio movement. He soon became involved with the nascent community, which he regarded as "another Gospel and another Church."[2139] In 1977, aged twenty-two, he completed a degree in literature and philosophy at La Sapienza University in Rome, with a thesis on the life of Cardinal Alfredo Ildefonso Schuster.[2140] He then entered a seminary in the

---

[2137] In 2010, a selection of his father's professional and personal correspondence, which included eight letters from Giovanni Battista Montini (whom Enrico had met during his university years while serving in the Catholic apostolate on the peripheries of Rome) and eighty letters to Carla during their engagement and marriage, was published in a book titled *You Have Filled the Abyss of My Heart*. With a foreword by Cardinal Achille Silvestrini (an occasional collaborator of *L'Osservatore della Domenica* during the Enrico Zuppi years), the book was presented in Rome in November 2010. Andrea Riccardi, founder of the Sant'Egidio community, and Giovanni Maria Vian, then editor-in-chief of *L'Osservatore Romano*, were featured speakers at the launch. Marco Roncalli, "Enrico Zuppi, lettere 'luminose' alla moglie Carla, Avvenire, 10 November 2010, http://www.edizionistudium.it/sites/default/files/zuppi_presentazione_e_recensione_avvenire.pdf.

[2138] Virgilio High School, located on the well-known via Giulia in historic Rome.

[2139] Simonetta Pagnotti, "Monsignor Matteo Zuppi: 50 Anni Dalla Parte Degli Ultimi," *Famiglia Cristiana*, 1 March 2018, https://m.famigliacristiana.it/articolo/monsignor-matteo-zuppi-50-anni-dalla-parte-degli-ultimi.htm.

[2140] Archbishop of Milan from 1929 to 1954. Regarding his thesis, Archbishop Zuppi has said that "getting to know him has greatly helped me to understand the complexity of the Church. I saw him as an exponent of a Church that was weak against fascism. In reality, I discovered exactly the opposite, that is, a very beloved father of his diocese, who was anything but subservient to power. It was Fr. David Maria Turoldo, who when he was very young preached in Milan at the request of the cardinal, who helped me to discover this aspect of Schuster.... They were extremely different, they had ways and sensibilities that were almost opposite, and yet Turoldo loved Schuster and felt understood by him. This taught me that the Church is a much more complex reality than our ideas and some of our ideological readings of it." Roberto Zichittella, "Voglio una Chiesa in cui tutti si sentano amati,"

suburban-Rome Diocese of Palestrina and studied for the priesthood at the Pontifical Lateran University, where he obtained a bachelor's degree in theology. Ordained a priest for the Diocese of Palestrina in 1981, he was first assigned as an assistant parish priest of Santa Maria in Trastevere under Msgr. Vincenzo Paglia. While there, he held a number of additional positions, including rector of a nearby church and head of a diocesan priestly council. In 1992, Fr. Zuppi played a key role in the Sant'Egidio-brokered peace accords with Mozambique, leading him to be made an honorary citizen of the country. In 2000, when Vincenzo Paglia was made bishop of Terni, Zuppi replaced him as parish priest of Santa Maria in Trastevere and as ecclesiastical assistant to Sant'Egidio.[2141] In 2006, Benedict XVI granted him the honorary title of Chaplain to His Holiness.[2142] In 2010, he was transferred to serve in one of Rome's largest parishes on the city's periphery, and in 2012, Benedict XVI appointed him auxiliary bishop of Rome. Archbishop Paglia was one of his co-consecrators. Pope Francis appointed Zuppi archbishop of Bologna in 2015, succeeding Cardinal Carlo Caffarra, and elevated him to cardinal in 2019.

SANCTIFYING OFFICE

Cardinal Matteo Maria Zuppi is known as a "street priest" and missionary to the peripheries and the marginalized.

Since his promotion to the Archdiocese of Bologna, the sanctifying office of Cardinal Zuppi could perhaps best be summed up as a commitment to implementing Pope Francis' call to "missionary conversion" in his 2013 Apostolic Exhortation *Evangelii Gaudium* (no. 30).

Famigila Cristiana, 31 October 2015, https://m.famigliacristiana.it/articolo/don-matteo-zuppi-a-bologna-per-una-chiesa-in-cui-tutti-si-sentano-amati.htm (translated from Italian).

[2141] Pagnotti, "Monsignor Matteo Zuppi."

[2142] Granting him the title of Monsignor. In 2014, Pope Francis abolished this title for diocesan priests under the age of sixty-five.

Eucharistic Congress

Archbishop Zuppi began to implement the pope's programmatic document within the first year of arriving in Bologna. In 2016, he announced that the forthcoming diocesan Eucharistic Congress would be themed "The Eucharist and the City of Men" and would be based on a reflection of *Evangelii Gaudium*. The archbishop said the preparatory year for the diocesan congress would be "a year of adoration to understand [Christ's] presence in the Eucharist and in the sacrament of our brother and the poor; a year of contemplation of the city of men, to look upon it with the eyes of the Lord, those of mercy; a year of a synodal search to respond to the crowd that surrounds us and which Jesus asks us, today, to give something to eat."[2143]

The four steps in the year of preparation for the 2017 diocesan Eucharistic Congress invited clergy and the faithful to reflect on several key passages from *Evangelii Gaudium*.[2144] (This will be discussed in greater detail later on.)

Liturgical Guidelines

In November 2019, new archdiocesan liturgical guidelines were issued that underlined a "synodal" approach to the liturgy and greater participation of the laity, drawing on *Sacrosanctum Concilium* interpreted in light of *Evangelii Gaudium*.[2145]

[2143] "Voi stessi date loro da mangiare," Parrocchia di Santi Vitale e Agricola in Arena, 13 November 2016 to 8 October 2017, http://www.santivitaleeagricolainarena.it/wp-content/uploads/2016/11/«Voi-stessi-date-loro-da-mangiare»-notificazione-e-lettera-del-Vescovo-Matteo.pdf (translated from Italian).

[2144] 2017 Diocesan Eucharistic Congress, Parrocchia di Santi Vitale e Agricola in Arena, 10 November 2016, https://www.santivitaleeagricolainarena.it/congresso-eucaristico-diocesano-2017/.

[2145] Diocese of Bologna Office for Liturgy, *La liturgia della "Chiesa in uscita,"* 18 November 2019, https://liturgia.chiesadibologna.it/wp-content/uploads/sites/6/2019/12/La-liturgia-della-22Chiesa-in-uscita22.-Promozione-liturgica-nelle-zone-pastorali.pdf (translated from Italian). The guidelines, entitled *The Liturgy of the "Church That Goes Forth": Considerations on the Celebrative Style of the Church in Her "Missionary Conversion"* (EG, 30), assert: "In our need to understand liturgical celebration ever better, it is necessary to

Cardinal Zuppi has expressed his views on the nature of the Mass, and the role the laity have in the liturgy, on other occasions. During the coronavirus pandemic, the cardinal was asked in an interview for Italian television if it was difficult for him not to have the faithful present at Mass (as public celebrations of the Eucharist were suspended, he celebrated them privately in the crypt of the cathedral, with livestreaming). Cardinal Zuppi replied by likening the absence of the faithful to a kind of Lenten fast. "In reality," he said, "it is not right because the Mass is for the people.... It is a fast because the community is fundamental in the Eucharistic celebration."[2146] The cardinal's view would appear to be at odds with that of Paul VI. In his encyclical on the Eucharist, *Mysterium Fidei*, he said that while "active participation by many faithful is of its very nature particularly fitting when Mass is celebrated," there is "no reason to criticize but rather only

keep as the horizon of our thinking the indications of *Sacrosanctum Concilium*, according to the understanding, revival and perspective that *Evangelii Gaudium* offers the Church today." Issued by the archdiocesan Office for Liturgy, the guidelines point to four characteristics of evangelization found in *Evangelii Gaudium*: the kerygmatic, mystagogical, synodal, popular.

Regarding the "synodal" way of celebration, the document asserts that the "tendency" in liturgy "to delegate the carrying out of the celebration to experts, to others who have to perform the rites, is an evil that has assailed us for centuries and from which we can be healed with difficulty." The document recalled *Sacrosanctum Concilium*'s reminder to the Church that all of the baptized have the "right and duty" to participate in the liturgy, not just "the clergy and some other 'altar boy.'"

According to the guidelines, a "synodal" way of celebrating the liturgy would mean the laity's being involved "not only in the preparation of the prayers of the faithful," but also "in the preparation of the Sunday readings, in the choice of the various options that the rite provides, and in some services, so that it appears that the entire assembly that God has gathered is made up of the whole People of God." The document asserts that when liturgies are prepared in such a "synodal manner" and "a large part of the People of God [feel] represented in the celebration," the rite more truly "manifests and expresses the real nature of the true Church."

[2146] Comunità di Sant'Egidio Liguria, "A Sua Immagine 22 marzo 2020 Intervista a SE Matteo Zuppi," YouTube video, 5:36, posted 22 March 2020, https://www.youtube.com/watch?v=rkB8EpNdz5c.

to approve a Mass that a priest celebrates privately." It brings "a rich and abundant treasure of special graces" to the priest, the faithful, the Church, and the whole world.[2147]

Popular Devotions

In an interview in 2018, then-Archbishop Zuppi, reflecting on an initial encounter with the Community of Sant'Egidio, said that "Sant'Egidio made me discover another Gospel and another Church, the Church of my friends and not of the priests, of spontaneous prayer instead of the Rosary."[2148]

In the same interview, reflecting back on his early days as a new priest in the early '80s, assigned to the Basilica of Santa Maria in Trastevere, Archbishop Zuppi said he initially found the "popular devotions" of the locals "not easy" to take, as he regarded them as "leftovers of the past." But he said he discovered their "spiritual depth" in their ability to respond to the laity's need for an "affective bond with the Church." By the time he

---

[2147] "It is also only fitting for us to recall the conclusion that can be drawn from this about 'the public and social nature of each and every Mass.' For each and every Mass is not something private, even if a priest celebrates it privately; instead, it is an act of Christ and of the Church. In offering this sacrifice, the Church learns to offer herself as a sacrifice for all and she applies the unique and infinite redemptive power of the sacrifice of the Cross to the salvation of the whole world. For every Mass that is celebrated is being offered not just for the salvation of certain people, but also for the salvation of the whole world. The conclusion from this is that even though active participation by many faithful is of its very nature particularly fitting when Mass is celebrated, still there is no reason to criticize but rather only to approve a Mass that a priest celebrates privately for a good reason in accordance with the regulations and legitimate traditions of the Church, even when only a server to make the responses is present. For such a Mass brings a rich and abundant treasure of special graces to help the priest himself, the faithful, the whole Church and the whole world toward salvation—and this same abundance of graces is not gained through mere reception of Holy Communion." Paul VI, Encyclical *Mysterium Fidei* (3 September 1965), http://www.vatican.va/content/paul-vi/en/encyclicals/documents/hf_p-vi_enc_03091965_mysterium.html (internal citations omitted).

[2148] Pagnotti, "Monsignor Matteo Zuppi."

arrived in Bologna, he appeared to have warmed to popular devotions, as his response to the coronavirus pandemic showed.

Liturgy and Sacraments during the Coronavirus

Each evening from March 8 to 16 during the pandemic, via livestreaming, the cardinal led a special novena in the cathedral.[2149] On March 17, he concluded the novena with a pilgrimage to the local Shrine of Our Lady of St. Luke.[2150] He told the faithful that the novena was meant to implore the Blessed Virgin to protect Bologna from evil. "For nine days," he said, "I invite you to pray the Holy Rosary wherever you are, united spiritually to her and among ourselves, one in prayer like the Apostles with Mary on the day of Pentecost."[2151] In a video message, he told the faithful of Bologna that only with "insistence more insistent than evil" is it possible to "fight evil and feel Mary's protection, feel the strength of the Lord who loves the lives of men." Cardinal Zuppi continued to pray (and livestream) the Rosary each evening throughout the coronavirus pandemic, from the diocesan cathedral or the archbishop's residence or a monastery of nuns.[2152]

During the coronavirus crisis, although Cardinal Zuppi suspended all public Masses, he opposed closing churches.

He also stressed the importance of attending to the vulnerable, particularly the elderly. On the feast of the Annunciation, he sent a letter to the elderly of the diocese, saying: "I would like to tell you that we love you, that no one is forgotten and that we are praying for you."

Following the recommendations of the Italian Bishops' Conference, Cardinal Zuppi also suspended funerals during the pandemic. Speaking to the Italian press, he recalled the suffering of those who die alone. "It's

[2149] "La Novena in tempo di epidemia," Chiesa di Bologna, 19 March 2020, https://www.chiesadibologna.it/la-novena-di-preghiera-alla-madonna-di-san-luca/.

[2150] Dodici Porte, "17/03/2020 Rosario dal Santuario di San Luca," You-Tube video, 54:49, posted 17 March 2020, https://www.youtube.com/watch?v=wLrWnVHwqGA.

[2151] "La Novena in tempo di epidemia" (translated from Italian).

[2152] "Il Rosario delle 19," Chiesa di Bologna, 21 March 2020, https://www.chiesadibologna.it/la-preghiera-delle-19/ (translated from Italian).

the greatest regret I have, and it's been a cause of great suffering," he said, adding, "Let's not overlook the absence of funerals: the communities were unable to say goodbye to their friends who have passed. Even the absence of funerals reminds us that we cannot but be a community."[2153] He repeated the concern in a joint video message with the mayor of Bologna, referring to the lack of last rites for many of those who died. The cardinal announced that church bells around the city would be rung "to remember all those we carry in our hearts and who have gone to heaven. It will be a moment of recollection and suffering for them, and also of consolation for those who remain."[2154]

During Holy Week, Cardinal Zuppi issued directives indicating that "the solemn liturgical celebrations foreseen by the Roman Missal for Palm Sunday and the Easter Triduum must take place in the churches, behind closed doors, with the minimum number of people present necessary for a worthy celebration."[2155] Churches would remain open for private prayer.

Regarding sacramental Confession, Cardinal Zuppi—who authored a pastoral work titled *Confession*[2156] to help people approach the sacrament—noted in his directives that "as far as possible, with the prescribed precautions (open space, distance of at least one meter, use of the mask) it will be good and commendable for those who can approach sacramental confession."[2157]

[2153] Domenico Agasso Jr., "Coronavirus, l'appello della Cei: 'Autorizzate funerali, battesimi e matrimoni,'" *La Stampa*, 16 April 2020, https://www.lastampa.it/cronaca/2020/04/16/news/coronavirus-dalla-cei-un-pacchetto-di-soluzioni-per-funerali-battesimi-e-matrimoni-1.38724572 (translated from Italian).

[2154] Matteo Maria Cardinal Zuppi, 25 March 2020, https://www.chiesadibologna.it/wp-content/uploads/sites/2/2020/03/Lettera-Zuppi-agli-anziani.pdf (translated from Italian).

[2155] "Disposizioni nell'Arcidiocesi di Bologna per la Settimana Santa 2020," Chiesa di Bologna, 27 March 2020, https://www.chiesadibologna.it/wd-doc-ufficiali/disposizioni-nellarcidiocesi-di-bologna-per-la-settimana-santa-2020/ (translated from Italian).

[2156] Matteo Zuppi, *La confessione. Il perdono per cambiare* (Cinisello Balsamo: San Paolo Edizioni, 2016).

[2157] "Disposizioni nell'Arcidiocesi di Bologna."

The cardinal continued: "If the sick cannot confess their sins individually, but ask for sacramental absolution, priests may absolve them, after having invited them, as far as possible, to express repentance and the request for forgiveness." He gave provision for limited general absolution for the sick, health-care workers, and families, but reminded them of the need "once the emergency is over, to confess serious sins that have been absolved without being able to make individual confession." He also stipulated that "priests who have recourse to general absolution should inform the Archbishop."

Asked during the coronavirus pandemic if he could envision a "diaconate" being given to Catholic hospital workers, he replied: "Rather than the diaconate, one could confer a ministry of the Eucharist." He cited the example of a nurse in his diocese who was given "the faculty to bring Communion" to people in the COVID wards of the hospital where she works. "In reality I believe that many patients also asked her for blessings and prayers and at that point she became almost an established minister," Cardinal Zuppi said. "This is part of that enormous heritage of generosity, solidarity, closeness, attention to others, compassion, piety and sensitivity that these weeks of fighting the virus have shown."[2158]

Extraordinary Form

Cardinal Zuppi daily celebrates the Ordinary Form of the Roman Rite in the Bologna cathedral but in 2014, he won the appreciation of traditionalists for being the first auxiliary bishop of Rome to celebrate the Extraordinary Form of the Roman Rite since the promulgation of *Summorum Pontificum*.[2159] It was also the first time that an auxiliary of Rome, while in office, had celebrated Mass in the Extraordinary Form in a Roman parish since

---

[2158] "L'intervista al card. Matteo Zuppi," Chiesa di Bologna, 10 April 2020, https://www.chiesadibologna.it/lintervista-al-card-matteo-zuppi/ (translated from Italian).

[2159] Luigi Casalini, "Pontificale in Rito Antico del Vescovo Ausiliare di Roma Mons. Matteo Maria Zuppi nella Parr della Santissima Trinità dei Pellegrini," *Messainlatino*, 31 March 2014, http://blog.messainlatino.it/2014/03/30-marzo-2014-santa-messa-in-rito.html; New Catholic, "Images: Pontifical Laetare Sunday in Rome with Auxiliary Bishop Matteo Zuppi," *Rorate Caeli*,

the post-conciliar liturgical reforms began.[2160] In October 2015, the new archbishop of Bologna said he would celebrate the Extraordinary Form of the Roman Rite in the archdiocese if he were asked. Recalling past requests in Rome, he called it a "gesture of communion" and said he is "in favor of leaving behind every form of being closed."[2161] There is no record of Cardinal Zuppi's ever having celebrated the Extraordinary Form of the Mass after these remarks.

Interreligious Prayer with Muslims

Zuppi has also led interreligious prayer services with the Muslim community in Bologna. On February 2, 2020—the Catholic feast of Candlemas and the close of the Christmas Season—the youth branch of the archdiocesan Catholic Action organized a day of prayer for peace.[2162] In the morning, the children and young adults were invited to attend Mass. In the afternoon, the group traveled to the Islamic Center to spend time with the Muslim community. The afternoon ended with an interreligious prayer service for Catholic and Muslim children, young adults, and their parents, led by Cardinal Zuppi and the president of the Islamic Center of Bologna.[2163]

31 March 2014, https://rorate-caeli.blogspot.com/2014/03/images-pontifical-laetare-sunday-in.html.

[2160] Gregory DiPippo, "A Bishop of Rome Celebrates Laetare Sunday with the FSSP," New Liturgical Movement, 31 March 2014, http://www.newliturgicalmovement.org/2014/03/a-bishop-of-rome-celebrates-laetare.html#.Xp7dky2B2gR.

[2161] Luigi Casalini, "Mons. Matteo Zuppi Arcivescovo di Bologna," Messainlatino, 27 October 2015, http://blog.messainlatino.it/2015/10/mons-matteo-zuppi-arcivescovo-di-bologna.html.

[2162] "Festa interreligiosa della pace—Bologna, 2 Febbraio 2020," Chiesa Cattolica Italiana, https://ecumenismo.chiesacattolica.it/2020/01/22/festa-interreligiosa-della-pace-bologna-2-febbraio-2020/.

[2163] Azione Cattolica Ragazzi Bologna, "Festa interreligiosa della pace," Ufficio Nazionale per L'ecumenismo e Il Dialogo Interreligioso, https://ecumenismo.chiesacattolica.it/wp-content/uploads/sites/32/2020/01/22/06Bologna.jpg.

GOVERNING OFFICE

Running One of the World's Wealthiest Dioceses

Cardinal Matteo Maria Zuppi may be known as a "street priest," but he governs one of the wealthiest dioceses in the world.

In 2012, Michelangelo Manini, the owner of FAAC,[2164] a leading international automatic-gate manufacturer, died, having bequeathed his estate, worth an estimated 1.7 billion euro ($1.85 billion), including the majority of FAAC shares (66 percent), to the Archdiocese of Bologna. After two years of legal proceedings and negotiations, the archdiocese acquired complete ownership of the company.[2165] Zuppi's predecessor, Cardinal Carlo Caffarra, established a trust and appointed three professionals to manage the company, directing a percentage of its annual earnings to the archdiocese. In 2014, the company had a thousand employees and 284 million euro ($309 million) in sales. One of Cardinal Caffarra's final acts as archbishop of Bologna, in late 2015, was to allocate 5 million euro ($5.4 million) to the local Caritas for families who were in difficulty or unemployed.[2166]

When Matteo Zuppi took possession of the Archdiocese of Bologna in 2015, he confirmed the trust's administrators in their position. He also

---

[2164] Fabbrica Automatismi Apertura Cancelli (Factory for automatic gate opener), https://faac.it.

[2165] S. Salvemini, "FAAC: Governance from on High," SDA Bocconi, 23 March 2020, https://www.sdabocconi.it/en/sda-bocconi-insight/faac-governance-from-on-high.

[2166] "I am not doing it for the money," Cardinal Caffarra said on accepting the FAAC inheritance. "I am doing it for the 300 families of the Bologna company who represent the heart and mind of FAAC. If we let it go they will all be absorbed by the new owners who may transfer the headquarters elsewhere. I cannot allow it. I stand with the families." Ilaria Venturi, "Caffarra dona ai poveri 5 milioni del lascito Faac," *Bologna*, 22 November 2015, https://bologna.repubblica.it/cronaca/2015/11/22/news/caffarra_dona_ai_poveri_5_milioni_del_lascito_faac-127879220/.

credited Cardinal Caffarra with the decision to reserve the profits for the poor. "This has made it possible to distribute millions in charity, not for worship, culture and as a means of support [for the diocese]," he said.[2167] By 2017, FAAC had grown to 2,500 employees on five continents and in twenty-four countries, and closed 2017 with 428 million euro ($465 million) in sales, zero debt, and a net profit of 43 million euro ($47 million). In 2015, 5 million euro ($6 million) was given to the Archdiocese of Bologna. By 2019, that figure doubled to 10 million euro ($11 million).[2168] From the latter amount, 6.5 million euro was allocated to several entities: approximately 1.5 million euro went to the diocesan Caritas to help families with rent, bills, and health care; 1.3 million euro was allocated for schooling and educational grants; 1 million euro went to "Together for Work," a collaborative project launched by the Archdiocese of Bologna and the local government;[2169] and a commission chaired by Archbishop Zuppi distributed the remaining 2.7 million to a variety of causes, including projects to help migrants, the homeless, and the reintegration of released prisoners. The remaining millions were placed in an emergency fund.[2170]

In April 2020, during the coronavirus pandemic and following Cardinal Carlo Caffarra's example during the 2008 economic crisis, Cardinal Zuppi donated one million euro in FAAC dividends to establish the San

---

[2167] Marco Roncalli, "Matteo Zuppi visto da vicino," *La Stampa*, 15 September 2019, https://www.lastampa.it/vatican-insider/it/2019/09/15/news/matteo-zuppi-visto-da-vicino-1.37455500?refresh_ce.

[2168] Domenico Affinito and Milena Gabanelli, "Faac: il 'capitalismo nel nome di Dio' funziona," *Corriere della Sera*, 8 November 2018, https://www.corriere.it/dataroom-milena-gabanelli/faac-capitalismo-nome-dio-funziona/b7fcc536-e2a5-11e8-86b9-0879a24c1aca-va.shtml?fbclid=IwAR3UsxgraSFdgScYri0euRqcTUORuZyPpIbfSOAhDvLIMd4s6qwpoeqAMkA; "Bologna: La Curia incassa 10 mln dai dividendi faac," TR 24, 20 November 2019, https://www.teleromagna24.it/attualità/bologna-la-curia-incassa-10-mln-dai-dividendi-faac-video/2019/11.

[2169] Insieme per il Lavoro, https://www.insiemeperillavoro.it

[2170] "Bologna incassa dieci milioni di dividendi dalla Faac," *Bologna*, 20 November 2019, https://bologna.repubblica.it/cronaca/2019/11/20/news/faac_la_curia_di_bologna-241499127/.

Petronio Fund to provide financial assistance to families and individuals who were out of work due to the pandemic.[2171]

Influence of Sant'Egidio

"If I am here today," then-Archbishop Zuppi said on the Community of Sant'Egidio's fiftieth anniversary in 2018, "I owe it to Sant'Egidio."[2172]

To understand better Cardinal Matteo Zuppi's priorities in governing, it is important to assess the influence of Sant'Egidio in his life.

A worldwide Catholic lay movement founded in Rome in 1968 by Andrea Riccardi,[2173] Sant'Egidio is a fruit of the Second Vatican Council and focuses on care of the needy and on mediating conflicts. It is respected for its work for the poor and the elderly as well as its pioneering DREAM program for treating HIV and AIDS sufferers, especially in Africa. It cares for gypsies, runs soup kitchens for the homeless, and has for many years opened up the nave of the Basilica of Santa Maria in Trastevere to serve Christmas lunch to the dispossessed. It has led long-running campaigns to end the death penalty and more recently to push for a debt moratorium for Africa. The community was also responsible for the famous Assisi meeting of interreligious leaders in 1986 and regularly organizes a "Spirit of Assisi" conference in different parts of the world. Its emphasis on social justice has given it a distinctly political rather than spiritual focus, and it has become closely allied with Italy's political left while maintaining great adaptability to the papacy.[2174]

[2171] "Fondo San Petronio: un aiuto a chi è in difficoltà," Chiesa di Bologna, 26 April 2020, https://www.chiesadibologna.it/fondo-san-petronio-un-aiuto-a-chi-e-in-difficolta/.

[2172] Pagnotti, "Monsignor Matteo Zuppi."

[2173] Today the Community of Sant'Egidio is present in more than seventy countries, in Europe (twenty-three), Africa (twenty-nine), Asia (seven), North America (eight), and South America (five).

[2174] Andrea Riccardi served as minister for international cooperation in the cabinet of Italian prime minister Mario Monti (2010-2013), and in 2013 Riccardi was president of Scelta Civica (Civic Choice), a centrist political party. In March 2015, Riccardi was elected president of the Dante Alighieri Society,

Shortly before taking possession of the Archdiocese of Bologna, Matteo Zuppi explained that his vocation was "born inside the Community of Sant'Egidio, to which I have belonged from the age of 15."[2175] Three years later, in an interview commemorating the fiftieth anniversary of Sant'Egidio, he said he came from a "very religious family that my father had wanted to build around the Gospel, but those were the years after the Council and, as happened to many, this [was] overwhelmed by all the aspirations, naïveté and even the contradictions that ran through the student world." He said the education he had received "seemed to me obsolete and moralistic,"[2176] whereas Sant'Egidio made him "discover another Gospel and another Church" that attracted him "much more than a faith, however deep, like that of my parents."[2177]

Due to Sant'Egidio's influence, he said his vocation "was born as a service to the Church and the Community."[2178] Growing in a lay community, Zuppi said, "helped me greatly to live out a priestly role that isn't too clerical and, as the Pope says, clericalism is a sickness of the Church." He said he "learned to live [his] ministry together with lay brothers and sisters, discovering the enormous richness of the Church and the different charisms" that are all necessary in communion. "That said," he added,

---

receiving "best wishes for fruitful work" from the Grand Orient of Italy Palazzo Giustiniani Masons. "Andrea Riccardi nuovo presidente della Dante Alighieri," Grand Orient of Italy, https://www.grandeoriente.it/andrea-riccardi-nuovo-presidente-della-dante-alighieri/. Historically, the leadership of the Dante Alighieri Society is given only to Freemasons. "Società Dante Alighieri, Riccardi presidente. Con tanti auguri dalla massoneria," Corrispondenza Romana, 26 March 2015, https://www.corrispondenzaromana.it/notizie-brevi/societa-dante-alighieri-riccardi-presidente-con-tanti-auguri-dalla-massoneria/.

[2175] Roberto Zichittella, "Voglio una Chiesa in cui tutti si sentano amati," *Famiglia Cristiana*, 31 October 2015, https://m.famigliacristiana.it/articolo/don-matteo-zuppi-a-bologna-per-una-chiesa-in-cui-tutti-si-sentano-amati.htm (translated from Italian).

[2176] Pagnotti, "Monsignor Matteo Zuppi."

[2177] Ibid.

[2178] Zichitella, "Voglia una Chiesa."

"it's clear that I will not be the Bishop of Sant'Egidio but the Bishop of Bologna."[2179]

In 1992, Fr. Zuppi, who was responsible for Sant'Egidio's peace efforts in Africa, worked with Andrea Riccardi on conflict-resolution talks that would lead to the Rome General Peace Accords, ending a fifteen-year civil war in Mozambique. The community's role in brokering the accord, signed at the Sant'Egidio headquarters in Rome, earned the community the name "the UN of Trastevere."

Yet as Sant'Egidio gained a worldwide reputation as peacemakers in warzones and as bridge builders between religions,[2180] by 1998, when Vincenzo Paglia was the community's ecclesiastical assistant, reports of serious moral, liturgical, and sacramental problems within the community began to emerge.[2181] In 2003, an important member of Sant'Egidio, who had been with the community for twenty-five years, reportedly lifted the veil on aspects of its inner life, testifying that leaders had used coercion to arrange marriages between lay members and were wielding their authority to dictate if and when married couples in the community could have children.[2182]

In 2011, Cardinal Francis George of Chicago warned the Vatican about the community's willingness to compromise on the nonnegotiable values of life and marriage.[2183] One year later, the Community of Sant'Egidio came

---

[2179] Ibid.

[2180] Sant'Egidio has organized the annual interreligious meetings in Assisi since the first famous interreligious meeting in 1986.

[2181] Sandro Magister, "The Story of Sant'Egidio. The Great Bluff," chiesa.espressonline.it, 9 April 1998, http://chiesa.espresso.repubblica.it/articolo/6878bdc4.html?eng=y.

[2182] Ibid.

[2183] Cardinal George took issue with the community's granting Illinois governor Pat Quinn an award for abolishing the death penalty, even though he had signed into law same-sex "marriage" and supported legalized abortion. The cardinal's concerns were raised in an encrypted cable from the apostolic nunciature in Washington, D.C., to the Vatican, later revealed in Vatileaks. Manya A. Brachear, "Cardinal George Exposed in 'Vatileaks' Scandal," *Chicago Tribune*, 4 June 2012, https://www.chicagotribune.com/news/ct-xpm-2012-06-04-chi-cardinal-george-could-play-minor-role-in-vatileaks-20120604-story.

under fire from Cardinal Joseph Zen Ze-kiun, who accused the community of taking a submissive stance toward Communist China[2184]—a position that does not appear to have changed.[2185] Former cardinal Theodore McCarrick also had a long relationship with the Community of Sant'Egidio and was a featured speaker at their conferences, particularly from 2008 to 2010.[2186]

Criticism has also been leveled against the community for their involvement in politics in Italy[2187] and abroad,[2188] and they have entertained

---

html; "Vatican Diary/Double slap, for Saint Egidio and for the Jesuits," chiesa.espressonline.it, 7 June 2012, http://chiesa.espresso.repubblica.it/articolo/1350261bdc4.html?eng=y.

[2184] Cardinal Zen criticized the community for inviting to their 2011 interreligious meeting in Munich a Chinese bishop in grave disobedience to the pope for his participation in the ordination of a bishop imposed by the Chinese authorities. Sandro Magister, "China. Cardinal Zen against Saint Egidio," chiesa.espressonline.it, 9 February 2012, http://chiesa.espresso.repubblica.it/articolo/1350164bdc4.html?eng=y.

[2185] In September 2019, Andrea Riccardi and Marco Impagliazzo, president of the Community of Sant'Egidio, together with former Italian MP from Emilia-Romagna, Romano Prodi, along with Cardinal Claudio Maria Celli and Fr. Federico Lombardi, were featured speakers at the launch of a new book lauding the Holy See's secret agreement with the Chinese communist government. The foreword to the book was written by Vatican secretary of state Cardinal Pietro Parolin. Cindy Wooden, "China-Vatican Accord Promotes Church's Pastoral Work, Speakers Say," *Crux*, 28 September 2019, https://cruxnow.com/church-in-asia/2019/09/china-vatican-accord-promotes-churchs-pastoral-work-speakers-say/; Alessandro Gisotti, "The Holy See and China: The Door Is Open," Vatican News, 27 September 2019, https://www.vaticannews.va/en/vatican-city/news/2019-09/vatican-china-holy-see-gisotti.html.

[2186] Paolo Facciotto, "C'e anche Sant'Egidio nella McCarrick Connection," *La Nuova Bussola Quotidiana*, 5 September 2018, https://www.lanuovabq.it/it/ce-anche-santegidio-nella-mccarrick-connection.

[2187] Sandro Magister, "Between 'Gay' Marriage and Elections. Can the Pope Trust Andrea Riccardi?," chiesa.espressonline.it, 10 January 2013, http://chiesa.espresso.repubblica.it/articolo/1350400bdc4.html?eng=y.

[2188] Sandro Magister, "St. Egidio and Algeria. An Ambassador's Disturbing Revelations," chiesa.espressonline.it, 29 December 2003, http://chiesa.espresso.repubblica.it/articolo/7005bdc4.html?eng=y.

controversial figures at their "Spirit of Assisi" annual meetings, including speakers such as population-control advocate Jeffrey Sachs.[2189]

Ties to the Political Left

Archbishop Zuppi is the first non-Northern Italian to be appointed to the Metropolitan See of Bologna since 1894. Italy's political left enthusiastically welcomed his elevation to the cardinalate in 2019,[2190] with socialist politicians lauding the choice on social media and headlines reading "The Chaplain of the Pd Has Become a Cardinal"[2191] — the Pd (Partito democratico) being Italy's largest center-left social-democratic party.

[2189] Jeffrey Sachs has had an increasingly influential role at the Pontifical Academy of Sciences under the leadership of Bishop Marcelo Sánchez Sorondo. In his talk to Sant'Egidio in 2019, Sachs spoke of Jesus Christ as a historical figure on a par with Immanuel Kant, saying: "We are the heirs of Plato and Aristotle, who championed the gift of reason; of Jesus, who proclaimed that peacemakers are the children of God; of Immanuel Kant, who envisioned a union of republics to secure perpetual peace; of Franklin Roosevelt, who launched the United Nations after World War II to put Kant's vision into effect; of John F. Kennedy and Nikita Khrushchev, who signed the Partial Nuclear Test Ban Treaty at the height of the Cold War, and thereby showed the path to peace; and of Martin Luther King, Jr., who reminded us that 'the arc of the moral universe is long, but it bends towards justice.'" "Speech of Jeffrey Sachs," Sant'Egidio, 15 September 2019, https://preghieraperlapace.santegidio.org/pageID/31024/langID/en/text/3172/MADRID-2019-PEACE-WITHOUT-BORDERS.html; "'Pace senza confini': Comunità di Sant'Egidio, da domenica a Madrid l'incontro internazionale nello 'spirito di Assisi,'" SIR, 11 September 2019, https://www.agensir.it/quotidiano/2019/9/11/pace-senza-confini-comunita-di-santegidio-da-domenica-a-madrid-lincontro-internazionale-nello-spirito-di-assisi/.

[2190] Andrea Zambrano, "'Abbiamo un cardinale.' Che festa il Pd unito da Zuppi," *La Nuova Bussola Quotidiana*, 2 September 2019, https://lanuovabq.it/it/abbiamo-un-cardinale-che-festa-il-pd-unito-da-zuppi.

[2191] Pasquale Napolitano, "Il cappellano del Pd è diventato cardinale: sinistra e comunità Lgbt già fanno festa," *Il Giornale*, 3 September 2019, https://www.ilgiornale.it/news/politica/cappellano-pd-diventato-cardinale-sinistra-e-comunit-lgbt-gi-1747705.html.

In view of these allegiances,[2192] Cardinal Zuppi inevitably clashed with Matteo Salvini, leader of the right-wing Lega Party and Italy's deputy prime minister (2018-2019), particularly on immigration. Speaking at a book launch in Rome in February 2019, Zuppi argued that "populism and sovereignty are intolerant toward [certain] groups that are, instead, the guarantee against totalitarianism: saying us first and then them, first our own and then the others, sends everyone backward, while if you say the others first, then everyone comes." For him, the Church is tasked with proposing as an antidote to populism "humanism and humanitarianism, which is not synonymous with do-goodery or naïveté" but "is behaving like the Good Samaritan in the parable, i.e., looking at politics as a response to suffering."[2193]

Cardinal Zuppi has spoken at numerous Pd conferences and events,[2194] and he wrote the foreword to a book by the former communist, ex–Rome mayor, and founding leader of the Pd, Walter Veltroni.[2195]

In December 2019, at a dinner held in the nave of one of the archdiocesan churches (a tradition pioneered by the Sant'Egidio community as a service to the poor), Archbishop Zuppi was photographed warmly greeting Mattia Santori, the thirty-two-year-old Bologna native and founder of the

---

[2192] Franca Giansoldati, "Il Papa chiude il Sinodo delle divisioni con un forte appello all'unità," *Il Messaggero*, 27 October 2018, https://www.ilmessaggero.it/vaticano/papa_francesco_sinodo_chiesa_vigano_votazioni_cardinali_persecuzioni_satana-4068283.html.

[2193] Michele Altoviti, "Zuppi: la politica 'ritrovi la sua "p" maiuscola,'" *Roma-Sette*, 5 February 2019, https://www.romasette.it/zuppi-la-politica-ritrovi-la-sua-p-maiuscola/.

[2194] Francesco Boezi, "Bologna, l'arcivescovo pro migranti a convegno col Partito Democratico," *Il Giornale*, 1 February 2019, http://www.ilgiornale.it/news/politica/bologna-larcivescovo-pro-migranti-convegno-col-partito-1637253.html.

[2195] Matteo Zuppi, "La politica ha bisogno di artigiani del bene comune," *Avvenire*, 3 June 2019, https://www.avvenire.it/agora/pagine/zuppi-veltroni. Veltroni, the former mayor of Rome, is perhaps more famous for having married George Clooney and Amal Alamuddin in a civil ceremony in Venice.

Sardines movement, a grassroots anti-Salvini group. Santori has become a symbol of the left's anti-populist movement.[2196]

A proponent of dialogue, Zuppi is known also to attend right-leaning meetings if invited.

At the death of politician and activist Giacinto (Marco) Pannella, founder of Italy's Radical Party, who fought for legalized divorce and abortion and who, together with Emma Bonino, pushed for the 2016 law legalizing same-sex civil unions, Archbishop Zuppi called him "an honest and generous man, even if he wasn't always right."[2197] Archbishop Vincenzo Paglia, whom Zuppi has known almost all his life through Sant'Egidio, praised Panella as a friend.[2198]

Archbishop Zuppi said that he and Pannella shared some common battles, such as the abolition of the death penalty—a key Sant'Egidio cause—and prisoners' rights.[2199] Asked by a reporter which of Pannella's battles he found unacceptable, the archbishop responded: "All those that led to the paradox that freedom can surpass the rights of the human person." Puzzled, the reporter said he expected a bishop to name abortion or divorce. Archbishop Zuppi replied: "Taking the life of a person who has yet to be born is part of this paradox. I would add that my knowledge of Pannella leads me to say that he would not have asked his companion to

[2196] Andrea Zambrano, "La sardina e il cardinale," *La Nuova Bussola,* 23 December 2019, https://www.lanuovabq.it/it/la-sardina-e-il-cardinale-la-chiesa-cucina-passa-in-salotto.

[2197] Massimo Selleri, "Pannella, il ricordo di Zuppi: 'Le sue lotte erano genuine,'" *il Resto del Carlino,* 20 March 2016, https://www.ilrestodelcarlino.it/bologna/cronaca/zuppi-pannella-lotte-genuine-1.2176643.

[2198] Jeanne Smits, "Pontifical Academy for Life Chief Glorifies Radical Culture of Death Devotee," LifeSite News, 27 February 2017, https://www.lifesite-news.com/blogs/pontifical-academy-for-life-chief-glorifies-departed-italian-radical-dissen.

[2199] "L'Arcivescovo di Bologna Mons. Matteo Zuppi ai nostri microfoni ricorda Marco Pannella," ÈTV video, posted 20 May 2016 on Facebook, https://www.facebook.com/watch/?v=1087467574658379.

have an abortion; he was interested in the fact that she could do so, because he considered it an inalienable right."[2200]

In September 2019, Cardinal Zuppi, with the permission of the Congregation for the Clergy, incardinated into the Archdiocese of Bologna Eugenio Melandri, the "red priest" whom John Paul II suspended *a divinis* (a suspension that lasted twenty-eight years) after he ran in the 1989 European elections as a member of the Proletarian Democracy Party, a far-left Italian political party.[2201]

In 1992, Melandri was elected to the Italian Parliament for the Communist Reform Party. He was also the cofounder of Senza Confini (Without Borders), an association that works to promote the rights of immigrants and refugees and integrate them into Italian society. On October 20, 2019, Melandri celebrated Mass for the first time since his suspension, but he died one week later, at the age of seventy-one, after a long illness. One year earlier, he was received in Casa Santa Marta by Pope Francis, who had him serve his Mass.[2202] There are no reports of his renouncing his communist affiliations before he died.

In 2014, as auxiliary bishop of Rome, Zuppi was a featured speaker at a launch of the autobiography of another dissident Catholic priest, Dom Giovanni Frazoni.[2203] In 1964, as a young Benedictine abbot, Frazoni took part in Vatican II. In 1976, he was reduced to the lay state for his support of divorce legislation, and openly supporting the Italian Communist Party (Pdi). Frazoni, who died in 2017 at the age of eighty-eight, was in favor of

---

[2200] Selleri, "Pannella, il ricordo di Zuppi."

[2201] Enea Conti, "Il 'prete rosso' sull'altare. Zuppi lo riabilita sacerdote," *Corriere di Bologna*, 19 September 2019, https://corrieredibologna.corriere.it/bologna/cronaca/19_settembre_19/bologna-08-ddcorrierebologna-web-bologna-37ba0826-dabf-11e9-9846-a749315dbf5b.shtml.

[2202] Redazione, "Reintegrato il comunista don Melandri," *Radiospada*, 19 September 2019, https://www.radiospada.org/2019/09/reintegrato-il-comunista-don-melandri/.

[2203] Autobiografia di un cattolico marginale – presentazione del libro di Giovanni Frazoni, Radio Radicale, 20 May 2014, http://www.radioradicale.it/scheda/411761/autobiografia-di-un-cattolico-marginale-presentazione-del-libro-di-giovanni-franzoni.

abortion and euthanasia,[2204] saw artificial birth control as consistent with the Gospel, and supported the abolition of both the priesthood and the papal Magisterium.[2205]

Bologna's Eucharistic Congress

Cardinal Zuppi's exercise of his governing office in the Archdiocese of Bologna is also closely connected to *Evangelii Gaudium*.

Within a year of taking possession of the Archdiocese of Bologna, Archbishop Zuppi was tasked with organizing Bologna's tenth diocesan Eucharistic Congress.[2206] The congress, held every ten years, with a year of preparation culminating in a weeklong conference, took place from November 2016 to October 2017. Its theme was "Give them something to eat (Mt 14:16): The Eucharist and the City of Men." The Scripture passage is taken up in paragraph 49 of *Evangelii Gaudium*.

Cardinal Carlo Caffarra had always given the congress an emphasis on the poor but kept the main focus on the Blessed Sacrament. In his letter to the diocese on the congress, Archbishop Zuppi placed far more emphasis on poverty and social justice. He wrote: "Jesus (Mt 14:13-21) involves us in his emotion for the crowd and teaches everyone to respond to the hunger of so many. To do this, we must not look for particular abilities or extraordinary possibilities, which we will never have, but only offer the little we have and share it, offer it to his love so that all may be satisfied, we and our neighbor." The archbishop continued: "We ourselves can give to eat if, like Jesus, we do not remain distant from the condition of others. This is the goal that we want to achieve in the year of the Eucharistic Congress,

---

[2204] Dom Giovanni Frazoni: un cattolico "marginale," *Compagnia della Speranza*, 4 June 2014, http://gruppodelguado.blogspot.com/2014/06/dom-giovanni-franzoni-un-cattolico.html.

[2205] "Vatican II: Lost and Betrayed: Giovanni Frazoni," Association of Catholic Priests, 24 September 2011, https://www.associationofcatholicpriests.ie/2011/09/vatican-ii-lost-and-betrayed-giovanni-franzoni/.

[2206] The Archdiocese of Bologna has held a Eucharistic Congress every ten years since 1947. The previous Eucharistic Congress was held in 2007 and was organized by Cardinal Carlo Maria Caffarra.

through a synodal journey that involves all the Christian communities that are gathered around the Lord, always looking toward the horizon of the crowd that Jesus wants to feed."[2207]

To this end, he announced that the 2016-2017 year of preparation would comprise four steps centered on a "synodal" reflection on *Evangelii Gaudium* that would set in motion a plan of diocesan and "even structural" renewal.

The first step was to be a time for *lectio divina* on Matthew 14:13-21 and reflection on paragraph 49 of *Evangelii Gaudium*, which speaks against being confined to structures and rules that "make us harsh judges."[2208] It featured two meetings: the formal announcement of the Eucharistic Congress and the closing of the Year of Mercy called by Pope Francis, with which it coincided.

The second step, from Advent to Lent, was dedicated to "analyzing the local situation" and reflection on paragraph 27 of *Evangelii Gaudium* — Francis' dream of a missionary option suited to today's world.[2209] The faithful were invited to ask themselves: "If I put myself in the perspective of those on the 'peripheries' of the Christian community, what must we change and what missionary choices can we think about to initiate renewal?" That stage included participation in two meetings: a "national march for peace" in December, and the "Week of Prayer for Christian Unity in the Fifth Centenary of the Lutheran Reformation."

[2207] "Congresso Eucaristico Diocesano 2017," Chiesa di Bologna, https://web.archive.org/web/20161118165855/https:/www.chiesadibologna.it/congresso-eucaristico-diocesano-2017.html.

[2208] "More than by fear of going astray, my hope is that we will be moved by the fear of remaining shut up within structures which give us a false sense of security, within rules which make us harsh judges, within habits which make us feel safe, while at our door people are starving and Jesus does not tire of saying to us: 'Give them something to eat' (Mark 6:37)."

[2209] "I dream of a 'missionary option,' that is, a missionary impulse capable of transforming everything, so that the Church's customs, ways of doing things, times and schedules, language and structures can be suitably channeled for the evangelization of today's world rather than for her self-preservation. The renewal of structures demanded by pastoral conversion can only be understood in this light: as part of an effort to make them more mission-oriented."

The third step, during Lent, was centered on "rediscovering the center of everything: the quality of our Eucharistic celebrations" and focused on paragraph 24 of *Evangelii Gaudium*—the joy of evangelization and the importance of the beauty of the liturgy.[2210] The faithful were invited to ask themselves: "In the perspective of a missionary conversion, what are the elements of joy and fatigue at our Sunday Masses?"

The fourth step, from Easter to Corpus Christi, focused on the "missionary subject."[2211] The faithful were invited to consider: "Who are the disciples to whom Jesus says, 'You give them something to eat'? How do we involve everyone and the whole Christian community?" Common meetings included a May celebration in honor of Our Lady of San Luca, patroness of Bologna; Pentecost; and Corpus Christi.

A month before the congress, on September 6, 2017, Cardinal Carlo Maria Caffarra died. Archbishop Zuppi celebrated his funeral Mass in Bologna's Cathedral of St. Peter.

Closing celebrations for the 2017 diocesan Eucharistic Congress included a visit from Patriarch Bartholomew of Constantinople and Cardinal Luis Antonio Tagle, head of Caritas Internationalis,[2212] and a one-day pastoral visit from Pope Francis.

[2210] "Finally an evangelizing community is filled with joy; it knows how to rejoice always. It celebrates every small victory, every step forward in the work of evangelization. Evangelization with joy becomes beauty in the liturgy, as part of our daily concern to spread goodness. The Church evangelizes and is herself evangelized through the beauty of the liturgy, which is both a celebration of the task of evangelization and the source of her renewed self-giving."

[2211] "Evangelization is the task of the Church. The Church, as the agent of evangelization, is more than an organic and hierarchical institution; she is first and foremost a people advancing on its pilgrim way towards God. She is certainly a mystery rooted in the Trinity, yet she exists concretely in history as a people of pilgrims and evangelizers, transcending any institutional expression, however necessary. I would like to dwell briefly on this way of understanding the Church, whose ultimate foundation is in the free and gracious initiative of God."

[2212] Dodici Porte, "Il cardinale Tagle a Bologna (intervento integrale)," YouTube video, 46:32, posted 26 September 2017, https://www.youtube.com/watch?v=FokXELEtqOs.

Papal Visit

On October 1, 2017, at the culmination of preparations for the Eucharistic Congress, Archbishop Zuppi welcomed Pope Francis to Bologna for an apostolic visit. The pope's first scheduled meeting was with migrants and care workers at the "Regional Hub" migrant reception center. He next met with representatives of the world of work, the unemployed, and members of trade unions. Archbishop Zuppi then invited the Holy Father to join a Sant'Egidio-style "solidarity lunch with poor people, refugees and prisoners" in the nave of Bologna's patronal basilica. An estimated one thousand people were in attendance. After lunch, the pope made a customary visit to priests, religious, and seminarians, then met with students and representatives of the academic world, and concluded the day with Holy Mass.[2213]

First Pastoral Letter

At the close of the Eucharistic Congress, and following Pope Francis' pastoral visit to Bologna, Archbishop Zuppi issued his first pastoral letter, titled *Were Not Our Hearts Burning within Us?*[2214] The seventy-nine-page missive, based on the Gospel account of the disciples on the road to Emmaus, focused on the importance of traveling along a "synodal path" in communion and mission.[2215] It also stressed the importance of the Eucharist, Word, and charity—hearkening to Pope Francis' exhortation to the faithful of Bologna to remember the "three Ps": in Italian, *Pane, Parola, Poveri.*[2216]

[2213] Pope Francis, "Schedule of Pastoral Visit to Bologna," Vatican, 1 October 2017, http://w2.vatican.va/content/francesco/en/travels/2017/inside/documents/papa-francesco-cesena-bologna_2017.html.

[2214] Matteo Maria Zuppi, *Non Ci Ardeva Forse il Cuore* (4 October 2017), http://www.santamariadifossolo.it/wp-content/uploads/2019/05/Lettera-Pastorale-Zuppi-Arcivescovo-Bologna-non-ci-ardeva-forse-il-cuore.pdf.

[2215] In March 2020, Pope Francis chose as the theme of the XVI Ordinary General Assembly of the Synod of Bishops, "Towards a Synodal Church: Communion, Participation and Mission."

[2216] Pope Francis, "The Bread, the Word, the Poor," homily during the 2017 Eucharistic Congress, Bologna, 1 October 2017, http://www.vatican.va/content/francesco/it/homilies/2017/documents/papa-francesco_20171001_omelia-visitapastorale-bologna.html.

Reorganizing the Archdiocese

Pope Francis' "dream of a missionary option" also inspired Cardinal Zuppi's restructuring of the Archdiocese of Bologna. In July 2018, the cardinal issued a pastoral note, reorganizing the diocese into fifty "pastoral regions" consisting not only of parishes but also of monasteries, convents, religious houses, and headquarters of ecclesial associations and movements.[2217] The reorganization was based on the work and counsel of Cardinal Zuppi's "vicar for synodality" and input from archdiocesan priests. A moderator was appointed to each pastoral zone for a three-year term and was tasked with convening a "regional assembly." Cardinal Zuppi said these regional assemblies were "inspired" by Pope Francis' "dream" in *Evangelii Gaudium*, paragraph 27.

In his pastoral note to the archdiocese, Cardinal Zuppi urged the faithful of Bologna to move away from "self-sufficient" parishes that make the faithful feel at home to "a communion of parishes." "We become saints in community because sanctification is a community journey, to be undertaken two by two," he wrote.[2218] He also said the year would be dedicated to "continuing the synodal journey" indicated in *Evangelii Gaudium*.

Pastoral Visit

In keeping with canon law,[2219] on the solemnity of Pentecost in 2019, Cardinal Zuppi announced his plan to visit the various regions of the diocese over a five-year period. The theme of the visit—"Now you are the body of Christ and individually members of it" (1 Cor. 12:27)—was inspired by Pope Francis' apostolic visit to Bologna in October 2017, particularly his stress on actively belonging to the diocese and his calls for an outgoing, missionary Church in *Evangelii Gaudium*.

[2217] Matteo Maria Zuppi, *Ciascuno li udiva parlare nella propria lingua*, Chiesa di Bologna, 1 July 2018, https://www.chiesadibologna.it/wp-content/uploads/sites/2/2019/12/Lettera-Pastorale-Zuppi-Arcivescovo-Bologna-Tutti-missionari-Zone-Pastorali.pdf.pdf (translated from Italian).

[2218] Ibid.

[2219] CIC/83 can. 396 § 1.

In his letter to the archdiocese, Cardinal Zuppi said "the aim of this pastoral visit will be to grow in communion and live out missionary conversion."[2220] He added: "The Church does not want to live for herself, and her vocation is to serve man and labor in the harvest of the world, without boundaries, as the Lord Jesus asked." By "making us all feel part of a body, all important and full of the same Spirit of love," the cardinal said the pastoral visit would be the "exact opposite" of the archdiocese's worst enemy, "what Pope Francis calls 'postmodern and globalized individualism (EG 67).'" Each visit, beginning on Thursday and ending on Sunday, would include the celebration of the Liturgy of the Hours, a moment of prayer and fraternity with the priests, group *lectio divina*, a vocational-missionary prayer vigil, initiatives specific to each region, and the Sunday Eucharistic liturgy.[2221]

Amoris Laetitia *Guidelines and the Synod of Bishops*

Cardinal Zuppi is the president of the Bishops' Conference of Emilia-Romagna, a possible step, some observers believe, to heading Italy's bishops' conference.[2222] As president, he took a leading role in formulating and promulgating episcopal guidelines for the controversial chapter 8 of *Amoris Laetitia* (the guidelines, issued in 2018, are discussed in the next section). The bishops' document, under Cardinal Zuppi's leadership, referred to sexual relations in a second, unmarried union not as adultery, as the Church has traditionally taught, but as "conjugal acts" that are sometimes needed to preserve the "new union" and therefore the "good of the children."

Zuppi is also a member of the Council of the Secretariat of the Synod of Bishops at the Vatican, a position giving him some influence on the organization of synods. He was elected to the council at the conclusion of the Synod on Youth in October 2018.

[2220] Matteo Zuppi, *Voi siete corpo di Cristo e sue membra, ognuno secondo la propria parte*, Chiesa di Bologna, 9 June 2019, https://www.chiesadibologna.it/wp-content/uploads/sites/2/2019/12/Indizione-della-Visita-pastorale-al-le-Zone-della-Diocesi-Zuppi-2019.pdf.

[2221] Ibid.

[2222] According to multiple sources, including Sandro Magister, Cardinal Zuppi is a likely contender to be the next president of the Italian Bishops' Conference.

Coronavirus

As mentioned above, Cardinal Zuppi never closed the churches in Bologna but suspended all public celebrations of the Mass, including funerals, following the provisions of the bishops' conference. He did not prohibit sacramental Confession, the Anointing of the Sick, and Baptisms but ordered that priests observe precautions.[2223]

In an interview with *La Repubblica* in early April, the cardinal intimated that he would have liked to have celebrated the Holy Week and Easter liturgies but that the risks were too "dangerous" and the "rules must be respected."[2224] He continued to livestream liturgies during Holy Week and Easter. The cardinal said that when, at the beginning of the crisis, he saw restaurants open but Masses banned, he initially found it "very hard to understand the government's decision and asked [himself] many questions."

"We need God as well as scientists and doctors," he said, adding that even under lockdown it is important to "strengthen communion between people and the awareness that the community needs the Eucharist and vice-versa." Cardinal Zuppi also stressed that the elderly "are not objects" but "indispensable people" who face a double burden of isolation. "It is not acceptable that age should become a discriminating factor to save or condemn a life," he said.

The cardinal said it is a regrettable reality that too little is done to care for parents and grandparents and to support them at home. If more of the elderly had been able to "stay at home," they would have been better protected, he said. This crisis, he noted, is teaching a lesson on how to treat the weakest. "If it's true that nothing will be like before, we too must be better," he said.[2225]

[2223] "Disposizioni nell'Arcidiocesi di Bologna."

[2224] Edward Pentin, "Coronavirus Latest from Rome," *National Catholic Register*, 6 April 2020, https://www.ncregister.com/blog/edward-pentin/coronavirus-latest-italys-bishops-call-for-all-churches-to-be-closed.

[2225] Ilaria Venturi, "Il cardinale Zuppi: 'Anch'io vorrei celebrare la messa ma ci sono rischi e le regole vanno rispettate,'" *La Repubblica*, 5 April 2020, https://rep.repubblica.it/pwa/intervista/2020/04/05/news/zuppi_chiese_aperte_salvini-253247475/.

Communications

Cardinal Zuppi, who won the affection of many Romans, has become well known to Italians through his many appearances on national television and in print. Perhaps influenced by Sant'Egidio's effective employment of public relations, Zuppi also makes maximum use of the media.

He uses the diocesan television program *12 Porte* (Twelve Doors) to broadcast video messages to the faithful of Bologna or special events, such as the diocesan train ride to Rome when he was created a cardinal.

Cardinal Zuppi has also had a "docufilm" made about him, called *The Gospel according to Matteo Z.*[2226] Produced by Italian journalist Emilio Marrese and described as a "rock documentary," it aims at telling the story of the bicycle-riding "street bishop" who is "changing Bologna, dialoguing with everyone and incarnating the open and reforming vision of Pope Francis."[2227] The docufilm was released on December 17, 2019.[2228]

An effective communicator, Cardinal Zuppi regularly appears on TV2000, the official television station of the Italian bishops, as well as on popular talk shows. He is also regularly featured on a program broadcast by the Italian public broadcasting system (RAI) called *A Sua Immagine* (In His Image) to comment on the Gospel and highlight how it is being lived out in the Archdiocese of Bologna. For example, on March 3, 2020, he traveled

[2226] "Il Vangelo secondo Matteo Z.—Professione Vescovo," Facebook video, 2:00, posted 1 December 2019, https://www.facebook.com/100733861410519/videos/550740638839292/.

[2227] "Il Vangelo secondo Matteo Z.—Professione Vescovo," https://www.facebook.com/pg/Il-Vangelo-secondo-Matteo-Z-Professione-Vescovo-100733861410519/reviews/?ref=page_internal.

[2228] "'Il Vangelo secondo Matteo Z': il docufilm sul Cardinale Matteo Maria Zuppi," *Bologna Today*, 2 December 2019, http://www.bolognatoday.it/eventi/matteo-zuppi-docufilm-marrese.html. The film synopsis reads: "Don Matteo (as he prefers to be called) is one who rides a bike and lives in a retirement home for priests, one who quotes Alda Merini and Saint Francis, the Gospel and the Constitution, John XXIII and Guccini. He was the first bishop of Bologna to speak on the May Day stage, to enter a social center, to dialogue with the LGBTI community and to let refugees dance in the Basilica of San Petronio during the Mass for their Patron Saint."

to a monastic community in the mountains of Bologna to comment on the Transfiguration.[2229] On another occasion, he visited a former hermitage that had been transformed into a home for young migrants and refugees.[2230]

On October 5, 2019, Pope Francis created Archbishop Zuppi a cardinal in St. Peter's Basilica; he was assigned the church of St. Egidio as his titular church. He is a member of the Dicastery for Promoting Integral Human Development[2231] and of the Administration of the Patrimony of the Apostolic See (APSA).[2232]

TEACHING OFFICE

Attitude toward the Second Vatican Council

Cardinal Zuppi was born on October 11, 1955, the traditional liturgical feast of the Motherhood of the Blessed Virgin Mary. Seven years later to the day would mark the solemn opening of the Second Vatican Ecumenical Council.

Shortly before taking possession of the Archdiocese of Bologna in December 2018, Archbishop Zuppi was asked what he would be "carrying in his bag" to help him fulfill his episcopal responsibilities. He replied: "Other than the Gospel, which we must never forget … there is my story, the Council, and the Apostolic Exhortation *Evangelii Gaudium*, which is the program of Pope Francis."[2233]

For Cardinal Zuppi, the Council "brought about a profound change in the Church which has begun to listen again to the many questions of the world." Beginning again with mercy, he said, means "implementing Vatican II, because mercy represents the attitude of the post-conciliar Church." It

---

[2229] *A Sua immagine*, 7 March 2020, Raiplay, https://www.raiplay.it/video/2020/03/A-sua-Immagine-2dbc5bd7-aa10-4a76-894e-f808cdfcdcff.html.

[2230] *A Sua immagine*, 27 April 2019, Raiplay, https://www.raiplay.it/video/2019/04/A-Sua-immagine-a1a1272d-f51f-4585-8f99-a944888716dc.html.

[2231] Appointed by Pope Francis on 21 February 2020.

[2232] Appointed by Pope Francis on 18 April 2020.

[2233] Zichittella, "Voglio una Chiesa."

means "putting into practice exactly what the Council wanted" and "looking sympathetically at the world and its inhabitants, and then answering the many questions that the world itself poses to the Church."[2234]

Zuppi has another natural connection to Vatican II—namely, through his father, who knew and worked for Giovanni Battista Montini (the future Paul VI).

Cardinal Zuppi often cites Paul VI. In a TedxYouth talk titled "What Unites Heaven and Earth," delivered in Bologna in 2018, he said that what unites them is "the horizon." He said he believes that "for each of us, looking at the horizon also means understanding what unites us, what unites earth and heaven (sky), and we can't understand what we are doing here on earth without measuring ourselves against the greatness of heaven (the sky) itself."[2235]

"We are born in one place but have to learn to be anywhere," he said, adding that Paul VI had a beautiful expression: *La stanza del mondo* (the room of the world). "It's one room," the cardinal told young people, and "many times we believe more in division and can't see the room anymore, and it's terrible because we don't understand anymore who we are." He noted that Pope Francis "uses a similar expression, 'common home,' and invites us all to remember that the house is one … and that we are all called to be citizens of the world, an expression that was very fashionable in the 1960s, when people saw the terrible effects of nationalism." We need to learn to live with others, to see others, or else we become enclosed in our own little world, he said. Addressing the inequality of resources in the world, Zuppi told young people that "we need to adjust the room" and said this begins with each of us, through solidarity.

[2234] Alessandra Stoppini, "Si apre il Giubileo. Matteo Zuppi, arcivescovo di Bologna: 'Ripartire dalla Misericordia vuol dire attuare il Concilio,'" Santalessandro, 3 December 2015, http://www.santalessandro.org/2015/12/parte-il-giubileo-matteo-zuppi-arcivescovo-di-bologna-ripartire-dalla-misericordia-vuol-dire-attuare-il-concilio/.

[2235] TEDxTalks, "Quello che unisce cielo e terra Matteo Zuppi TEDxYouth@Bologna," YouTube video, 7:11, posted 1 March 2018, https://www.youtube.com/watch?v=lK9namAm1so.

In his TedxYouth talk, Cardinal Zuppi mentioned neither God nor Jesus, nor heaven in any supernatural sense.[2236]

On Hell

During an in-studio appearance on an Italian television program in October 2019, Cardinal Zuppi was asked by the presenter: "Do you believe in hell, or does the mercy of God exclude it?" Cardinal Zuppi answered: "Hell is something we have to contend with seriously." He added: "I believe that hell is, for example, when you are so distrustful that you no longer believe in love, or you construct a completely autonomous world where mercy can

---

[2236] Yet when Paul VI used the expression *stanza del mondo* (room of the world), he used it entirely in reference to Christ, the true Light, who shines into "the room," illumining nations, and giving beauty and brightness, meaning and the splendor of supernatural life, to every soul who welcomes Him. The original text of Paul VI's words: "There resound in Our spirit the words of the Gospel that yesterday, on the feast of the Presentation of the Child Jesus in the Temple, and the Purification of Mary Most Holy, the liturgy offered to Our meditation, proclaiming Jesus the Messiah of the Lord 'Christum Domini,' the salvation of all peoples, 'salutare … omnium populorum,' the light to illumine the nations 'lumen ad revelationem gentium' (Lk. 2:30-32)…. Jesus is at the summit of human aspirations, He is the end of our hopes and prayers, He is the focal point of the desires of history and civilization, He is the Messiah, the center of humanity, He who gives meaning to human events, He who gives value to human actions, He who forms the joy and fullness of the desires of all hearts, the true man, the type of perfection, beauty, and holiness, placed by God to embody the true model, the true concept of man, the brother of all, the irreplaceable friend, the only one worthy of all trust and all love: He is the Christ-man. And at the same time Jesus is at the source of all our true good fortune, He is the light through which the room of the world takes proportions, form; beauty and shadow; He is the word that defines everything, explains everything, classifies everything, redeems everything; He is the principle of our spiritual and moral life; He says what must be done and gives the strength and grace to do it; His image, indeed His presence, reverberates in every soul that becomes a mirror to welcome His ray of truth and life, that is, who believes in Him and welcomes His sacramental contact; He is the Christ-God, the Master, the Savior, the Life." Paul VI, *Udienza Generale* (3 February 1965), http://www.vatican.va/content/paul-vi/it/audiences/1965/documents/hf_p-vi_aud_19650203.html.

no longer enter in, because you do everything alone. Individualism leads to this. You also think you can judge everything yourself, and so you remain alone with your judgment, surrounded by mirrors … but you're alone. I think this is what hell is." Cardinal Zuppi smiled and added: "And when mercy can't enter in, then I believe mercy is able to do the impossible."[2237]

On the Death Penalty

Consistent with his close association with the Community of Sant'Egidio, Cardinal Zuppi has long favored a universal ban on the death penalty. Speaking in Bologna, at the 2016 launch of the book *From Cain to Caliphate: Towards a World without the Death Penalty*,[2238] Cardinal Zuppi asserted that the death penalty is "born out of the feelings of revenge that underlie punitive justice." This concept, he said, is the "the exact opposite of what justice must really be." Supporting Pope Francis' statements on the subject, Cardinal Zuppi said that "to speak of the death penalty is actually to speak of imprisonment, because, for example, life imprisonment is in fact a kind of masked death penalty. The penalty, instead, must be a path of rehabilitation."[2239]

The cardinal praised the United Nations for seeking (with Sant'Egidio) a moratorium on capital punishment, saying to fight for a world without the death penalty "is a duty of our generation." It is a commitment, he believes, "to the culture of life," whereas "the death penalty turns us from victims into executioners without realizing it."[2240]

[2237] RaiPlay, "Il Cardinal Matteo Zuppi - Che tempo che fa," YouTube video, 21:38, posted 27 October 2019, https://www.youtube.com/watch?v=GAOu_ZIVLNI (translated from Italian).

[2238] "Life: presentazione del libro di Marazziti contro la pena di morte. Presente l'Arcivescovo Zuppi," Sant'Egidio, 23 January 2016, https://www.santegidio.org/pageID/30284/langID/fr/itemID/15088/Life-presentazione-del-libro--di-Marazziti-contro-la-pena-di-morte-Presente-l-Arcivescovo-Zuppi.html.

[2239] "Pena di morte: Monsignor Zuppi e Prodi con Sant'Egidio," Sant'Egidio, 24 January 2016, https://www.santegidio.org/pageID/30468/langID/es/itemID/21476/Pena-di-morte-monsignor-Zuppi-e-Prodi-con-Sant-Egidio.html (translated from Italian).

[2240] Emilio Marrese, "Il vescovo di Bologna e i killer della Uno Bianca: 'Uno della banda mi ha chiesto perdono,'" *Bologna*, 25 September 2016, https://

Amoris Laetitia

As mentioned above, as president of the Bishops' Conference of Emilia-Romagna, Cardinal Zuppi played a key role in developing pastoral guidelines for chapter 8 of *Amoris Laetitia*. Issued in 2018, the guidelines appear to depart from traditional Church teaching on admission of the divorced and "remarried" to Holy Communion. The document argues that chastity is not the only possible option for "remarried" divorcees, "since the new union and therefore also the good of the children could be put at risk in the absence of conjugal acts." The document adds that it is a "delicate matter" of that discernment in the "internal forum."

Regarding possible readmission to the sacraments, the guidelines state "it will be opportune to establish the modalities, in order to avoid, on the one hand, situations of conflict and scandal and, on the other, the feeling that readmission represents a private matter and a sort of 'exception' granted to some."[2241]

Humanae Vitae

Cardinal Zuppi has expressed support for Pope Paul VI's Encyclical *Humanae Vitae* but has not explicitly endorsed its teaching against the use of contraception. In October 2018, Zuppi was a featured speaker at a conference to mark the fiftieth anniversary of *Humanae Vitae*.[2242] During his

---

bologna.repubblica.it/cronaca/2016/09/25/news/il_vescovo_di_bolo-gna_e_i_killer_della_uno_bianca_uno_di_loro_mi_ha_chiesto_per-dono_-148455293/ (translated from Italian).

[2241] Episcopal Conference of Emilia-Romagna, "Indications on Chapter 8 of *Amoris Laetitia*" (15 January 2018), no. 9, https://www.viandanti.org/sito/wp-content/uploads/2016/11/Conferenza-episcopale-ER_Indicazioni-sul-capVIII-di-Amoris-laetitia.pdf (translated from Italian).

[2242] The one-day conference, sponsored by numerous pro-life, pro-family organizations, was titled "*Humanae Vitae*: Natural Methods: A Road to Happiness." It also featured a talk by wife, mother, and journalist Costanza Miriano on "How *Humanae Vitae* Saved My Life." "A Bologna si fa festa per Humanae Vitae," Confederazione Italiana dei Centri per la Regolazione Naturale della Fertilità, 1 October 2018, https://www.confederazionemetodinaturali.it/a-bologna-si-fa-festa-per-humanae-vitae/s1b2057e5.

talk, titled "What Are the Ways to Welcome Pope Francis' Invitation to Rediscover *Humanae Vitae*?," Cardinal Zuppi, who is one of six children, praised a pro–*Humanae Vitae* talk and stressed that the "beauty" of marriage set forth in the encyclical needs to be rediscovered today, in a world where so many people grow up in unstable families and relationships. Cardinal Zuppi, who prefers not to take sides and seeks conciliatory positions as much as possible, cautioned against polemics in the Church. He said he believed Pope Francis had sought to relaunch the teaching of *Humanae Vitae* in *Amoris Laetitia*.[2243]

Homosexuality

Shortly after Zuppi's promotion to Bologna in 2015, *Famiglia Cristiana* published an article noting that, as auxiliary bishop in Rome, Cardinal Zuppi was "sensitive to the paths of welcoming 'marginalized' people into the community."[2244] It added that, with his support, the Jesuits of San Saba, Rome, had organized a group called "Church: A Home for All," whose meetings were "attended mainly by remarried divorcees and homosexuals."[2245]

In 2016, in Bologna, Cardinal Zuppi said that "the fight against homophobia … will find us close."[2246]

[2243] Dodici Porte, "Zuppi: Riscoprire Humanae Vitae," YouTube video, 45:06, posted 31 October 2018, https://www.youtube.com/watch?v=UuxTdUW5eeU.

[2244] Vittoria Prisciandaro, "A Bologna Don Matteo Zuppi, il missionario delle periferie," *Famiglia Cristiana*, 27 October 2015, https://www.famigliacristiana.it/articolo/a-bologna-don-matteo-zuppi-il-missionario-delle-periferie.aspx.

[2245] "Chiesa casa per tutti" (Church: home for all) aims at being an opportunity to experience an inclusive way of being "Church" that is open to all; an ecclesial space where one can get to know, tell, and share one's spiritual experience with others starting from the condition that each one lives: lay or religious, old or young, homosexual or straight, single or married, living together or divorced. "Gli incontri 'Chiesa casa per tutti,'" Parrocchia di San Saba, https://sansaba.gesuiti.it/chiesa-casa-per-tutti/ (translated from Italian).

[2246] Redazione, "Zuppi alla festa della Fiom: 'Sempre contro omofobia e violenza sulle donne,'" *Bologna Today*, 16 June 2016, http://www.bolognatoday.it/cronaca/festa-fiom-zuppi-bologna.html.

Cardinal Zuppi's views on homosexuality are ambiguous; he has shown support for divergent stances in writing the prefaces to two books with opposing perspectives on the pastoral care of persons who experience same-sex attraction. The first was written for the Italian edition of *Same-Sex Attraction: Catholic Teaching and Pastoral Practice*, originally published by the Knights of Columbus Supreme Council in 2007.[2247]

Cardinal Zuppi, who has firsthand experience of the AIDS epidemic through his work in Africa with Sant'Egidio, wrote that pastoring to homosexuals means risking to go to the peripheries, to those "who feel rejected by family or society; it implies a presence in areas at risk, where—as in a 'field hospital' of a 'throw-away society'—there are deaths and injuries to be healed." And he says that this is not meant figuratively but relates to those homosexuals who have died of HIV or AIDS.

He wrote that "no obvious pastoral solutions" exist in this area, adding that the Church "does not build walls" or create "categories of people according to sexual orientation, because, before having a particular sexual attraction, they are people." He added that it was "pleasing" to see people with homosexual tendencies help each other to live a "full Christian life" and acquire "a deep sense of Mercy, close to the sacraments," where "God's abundant grace will help, I am sure," to direct "so many souls towards the happiness of Love."

But Zuppi also wrote the preface for *Building a Bridge*, the controversial book[2248] by Fr. James Martin, S.J., praised by those pushing for greater LGBT acceptance in the Church, but criticized for its failure to stress the importance of celibacy and chastity and to acknowledge Catholic homosexuals trying to live in obedience to Church teaching.[2249]

[2247] See https://www.kofc.org/un/en/resources/cis/cis385.pdf; Italian edition here: https://www.edizionistudiodomenicano.it/Libro.php?id=923.

[2248] Matteo Zuppi, "Italian Archbishop Endorses a 'New Pastoral Attitude' for L.G.B.T Catholics," *America*, 21 May 2018, https://www.americamagazine.org/faith/2018/05/21/italian-archbishop-endorses-new-pastoral-attitude-lgbt-catholics.

[2249] Adelaide Mena, "Fr. James Martin's LGBT Book: Where It's Strong, Where It Falls Short," Catholic News Agency, 29 July 2017, https://www.

Drawing on Pope Francis' writings, he urged "a true and patient *accompaniment* (*'To accompany, To discern; To integrate …'*), one that favors the comprehension and vital engagement of the Gospel message on the part of every person, but without reducing it." He supported "a wise pedagogy of gradualism," taking the particular circumstances of each person into account, but not taking "anything away from the integrity of faith and doctrine." He said Fr. Martin's book was "useful for encouraging dialogue, as well as reciprocal knowledge and understanding, in view of a new pastoral attitude that we must seek together with our LGBT brothers and sisters." And he supported Cardinal Kevin Farrell's endorsement of the book: that it was "much-needed" and would be of help to Church leaders to "compassionately minister to the LGBT community" and make them "feel more at home" in the Church.[2250] Some argue that by merely using the acronym LGBT, a politically loaded term, Zuppi was signaling his support for their agenda. Certainly, this was how Fr. Martin saw it, tweeting on the day he was announced a new cardinal that Zuppi is a "great supporter of #LGBT Catholics."[2251]

In May 2020, Cardinal Zuppi wrote a third preface to a book on the same topic, this one called *Church and Homosexuality: An Inquiry in Light of Pope Francis' Magisterium*. Written by Luciano Moia, editor-in-chief of *Avvenire*'s monthly magazine, the book aims to "define better" the boundaries of a new pastoral approach to homosexuality. Zuppi's endorsement amounted to a "new offensive for the legitimization of homosexuality in the Church" under the "guise of welcoming people," wrote Riccardo Cascioli, editor of the Italian Catholic daily *La Nuova Bussola Quotidiana*.[2252]

---

catholicnewsagency.com/news/fr-james-martins-lgbt-book-where-its-strong-where-it-falls-short-18695.

[2250] Zuppi, "New Pastoral Attitude."

[2251] James Martin, SJ (@JamesMartinSJ), "Pope Francis has also named Archbishop Matteo Zuppi of Bologna as a cardinal! He is a great supporter of #LGBT Catholics," Twitter, 1 September 2019, 3:43 a.m., https://twitter.com/jamesmartinsj/status/1168112047508328448?s=21.

[2252] Riccardo Cascioli, "Catto-gay Connection, come ti promuovo l'omosessualità," *La Nuova Bussola Quotidiana*, 25 May 2020, https://lanuovabq.it/it/catto-gay-connection-come-ti-promuovo-lomosessualita#.XstqUn-xRm8.twitter.

Civil Unions

In January 2016, just months before Italy legally recognized same-sex civil unions, Archbishop Zuppi said he agreed with Cardinal Angelo Bagnasco, then president of Italy's bishops' conference, that "there are other priorities that must be faced." Zuppi added, "There are different sensibilities. We hope we can find solutions that bring these sensitivities together without upsetting the fundamental lines of the family that we all want."[2253]

Speaking in August 2016, three months after the Cirinnà law passed, legalizing same-sex civil unions, Archbishop Zuppi said: "Having clarified the aspects that have most concerned the Church, that is, the confusion with marriage and the family, these are brothers and sisters whom we will love. And with them we will try to live and walk together."

Regarding the possibility of homosexual couples' adopting children, he said the real concern of the Italian bishops is that "there aren't adequate defenses for the family," and the "contradiction" that those who have more children pay more. "We are far behind on this front," he said, adding: "I believe that the task of the Church will be more *for* than *against* something—to give the family back the indispensable role it actually has, otherwise with the economic crisis there will be further consequences of impoverishment."[2254]

Interreligious Dialogue

As a long-serving member of the Community of Sant'Egidio—which for decades has promoted the spirit of the 1986 World Day of Prayer for Peace in Assisi through its own international Meetings of Prayer for Peace—Cardinal

---

[2253] "Unioni civili: Zuppi, ha ragione Bagnasco," *ANSA*, 20 January 2016, https://www.ansa.it/sito/notizie/politica/2016/01/20/unioni-civili-zuppiha-ragione-bagnasco_f51f47e0-4800-492c-97e0-ecabf1d6b75d.html.

[2254] "Zuppi: in città tanta solitudine. Unioni civili: fratelli e sorelle a cui vogliamo bene," *FarodiRoma*, 16 August 2016, http://www.farodiroma.it/zuppi-in-citta-ce-tanta-solitudine-sulle-unioni-civili-sono-fratelli-e-sorelle-a-cui-vogliamo-bene/.

Zuppi is unsurprisingly a keen promoter of interreligious dialogue.[2255] The 1986 Assisi meeting gathered 160 religious leaders who spent the day together in prayer to God or their gods. While supporters see the meetings as vital for ensuring peace among men, critics believe the Assisi meeting and other similar initiatives relativize the uniqueness of Christ and His Church for the salvation of souls.[2256]

Cardinal Zuppi has been a regular participant at the annual "Spirit of Assisi" meetings, which are held in a different city each year and seek to continue the essence of the 1986 meeting. The 2018 meeting was organized by the Community of Sant'Egidio in Bologna. Speaking to representatives of the great world religions, Zuppi said Bologna's "magnificent towers" symbolized man's "desire for heaven" but that people cannot live "enclosed in towers" and be a "collection of isolated individuals."[2257]

[2255] "The Spirit of Assisi: 25 Years of Prayer for Peace," Sant'Egidio, https://archive.santegidio.org/index.php?staticURL=pageID/2535/langID/en/The-Spirit-of-Assisi-25-Years-of-Prayer-for-Peace.html.

[2256] In 2011, Benedict XVI eliminated common prayer so as not to give the impression that theological differences have been reduced or are inconsequential.

[2257] "Participants in the Bologna meeting included the founder of the Community of Sant'Egidio, Andrea Riccardi; the grand imam of Al-Azhar, Ahmad Al-Tayyeb; the Syrian Orthodox patriarch, Ignatius Aphrem II; the chief rabbi of France, Haïm Korsia; the president of the European Parliament, Antonio Tajani; and the former president of the European Commission, Romano Prodi. Also participating were three bishops from the People's Republic of China: Joseph Shen Bin, bishop of Haimen; Anthony Dang Mingyan, bishop of Xi'an; and Joseph Yang Yongqiang, bishop of Zhoucun. Among the other important personalities were Bernice King, daughter of Martin Luther King and guardian of his "dream" of a world without discrimination; Fr. Solalinde, who in Mexico defends migrants and takes young people away from the network of drug traffickers; and the Beninese Grégoire Ahongbonon, who fights for the dignity and care of the mentally ill in West Africa. "Zuppi: non si può vivere nelle torri, a Bologna ci sono i portici che uniscono. Aperto il meeting promosso da S. Egidio," *FarodiRoma*, 14 October 2018, http://www.farodiroma.it/zuppi-non-si-puo-vivere-nelle-torri-a-bologna-ci-sono-i-portici-che-uniscono-aperto-il-meeting-promosso-da-s-egidio/.

The meetings often draw controversial guests and speakers advocating a more globalist world. Among those attending that year were three Chinese bishops, two of whom were vice presidents of the communist-run Chinese church, the Chinese Patriotic Catholic Association (underlining Sant'Egidio's close ties with China and its state-run church), and UN adviser and population-control proponent Jeffrey Sachs, who spoke at the 2013, 2014, 2017, and 2019 gatherings.[2258]

In an interview at the 2019 meeting, held in Madrid and themed "Peace with No Borders," Cardinal Zuppi said that more than three decades after their inception, the international meetings are still very "forward" in their vision. "It is an event that helps us to glimpse the future that awaits us." This future, he said, "will not be the 'supermarket of religions'; the future will not be a 'super-religion'!"

Instead, he said "individual religions will point their faithful to the future reality of our entire planet, that is, living together and thinking of each other … in this unique, extraordinary home that is earth. Each religion has the duty to teach its faithful how to live together with others."

Cardinal Zuppi acknowledged that "a kind of UN of religions might frighten some, since it would mean that then there is also a 'super-religion' above all others." Better, he said, is "a meeting between a friend who invites his friend, rather than a cold institution." At the international Meetings of Prayer for Peace, he said "there is a lot of friendship. Everyone knows who has invited them, who else comes … everyone feels at home."[2259]

[2258] "Sachs, Jeffrey D.," Sant'Egidio, September 2019, https://preghieraperlapace. santegidio.org/pageID/31024/langID/en/orator/993/Sachs-Jeffrey-D.html. Sachs has gained increasing influence in the Vatican's Pontifical Academy of Sciences and drew attention in 2020 for his tirade against U.S. President Donald Trump at an academy meeting, to the applause of many attending, including academy chancellor Bishop Marcelo Sánchez Sorondo.

[2259] Deborah Castellano Lubov, "EXCLUSIVE INTERVIEW: Cardinal-Elect Zuppi: Peace Begins with One-on-One Encounter," Zenit, 4 October 2019, https://zenit.org/articles/interview-cardinal-elect-zuppi-peace-begins-with-one-on-one-encounters-2/.

Islam

For Cardinal Zuppi, one of the good fruits of the 1986 Assisi meeting is the controversial "Document on Human Fraternity for World Peace and Living Together," signed by Pope Francis and the grand imam of Al-Azhar, Ahmad Al-Tayyeb, on February 4, 2019 in Abu Dhabi.[2260]

Speaking to Catholic and Muslim university students at a summer school in early September 2019, he said we are "indebted" to the first Assisi meeting for the Abu Dhabi document.[2261] During the weekend event, Catholic students were invited to participate in Muslim Friday prayers, and Muslim students were invited to participate in Catholic Sunday Mass.[2262]

Cardinal Zuppi told the young people: "If there is no dialogue, there is division. If there is no fraternity, there is indifference. When one does not understand the other, there is prejudice. Dialogue is often seen as dangerous, in the sense that it discolors identities, but this is a contradiction. Faith helps us to understand, makes us rejoice in diversity and expresses

---

[2260] The Abu Dhabi document sparked controversy for stating: "The pluralism and the diversity of religions, color, sex, race and language are willed by God in His wisdom, through which He created human beings." Diane Montagna, "Pope Francis under Fire for Claiming 'Diversity of Religions' Is 'Willed by God,'" LifeSite News, 5 February 2019, https://www.lifesitenews.com/news/pope-francis-under-fire-for-claiming-diversity-of-religions-is-willed-by-go.

[2261] The summer school, held in the Archdiocese of Bologna, was an initiative promoted by the National Office for Ecumenism and Interreligious Dialogue (UNEDI) of the Italian Episcopal Conference (CEI) in collaboration with the Italian Islamic Religious Community (COREIS), the Union of Islamic Communities and Organizations in Italy (UCOII), and the Italian Islamic Confederation (CII). "Dialogo interreligioso: mons. Zuppi, (Bologna), 'la fratellanza abbatte l'indifferenza che spesso è al limite dell'intolleranza,'" SIR, 5 September 2019, https://www.agensir.it/quotidiano/2019/9/5/dialogo-interreligioso-mons-zuppi-bologna-la-fratellanza-abbatte-lindifferenza-che-spesso-e-al-limite-dellintolleranza/.

[2262] Ufficio Nazionale per l'ecumenismo e il Dialogo Interreligioso, *2ᵃ Edizione Summer School* (Rome: Ufficio Nazionale per l'ecumenismo e il Dialogo Interreligioso, 2019), https://ecumenismo.chiesacattolica.it/wp-content/uploads/sites/32/2019/07/29/Brochure_SummerSchool.pdf.

fraternity."[2263] No distinction between supernatural Christian faith and natural faith appeared to have been made.

Cardinal Zuppi's embrace of the Abu Dhabi document is consistent with his approach to the growing Islamic presence in Bologna. In March 2016, at a conference on the local Muslim community, sponsored by George Soros' Open Society Foundation,[2264] Cardinal Zuppi called for a mosque to be built in Bologna. "Rome has had a mosque since the 1970s, and I believe it is an important place. Some people think otherwise, but they are wrong," he said. The fact that Islamic countries forbid the construction of Catholic churches, he added, should "commit us all the more to allow believers to pray."[2265]

At the meeting, Cardinal Zuppi also expressed his hope that "some Islamic feasts will be welcomed in schools." Citing Pope Francis, he said "we need to build bridges between different cultures."[2266] The one-day conference, titled "For a Politics of Inclusion of Islam and Muslims in Bologna," was based on the findings of a report by the same title, also funded by the Open Society Foundation.[2267]

One month later, in April 2016, Cardinal Zuppi visited one of the many small mosques in Bologna and reminded the media and all those present of Pope Francis' call to "build bridges" and not "walls."[2268] Noting the upcoming feast of the Blessed Virgin of San Luca, the cardinal invited

[2263] "Dialogo interreligioso."

[2264] Le Comunità Musulmane a Bologna, "Per una politica di inclusione dell'-Islam e dei Musulmani," 4 March 2016, http://www.comune.bologna.it/sites/default/files/documenti/Programma%20seminario.pdf.

[2265] "Islam, il vescovo di Bologna: 'Sì alla moschea e feste musulmane nelle scuole,'" *Bologna*, 4 March 2016, https://bologna.repubblica.it/cronaca/2016/03/04/news/islam_il_vescovo_di_bologna_si_alla_moschea_e_feste_musulmane_nelle_scuole_-134784563/.

[2266] Ibid.

[2267] See *Per una politica dell'inclusione dell'Islam e dei Musulmani a Bologna: Rapporto conclusivo*, http://www.amitiecode.eu/sites/default/files/uploads/rapporto_conclusivo_-_lislam_e_i_musulmani_a_bologna.pdf.

[2268] Moschea di via Ranzani, L'intervento di Monsignor Maria Zuppi (arcivescovo di Bologna) nell'evento di sabato 23 aprile giornata storica per l'incontro

the imam to "contemplate the profound faith of the city, which is not a faith against the others and without the others" but "helps us see in the other our brother." Recalling the thirtieth anniversary of the 1986 Assisi meeting, Cardinal Zuppi also said he hoped a similar meeting could be organized in Bologna.

In May 2019, Cardinal Zuppi visited the Islamic Center of Bologna (established to unite the majority of smaller mosques in the city) for the first Friday of Ramadan.[2269] He told reporters that "when you don't know one another or [when you] look at one another only from afar, you often think there is an enemy." Getting to know one another, he said, will "help us commit to living in the reality" of Bologna and Italy. "This is what all Muslims want—to insert themselves, to live fully in the culture and rights and duties of our countries," he said. "It's clear that we are experiencing something new. It's the first time that there is such a constant presence of Islamic communities in our country—in wider Europe it's already been this way for some time—but we need to be more ourselves and dialogue so that this presence is a sign of respect and humanism that we live."[2270]

Also in the spirit of the Abu Dhabi document, Cardinal Zuppi has attended and encouraged participation in a public celebration of *iftar*, the evening meal with which Muslims break their fast during Ramadan.[2271] In May 2019, he supported the celebration of *iftars* in front of the Catholic

---

tra moschea e chiesa, Facebook video, 3:42, posted 24 April 2016, https://www.facebook.com/117543428411224/videos/588688204630075/.

[2269] "Zuppi in visita al centro islamico di Bologna per il ramadan," *Bologna*, 10 May 2019, https://bologna.repubblica.it/cronaca/2019/05/10/foto/zuppi_in_visita_al_centro_islamico_di_bologna_per_il_ramadan-225942043/1/#1.

[2270] Antonella Scarcella, "Dialogare contro odio, fa paura ciò che non si conosce," *Bologna Today*, 10 May 2019, http://www.bolognatoday.it/cronaca/zuppi-visita-moschea-ramadan.html.

[2271] "Diocesi: Bologna, a fine Ramadan momenti di scambio e incontro come Iftar pubblici nella zona Barca, in via Torleone e piazza Marzabotto," SIR, 28 May 2019, https://www.agensir.it/quotidiano/2019/5/28/diocesi-bologna-a-fine-ramadan-momenti-di-scambio-e-incontro-come-iftar-pubblici-nella-zona-barca-in-via-torleone-e-piazza-marzabotto/; Centro Interculturale Zonarelli Bologna, "Grande iftar—cena di Ramadan a Bologna," Facebook, 7 June

church in Marzabotto (Diocese of Bologna), even though the parish priest had suggested the square in front of the town hall was a more suitable and less controversial location. A letter from the archdiocesan office of ecumenism and interreligious dialogue said the decision was in harmony with the Abu Dhabi document.[2272]

Controversy erupted in October 2019 when reports emerged that Cardinal Zuppi had ordered a chicken-variation of the traditionally pork-filled tortellini customarily eaten at Bologna's patronal feast to be provided for the sake of Muslim guests. In a statement, the archdiocese called the reports "fake news," saying that Cardinal Zuppi learned of the news from the media. The archdiocese did confirm that non-pork tortellini would be provided, saying the decision was made so that "everyone can participate in the feast, even those who have problems or other dietary needs or religious reasons."[2273]

More recently, on February 2, 2020, the Catholic feast of Candlemas, Cardinal Zuppi together with the president of the local Islamic community, led an interreligious prayer service for peace with Catholic and Muslim children and young people at the Islamic Cultural Center of Bologna.[2274] Cardinal Zuppi told local media: "This is a right and important method

2018, https://www.facebook.com/centrointerculturale.zonarellibologna/photos/a.646102358849020/1637685103024069/?type=3&theater.

[2272] Associazione islamica di Marzabotto, Archdiocese of Bologna Press Statement, Facebook, 28 May 2019, https://www.facebook.com/AssociazioneIslamicadiMarzabotto/photos/a.1130504287065896/2201715536611427/?type=3&theater.

[2273] "Tortellini al pollo: Bologna, l'arcivescovo Zuppi 'all'oscuro' dell'iniziativa. Ma la diocesi precisa, 'normale regola di accoglienza,'" SIR, 1 October 2019, https://www.agensir.it/quotidiano/2019/10/1/tortellini-al-pollo-bologna-larcivescovo-zuppi-alloscuro-delliniziativa-ma-la-diocesi-precisa-normale-regola-di-accoglienza/.

[2274] Centro Cultura Islamica Bologna, Il cardinale Matteo Zuppi, arcivescovo di Bologna, ospite della moschea Annur per la Festa Interreligiosa della Pace, Facebook video, 1:59, posted 3 February 2020, https://www.facebook.com/watch/?v=583516385827433.

for living together, without confusion and without syncretism, without yielding. This is important as we look to the future."[2275]

During the coronavirus pandemic, Cardinal Zuppi sent a message to the Muslim community in Bologna for Ramadan, telling them: "This emergency can strengthen the bonds of solidarity between us."[2276]

Immigration

Cardinal Zuppi is a staunch supporter of the need to welcome and integrate into Italian society migrants and refugees fleeing war, violence, and poverty. His positions on migration led to sharp clashes with the Salvini populist movement.

In November 2019, shortly after it was announced that Pope Francis had chosen to elevate him to the College of Cardinals, Cardinal Zuppi published a book exploring what he believes are the root causes of the opposition to the mass migration Europe has been experiencing in recent years: fear, individualism, and an unwillingness to see the "other" as one's brother. The summary of the book, titled *You Shall Hate Your Brother: Why We Have Forgotten Fraternity*, says that Matteo Zuppi considers it "urgent to address the issue of hatred, a feeling that dehumanizes us and condemns us to loneliness." He criticizes in the book "unbridled individualism" that makes people "impervious to the suffering of others, but also more fragile and incapable of thinking about themselves in relation to others." Hate, he wrote, must be rejected, and the antidote is love and fraternity. The book says Zuppi calls for the rediscovery of "authentic solidarity," to see religious pluralism "as an opportunity to rediscover the reasons for one's faith" and to be open to love and so be capable of "great things."[2277]

[2275] Ibid.

[2276] "Il messaggio del cardinale Zuppi per il Ramadan," Chiesa di Bologna, 24 April 2020, https://www.chiesadibologna.it/il-messaggio-del-cardinale-zuppi-per-il-ramadan/.

[2277] Matteo Maria Zuppi, *Odierai il prossimo tuo: Perché abbiamo dimenticato la fraternità. Riflessioni sulle paure del tempo presente* (Segrate: Edizioni Piemme,

SUMMARY

A much-loved prelate in his native Rome with a lifelong concern for the poor and marginalized, forged through his close connections with the Sant'Egidio community, Matteo Zuppi reveals himself to be a true son of the spirit of Vatican II, someone who seeks to engage constantly with the modern world and implement the "profound change" that he believes the Council wanted for the Church.

That means helping the Church to "listen again to the many questions of the world," beginning with a concept of mercy, which, he says, "represents the attitude of the post-conciliar Church." His approach is about "rejecting hate," engendering "authentic solidarity," embracing religious pluralism and "fraternity,"[2278] and going out to the peripheries to help the poor and the marginalized—whether they be destitute drug addicts, impoverished gypsy children, or elderly persons who have been abandoned—earning him the moniker "street priest." He also strives to include same-sex-attracted people and the divorced and civilly "remarried," and engage Muslims, Jews, and the concerns of migrants.

Appointed archbishop and created cardinal by Pope Francis, Matteo Zuppi shows himself to be fully committed to adhering to the vision of this pontificate and seeing it to fruition, beginning with Francis' Apostolic Exhortation *Evangelii Gaudium* and including the pontificate's seminal and controversial interreligious document on human fraternity, signed in Abu Dhabi in 2019.

For Zuppi, community, activism, and mission come first. He has a devotion to Our Lady and values prayer, on which he places considerable importance, but his emphasis on social justice and equality has inevitably brought him into alliances with Italian leftist politics. So much so, that

---

2019), https://www.amazon.com/Odierai-prossimo-tuo-dimenticato-fraternità-ebook/dp/B081ZLK4V1.

[2278] "Le tre religioni invitano alla preghiera," Chiesa di Bologna, 28 March 2020, https://www.chiesadibologna.it/le-tre-religioni-invitano-alla-preghiera/.

when Francis announced that he was elevating Zuppi to the College of Cardinals, the Italian media joked that the "chaplain" of Italy's leading socialist party was to become a cardinal. Zuppi has also had connections with a movement opposed to Matteo Salvini, the populist leader of Italy's Lega Party; eulogized a far-left, pro-abortion Italian radical; and even incardinated into the Bologna Archdiocese a communist priest who ran for a seat in the European Parliament.

But despite his leftist political leanings, he also tries to dialogue with those on the right and those in favor of Church tradition, having celebrated Mass in the Extraordinary Form on at least two occasions.

Incongruous with his humble "street priest" persona is the fact that he heads one of the world's wealthiest dioceses, thanks to an astonishingly generous endowment of $1.8 billion to the Archdiocese of Bologna made just a few years prior to his appointment.

It is not always easy to know exactly where Zuppi, an intelligent prelate with a sharp mind, stands on doctrine and other issues, as he has shown himself able to tailor his message to his audience or his pope. A number of views on Church teaching, such as on the indissolubility of marriage and on hell, appear distinctly unorthodox. His supporters would say this makes him able to tackle the complexities of the modern world; his critics might describe him as a clever, archetypal modernist.

SERVICE TO THE CHURCH

Ordination to the Priesthood: 9 May 1981
Incardinated in Rome: 15 November 1988
Ordination to the Episcopate: 31 January 2012
Elevation to the College of Cardinals: 5 October 2019

Education
- Virgilio Lyceum, Rome

- 1977: University of Rome "La Sapienza"; License in letters and philosophy
- Palestrina Seminary
- Pontifical Lateran University; Theology (B.A.)

Assignments
- 1981-2000: Vicar to Msgr. Vincenzo Paglia, Basilica of Santa Maria in Trastevere
- 1983-2012: Rector, Church of Santa Croce alla Lungara
- 2000-2012: General ecclesiastical assistant, Sant'Egidio community
- 2000-2010: Parish priest, Basilica of Santa Maria in Trastevere
- 2005-2010: Prefect of the third prefecture of Rome
- 2010-2012: Parish priest of Santi Simone e Giuda Taddeo a Torre Angela, Rome
- 2011-2012: Prefect of the seventeenth prefecture of Rome
- 2015-present: President of Emilia-Romagna Bishops' Conference

Episcopacy
- 2012-2015: Auxiliary bishop of Rome, titular bishop of Villanova
- 2015-present: Archbishop of Bologna

Membership
- 1990s-present: Member of Sant'Egidio community
- 1995-2012: Member of diocesan presbyteral council
- Member of Dicastery for Promoting Integral Human Development
- Member of Administration of the Patrimony of the Apostolic See

INDEX

ABOUT THE AUTHOR

EDWARD PENTIN HAS REPORTED ON THE VATICAN since 2002, beginning with Vatican Radio before moving on to become the Rome correspondent for the *National Catholic Register*. He has also reported on the Holy See and the Catholic Church for a number of other publications, including *Newsweek*, *Newsmax*, and *Foreign Affairs*. He is the author of *The Rigging of a Vatican Synod? An Investigation into Alleged Manipulation at the Extraordinary Synod on the Family*, published by Ignatius Press (2015).

Sophia Institute

Sophia Institute is a nonprofit institution that seeks to nurture the spiritual, moral, and cultural life of souls and to spread the Gospel of Christ in conformity with the authentic teachings of the Roman Catholic Church.

Sophia Institute Press fulfills this mission by offering translations, reprints, and new publications that afford readers a rich source of the enduring wisdom of mankind.

Sophia Institute also operates the popular online resource Catholic-Exchange.com. *Catholic Exchange* provides world news from a Catholic perspective as well as daily devotionals and articles that will help readers to grow in holiness and live a life consistent with the teachings of the Church.

In 2013, Sophia Institute launched Sophia Institute for Teachers to renew and rebuild Catholic culture through service to Catholic education. With the goal of nurturing the spiritual, moral, and cultural life of souls, and an abiding respect for the role and work of teachers, we strive to provide materials and programs that are at once enlightening to the mind and ennobling to the heart; faithful and complete, as well as useful and practical.

Sophia Institute gratefully recognizes the Solidarity Association for preserving and encouraging the growth of our apostolate over the course of many years. Without their generous and timely support, this book would not be in your hands.

www.SophiaInstitute.com
www.CatholicExchange.com
www.SophiaInstituteforTeachers.org

Sophia Institute Press® is a registered trademark of Sophia Institute.
Sophia Institute is a tax-exempt institution as defined by the
Internal Revenue Code, Section 501(c)(3). Tax ID 22-2548708.